ን

1   pg 38
2 - chpt 6
3 - App F.2
4 - App K
5- App F.13
6   chpt 9, app F
7 - chpt 11
8 - pg 43
9 - pg 40
10 - App F.1
11 - App L
12 - App P
13   App F.1
14 - App H
15   Ap F.37

Introduction to Computing

Structured Problem Solving Using WATFIV-S

by

V.A. Dyck, J.D. Lawson, J.A. Smith all of University of Waterloo

Reston Publishing Company, Inc.
A Prentice-Hall Company
Reston, Virginia

Library of Congress Cataloging in Publication Data

Dyck, V   A
   Introduction to computing.

      Includes bibliographies.
      1. Electronic digital computers—Programming.
   2. FORTRAN (Computer program language) 3. Mathematics—Data processing. I. Lawson, John Douglas,
   1937   joint author. II. Smith, J. A.,
   joint author. III. Title.
   QA76.6.D93   001.6'42   79-12466
   ISBN 0-8359-3158-7

© 1979 by
Reston Publishing Company, Inc.
A Prentice-Hall Company
Reston, Virginia

10   9   8   7   6   5   4   3   2

Printed in the United States of America

Contents

Dedication

To Lou, Jacquie, and Ann

Preface

Computer use continues to grow explosively because of the indispensible role which computers play in daily life. This pervasive aspect of computation makes it critical that all educated people have some exposure to the serious use of computers. This text is intended as an introduction to computing for those students who will have occasion to make use of a computer in a mathematical or scientific context. That is to say, it is intended for future scientists, engineers, mathematicians, economists, and indeed any student for whom work with mathematical models will be of any importance. There is a need to provide students with basic mathematical skills and a knowledge of how these skills relate to the computer. Because the problems which justify computer solution are often large, it is very important that the student should also learn a formal organized approach to problem solving.

On most general purpose computing systems, efficient mathematical routines exist in program libraries to help problem solvers in their task. As a result, the intent in teaching such problem solving is not to create expert mathematical programmers, but rather to create intelligent users who are familiar with good programming practices. That is our aim in writing this text.

A common approach to teaching introductory computer courses has been to get the students on the computer immediately. Although this approach was valid when a prime objective was to teach a computer programming language (and this text certainly could be used in this way), the authors feel that this approach encourages poor programming practices. It has been our observation that students tend to neglect the design phase of program development and to rely instead on ad hoc incremental changes over many trial computer runs, which is wasteful of both human time and computer resources. We do agree that students should get some early exposure to the computer for motivation, excitement, and a sense of achievement. However, we would argue that some minimum level (say a few lectures) of instruction on algorithm design should be undertaken first.

As has been recognized in business and industry, the major effort in a programming exercise should be spent in the design process. Thus, it follows that the major effort in a programming course should be spent in teaching students techniques to facilitate this design process — techniques which are applicable regardless of which computer programming language is to be used. In programming, the major creative task is the algorithm design. Conversion to a computer program is then a routine, albeit painstaking matter.

In terms of the design process, a major step forward was the identification and development of the concepts which are referred to as *structured programming*. Many definitions for structured programming exist but all imply an organized approach to the design, implementation, and testing of computer software. For the purposes of this introductory text, we consider structured programming to be:

a) the use of *top-down design techniques*,
b) the use of *structured language constructions*, and
c) the use of *good coding style*.

It is not intended that this be a text on structured programming but rather a text that illustrates a structured approach to the development of solutions to problems of a mathematical nature.

The emphasis in this text is placed on the development of algorithms and the translation of these algorithms into computer programs. A simple *pseudo-code* language is used for the systematic development of algorithms using step-wise refinement.

The use of pseudo code for algorithmic descriptions allows a student to concentrate on algorithm development at varying levels of abstraction without having to worry about the more complicated syntactic details of a particular programming language. The pseudo-code language used in the text has a precise definition which makes for easy translation into a computer program. This preciseness is useful so that a beginning student may know what constitutes an acceptable algorithm. The pseudo code allows the control structures of sequence, **while-do** and **if-then-else**. Provision also exists for module definition and subscripted storage.

WATFIV-S,[1] a structured version of WATFIV is used as the programming language. For those institutions without access to WATFIV-S, a portable (ANSI standard FORTRAN) preprocessor is available. It accepts as input the structured WATFIV-S language and generates as output an ANSI standard FORTRAN program.

This book is designed as the text for a first course in computing offered to students with good high-school mathematics backgrounds. There is more material than may reasonably be covered in a first course. However, many students have had some high-school computing experience and may then find the extra material worthwhile. Instructors may also find that very little supplementary material is needed for a two-semester introductory sequence.

---

[1] Trademark - A fast **FORTRAN IV** debugging compiler available for IBM 360/370 computers and UNIVAC 9000-OS3 computers. A subset of this language is available as WATFOR11-S which runs on PDP-11 mini-computers. This language is identical to WATFIV-S for the purposes of this text, with the exception of a brief reference to **CHARACTER** variables in Chapters 12 and 13. Both compilers are distributed by the Computer Systems Group at the University of Waterloo.

Organization of the Text

This text is divided into four parts. The first introduces the basic concepts of algorithms, their design, and their translation into WATFIV-S. The other three parts deal with the development of mathematical tools and programming techniques for use in applications. As they become necessary for the applications, more advanced algorithmic techniques are introduced and discussed.

In the first part, Chapter 1 provides a perspective on problem solving and introduces the basic actions needed for describing algorithms. Chapter 2 describes how these basic actions may be written in pseudo code and gives examples of simple algorithms to illustrate these actions. Chapter 3 discusses conversion of pseudo-code algorithms into WATFIV-S. Additional techniques for developing pseudo-code algorithms are given in Chapter 4 and the efficiency of such algorithms is discussed in Chapter 5.

The second part is concerned with determining characteristics of mathematical functions and how to organize algorithms and programs in terms of modules. Chapter 6 looks at tabulation and plotting as initial ways of determining characteristics of functions. Chapters 7 and 8 describe methods for finding the zeros of functions and for the computation of areas. The use of modules in the development of algorithms and programs is described in Chapters 9 and 10.

The theme of the third part is the problem of dealing with large masses of data. Chapter 11 discusses some general ideas concerned with storing and manipulating large quantities of data. Chapter 12 discusses internal sorting and searching algorithms. These aid in the organization of data and the extraction of information from it. Statistical techniques for summarizing the characteristics of masses of data are described in Chapter 13. Chapter 14 deals with vectors, matrices, and linear equations.

The fourth part is concerned with the use of simulation techniques to predict the behaviour of models of physical systems. Chapter 15 describes basic deterministic simulation techniques which are used for systems whose behaviour is predetermined by a set of fixed equations. Chapter 16 describes probabilistic simulation techniques which are used when the changes in a system are subject to some randomness.

Preparation of the Text

This text was developed at the University of Waterloo over a two-year period. During this time, the manuscript has received intensive testing in a variety of introductory courses which have included students in Architecture, Computer Science, Engineering, Kinesiology, Mathematics, and Science.

Draft versions of the manuscript were prepared in machine-readable form and formatted for the line printer using the SCRIPT[2] processor. All computer programs have been machine tested. The resulting computer output has been captured and is reproduced in the text with a minimal amount of editing, namely, the condensing of blank lines and spaces to conform to the size limitations of a textbook page. This final version of the book has been produced at the University of Waterloo from the machine-readable text files. The computing for the typesetting was performed at the Mathematics Faculty Computing Facility.

---

[2] SCRIPT is a text-formatting processor distributed by the Computer Systems Group at the University of Waterloo.

The authors have created a discipline for representing the three stages of problem solving: development of the mathematical model, creation of a pseudo-code algorithm, and the translation to a programming language (WATFIV-S). Unique type styles have been adopted for each of these stages to allow the reader to distinguish between them, and to emphasize references to the stages in the narrative description. For all pseudo-code references, a distinctively simple typeface has been chosen. Furthermore, different weights have been selected for comments and unrefined pseudo-code, for pseudo-code variables and constants, and for pseudo-code keywords. Finally, the WATFIV-S programs, the output they produce, as well as references to WATFIV-S entities have been typeset in a monospace typeface simliar to that found on many computer line printers.

The authors trust that the presentation of accurate computer programs, virtually exact computer output, and the discipline in typesetting will enhance the reader's confidence and understanding of the material.

Acknowledgements

The authors would like to thank the many instructors, teaching assistants, and students who have assisted in debugging the text material. Thanks are also due to members of the University of Waterloo Department of Computing Services, who assisted the authors in the use of SCRIPT in the preparation of draft versions of this manuscript. We also thank our colleagues for their help and constructive comments over the course of development of this text.

Finally, the authors gratefully acknowledge the efforts of Richard Beach who supervised the preparation and phototypesetting of the final manuscript, and the efforts of his hard-working staff.

V. A. Dyck
J. D. Lawson
J. A. Smith
University of Waterloo

1
Introduction to Problem Solving

1.1 Computers in Perspective

Computers are an important part of our everyday life. There is such a variety of computer applications that computers affect everyone either directly or indirectly. It is the assistance of computers, their speed, accuracy, and reliability that allows us to solve many problems that were previously difficult or even impossible.

In today's society computers are used in many areas. Business data processing applications include payroll, inventory, and billing systems. Scientists and engineers rely heavily on computers to assist in design and simulation studies. Computers also facilitate the use of the data "banks" found, for example, in medical information systems and airline reservation systems. Physical events, such as the changing of traffic lights and the movement of subway trains, are monitored and controlled by computer. The preparation of letters, reports, books, and newspapers is often accomplished with the aid of a computer. These are but a few of the many applications.

Although computers as we know them are a relatively recent invention, the use of devices to help solve numerical problems is far from new. Most of us have heard of the Chinese abacus, if not of its relative, the Japanese soroban, which were two of the earliest aids to calculations.

Later examples of computing aids included the mechanical adder built by Blaise Pascal in 1642 (to assist in adding long columns of numbers common in his father's tax accounting office) and the stepped-wheel machine of Gottfried Wilhelm Leibniz in 1694. This machine could be used to multiply and divide numbers as well as add them. The "difference" and "analytical" engine designs of Charles Babbage were noteworthy for their time, 1822, even though his ideas were ahead of the available technology, and the devices could never be actually constructed.

Punched card technology was first introduced in 1801 as a mechanism for controlling the complex weaving patterns in the Jacquard loom and later was used for numerical computation by Dr. Herman Hollerith of the United States. Dr. Hollerith, a statistician, was faced with the task of analyzing the 1890 census before it was time for the next census. Recording of information in this medium and performance of numerical calculations under control of punched cards were widely used aids to business data processing and indeed scientific calculations for the next several decades.

Much of the basic computer development took place in the 1930's and 1940's, in many cases in response to problems that arose in the war effort. Ballistic computations and code-breaking were two very important stimuli.

Many technological advances have led to improved versions of these early computers. The vacuum tubes that were important components of the "first generation" machines were bulky, very sensitive to temperature, and quite unreliable. The transistor based "second generation" computers of the 1960's were much more compact and reliable. Transistors in turn gave way to the integrated circuits of today's "third generation" computers. The current components are so small and inexpensive that they have been adapted for use in everyday pocket calculators. In fact whole computers (called microcomputers) may now be constructed on a single "chip," roughly the size of a small finger nail.

1.2   Transition: Computers and Problem Solving

Counting devices, mechanical, and electrical calculators, and finally computers arose out of the need to solve problems. In fact, that is still the primary motivation today. Given a problem that is either too lengthy or too large to solve manually, one turns to a computer for assistance.

In order to make use of a computer, it is necessary to describe in an explicit manner exactly what operations are to be performed. These operations must be described to the computer in what is referred to as a *computer programming language*. The collection of operations is called a *computer program*. Many such languages exist for computers. In most cases these languages are best suited to one particular application area.

To use a computer, then, it is necessary to learn something about that computer, specifically, to choose and to learn a language for one's application. Generally, these languages are well defined and not too difficult to master. The much more difficult process involves developing the problem to the point where it can easily be expressed in this computer language — this is where the problem solving takes place.

1.3   What is Problem Solving?

The term "problem solving" can be used in many different contexts and therefore can be defined in various ways. In this context, it will be taken to mean the provision of a quantitative answer to some question posed in physical terms. As an example, suppose the question were, "What will the weather be like next Friday?" A quantitative answer might be "With a probability of .4, it will be sunny; with a probability of .4, it will be overcast; and with a probability of .2, it will be raining;" whereas a response like "It likely won't rain" would be a nonquantitative answer.

Typically, the steps leading from the initial question to the quantitative answer require one to:

- analyze the information given in the question
- express the question in mathematical terms
- develop techniques to deal with this mathematics
- interpret the results.

It is impossible to solve a problem correctly until one understands exactly what information is given and what needs to be found. Although this statement may seem obvious, too often a person begins to solve a problem without taking the time to arrive at an adequate definition of the problem. As a result, the problem is rarely solved correctly on the first attempt, and much time and effort is wasted iterating toward a solution.

In order to quantify our problem definition, a mathematical statement of the problem is sought. Solution of this mathematical problem, possibly aided by a computer, leads to quantitative answers to the original question. At this stage, these answers may be found to be unsatisfactory, thus requiring a redefinition of the problem.

1.4 The Mathematical Problem-Solving Process

Obtaining a solution to a mathematical problem involves the two processes of *development* and *application*. The first process refers to the development of a procedure that describes how a problem or subproblem may be solved. The second process refers to the application of the problem-solving procedure on a given set of data.

When describing such a procedure, the detail given must be sufficient for it to be followed, either manually or mechanically. The more sophisticated the procedure follower, the less detail is needed in the procedure.

If a problem is to be solved manually, the problem-solving procedure is generally *developed and applied* concurrently in a step by step manner. Often the result of a given step determines the nature of the subsequent step. This approach is possible since both the development and application of the problem-solving procedure are performed by the human problem solver.

When a computer is introduced into problem solving, it assists in the application process. However, the procedure must be more fully developed before it can be followed by the computer. As a result, the procedure must allow for the occurrence of all possible outcomes. Development of such a complete procedure is frequently far from trivial.

Hence, the loss involved in moving from the manual approach to the computer approach is a sacrifice of the versatility inherent in the concurrent development and application of a procedure. The gain is in the speed, accuracy, and storage capabilities of the computer. In addition, once a program has been written, it may be reused easily for different sets of data without further development.

1.5   Problem-Solving Procedures

A problem-solving *procedure,* often called an *algorithm,* specifies a set of operations that may be followed in order to solve the problem. Although there are many possible ways in which algorithms could be described, two common methods involve using a *pseudo-code* description or a *flowchart* diagram.

A pseudo-code description uses English, mathematical notations, and a limited set of special commands to describe the actions of an algorithm. A flowchart diagram provides exactly the same information graphically, using diagrams with a limited set of symbols in the place of the more elegant features of the pseudo code.

Unfortunately, neither pseudo code nor flowcharts are directly understood by a computer. However, the translation from either pseudo code or a flowchart to a computer programming language is relatively easy to learn.

In the description of an algorithm, there are a number of basic actions involved. Typically, it is necessary to find a means of expressing the following six basic activities:

1) specifying data values
2) recording results
3) performing calculations and assigning values
4) testing quantities and selecting alternate courses of actions
5) repeating actions
6) terminating the algorithm

In addition, it is sometimes desirable to have more sophisticated combinations or enhancements, but these activities will be introduced later as they become necessary.

1.6   Summary

The motivation for developing and using computing devices has been, and continues to be, providing assistance in the solution of problems. However, before a computer can be of such assistance, a problem must be formulated precisely. Then it is necessary to develop an algorithm that describes, in a step by step manner, precisely how the problem may be solved. Following this, the algorithm is translated into a computer programming language, and the resulting program is prepared in machine readable form. Finally, the program is read by the computer and applied to a set of data values.

The above steps will be expanded upon in more detail in succeeding chapters.

1.7   References

Huskey, H.D. and Huskey, V.R. "Chronology of Computing Devices." *IEEE Transactions on Computers* 25(1976):1190-1199. (This article provides an excellent summary of the development of computing devices, beginning with the abacus, through desk calculators and analog computers, and, finally, stored program automatic digital computers.)

Rosen, S. "Electronic Computers: A Historical Survey." *Computing Surveys* 1(1969):7-36.

Squires, E. *The Computer – An Everyday Machine.* Reading, Mass.: Addison-Wesley Publishing Co., 1977.

Wilkes, M.V. "Computers Then and Now." *Journal of the ACM* 15(1968):1-7.

1.8   Exercises

1.1 Name several other uses of computers that affect your life.

1.2 What are several future applications of computers that you can think of?

1.3 What are some examples of algorithms that you encounter in everyday life? These algorithms need not be mathematically oriented.

1.4 Describe an algorithm for an everyday task such as brushing your teeth, tying your shoes, or putting on a coat. Have a friend follow your instructions *explicitly.*

1.5 In any group, there will be people of various shapes and sizes. Describe how you would find the tallest person in a group. How would you find the heaviest person in the group? Describe how your above methods would change if you could look at only two people at any one time.

1.6 Describe an algorithm for finding the roots of the quadratic equation $ax^2+bx+c = 0$ using only very simple mathematical operations.

2
Problem Solving and Algorithms

2.1 Introduction

Pseudo code is a language for describing algorithms. Many variations of pseudo code exist as people often develop their own version to suit their particular needs. A pseudo-code algorithm consists of a series of statements or instructions which, when followed, will solve a particular problem. These instructions may be regarded as a means of being precise about the required calculations and related activities so that the person or even an assistant could follow them. Eventually, of course, the "assistant" will be a computer for which instructions are called *code*. Thus, the term pseudo code is used for these instructions.

The pseudo code described in this chapter has been designed to parallel the features found in modern programming languages in order that the transition from a pseudo-code algorithm to a computer program can be made easily.

2.2 Pseudo Code

Pseudo code must be capable of describing the six basic actions of algorithms. The actions and corresponding pseudo-code features are listed below.

	Action		Pseudo-Code Feature
1)	specifying data		**get**
2)	recording results		**put**
3)	performing calculations and assigning values		assignment operation
4)	testing quantities and selecting alternate courses of action		**if-then-else**
5)	repeating actions		**while-do**
6)	terminating an algorithm		**stop**

A pseudo-code algorithm is composed of a set of actions or statements, specified in terms of the above features. The actions are performed sequentially, starting with the first action, and proceeding until termination. In order for a pseudo-code algorithm to be correct, it must terminate after a finite number of steps. Any group of actions listed sequentially will be referred to as an *action sequence*. Such a sequence may contain any combination of the above six actions.

2.3   The Basics — A First Algorithm

To introduce how the pseudo-code actions may be used to describe an algorithm, a simple problem will be discussed. The problem is that of converting temperatures expressed in Fahrenheit degrees to temperatures in Celcius degrees. Mathematically, this conversion is expressed in terms of the following formula.

$$c = (f-32)\frac{5}{9}$$

In algebra, the symbols c and f are called "unknowns" and are used to represent the unknown numeric values of temperature in degrees Celcius and Fahrenheit, respectively. Substitution of a Fahrenheit temperature value, f, into the formula will give the corresponding Celcius temperature for c.

The first algorithm will formalize the steps to be followed to perform a single temperature conversion using the above formula. This problem is stated below.

Example 2.1

Develop an algorithm to take the single Fahrenheit temperature reading, 68°F, and convert the reading to degrees Celcius.

Since the formula for conversion is already known, the solution to this problem is straightforward. The pseudo-code algorithm, appearing in Figure 2.1, gives the steps which may be followed or *executed* to perform the necessary conversion. These steps are to be followed sequentially, from top to bottom. The first two statements are assignment operations and are used to express the necessary calculations. The first gives the constant value 68 to the symbol f while the second computes (f−32)*5/9 as (68−32)*5/9 = 36*5/9 = 180/9 = 20 which becomes the value of the symbol c. Notice the use of an asterisk for multiplication and a slash for division. The third statement directs that the results of the algorithm be recorded, that is, that the values of f and c, 68 and 20

Figure 2.1   Pseudo-code algorithm to convert from Fahrenheit to Celcius.

```
f ← 68
c ← (f − 32)*5/9
put f, c
stop
```

---

respectively, are to be written on a separate sheet of paper. Finally, the **stop** statement indicates the conclusion of the algorithm.

Contained in this simple algorithm are many important concepts and features of pseudo code. These are described in the following subsections.

2.3.1 Variables

A fundamental idea in the algorithm is the use of the symbols c and f. In pseudo code such quantities are called *variables*. Unlike algebra, variables are used to represent known numeric values. In this algorithm the variable f is assigned the Fahrenheit temperature, 68. Likewise the variable c is assigned the result of the expression which gives the equivalent Celcius temperature, 20.

In general, variables in pseudo code may consist of any group of alphanumeric characters, that is, letters of the alphabet (a-z) or digits (0-9). The first symbol should be an alphabetic character to avoid confusion with numeric quantities. Listed below are examples of valid and invalid variables.

Valid Variables	*Invalid Variables*
f	2f
c	456
celcius	c+f
dollar	dollar−sign
r2d2	3peeoh

Variables are *undefined* until they have been assigned a value. An undefined variable may not be used in an arithmetic operation. Furthermore, a variable can only have one numeric value at any given time. Once a variable has been given a value, it retains that value until it is explicitly changed.

2.3.2 Constants

As well as variables, the algorithm uses numeric quantities called constants. Constants are simply numbers, such as:

68   32   5   9   −12.34   +3.14159   0. $2.99776*10^{10}$

Constants may be positive (with or without the + sign) or negative, and may be written in exponent form to save writing a long string of zeros.

2.3.3   Assignment Operations

The first two statements in the algorithm in Figure 2.1 are called assignments. The first line f ← 68 is read "f is assigned the value 68." Similarly, line 2 means "c is assigned the numerical value of the expression (f−32)*5/9."

The assignment operation is the backbone of mathematical algorithms. It is used to express the evaluation of arithmetic expressions and the storage of intermediate results for future use. The general form of the assignment operation is:

variable ← expression

where variable is the name chosen to represent the result and expression indicates the arithmetic operations that are required in the calculation. The ← symbol is the assignment operator and indicates that the expression on the right-hand side (RHS) is to be calculated and *then* its value is to be assigned to the variable on the left-hand side (LHS).

An arithmetic expression can be a single constant; a single variable; or a combination of constants, variables, and the following arithmetic operators, used to express addition, subtraction, multiplication, and division.

+   −   *   /

Parentheses may also be used to order operations within an expression. Listed below are several arithmetic expressions and their evaluation. Notice that expressions are usually evaluated from left to right, but that, given a choice between adjacent operations, exponentiation is completed first and multiplication or division precedes addition or subtraction. The → symbol is used informally to mean "evaluates to."

Expression	*Evaluation*
$2 + 3*4$	$2 + 12 \rightarrow 14$
$2.5 + 3^3/4$	$2.5 + 27/4 \rightarrow 2.5 + 6.75 \rightarrow 9.25$
$1.1 + 2.2 - 3.3$	$3.3 - 3.3 \rightarrow 0$
$(4 + 5)*3$	$9*3 \rightarrow 27$

2.3.4   The put Action

When the actions of an algorithm are performed, many values may be calculated. In most cases these values will represent intermediate results which need not be recorded permanently as part of the solution to the problem. Therefore, an action is required to indicate those values that are important enough to be recorded. The **put** action is used for this purpose and its general form is:

put output list

where the output list contains messages and/or variables whose values are to be recorded. An output list may contain many such elements separated by commas.

In the previous algorithm, the statement **put** f, c states that the values of f and c are to be written on a separate sheet of paper. Since the numbers by themselves may be difficult to interpret, it is best to include a message to identify them. Thus, a modified **put** statement might be written as:

   put f, 'degrees Fahrenheit is', c, 'degrees Celcius'

Note that messages are differentiated from variables by placing a single quote on either side. Assuming that f and c have been assigned the values 68 and 20, the message written when this statement is performed is

   68 degrees Fahrenheit is 20 degrees Celsius

2.3.5   The **stop** Action

Since all algorithms must halt, it is necessary to include a statement to indicate when this termination is to happen. The pseudo-code statement **stop** is used to terminate an algorithm and thus is always the last action performed. Its general form is:

   stop

Though the **stop** statement may appear many times and anywhere in an algorithm, good usage limits the number of occurrences to one, appearing as the last statement of the algorithm. Such usage removes any doubt about where an algorithm terminates.

2.4   Repetition — A Second Algorithm

The example in the previous section investigated how a single temperature might be converted. A more likely task requiring an algorithm is the production of a conversion table. A formal statement of such a request follows.

Example 2.2
   Develop an algorithm to produce a table of Fahrenheit and the equivalent Celcius temperatures for 0°F, 1°F, 2°F, . . . , 212°F.

Having accomplished the task of conversion for a single temperature, the solution to this problem would appear to be automatic. The steps for each degree could be written out as:

```
f ← 0
c ← (f − 32)*5/9
put f, c

f ← 1
c ← (f − 32)*5/9
put f, c

    ⋮

f ← 212
c ← (f − 32)*5/9
put f, c

stop
```

Several things quickly become apparent about this approach. The task is tedious and there is a great deal of duplication. In fact, it probably takes longer to *describe* the calculations than to do them by hand. Since repetition in some form or other is necessary in a large number of calculations, a special pseudo-code feature, called the **while-do**, exists. Figure 2.2 illustrates its use in solving this problem.

Figure 2.2   Pseudo-code algorithm to produce a Fahrenheit to Celcius conversion table.

```
* Generate a conversion table from Fahrenheit to Celcius
* for 0°F to 212°F in 1°F increments.

* Variables used:
* f - the Fahrenheit temperature
* c - the Celcius temperature
f ← 0        ← initialization step
while f ≤ 212 do
    ⎡  c ← (f − 32)*5/9
    ⎢  put f, '°F is', c, '°C'
    ⎣  f ← f + 1    ← changes value of f

stop
```

assignment of position

The **while-do** statement specifies that the sequence of statements indicated by the indentation and the brace are to be repeated as long as f ≤ 212. The variable f is assigned the value 0 prior to the **while** and is increased by 1 each time through the sequence. These two steps are an integral part of the **while-do** feature.

In the discussion of the previous algorithm, it was mentioned that messages should be included to identify the output. The **put** statement for this algorithm includes an abbreviation of the suggested messages for the previous example.

This algorithm also includes several lines that begin with an asterisk. These lines are called *comment* statements and provide an English description of the algorithm to help the person reading the algorithm to understand the significance of the pseudo-code statements. In this example, the first two lines simply state the purpose of the algorithm. Following the purpose is a list of variables and how they are used in the algorithm to follow.

Portions of the application of this algorithm are given in Figure 2.3. A total of 855 statements are performed to complete the algorithm.

Figure 2.3 Step-by-step application of the Fahrenheit to Celcius conversion table algorithm of Figure 2.2.

Step	Statement Performed	Action Specified
1)	f ← 0	f is assigned the value 0
2)	**while** f ≤ 212 **do**	Since f is 0 and ≤212, perform the statements in the brace.
3)	c ← (f − 32)*5/9	compute (f−32)*5/9 → (0−32)*5/9 → (−32)*5/9 → (−160)/9 → −17.778 Assign −17.778 to c.
4)	**put** f, '°F is', c, '°C'	Write the values of f and c, 0 and −17.778, and the messages on a separate piece of paper.
5)	f ← f + 1	Compute f+1 → 0+1 → 1 and assign 1 to f.
6)	**while** f ≤ 212 **do**	Since f is 1 and ≤212, perform the statements in the brace.
7)	c ← (f−32)*5/9	Compute (f−32)*5/9 → −17.222 Assign −17.222 to c.
8)	**put** f, '°F is', c, '°C'	Write the values of f and c, 1 and −17.222, and the messages on the piece of paper.
9)	f ← f + 1	Compute f+1 → 2 and assign 2 to f.
10)	**while** f ≤ 212 **do**	Since f is 2 and ≤212, perform the statements in the brace.
⋮	⋮	⋮
850)	**while** f ≤ 212 **do**	Since f is 212 and ≤212, perform the statements in the brace.
851)	c ← (f−32)*5/9	Compute (f−32)*5/9 → 100 Assign 100 to c.
852)	**put** f, '°F is', c, '°C'	Write the values of f and c, 212 and 100, and the messages on the piece of paper.
853)	f ← f + 1	Compute f+1 → 213 and assign 213 to f.
854)	**while** f ≤ 212 **do**	Since f is 213 and >212, continue with the first statement beyond the brace.
855)	**stop**	Terminate the application process.

The process exhibited in this diagram is sometimes called *stepping through* the algorithm. It is a worthwhile exercise to test an algorithm in this way for a few steps before converting it to a computer program. The output that this process produces is illustrated below, as Figure 2.4.

Figure 2.4 Partial output from the Fahrenheit to Celcius conversion table algorithm from Figure 2.2.

```
  0°F  is  −17.778°C
  1°F  is  −17.222°C
⋮
212°F  is  100°C
```

The next subsection will explore the details of the **while-do** feature.

2.4.1   The **while-do** Action

In the previous example, the **while-do** feature was used to specify repetition of actions. Its general form follows:

while condition **do**

$$\left[\; \mathsf{S} \right.$$

S is an action sequence, the set of statements to be repeated. A brace or bracket as well as indentation is used to group the statements that form S. This group of statements is called the *range* of the **while** loop. In the previous example, the action sequence consisted of the three statements:

```
c ← (f − 32)*5/9
put f, c
f ← f + 1
```

The condition is a *logical expression* which tests the relationship between one or more pairs of arithmetic expressions and has a value of **true** or **false**. The relationship between two arithmetic expressions may be tested using one of the following operators, called *relational operators*.

$$= \; \neq \; < \; \leq \; > \; \geq$$

The condition in the previous example was $f \leq 212$. Any variables contained in the condition are called *control variables* of the **while-do** action. In the example, f was the sole control variable.

The operation of the **while-do** feature may be understood by following the arrows in the picture in Figure 2.5. Starting at the top of the picture, the arrow points to a diamond-shaped box containing the condition from the **while-do** statement. Thus, the first step is to evaluate the condition. If the condition is **true**, the exit arrow labeled **true** is taken from the diamond box to the rectangular box containing the action sequence S. Following the completion of the action sequence, the arrow points back to the condition in the diamond box. The condition is reevaluated and the decision is made again. As long as the condition is **true**, the action sequence is repeated. If the value of the condition is **false**, either initially or following the completion of S, execution continues with the statements following the **while-do** action, that is, the first pseudo-code statement following the brace.

In order to use **while-do** actions in an algorithm, however, more information must be specified. In fact, each **while-do** has associated with it three important operations. Each operation is *essential* for the **while-do** action to function correctly. The operations are:

1) The initialization of the **while-do** control variables in actions preceding the **while-do** itself. (The condition may not be evaluated unless its control variables have values.)
2) The condition evaluation, which controls termination of the **while-do** repetition.

Figure 2.5   Operation of the **while-do** action.

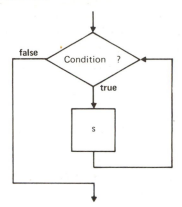

3) The action sequence S which must change at least one **while-do** control variable. (If no control variable is ever changed by the action sequence, the **while-do** will never terminate.)

A careful analysis of the algorithm of Figure 2.2 reveals that all three of the above operations are present. The control variable, f, is assigned a value prior to the **while-do**. The condition involves evaluating f ≤ 212. Within the action sequence, the value of f is increased by 1. Thus, all three elements are accounted for.

2.5   Specifying Data — A Third Algorithm

The algorithm of Figure 2.1 was written to convert a single temperature reading from Fahrenheit to Celcius. The next algorithm in Figure 2.2 performed a similar conversion for the specific range 0°F to 212°F. Frequently, an algorithm is to be applied to a number of values that either are not known in advance or are difficult to generate in an assignment action. Thus, a mechanism is required to supply the algorithm with the necessary values, referred to as *data*. The next example illustrates such a situation.

Example 2.3
Temperature readings from countries using the metric system are given in degrees Celcius. Develop an algorithm that will convert the Celcius temperature readings from 7 foreign locations to Fahrenheit degrees.

The formula for this conversion may be obtained by rearranging the previous formula as follows.

$$f = \frac{9}{5}c + 32$$

The definition of the problem implies that this conversion is to be applied repetitively to 7 unknown values. As was seen earlier, a convenient way to repeat such an operation is to make it part of a **while-do** action. Figure 2.6 illustrates this feature in solving Example 2.3. To accomplish the repetition 7 times, the variable count acts as a counter. It is assigned the initial value 1 and increased by 1 each time a conversion takes place. To obtain the 7 values, the **get** action is used. The statement **get** c is an instruction to find a value for c from a data list. This data list is usually placed immediately following the **stop** statement. In this case, the Celcius temperatures to be converted are 15, 18, 22, 25, 10, 8, and 15.

Previous examples discussed the benefits of identifying numerical output from an algorithm with appropriate messages. In this algorithm, a **put** statement to record the meaning of the numbers is located before the **while** loop. As a result, the words Fahrenheit and Celcius are recorded only once, before the numbers produced inside the **while** loop. Thus, these words will appear as column headings.

Figure 2.6   Pseudo-code algorithm to convert 7 temperatures from Celcius to Fahrenheit.

```
* Convert 7 temperatures from Celcius to Fahrenheit.

* Variables used:
* c - the Celcius temperature
* f - the Fahrenheit temperature
* count - the counter for number of values processed
put 'Celcius', 'Fahrenheit'
count ← 1
while count ≤ 7 do
      get c
      f ← (9/5)*c + 32
      put c, f
      count ← count + 1
stop
15,18,22,25,10,8,15
```

The table in Figure 2.7 indicates the action of the **get** statement on the data list and the values that the variables are given as the algorithm is performed. The values of c are changed by the **get** statement; f is changed by the conversion formula. The initial value of count is obtained through the statement count ← 1 and all remaining values from the statement count ← count + 1. Note that before the algorithm is started, all variables are undefined.

Finally, the output that would result from applying the algorithm is listed in Figure 2.8. The next section will formalize the action of the **get** statement.

Figure 2.7   Table of values for the Celcius to Fahrenheit conversion algorithm of Figure 2.6.

count	c	f	data list remaining
undefined	undefined	undefined	15,18,22,25,10,8,15
1	15	59	18,22,25,10,8,15
2	18	64.4	22,25,10,8,15
3	22	71.6	25,10,8,15
4	25	77	10,8,15
5	10	50	8,15
6	8	46.4	15
7	15	59	
8	→ exit from the **while** loop and perform the **stop**		

Figure 2.8   Output from the Celcius to Fahrenheit conversion algorithm of Figure 2.6.

Celcius	Fahrenheit
15	59
18	64.4
22	71.6
25	77
10	50
8	46.4
15	59

2.5.1   The get Action

The pseudo-code feature designed for specifying data values is called the **get** statement and has the following general form:

>   **get** input list

where the input list consists of one or more variables for which values are required. The variables in the list are separated from each other by commas. The **get** action is, in fact, just another way of assigning values to variables. The assigned values are selected sequentially from the *data list*. Naturally, for an algorithm to be considered correct, a **get** action cannot require more data values than are provided in the list.

By convention the list of data values for an algorithm is placed immediately after the **stop** statement. Each time a **get** is performed, the next unused value on the data list is selected and assigned to the next variable in the input list.

2.6   Selecting Alternatives — A Fourth Algorithm

In learning to live with a new system of measurement, such as temperatures given in Celcius rather than Fahrenheit, the crux of the problem is to develop a feeling for the new system. If the temperature for tomorrow is forecast to be 25°C, will that temperature be comfortable or not? The next example will attach such a relative measure to several temperatures. Since being comfortable is relative to the individual, the problem requires specification of both a lower and an upper temperature limit for comfort. Temperatures outside these limits are rated uncomfortable while those within are rated comfortable.

Example 2.4

Develop an algorithm that, given a lower and upper bound for temperatures that are comfortable (in °F) and given a specified number of Celcius temperature readings, will rate each temperature reading as comfortable or uncomfortable.

The solution to this problem, given in Figure 2.9, demonstrates the selection of alternatives using the **if-then-else** feature.

Figure 2.9   Pseudo-code algorithm to rate several Celcius temperatures.

```
* Given limits for what temperatures are comfortable,
* produce a comfort rating for several temperatures.

* Variables used:
* flo - low comfortable temperature (°F)
* clo - low comfortable temperature (°C)
* fhi - high comfortable temperature (°F)
* chi - high comfortable temperature (°C)
* num - number of temperature readings to process
* count - count of readings
* c — given temperature reading (°C)

* Obtain the Fahrenheit comfort limits and convert to Celcius.
get flo, fhi
clo ← (flo − 32)*5/9
chi ← (fhi − 32)*5/9
put 'The low comfortable limit is', flo, '°F', clo, '°C'
put 'The high comfortable limit is', fhi, '°F', chi, '°C'

* Obtain the number of readings to evaluate.
* Process each reading by recording an appropriate message.
get num
put 'The number of temperatures to process is', num
count ← 1
while count ≤ num do
    ┌ get c
    │ if c ≥ clo and c ≤ chi then
    │     ┌ put c, 'is comfortable'
    │   else
    │     ┌ put c, 'is uncomfortable'
    └ count ← count + 1
stop

68, 86, 10, 22, 31, 17, 20, 22, 30, 34, 39, 25, 12
```

The algorithm begins by obtaining the comfort limits (in °F), converting them to °C, and recording both. Next, the specific number of temperatures in the data list is obtained, assigned to num, and recorded. Finally, the counting loop is designed to repeat the rating process num times. Within the loop a Celcius temperature is taken from the data list and assigned to c. The value of c is then compared with the values of clo and chi. If c is both greater than or equal to clo and less than or equal to chi, the message is comfortable is written beside the value of c. Otherwise, c must be either less than clo or greater than chi, in which case the message is not comfortable is written beside the value of c. In this way the **if-then-else** feature allows for the selection of the appropriate action to take.

Listed in Figure 2.10 is a portion of the results of applying the algorithm of Figure 2.9 to the data given. The complete output is given in Figure 2.11.

Figure 2.10   Step-by-step application of the Celcius rating algorithm of Figure 2.9.

Step	Statement Performed	Action Specified
1)	**get** flo, fhi	$68 \rightarrow$ flo
		$86 \rightarrow$ fhi
2)	clo $\leftarrow$ (flo $-$ 32)*5/9	$20 \rightarrow$ clo
3)	chi $\leftarrow$ (fhi $-$ 32)*5/9	$30 \rightarrow$ chi
4)	**put** 'The low . . . '	Write out the message
		The low . . . is 68°F, 20°C
5)	**put** 'The high . . . '	Write out the message
		The high . . . is 86°F, 30°C
6)	**get** num	$10 \rightarrow$ num
7)	**put** 'The number of . . . '	Write out the message
		The number of . . . is 10
8)	count $\leftarrow$ 1	$1 \rightarrow$ count
9)	**while** count $\leq$ num **do**	$1 \leq 10$, therefore perform loop.
10)	**get** c	$22 \rightarrow$ c
11)	**if** c $\geq$ clo & c $\leq$ chi **then**	$22 \geq 20$ & $22 \leq 30$, therefore perform the statements in the range of the **then**.
12)	**put** c, 'is comfortable'	Write out: 22 is comfortable
13)	count $\leftarrow$ count + 1	$2 \rightarrow$ count
14)	**while** count $\leq$ num **do**	$2 \leq 10$, therefore perform loop.
15)	**get** c	$31 \rightarrow$ c
16)	**if** c $\geq$ clo & c $\leq$ chi **then**	$31 \geq 20$ but $31 > 30$, therefore perform the statements in the range of the **else**.
17)	**put** c, 'is uncomfortable'	Write out: 31 is uncomfortable
18)	count $\leftarrow$ count + 1	$3 \rightarrow$ count
19)	**while** count $\leq$ num **do**	$3 \leq 10$, therefore perform loop.
20)	**get** c	$17 \rightarrow$ c
21)	**if** c $\geq$ clo & c $\leq$ chi **then**	$17 < 20$, therefore perform the statements in the range of the **else**.
22)	**put** c, 'is uncomfortable'	Write out: 17 is uncomfortable
23)	count $\leftarrow$ count + 1	$4 \rightarrow$ count
⋮	⋮	⋮

2.6.1   Conditions and Logical Operators

There are three *logical operators* for manipulating logical quantities found in the conditions of the **while-do** and **if-then-else**. These logical quantities are normally the result of comparing arithmetic expressions using the relational operators, $=$, $\neq$, $<$, $\leq$, $>$, and $\geq$. The three logical operators are *not*, *and*, and *or* and are represented in pseudo

---

Figure 2.11   Output produced by applying the Celcius rating algorithm of Figure 2.9.

```
The low comfortable limit is 68°F 20°C
The high comfortable limit is 86°F 30°C
The number of temperatures to convert is 10
22 is comfortable
31 is uncomfortable
17 is uncomfortable
20 is comfortable
22 is comfortable
30 is comfortable
34 is uncomfortable
39 is uncomfortable
25 is comfortable
12 is uncomfortable
```

---

code by the following symbols.

Logical Operation	Pseudo Code Operator	Alternate Pseudo Code Symbol
not	**not**	¬
and	**and**	&
or	**or**	∨

The **and** (&) and **or** (∨) operators are called *binary* operators since they require a logical expression on either side. The **not** (¬) operator is a *unary* operator and the single operand is placed to the right. The result of an **and** operation is **true** if and only if the values of the logical expressions on both sides are **true**. If either or both is **false**, the result is **false**. The result of an **or** operation is **true** if either or both of its operands are **true**. Thus, the result is **false** only if both operands are **false**. Finally, the **not** operator negates its operand. If the operand is **true**, the result is **false**. If the operand is **false**, the result is **true**.

If several logical operators appear in the same expression, the highest priority is given to a **not** operator, the lowest priority is given to the **or** operator. In the general scheme of expression evaluation, logical operators are the last to be performed. Listed below are several examples and their evaluation.

Expression	Evaluation
not 2>3	**not false** → **true**
2>3 & 3>1	**false** & 3>1 → **false** & **true** → **false**
2>3 **or** 3>1	**false or** 3>1 → **false or true** → **true**
not 2>3 **and** 3>1	**not false and** 3>1 → **true and** 3>1
	→ **true and true** → **true**

2.6.2   The **if-then-else** Action

The selection of alternate courses of action based on the relationship between quantities is accomplished using the **if-then-else** feature.

> **if** condition **then**
>
> $\Bigl[\;$ S$_1$
>
> **else**
>
> $\Bigl[\;$ S$_2$

In its general form, the condition is a logical expression having a value of **true** or **false** and S$_1$ and S$_2$ signify *action sequences*. The action sequence S$_1$ may contain one or more actions while S$_2$ may contain zero or more actions. The first brace encloses the statements that form S$_1$, that is, the range of the **then**. The second brace encloses the statements that form S$_2$, that is, the range of the **else**.

Figure 2.12   Operation of the **if-then-else** statement.

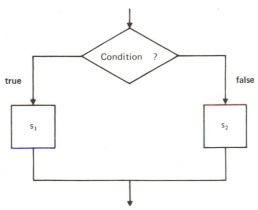

The operation of the **if-then-else** action is described in Figure 2.12. The first stage of the **if-then-else** statement is to evaluate the condition. If the value of the condition is **true**, the action sequence S$_1$ is performed. If the value of the condition is **false**, the action sequence S$_2$ is performed. After the completion of either S$_1$ or S$_2$, the action following the **if-then-else** is performed. It is important to note that the **if-then-else** does *not* perform any repetition by itself; only one of the action sequences, either S$_1$ or S$_2$, will be selected in one particular execution of the **if-then-else** action.

2.6.3   The **if-then** Action

There is a second form of the **if-then-else** which is used when the action sequence S$_2$ is null. This means that the **else** portion may be omitted, resulting in an **if-then** action. The general form of the **if-then** statement is given below,

if condition **then**

$$\left[\; S_1 \right.$$

where condition and S_1 are the same as for the **if-then-else** action. In the operation of an **if-then** statement, the condition is evaluated. If the result is **true**, action sequence S_1 is executed, then the statements following the **if-then**. However, if the result is **false**, execution continues immediately with the statements following the **if-then**.

2.7   Ups and Downs at the Indianapolis 500

The algorithms developed thus far in this chapter have been relatively straightforward. The formal topic of algorithm development is discussed in Chapter 4. In the meantime, it is useful to introduce several elementary techniques that are commonly used in solving problems. The next problem will introduce several new ideas. The problem makes use of the table of winning speeds at the Indianapolis 500 race, contained in Appendix N.

Example 2.5
   Develop an algorithm to list the winning speeds at the Indianapolis 500 race and to indicate the amount that each speed is up or down from the previous race.

The basic idea of this problem appears to be similar to that of the previous problem. Several data values are to be obtained and processed. The solution to Example 2.4 assumed that the data values to be processed were preceded by a count of how many follow. Often it is a nuisance to count such values. Another technique involves the addition of a specific data value, called an *end-of-file sentinel* or *flag,* to the end of the list of values. Usually this value is chosen so that it could not possibly be a valid entry earlier in the data list. This technique is used in solving Example 2.5.
   In order to decide whether a specific speed is up or down, it is necessary to retain the speed from the previous race. Thus, the algorithm must always retain the winning speeds for two consecutive races. This technique is also demonstrated in the solution presented in Figure 2.13.
   Several points should be noted about the algorithm. Only the previous winning speed needs to be retained; the year is not used subsequently. If the winning speed decreased from the previous race, the sign of the change is made positive before the value is recorded. This is done by replacing change by −change. In this expression, the subtraction operator is used as a *unary* operator, requiring only a single operand to the right. Normally, subtraction is a *binary* operator, requiring an operand on both sides. Finally, the sentinel values chosen are −1 and −1. The application of the algorithm to the data is suggested as an exercise at the end of the chapter (see Exercise 2.3).

Figure 2.13   Pseudo-code algorithm to list speeds and ratings for the Indianapolis 500 race.

```
* Given the winning speeds for the Indianapolis 500 race, list each winning speed
* and the amount by which it is up or down over the previous race.

* Variables used:
* year - the year of the current race
* newspeed - the winning speed for the current race
* oldspeed - the winning speed for the previous race
* change - the amount of change from the previous race

* Record titles for the output columns, then obtain and record the first winning speed.
put 'Year', 'Speed', 'Up or Down'
get year, oldspeed
put year, oldspeed

* Obtain the next year's race data and keep processing
* as long as the year and speed are positive.

get year, newspeed
while year > 0 and newspeed > 0 do
      change ← newspeed − oldspeed
      if change < 0 then
            change ← −change
            put year, newspeed, 'down', change
        else
            put year, newspeed, 'up', change
      * Remember the current speed and obtain the next.
      oldspeed ← newspeed
      get year, newspeed
stop
1919, 88.05, 1920, 88.62, 1921, 89.62, 1922, 94.48,
1923, 90.95, . . . , 1977, 161.33, −1, −1
```

2.8   The Money Changing Problem

The intention of pseudo code is to provide an easy language for describing an algorithm, free of the restrictive details necessary in a programming language. At the same time, it is useful to express algorithms in terms of the six features described in this chapter since this facilitates the eventual translation to a programming language.

Within the structure of these six features, it is quite legitimate to improvise and to define symbols or specific expressions to make the design of an algorithm easier. Listed below are several examples of such useful short-hand notation. The letters exp are used to indicate an *arithmetic expression.*

Abbreviation	*Meaning*
$\sqrt{\text{exp}}$ or sqrt(exp)	the square root of the expression
|exp| or abs(exp)	the absolute value of the expression
int(exp)	the integral portion of the value of the expression
$\lfloor$ exp $\rfloor$ or floor(exp)	the largest integer in magnitude less than the value of the expression
$\lceil$ exp $\rceil$ or ceiling(exp)	the smallest integer in magnitude greater than the value of the expression
quotient(exp1,exp2)	the integer quotient resulting when the first expression is divided by the second
rem(exp1,exp2)	the remainder resulting when the first expression is divided by the second

Several of these abbreviations are used in solving the following money changing problem.

Example 2.6

Given several amounts of money, each less than one dollar, determine the minimum number of coins (quarters, dimes, nickels, and pennies) that are neccessary to make up each amount.

The amounts of money to be processed are assumed to be supplied in a data list. Since no information is given about how many amounts there will be, it is again appropriate to use an end-of-file sentinel. A value greater than 100 could be used since the problem definition indicates that such a value should not be processed. Next, consider the problem of determining the number of coins needed. The first step is to calculate the necessary number of quarters. One possibility is to keep adding 25 to a sum until the sum is greater than the amount. The number of 25's added, less one, would be the number of quarters needed. A more elegant approach is to determine the quotient when the amount is divided by 25. The amount leftover is simply the remainder of this division. This same technique, applied successively to the remaining amounts, can be used to calculate the number of dimes, nickels, and pennies. This approach is used in the solution to this problem presented in Figure 2.14. Notice that the variable left is used repeatedly to contain the amount left over after each computation. Again, the application of this algorithm is left as an exercise (see Exercise 2.4).

2.9   The Structure of Algorithms

All algorithms and programming languages must have some method, either implicit or explicit, of controlling the order in which the statements are to be executed. The term used to describe this feature is *control structures*.

In pseudo code, there are really only three control structures, sequence, **while-do**, and **if-then-else**. The diagrams for these control structures are repeated in Figure 2.15.

Figure 2.14   Pseudo-code algorithm for the money changing problem.

```
* Determine the minimum number of coins needed
* to give change for a variable number of amounts.

* Variables used:
* amount - the given amount
* quarters - the number of quarters required
* dimes - the number of dimes required
* nickels - the number of nickels required
* pennies - the number of pennies required
* total - the total number of coins required
* left - the amount left at each stage

* Record titles for the output.
put 'Amount Quarters Dimes Nickels Pennies Total'

* Obtain the first amount, then keep processing
* as long as an amount < 100 is obtained.
get amount
while amount < 100 do
    ┌  quarters ← quotient(amount,25)
    │  left ← rem(amount,25)
    │  dimes ← quotient(left,10)
    │  left ← rem(left,10)
    │  nickels ← quotient(left,5)
    │  pennies ← rem(left,5)
    │  total ← quarters + dimes + nickels + pennies
    │  put amount, quarters, dimes, nickels, pennies, total
    └  get amount
stop
77, 89, 13, 67, 99, 100
```

As implied by the diagram, a sequence structure is entered from the top and left from the bottom. The language features **get**, **put**, assignment, and **stop** obviously have this structure. The **while-do** and **if-then-else** control structures are somewhat more complicated as they control repetition and selection, respectively. These three control structures are all that are needed to describe algorithms.

As has been seen, the **while-do** and **if-then-else** structures provide much power in describing algorithms. Since these structures, taken as a whole, have only one entrance and one exit, they may also be regarded as sequences. This is illustrated in Figure 2.16.

Figure 2.15   Diagrams for the three control structures.

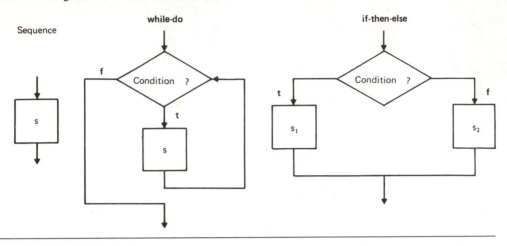

Figure 2.16   The **while-do** and **if-then-else** as sequence structures.

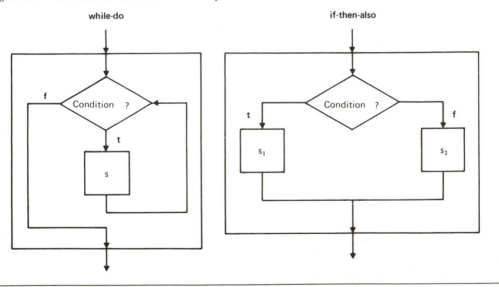

This observation makes it clear that the **while-do** and **if-then-else** may be placed anywhere that a sequence is legal. This means that it is possible to *nest* these structures to any level. That is, a **while-do** may appear in the sequence block of another **while-do**, or in the **then** and/or the **else** sequence block of an **if-then-else**. Examples of an **if-then-else** nested within a **while-do** were already seen in the examples earlier in the chapter.

Looking at this sequence concept from the point of the entire algorithm, an algorithm can be considered as just a series of sequence blocks with one starting point and one ending point. Or, taking the concept even further, an algorithm can be considered to be just one large block. This situation is illustrated in the diagrams or *flowcharts* of Figure 2.17. This point can be made even more strongly by drawing a flowchart of the structure of the algorithm of Figure 2.13 as shown in Figure 2.18.

Figure 2.17   Algorithms as sequence blocks.

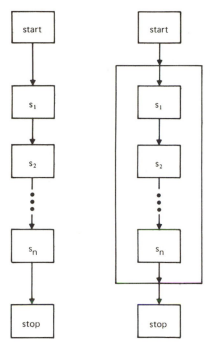

The restriction that control structures have but one entrance and one exit permits all algorithms to be regarded as simple sequences. This observation suggests a possible approach to the development of algorithms. One begins with a simple description of the sequence of major tasks to be performed by the algorithm. At each stage of the development, such sequences may be broken into a series of subsequences, until each sequence contains a basic pseudo-code structure. This method of solving problems will be demonstrated in Chapter 4.

2.10   Summary

This chapter has introduced pseudo code as a means of describing mathematical algorithms. Even though the number of pseudo-code actions introduced so far is quite small, it is sufficient to allow algorithms of great complexity to be expressed. An important consideration in the design of the pseudo-code actions was the ability to translate them easily into a computer program. That this objective was achieved will be demonstrated in Chapter 3.

Figure 2.18 The structure of the Indianapolis 500 algorithm of Figure 2.13.

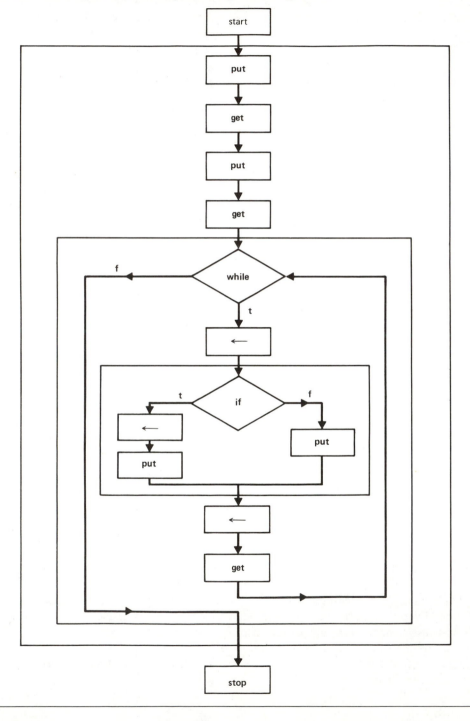

2.11   Exercises

2.1 Develop an algorithm to produce a table of Celcius and the equivalent Fahrenheit temperatures for 0°C, 1°C, 2°C, . . . , 100°C.

2.2 Modify the algorithm for Example 2.4 to be more explicit about temperatures that are uncomfortable, that is, to rate the temperatures less than the lower limit as too cool and those greater than the upper limit as too warm.

2.3 Manually apply the algorithm of Figure 2.13 for the first 10 years of the Indianapolis 500 race. Your solution should be similar to the table in Figure 2.10 which illustrated the application of the algorithm of Figure 2.9. Use a separate sheet of paper for the output.

2.4 Manually apply the algorithm of Figure 2.14 for the data values given. Your solution should be similar to the table in Figure 2.10 which illustrated the application of the algorithm of Figure 2.9. Use a separate sheet of paper for the output.

2.5 Develop a pseudo-code algorithm to determine the minimum number of bills (ones, twos, fives, tens, or twenties) to give exact change for a given amount of money. Assume that the amount is an integral number of dollars.

2.6 a) Develop a pseudo-code algorithm to convert any given number of hours into an equivalent grouping of weeks, days, and hours. In the grouping, the number of days should be ≤6 and the number of hours should be ≤23.

   b) Develop a similar pseudo-code algorithm to convert any given number of seconds into an equivalent grouping of days, hours, minutes, and seconds. In this grouping, the number of hours should be ≤23, the number of minutes should be ≤59, and the number of seconds should be ≤59.

2.7 Modify the algorithm of Figure 2.14 to produce a table of the minimum number of coins necessary to give exact change for each amount from 1¢ to 99¢. The table should list the required number of pennies, nickels, dimes, quarters, and total number of coins for each amount.

2.8 Modify the algorithm of Figure 2.13 to also record the year of the race that showed the most improvement over the previous race.

2.9 The following sequence of numbers, called the Fibonacci sequence,

   1, 1, 2, 3, 5, 8, 13, 21, · · ·

   has the property that each term after the first two is the sum of the two preceding terms. Develop a pseudo-code algorithm to generate the first 50 terms of this sequence.

2.10 Manually apply the following pseudo-code algorithm.

```
whatisit ← 0
i ← 1
while i ≤ 15 do
    ┌ whatisit ← whatisit + i
    └ i ← i + 2
put 'The final answer is', whatisit
stop
```

What is the recorded output? What would the output be if the 15 were changed to 100? What is the algorithm designed to do?

2.11 Develop a pseudo-code algorithm to arrange a set of 3 numbers in ascending order. Design your algorithm to handle several sets of input data.

2.12 Assume that you are given a set of positive data values that supposedly have been arranged in ascending order. Develop and test a pseudo-code algorithm which will check the ordering of these data values and record an appropriate message about the results. Use a suitable technique to terminate your algorithm after all values have been tested. Is it possible to also identify any values that are out of order? Explain your answer.

2.13 It is often necessary to be able to determine the maximum and minimum values of an unordered set of data. Develop a pseudo-code algorithm that will perform this operation.

2.14 The linear equations

$$ax+by = c$$

$$dx+ey = f$$

have the solution $x = (ce-fb)/(ae-bd)$ and $y = -(af-dc)/(ae-bd)$ provided that the equations are not linearly dependent (that is, $ae \neq bd$). Develop a pseudo-code algorithm which will solve the above equations. If a solution does not exist, the algorithm should record an appropriate message. Test your algorithm on the following coefficients:

a) $a = 5, b = 7, c = 31, d = 1, e = 2, f = 9$
b) $a = 3, b = 6, c = 42, d = 2, e = 4, f = 28$

2.15 It has been conjectured that for any positive integer n, n^2+3n+5 is never divisible by 121. Develop a pseudo-code algorithm which will test this conjecture for the integers from 1 to 10,000. Your algorithm should record an appropriate message as to whether the conjecture is true or false over the range of numbers.

2.16 A geometric progression is defined to consist of a sequence of terms in which each term is derived from the previous term by the multiplication of the same constant factor. The following is a geometric progression.

$$a, ar, ar^2, ar^3, \cdots$$

Develop a pseudo-code algorithm which will compute and record the first n terms of the above progression. Test your algorithm for $a = 3, r = 2$ and $n = 1,2,5$.

2.17 The factorial of a number n, written as $n!$, is given by the following scheme:

$$0! = 1$$

$$1! = 1$$

$$2! = 2 \times 1$$

$$3! = 3 \times 2 \times 1$$

$$\vdots$$

$$n! = n \times (n-1) \times (n-2) \times (n-3) \times \cdots \times 3 \times 2 \times 1$$

Develop a pseudo-code algorithm that will, for a given number n, compute its factorial. Test your algorithm on 4! and 7!.

2.18 Develop a pseudo-code algorithm to tabulate the function:

$$\frac{1}{x!}$$

for $x = 0,1,2, \cdots ,10$. Note that each successive value of the function can be obtained from the previous value using a single multiplication, that is,

$$\frac{1}{x!} = \frac{1}{(x-1)!} \times \frac{1}{x}.$$

Incorporate this idea into the algorithm.

2.19 Suppose that a set of three numbers is to represent the lengths of three line segments. Develop a pseudo-code algorithm that will determine if such a set of numbers:

- does not represent the sides of a triangle
- represents the sides of a triangle which is neither an isosceles nor equilateral triangle
- represents the sides of an isosceles triangle
- represents the sides of an equilateral triangle.

3
Algorithms and
WATFIV-S

3.1 Introduction

Pseudo code has been introduced as a means of expressing algorithms. Though it is suited to developing algorithms and applying them manually, pseudo code is not directly understood by a computer.

Before a computer may apply a procedure, the procedure must be described in a manner which the computer can understand. Thus, a pseudo-code algorithm must be translated into a programming language. Following this translation, the statements in this language must be prepared in machine-readable form for processing by a computer. Once in machine-readable form, the program can be submitted to the computer for processing.

There are many different programming languages. For mathematical and scientific applications, the most popular language continues to be FORTRAN IV. Developed initially in the mid-1950's, FORTRAN, an acronym for FORmula TRANslation, has undergone many evolutionary changes. Though international standards have been established, many dialects of FORTRAN are in common use. WATFIV-S or structured WATFIV is such a dialect particularly suited to learning about the language and to expressing algorithms clearly and elegantly.

3.2 Translation From Pseudo Code to WATFIV-S

Several comments have been made concerning the ease with which pseudo code can be translated to a computer programming language. In most cases, there is a direct correspondence between each pseudo-code construct and equivalent statements in a programming language. The intent of this chapter is to introduce the essential details of this correspondence with adequate but not overly complicated information about rules and regulations. Additional reference material is provided in the appendices for the interested reader.

Perhaps the best way to illustrate the translation to WATFIV-S is to look at an example. Consider one of the algorithms discussed in Chapter 2.

Example 3.1

Translate the pseudo code for Example 2.4 into WATFIV-S. Recall that this algorithm was designed to rate a list of Celcius temperature readings according to whether each was comfortable or uncomfortable.

The required program is shown in Figure 3.1. A number of characteristics are immediately obvious. Several of the lines begin with a dollar sign. These lines are not really part of the WATFIV-S language proper. Such lines are called *control statements* or *control cards* and are a necessary part of almost all computer systems. The $JOB WATFIV statement identifies the start of a WATFIV-S program or *job* while the $ENTRY line signals the end of the program and the start of the data list. The number and type of control cards needed to have the computer process a program will vary from one installation to another. It is therefore a good idea to determine the intricacies for your particular computer system. A thorough description of the control cards available for use with WATFIV-S is given in Appendix E.

Lines beginning with the letter "c" are comment lines and have no affect on the flow of the program. They are included to explain the program logic for the benefit of anyone reading the program. Normally, all WATFIV-S statements use only capital letters; lower-case letters have been used in these comments simply to improve the readability of the remaining statements. As a matter of style, comments, also called *program documentation,* should include:

- an initial statement of the problem to be solved by the program,
- a list of the major variables and their purpose in the program,
- a brief running commentary on each major section of the program.

These three aspects of documentation are demonstrated in the sample program.

The positioning of commands on each line is very important. In general, WATFIV-S statements are placed in columns 7 through 72 of each line. Within these columns, blanks may be used liberally to improve readability and do not normally affect the statements. In structured WATFIV, columns 1-6 are usually left blank, though their use is common in standard FORTRAN and standard WATFIV. The data for a program may be placed anywhere from column 1 through 80, inclusive.

Upon closer inspection, the meaning of some of the WATFIV-S statements is immediately obvious. The assignment statement, similar in format to the pseudo-code versions, uses the = character in place of the ← symbol as the assignment operator. The actions **get** and **put** are represented by READ and PRINT statements, respectively. Though the layout is obviously different, the **while-do** and **if-then-else** actions can also be recognized easily. Finally, there are a number of statements that are clearly additions to the pseudo-code actions.

```
$JOB    WATFIV
C****************************************************************
C Figure 3.1 -- Given limits for what temperatures are comfort-
C               able, produce a comfort rating for several
C               temperatures.
C****************************************************************
C FLO    - low comfortable temperature (Fahrenheit)
C CLO    - low comfortable temperature (Celcius)
C FHI    - high comfortable temperature (Fahrenheit)
C CHI    - high comfortable temperature (Celcius)
C NUM    - number of temperature readings to process
C COUNT  - count of readings
C C      - given temperature reading (Celcius)
C****************************************************************
        INTEGER NUM, COUNT
        REAL FLO, CLO, FHI, CHI, C
C Obtain the Fahrenheit comfort limits and convert to Celcius.
        READ, FLO, FHI
        CLO = (FLO - 32.0)*5.0/9.0
        CHI = (FHI - 32.0)*5.0/9.0
        PRINT, 'THE LOW COMFORTABLE LIMIT IS', FLO, 'F', CLO, 'C'
        PRINT, 'THE HIGH COMFORTABLE LIMIT IS', FHI, 'F', CHI, 'C'
        PRINT, ' '
C Obtain the number of readings to evaluate.
C Process each reading by recording an appropriate message.
        READ, NUM
        PRINT, 'THE NUMBER OF TEMPERATURES TO PROCESS IS', NUM
        PRINT, ' '
        COUNT = 1
        WHILE(COUNT .LE. NUM) DO
            READ, C
            IF(C .GE. CLO .AND. C .LE. CHI) THEN DO
                    PRINT, C, 'IS COMFORTABLE'
                ELSE DO
                    PRINT, C, 'IS UNCOMFORTABLE'
            END IF
            COUNT = COUNT + 1
        END WHILE
        STOP
        END
$ENTRY
68.0, 86.0
10
22.0
31.0
17.0
20.0
22.0
30.0
34.0
39.0
25.0
12.0
```

Converting an algorithm to a program requires careful attention to detail. There are specific rules, which must be strictly adhered to, which establish the correct form of statements in a language (the *syntax* of the language). The basic syntax rules for WATFIV-S will be summarized in succeeding sections of this chapter.

3.3   Processing a WATFIV-S **Program**

The previous section briefly introduced the topic of translation of a pseudo-code algorithm into WATFIV-S. Once the translation is complete, the resulting program must be prepared in machine-readable form.

Historically, the most common medium has been the *punched card.* A punched card consists of 80 columns, each capable of representing a single character by a series of rectangular holes. The process of coding a character by punching the necessary holes is accomplished by a primarily mechanical device called a *keypunch.* Normally, each line of the program and each line of data is keypunched on a separate card.

Programs can also be prepared for computer processing using a more modern *text-preparation* or *text-editing* system. In such a system, programs are entered at special typewriters or cathode-ray tube devices called *computer terminals.*

Once a program is in machine-readable form, it is ready for computer processing. Though programming languages such as WATFIV-S are relatively natural and easy for humans to use, these languages are not the language of the computer. The computer's language, called *machine language,* is a purely numeric, binary-based language. In order to process programs written in WATFIV-S, a special computer program called a *compiler* is used to translate the program into the machine's language. Once the program has been translated, the resulting translation is submitted to the computer for processing. Thus, a program goes through two phases, a translation or *compilation phase* and an *execution phase.*

A copy of the computer output listing produced for the program in Figure 3.1 is given as Figure 3.2.[1] The lines from $JOB WATFIV through $ENTRY are printed by the compiler as it translates each line. It assigns the numbers at the left to use as a reference in case an error occurs. Errors can occur during either of the two phases of processing. If an error occurs during the translation, an appropriate message is printed under the offending line and the program is not allowed to execute. Errors, such as an attempt to divide by zero, can occur during the execution phase. Such errors are also indicated by an error message, referring to the offending line if possible, and execution is immediately terminated. A complete list of WATFIV-S error messages is provided for reference in Appendix Q.

The output lines following the $ENTRY and before STATEMENTS EXECUTED= are produced by the program itself, during the execution phase. Notice that the output from each PRINT statement appears on a separate line and that the numeric values appear in a different notation than before. These features will be explained later in the chapter.

The last few lines of output are printed by the compiler. Though not all of these lines are relevant at this stage, they should, nevertheless, not be ignored. The first line states that 61 statements were executed by the program. The second line and its continuation specifies the amount of storage space, in units called bytes, that were used by the program. The third line (and its continuation) gives diagnostic messages, namely, the number of errors, warnings, and extensions detected. Errors represent invalid conditions that prohibit the execution of the program. Warning messages are just that, a

---

[1]Due to the width of a computer printer page, which exceeds the margins of this book, the last portion of some long lines has been placed on the line following.

Figure 3.2   Computer output list from the program of Figure 3.1.

```
        $JOB    WATFIV  *************
        C************************************************************

        C Figure 3.1 -- Given limits for what temperatures are comfort-
        C               able, produce a comfort rating for several
        C               temperatures.

        C************************************************************

        C FLO     - low comfortable temperature (Fahrenheit)
        C CLO     - low comfortable temperature (Celcius)
        C FHI     - high comfortable temperature (Fahrenheit)
        C CHI     - high comfortable temperature (Celcius)
        C NUM     - number of temperature readings to process
        C COUNT   - count of readings
        C C       - given temperature reading (Celcius)

        C************************************************************
   1            INTEGER NUM, COUNT
   2            REAL FLO, CLO, FHI, CHI, C

        C Obtain the Fahrenheit comfort limits and convert to Celcius.

   3            READ, FLO, FHI
   4            CLO = (FLO - 32.0)*5.0/9.0
   5            CHI = (FHI - 32.0)*5.0/9.0
   6            PRINT, 'THE LOW COMFORTABLE LIMIT IS', FLO, 'F', CLO, 'C'
   7            PRINT, 'THE HIGH COMFORTABLE LIMIT IS', FHI, 'F', CHI, 'C'
   8            PRINT, ' '

        C Obtain the number of readings to evaluate.
        C Process each reading by recording an appropriate message.

   9            READ, NUM
  10            PRINT, 'THE NUMBER OF TEMPERATURES TO PROCESS IS', NUM
  11            PRINT, ' '
  12            COUNT = 1
  13            WHILE(COUNT .LE. NUM) DO
  14               READ, C
  15               IF(C .GE. CLO .AND. C .LE. CHI) THEN DO
  16                    PRINT, C, 'IS COMFORTABLE'
  17                  ELSE DO
  18                    PRINT, C, 'IS UNCOMFORTABLE'
  19               END IF
  20               COUNT = COUNT + 1
  21            END WHILE

  22            STOP
  23            END
        $ENTRY
THE LOW COMFORTABLE LIMIT IS     0.6800000E 02 F    0.2000000E 02 C
THE HIGH COMFORTABLE LIMIT IS    0.8600000E 02 F    0.3000000E 02 C

THE NUMBER OF TEMPERATURES TO PROCESS IS         10

    0.2200000E 02 IS COMFORTABLE
    0.3100000E 02 IS UNCOMFORTABLE
    0.1700000E 02 IS UNCOMFORTABLE
    0.2000000E 02 IS COMFORTABLE
    0.2200000E 02 IS COMFORTABLE
    0.3000000E 02 IS COMFORTABLE
    0.3400000E 02 IS UNCOMFORTABLE
    0.3900000E 02 IS UNCOMFORTABLE
    0.2500000E 02 IS COMFORTABLE
    0.1200000E 02 IS UNCOMFORTABLE

STATEMENTS EXECUTED=       61
CORE USAGE       OBJECT CODE=    1136 BYTES,ARRAY AREA=        0 BYTES, . . .
                             . . . TOTAL AREA AVAILABLE=   51200  BYTES
DIAGNOSTICS       NUMBER OF ERRORS=      0, NUMBER OF WARNINGS=       0,
                             . . . NUMBER OF EXTENSIONS=          2
COMPILE TIME=      0.21 SEC,EXECUTION TIME=      0.06 SEC, . . .
         . . . 20.53.29    SATURDAY    24 JUN 78    WATFIV - JUN 1977 V1L6
```

warning that something unusual was detected but that processing could still continue. Finally, the number of WATFIV-S extensions to the FORTRAN language is recorded, but messages for these are not printed unless requested (see Appendix E). The final line of output specifies timing considerations. This particular program required 0.21 seconds to compile, required 0.06 seconds to execute, was processed at 20.53.29 hours on Saturday, June 24, 1978, and was processed by the WATFIV compiler of June, 1977 which is Version 1, Level 6 of the compiler.

3.4 Expressing Constants and Variables

In pseudo-code descriptions of algorithms, constants and variables were used to specify and remember numeric values, respectively. In WATFIV-S, the corresponding quantities are also called constants and variables, but must be expressed somewhat more formally since computers are capable of storing information in several different ways. The most useful are representations of integer and decimal numbers.

In WATFIV-S, the terms INTEGER and REAL are used, thus giving integer and decimal constants as well as integer and decimal variables. Constants which include a decimal point are of type REAL. Such constants may also be written in exponent notation to save writing many zeros. The general form of a REAL constant in exponent notation is:

```
±xxxxx.xxxxxE±yy
└─────────┘└───┘
 mantissa  exponent
```

where the x's and y's are digits (0-9) and the letter "E" is read "times 10 to the power". Thus, for example, 12.34 could be written as 12.34E 00 or 12.34E0 or 0.1234E 02 or .1234E2 or 1234.0E-02. The absence of a decimal point makes a constant an INTEGER. The table below illustrates several valid constants of each type.

Valid INTEGER *Constants*	*Valid* REAL *Constants*
32	32.
-5	-5.0
0	0.
-1234	+3.14159
2147483647[a]	0.5397605E-78[b]
-2147483648[c]	0.7237005E 76[d]

[a] the largest positive INTEGER
[b] the smallest positive REAL constant
[c] the largest negative INTEGER constant
[d] the largest REAL constant

Notice that the range and number of significant digits differ between INTEGER and REAL constants. Because of storage considerations, there is a limit to the range and accuracy in the values that are represented in a computer. The limits illustrated above are those for the IBM 360/370 series of computers. These machines are capable of achieving a maximum accuracy of 10 significant digits with integer arithmetic and 7 significant digits with real arithmetic. Further insight into the question of accuracy is given in Chapters 6, 7, and 8 as well as in Appendix E.

Variable names in WATFIV-S must be chosen in accordance with the following rules. Variable names must:

1) be from 1 to 6 characters long
2) begin with a letter of the alphabet
3) consist of characters chosen from: letters A-Z, digits 0-9

Listed below are several examples of valid and invalid variables.

Valid Variables	Invalid Variables
C	2C
CLO	456
CELCIS	CELCIUS
DOLLAR	DOLLAR-SIGN
R2D2	3PEEOH

As in pseudo code, variables are undefined until thay have been assigned a value, either via an assignment operation or a READ statement. WATFIV-S will detect an undefined variable and will issue an error message before terminating the execution of the program.

Before a variable of either type can be used in a program, good practice dictates that its type be declared in a declaration statement as illustrated below.

```
INTEGER variable list
REAL variable list
```

Each declaration statement begins with the variable type (INTEGER or REAL) and is followed by a list of all names that are to be of that type. Commas are used to separate the names in the variable list. Normally, all such declarations are grouped at the beginning of the program as demonstrated in the sample program. The statements:

```
INTEGER NUM, COUNT
REAL FLO, CLO, FHI, CHI, C
```

define NUM and COUNT to be variables of type INTEGER and FLO, CLO, FHI, CHI, and C to be REAL variables.

When assigning values to a variable or when using both constants and variables in arithmetic expressions, the numbers should be expressed consistently. Thus, REAL constants should always include a decimal point whereas INTEGER constants should not. In the sample program, the conversion from Fahrenheit to Celcius involves only REAL variables and therefore the constants 32.0, 5.0, and 9.0 have been written with decimal points. Conversely, statements involving the INTEGER variable COUNT use constants without a decimal.

3.5   Arithmetic Expressions and Assignment Statements

The use of arithmetic expressions in programming languages is very natural and parallels their use in pseudo code. In WATFIV-S, the symbols used for the various arithmetic operations are summarized in the following table:

Symbol	Operation
**	exponentiation
*	multiplication
/	division
+	addition
–	subtraction

In addition, parentheses may be used to group subexpressions. A valid arithmetic expression may consist of a single constant, a single variable, or a combination of constants and/or variables separated by any of the five arithmetic operators.

Listed below are several examples of valid arithmetic expressions taken from the program in Figure 3.1.

```
(FLO - 32.0)*5.0/9.0
COUNT + 1
COUNT
1
```

Arithmetic expressions in WATFIV-S are evaluated much like pseudo-code arithmetic expressions, according to the following scheme.

1) The expression is scanned from left to right.
2) Whenever an operand (constant or variable) has an operator on both sides, a priority scheme is applied. Exponentiation has the highest priority, multiplication and division have the next priority, and addition and subtraction have the same, lowest priority.
3) Parentheses may be used to remove ambiguity or to change the normal pattern of evaluation. Expressions within parentheses are evaluated as they occur in the scanning process.
4) Consecutive exponentiation operations are performed from *right* to *left*.
5) Consecutive multiplication and/or division operations are performed from *left* to *right*.
6) Consecutive addition and/or subtraction operations are performed from *left* to *right*.

The following examples illustrate the application of the above rules to evaluating several arithmetic expressions.

Expression	*Evaluation*
2 + 3*4	2 + 12 → 14
2 + 3**3/4	2 + 27/4 → 2 + 6 → 8
1.1 + 2.2 - 3.3	3.3 - 3.3 → 0.0
1 + 2 - 3	3 - 3 → 0
(4.1 + 5.2)*3.0	9.3*3.0 → 27.9
5*6*7	30*7 → 210
2**3**2	2**9 → 512

Notice that arithmetic involving REAL values always produces a REAL result and that arithmetic involving INTEGER constants always results in an integer, even if a fractional value must be dropped or *truncated,* as may occur with division. While WATFIV-S does allow a mixture of INTEGER and REAL values, such instances should usually be avoided. The rules for such expressions are described under "Arithmetic Expressions" in Appendix F.

In WATFIV-S, the assignment operator, =, is used in place of the ← used in pseudo code to imply that the value of the arithmetic expression to the right is to be assigned to the variable on the left. The following four examples are taken from the sample program in Figure 3.1.

```
CLO = (FLO - 32.0)*5.0/9.0
CHI = (FHI - 32.0)*5.0/9.0
COUNT = 1
COUNT = COUNT + 1
```

3.6   Expressing the get Action

In WATFIV-S, the simplest form of the **get** action is:

```
READ, input list
```

The word READ is followed by the list of variables requiring values. The data values are placed after the $ENTRY control card.

In pseudo code, the data was listed after the stop action, on one line, if possible. As each **get** statement was performed, the next numbers on the list were obtained and assigned to the variables in the list following the word **get**. While a similar operation takes place in WATFIV-S, the numeric values are placed on succesive punched cards or lines following the $ENTRY. Care must be used in determining how many values must be placed on each card.

Each READ statement causes the next punched card to be physically read by the card reader. Thus, the data for an individual READ statement must always begin on a new card. When a card is read, it is scanned from left to right, looking for constants to assign to the variables in the input list. As each constant is found, it is assigned to the corresponding variable. The reading and scanning of cards continues until a value has been found for each variable.

Naturally, the type of each constant in the data must correspond to the type of the variable in the list. Failure to do so will result in an error and termination of the program. Similarly, if an insufficient number of values are given for a program, an error message is issued and the program is halted. If several values are placed on the same data card, they must be separated by a single comma, or at least one blank, or a single comma and one or more blanks.

Listed below is a summary of the operation of the READ statements in the sample program.

Next READ *Statement*	*Next Data Card*	*Resulting Assignments*
READ, FLO, FHI	68.0, 86.0	68.0 → FLO
		86.0 → FHI
READ, NUM	10	10 → NUM
READ, C	22.0	22.0 → C
READ, C	31.0	31.0 → C
⋮	⋮	⋮
READ, C	12.0	12.0 → C

Note that the scanning always begins with the next line or card. Furthermore, the values given correspond in type to the variable in the list.

3.7   Expressing the put Action

In WATFIV-S, the simplest form of the **put** action is:

```
PRINT, output list
```

Messages as well as variable names may be included in the output list as illustrated in Figure 3.1. As in pseudo code, messages must include a single quote on either side; and successive messages and variables in the list are separated by commas.

Execution of a PRINT statement causes the messages and the values of each variable to be displayed on the printer. Each PRINT statement always begins a new line of output. WATFIV-S uses a standard number of output columns and accuracy to express the value of each variable. By default, REAL values are normally expressed in exponent notation. A simple facility to circumvent this standard will be discussed later in this chapter. Though the facility exists for the programmer to control the output layout, that aspect of WATFIV-S is beyond the scope of this introduction. A more complete discussion of this topic is given in Appendix H.

3.8   Expressing Conditions

Conditions form an integral part of the **if-then-else** and **while-do** actions. In WATFIV-S, all conditions are placed in parentheses. To compare two numeric quantities, the general form of a condition is:

```
( arithmetic-expression   operator   arithmetic-expression )
```

Naturally, the arithmetic expressions used may be a single variable or constant as well as combinations of variables and constants. The `operators`, called *relational operators,* must be chosen from the list of six given below. Notice that each pseudo-code symbol is represented by a two-letter code surrounded by periods.

Pseudo-Code Symbol	WATFIV-S *Relational Operator*
=	.EQ.
≠	.NE.
>	.GT.
≥	.GE.
<	.LT.
≤	.LE.

It is also possible to express more complex conditions using *logical operators.* WATFIV-S provides the same three logical operators as pseudo code, but uses a different notation to express them.

Pseudo-Code Symbol	WATFIV-S *Logical Operator*
not	.NOT.
and	.AND.
or	.OR.

The following conditions were demonstrated in the sample program of Figure 3.1.

```
(COUNT .LE. NUM)
(C .GE. CLO .AND. C .LE. CHI)
```

In the general scheme of expression evaluation, relational operators have a priority below that of the arithmetic operators while the logical operators have a lower priority still, in the order listed above. This priority scheme is illustrated below for several simple expressions.

Expression	*Evaluation*
.NOT. 2 .GT. 3	.NOT. **false**
	→ **true**
2.0.GT.3.0 .AND. 3.LT.4	**false** .AND. 3.LT.4
	→ **false** .AND. **true**
	→ **false**
2.0.GT.3.0 .OR. 3.LT.4	**false** .OR. 3.LT.4
	→ **false** .OR. **true**
	→ **true**
.NOT. 2.GT.3 .AND. 3.LT.4	.NOT. **false** .AND. 3.LT.4
	→ **true** .AND. 3.LT.4
	→ **true** .AND. **true**
	→ **true**

3.9 The **while-do** Action

The expression of the **while-do** action in WATFIV-S is illustrated below:

```
WHILE condition DO
   ⋮ statements in the range of the while
END WHILE
```

As in pseudo code, the condition is surrounded by the words WHILE and DO. However, the end of the action sequence is indicated by the statement END WHILE in WATFIV-S rather than with a brace as in pseudo code. Statements within this range are usually indented, say 3 spaces, as a matter of style. This spacing is important for readability since the consistent indentation clearly indicates to the reader which statements are to be repeated.

The WHILE-DO in the sample program was designed to repeat as long as the counter, COUNT, is less than or equal to the number of data entries to process, NUM. This was written as:

```
WHILE(COUNT .LE. NUM) DO
```

The statements between this line and the END WHILE statement are considered to be in the range of the WHILE-DO.

3.10 The **if-then-else** Action

The WATFIV-S version of the **if-then-else** appears much like the pseudo-code construct with the inclusion of the word DO following the words THEN and ELSE. In addition, the statement END IF must be placed after the sequence of statements in the ELSE.

```
IF condition THEN DO
     : statements in the range of the then
  ELSE DO
     : statements in the range of the else
END IF
```

For emphasis and readability, the two ranges are indented to indicate their inclusion as part of the **then** or the **else**. Naturally, the **else** sequence may be omitted but the END IF statement must still be supplied.

In a similar fashion to the pseudo code, the **if-then-else** construct in the sample program was the following, used to select which of the two messages is to be printed:

```
IF(C .GE. CLO .AND. C .LE. CHI) THEN DO
     PRINT, C, 'IS COMFORTABLE'
  ELSE DO
     PRINT, C, 'IS UNCOMFORTABLE'
END IF
```

3.11   The STOP and END Statements

The termination of a pseudo-code algorithm was indicated by the **stop** action. A WATFIV-S program must indicate where the two phases, compilation and execution, terminate. The compilation phase is terminated by the END statement. Naturally, the END statement must always be the last WATFIV-S statement in the program. The completion of execution is indicated by the STOP statement. The STOP statement thus corresponds in function to the pseudo-code **stop** statement.

3.12   Additional Examples of Translation

To further illustrate the process of translation to WATFIV-S, programs for the last two examples in Chapter 2 will also be presented.

3.12.1   Ups and Downs at the Indianapolis 500

The topic of Example 2.5 was a simple analysis of the winning speeds at the Indianapolis 500 race. A program to correspond to the algorithm in Figure 2.12 is presented in Figure 3.3. Variable YEAR was chosen to be INTEGER while NSPEED, OSPEED, and CHANGE are defined to be REAL. Notice the abbreviation to six letters. Care must also be exercised to ensure that the titles appear directly over the intended columns of numbers. Careful counting is required for this purpose. The remaining statements of the program are primarily direct translations of the pseudo code.

The output produced by this program is presented in Figure 3.4. Notice again that the REAL values are printed in exponential notation. Since this notation frequently clouds the significance of the output, REAL values can be printed in the standard decimal form by using a C$OPTIONS DECIMAL control card which is inserted immediately after the $JOB card. The majority of subsequent programs demonstrate its placement. The revised output appears in Figure 3.5.

```
$JOB    WATFIV
C****************************************************************
C Figure 3.3 -- Given the winning speeds for the Indianapolis 500
C               race, list each winning speed and the amount by
C               which it is up or down over the previous race.
C****************************************************************
C YEAR   - the year of the current race
C NSPEED - the winning speed for the current race
C OSPEED - the winning speed for the previous race
C CHANGE - the amount of change from the previous race
C****************************************************************
      INTEGER YEAR
      REAL NSPEED, OSPEED, CHANGE
C Record titles for the output columns,
C then obtain and record the first winning speed.
      PRINT, '        YEAR           SPEED         UP OR DOWN'
      PRINT, ' '
      READ, YEAR, OSPEED
      PRINT, YEAR, OSPEED
C Obtain the next year's race data and keep processing
C as long as the year and speed are positive.
      READ, YEAR, NSPEED
      WHILE(YEAR .GT. 0 .AND. NSPEED .GT. 0.0) DO
         CHANGE = NSPEED - OSPEED
         IF(CHANGE .LT. 0.0) THEN DO
              CHANGE = - CHANGE
              PRINT, YEAR, NSPEED, 'DOWN', CHANGE
           ELSE DO
              PRINT, YEAR, NSPEED, 'UP  ', CHANGE
         END IF
C        Remember the current speed and obtain the next.
         OSPEED = NSPEED
         READ, YEAR, NSPEED
      END WHILE
      STOP
      END
$ENTRY
1919    88.05
1920    88.62
1921    89.62
1922    94.48
  :       :
1977   161.33
  -1    -1.00
```

Figure 3.4   Output from the Indianapolis 500 program of Figure 3.3 using the default exponential form.

YEAR	SPEED		UP OR DOWN
1919	0.8805000E 02		
1920	0.8862000E 02	UP	0.5699921E 00
1921	0.8962000E 02	UP	0.1000000E 01
1922	0.9448000E 02	UP	0.4860001E 01
1923	0.9095000E 02	DOWN	0.3529999E 01
1924	0.9823000E 02	UP	0.7279999E 01
⋮	⋮	⋮	⋮
1972	0.1629600E 03	UP	0.5220001E 01
1973	0.1590400E 03	DOWN	0.3920013E 01
1974	0.1585900E 03	DOWN	0.4499969E 00
1975	0.1492100E 03	DOWN	0.9379990E 01
1976	0.1487300E 03	DOWN	0.4800110E 00
1977	0.1613300E 03	UP	0.1260001E 02

Figure 3.5   Output from the Indianapolis 500 program of Figure 3.3 using the optional decimal form.

YEAR	SPEED		UP OR DOWN
1919	88.05000000		
1920	88.61999000	UP	0.56999200
1921	89.61999000	UP	1.00000000
1922	94.47999000	UP	4.86000000
1923	90.94999000	DOWN	3.52999800
1924	98.22999000	UP	7.27999800
⋮	⋮	⋮	⋮
1972	162.96000000	UP	5.22000100
1973	159.03990000	DOWN	3.92001300
1974	158.58990000	DOWN	0.44999690
1975	149.21000000	DOWN	9.37998900
1976	148.72990000	DOWN	0.48001090
1977	161.33000000	UP	12.60000000

3.12.2   The Money Changing Problem

The final example is the money changing algorithm of Figure 2.14. The translation of this algorithm requires a little more caution since some abbreviations were used in expressing the algorithm. Fortunately, WATFIV-S also includes abbreviated ways to compute many common scientific and mathematical functions. In fact, these functions are called *built-in functions*. A complete list of the functions available is given in Appendix P.

The quotient function used in pseudo code does not require a built-in function since the division of one integer by another automatically results in an integer quotient. While it is possible to isolate the remainder of such a division by arithmetic means, it is also possible to use the built-in MOD function. The result of MOD(A,B) is A modulus B. For positive numbers, this is equivalent to the remainder when A is divided by B. Since the MOD function produces an integer-valued result, MOD is included in the INTEGER declarations. These features are illustrated in the translation in Figure 3.6. Notice again the necessary restriction in the length of variable names. Also of note is the statement to print the titles. Since the title message is too long to be punched on one card, a continuation card has been used. In order to indicate that a card is a continuation of the previous card, a nonblank character is placed in column 6. This indicates that columns

7-72 are to be considered as following column 72 of the previous card. This program and its output are listed as Figures 3.6 and 3.7. Be aware that the output has been compressed horizontally to fit into a textbook page. This practice is continued throughout the remainder of this text.

```
$JOB     WATFIV
C$OPTIONS DECIMAL
C**************************************************************
C Figure 3.6 -- Determine the minimum number of coins needed
C                 to give change for a variable number of amounts.

C**************************************************************
C AMOUNT - the given amount
C QURTRS - the number of quarters required
C DIMES  - the number of dimes required
C NICKLS - the number of nickels required
C PENIES - the number of pennies required
C TOTAL  - the total number of coins required
C LEFT   - the amount left at each stage

C MOD    - the built-in modulus function

C**************************************************************
      INTEGER AMOUNT, QURTRS, DIMES, NICKLS, PENIES, TOTAL, LEFT
      INTEGER MOD
C Record titles for the output.
      PRINT, '     AMOUNT     QUARTERS       DIMES        ',
     +      'NICKELS      PENNIES        TOTAL'
      PRINT, ' '
C Obtain the first amount, then keep processing
C as long as an amount less than 100 is obtained.
      READ, AMOUNT
      WHILE(AMOUNT .LT. 100) DO
         QURTRS = AMOUNT/25
         LEFT = MOD(AMOUNT,25)
         DIMES = LEFT/10
         LEFT = MOD(LEFT,10)
         NICKLS = LEFT/5
         PENIES = MOD(LEFT,5)
         TOTAL = QURTRS + DIMES + NICKLS + PENIES
         PRINT, AMOUNT, QURTRS, DIMES, NICKLS, PENIES, TOTAL
         READ, AMOUNT
      END WHILE

      STOP
      END
$ENTRY
77
89
13
67
99
100
```

Figure 3.7   Output from the money changing program of Figure 3.6.

AMOUNT	QUARTERS	DIMES	NICKELS	PENNIES	TOTAL
77	3	0	0	2	5
89	3	1	0	4	8
13	0	1	0	3	4
67	2	1	1	2	6
99	3	2	0	4	9

3.13   Summary

The translation of an algorithm into a machine-readable program is necessary before a computer can process it. For the sake of convenience, it is desirable that this translation be as simple as possible. WATFIV-S, a dialect of FORTRAN, is a good choice for the programming language since it bears a close resemblance to the algorithm description. The translation process usually requires the provision of additional information such as declarations before the task is complete. For this reason it is still better to use pseudo code as the vehicle for algorithm development.

If necessary, a WATFIV-S program may be converted either manually or mechanically into a standard WATFIV or FORTRAN program. The techniques involved in this process are given in Appendix D.

3.14   References

Though there are a large number of introductory texts for standard FORTRAN and standard WATFIV, the number of texts fully integrating structured WATFIV is limited. The texts in the following list present a variety of approaches as indicated by the annotations.

Cress, P.; Dirksen, P.H.; and Graham, J.W. FORTRAN IV *with* WATFOR *and* WATFIV. Englewood cliffs, N.J.: Prentice-Hall, 1970. (Standard WATFIV only.)

Holt, R.C. and Hume, J.N.P. *Fundamentals of Structured Programming using* FORTRAN *with* SF/k *and* WATFIV-S. Reston Va.: Reston Publishing Co., 1977. (Structured FORTRAN is introduced in a series of subsets called SF/1, SF/2, etc.. All sample programs are WATFIV-S compatible.)

Moore, J.B. and Makela, L.J. *Structured* FORTRAN *with* WATFIV. Reston Va.: Reston Publishing Co., 1978.

3.15   Exercises

3.1 a)   Develop a pseudo-code algorithm to tabulate the function

$$k = 2^n$$

for $n = 1, 2, 3, \cdots, 50$. Notice that each term can be obtained from the previous term using a single multiplication. Incorporate this feature into the algorithm.

b) Translate the algorithm of part a) into WATFIV-S and run the program on the computer. Use only INTEGER arithmetic. Study and explain the output.

c) Change the program of part b) to use REAL arithmetic and run this program on the computer. Compare the output with that obtained in part b).

d) Revise the algorithm of part a) and the program of part b) to tabulate the first 50 powers of 3. Run the resulting program and compare the results with part b).

3.2 If S_n is defined as the sum of the first n terms of the following series:

$$\frac{1}{1^3} - \frac{1}{3^3} + \frac{1}{5^3} - \frac{1}{7^3} + \cdots$$

a) Develop an expression for the nth term of the given series (call this term t_n).

b) Devise a pseudo-code algorithm and write the corresponding WATFIV-S program to tabulate t_n and S_n for $n = 1, 2, 3, \cdots, 50$.

c) The algorithm in part b) was designed to compute S_{50} by adding the terms $t_1, t_2, \cdots, t_{50}$. Alternatively, the algorithm could be designed to sum the series in reverse order. Revise the algorithm of part b) to compute S_{50} by summing the terms in reverse order. Translate this algorithm into WATFIV-S and run the program.

d) Examine the output listings from the programs for part b) and c). Are the answers for S_{50} identical? Why? Which answer would you expect to be more accurate?

3.3 The squares of the integers 1, 2, 3, . . . can be generated by a method that involves adding successive odd numbers to the previous square, that is:

$$1^2 = 0+1 = 1$$
$$2^2 = 1+3 = 4$$
$$3^2 = 4+5 = 9$$

or in general

$$(k+1)^2 = k^2 + (2k+1)$$

Develop a pseudo-code algorithm which uses this technique to generate the squares of the integers from 1 to a given number n. Translate the algorithm to a WATFIV-S program and run it on the computer.

3.4 A method of multiplying two numbers that requires only multiplication and division by two is called "Russian peasant" multiplication. The two numbers are placed at the top of 2 columns. The numbers in the first column are successively divided by 2; the numbers in the second column are successively multiplied by 2. Whenever the number in the first column is odd (that is, whenever the division in the first column results in a remainder), the corresponding number in the second column is added to a sum. The final sum represents the product of the two original numbers. The example below follows this algorithm for multiplying 37 times 41.

first number	*second number*	*product*
37	41	→ 41 + 0 = 41
18	82	
9	164	→ 164 + 41 = 205
4	328	
2	656	
1	1312	→ 1312 + 205 = 1517

Develop a pseudo-code algorithm to use this method to multiply successive pairs of numbers until both numbers in the pair are zero. Translate the algorithm to a WATFIV-S program and run it on the computer.

3.5   The following formulae can be used to calculate the area of a triangle having sides *a*, *b*, and *c*:

$$s = semiperimeter = (a+b+c)/2$$

$$a = area = \sqrt{s(s-a)(s-b)(s-c)}$$

Develop a pseudo-code algorithm to find the area of a triangle given the lengths of its 3 sides. The algorithm should be designed to handle sets of input data until any one of the lengths is zero. Translate the algorithm to WATFIV-S and run it on the computer.

3.6   The square root of a number may be found using an algorithm called Newton's method. Successive values of *x* are produced by the following equations and will converge to the square root of *a*.

$$x_0 = \frac{a}{2}$$

$$x_{i+1} = \frac{1}{2}(x_i + \frac{a}{x_i}) \quad \text{for } i = 0, 1, 2, 3, \cdots.$$

Develop a pseudo-code algorithm that will repeat this calculation five times. Translate the algorithm to WATFIV-S and run the program on the computer.

3.7   The cube root of a number may also be found using Newton's method. The successive values of *x* which are produced by the following equations will converge to the cube root of *a*.

$$x_0 = \frac{a}{3}$$

$$x_{i+1} = \frac{1}{3}(2x_i + \frac{a}{x_i^2}) \quad \text{for } i = 0, 1, 2, 3, \cdots.$$

Develop a pseudo-code algorithm that will perform this calculation until two successive values of *x* differ by less than 0.001. Translate the algorithm to WATFIV-S and run the program on the computer.

3.8 The value of a sum of money a, when invested at an interest rate of $p\%$ compounded annually, may be determined using $r = p/100$ as follows:

Number of Interest Periods	*Amount*
1	$a + (r \times a) = a(1+r)$
2	$a(1+r) \times (1+r) = a(1+r)^2$
3	$a(1+r)^2 \times (1+r) = a(1+r)^3$
$\vdots$	$\vdots$
n	$a(1+r)^{n-1} \times (1+r) = a(1+r)^n$

Develop a pseudo-code algorithm that will perform the above tabulation. Test your algorithm on a $1000 investment at 10% interest over 5 years. Translate the algorithm to WATFIV-S and run the program on the computer.

3.9 Modify the pseudo-code algorithm developed in Exercise 3.8 to perform the same tabulation when the interest is compounded semiannually. Test your algorithm with the same values and compare the results. Translate the algorithm to WATFIV-S and run the program on the computer.

3.10 A loan of x dollars with an interest rate of $r\%$ compounded monthly ($r/12\%$ per month on the outstanding balance) is to be repaid in monthly payments of y dollars. Develop a pseudo-code algorithm that will generate a table of payments. Be sure to account for the fact that the last month's payment will be less than y dollars. Test your algorithm on a loan of $100 at 10% interest with monthly payments of 10 dollars. Translate the algorithm to WATFIV-S and run the program on the computer.

3.11 Develop a pseudo-code algorithm that will perform the same tabulation as the previous question when the interest is compounded semiannually. Test your algorithm with the same values and compare the results. Translate the algorithm to WATFIV-S and run the program on the computer.

3.12 The monthly payments on a mortgage will change with the amortization period (time over which the loan is to be repaid). Develop a pseudo-code algorithm which will determine the amount of the monthly payments if a mortgage of x dollars is to be repaid over a period of n years. Your algorithm should also compute and record the cost of the loan. Test your algorithm by computing the monthly payments for a $10,000 mortgage at 10% interest compounded semiannually for amortization periods of 5, 10, 15, 20, and 25 years. Translate the algorithm to WATFIV-S and run the program on the computer.

3.13 A formula for computing the day of the week for any given day of the Gregorian calendar was developed by a Reverend Zeller. The input to the algorithm is specified in the following manner:

- let *m* be the month of the year, starting with March as $m = 1$. January and February are months 11 and 12 of the previous year.
- let *d* be the day of the month.
- let *y* be the year of the century.
- let *c* be the previous century.

For example, to convert April 1, 1979, $m = 2$, $d = 1$, $y = 79$, and $c = 19$. To compute the day of the week on which the day falls,

a) Take the integer part of the ratio $(13m-1)/5$. Call this *A*.
b) Take the integer part of the ratio $y/4$. Call this *B*.
c) Take the integer part of the ratio $c/4$. Call this *C*.
d) Compute $D = A+B+C+d+y-2c$.
e) Divide the resulting *D* by 7 and keep the remainder, *R*.
f) If *R* is 0, the day is Sunday, if *R* is 1, the day is Monday, . . . , and if *R* is 6, the day is Saturday.

Describe this algorithm in pseudo code, then translate it to WATFIV-S and run it on the computer.

3.14 Develop a pseudo-code algorithm to find all positive integers less than 1000 which do not end in zero and have the property that if the rightmost digit is deleted, the integer obtained divides into the original evenly. For example, 39 is such an integer since 3 remains after deleting the rightmost digit, and 3 divides 39 evenly. Translate the algorithm into WATFIV-S and run it on the computer.

3.15 The four-digit number 3025 has the following property: if the number formed by considering only the first two digits (30) is added to the number formed by considering only the last two digits (25), (the total will be 55), and if this number (55) is squared, the result will be the original number. Develop a pseudo-code algorithm to find all four-digit numbers having this property, then translate the algorithm to WATFIV-S and run it on the computer.

3.16 Develop a pseudo-code algorithm to reverse the order of the digits in any positive integer. The algorithm should output both versions and be designed to handle a variable number of integers. Translate the algorithm to WATFIV-S and run it on the computer.

3.17 It is fairly common practice in business to devise account numbers for things like credit cards so that the number is self-checking. This usually means that one of the digits is assigned to provide a certain amount of protection against fraud and clerical errors. This digit is assigned by some fixed sequence of operations on the other digits.

  As an example, consider an environment which uses a nine-digit account number with the rightmost digit acting as the "check" digit. This digit is computed when the number is assigned. It is the rightmost digit of the sum formed by adding all of the remaining digits of the account number.

For example, if the first 8 digits are 12345678

1+2+3+4+5+6+7+8 = 36

and the account number would be 123456786.

Develop a pseudo-code algorithm to compute the complete account number for a series of n eight-digit numbers, where the value of n is supplied as data to the algorithm. Translate the algorithm to WATFIV-S and run the program on the computer.

4
Design of Algorithms

4.1 Introduction

In the previous chapters, many examples of algorithms were given. However, the question of how to develop an algorithm remains to be discussed. For simpler problems, algorithms may be developed easily without reference to any formal techniques. More complicated problems require some formal method or approach, other than trial and error, so that correct algorithms may be developed in a reasonable amount of time. There are several ways of approaching algorithm development. The one to be discussed here is called *top-down design* using *step-wise refinement*.

4.2 Top-Down Design of Algorithms

Development of algorithms for large problems is difficult because of the vast amount of detail that must be managed. Top-down design is a constructive approach to algorithm development which establishes a hierarchy of algorithmic operations, describing the relationship of these operations to each other. Thus, one is forced to resolve major design issues early in the design process. This allows the designer to concentrate on the problem at various levels of abstraction and keep to a minimum the number of details which must be considered at any one time. Hopefully, this technique allows the whole design process to become what has been called "intellectually manageable."

The top-down design process is a divide-and-conquer approach, which involves decomposing the original problem into several subproblems, each of which is easier to deal with. Since the relationships between these subproblems are also established at this time, each subproblem may be considered in isolation. As the decomposition proceeds, the algorithm becomes more and more detailed in describing how to solve the problem.

Problem decomposition is probably the most important aspect of the design process since the form of the final algorithm depends upon the choices made in the decomposition. Fortunately, this task becomes easier with experience as one acquires knowledge of algorithm development techniques.

There are many vehicles which may be used to implement the top-down design process. Step-wise refinement using pseudo code is one which has met with some success and is the one to be used here.

4.3   Step-Wise Refinement Using Pseudo Code

The basic notion of step-wise refinement is to start with a simple generalized description of an algorithm which is known to be correct, and expand it through several stages until a detailed version of the algorithm is produced. At each stage, one step or action of the algorithm is chosen for expansion. This step is decomposed into several more detailed substeps. Any step that is too vague for the algorithm follower is a candidate for expansion. Expansion terminates when all steps are sufficiently detailed. For this discussion it will always be assumed that the computer will eventually be the algorithm follower. Thus, the final version of the algorithm should be in terms of the basic pseudo-code actions, all of which can easily be translated into a programming language. The restriction, in Chapter 2, of the pseudo code to the three control structures of sequence, repetition, and alternation, aids in reducing the complexity of the step-wise refinement.

If the original statement of the problem is correct and if the expansions at each stage of the step-wise refinement are correct, then the final algorithm will also be correct. Thus, it is important to keep these expansions small enough that their correctness is easily maintained. This is not meant to imply that maintaining correctness at each stage is an easy task. It requires attention to detail and a careful investigation of the mathematical principles which are being used. If an incorrect decomposition is made at any stage and is not discovered until much later in the refinement, it is necessary either to backtrack and try a different decomposition or to change some part of the algorithm which was assumed to be complete.

Step-wise refinement is an organized approach to algorithm development, which by its nature aids in producing correct algorithms. This does not imply that the resulting algorithm will be the most efficient. Algorithm efficiency is discussed in Chapter 5.

4.4   Techniques of Step-Wise Refinement

The main power of step-wise refinement is that one is dealing with a very small number of problems at any one time and attention is usually focused on refinement of only one problem. Each such refinement has one of the following results:

1) the problem is decomposed into subproblems
2) the problem is translated directly into pseudo code
3) the problem is decomposed into some pseudo code and some subproblems.

The process is then repeated in turn on each of the subproblems.

During the refinement process it is usually convenient to isolate a problem and work on it. After all refinements are finished, the generated pseudo code must be collected to form the final algorithm. To facilitate refinement and the subsequent recombination, a label will be associated with each subproblem. The relative positions of the subproblems will be recorded through the use of index levels in the label.

The following diagram illustrates the labeling scheme. Each number signifies a problem still to be refined and the arrows indicate the result of a decomposition or refinement. As each problem is decomposed, another numeric index level is added to the original label as illustrated in Figure 4.1. In this diagram, the original problem is decomposed into three subproblems, labeled **1.**, **2.**, **3.**, and some pseudo code. The order in which the subproblems and the pseudo code are placed indicates the order in which they must be performed in the algorithm. When problem **1.** is decomposed, two subproblems labeled **1.1** and **1.2** result. This labeling indicates that these subproblems are the first and second subproblems respectively of problem **1.** Subsequent refinement of problem **1.1** results in subproblems **1.1.1**, **1.1.2**, and **1.1.3**, each of which is refined further into pseudo code. On the other hand, problem **1.2** needs no further decomposition and is refined directly into pseudo code.

Figure 4.1   An example of the step-wise refinement labeling scheme.

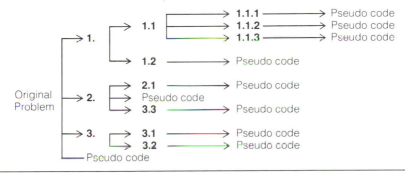

When a problem is decomposed, it may be possible to make use of an algorithm that was developed at some earlier time. For example, if a problem requires testing if a number is a prime, and such an algorithm has been done before, then the previous results may be used without going through a formal development of this segment of the algorithm again.

Although it may seem that the first decomposition should be difficult, in fact the opposite is usually true. Almost all mathematical algorithms will, in one way or another, perform:

- the acquisition of parameters for a computation,
- some computations on these parameters,
- recording of some results, and
- termination of the algorithm.

Thus, an initial decomposition which performs these operations is always a good first try. If the problem has only one set of input parameters, then a good first attempt at

---

Figure 4.2   Version 1 of an algorithm when using initial decomposition #1.

1. Acquire values for parameters.

2. Perform required computations and record results.

stop

---

decomposition is illustrated in a general manner in Figure 4.2. On the other hand, if the problem has many sets of input parameters which are to be processed then some form of repetition is required. For this case Figure 4.3 illustrates a good first attempt at

---

Figure 4.3   Version 1 of an algorithm when using initial decomposition #2.

1. **while** input data remains **do**
  ⌈ Perform the required computations and record the results.

stop

---

decomposition. Notice that this second decomposition does not explicitly specify the acquisition of values for the parameters but assumes this action is implicit in the **while-do** condition. The reason for this is to maintain as much generality as possible since parameter acquisition and termination of the **while** loop are interrelated and may be accomplished in many different ways. The **while** loop as a whole is given the label **1.**

In both of the above decompositions the computation and the recording of results are grouped together initially. Experience indicates that this aids the step-wise refinement. The labels are used as a reminder that steps **1.** and **2.** of decomposition #1 and step **1.** of decomposition #2 require further refinement. Of course, when dealing with an actual problem, these steps would be more specific as to the actual computation that is to be performed.

The use of pseudo-code comments is important to document the purpose and behaviour of an algorithm. Many of these comments can be generated quite naturally as part of the step-wise refinement by merely converting the step descriptions into comments when the step is decomposed into pseudo code. These descriptions are usually the most appropriate comments possible because they describe exactly what the generated pseudo code is supposed to do. This technique will be demonstrated in the following examples.

4.5   Finding All Factors of a Number

As the first example of a step-wise refinement, consider the problem of finding all distinct, nontrivial factors of a positive number *n*. The initial version of the algorithm, which will be called version 0, is merely the statement of the problem itself and is given as Figure 4.4. Clearly, this request is a correct algorithm in its own right and would be detailed enough for a human problem solver familiar with elementary mathematics. However, for computer application, this algorithm must be refined into basic pseudo code before it may be translated into a computer program. Before proceeding with the refinement, it is a good idea to review the mathematical aspects of the current problem.

Figure 4.4   Version 0 of the factoring algorithm.

Find all distinct, nontrivial factors of a positive number **n**.

a) Some Mathematical Background   An integer *m* will be a *nontrivial* factor of *n* if $1 < m < n$ and *m* divides into *n* evenly. (The trivial factors of *n* are 1 and *n*.) Thus, the algorithm must decide which values of *m* in the specified range divide into *n* evenly.

b) Selecting an Initial Decomposition   Since the algorithm must work on only one set of input parameters, consisting of one value n, the first initial decomposition may be used. Modifying it to reflect the current problem results in version 1 of the algorithm shown in

Figure 4.5   Version 1 of the factoring algorithm.

* Find all distinct, nontrivial factors of a positive number.

1.   Acquire a value for **n**.

2.   Find and record all factors of **n**.

stop

Figure 4.5. The decomposition from version 0 to version 1 of the algorithm is straightforward and simple enough that this version of the algorithm should also be correct. Also, the statement of the problem has been included as the initial comment. Now each of the labeled steps must be refined.

c) Refining Step **1.**   For this step a decision must be made as to how to assign a value to n. Of the two possible ways, either using an assignment operation or a **get** action, the latter was chosen to make the algorithm more general. A **put** statement has been added to echo the value of the number to be tested. Thus, the refinement of step one will result in:

```
* Acquire a value for n.
get n
put 'The number being factored is', n
```

Since this refinement has generated only basic pseudo code, no further refinements are necessary.

*d) Refining Step **2.***   Finding all factors of n may be done by considering the values of m = 2, 3, . . . , n−1 as possible factors. This implies a need for repetition in the algorithm, which may be achieved through the use of a **while-do** loop. Using this as the basis for the refinement we get:

```
* Find and record all factors of n by
* dividing it by all m from 2 to n−1.
m ← 2
while m ≤ n−1 do
   ⌈  2.1 Test if m is a factor and, if so, record it.
   ⌊  m ← m + 1
```

This algorithmic segment now performs the correct iteration of m. The actual test has been labeled as step **2.1** since it is still not specific enough.

*e) Refining Step **2.1***   A value of m will be a factor of n, if m divides evenly into n, that is, if the remainder of n/m is zero. The remainder of this division may be denoted using the notation rem(n,m) of Chapter 2, or the modulus notation n(mod m). For example, 5(mod 3)=2, 8(mod 3)=2, and 6(mod 3)=0. Thus, step **2.1** becomes:

```
if n(mod m) = 0 then
   ⌈  put m, 'is a factor'
```

All steps have now been refined into basic pseudo code so the refinement is finished. The next operation involves combining the pseudo code steps to form the final algorithm.

f) The Final Algorithm   Using the labels as a guide, the generated pseudo code may be recombined to give the algorithm of Figure 4.6. A sample data value for the algorithm is also included. Notice how the step descriptions have been carried through the step-wise refinement as comments.

This algorithm obtains a number n from a data list and then tests all numbers m, 2 ≤ m ≤ n−1, to see if they are factors of n. When a factor is found, its value is recorded with an appropriate message. The step-wise development of this algorithm was straightforward and since the steps were small at each stage, correctness was easily maintained.

The above algorithm is currently designed to record the number being factored followed by information about its factors. An improvement to this algorithm would have it record a message if no factors exist for the number (see Exercise 4.2).

Figure 4.6   Final version of the factoring algorithm.

```
* Find all distinct, nontrivial factors of a positive number.

* Variables used:
* n - the given number
* m - trial divisors

* Acquire a value for n.

get n
put 'The number being factored is', n

* Find and record all factors of n by
* dividing it by all m from 2 to n−1.

m ← 2
while m ≤ n−1 do
   ┌  if n(mod m) = 0 then
   │     ┌  put m, 'is a factor'
   │  m ← m + 1
   └
stop
1820
```

This algorithm can also be improved with respect to efficiency since it performs more calculations than are necessary. For instance, when a factor is found, it is also possible to calculate its *cofactor*. (Note that the product of a factor and its cofactor produces the original number.) This technique drastically reduces the number of iterations through the loop. This and other changes to the algorithm are developed in Chapter 5.

4.6   Prime Number Algorithm

As a second example, consider the problem of testing many positive numbers to determine if they are prime or composite. Again the initial version of the algorithm is simply the problem statement itself as given in Figure 4.7.

Figure 4.7   Version 0 of the prime/composite number algorithm.

Determine if individual numbers in a set of positive values are prime or composite.

a) Some Mathematical Background A number is said to be prime if it has no nontrivial factors. Conversely, a number is said to be composite if it has any nontrivial factors.

b) Selecting an Initial Decomposition This problem requires the application of a prime number computation to many sets of input parameters. Thus, the second initial decomposition technique may be used. Modifying it to reflect the current problem gives the version in Figure 4.8.

Figure 4.8 Version 1 of the prime/composite number algorithm.

* Determine if individual numbers in a set of positive values are prime or composite.

1. **while** input data remains **do**

> Acquire the current number, determine if it is prime or composite, and record the result.

stop

---

c) Refining Step **1.** When dealing with many sets of input parameters, the values must be provided in a data list. One way to keep the algorithm general is to assume that the data list is preceded by a data count. Thus, step **1.** must obtain the data count and use it to control loop termination. This step must also obtain the input parameters themselves. Expressing these notions in pseudo code gives the following.

> * Acquire a count of the numbers in the set.
>
> **get** count
> **put** 'There are', count, 'numbers to be tested'
> index ← 1
> **while** index ≤ count **do**
>
> > * Acquire the current number.
> >
> > **get** n
> >
> > **1.1** Determine if n is prime or composite, and record the result.
> >
> > index ← index + 1

In this portion of the algorithm, the statement **get** count will obtain the data count from the data list and assign it to the variable count. The control variable, index, is used in the **while** loop to control termination. The statements within the range of the **while** obtain one input value at a time from the data list, perform the prime/composite calculations, and then increment index. When index exceeds count, the **while** loop terminates. In the above algorithm, only step **1.1** requires further refinement.

d) Refining Step **1.1**   This step seems reasonably simple, and a *first* attempt at a refinement is shown below.

```
if n is prime then
    ┌ put n, 'is prime'
else
    ┌ put n, 'is composite'
```

If this refinement is used, the remaining problem to be solved is to decide whether n is prime. However, it is then necessary to be able to solve this problem in the pseudo-code condition. Unfortunately, this is not possible with the current pseudo-code definitions. Thus, this first attempt at refinement is not satisfactory, and it is necessary to backtrack and try a different refinement.

The *second* refinement attempt, as given below, has step **1.1** decomposed into two subproblems. The first determines if n is a prime and the second uses this result to record the proper message. Decompositions such as this are common in algorithm development. They are characterized by a sequence of actions that determines which of many possible conditions has occurred and then a test to record that fact.

1.1.1 Determine if n is prime or composite.

* Record the result.

1.1.2 if n is prime **then**
```
    ┌ put n, 'is prime'
else
    ┌ put n, 'is composite'
```

This decomposition will require some communication between steps **1.1.1** and **1.1.2** as to the status of the number n. The communication can be done by simply setting a variable to a particular value. This method will be used in the subsequent refinements.

e) Refining Step **1.1.1**   To determine whether n is prime or not involves determining if it has any nontrivial factors. This task appears similar to that of the previous algorithm of Figure 4.6. The only difference is that for this application, it is only necessary to determine whether or not a single nontrivial factor exists. Thus, the algorithm can be changed to indicate whether or not the number has a factor. One way to do this is to assume one of the two situations is true and to then revise this decision if calculations prove otherwise. This status is maintained by what is called a *flag* or *switch*. In pseudo code, a variable is used for this purpose. Adapting the algorithm of Figure 4.6 for use here gives the following algorithmic segment which assumes the number being tested is prime (prime←1) and then changes its status if a factor is found (prime←0). Thus, the variable prime is used to contain the flag. The value of prime will then be tested in the **if** statement in order that the correct message be recorded.

* Determine if **n** is prime or composite by dividing it by all **m** from 2 to n−1.
* Set the flag **prime** accordingly.

```
prime ← 1
m ← 2
while m ≤ n−1 do
      if n(mod m) = 0 then
            prime ← 0
      m ← m + 1
```

f) Refining Step **1.1.2**   In the previous refinement, the flag prime is used to indicate whether or not the number is a prime. Using it in this refinement gives the following algorithmic segment.

* Test the flag **prime** to record the results.

```
if prime = 1 then
      put n, 'is prime'
else
      put n, 'is composite'
```

This completes the refinement as all steps are now expressed in basic pseudo code.

g) The Final Algorithm   Combining the pseudo-code refinements gives the final version of the algorithm illustrated in Figure 4.9. This algorithm solves the problem of determining if the numbers of a set are prime or composite. It uses a data count to indicate the number of values in the set. Each of these values is processed sequentially; and each value and its status, prime or composite, is recorded. The sample data list shown contains four numbers to be tested. As with the previous problem, the efficiency of this algorithm may also be improved. The inner **while** loop, which determines whether n has a factor, performs too many iterations when n is a prime and even keeps iterating after a factor is found. An improved version of this algorithm will be given in Chapter 5.

4.7   An Algorithm for Solving $ax^2+bx+c = 0$

As a third example of step-wise refinement, consider the problem of solving all equations of the form $ax^2+bx+c = 0$ for several given sets of a, b, c values. Version 0 of the algorithm appears in Figure 4.10.

Figure 4.9   Final version of the prime/composite number algorithm.

* Determine if individual numbers in a set of positive values are prime or composite.

* Variables used:
* **count** - count of numbers in set
* **index** - number of current set
* **n** - individual numbers
* **m** - potential divisors
* **prime** - prime flag - **0** means composite; **1** means prime

* Acquire a count of the numbers in the set.

get count
put 'There are', count, 'numbers to be tested'
index ← 1
while index ≤ count **do**

> * Acquire the current number.
>
> **get** n
>
> * Determine if **n** is prime or composite by dividing it by all **m** from 2 to n−1.
> * Set the flag **prime** accordingly.
>
> prime ← 1
> m ← 2
> **while** m ≤ n−1 **do**
>
> > **if** n(mod m) = 0 **then**
> >
> > > prime ← 0
> >
> > m ← m + 1
>
> * Test the flag **prime** to record the results.
>
> **if** prime = 1 **then**
>
> > **put** n, 'is prime'
>
> **else**
>
> > **put** n, 'is composite'
>
> index ← index + 1

stop

4, 37, 51, 143, 113

Figure 4.10   Version 0 of the quadratic equation solving algorithm.

Solve all equations of the form $ax^2+bx+c=0$ for several sets of **a**, **b**, **c** values.

a) Mathematical Background   The equation $ax^2+bx+c = 0$ is a quadratic equation if $a{\neq}0$ and has two roots which are given by the formulas

$$root1 = \frac{-b+\sqrt{b^2-4ac}}{2a}; \quad root2 = \frac{-b-\sqrt{b^2-4ac}}{2a}.$$

These two roots will be complex if b^2-4ac is less than zero. If $a = 0$, then the equation becomes linear, $bx+c = 0$ ($b{\neq}0$), which has a single root given by

$$root = -\frac{c}{b}$$

If $a = 0$ and $b = 0$, then the coefficients do not form an equation.

b) Selecting an Initial Decomposition   This problem requires the solution of the equation for several sets of a, b, c values. Thus, the second initial decomposition may be used as demonstrated in Figure 4.11.

Figure 4.11   Version 1 of the quadratic equation solving algorithm.

* Solve all equations of the form $ax^2+bx+c=0$ for several sets of a, b, c values.

1.   **while** input data remains **do**

> Solve $ax^2+bx+c=0$ for the current a, b, c values
> and record the results.

stop

---

c) Refining Step **1.**   Each set of input parameters will contain three values, one each for a, b, and c. For variety, assume in this problem that an end-of-data flag, consisting of three zero values, follows the data list. These special values are to be used to terminate the data list processing. These refinements are indicated below.

> * Process equations until a=b=c=0.
>
> **get** a, b, c
> **while not** (a=0 **and** b=0 **and** c=0) **do**
>
> > **put** 'The coefficients of the equation are', a, b, c
> >
> > **1.1** Solve $ax^2+bx+c=0$ for the current a, b, c values and record the results.
> >
> > **get** a, b, c

This portion of the algorithm first obtains a set of a, b, c values from the data list and then uses a **while** loop to perform the testing and calculations. The termination condition of the **while** loop was arrived at using the following reasoning. If the **while** should terminate when a, b, and c are all zero, that is, (a=0 **and** b=0 **and** c=0), then the reverse of this is that the **while** should continue looping when a, b, and c are not all zero. This condition may be written as **not** (a=0 **and** b=0 **and** c=0). Notice that a **put** statement has been inserted within the range of the **while** to record all values of a, b, and c except for the end-of-data flag.

d) Refining Step **1.1**   This step is quite complicated and will require a careful refinement to ensure correctness. There are many possible decompositions so perhaps listing the alternatives would be helpful. The equation $ax^2+bx+c = 0$ may have

- two roots
- one root
- no roots.

Taking these one at a time, the following algorithmic segment isolates the cases which have two roots.

> **if** a=0 **then**
>> **1.1.1** Solve **bx+c=0** and record the results.
>
> **else**
>> **1.1.2** Solve **ax²+bx+c=0** for two roots and record the results.

e) Refining Step **1.1.1**   This problem concerns solving the equation $bx+c = 0$ which may have either a single root or no roots at all. The algorithmic segment to distinguish between these two situations is given below.

> * Solve **bx+c=0** and record the results.
>
> **if** b=0 **then**
>> **put** 'Not an equation'
>
> **else**
>> root ← −(c/b)
>> **put** 'Single root', root

f) Refining Step **1.1.2**   For this problem it is known that two roots exist, but whether they are real or complex must still be decided. The algorithmic segment given below performs this classification.

> * Solve for 2 roots and record the results.
>
> **if** b²−4ac ≥ 0 **then**
>> root1 ← (−b+√b²−4ac)/2a
>> root2 ← (−b−√b²−4ac)/2a
>> **put** 'Two roots', root1, root2
>
> **else**
>> **1.1.2.1** Solve for complex roots and record them.

g) Refining Step **1.1.2.1**   Finding the complex roots involves isolating the real and imaginary parts of the roots as illustrated in the following pseudo code.

```
* Solve for complex roots and record them.
real1 ← −(b/2a)
imag1 ← +√‾4ac−b²/2a
real2 ← −(b/2a)
imag2 ← −√‾4ac−b²/2a
put 'Complex roots', real1, imag1, real2, imag2
```

h) The Final Algorithm   All of the refined steps have been combined to form the final version of the algorithm given in Figure 4.12. This algorithm, which in total turns out to be reasonably complicated, evolved from a simple statement of the problem. The algorithm determines, records, and identifies the roots of any equation of the form $ax^2+bx+c = 0$. If the coefficients of the equation do not form an equation, then this fact is noted by the algorithm. A data list for three sets of a, b, c values is included following the algorithm.

4.8   Correctness of Algorithms

The previous sections have discussed in detail how to develop algorithms using a top-down approach with structured language constructs. Although this approach generally results in a final algorithm which is more often correct than one developed in a less organized way, correctness is not guaranteed.

The topic of algorithm correctness is receiving much attention in the current literature. People are beginning to realize that the time spent in assuring that an algorithm is correct is repaid many fold in terms of both human and computer time when errors are corrected at the program level. For the relatively small problems encountered in this text, it is better to spend 5 to 10 minutes verifying an algorithm manually rather than an hour or more removing such errors as they are discovered in successive computer runs.

Formal algorithm verification methods are based upon mathematical proof techniques. Some assertions are made about how the algorithm should perform, and then it is proved whether or not the algorithm fulfils these assertions. An algorithm is considered correct if it performs properly according to these assertions and produces no undesirable side effects.

Even though the limited number of language constructs aid in these mathematical proofs, the proofs are still quite involved. Also, it is possible to make a mistake in stating the assertions. Thus, mathematical proofs of algorithm correctness are difficult and not routinely done in algorithm development. This situation may improve in the future as research progresses into automated verification techniques.

One way to achieve a degree of correctness is to use manual test techniques on the algorithm before it is translated into a computer program.

Figure 4.12   Final version of a quadratic equation solving algorithm.

* Solve all equations of the form $ax^2+bx+c=0$ for several sets of a, b, c values.

* Variables used:
* **root** - root of $bx+c=0$
* **root1/2** - two real roots
* **real1/2** - real part of complex roots
* **imag1/2** - imaginary part of complex roots

* Process equations until $a=b=c=0$.

get a, b, c
while not(a$=$0 **and** b$=$0 **and** c$=$0) **do**

  put 'The coefficients of the equation are', a, b, c
  if a$=$0 **then**

    * Solve $bx+c=0$ and record the results.

    if b$=$0 **then**
      put 'Not an equation'
    else
      root $\leftarrow$ $-(c/b)$
      put 'Single root', root

  else

    * Solve for 2 roots and record the results.

    if $b^2-4ac \leq 0$ **then**

      * Solve for real roots and record them.

      root1 $\leftarrow$ $-b+\sqrt{b^2-4ac}/2a$
      root2 $\leftarrow$ $-b-\sqrt{b^2-4ac}/2a$
      put 'Two roots', root1, root2

    else

      * Solve for complex roots and record them.

      real1 $\leftarrow$ $-(b/2a)$
      imag1 $\leftarrow$ $+\sqrt{4ac-b^2}/2a$
      real2 $\leftarrow$ $-(b/2a)$
      imag2 $\leftarrow$ $-\sqrt{4ac-b^2}/2a$
      put 'Complex roots', real1, imag1, real2, imag2

  get a, b, c
stop

1, -5, 6, 0, 5, -15, 1, 3, 4, 0, 0, 0

4.8.1 Manual Testing of Algorithms

Manual testing of algorithms may be done by taking the algorithm (or sections of it) and following the algorithm through for some actual data. Simple examples of manual testing were introduced in Chapter 2.

One of the first rules in the manual execution of an algorithm is to do exactly what the algorithm specifies at each stage. Do not assume that any section of the algorithm is working correctly until it has actually been tested.

The algorithm should be manually executed for the kind of data that the algorithm is designed to handle. Algorithms are not written in a vacuum. Algorithm designers should always know what problem they are trying to solve and thus have an idea of the expected outputs for at least several sets of input data. (If this is not true, then the algorithm design should not have been started. The designers should go back to the problem statement until they do understand it.)

Assuming then that something is known about the expected output of the algorithm for a given input, one may test the algorithm using this input data. If the algorithm is followed precisely and the output is incorrect, then the algorithm is in error. Unfortunately, even if this output is correct, there is no guarantee that the algorithm will be correct for all possible input data. The best one can say is that the output is correct for the given input. (There could be numerous other input data for which the algorithm would fail.) Thus, the objective is to select several sets of input data which will test all aspects of the algorithm. For example, in the algorithm of Figure 4.9 the algorithm should be tested with numbers that are prime and numbers that are composite. In the algorithm of Figure 4.12 zero and nonzero combinations of the a, b, c coefficients should be tried. The possible combinations are shown below.

a	b	c
0	0	0
0	0	**not** 0
0	**not** 0	0
0	**not** 0	**not** 0
not 0	0	0
not 0	0	**not** 0
not 0	**not** 0	0
not 0	**not** 0	**not** 0

In general, finding such sets of data may be a nontrivial, but necessary, task.

Testing one's own algorithm has a basic weakness; if bad assumptions were made in designing an algorithm, these assumptions will probably carry over into the testing phase and the error situations may not be discovered. One common, effective, and often humbling solution to this latter difficulty is to have someone else test the algorithm. This works quite well since it is unlikely that another person will make the same assumptions in testing it.

Further tests of an algorithm may involve breaking it apart into sections and examining these sections to convince oneself that the individual sections are working for all possible data values. Then one may determine that the sections are working together correctly. Conversely, one can even determine the circumstances under which a section of an algorithm will fail and then assure oneself that because of the way other sections are designed, those circumstances will not occur.

There are several common errors to check for. For instance, some of the most common errors involve **while** loops which do not terminate, perform one iteration too few, or perform one iteration too many. Another common mistake is the omission of statements to initialize variables. One of the more convenient ways to detect these errors is to keep track of the state of the algorithm by using a table of variable values.

To illustrate algorithm testing, the algorithm of Figure 4.9 will be used. This algorithm determines if count individual numbers are prime or composite. This algorithm can be tested as a complete unit or broken up for testing in a number of ways. The approach to be used here will break the algorithm into three sections. The first section will be the outer **while** loop. The second section will be the statements to get the number and test it for primeness. The third section will be the statements that print out the message that the number is prime or composite.

a) The outer **while** loop must be tested to ensure that it repeats correctly. This loop is shown below with all the statements that affect it. In addition, the **stop** statement is included so that a test for algorithm termination may also be made.

```
get count
index ← 1
while index ≤ count do
    ⎡ ⋮
    ⎣ index ← index + 1
stop
```

This section of algorithm is tested for several values of count as shown in the table of Figure 4.13. The arrows indicate the order in which the actions take place when the algorithm is followed. As can be seen from the table, the **while** loop performs the correct number of iterations, and the algorithm stops in each case. Thus, this section of the algorithm is correct.

b) The statements that obtain the number and determine if the number is prime or composite are shown below.

```
get n
prime ← 1
m ← 2
while m ≤ n−1 do
    ⎡ if n(mod m) = 0 then
    ⎢     ⎡ prime ← 0
    ⎣ m ← m + 1
```

This section of code has two possible outcomes. If the number is prime, then the variable prime should be 1. If the number is composite, the variable prime should be 0. Both of these possible outcomes should be tested.

Figure 4.13 Table to illustrate the testing of the outer **while** loop in the prime/composite number algorithm of Figure 4.9.

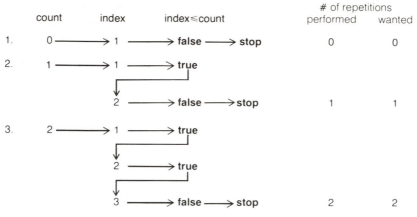

Suppose that the number 5 is to be tested for primeness. Since this value is prime, the algorithmic section should end with prime having the value 1. The table in Figure 4.14 shows the results as the algorithm is executed. The **get** statement sets n to 5

Figure 4.14 Testing the prime number 5 in the body of the outer **while** loop in the prime/composite number algorithm of Figure 4.9.

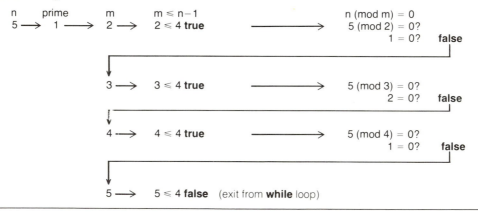

initially. When the **while** loop is finished the variable prime still has the value 1. Thus, this algorithmic section correctly determined that 5 is a prime number.

To test the other possible outcome of this algorithmic section, the composite value 4 will be used. In this case the variable prime should have the value 0 when this algorithmic section is finished. The table in Figure 4.15 gives the results of this test. When this algorithmic section ends, the value of prime is 0. Thus, it correctly determined that 4 is a composite number.

Figure 4.15   Testing the composite number 4 in the body of the outer **while** loop in the prime/composite number algorithm of Figure 4.9.

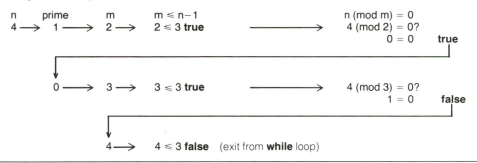

From the above two examples it seems that the prime number determination performs correctly. It sets prime to 1 when the number is prime and prime to 0 when the number is composite. Also, there is no way for prime to receive any value other than 0 or 1. Although other numbers could be tested, in this case there is no reason to believe that the results would be different.

c)   The remaining section of the algorithm to be tested is the statements which print the message describing the outcome. These statements follow:

```
if prime = 1 then
    [ put n, 'is prime'
else
    [ put n, 'is composite'
```

This section of algorithm will record the message that the number is a prime when prime has the value 1 and that the number is composite when the value of prime is 0. This is exactly what was wanted, and thus this section is correct.

d)   The individual sections of the algorithm were tested and are correct for the cases tried. The sections of the algorithm that interact were discussed, and the interactions are correct.

4.8.2   Testing of Programs
The fact that an algorithm has been tested and appears to be correct does not, unfortunately, guarantee that the corresponding program is correct. There are many reasons for this. Some errors may be introduced in translating the algorithm into a program or by mistyping the program. Other errors result from intrinsic limitations of computers. For instance, computers have a limitation on the number of significant digits they may store. This limitation on precision can cause problems in arithmetic which may not have been anticipated at the algorithm design stage. The process of detecting, isolating, and correcting the errors in a program is called *debugging*.

Debugging a program is greatly facilitated by a compiler that detects and identifies errors. The WATFIV-S processor catches, among other things, statements that may not be executed and undefined variables. In addition, arithmetic operations which generate numbers too large or too small to be stored in the computer are detected. Even though the reasons why these conditions exist may not be immediately obvious, one at least knows something is wrong with the program.

Unfortunately, not all mistakes are detectable by a compiler. The only effect some mistakes have is to produce erroneous results. If these results are grossly wrong, then the programmer can easily recognize the situation. A more difficult case arises if some results are wrong but not blatantly so. Errors of this subtle type may require careful checking before they are discovered. The usual procedure is to run the program first on at least one problem for which the *exact* solution is known. Under these circumstances, small discrepancies will be noticeable. When the program performs correctly on these problems, one may have more confidence in it for other problems.

Once it has been established that a program does contain an error, it is necessary to determine what caused the error. An erroneous result can potentially be caused anywhere in the calculations or even by something as subtle as declaring a variable to be the wrong type. Thus, isolation of the error may be complicated. A common isolation technique is to insert PRINT statements to output intermediate results for checking against manual calculations. In large programs it is a good idea to leave these debugging PRINT statements in the program. They may be part of an IF statement such that they may be turned on and off as desired. For example, the following debugging statements allow the PRINT statement to be executed whenever the variable TRACE has the value 1 and to be ignored when TRACE is not 1.

```
        :
READ, TRACE
        :
IF(TRACE .EQ. 1) THEN DO
        PRINT, X, Y, I, J
END IF
        :
```

The WATFIV-S compiler assists in the debugging process by performing extensive error checking. It also allows a program to be cross-referenced, traced, and profiled automatically. See Appendix E, Sections E.3, E.4, and E.5 for more information and examples of these features.

Note that when an algorithm is translated into a computer program, the correctness issue expands to become one of *software reliability*. This phrase has been defined as including the concepts of *correctness* and *robustness*. The concept of program correctness is similar to that of algorithm correctness. Program robustness is concerned with the ability of a program to continue functioning in the presence of unforeseen events such as hardware failure or bad data. For example, when some compilers detect an undefined variable, a warning message is issued, the variable is set to 0, and the program continues execution.

4.9   Summary

The development of large algorithms is a difficult task because of the vast amount of detail that must be maintained. The method of top-down design using step-wise refinement provides an orderly way to approach the development of both small and large algorithms. It establishes a hierarchy of algorithmic operations by performing successive decompositions of problems into subproblems.

Although a top-down design approach aids in producing correct algorithms, it is still possible for an incorrect algorithm to result. Manual testing of the algorithm is a good way to detect many of these incorrect situations.

4.10   References

Brown, A.R. and Sampson, W.A. *Program Debugging.* Computer Monograph Series, New York: Elsevier-North Holland Pub. Co., 1973.

Dahl, O.J.; Dijkstra, E.W.; and Hoare, C.A.R. *Structured Programming.* New York: Academic Press, 1972.

Freeman, P. "Software Reliability and Design: A Survey." *13th Design Automation Conference,* New York: IEEE Computer Society and Association for Computing Machinery, 1976. (An excellent and very readable survey on the state of software reliability.)

Hughes, J.K and Michton, J.I. *A Structured Approach to Programming.* Englewood Cliffs, N.J.: Prentice-Hall, 1977.

McGowan, C.L. and Kelly, J.R. *Top-Down Structured Programming Techniques.* New York: Petrocelli Charter, 1975.

Wirth, N. *Systematic Programming: An Introduction.* Englewood Cliffs, N.J.: Prentice-Hall, 1973.

4.11   Exercises

4.1 a) Translate the final version of the algorithm of Figure 4.6. into a WATFIV-S program and test it on the computer.

  b) Translate the final version of the algorithm of Figure 4.9. into a WATFIV-S program and test it on the computer.

  c) Translate the final version of the algorithm of Figure 4.12. into a WATFIV-S program and test it on the computer. Be sure to try test data that will cause all possible messages to be printed.

4.2 Develop a pseudo-code algorithm, using the step-wise refinement technique, that will determine all distinct, nontrivial factors of a number. If no factors exist for a given number, the algorithm should put out an appropriate message. (See Section 4.5.)

4.3 Develop a pseudo-code algorithm, using the step-wise refinement technique, that will test each number in a set to determine if it is prime or composite. The algorithm should handle negative numbers as well as positive numbers. Negative numbers are not prime. (See Section 4.6.)

4.4 Develop a pseudo-code algorithm, using the step-wise refinement technique, that will determine the prime factors of a number *n*. Translate your algorithm into WATFIV-S and test it on the computer.

4.5 Develop a pseudo-code algorithm, using the step-wise refinement technique, that will identify all three digit numbers (numbers between 100 and 999) whose digits when cubed, sum to the number itself. For example the number 153 has this property since $1^3+5^3+3^3 = 153$. Translate your algorithm into a WATFIV-S program and test it on the computer.

4.6 The greatest common divisor (GCD) of two numbers is the largest factor of both numbers. For example the GCD of 54 and 63 is 9. Develop a pseudo-code algorithm, using the step-wise refinement technique, that will compute the GCD of any two given numbers. Translate your algorithm into a WATFIV-S program and test it on the computer.

4.7 The least common multiple (LCM) of two numbers is the smallest integer evenly divisible by both numbers. For example, the LCM of 9 and 12 is 36. Develop a pseudo-code algorithm, using the step-wise refinement technique, that will find the LCM of any two given numbers. Translate your algorithm into a WATFIV-S program and test it on the computer.

4.8 Two numbers are said to be relatively prime if they do not have any common, nontrivial factors (Section 4.5 a). For example, 9 and 16 are relatively prime whereas 15 and 21 are not since they have a common factor of 3. Develop a pseudo-code algorithm, using the step-wise refinement technique, that will determine if any two given numbers are relatively prime. Translate your algorithm into a WATFIV-S program and test it on the computer.

4.9 Develop a pseudo-code algorithm, using the step-wise refinement technique, that will find and record the first 50 positive integers which have no prime factors other than 2, and/or 3, and/or 5. (Numbers in this category include: 2 (factor is 2), 3 (factor is 3), 5 (factor is 5), 6 (factors are 2 and 3), 10 (factors are 2 and 5), . . . , 120 (factors are 2, 3, and 5), ... Translate your algorithm into a WATFIV-S program and test it on the computer.

4.10 A number is said to be a perfect number if it is equal to the sum of its factors other than itself. For instance, the number 28 is a perfect number since $1+2+4+7+14 = 28$. Develop a pseudo-code algorithm, using the step-wise refinement technique, that will test a given number to determine if it is a perfect number. Translate your algorithm into a WATFIV-S program and run it on the computer.

4.11 Extend the algorithm of Exercise 4.10 such that the algorithm will test all numbers in the range 25 to 300 for perfectness. Translate your algorithm into a WATFIV-S program and run it on the computer.

4.12 Two positive integers are said to be friendly if each one is equal to the sum of the divisors (including 1, excluding the number itself) of the other. For example the numbers 220 and 284 are friendly since:

divisors of 220: 1+2+4+5+10+11+20+22+44+55+110 = 284
divisors of 284: 1+2+4+71+142 = 220.

Develop a pseudo-code algorithm, using the step-wise refinement technique, that will find all pairs of friendly numbers such that both numbers are less than 1500. Translate your algorithm into a WATFIV-S program and test it on the computer.

4.13 It has been conjectured that the product of two consecutive numbers lies between two odd numbers of which at least one is prime. Develop a pseudo-code algorithm, using the step-wise refinement technique, that will test this conjecture for all pairs of consecutive positive integers such that both are in the range from 1 to 100 inclusive. Translate your algorithm into a WATFIV-S program and test it on the computer.

4.14 Twin primes are defined to be two consecutive odd numbers which are both primes. For example, 11 and 13 are twin primes. Develop a pseudo-code algorithm, using the step-wise refinement technique, which will generate all of the twin primes in the set of numbers less than 200. Translate your algorithm into a WATFIV-S program and test it on the computer.

4.15 Pairs of prime numbers exist such that the larger prime is just 1 more than twice the smaller prime. For example, 3 and 7 form such a pair. Develop a pseudo-code algorithm, using the step-wise refinement technique, which will find all such pairs of prime numbers from the set of numbers less than 200. Translate your algorithm into a WATFIV-S program and test it on the computer.

4.16 If the sides of a right-angled triangle are restricted to be of integral lengths, then only certain triplets of integers will form such a triangle. Develop separate pseudo-code algorithms, using the step-wise refinement technique, that will produce all triplets of integers which represent the sides of a right-angled triangle:

a)   whose hypotenuse is < 100,
b)   whose perimeter is < 100.

Recall that for a right-angled triangle, the hypotenuse squared is equal to the sum of the squares of the other two sides (Pythagorean Identity). Translate your algorithms into WATFIV-S programs and test them on the computer.

4.17 Every integer has the property that it is divisible by 9 if and only if the sum of its digits is divisible by 9. For example, 4520 is not divisible by 9 since 4+5+2+0=11 is not divisible by 9; 4527 is divisible by 9 since 4+5+2+7=18 is divisible by 9. Develop a pseudo-code algorithm, using the step-wise refinement technique, to test a variable number of integers for divisibility by 9 using this test. The algorithm should output an appropriate message for each integer. Translate your algorithm into a WATFIV-S program and test it on the computer.

4.18 In the following number problems, the letters take the place of digits and each distinct letter represents a different digit.

```
      I           IS
    +AM          +IT
    -------      -------
     OK           OK
```

Develop a separate pseudo-code algorithm, using the step-wise refinement technique, for each of the above puzzles, which will determine all possible combinations of digits for the letters such that the arithmetic holds. Translate your algorithms into WATFIV-S programs and test them on the computer.

5
Efficiency of Algorithms

5.1 Introduction

As was intimated in the last chapter, the development of a correct algorithm does not automatically mean that the algorithm is efficient. Despite the tremendous advances being made in the power and size of computers, the topic of algorithm efficiency is still important. Awaiting any advances in computing speed are larger and larger problems to be solved. In terms of efficiency, the difference between a good algorithm and a bad algorithm can make even the computer solution of a problem entirely intractable.

In the simplest of terms, achieving efficiency usually means performing a minimum number of operations to compute the required result. Once an algorithmic technique is known to be efficient for certain tasks, that technique may be used in similar situations.

It is the intent of this chapter to provide only a brief introduction to the topic of efficiency and how efficiency is measured. An extensive discussion of *algorithm complexity,* as it is called, is certainly beyond the scope of an introductory course. There are excellent texts which pursue this topic further, and the interested reader is directed to the references at the end of this chapter.

5.2 Measures of Efficiency

The efficiency of an algorithm is usually measured in terms of the rate of growth of its time and space requirements with an increase in the size of the problem. That is, if an algorithm is to operate on a problem of twice a previous size, how many more operations (time) will the algorithm have to perform, and how much more data will have to be stored (space)? The answer to this question gives a method of predicting and comparing algorithm efficiency.

The size of a problem is denoted by n. In a general sense, n represents the amount of data to be processed. For the factoring algorithm of Figure 4.6, n would be the number being factored, and of concern would be how does the number of operations increase as this number gets larger. For the prime number algorithm of Figure 4.9, n would also represent the number being tested. For the quadratic equation algorithm of Figure 4.12, the number of a, b, c groups is the problem size n.

The usual measure for the efficiency of an algorithm is called the *order* of the algorithm. If the size of a problem doubles and the time to solve this new problem also doubles, then the algorithm is said to be linear and of order n, written $O(n)$. An algorithm of $O(n^2)$ is one for which every doubling of the problem size roughly quadruples the solution time.

The diagrams in Figure 5.1 illustrate possible time complexities for different algorithms. Figure 5.1 a) shows the time growth curves for two different algorithms. The curves are straight lines with equations of the form:

$$time_1 = a_1 + b_1 \times x$$

for algorithm 1, and

$$time_2 = a_2 + b_2 \times x$$

for algorithm 2. The slope of the line gives the linear factor. If these algorithms performed the same computations, then algorithm 2 would be preferred to algorithm 1 on a time complexity basis, since its rate of growth is smaller ($b_2 < b_1$). (If the problem size is sufficiently small, it may be necessary to compare a_1 and a_2.) Figure 5.1 b) shows a graph for an algorithm of complexity $O(n^2)$. The equation of this curve is of the form:

$$time = a + bx + cx^2$$

Figure 5.1   Examples of time complexity graphs.

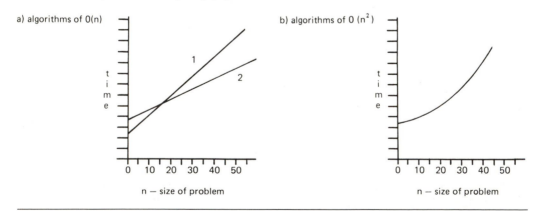

a) algorithms of O(n)

1

2

t
i
m
e

0   10   20   30   40   50

n — size of problem

b) algorithms of 0 (n^2)

t
i
m
e

0   10   20   30   40   50

n — size of problem

It is important to note that the order of an algorithm does not indicate that the algorithm is necessarily the best choice over the entire range of problem sizes. For instance, Figure 5.2 illustrates possible time complexities for two different algorithms which perform the same computation. According to these graphs, the algorithm of $O(n^2)$ is better than the algorithm of $O(n)$ for an initial range of problem sizes less than forty.

Figure 5.2   Time complexity curves for two algorithms performing the same computation.

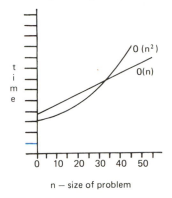

It should also be noted that, for a problem of a given size, the actual data may be different, and this can have an effect on the number of computations performed. In these cases some assumptions must be made about the occurrences and distribution of the data to aid in the estimation of complexity. Through these assumptions, it is often possible to compute a best, an average, and a worst case complexity.

There are essentially two levels at which both time and space efficiency may be examined and discussed. At the first level, the concern is with the overall efficiency of the mathematical technique that the algorithm uses. Attention is usually paid to the computational approach and the organization and access of data. There is usually a tradeoff with respect to time and space. The time efficiency may often be improved by using more space to store data and by arranging data in a readily accessible manner. These latter points will become clearer with the discussions on applications which appear in later chapters. The order of an algorithm is usually a function of the level one efficiency.

At the second level, one examines the chosen algorithm to eliminate unnecessary duplication of computations. Unfortunately, it is all too easy to implement an efficient algorithm in an inefficient manner. The space/time tradeoff is also present at this level, but usually to a lesser extent.

In general, the greatest gain in efficiency will be obtained at the level one stage, and this is where the major effort in the design process should be expended. Since the step-wise refinement process does not guarantee an efficient algorithm, it is often necessary to modify the algorithm to improve the level one efficiency. The initial effort spent in developing the algorithm is definitely not wasted, since the experience gained should greatly facilitate these modifications. In most cases, improvement at the level two stage may be performed independently of the level one design.

When optimizing a problem, the level at which the optimization is being done is often not obvious. Since both levels have the same objective of producing a more efficient algorithm, a distinction is not usually necessary.

In most of the problems discussed in this and succeeding chapters, the major concern will be with time complexity. Thus, unless otherwise stated, all references to complexity will be taken to mean the time complexity.

5.3   Determining Efficiency

Evaluating the efficiency of an algorithm involves determining the number of operations performed for a problem of size n. The order of an algorithm can often be obtained without an extensive analysis. To illustrate how efficiency may be measured, the factoring algorithm of Figure 4.6 and the prime number algorithm of Figure 4.9 are examined below. The efficiency discussions lead to improved versions of the algorithms.

5.3.1   Efficiency of the Factoring Algorithm
This first example deals with the algorithm of Figure 4.6 of the previous chapter. This algorithm, repeated in an abbreviated form in Figure 5.3, finds all distinct, nontrivial factors of a given positive number. To obtain a measure of its complexity, it is necessary to consider the number of operations performed for different values of n.

Figure 5.3   Factoring algorithm — no optimizations.

```
* Find all distinct, nontrivial factors of a positive number.
* Test for divisibility by all m from 2 to n−1.

get n
put 'The number being factored is', n
m ← 2
while m ≤ n−1 do
    ⌈  if n(mod m) = 0 then
    |      ⌈ put m, 'is a factor'
    |  m ← m + 1
stop
```

Analyzing the algorithm one can see that, for any n ($n \geq 2$) the **while** loop will be repeated $n-2$ times. The number of operations performed each time through the loop is essentially constant. The algorithm will perform an extra operation, namely the **put**, for each factor, but the maximum number of times that this will occur is once per iteration. Thus, the maximum number of operations performed by the algorithm is the maximum number of operations in the loop (call it c) times the number of repetitions of the loop ($n-2$) plus the number of operations outside the loop (call it d). This gives the expression $c(n-2)+d = cn+(d-2c)$. Since c and d are essentially constant, this expression varies as n, and thus the algorithm is linear or $O(n)$.

As was mentioned in the last chapter, this algorithm may be improved by recording both the factor and its cofactor at the same time. The benefit to be derived from this approach is that the algorithm would only need to test m in the range $2 \leq m \leq \sqrt{n}$ since for every factor $m \leq \sqrt{n}$ there exists a cofactor $c \geq \sqrt{n}$ which may be found at the same time. Such a change, shown in the algorithm of Figure 5.4, can be considered a level one optimization. For a given n, this algorithm performs $\lfloor \sqrt{n} \rfloor - 1$ iterations through the **while** loop. (The notation $\lfloor \sqrt{n} \rfloor$ refers to the floor function applied to the square root of n.) For each factor an extra division and assignment operation are now performed, but again they may be performed at most once for each iteration. Thus, this algorithm is of $O(\sqrt{n})$, which indicates a substantial reduction in computation time when n is large. The increase in space required by this change is negligible.

Figure 5.4   Factoring algorithm — optimized version 1.

* Find all distinct, nontrivial factors of a positive number.

* Test for divisibility by all **m** from 2 to $\sqrt{n}$ and record the cofactor as well as factor.

```
get n
put 'The number being factored is', n
m ← 2
while m ≤ √n do
    ⎡ if n(mod m) = 0 then
    ⎢     ⎡ c ← n/m
    ⎢     ⎣ put m, c, 'are factors'
    ⎣ m ← m + 1
stop
```

Upon examining the algorithm of Figure 5.4 closely, there is one more change that may be made. Since the condition of a **while** loop is evaluated on every iteration, the condition $m \leq \sqrt{n}$, when taken literally, implies that the square root of n must be evaluated each time. Since n does not change, the square root computation may be moved outside the loop as in the algorithm of Figure 5.5. Now the algorithm performs only one square root calculation instead of $\lfloor \sqrt{n} \rfloor - 1$ of them. This is a level two change and does not change the order of the algorithm. Again, the space increase is negligible.

For the above algorithms, it was possible to establish their order without doing a detailed analysis. However, sometimes a detailed computation count is necessary to gain better insight into the effect of the optimizations. To facilitate this process, all arithmetic operations and the assignment operation may be normalized to the time of an addition operation. The table in Figure 5.6 gives reasonable normalization factors for present day computers. The expression n (mod m) = 0 which appears in the table may be evaluated using integer arithmetic as $n - n/m \times m = 0$, which accounts for the equivalent six add operations. (In many cases, the mod operation may be performed internally in the computer by using only an integer division, and thus the mod operation could be as fast as two equivalent add operations.)

Figure 5.5   Factoring algorithm — optimized version 2.

```
* Find all distinct, nontrivial factors of a positive number.
* Test for divisibility by all m from 2 to √n and record the cofactor as well as factor.
* Move the square root out of the loop.
get n
put 'The number being factored is', n
m ← 2
k ← √n
while m ≤ k do
      ┌ if n(mod m) = 0 then
      │       ┌ c ← n/m
      │       └ put m, c, 'are factors'
      └ m ← m + 1
stop
```

Figure 5.6   Normalization factors for algorithmic operations.

Operation	Time equivalent (number of adds)
←	1
−	1
*	2
/	2
<, ≤, =, ≠, >, ≥	1
¬, &, ∨	1
√n	10
n(mod m) = 0	6

The **get** and **put** operations are more difficult to normalize so they will be counted separately.

The following tables give a detailed breakdown of the actual number of computations performed by the algorithms of Figures 5.3, 5.4, and 5.5. The column entitled *cost* contains either the normalized operation count or a code to indicate a **get** or a **put** operation. It has been assumed that the difference between recording one value and two values in a **put** operation is negligible. The repetition factor indicates the number of times the operations are repeated.

The first table in Figure 5.7 provides a count of each operation in the algorithm of Figure 5.3. To obtain this complete analysis, it was necessary to make an assumption about the number of factors that any number may have. As a first estimate, the number of distinct, nontrivial factors cannot exceed $n-2$ since this is the length of the range between 1 and n. A little more thought though will reveal that in fact $2(\lfloor\sqrt{n}\rfloor-1)$ is a tighter upper bound on the number of factors. All factors may be obtained by finding the factors $m\leq\sqrt{n}$ ($\lfloor\sqrt{n}\rfloor-1$ possible factors) and for each of these a cofactor may be found (another $\lfloor\sqrt{n}\rfloor-1$ possible factors). Thus, the total number of factors must be less than or equal to $2(\lfloor\sqrt{n}\rfloor-1)$.

Figure 5.7   Operation count for the factoring algorithm of Figure 5.3.

	Cost	*Repetition factor*	*Total operations*
get	g	1	g
put	p	1	p
m ← 2	1	1	1
m ≤ n−1	2	$n-2$	$2n-4$
n(mod m) = 0	6	$n-2$	$6n-12$
put	p	$2(\lfloor\sqrt{n}\rfloor-1)$	$2p(\lfloor\sqrt{n}\rfloor-1)$
m ← m+1	2	$n-2$	$2n-4$
		worst case	$10n+g+2p\lfloor\sqrt{n}\rfloor-p-19$

The table of Figure 5.8 gives an analysis of the algorithm of Figure 5.4. For this algorithm, the number of iterations through the **while** loop is $\lfloor\sqrt{n}\rfloor-1$, as determined by the **while** condition. Since the maximum number of factors in this range is also $\lfloor\sqrt{n}\rfloor-1$, the statements within the **if** action are performed a maximum of $\lfloor\sqrt{n}\rfloor-1$ times.

Figure 5.8   Operation count for the factoring algorithm of Figure 5.4.

	Cost	*Repetition factor*	*Total operations*
get	g	1	g
put	p	1	p
m ← 2	1	1	1
m ≤ $\sqrt{n}$	11	$\lfloor\sqrt{n}\rfloor-1$	$11\lfloor\sqrt{n}\rfloor-11$
n(mod m) = 0	6	$\lfloor\sqrt{n}\rfloor-1$	$6\lfloor\sqrt{n}\rfloor-6$
c ← n/m	3	$\lfloor\sqrt{n}\rfloor-1$	$3\lfloor\sqrt{n}\rfloor-3$
put	p	$\lfloor\sqrt{n}\rfloor-1$	$p(\lfloor\sqrt{n}\rfloor-1)$
m ← m+1	2	$\lfloor\sqrt{n}\rfloor-1$	$2\lfloor\sqrt{n}\rfloor-2$
		worst case	$22\lfloor\sqrt{n}\rfloor+g+p\lfloor\sqrt{n}\rfloor-21$

Figure 5.9 gives the operation counts for the algorithm of Figure 5.5. Remember that the major difference between this algorithm and the previous one is that the square root calculation has been moved outside of the loop. As may be seen from the table, the effect of this change is to reduce the operation count by a total of $10\lfloor\sqrt{n}\rfloor-21$ equivalent add operations.

Although the above tables give a worst case estimate of the time efficiency for each algorithm, the efficiencies implied by these formulas are still a bit intangible. Better insight may be achieved by tabulating these formulas for different problem sizes. The table in Figure 5.10 shows the operation counts in terms of the number of normalized add operations and the number of **get** and **put** actions for different values of n.

Figure 5.9 Operation count for the factoring algorithm of Figure 5.5.

	Cost	*Repetition factor*	*Total operations*
get	g	1	g
put	p	1	p
m ← 2	1	1	1
k ← $\sqrt{n}$	11	1	11
m ≤ k	1	$\lfloor \sqrt{n} \rfloor - 1$	$\lfloor \sqrt{n} \rfloor - 1$
n(mod m) = 0	6	$\lfloor \sqrt{n} \rfloor - 1$	$6 \lfloor \sqrt{n} \rfloor - 6$
c ← n/m	3	$\lfloor \sqrt{n} \rfloor - 1$	$3 \lfloor \sqrt{n} \rfloor - 3$
put	p	$\lfloor \sqrt{n} \rfloor - 1$	$p(\lfloor \sqrt{n} \rfloor - 1)$
m ← m+1	2	$\lfloor \sqrt{n} \rfloor - 1$	$2 \lfloor \sqrt{n} \rfloor - 2$
		worst case	$12 \lfloor \sqrt{n} \rfloor + g + p \lfloor \sqrt{n} \rfloor$

Figure 5.10 Operation counts for different factoring problem sizes.

n	Algorithm of Figure 5.3 $10n + g + 2p \lfloor \sqrt{n} \rfloor - p - 19$	Algorithm of Figure 5.4 $22 \lfloor \sqrt{n} \rfloor + g + p \lfloor \sqrt{n} \rfloor - 21$	Algorithm of Figure 5.5 $12 \lfloor \sqrt{n} \rfloor + g + p \lfloor \sqrt{n} \rfloor$
4	$21 + g + 3p$	$23 + g + 2p$	$24 + g + 2p$
10	$81 + g + 5p$	$45 + g + 3p$	$36 + g + 3p$
100	$981 + g + 19p$	$199 + g + 10p$	$120 + g + 10p$
500	$4981 + g + 43p$	$463 + g + 22p$	$264 + g + 22p$
1000	$9981 + g + 61p$	$661 + g + 31p$	$372 + g + 31p$

As may be seen from this table, the optimizations result in a substantial reduction in the number of required operations. The worst case estimate of the number of operations to find all the distinct, nontrivial factors of the number 1000 has been reduced by 9609 equivalent add operations, and the number of **put** operations has been reduced by half.

5.3.2 Efficiency of the Prime Number Algorithm

The prime number algorithm of Figure 4.9 processed many numbers to determine whether they were prime or composite. The most interesting part of that algorithm is the body of the outer **while** loop which performs the actual prime/composite calculation. This section of pseudo code has been chosen as a second example and is shown, in an abbreviated form, in Figure 5.11.

Since part of this algorithm was derived from the algorithm of Figure 4.6, the optimizations applied to that algorithm may be used here. In addition, as was mentioned in Chapter 4, the above algorithm may be improved in at least one other respect. The whole purpose of this algorithm is to determine if the number n has a factor. This algorithm does do this, but after it has found one factor it still looks for more. If the **while** loop could be made to cease iterating after the first factor was found, many computations could be avoided. To achieve early termination of the **while** loop requires modification of the loop condition.

Figure 5.11   Prime number algorithm — no optimizations.

* Determine if a number is prime or composite.
* Test all divisors from 2 to n−1 inclusive.

get n
prime ← 1
m ← 2
while m ≤ n−1 **do**
    if n(mod m) = 0 **then**
        prime ← 0
    m ← m + 1
if prime = 1 **then**
    put n, 'is prime'
  else
    put n, 'is composite'
stop

In this algorithm, the presence or absence of a factor is indicated by the variable prime. If prime is zero then a factor has occurred, and if prime is one then a factor has not been found. Thus, the **while** loop should be terminated if prime has the value zero. Conversely, the **while** loop should continue repeating while prime is not zero. These changes have been incorporated into the algorithm of Figure 5.12. The **while** loop of this algorithm will now terminate after the first factor is found.

With respect to the efficiency of this algorithm, if the number being tested is a prime then the **while** loop will still test all values of $m \leq \sqrt{n}$ before terminating. Thus, the worst case efficiency (when n is prime) has not been improved. If the number is composite, fewer calculations will be performed in almost all circumstances. Thus, it is the average and the best case efficiencies that are improved.

An analysis of the average complexity of the above algorithm is quite complicated. It depends upon the numbers being tested, and no information about them has been given. An analysis of the average efficiency would require some knowledge of the expected distribution of primes versus nonprimes in the numbers to be tested.

Figure 5.12   Prime number algorithm — optimized version 1.

* Determine if a number is prime or composite.
* Test all divisors from 2 to $\sqrt{n}$ inclusive.

get n
prime ← 1
m ← 2
k ← $\sqrt{n}$
while m ≤ k **and** prime ≠ 0 **do**

    if n(mod m) = 0 **then**

        prime ← 0

    else

        m ← m + 1

if prime = 1 **then**

    put n, 'is prime'

  else

    put n, 'is composite'

stop

The next improvement to this algorithm also reduces the number of **while** loop iterations. If the number *n* is even, then it is not prime since it is evenly divisible by two. If *n* is not divisible by two, then only odd numbers need be used as divisors. Using only odd numbers will reduce the number of loop iterations by approximately half. The algorithm of Figure 5.13 incorporates this idea. It first tests if the number is even, and if it is simply records the correct message. If it is not even, then the algorithm proceeds to divide by the odd numbers $m = 3,5,7, \cdots$, etc..

The tables in Figures 5.14, 5.15, and 5.16 give a detailed analysis of the above three algorithms. In Figure 5.14 the operation counts are given for the unoptimized, prime/composite algorithm of Figure 5.11. The table gives a worst case analysis, which occurs when the number *n* is prime. This means that the algorithm will perform *n*−2 test divisions, and that the statement prime ← 0 will not be performed.

Figure 5.13   Prime number algorithm — optimized version 2.

* Determine if a number is prime or composite.
* Test for divisibility by 2, then check all odd numbers from 3 to $\sqrt{n}$.

get n
prime ← 1
if n(mod 2) = 0 **and** n ≠ 2 **then**
   [prime ← 0
  else
   [m ← 3
    k ← $\sqrt{n}$
    while m ≤ k **and** prime ≠ 0 **do**
     [**if** n(mod m) = 0 **then**
       [prime ← 0
      else
       [m ← m + 2

if prime = 1 **then**
   [**put** n, 'is prime'
  else
   [**put** n, 'is composite'
stop

Figure 5.14   Operation count for the prime number algorithm of Figure 5.11.

	Cost	Repetition factor	Total operations
get	g	1	g
prime ← 1	1	1	1
m ← 2	1	1	1
m ≤ n−1	2	n−2	2n−4
n(mod m) = 0	6	n−2	6n−12
prime ← 0	1	0	0
m ← m+1	2	n−2	2n−4
prime = 1	1	1	1
put	p	1	p
		worst case	10n+g+p−17

A worst case analysis for the prime/composite algorithm of Figure 5.12 is given in Figure 5.15. This algorithm contained two changes from the previous one. First, for prime numbers the algorithm divides by numbers only up to the square root of *n*. Second, for composite numbers the algorithm will terminate immediately after the first factor is found. The worst case analysis assumes that *n* is a prime number. Again, the statement prime ← 0 will not be executed.

Figure 5.15   Operation count for the prime number algorithm of Figure 5.12.

	Cost	Repetition factor	Total operations
get	g	1	g
prime ← 1	1	1	1
m ← 2	1	1	1
k ← $\sqrt{n}$	11	1	11
m ≤ k & prime ≠ 0	3	$\lfloor \sqrt{n} \rfloor - 1$	$3 \lfloor \sqrt{n} \rfloor - 3$
n(mod m) = 0	6	$\lfloor \sqrt{n} \rfloor - 1$	$6 \lfloor \sqrt{n} \rfloor - 6$
prime ← 0	1	0	0
m ← m+1	2	$\lfloor \sqrt{n} \rfloor - 1$	$2 \lfloor \sqrt{n} \rfloor - 2$
prime = 1	1	1	1
put	p	1	p
		worst case	$11 \lfloor \sqrt{n} \rfloor + g + p + 3$

Figure 5.16 gives a worst case analysis for the algorithm of Figure 5.13. The optimizations in this case allowed the **while** loop to consider only odd divisors.

Figure 5.16   Operation count for the prime number algorithm of Figure 5.13.

	Cost	Repetition factor	Total operations
get	g	1	g
prime ← 1	1	1	1
n(mod2) = 0 **and** n ≠ 2	8	1	8
prime ← 0	1	0	0
m ← 3	1	1	1
k ← $\sqrt{n}$	11	1	11
m ≤ k & prime ≠ 0	3	$(\lfloor \sqrt{n} \rfloor - 1)/2$	$3(\lfloor \sqrt{n} \rfloor - 1)/2$
n(mod m) = 0	6	$(\lfloor \sqrt{n} \rfloor - 1)/2$	$6(\lfloor \sqrt{n} \rfloor - 1)/2$
prime ← 0	1	$(\lfloor \sqrt{n} \rfloor - 1)/2$	$(\lfloor \sqrt{n} \rfloor - 1)/2$
m ← m+2	2	$(\lfloor \sqrt{n} \rfloor - 1)/2$	$2(\lfloor \sqrt{n} \rfloor - 1)/2$
prime = 1	1	1	1
put	p	1	p
		worst case	$6 \lfloor \sqrt{n} \rfloor + g + p + 16$

The worst case expressions from the above tables have been evaluated for different values of n and listed in Figure 5.17. Each value of n in this table is a prime number. The calculated values in the table give the exact number of operations required to verify that the values of n are prime. As may be seen from the table, the optimizations reduced tremendously the number of required operations. The number of equivalent add operations required to verify that the number 1013 is prime has been reduced to approximately 1/50 of its previous value.

Figure 5.17 Operation counts for different prime number problem sizes.

n	Algorithm of Figure 5.3 $10n+g+p-17$	Algorithm of Figure 5.4 $11\lfloor\sqrt{n}\rfloor+g+p+3$	Algorithm of Figure 5.5 $6\lfloor\sqrt{n}\rfloor+g+p+16$
5	$33+g+p$	$25+g+p$	$28+g+p$
11	$93+g+p$	$36+g+p$	$34+g+p$
101	$993+g+p$	$113+g+p$	$76+g+p$
503	$5013+g+p$	$245+g+p$	$148+g+p$
1013	$10113+g+p$	$344+g+p$	$202+g+p$

5.4 Optimizations in General

The above examples have illustrated that the efficiency of some algorithms may be improved greatly by relatively simple optimizations. The largest gains in efficiency were achieved by reducing the number of **while** loop iterations. The remaining gains were accomplished by minimizing the number of operations performed within the **while** loops. The design of an efficient algorithm is the first step towards achieving an efficient computer program.

When large computer programs are being designed, it is not clear as to how much time should be spent performing extensive algorithm optimizations. The reason for this uncertainty is that in large systems it is not easy to predict in advance which parts of the system will be used most. In some systems, a small amount of code, say 10%, may consume a large percentage of the execution time, up to 90%. Thus, an extensive optimization effort would be best performed on that 10% of code.

One method of measuring the activity of a program is called *profiling*. In the simplest sense, a profile of a program gives the number of times each statement is executed. Thus, by comparing these numbers the sections of a program which are executed the most may be found. Special programs, called *profilers,* exist to perform these measurements. WATFIV-S has a built-in profiler. The use and output of this profiler option in WATFIV-S is illustrated in Appendix E.

The intended use of a program also affects the optimization effort. If a program is only going to be used once, then extensive optimization may not be warranted. On the other hand, a program that is liable to undergo very frequent use should be made as efficient as possible.

5.5 Summary

This chapter has given a brief introduction to the topic of algorithm and program efficiency. This is an important topic as more people are using the computer, and the problems to be solved are becoming larger.

For the size of problems and algorithms presented here, a simple way to determine and compare the efficiencies is to count the number of operations each algorithm performs. The result of such analysis allows insight into the relative performance of algorithms and can determine which algorithm is best for the current problem.

Measurements of programs can be performed in a somewhat more automatic manner using computer profiling techniques. These measurements allow one to obtain precise information on the program to identify the heavily used parts. However, the ability to analyze programs in this manner does not remove the necessity for algorithm analysis. An algorithm analysis can remove the need for programming the various alternates.

5.6   References

Aho, A.V.; Hopcroft, J.E.; and Ullman, J.D. *The Design and Analysis of Computer Algorithms*. Reading, Mass.: Addison-Wesley Pub. Co., 1974.

Van Tassel, D. *Program Style, Design, Efficiency, Debugging, and Testing*. Englewood Cliffs, N.J.: Prentice-Hall, 1974.

Weide, B. "A Survey of Analysis Techniques for Discrete Algorithms." *Computing Surveys* 9(1977): 291-313.

5.7   Exercises

5.1 If two different algorithms for the same problem have the following equations for the number of equivalent add operations, which algorithm would you prefer? Discuss your answer.

   a)   algorithm 1: $x-10y+50$
   b)   algorithm 2: $x-2y+2$

5.2 The equivalent operation counts for three versions of the factoring algorithm are shown in Figure 5.10. Ignoring the **get** and **put** counts, plot the operation counts versus the problem size and compare the resulting curves.

5.3 Determine the expression for the equivalent number of add operations for the algorithms of Figures 5.3, 5.4, and 5.5 assuming that the modulus operation $n\,(\text{mod}\,m)$ is equivalent to only two add operations.

5.4 Determine the number of equivalent add operations (worst case) that the quadratic equation algorithm of Figure 4.12 will require for:

   a)   one set of a, b, c values,
   b)   two sets of a, b, c values,
   c)   three sets of a, b, c values.

   Plot a graph of the above counts versus the problem size (1, 2, and 3) ignoring the **get** and **put** counts.

5.5 The following algorithm determines the sum of a set of numbers in a data list. A data count indicates the number of values to be summed.

```
*  Algorithm to sum the numbers in a data list.
get n
sum ← 0
i ← 0
while i < n do
    ┌  get value
    │  sum ← sum + value
    └  i ← i + 1
put 'The sum of the', n, 'values is', sum
stop
```

Determine the number of equivalent add operations required by this algorithm to sum 10, 15, 20, and 25 numbers. Plot the operation count versus the size of the problem.

5.6 The following algorithm calculates the factorial of a given number. Determine an expression that gives the number of equivalent add operations that the algorithm performs for a number n.

```
*  An algorithm to calculate the factorial of n.
get n
prod ← 1
i ← 1
while i ≤ n do
    ┌  prod ← prod*i
    └  i ← i + 1
put 'The factorial of', n, 'is', prod
stop
```

Plot the number of operations required versus the problem size when $n = 5, 10, 15, 20$ (ignore the **get** and **put** times). Is this algorithm linear with respect to its time?

5.7 Develop an algorithm, using step-wise refinement, which will test the integer numbers from 2 to n to determine if they are prime or composite. For the algorithm as a whole, determine the equivalent number of add operations the algorithm would require.

a) if the prime number computation technique of Figure 4.9 is used,
b) if the prime number computation of Figure 5.13 is used.

Is the difference significant in this case? Discuss your answer.

5.8   The following algorithm calculates n terms of the following series.

$$x+x^2+x^3+x^4+ \cdots +x^n$$

in a somewhat inefficient manner.

```
* Algorithm to evaluate n terms of a series whose general term is xⁿ.

get n, x
put 'The values for n and x are', n, x
sum ← 0
i ← 1
while i ≤ n do
    ┌ prod ← 1
    │ j ← 1
    │ while j ≤ n do
    │     ┌ prod ← prod*x
    │     └ j ← j + 1
    │ sum ← sum + prod
    └ i ← i + 1
put 'The sum of the series is', sum
stop
```

a)   Determine the expression for the equivalent number of add operations for the algorithm.

b)   Rewrite the algorithm to make it more efficient and determine its equivalent add expression. Compare your answer to that of part a).

5.9   By inserting additional pseudo-code statements in the algorithm of Figure 5.3, it is possible to change it to perform the **put** operation of two factors at a time. Such a change will reduce the number of **put** operations by half.

a)   Change the algorithm of Figure 5.3 such that it will perform one half the number of **put** operations.

b)   Analyze your new algorithm and determine the number of additional equivalent add operations that it requires.

c)   In terms of equivalent add operations per **put** operation, at what point would such a scheme be worthwhile for this algorithm?

d)   Can the above method be easily extended to further reduce the number of **put** operations in any of the three algorithms? Discuss your answer.

6
Characteristics of Mathematical Functions

6.1 Introduction

Mathematics is playing an increasingly important role in helping to study complex phenomena in today's society. Mathematical models are used to describe relationships in a variety of fields including not only traditional areas such as physics, chemistry, and engineering, but also in relatively new fields such as economics, sociology, biology, and ecology.

In many of these studies, physical relationships are expressed in terms of mathematical formulas or equations. A very basic notion is that of the dependence of one quantity upon another, referred to mathematically as a functional relationship. The task of understanding these physical phenomena is facilitated by using a computer to manipulate the mathematical functions.

This chapter discusses several common characteristics of functions and examines tabulation and plotting as means of studying them.

6.2 Functional Characteristics

There are a number of characteristics of these mathematical relationships or functions that are of interest. Some of the questions often asked are listed below.

- What does the function look like for a given range of arguments? Figure 6.1 illustrates two common functions graphically, a hyperbola and a polynomial.
- Does the function have more than one value for a particular argument? The illustrated polynomial is single-valued for all values of x. The hyperbola has two values for $|x| \geq b$.

Figure 6.1 Graphs illustrating characteristics of functions.

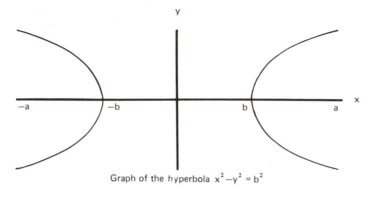

Graph of the hyperbola $x^2 - y^2 = b^2$

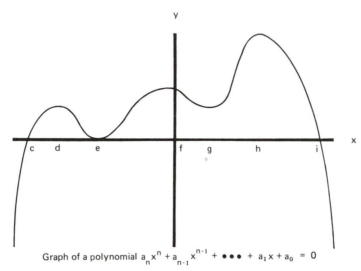

Graph of a polynomial $a_n x^n + a_{n-1} x^{n-1} + \bullet\bullet\bullet + a_1 x + a_0 = 0$

- Is the function defined over a given range or do arguments exist for which the function is undefined? The hyperbola, for example, is undefined for values of x between $-b$ and $+b$.
- Is the function continuous? The polynomial is continuous for all values of x.
- Are there arguments for which the function is zero? The hyperbola is zero for $x = -b$ and $x = +b$ while the polynomial function is zero for $x = c$, $x = e$, and $x = i$. In fact the polynomial has a double zero at $x = e$.
- Does the function have a maximum or minimum? If so, what and where are the maximum and minimum values? For example, the polynomial has two relative maxima at $x = d$ and $x = f$ and an absolute maximum at $x = h$, as well as two relative minima at $x = e$ and $x = g$.
- For what values of x is the function increasing or decreasing?

The answers to the above questions are often necessary in mathematical problem solving. In many cases it is relatively easy to develop algorithms and write computer programs to assist in answering these questions. A selection of these problems will be discussed in sections of this and subsequent chapters.

6.3   Function Tabulation

Perhaps the simplest technique used to study the characteristics of a function is to evaluate that function at a given set of values of the independent variable. Normally this evaluation begins with one specific value and proceeds to a final value using a constant step-size or increment. Consider a specific example.

Example 6.1
    Tabulate $y = x^3 + x^2 - 37x + 35$ from -10 to $+10$ in steps of 1.

The pseudo-code algorithm for this example, shown in Figure 6.2, is straightforward and similar to several examples presented in Chapter 2.

Figure 6.2   Pseudo-code algorithm for Example 6.1.

```
* Tabulate the polynomial y = x³+x²-37x+35 from -10 to +10 in steps of 1.
* Variables used:
* x - current x-value
* y - current y-value

* Initialize x and record column titles.
x ← -10
put ' x ', ' y '
* Keep tabulating points as long as x ≤ 10.
while x ≤ 10 do
    ⎡ y ← x³+x²-37x+35
    ⎢ put x, y
    ⎣ x ← x + 1
stop
```

A WATFIV-S program for this algorithm is given in Figure 6.3, and several points regarding the conversion are made in the notes section following the program.

The output produced by this program is given in Figure 6.4. By scanning this table of values several points of special interest may be observed. The value of y changes sign between x=-8 and x=-6, and a zero of the function occurs at x=-7. Additional zeros can be found at x=1 and x=5. A relative maximum can be detected near x=-4 since at that point y=135 while points on either side yield smaller functional values. Similarly, there is a relative minimum near x=3.

```
$JOB    WATFIV
C$OPTIONS DECIMAL
C*******************************************************************
C Figure 6.3 -- Tabulate the polynomial x**3 + x**2 - 37x + 35
C               from -10 to +10 in steps of 1.
C*******************************************************************
C X - current x-value
C Y - current y-value
C*******************************************************************
      REAL X, Y
C Initialize X and record column titles.
      X = -10.0
      PRINT, '            X                    Y'
      PRINT, ' '
C Keep tabulating points as long as X less or equal 10.
      WHILE(X .LE. 10.0) DO
         Y = X**3 + X**2 - 37.0*X + 35.0
         PRINT, X, Y
         X = X + 1.0
      END WHILE
      STOP
      END
$ENTRY
```

Program Notes

- Though all values in the program will be integers, it is desirable to be able to change the program to use fractional limits or increments. Thus, both X and Y are declared as REAL variables.
- In order to make the output readable, blanks are needed to position the letters X and Y over the two output columns, and a blank message provides vertical spacing.
- For the most part, constants are written with decimal points to be consistent with X and Y as REAL quantities, in keeping with good programming practice. However, there are exceptions in the line:

```
      Y = X**3 + X**2 - 37.0*X + 35.0
```

The two exponents, 3 and 2, are expressed as INTEGER constants. The reason stems from the way WATFIV-S performs exponentiation. If the exponent is a REAL constant or variable, WATFIV-S takes the logarithm of the base, multiplies by the exponent, and then uses antilogarithms to determine the result. If, however, the exponent is INTEGER, WATFIV-S uses successive multiplication by the base to calculate the answer. In addition to simplicity, using INTEGER exponentiation is sometimes necessitated when the base could be negative since logarithms are not defined for numbers less than or equal to 0.

Figure 6.4   Tabulation of the polynomial $x^3+x^2-37x+35$, output from the program of Figure 6.3.

X	Y
-10.00000000	-495.00000000
-9.00000000	-280.00000000
-8.00000000	-117.00000000
-7.00000000	0.00000000
-6.00000000	77.00000000
-5.00000000	120.00000000
-4.00000000	135.00000000
-3.00000000	128.00000000
-2.00000000	105.00000000
-1.00000000	72.00000000
0.00000000	35.00000000
1.00000000	0.00000000
2.00000000	-27.00000000
3.00000000	-40.00000000
4.00000000	-33.00000000
5.00000000	0.00000000
6.00000000	65.00000000
7.00000000	168.00000000
8.00000000	315.00000000
9.00000000	512.00000000
10.00000000	765.00000000

6.4   Evaluating Polynomials: Horner's Rule

In the previous example, the evaluation of the polynomial

$$x^3+x^2-37x+35$$

involved two multiplications to get x^3, one to compute x^2, and a fourth to calculate $37x$. To reduce this amount of arithmetic, computer scientists often evaluate polynomials in a slightly different manner using a technique called Horner's Rule. For the current example, the polynomial would be rewritten as

$$((x+1)x-37)x+35$$

Figure 6.5 compares the steps involved for evaluating the function at $x = 2$.

Figure 6.5   Example comparing evaluation of polynomials.

Step	$x^3+x^2-37x+35$	$((x+1)x-37)x+35$
1	$4x+x^2-37x+35$	$((3)x-37)x+35$
2	$8+x^2-37x+35$	$(6-37)x+35$
3	$8+4-37x+35$	$(-31)x+35$
4	$8+4-74+35$	$-62+35$
5	$12-74+35$	-27
6	$-62+35$	
7	-27	

Seven steps are required to evaluate the polynomial the standard way, whereas Horner's Rule involves only five steps. Though Horner's Rule is generally more efficient, for clarity of presentation succeeding examples involving the evaluation of polynomials will not always use Horner's Rule. However, it is recommended as a useful device for improving efficiency. In terms of Chapter 5, Horner's Rule is a level two optimization.

6.5   Trials and Tribulations of Function Evaluation

In the previous section, a polynomial function was tabulated and studied. Unfortunately, not all function evaluations are as straightforward. A variety of problems must be solved as functions become more complicated. This section will deal with difficulties as they arise in two specific areas, the evaluation of transcendental functions and rational functions.

6.5.1   Transcendental Functions

Many physical relationships are expressed using more complicated mathematical tools such as the trigonometric or exponential functions, which are classified as *transcendental* functions. In addition to problems in obtaining values for such functions, complications arise due to the limitations and peculiarities of computer arithmetic. Consider the following example.

Example 6.2
      Tabulate $\sqrt{x} \sin (\pi x)$ for x from 0 to 3 in steps of 0.2.

      The pseudo-code algorithm for this example, given in Figure 6.6, is a slightly more general form of the algorithm presented for Example 6.1. In this case, the initial value of x, the increment in x, and the final value of x are obtained via the **get** action, thus allowing for more flexibility. Should the first range of x not indicate sufficient information about the function, it is only necessary to change the input list and try the algorithm again for a different range.
      To follow this algorithm manually would require considerable effort. For each value of x, it would be necessary to search a table of values for the appropriate sine and square root values. Not only would this process be time consuming and prone to error, but the values of these functions are likely to be expressed to 4 or 5 decimal places and further arithmetic would tend to be cumbersome. Since FORTRAN was designed to facilitate scientific calculations, functions such as SIN and SQRT were built into the language and can be used simply by specifying the correct name for the function together with a value in parentheses as the *argument*. A large number of such *built-in functions* are provided by WATFIV-S. A complete list is presented in Appendix P. The resulting WATFIV-S implementation is shown in Figure 6.7.

Figure 6.6   Pseudo-code algorithm for Example 6.2.

```
*  Tabulate the transcendental function √x sin (πx )
*  from 0 to 3 in steps of 0.2.

*  Variables used:
*  x - current x-value
*  xfirst - initial x-value
*  xincr - increment in x-value
*  xlast - terminal x-value
*  y - current y-value

*  Obtain and record the tabulation parameters.

get xfirst, xincr, xlast
put 'The initial x-value is', xfirst
put 'The increment in x-value is', xincr
put 'The terminal x-value is', xlast

*  Record column titles and initialize x.

put '  x  ', '  y  '
x ← xfirst

*  Keep tabulating points as long as x ≤ xlast.

while x ≤ xlast do
   ⎡  y ← √x sin (πx )
   ⎢  put x, y
   ⎣  x ← x + xincr
stop

0, .2, 3
```

The output for the program is listed in Figure 6.8. A close look at this output reveals some disturbing news. The x values printed do not appear as expected. The second value of x is 0.1999999 rather than 0.2. All subsequent values of x also seem to be incorrect. Underlying this "inaccuracy" is the method used by computers to store floating-point numbers. Firstly, numbers in a computer are usually represented in a binary-based number system. Secondly, a computer only retains a fixed number of digits when storing a number. Thus, seemingly innocuous numbers such as 0.2 cannot be represented exactly and, as a consequence, 0.2+0.2+0.2+0.2+0.2 only approximates 1.0. This type of error is referred to as *roundoff* error. The same problem arises in other number systems. In base 10 for example, 1/3 represented to 5 decimal places is 0.33333. Adding three such approximations produces 0.99999 instead of 1.00000.

```
$JOB    WATFIV
C$OPTIONS DECIMAL
C************************************************************
C Figure 6.7 -- Tabulate the function sqrt(x)*sin(pi*x).
C************************************************************
C X      - current x-value
C XFIRST - initial x-value
C XINCR  - increment in x-value
C XLAST  - terminal x-value
C Y      - current y-value
C PI     - the numerical constant 3.141593
C************************************************************
        REAL X, XFIRST, XINCR, XLAST, Y, PI, SQRT, SIN
        PI = 3.141593
C Obtain and record the tabulation parameters.
        READ, XFIRST, XINCR, XLAST
        PRINT, 'THE INITIAL X-VALUE IS       ', XFIRST
        PRINT, 'THE INCREMENT IN X-VALUE IS  ', XINCR
        PRINT, 'THE TERMINAL X-VALUE IS      ', XLAST
C Record column titles and initialize X.
        PRINT, ' '
        PRINT, '            X                    Y'
        PRINT, ' '
        X = XFIRST
C Keep tabulating points as long as X less or equal XLAST.
        WHILE(X .LE. XLAST) DO
           Y = SQRT(X) * SIN(PI*X)
           PRINT, X, Y
           X = X + XINCR
        END WHILE
        STOP
        END
$ENTRY
0.0, 0.2, 3.0
```

Program Notes

- The built-in functions SIN and SQRT are used in evaluating the required mathematical function. Notice that an arithmetic expression may be placed within the parentheses for the sine function. This *argument* of the function is evaluated before the function is invoked to compute the desired sine. The arguments for these and most other commonly used mathematical functions must be of type REAL. Note that an approximate value for the numerical constant π must be explicitly given.

Thus, the output illustrates the fact that some computations may only approximate the values which are expected. In most cases, however, the information produced is sufficient for scientific purposes.

The above problem may often be avoided by choosing interval endpoints and increments which are either whole numbers or powers of 2, both of which can be represented accurately in the computer. In the above example, if the increment were changed to 0.25 ($1/2^2$), 0.1875 ($3/2^4$), or even 0.125 ($1/2^3$), the x values would not exhibit the roundoff difficulty. This is demonstrated in Figure 6.9. Though the values of x are now exact, the values of the function at x=1, 2, and 3 should be zero. Instead, they

Figure 6.8   Tabulation of the function $\sqrt{x} \sin(\pi x)$, output from the program of Figure 6.7.

THE INITIAL X-VALUE IS   0.00000000
THE INCREMENT IN X-VALUE IS   0.19999990
THE TERMINAL X-VALUE IS   3.00000000

X	Y
0.00000000	0.00000000
0.19999990	0.26286540
0.39999990	0.60150070
0.59999990	0.73668510
0.79999990	0.52573090
0.99999990	0.00000063
1.19999900	-0.64388580
1.39999900	-1.12530300
1.59999900	-1.20300100
1.79999900	-0.78859900
1.99999900	-0.00000447
2.19999800	0.87182250
2.39999800	1.47336700
2.59999800	1.53353300
2.79999800	0.98355880
2.99999800	0.00000987

are computed as very small numbers close to zero. This is partly a function of the approximation used for defining the constant π and the roundoff error inherent in the routines that compute the sine of πx.

Figure 6.9   Revised tabulation of the function $\sqrt{x} \sin(\pi x)$, output from the program of Figure 6.7.

THE INITIAL X-VALUE IS   0.00000000
THE INCREMENT IN X-VALUE IS   0.12500000
THE TERMINAL X-VALUE IS   3.00000000

X	Y
0.00000000	0.00000000
0.12500000	0.13529890
0.25000000	0.35355340
0.37500000	0.56575810
0.50000000	0.70710670
0.62500000	0.73039080
0.75000000	0.61237230
0.87500000	0.35796730
1.00000000	-0.00000033
1.12500000	-0.40589620
1.25000000	-0.79056870
1.37500000	-1.08334300
1.50000000	-1.22474300
1.62500000	-1.17771900
1.75000000	-0.93541350
1.87500000	-0.52400980
2.00000000	0.00000092
2.12500000	0.55785190
2.25000000	1.06065900
2.37500000	1.42379300
2.50000000	1.58113700
2.62500000	1.49685400
2.75000000	1.17260200
2.87500000	0.64886980
3.00000000	-0.00000169

6.5.2   Evaluating Rational Functions

In the previous example the limitations of computer representation of numbers was only an inconvenience. Sometimes, however, the problems created are more serious. Consider an example involving two polynomials.

Example 6.3

Tabulate the following function for a given set of values.

$$\frac{x^3+2x^2-7x-10}{x^2-x-2}$$

Unlike the examples thus far, evaluating this function requires a little more care. Values of x that cause the denominator to be zero must be avoided since the function is undefined at these points. This can be accomplished in several ways, either by checking for specific x values or by checking for a zero denominator. For generality, the latter technique is usually preferred. The pseudo-code algorithm incorporating such a check is given in Figure 6.10.

Converting this algorithm to a WATFIV-S program presents some practical problems. Specifically, how does one check for a zero denominator? Because of roundoff error, the specific values of x that cause a zero denominator may or may not be encountered. Even if this x value is computed exactly, the corresponding denominator may not be quite zero due to roundoff error. Again, because a computer only retains a fixed number of digits in its arithmetic and its representations, the result of a computation such as $(2.000005)^2-4.0$ could be zero. The safest check, therefore, involves looking for absolute values of the denominator which are less than some arbitrarily small number. This feature is illustrated in the program of Figure 6.11. All denominators between -0.00005 and +0.00005 are avoided. The program uses the built-in function, ABS, to find the absolute value of the denominator.

Figure 6.10   Pseudo-code algorithm for Example 6.3.

```
* Tabulate the rational function

*     x³+2x²−7x−10
      ────────────
        x²−x−2

* Variables used:
* x - current x-value
* xfirst - initial x-value
* xincr - increment in x-value
* xlast - terminal x-value
* y - current y-value

* Obtain and record the tabulation parameters.

get xfirst, xincr, xlast
put 'The initial x-value is', xfirst
put 'The increment in x-value is', xincr
put 'The terminal x-value is', xlast

* Record column titles and initialize x.

put '  x  ', '  y  '
x ← xfirst

* Keep tabulating points as long as x ≤ xlast.

while x ≤ xlast do
   ┌ denom ← x²−x−2
   │ if denom = 0 then
   │    ┌ put x, 'y is undefined'
   │  else
   │    ┌ y ← (x³+2x²−7x−10)/denom
   │    └ put x, y
   └ x ← x + xincr
stop
−4, .25, 3
```

The corresponding output appears in Figure 6.12. The function is undefined in the neighbourhood of x=1 and also x=2. Zeros of the function can be detected between -3.25 and -3.0, -1.5 and -1.25, and 2.25 and 2.5.

```
$JOB    WATFIV
C$OPTIONS DECIMAL
C************************************************************
C Figure 6.11 -- Tabulate x**3+2x**2-7x-10 / x**2-x-2.
C************************************************************
C X      - current x-value
C XFIRST - initial x-value
C XINCR  - increment in x-value
C XLAST  - terminal x-value
C Y      - current y-value
C DENOM  - denominator of the function
C************************************************************
        REAL X, XFIRST, XINCR, XLAST, Y, DENOM, ABS
C Obtain and record the tabulation parameters.
        READ, XFIRST, XINCR, XLAST
        PRINT, 'THE INITIAL X-VALUE IS       ', XFIRST
        PRINT, 'THE INCREMENT IN X-VALUE IS  ', XINCR
        PRINT, 'THE TERMINAL X-VALUE IS      ', XLAST
C Record column titles and initialize X.
        PRINT, ' '
        PRINT, '           X                   Y'
        PRINT, ' '
        X = XFIRST
C Keep tabulating points as long as X less or equal XLAST.
C Avoid values of X when the denominator is almost zero.
        WHILE(X .LE. XLAST) DO
            DENOM = X**2 - X - 2.0
            IF(ABS(DENOM) .LE. 0.00005) THEN DO
                PRINT, X, '          Y MAY BE UNDEFINED'
              ELSE DO
                Y = (X**3 + 2.0*X**2 - 7.0*X - 10.0) / DENOM
                PRINT, X, Y
            END IF
            X = X + XINCR
        END WHILE
        STOP
        END
$ENTRY
-4.0, 0.25, 3.0
```

6.5.3   Functions in General

The preceding two subsections have dealt specifically with transcendental and rational functions. The difficulties exhibited by the examples are also evident in evaluating functions in general. Though a detailed study of pitfalls in numerical computations is beyond the scope of this introduction, references are given at the end of the chapter for those interested in pursuing this topic further.

Figure 6.12   Tabulation of a rational function, output from the program of Figure 6.11.

THE INITIAL X-VALUE IS	-4.00000000
THE INCREMENT IN X-VALUE IS	0.25000000
THE TERMINAL X-VALUE IS	3.00000000

X	Y
-4.00000000	-0.77777770
-3.75000000	-0.52865610
-3.50000000	-0.28181810
-3.25000000	-0.03835979
-3.00000000	0.19999990
-2.75000000	0.43045100
-2.50000000	0.64814810
-2.25000000	0.84411760
-2.00000000	1.00000000
-1.75000000	1.07222100
-1.50000000	0.92857140
-1.25000000	-0.09615380
-1.00000000	Y MAY BE UNDEFINED
-0.75000000	5.88636300
-0.50000000	4.89999900
-0.25000000	4.82407300
0.00000000	5.00000000
0.25000000	5.30714200
0.50000000	5.72222100
0.75000000	6.26428500
1.00000000	7.00000000
1.25000000	8.10185100
1.50000000	10.09999000
1.75000000	15.65909000
2.00000000	Y MAY BE UNDEFINED
2.25000000	-5.21153800
2.50000000	0.35714280
2.75000000	2.37222100
3.00000000	3.50000000

6.6   Plotting a Single Function

The discussion in the previous sections of this chapter has been concerned with tabulating functions of various complexities and then studying the tables of values. There is an old adage which states that a picture is worth a thousand words. In a similar vein, a graph would be worth a thousand(?) tabulated points. Is there some method of having the computer generate a graph for a function?

To answer this question, consider how a graph might be drawn manually for a sample cubic polynomial.

Example 6.4

Plot a graph for the cubic polynomial x^3-2x^2-5x+6 from -2.5 to $+3.5$ with points plotted at intervals of 0.25.

The general structure of the algorithm would be very similar to the algorithm for tabulating the function. Some initial decisions would be necessary about the overall size of the graph and how the points should be kept. As the function is evaluated repetitively, each x value and corresponding functional value must be retained for future plotting. After the points have been tabulated, it is necessary to scan the table to determine the range of functional values. This range would be used to determine the scale factors necessary to produce a graph of the correct size. Next, each pair of values must be scaled to size and positioned on the graph. These steps are crudely incorporated into the general algorithm in Figure 6.13.

Figure 6.13   Pseudo-code algorithm for Example 6.4.

```
* Plot a graph for the cubic polynomial x³−2x²−5x+6

* Variables used:
* x - current x-value
* xfirst - initial x-value
* xincr - increment in x-value
* xlast - terminal x-value
* y - current y-value

* Obtain and record the plotting parameters.
get xfirst, xincr, xlast
put 'The initial x-value is', xfirst
put 'The increment in x-value is', xincr
put 'The terminal x-value is', xlast
x ← xfirst

"Prepare to record (x,y) pairs"
"Choose the graph size"

while x ≤ xlast do
    ┌  y ← x³−2x²−5x+6
    │  "Retain the (x,y) pair for plotting"
    └  x ← x + xincr

"Determine the range of values"
"Compute the scale factors"
"Scale and plot each (x,y) pair"

stop

−2.5, 0.25, 3.5
```

Though this algorithm may provide sufficient detail if applied manually, some big questions exist if the algorithm were to be applied by a computer. And although it would be possible to refine this algorithm to make it specific enough for translation into a computer program, fortunately this is not necessary. Since plotting is a commonly desired feature, provision already exists to help draw graphs by taking advantage of procedures already developed by other programmers.

Such commonly used programs are typically retained in a *program library* maintained by each individual computing facility. By properly referring to the appropriate program, it may be possible to solve problems more easily.

The WATFIV-S program in Figure 6.14 illustrates the use of a package of four such programs developed for plotting elementary graphs on an ordinary line printer (see Appendix M for a complete description). The four programs are special WATFIV-S *subprograms* called *subroutines*. As subprograms, they can not be used on their own, but must be referenced by other programs. Each routine is invoked by a CALL statement having the general form:

```
CALL name (argument list)
```

where name is replaced by the WATFIV-S name given to the subroutine in the library and where any arguments to the subroutine are placed in parentheses following the name. If there are several arguments in the list, they are separated by commas.

The preparation for plotting and recording (x,y) pairs is performed by the SETPLT subroutine. This subroutine does not have any arguments. Naturally, it must be the first of these routines to be executed and should only be executed once for each graph.

As an optional feature, it is possible to change the size of the plotting surface of the graph using the SETSIZ subroutine. The package will plot a graph with x coordinates spread across the printed page and with y coordinates down the page. By default, the limits are set to 51 lines in the y direction and 101 characters in the x direction. The call to subroutine SETSIZ in the program changes these values to 31 lines and 41 characters respectively. Valid sizes in the y direction are 11, 21, 31, 41, or 51, while in the x direction valid sizes are 11, 21, 31, . . . , or 101.

The STOPNT routine is used to retain or STOre PoiNTs for future plotting, to a maximum of 1000 points. For example, execution of the statement:

```
CALL STOPNT(X,Y,'C')
```

causes the values of x and y and the letter c to be remembered for plotting later. Notice that the desired character to be placed in the specified position is written between single quotes.

After all points to be plotted have been collected, several major steps in the plotting process remain. It is necessary to determine the range of values and compute the scale factors. Finally, each point must be scaled and plotted. All of these functions are accomplished by the PLOTC subroutine. The single parameter for this subroutine determines the type of graph, a value of 0 implying that no grid should be printed while a value of 1 causes an equally spaced grid to be superimposed on the plotted points.

The output produced by the sample plotting program is included in Figure 6.15. The message above the graph states that all 25 of the points submitted were plotted. The graph itself includes the scale of y values at regular intervals in a column to the left. The scale in the x direction is printed in a line at the bottom of the graph. For reference, the scale factors for the ordinate or y coordinates and for the abscissa or x coordinates are printed following the graph.

```
$JOB    WATFIV
C$OPTIONS DECIMAL
C**********************************************************
C Figure 6.14 -- Plot a graph for x**3-2x**2-5x+6
C**********************************************************
C X      - current x-value
C XFIRST - initial x-value
C XINCR  - increment in x-value
C XLAST  - terminal x-value
C Y      - current y-value
C**********************************************************
      REAL X, XFIRST, XINCR, XLAST, Y
C Obtain and record the plotting parameters.
      READ, XFIRST, XINCR, XLAST
      PRINT, 'THE INITIAL X-VALUE IS      ', XFIRST
      PRINT, 'THE INCREMENT IN X-VALUE IS ', XINCR
      PRINT, 'THE TERMINAL X-VALUE IS     ', XLAST
C Initialize X and the plotting routines.
      X = XFIRST
      CALL SETPLT
      CALL SETSIZ(31,41)
C Keep tabulating points as long as X less or equal XLAST.
      WHILE(X .LE. XLAST) DO
         Y = X**3 - 2.0*X**2 - 5.0*X + 6.0
         CALL STOPNT(X,Y,'C')
         X = X + XINCR
      END WHILE
C Plot the graph.
      CALL PLOTC(0)
      STOP
      END
$ENTRY
-2.5, 0.25, 3.5
```

Though limited by the accuracy of character positions on a printer, the graph does give a reasonable characterization of the function. The function appears to be continuous. It increases from x=-2.5 to about x=-1, then decreases to a relative minimum near x=+2 before increasing until at least the edge of the graph at x=+3.5. Approximating by eye, the maximum value near x=-1 appears to be about 8 while the minimum value near x=2 is about −4.

As indicated above, the package of printer-plot routines offers a more convenient way to study mathematical functions than simple tabulation. As with many routines written by other programmers, the subroutines may not offer all of the flexibility a user might desire. In some cases it is necessary to rewrite the programs; in others, it is more desirable to mold the routines to the task at hand. In the previous example, the zeros of the function are somewhat difficult to pinpoint. Molding the routines to improve the graph will be discussed in the next two sections.

Figure 6.15   Graph of the polynomial x^3-2x^2-5x+6, output from the program of Figure 6.14.

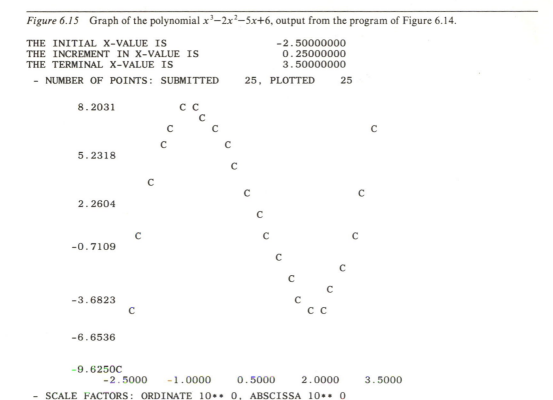

```
THE INITIAL X-VALUE IS                 -2.50000000
THE INCREMENT IN X-VALUE IS             0.25000000
THE TERMINAL X-VALUE IS                 3.50000000
 - NUMBER OF POINTS: SUBMITTED     25, PLOTTED     25


     8.2031           C C
                       C
                    C     C                          C
                    C       C
     5.2318                C
              C
                       C          C
     2.2604         C
              C          C          C
    -0.7109             C
                     C           C
                    C          C
    -3.6823             C
       C                C C

    -6.6536


    -9.6250C
        -2.5000    -1.0000    0.5000    2.0000    3.5000
 - SCALE FACTORS: ORDINATE 10** 0, ABSCISSA 10** 0
```

6.7   Plotting Several Functions

In the previous section, a program was developed to plot a single function. It is often desirable to plot two functions on the same graph, perhaps to determine their points of intersection. Consider such an example.

Example 6.5

Plot a single graph for the polynomial $y = x^3-2x^2-5x+6$ and the straight line $2y = 8-5x$ from -2.5 to $+3.5$ with points at intervals of 0.25.

Since the plotting routines simply remember points to be plotted, incorporating a second function on the same graph simply involves including a second loop in the program of Figure 6.14 to tabulate and store points on the straight line. The **while** loop:

```
X = XFIRST
WHILE(X .LE. XLAST) DO
   Y = 4.0 - 2.5*X
   CALL STOPNT(X,Y,'L')
   X = X + XINCR
END WHILE
```

could be inserted immediately following the END WHILE statement in the previous program. The resulting graph appears in Figure 6.16. Notice that the letter L was used for points on the line. The plotting package places an asterisk wherever the two curves intersect.

Figure 6.16   Graph of the polynomial and straight line, output from a modified program of Figure 6.14.

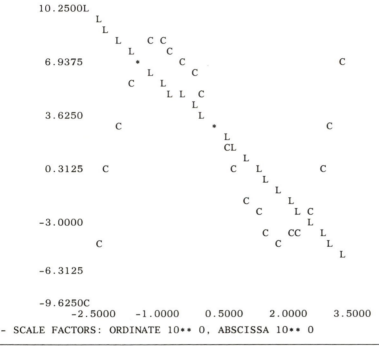

```
THE  INITIAL  X-VALUE  IS                    -2.50000000
THE  INCREMENT  IN  X-VALUE  IS               0.25000000
THE  TERMINAL  X-VALUE  IS                    3.50000000
 -  NUMBER  OF  POINTS:  SUBMITTED     50, PLOTTED     50


      10.2500L
              L
               L
                 L      C C
                   L      C
       6.9375       *      C                                  C
                     L      C
              C      L
                  L L  C
                        L
       3.6250          L
            C              *                      C
                        L
                        CL
                          L
       0.3125    C           C   L               C
                             L
                              L
                       C        L
                        C      L C
      -3.0000                   L
                        C   CC   L
              C                C     L
                                      L

      -6.3125


      -9.6250C
           -2.5000    -1.0000    0.5000    2.0000    3.5000
 -  SCALE  FACTORS:  ORDINATE  10** 0, ABSCISSA  10** 0
```

6.7.1 Adding an *x* Axis

Since including a second function on the same graph was so easy, why not include the *x* axis as well? After all, the *x* axis is simply the straight line with equation $y = 0$. A program combining all three functions is given in Figure 6.17. Since all three functions are being evaluated for the same set of *x* values, the three evaluations have been incorporated into a single loop. The letter c is used for the cubic polynomial, the letter L for the straight line, and a dash for the *x* axis.

```
$JOB     WATFIV
C$OPTIONS DECIMAL
C**************************************************************
C Figure 6.17 -- Plot a graph for x**3-2x**2-5x+6 and 2y=8-5x.
C                Include the x-axis on the graph.
C**************************************************************
C X       - current x-value
C XFIRST  - initial x-value
C XINCR   - increment in x-value
C XLAST   - terminal x-value
C YCUBIC  - current y-value for the cubic polynomial
C YLINE   - current y-value for the straight line
C**************************************************************
      REAL X, XFIRST, XINCR, XLAST, YCUBIC, YLINE
C Obtain and record the plotting parameters.
      READ, XFIRST, XINCR, XLAST
      PRINT, 'THE INITIAL X-VALUE IS       ', XFIRST
      PRINT, 'THE INCREMENT IN X-VALUE IS  ', XINCR
      PRINT, 'THE TERMINAL X-VALUE IS      ', XLAST
C Initialize X and the plotting routines.
      X = XFIRST
      CALL SETPLT
      CALL SETSIZ(31,41)
C Keep tabulating points as long as X less or equal XLAST.
      WHILE(X .LE. XLAST) DO
          YCUBIC = X**3 - 2.0*X**2 - 5.0*X + 6.0
          CALL STOPNT(X,YCUBIC,'C')
          YLINE = 4.0 - 2.5*X
          CALL STOPNT(X,YLINE,'L')
          CALL STOPNT(X,0.0,'-')
          X = X + XINCR
      END WHILE
C Plot the graph.
      CALL PLOTC(0)
      STOP
      END
$ENTRY
-2.5, 0.125, 3.5
```

The final graph is shown in Figure 6.18. From this graph, the points of intersection are easier to see. Estimating by eye (using the scales on the graph), the three points of intersection are near (-1,7), (0.5,3.5), and (2.75,-3). In addition, it is possible to approximate the zeros of the cubic as -2.0, 1.0, and 3.0, a fact that in this case can be checked analytically by factoring the polynomial as $(x+2)(x-1)(x-3)$.

6.8   Summary

This chapter has provided an introduction to the study of several characteristics of mathematical functions. Examples have been demonstrated for tabulating and plotting elementary functions. It is possible to design many other algorithms to assist in understanding the functions being studied. Some of these are suggested in the exercises

Figure 6.18   Final graph of the polynomial, straight line, and *x* axis, output from the program in Figure 6.17.

```
THE INITIAL X-VALUE IS                    -2.50000000
THE INCREMENT IN X-VALUE IS                0.12500000
THE TERMINAL X-VALUE IS                    3.50000000
 - NUMBER OF POINTS: SUBMITTED   147, PLOTTED    147

      10.2500LL
             LL
             LL
             LL     CCCC
                 LLC    CC
       6.9375     *L        C                        C
                 C LL      CC
                 C     LL      C
                     LLL   C                       C
                 C         LL
       3.6250              LC
                 C         L*                    C
                              *L
                 C          CL                   C
                            CLL
       0.3125---*--------------------*--**----------*---
                            L
                          C   LLL    C
              C           C        LL
                          CC       LLC
      -3.0000             C      CLL
                          CC  CC  LL
              C              CC     LL
                                    L
      -6.3125
              C

      -9.6250C
          -2.5000   -1.0000    0.5000    2.0000    3.5000
 - SCALE FACTORS: ORDINATE 10** 0, ABSCISSA 10** 0
```

to follow. Other specific problems such as determining zeros of a function and finding areas between a curve and the *x* axis will be discussed in succeeding chapters.

6.9   References

Abramowitz, M. and Stegun, I., ed. *Handbook of Mathematical Functions with Formulas, Graphs, and Mathematical Tables.* National Bureau of Standards Applied Mathematics Series, vol. 55. Washington, D.C.: Government Printing Office, (1964). Also available as a paperback reprint through Dover, New York.

Peterson, T.S. *Elements of Calculus.* New York: Harper and Row, 1960.

Stanton, R.G. and Fryer, K.D. *Algebra and Vector Geometry.* New York: Holt, Rinehart and Winston, (1965).

6.10   Exercises

In most of the following exercises a program is requested to solve a specific problem. For each problem it is recommended that step-wise refinement be used in developing a pseudo-code algorithm to solve the problem. This algorithm should then be translated into WATFIV-S and run on the computer. Where appropriate, the program should be tested with a variety of data sufficient to ensure that the program does what it is supposed to do.

6.1 Tabulate each of the following functions over a suitable range of values. Use the resulting table of values to discuss properties of the function.

a) $x^4-6x^3-6x^2-70x+9$
b) $x^4+3x^3-3x^2-6x+2$
c) $x^4+3x^3-3x^2-6x+4$
d) $x^4+3x^3-3x^2-6x+6$
e) $x^4-x^3-85x^2-403x+200$
f) $(\sqrt{\sin x+3}+\sqrt[4]{|\cos x|})/(2x^2-2x-3)$
g) $(|\sin x|+12)^{1/12}/(tan[x+4\sqrt{x}+2])$
h) $\dfrac{e^{-m}m^k}{k!}$ for given values of m and $k=0,1,2,\ldots,12$.

6.2 Plot each of the following functions over a suitable range of values. On the graph, indicate the noticeable properties of the function. Estimate each zero and relative maxima or minima.

a) $2x^3-15x^2+26x+7$
b) $x^4-5x^3-8x^2-7x+55$
c) $x^4-x^3-3x^2+5x-2$
d) x^4-2x^3-x-2
e) x^4-10x^2+25
f) $x^5+x^4+2x^3+2x^2-8x-8$
g) $2x^4-14x^3-2x^2+68x+56$
h) $(\sin x/\cos x)-x$
i) $\sqrt{x-1}+(x+e^{-x})/\sqrt{x}$

6.3 Develop a program to study each of the following limits.

a) $\lim\limits_{t\to0}[\cos 2t]\dfrac{1}{t^2}$

b) $\lim\limits_{t\to0}\left[\dfrac{1+t}{t}-\dfrac{1}{log(1+t)}\right]$

c) $\lim\limits_{t\to\infty}\left[\dfrac{3x^3-2x+4}{2-3x^2-2x^3}\right]$

d) $\lim\limits_{n\to\infty}\left[\dfrac{\left(1+\dfrac{1}{n^2}\right)^{\frac{1}{2}}}{1+\dfrac{1}{n}}\right]$

6.4 Series expansions are often used to generate values for commonly used mathematical functions. In many cases, a term in the series can be derived from the previous term by several simple arithmetic operations rather than by evaluating a general form of the term. Develop programs to evaluate each of the following series for a given range of x.

a) $\dfrac{1}{1+x} = 1-x+x^2-x^3+\cdots$

b) $\sqrt{1+x} = 1+\dfrac{1}{2}x-\dfrac{1}{8}x^2+\dfrac{1}{16}x^3-\cdots$

c) $\ln(1+x) = x-\dfrac{x^2}{2}+\dfrac{x^3}{3}-\dfrac{x^4}{4}+\cdots$

d) $e^x = 1+x+\dfrac{x^2}{2!}+\dfrac{x^3}{3!}+\cdots$

e) $\sin x = \dfrac{x^1}{1!}-\dfrac{x^3}{3!}+\dfrac{x^5}{5!}-\dfrac{x^7}{7!}+\cdots$

f) $\cos x = 1-\dfrac{x^2}{2!}+\dfrac{x^4}{4!}-\dfrac{x^6}{6!}+\cdots$

6.5 Polar coordinates are a useful tool for studying a variety of mathematical functions.

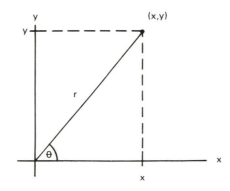

For any point (x,y) on the coordinate plane, $x = r\cos\theta$ and $y = r\sin\theta$. Make use of polar coordinates to plot the following functions. The letters a and b are given constants.

Hint: Vary the angle θ to calculate successive values for r and subsequently x and y.

a) A parabolic arc, $x^{1/2}+y^{1/2} = a^{1/2}$.
b) The folium of Descartes, $x^3+y^3-3axy = 0$.
c) The cissoid of Diocles, $y^2 = x^3/(2a-x)$.
d) An astroid, $x^{2/3}+y^{2/3} = a^{2/3}$.
e) The witch of Agnesi, $x^2y = 4a^2(2a-y)$.
f) A strophoid, $y^2 = x^2(a+x)/(a-x)$.
g) A cardioid, $r = a(1-\cos\theta)$.
h) A limacon, $r = b-a\cos\theta$, $(b < a)$.
i) The spiral of Archimedes, $r = a\theta$.
j) A hyperbolic spiral, $r\theta = a$.
k) The lemniscate of Bernoulli, $r^2 = a^2\cos2\theta$.
l) A three-leaved rose, $r = a\sin3\theta$.
m) A four-leaved rose, $r = a\sin2\theta$.
n) A cycloid, $x = a(\theta-\sin\theta)$, $y = a(1-\cos\theta)$.
o) A trochoid, $x = a\theta-b\sin\theta$, $y = a-b\cos\theta$, for values of $a < b$.

6.6 The following two functions intersect in two places.

$$f_1(x) = \sqrt{4-x^2}$$

$$f_2(x) = 1+x^2$$

Plot a graph of the functions which clearly illustrates the points of intersection and approximate their coordinates.

6.7 Develop a program to draw a straight line between any two points, (x_1,y_1) and (x_2,y_2). The resulting graph should include both an x axis and a y axis.

6.8 Develop a program to draw a circle of given radius and given center. The resulting graph should include both an x axis and a y axis.

6.9 Under ideal conditions, a bullet fired into the air will travel a horizontal distance d in a time t as described by the following equations.

$$d = \frac{v^2\sin2\theta}{g}$$

$$t = \frac{2v\sin\theta}{g}$$

where v is the initial velocity, θ is the angle of inclination and g, the force due to gravity, is 9.8 meters/second^2. Develop a program to produce a single graph of both d and t as a function of θ as θ ranges from 0° to 90°. Arrange to input a value for v.

6.10 A law of optics states that:

$$\frac{1}{a}+\frac{1}{b} = \frac{1}{f}$$

where f is the focal length of the lens, a is the distance from the lens to the object, and b is the distance from the lens to the image. If b is positive, then the image is a real image. If b is negative, then the image is said to be virtual. However, if

$1/b = 0$, then there is no image. Develop a program which tabulates the image distance, b, for all values of $a = 1, 2, 3, \ldots ,10$ and $f = 1, 2, 3, \ldots ,10$. The program should record an appropriate message beside each value of b.

6.11 Consider the diagram in Figure 6.19.

Figure 6.19 Banded area for Exercise 6.11.

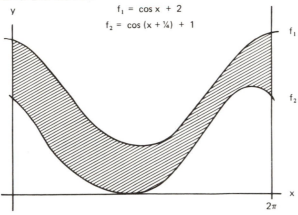

Develop a program to plot the pictured band. The area between the two curves should be filled with slashes.

6.12 Through the use of attached plotters and cathode-ray tube terminals, computers have the ability to provide graphical output in addition to the regular alphanumeric printouts. For some applications, the information to be drawn does not always fit in the limited drawing or viewing area. Thus, a method of trimming the drawing information must be used.

Figure 6.20 Drawing information doesn't always fit (Exercise 6.12).

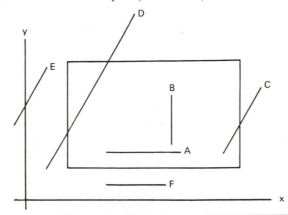

Figure 6.20 illustrates a situation for which the drawing information (straight lines) does not fit completely within the drawing area. The lines A and B are within the area, the lines C and D are partially within the area and must be trimmed, and the lines E and F lie outside the area and may be discarded. Develop a program that will take a specified viewing area, and for each of a series of lines with given endpoints, (x_1,y_1) and (x_2,y_2), determine if the line

a)   is within the drawing area
b)   is outside the drawing area
c)   pierces the drawing area (one end in, one end out)
d)   cuts the drawing area (similar to D in the diagram).

The program should record an appropriate message in each case.

6.13 The problem of finding a maximum point of a function can usually be solved analytically but must occasionally be solved numerically with the aid of a computer. Consider the following numerical technique. The continuous function $f(x)$ is known to have a single relative maximum in the interval $[a,b]$. Divide the interval $[a,b]$

Figure 6.21   Finding a maximum of a function (Exercise 6.13).

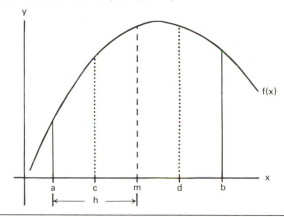

into four equal subintervals as shown in Figure 6.21. If $f(c) > f(m)$, then the maximum must be in the subinterval $[a,m]$. If $f(d) > f(m)$, then the maximum must be in the subinterval $[m,b]$. Otherwise, the maximum must lie in the subinterval $[c,d]$. In any case, the search is refined to the new subinterval and the procedure is repeated, this time with a smaller value of h. The algorithm continues until h, half the interval size, is sufficiently small, that is, $h \le \epsilon$. Develop a program to use this method to find the maximum value of $f(x) = 2.25x - x^3$ in the interval $[0,1]$ with ϵ equal to 0.5×10^{-8}. Compare the resulting approximation with that obtained by applying analytical methods.

6.14 Biorhythm theory originated in Europe toward the end of the last century. According to this theory, each person has a set of life rhythms or life cycles which begin on the day a person is born. There are three such rhythms known as the physical, emotional, and intellectual cycles. Each of these cycles takes the form of a sine wave with the following periods.

- physical cycle (23 days)
- emotional cycle (28 days)
- intellectual cycle (33 days)

In the case of the physical cycle, the theory proposes that in the first half, or positive portion, of the cycle, one's physical well-being is enhanced as opposed to the second half, or negative portion, of the physical cycle. Similar reasoning is applied to the emotional and intellectual cycles. The worst days are the critical days when any one of the three rhythms switch from negative to positive or vice versa.

The calculation of a person's biorhythm requires knowing the number of days since they were born. This may be determined by calculating the Julian Day number of the date of birth and the Julian Day number of the required day and subtracting them. The Julian Day number for a given day may be calculated by the following formula (valid for all dates A.D.).

$$\text{Julian Day} = 1721060 + 365y + 31(m-1) + d + \lfloor y'/4 \rfloor - \lfloor y'/100 \rfloor + \lfloor y'/400 \rfloor - x$$

where $\lfloor z \rfloor$ = the largest integer $\leq z$, y = the year, m = the month, d = the day, and for $m \leq 2$, $x = 0$ and $y' = y - 1$, for $m > 2$, $x = \lfloor .4m + 2.3 \rfloor$ and $y' = y$.

Once the number of days is known, it may be divided by the length of each cycle to determine the status of the cycles on the required day.

Develop a program that will generate a plot of the biorhythm cycles for a given person over a specified period of time. The input for the program should be the person's birthdate, the date the plot is to start, and the date the plot is to end. The dates may be given in the form YYYY MM DD. The output from the program should be be a plot containing the three biorhythm curves, using the characters P, E, and I for the respective curves, versus the Julian Day number. To the diagram add markings by hand to indicate the days of the month.

7
Locating Zeros and Root Finding

7.1 Introduction

In a number of examples in the previous chapter, it was noted that the value of a function could become zero for a certain specific value of its argument. Such a value of x, for which $f(x)$ is 0, is called a *zero* of $f(x)$. Similarly, one refers to the solution of an equation $f(x) = 0$ as a *root* of the equation. In this case the root of the equation and the zero of the function coincide and this leads to some confusion between the two terms. For example, a root of the equation $f(x) = a$ is not a zero of the function $f(x)$, unless $a = 0$.

Historically, mathematicians sought ways of solving for the roots of equations by explicit formulas, such as the quadratic formula discussed in Chapter 4. Later on, it was shown that such formulas are impossible to obtain for polynomial equations of degree greater than four and for virtually all transcendental equations. The need to have *approximate* methods for finding the roots of equations was recognized and studied over three centuries ago, and aspects of such methods still attract the attention of eminent scientists. In this chapter, various techniques for approximating the location of zeros are discussed and several algorithms are developed.

7.2 Graphical Search for a Zero

A sound way to approach the problem of locating a zero of $f(x)$ is to start with a *graph* of the function. From such a graph, one may be able to identify the location of a zero well enough for the purpose at hand. At the very least one can conclude that a zero lies in some rough interval, say $a \leq x \leq b$. Here a and b are two points between which it is certain that the values of $f(x)$ have changed sign.

(This implies the presence of a zero between them if $f(x)$ is continuous.)

The ability to draw a graph requires only values of the function for specific values of the independent variable. These are easy to obtain automatically by a function tabulation program as was illustrated in Chapter 6. The values may be plotted by hand but most computer systems have provision for automatic plotting, such as the program package of the previous chapter. In fact one may use plotting as the basis of an *algorithm* for the solution of the zero-finding problem to *any* accuracy required. The steps involved would be:

1)   graph $f(x)$ for $a \leq x \leq b$;
2)   estimate a better interval $[a',b']$ by eye;
3)   graph $f(x)$ for $a' \leq x \leq b'$;
4)   repeat 2) and 3) until the interval is small enough.

This algorithm may actually be quite useful to the scientist who needs a "quick and dirty" estimate of a zero for planning purposes, particularly if there is immediate access to interactive computing facilities.

As an illustration of how to apply this algorithm consider the function

$$f(x) = x^3 - 4x^2 - 4x + 15.$$

Figure 7.1 shows an initial printer-plot graph of this function in the range -3 to $+5$. This graph illustrates the rough location of all three zeros. Each of these zeros could be refined using the above algorithm. For example, consider applying this algorithm to the leftmost zero. In this case the rough interval $[-2.5, -1.5]$ may be used as a better interval for the next graph (top diagram of Figure 7.2). From this second graph, the zero can be seen to lie in the leftmost third of the interval $[-2.0, -1.75]$ so a third attempt plots the function between $x = -2.0$ and $x = -1.92$ (bottom diagram of Figure 7.2). From this graph, the zero would appear to be close to -1.96. Of course, this procedure could be continued to approximate the zero more accurately if desired.

Figure 7.1 Initial graph of the function $f(x) = x^3 - 4x^2 - 4x + 15$.

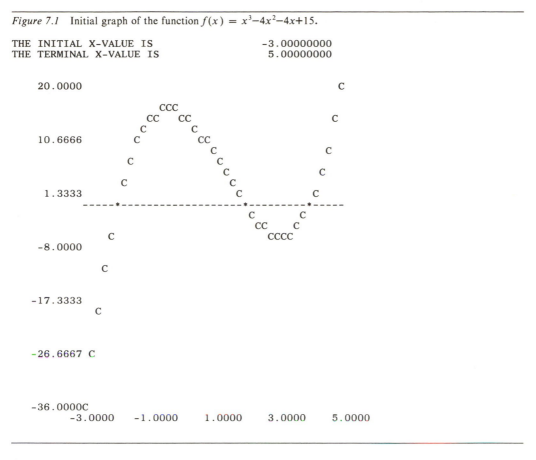

```
THE INITIAL X-VALUE IS                    -3.00000000
THE TERMINAL X-VALUE IS                    5.00000000


    20.0000                                          C

                          CCC
                       CC     CC                       C
                        C       C
    10.6666            C         CC                    C
                                   C                 C
                  C                C
                                    C                C
                C                    C
     1.3333                          C               C
             -----*--------------------*---------*-----
                                    C           C
                                  CC        C
               C                  CCCC
    -8.0000

              C


   -17.3333
               C


   -26.6667 C


   -36.0000C
        -3.0000    -1.0000    1.0000    3.0000    5.0000
```

As demonstrated above, this method provides one way to determine a zero of a function. It may be performed entirely by hand or with the assistance of the computer. However, even with the aid of a computer, the necessity for human involvement makes this algorithm tedious to implement, particularly if a high degree of accuracy is desired.

7.3   Automatic Search for a Zero

A simple-minded approach to an automatic search for a zero might be to evaluate the function over a set of points, checking for a point at which the function is exactly zero. The difficulty with such a technique is that the zeros of functions studied in real applications rarely have integer or simple fractional values such as those sometimes encountered in classroom and textbook examples. Thus, choosing appropriate points to "hit" a zero exactly is virtually impossible. In addition, when using a computer, round-off errors in the computation of $f(x)$ would probably cause nonzero values for $f(x)$ even if one did hit the theoretical zero of the function.

Figure 7.2 Second and third graphs of the function $f(x) = x^3 - 4x^2 - 4x + 15$.

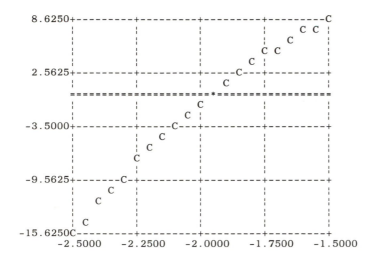

```
THE  INITIAL  X-VALUE  IS                    -2.50000000
THE  TERMINAL X-VALUE  IS                    -1.50000000
```

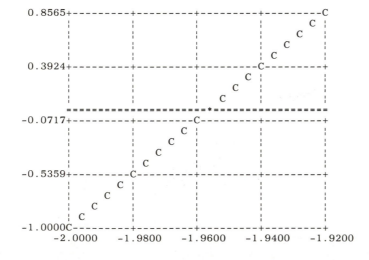

```
THE  INITIAL  X-VALUE  IS                    -2.00000000
THE  TERMINAL X-VALUE  IS                    -1.92000000
```

The best result which one should expect to achieve, therefore, is the identification of an *interval* containing a zero. That is, one should be able to find two successive values of x such that the corresponding values of $f(x)$ differ in sign. Such an algorithm, given in Figure 7.3, breaks the original interval [xfirst,xlast] into nsteps smaller intervals of length xstep, which are scanned from left to right. In each small interval, the algorithm checks for a change in the sign of $f(x)$ and writes out the values of the endpoints of the first small interval in which a sign change is detected. Note that although a change in sign could be detected by:

```
if f(xl) ≤ 0 and f(xr) ≥ 0 or f(xl) ≥ 0 and f(xr) ≤ 0 then
    put 'There is a sign change'
```

it is more elegant and efficient to observe that there will be a sign change whenever

```
f(xl)*f(xr) ≤ 0
```

This simpler test is used in the algorithm.

Figure 7.3   Scan for the first interval containing a sign change.

```
* Algorithm to look for the first sign change in f(x)

* Variables used:
* xfirst,xlast - initial interval
* nsteps - number of steps
* xstep - size of each step
* xl,xr - endpoints of successive subintervals

* Initialize the parameters and the subinterval endpoints.

get xfirst, xlast, nsteps
put 'The initial interval is', xfirst, xlast
put 'The number of steps to be used is', nsteps
xstep ← (xlast − xfirst)/nsteps
xl ← xfirst
xr ← xl + xstep

* Loop to scan successive small intervals.
* Reset the endpoints and check for a sign change.
while f(xl)*f(xr) > 0 do
    xl ← xr
    xr ← xr + xstep
put 'There is a zero between', xl, xr
stop
```

Since this algorithm determines an interval of width xstep which contains a zero, *either endpoint* of the interval is an approximation to the zero within a tolerance of xstep. Thus, arbitrarily high accuracy could be achieved by taking a small enough xstep (that is, a large enough nsteps). However, this would be very inefficient in that three digit accuracy, for example, would require several thousand function evaluations, many more than the 100 or so required to achieve the same accuracy by plotting 3 or 4 graphs, each of 30 or 40 points.

7.4 Systematic Refinement of the Zero Estimate

It was observed that three-digit accuracy in a zero estimate could be achieved graphically in about 100 function evaluations by repeatedly "blowing up" the graph at the point of interest. If a similar strategy were adopted in an automatic approach, then perhaps a similar saving might result. Such a scheme is, in fact, possible by simply applying successively the search algorithm of Figure 7.3. The recorded output from one application would become the input to the next.

The algorithm in Figure 7.4 automatically performs this repetition until the desired tolerance is achieved. For each successive application, the initial interval is arbitrarily subdivided into 25 subintervals. At the end of each application, the resulting subinterval becomes the new interval to be divided and scanned.

The equivalent WATFIV-S program, presented in Figure 7.5, applies this algorithm to the polynomial

$$x^3 - 4x^2 - 4x + 15$$

Several improvements have been made to the algorithm in the process of translation. In moving from one small interval to the next, the previous right endpoint becomes the left endpoint of the new interval. For efficiency the value of $f(x)$ does not need to be recomputed, hence the use of variables FL and FR. The program also introduces the use of an arithmetic statement function so that the complete function need not be included each time it is referenced.

The output from this program is given in Figure 7.6. Compare the successive intervals with the graphs used earlier. The first subinterval chosen by the program is about [-1.98,-1.94], which is somewhat better than the one chosen graphically. Of course, the program continues to refine the interval to a greater tolerance. The guess of −1.96 made from the graph is relatively close to the zero estimate of -1.957587.

Figure 7.4   Algorithm to refine a zero estimate systematically.

* Algorithm to look for the first sign change in **f(x)** then repeatedly divide
* the subinterval by **25** until the zero is approximated to the desired tolerance.

* Variables used:
* **xfirst,xlast** - initial interval
* **xstep** - size of each step
* **xl,xr** - endpoints of successive subintervals
* **epsilon** - desired tolerance for root

* Obtain the initial interval and desired tolerance.

get xfirst, xlast, epsilon
put 'The initial interval is', xfirst, xlast
put 'The desired tolerance =', epsilon

* Verify that the interval contains a zero.

if f(xfirst)*f(xlast) > 0 **then**

> **put** 'No sign change in', xfirst, xlast

  else

>> * Refine the interval until its width is within the desired tolerance.
>>
>> **while** |xlast − xfirst| > epsilon **do**
>>
>>> * Search for the first subinterval [xl,xr] containing a sign change.
>>>
>>> xstep ← (xlast − xfirst)/25
>>> xl ← xfirst
>>> xr ← xl + xstep
>>> **while** f(xl)*f(xr) > 0 **do**
>>>
>>>> xl ← xr
>>>> xr ← xr + xstep
>>>
>>> * Reset the endpoints [xfirst,xlast] for the next refinement.
>>>
>>> xfirst ← xl
>>> xlast ← xr
>>
>> **put** 'There is a zero between', xfirst, xlast

stop

```
C Figure 7.5 -- Program to look for the first sign change in
C               the polynomial x**3 - 4x**2 - 4x + 15, then
C               repeatedly divide the subinterval by 25 until
C               the zero is found to the desired tolerance.

C*****************************************************************

C XFIRST - left end of initial interval
C XLAST  - right end of initial interval
C XSTEP  - size of step
C XL,XR  - endpoints of successive subintervals
C FL,FR  - function values at subinterval endpoints
C EPS    - desired tolerance
C F      - function to be evaluated

C*****************************************************************

      REAL XFIRST, XLAST, XSTEP, XL, XR, FL, FR, F, EPS, ABS

C Define the polynomial using an arithmetic statement function.

      F(X) = X**3 - 4.0*X**2 - 4.0*X + 15.0

C Obtain the initial interval and desired tolerance.

      READ, XFIRST, XLAST, EPS
      PRINT, 'THE INITIAL INTERVAL IS', XFIRST, XLAST
      PRINT, 'THE DESIRED TOLERANCE =', EPS
      PRINT, ' '

C Verify that the interval contains a zero.

      IF(F(XFIRST)*F(XLAST) .GT. 0.0) THEN DO
            PRINT, 'NO SIGN CHANGE IN THIS INTERVAL'
         ELSE DO

C            Refine the interval until its width is
C            within the desired tolerance.

            WHILE(ABS(XLAST - XFIRST) .GT. EPS) DO

C               Search for the first subinterval (XL,XR)
C               containing a sign change.

               XSTEP = (XLAST - XFIRST)/25.0
               FL = F(XFIRST)
               XR = XFIRST + XSTEP
               FR = F(XR)
               WHILE(FL*FR.GT.0.0)DO
                  XR = XR + XSTEP
                  FL = FR
                  FR = F(XR)
               END WHILE

C               Reset the endpoints (XFIRST,XLAST)
C               for the next refinement.

               XFIRST = XR - XSTEP
               XLAST = XR
               PRINT, 'THERE IS A ZERO BETWEEN', XFIRST, XLAST
               PRINT, ' '
            END WHILE
      END IF
      STOP
      END
$ENTRY
-2.5, -1.5, 1.0E-05
```

Figure 7.5   (continued)

Program Notes

- The polynomial is defined using an arithmetic statement function. Such statements are normally placed immediately following the declarations. Any further reference to the name F in the program causes the expression to the right of the = sign to be evaluated for the current argument supplied in brackets.
- FL and FR are used to retain the function values at each end of the interval. Each time the interval is advanced, the current value of FR is moved to FL and a new FR is computed.
- The PRINT statement has been moved inside the **while** loop in order to demonstrate how the successive intervals approach the zero. The original position might be better for a production version of the program.

Figure 7.6   Output from the systematic refinement program of Figure 7.5.

THE INITIAL INTERVAL IS	-2.50000000	-1.50000000
THE DESIRED TOLERANCE =	0.00001000	
THERE IS A ZERO BETWEEN	-1.98000000	-1.94000000
THERE IS A ZERO BETWEEN	-1.95759500	-1.95599600
THERE IS A ZERO BETWEEN	-1.95759400	-1.95753000
THERE IS A ZERO BETWEEN	-1.95758800	-1.95758600

In the example above, the algorithm required four refinements to achieve the desired tolerance. If it should be necessary for the entire interval to be scanned before finding the subinterval containing the zero, a total of 26 function evaluations would be required per pass. On the average, one would expect to scan only half of the interval, thus necessitating 26/2 or 13 evaluations per refinement step. Therefore, a total of about 52 (13×4) evaluations might be expected. The actual count in this case is 39, which was determined by adding a counter to the program and adding to it each time the function is evaluated.

7.5   Bisection

In the previous section an algorithm was created for refining the estimate of a zero of a function given an initial estimate in the form of an interval containing the zero. The search scheme involved a subtabulation of function values in a given interval such that the new interval of tabulation was 1/25th the size of the original. Thus, after one such search, the uncertainty in the location of a zero is reduced by the factor 1/25. As mentioned, one would expect to have to compute about 13 values of the function, on average, to achieve this improvement. It follows, then, that the average reduction in uncertainty for each evaluation of $f(x)$ is $(1/25)^{1/13}$, which is approximately 0.78. On the other hand, if only 2 steps rather than 25 steps had been used, the uncertainty may be reduced by the factor 0.5 for each additional evaluation of $f(x)$. Thus, the use of 2 steps is more efficient, in fact, the most efficient possible.

A search scheme to use only 2 steps is logically very simple. The function is computed at the midpoint of the interval, and either the left half or right half of the interval is retained, depending upon which half proves to have a sign change of $f(x)$ within it. This is called the *bisection algorithm*. It is illustrated graphically in Figure 7.7. and is given in pseudo-code form in Figure 7.8. The algorithm successively bisects the interval [xl,xr] with midpoint xmid until the condition |xl−xmid| ≤ epsilon. This test guarantees that xmid is an approximation to the zero with error less than the chosen tolerance. The algorithm also contains an initial test on fl*fr. If fl*fr≤0, the algorithm assumes that the interval has a single zero (in fact, there could be an odd number of zeros, but bisection will still find one of them). If fl*fr>0, the algorithm considers the interval to have no zeros. In fact, there could be an even number of zeros in the interval, but bisection can not be guaranteed to find one of them.

Figure 7.7   Geometry for bisection.

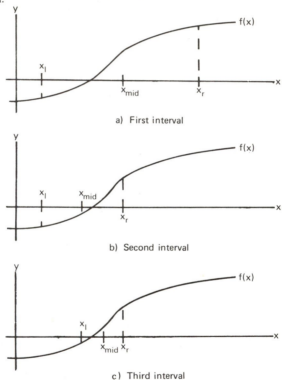

a) First interval

b) Second interval

c) Third interval

The WATFIV-S program in Figure 7.9 applies the bisection algorithm to find the leftmost zero of the same cubic polynomial example used earlier in this chapter.

The resulting output in Figure 7.10 demonstrates how 16 iterations (and their 16+2 original function evaluations) were required to achieve a tolerance of less than 10^{-5}. This compares quite favorably with the previous refinement process when 39 function evaluations were required to achieve the same accuracy.

Figure 7.8   The bisection algorithm.

* Bisection algorithm to approximate a zero of **f(x)**.

* Variables used:
* xl,xr - endpoints of successive intervals
* fl,fr - function values at the endpoints
* xmid - midpoint of the interval
* fmid - function value at the midpoint
* epsilon - desired tolerance

* Obtain the initial interval and tolerance.
* Compute **f(x)** at the interval endpoints.
get xl, xr, epsilon
put 'Initial interval,   xl =', xl, 'xr =', xr
put 'Tolerance =', epsilon
fl ← f(xl)
fr ← f(xr)

* Provided a zero exists in the given interval, bisect the interval and choose
* the subinterval with a sign change until the tolerance is reached.

if fl*fr > 0 **then**
    ⌈ **put** 'No sign change in this interval'
  else
    ⌈ xmid ← (xl + xr)/2
    | **while** |xl − xmid| > epsilon **do**
    | ⌈ fmid ← f(xmid)
    | | **if** fl*fmid ≤ 0 **then**
    | | ⌈ xr ← xmid
    | | **else**
    | | ⌈ xl ← xmid
    | | ⌊ fl ← fmid
    | ⌊ xmid ← (xl + xr)/2
    | **put** 'The zero in this interval =', xmid
    ⌊ **put** 'The function value there =', f(xmid)
stop

```
C Figure 7.9 -- Program to use bisection to find a zero of
C                the function x**3 - 4x**2 - 4x + 15.

C**************************************************************

C XL,XR   - endpoints of successive intervals
C FL,FR   - function values at the endpoints
C XMID    - midpoint of the interval
C FMID    - function value at the midpoint
C EPS     - desired tolerance
C F       - function to be evaluated

C**************************************************************

      REAL XL, FL, XR, FR, XMID, FMID, F, EPS, ABS
C Define the function to be evaluated.
      F(X) = X**3 - 4.0*X**2 - 4.0*X + 15.0
C Obtain the initial interval and tolerance.
C Compute F(X) at the interval endpoints.
      READ, XL, XR, EPS
      PRINT, 'INITIAL INTERVAL, XL =',XL,' XR =',XR
      PRINT, 'TOLERANCE =', EPS
      PRINT, ' '
      FL = F(XL)
      FR = F(XR)
C Provided a zero exists in the given interval,
C bisect the interval and choose the subinterval
C with a sign change until the tolerance is reached.
      IF(FL*FR .GT. 0.0) THEN DO
            PRINT, 'NO SIGN CHANGE IN THIS INTERVAL'
         ELSE DO
            XMID = (XL + XR)/2.0
            WHILE(ABS(XL - XMID) .GT. EPS) DO
               FMID = F(XMID)
               IF(FL*FMID .LE. 0.0) THEN DO
                     XR = XMID
                  ELSE DO
                     XL = XMID
                     FL = FMID
               END IF
               PRINT, 'CURRENT INTERVAL, XL =',XL,' XR =',XR
               XMID = (XL + XR)/2.0
            END WHILE
            PRINT, ' '
            PRINT, 'THE ZERO IN THIS INTERVAL =', XMID
            PRINT, 'THE FUNCTION VALUE THERE  =', F(XMID)
      END IF
      STOP
      END
$ENTRY
-2.5, -1.5, 1.0E-05
```

Program Notes

- Notice again the use of an arithmetic statement function to define F(X).
- A PRINT statement has been added to output the successive intervals obtained in the bisection process. This statement could be deleted in further uses of the program.

Figure 7.10   Output from the bisection program of Figure 7.9.

```
INITIAL INTERVAL, XL =              -2.50000000  XR =        -1.50000000
TOLERANCE =            0.00001000
CURRENT INTERVAL, XL =              -2.00000000  XR =        -1.50000000
CURRENT INTERVAL, XL =              -2.00000000  XR =        -1.75000000
CURRENT INTERVAL, XL =              -2.00000000  XR =        -1.87500000
CURRENT INTERVAL, XL =              -2.00000000  XR =        -1.93750000
CURRENT INTERVAL, XL =              -1.96875000  XR =        -1.93750000
CURRENT INTERVAL, XL =              -1.96875000  XR =        -1.95312500
CURRENT INTERVAL, XL =              -1.96093700  XR =        -1.95312500
CURRENT INTERVAL, XL =              -1.96093700  XR =        -1.95703100
CURRENT INTERVAL, XL =              -1.95898400  XR =        -1.95703100
CURRENT INTERVAL, XL =              -1.95800700  XR =        -1.95703100
CURRENT INTERVAL, XL =              -1.95800700  XR =        -1.95751900
CURRENT INTERVAL, XL =              -1.95776300  XR =        -1.95751900
CURRENT INTERVAL, XL =              -1.95764100  XR =        -1.95751900
CURRENT INTERVAL, XL =              -1.95764100  XR =        -1.95758000
CURRENT INTERVAL, XL =              -1.95761100  XR =        -1.95758000
CURRENT INTERVAL, XL =              -1.95759500  XR =        -1.95758000

THE ZERO IN THIS INTERVAL =            -1.95758800
THE FUNCTION VALUE THERE   =            -0.00001526
```

How efficient is this bisection algorithm? It may be shown that the number of calculations of the function $f(x)$ needed to achieve a particular error tolerance, ϵ, starting with $[x_l, x_r]$ is about

$$\log_2 \left[\frac{x_r - x_l}{\epsilon} \right]$$

For example, in the previous program, to locate a zero with error less than 10**-5, starting with the interval [0,1], requires 17 steps according to this formula as compared with the actual 18.

The efficiency of bisection is quite satisfactory in many applications since the cost of computing even rather complicated expressions is remarkably small. On a typical modern computer the cost of evaluating a polynomial of degree 10 or a trigonometric function may be only a few hundredths of a cent. Thus, the cost of finding a zero of such a function by bisection is usually less than one cent for the few milliseconds of machine resources needed.

7.6   Faster Algorithms

Some zero-finding problems involve functions which are very costly to compute. In other cases, the zero-finding process may be only a portion of some complex algorithm and may have to be performed thousands of times in one program. In such situations, it becomes important to reduce the number of function evaluations as much as possible. This is accomplished by the use of algorithms more sophisticated than bisection.

7.6.1 The Regula-Falsi Method

Historically, the regula-falsi method was proposed as an alternative to bisection. Like bisection, it retains an interval surrounding the zero. The function between the two endpoints of the interval is approximated by a straight line. The intersection of this line with the x axis rather than the midpoint is used as one of the endpoints of an improved interval. This is shown graphically in Figure 7.11.

Figure 7.11   Geometry for the regula-falsi method.

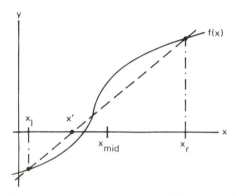

In this figure, $f(x)$ is shown, together with the straight line joining $(x_l, f(x_l))$ to $(x_r, f(x_r))$. This line intersects the x axis at x'. In general, the equation of the line passing through any two points (x_l, y_l) and (x_r, y_r) is given by

$$\frac{y - y_l}{x - x_l} = \frac{y_r - y_l}{x_r - x_l}$$

Notice that the right-hand side of this equation represents the slope of the line. By using this equation and solving for its intersection with the x axis $(y = 0)$, it is seen that

$$x' = x_l - f(x_l) \times \frac{x_r - x_l}{f(x_r) - f(x_1)}$$

Although the point x', found by the regula-falsi method, is closer to the actual zero of $f(x)$ than is the point x_{mid}, found by bisection, the interval which brackets the zero, namely $[x', x_r]$, is clearly longer than the interval $[x_l, x_{mid}]$. Therefore, in practice it is unwise to use the regula-falsi method as an interval shrinking algorithm. One end point of the interval may converge to a zero while the other end point remains fixed, even for very simple functions.

7.6.2 The Secant Method

The secant method is similar in principle to the regula-falsi method except that it does not maintain a bracketing of the zero; rather the points are used in the order in which they are generated. The initial points are labeled x_1 and x_2 with corresponding function values $f_1 = f(x_1)$ and $f_2 = f(x_2)$. A new point can be computed as

$$x_3 = x_2 - f_2 \times \frac{x_1 - x_2}{f_1 - f_2}$$

Regardless of whether or not they bracket a zero, the points x_2 and x_3, together with f_2 and f_3, are used to generate x_4, and so forth. The general formula for a new point is

$$x_{n+1} = x_n - f_n \times \frac{x_{n-1} - x_n}{f_{n-1} - f_n}$$

Note that in this case, the slope of the secant is

$$\frac{f_{n-1} - f_n}{x_{n-1} - x_n}$$

The geometrical motivation for this method is that the secant to a curve *ought* to cross the x axis somewhere close to the point at which the curve crosses the axis, namely, at a zero of the function. Figure 7.12 illustrates a possible sequence of points produced by the secant method.

Figure 7.12   Geometry for the secant method.

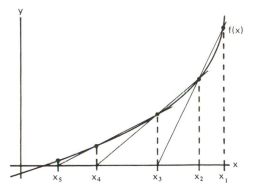

Since the idea of retaining a zero-containing interval at each stage has been abandoned in the secant method, there is no longer any guarantee that the process will converge. It is possible to find that at some stage of the scheme, f_{n-1} and f_n are nearly equal. This would obviously produce a nonsensical value for x_{n+1}.

A WATFIV-S implementation of the secant method is given in Figure 7.13. The algorithm itself is straightforward. The **while** loop proceeds to pass a secant line through successive pairs of points until the desired tolerance is achieved. The same polynomial example considered previously is used with starting points of -2.5 and -1.5.

The resulting output is presented in Figure 7.14 and illustrates successive values of the intercepts until the approximation is complete. Only six iterations are necessary to achieve the desired tolerance (a total of 8 function evaluations).

```
C Figure 7.13 -- Program to use the secant method to find a
C                 zero of the function x**3 - 4x**2 - 4x + 15.
C************************************************************
C X1      - 1st point near the zero
C X2      - 2nd point near the zero
C XNEW    - new estimate closer to the zero
C EPS     - desired tolerance
C F       - function to be evaluated
C F1      - function evaluated at X1
C F2      - function evaluated at X2

C************************************************************
      REAL X1, X2, XNEW, F, EPS, F1, F2, ABS
C Define the function to be evaluated.
      F(X) = X**3 - 4.0*X**2 - 4.0*X + 15.0
C Initialize the starting interval and tolerance.
      READ, X1, X2, EPS
      PRINT, 'STARTING VALUES,    X1 =',X1,' X2 =',X2
      PRINT, 'TOLERANCE =', EPS
      PRINT, ' '
C Compute the functional values at X1 and X2,
C then pass a line through (X1,F(X1)) and (X2,F(X2))
C using the x intercept to improve the estimate of the zero
C until the desired tolerance has been achieved.
      F1 = F(X1)
      F2 = F(X2)
      WHILE(ABS(X1 - X2) .GT. EPS) DO
          XNEW = X2 - F2*(X1 - X2)/(F1 - F2)
          PRINT, 'X INTERCEPT =', XNEW
          X1 = X2
          F1 = F2
          X2 = XNEW
          F2 = F(X2)
      END WHILE
      PRINT, ' '
      PRINT, 'THE ZERO IS', X2
      PRINT, 'F(X) IS    ', F2
      STOP
      END
$ENTRY
-2.5, -1.5, 1.0E-05
```

Program Notes

- Since only the most recent two points are needed at any one time, it is not necessary to retain all values of X. Thus, the program uses the variables X1 and X2 to label the current two points of interest. Each time a new secant is to be formed, X1 and F1 take on the old values of X2 and F2 while X2 takes on the value at XNEW.

7.6.3   Newton's Method

Newton's method has an ancient and honored place in the history of zero-finding methods. Geometrically, it is motivated by the same consideration as the secant method. The tangent to the graph of $f(x)$ ought to cross the x axis at a point close to the zero of $f(x)$. The slope of the tangent to $f(x)$ at x_n is $f'(x_n)$, so Newton's method becomes

Figure 7.14   Output from the secant method program of Figure 7.13.

```
STARTING VALUES,    X1 =            -2.50000000  X2 =            -1.50000000
TOLERANCE =          0.00001000
X INTERCEPT =       -1.85566900
X INTERCEPT =       -1.98185100
X INTERCEPT =       -1.95650500
X INTERCEPT =       -1.95757500
X INTERCEPT =       -1.95758700
X INTERCEPT =       -1.95758600

THE ZERO IS         -1.95758600
F(X) IS              0.00002289
```

$$x_{n+1} = x_n - \frac{f(x_n)}{f'(x_n)}$$

Notice that only one starting value is needed, but that a formula is required for the derivative as well as the function. As with the secant method, convergence cannot be guaranteed for starting values near points where $f'(x)$ vanishes.

Figure 7.15 illustrates a sequence of estimates of a zero produced by Newton's method.

Figure 7.15   Geometry for Newton's method.

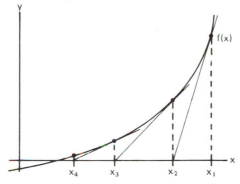

In Figure 7.16 a WATFIV-S program is presented for Newton's method. The great similarity to the program for the secant method should be noted.

The output from the Newton's method program in Figure 7.17 is very similar to the secant program output in Figure 7.14. This is a general observation — one should expect to see very little difference in the performance of the two methods. In this case, the four iterations involve 4 evaluations of the function plus 4 evaluations of its derivative.

```
C Figure 7.16 -- Program to use Newton's method to find a
C                zero of the function x**3 - 4x**2 - 4x + 15.
C******************************************************************
C X1      - initial point near the zero
C CORR    - correction to the current estimate (F(X1)/F'(X1))
C EPS     - desired tolerance
C F       - function to be evaluated
C DF      - derivative of the function
C******************************************************************
      REAL X1, CORR, F, DF, EPS, ABS
C Define the function and its derivative.
      F(X) = X**3 - 4.0*X**2 - 4.0*X + 15.0
      DF(X) = 3.0*X**2 - 8.0*X - 4.0
C Initialize the starting value and tolerance.
      READ, X1, EPS
      PRINT, 'STARTING VALUE, X1 =',X1
      PRINT, 'TOLERANCE =', EPS
      PRINT, ' '
C Pass a line through (X1,F(X1)) with slope F'(X1) using the
C x intercept to improve the estimate of the zero until the
C correction to the zero estimate is less than the tolerance.
      CORR = 2*EPS
      WHILE(ABS(CORR) .GE. EPS) DO
         CORR = F(X1)/DF(X1)
         X1 = X1 - CORR
         PRINT, 'X INTERCEPT =', X1
      END WHILE
      PRINT, ' '
      PRINT, 'THE ZERO IS', X1
      PRINT, 'F(X) IS    ', F(X1)
      STOP
      END
$ENTRY
-2.5, 1.0E-05
```

Program Notes

- Note the use of two arithmetic statement functions to define F(X) and its derivative.
- In order to enter the **while** loop, the correction to the zero estimate is initialized at double the tolerance.
- Once the previous value of X1 has been used to evaluate the function and its derivative, it is no longer needed. Thus, the new value is assigned directly.
- Again, note the extra PRINT statement to list intermediate X intercepts.

Figure 7.17 Output from the Newton's method program of Figure 7.16.

```
STARTING VALUE, X1 =            -2.50000000
TOLERANCE =           0.00001000

X INTERCEPT =         -2.05035900
X INTERCEPT =         -1.96104800
X INTERCEPT =         -1.95759200
X INTERCEPT =         -1.95758700

THE ZERO IS          -1.95758700
F(X) IS              -0.00000381
```

The authors have a small preference for the secant method in that one does not need to have an explicit formula for the derivative of the function whose zero is sought. It is somewhat difficult to compare function evaluations. Although Newton's method converges somewhat more quickly than the secant method, it requires evaluation of $f(x)$ and its derivative for each approximation.

7.6.4 Other Algorithms
Over the years, many zero-finding algorithms of great mathematical sophistication have been developed and used. Some are adapted to solve particular problems very well. A number of such methods are discussed in Ralston (1965).

For general use in finding a single real zero experts now recommend a variation of the simple methods which have been examined in this chapter. A particularly effective combination is the secant method and bisection method, which are the important components of Dekker's algorithm. A variation of this is given in Forsythe et al. (1977).

7.7 Summary

In this chapter, several simple methods have been developed to find a single zero of a given function. The bisection algorithm is very reliable, but may be somewhat slow to converge. Newton's method or the secant method are faster when they do work, but either method may fail completely.

The authors recommend the bisection algorithm for simple general purpose use unless speed is crucial. Then the choice would be the secant method or, better still, the use of a library program which implements a combination of these methods.

7.8 References

Barrodale, I.; Roberts, F.D.K.; and Ehle, B.L. *Elementary Computer Applications.* New York: John Wiley and Sons, 1971.

Forsythe, G.E.; Malcolm, M.A.; and Moler, C.B. *Computer Methods for Mathematical Computations.* Englewood Cliffs, N.J.: Prentice-Hall, 1977.

Ralston, A. *A First Course in Numerical Analysis.* New York: Mcgraw-Hill Book Co., 1965.

7.9 Exercises

In most of the following exercises a program is requested to solve a specific problem. For each problem it is recommended that step-wise refinement be used in developing a pseudo-code algorithm to solve the problem. This algorithm should then be translated into WATFIV-S and run on the computer. Where appropriate, the program should be tested with a variety of data sufficient to ensure that the program does what it is supposed to do.

7.1 The two curves $f(x) = 10-x^2$ and $g(x) = 5-(x-5)^2$ each have a zero in the interval $[2,4]$. Write a program to determine the distance between these zeros.

7.2 Consider the following polynomial.

$$f(x) = x^4+9.75x^3+17.75x^2-17.75x-26.25$$

a) Plot a graph of $f(x)$ exhibiting its 4 zeros.
b) Using graphical techniques, estimate the smallest zero (in magnitude) of $f(x)$, correctly rounded to three decimal places.
c) Prove that the estimate from b) is correct.
d) Use systematic refinement to estimate the remaining zeros of $f(x)$, correctly rounded to four decimal places.

7.3 For *each* value of $k = -1, -0.95, -0.9, -0.85, \cdots, 0.95, 1$, the equation $\tan x - kx = 0$ has one root $g(k)$ which lies between $\pi/2+\epsilon$ and $3\pi/2-\epsilon$ (where ϵ is an arbitrary small number). Write a program to use bisection to find each root, $g(k)$, over the given range of k and plot a graph of $g(k)$ versus k.

7.4 The following function has three real zeros.

$$f(x) = 8x^3+2x^2-5x+1$$

Plot a graph of the function which clearly shows all three zeros. From this graph obtain an interval around each zero, and use these as input to a single program which uses bisection to find the zeros more exactly.

7.5 Consider the following function.

$$f(x) = .05x+\sin x$$

Develop a program to find all zeros of the function between $x = -1$ and $x = 12$. Between these limits there is at most one zero in any interval of length π ($f(x)$ has a sinusoidal term). Generate the end points of intervals of length π starting with -1 and determine if a zero lies within the interval. If it does not, generate the next interval. If it does, use bisection to find the zero. The recorded output should include the intervals as well as the zeros contained within them.

7.6 Develop a program for the regula-falsi method and use it to approximate the zeros of the following function.

$$f(x) = x^4-10x^3+31x^2+312x+370$$

7.7 Use the secant method program to approximate the zeros of each of the following functions.

a) $f(x) = x^4-x^3-3x^2+5x-2$
b) $f(x) = x^4-10x^2+20$
c) $f(x) = x^4-10x^2+25$
d) $f(x) = x^5+x^4+2x^3+2x^2-8x-8$
e) $f(x) = 2x^4-14x^3-2x^2+68x+56$

7.8 Consider the following function.

$$f(x) = x^4 + 3x^3 - 3x^2 - 6x + 1$$

Changing the constant term by 1 has the effect of shifting the graph by 1 in the y direction. Modify the Newton's method program to determine the change in each zero as the constant term changes from 1 to 2, 2 to 3, and 3 to 4.

7.9 If a function is continuous and well behaved, the zero-finding method of successive substitution will converge to a zero faster than bisection. The use of this technique to find a solution of an equation, $f(x) = 0$, involves obtaining an expression which defines x in terms of itself. As an example, consider the following equation.

$$f(x) = x^3 - x^2 - x - 1 = 0$$

One simple rearrangement involves moving x across the equals sign.

$$x = x^3 - x^2 - 1$$

By starting with an initial estimate, say x_1, for the solution x and substituting into the right-hand side of the above expression, a new estimate of x, say x_2, is obtained. This procedure can be continued as follows.

$$x_2 = x_1^3 - x_1^2 - 1$$

$$x_3 = x_2^3 - x_2^2 - 1$$

$$x_4 = x_3^3 - x_3^2 - 1$$

$$\vdots$$

$$x_{n+1} = x_n^3 - x_n^2 - 1$$

This process may be continued until two consecutive estimates of the solution, x_{n+1} and x_n, differ by less than some epsilon.

a) Develop a program to apply successive substitution to the sample equation with a starting value of 2.0.

b) Modify the program to use the following rearrangement and to use the starting value 2.0.

$$x = 1 + \frac{1}{x} + \frac{1}{x^2}$$

c) Modify the program to approximate a zero of $f(x) = x^2 - 2x - 1$ using the following rearrangement and using 2.0 as the starting value.

$$x = x^2 - x - 1$$

8
Area Finding

8.1 Introduction

In this chapter another elementary problem related to the graph of a function $f(x)$ is examined. The area bounded by the graph of the function, the x axis, and two ordinates

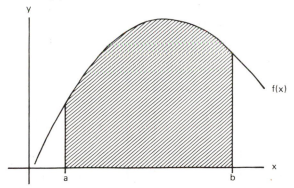

Figure 8.1 Area under a curve $f(x)$.

at $x = a$ and $x = b$ is sought, as shown in Figure 8.1. To the reader familiar with calculus, this is a *definite integral,* represented by

$$\int_a^b f(x)\, dx$$

Such problems arise in applications in a wide variety of contexts. One would need to solve this integration problem to calculate the strength of an aircraft wing, to compute the amount of earth to be moved in leveling out a hill during construction, to construct a fuel gauge for an irregularly shaped tank, or to decide whether a particular re-entry path will cause intolerable heat build-up in a space shuttle. The list is really endless since this is probably the most basic and frequently posed mathematical problem arising from the construction of mathematical models of the real world.

Historically, the mathematical treatment of this problem is old and well-developed, as is the development of computational tools for its approximate solution.

Simple mechanical devices called planimeters can be used to give a crude approximation to the area of a plotted curve. Of course, for a rough solution to the problem, one can always do the plot on squared graph paper and count the squares enclosed.

It is the intent of this chapter to give some tools which will enable most of the work in such integration problems to be passed over to the computer. Some elementary algorithms will be developed together with some methods for assuring that the answers produced are correct.

8.2   The Area Approximated by Sums

The symbol for the definite integral originated with the relationship of the integral to the sum of the areas of small rectangles of width $x_{i+1} - x_i$ and height $f(x'_i)$, where x'_i is any point between x_i and x_{i+1}. This sum is denoted as S_n.

$$S_n = \sum_{i=1}^{n} f(x'_i) \times (x_{i+1} - x_i)$$

Such a sum is illustrated in Figure 8.2. The integral is, in fact, defined as the *limiting value* of S_n as n, the number of rectangles, becomes large, but in such a fashion that the width of the largest rectangle shrinks to zero as n increases.

Figure 8.2   Area approximated by a sum of rectangles.

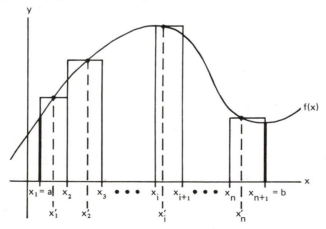

It should be observed that negative values of $f(x)$ subtract from the sum. Therefore, the integral will be interpreted as the difference between areas above and below the x axis should $f(x)$ have a zero between a and b.

8.3   Rectangle Rules

One of the simplest methods of approximating the desired area is derived from the definition of S_n. In fact, the diagram of Figure 8.2 suggests that there will always be one or more values, x', such that $S_1 = (b-a) \times f(x')$ will be precisely the area desired. Dressed up a bit, this is called the *mean-value theorem* of calculus. It assures that it is not necessary to take the limit of S_n to get the area if a clever choice is made for the point(s) at which $f(x)$ is computed. This is illustrated in Figure 8.3, where the area is seen to be $(b-a) \times f(x')$, assuming that the two shaded areas are equal.

Figure 8.3   Area calculation using one rectangle based on x'.

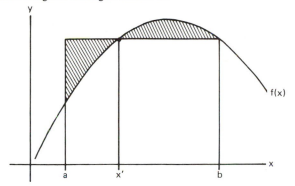

To compensate for the fact that the appropriate point is not known, a weighted average of values of $f(x)$ at a number of different points is computed, to give a formula of the form

$$S = (b-a) \times \sum_{i=1}^{n} w_i \times f(x_i), \quad \text{where} \quad \sum_{i=1}^{n} w_i = 1$$

One of the simplest such formulas involves choosing all weights to be equal, that is, $w_i = 1/n$, and choosing the x'_is to be the left (or right) endpoints of the i-th rectangle of width $(b-a)/n$. That is,

$$x_i = a + \frac{i \times (b-a)}{n}, \quad i = 0, 1, 2, \cdots, n-1, \text{ or}$$

$$x_i = a + \frac{i \times (b-a)}{n}, \quad i = 1, 2, \cdots, n.$$

Thus, the two rectangle formulas are:

$$R' = \frac{(b-a)}{n} \times \sum_{i=0}^{n-1} f(x_i), \text{ and}$$

$$R'' = \frac{(b-a)}{n} \times \sum_{i=1}^{n} f(x_i), \text{ respectively.}$$

For a function which increases as x increases from a to b, it may be seen that R' is always less than the actual area, and R'' is always greater. This is illustrated in Figure 8.4 for the case $n = 2$. R' is the darker shaded area, and R'' is the sum of the light and dark areas.

Figure 8.4   Geometry for the rectangle rules.

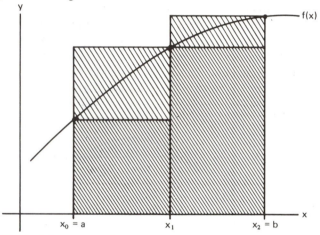

8.4   Trapezoidal Rule

From Figure 8.4, it is seen that the two Rectangle Rules respectively underestimate and overestimate the actual area, and by similar amounts. Averaging the two rules should have the effect of canceling the errors, and lead to a better formula. This averaging is indicated below.

$$T = \frac{R'+R''}{2}$$

$$= \frac{1}{2}\left[\frac{(b-a)}{n} \times \sum_{i=0}^{n-1} f(x_i) + \frac{(b-a)}{n} \times \sum_{i=1}^{n} f(x_i) \right]$$

$$= \frac{(b-a)}{2 \times n} \times \left[f(x_0) + 2\times \sum_{i=1}^{n-1} f(x_i) + f(x_n) \right]$$

$$= \frac{h}{2} \times \left[f(a) + 2\times \sum_{i=1}^{n-1} f(a+i\times h) + f(b) \right]$$

This is called the *Trapezoidal Rule* since the area under the curve is approximated by the area of a number of trapezoids, rather than rectangles. This is shown in Figure 8.5 for $n = 1$, and $n = 2$. The dark shading shows the area for one trapezoid. The light

Figure 8.5   Geometry for the Trapezoidal Rule with n = 1 and n = 2.

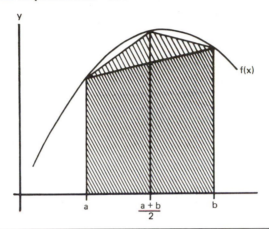

plus the dark shading is the area for two trapezoids. It is clear that this formula gives the exact value of the area if the graph of the function is a straight line between endpoints, since the actual figure is then a trapezoid. The area found by the Trapezoidal Rule will not be precisely right if $f(x)$ is curved, but it will be a *better approximation* than is provided by the Rectangle Rules.

It should also be observed from Figure 8.5 that the approximation using 2 trapezoids is substantially better than the result using 1. Just how much better is a question which will be examined after considering Figure 8.6 which gives a WATFIV-S program for the Trapezoidal Rule. This program tests the algorithm on a function $f(x) = 7-7x^6$, for which the area between $x = 0$ and $x = 1$ is known to be 6.0.

The output of this program is given in Figure 8.7 for the particular data presented. Such a single numerical output may be quite useless as an area estimate, since there is no assurance of its validity. Such assurance could come from a mathematical analysis or it could come from a better algorithm which incorporates an error estimation.

```
C Figure 8.6 -- Program to find areas using Trapezoidal Rule.
C               Apply it to 7 - 7x**6 from 0 to 1.
C*****************************************************************
C A,B      - endpoints of interval
C N        - number of subintervals for use in Trapezoidal Rule
C F        - function to be integrated
C H        - interval width
C SUM      - sum of values of F(X) at interior points
C AREA     - resulting area
C*****************************************************************
      REAL A, B, F, H, SUM , AREA, X
      INTEGER N, I
C Define the specific problem.
      F(X) = 7.0 - 7.0*X**6
      A = 0.0
      B = 1.0
C The input parameter N controls the accuracy of the solution.
      READ, N

      PRINT, 'THE INTERVAL IS', A, B
      PRINT, 'THE NUMBER OF SUBINTERVALS IS',N
      PRINT, ' '
C Check if the interval width is valid.
      IF(N .LE. 0) THEN DO
            PRINT, 'VALUE OF N INCORRECTLY SPECIFIED'
        ELSE DO
C           Calculate the interval width.
            H = (B - A)/N
C           Evaluate the formula for the area.
            I = 1
            SUM =  0.0
            WHILE(I .LE. N - 1) DO
               X = A + I*H
               SUM = SUM + F(X)
               I = I + 1
            END WHILE
C           Assemble the terms and record the resultant area.
            AREA = H*((F(A) + F(B))/2.0 + SUM)
            PRINT, 'THE AREA UNDER THE CURVE IS', AREA
        END IF
      STOP
      END
$ENTRY
16
```

Program Notes

- Note that the formula for T has been reorganized for efficiency. The arguments of F(X) are found by incrementing previous values, rather than recomputing a formula for the argument.
- An integer I is used to count the proper number of terms in the sum, rather than comparing the current argument X to the endpoint B. A comparison such as WHILE(X.LE.B) DO will be unreliable due to round-off errors for some values of A, B, and N.

Figure 8.7   Output from the Trapezoidal Rule program of Figure 8.6.

```
THE INTERVAL IS            0.00000000              1.00000000
THE NUMBER OF SUBINTERVALS IS            16
THE AREA UNDER THE CURVE IS        5.98634200
```

8.5   Error Estimation for the Trapezoidal Rule

The simplest way to increase confidence in the area estimate is to repeat the calculation with a larger number of intervals (say twice as many) and compare the results.

Figure 8.5 should convince us that, for small intervals and a smoothly varying function, the difference between the results for $2n$ and for n intervals (light shading) is larger than the difference between the true area and the result for $2n$ intervals (unshaded area).

This difference provides an error *estimate* which is quite reliable. To illustrate this, the previous program was modified to tabulate results for several values of n. The results are given together with the actual errors and the error estimates in Figure 8.8.

Figure 8.8   Trapezoidal Rule with errors tabulated.

n	T_n	Actual Error	Estimated Error $(T_n - T_{n/2})$
2	5.195312	0.804688	-----------
4	5.785766	0.214234	0.590454
8	5.945594	0.054406	0.159828
16	5.986342	0.013658	0.040748
32	5.996577	0.003423	0.010235

There are several observations which may be made from this table. The difference which was suggested as an error estimate grossly overestimates the actual error. Closer inspection shows that the estimate is about three times the error, particularly for large values of n.

The table also suggests the hypothesis that the size of the error decreases by a factor of four when n is doubled. That is, the error is very well described by the formula

$$\text{Error} \simeq \frac{c}{n^2},$$

where, in this case, c is about 3.5 but would assume other values for different functions. It may be shown by a mathematical analysis that this will always be the *form* of the error for large n and smooth $f(x)$.

More analysis would also establish that the relationship suggested in the table, namely,

$$\text{Error} \simeq \frac{T_n - T_{n/2}}{3},$$

follows from the above formula for the error, and is quite easy to compute by an additional application of the Trapezoidal Rule. In Figure 8.9, this estimate is compared to the actual error, for the previous example.

Figure 8.9 Comparison of error and error estimates for Trapezoidal Rule.

n	*Actual Error*	$\dfrac{T_n - T_{n/2}}{3}$
2	0.804688	----------
4	0.214234	0.196818
8	0.054406	0.053276
16	0.013658	0.013583
32	0.003423	0.003412

8.6   Simpson's Rule

Just as the Trapezoidal Rule could be obtained as an average of Rectangle Rules, the Trapezoidal Rule may also be manipulated to produce an improved formula. In the last section it was observed that the Trapezoidal Rule could be applied with n steps and with $2n$ steps to provide an error estimate $(T_{2n} - T_n)/3$. This error estimate may be visualized as an approximation to the area which lies between the graph of the function and the shaded area of the trapezoids (see Figure 8.5). An improved formula must surely result if this area is added to the area of the trapezoids. For the case of one and two trapezoids of Figure 8.5, the formula becomes:

$$S = T_2 + \frac{T_2 - T_1}{3}$$

$$= \frac{4}{3}T_2 - \frac{1}{3}T_1$$

$$= \frac{4}{3}\left[\frac{(b-a)}{4} \times \left(f(a) + 2f(\frac{a+b}{2}) + f(b)\right)\right] - \frac{1}{3}\left[\frac{(b-a)}{2} \times [f(a) + f(b)]\right]$$

$$= \frac{b-a}{6}\left[f(a) + 4 \times f(\frac{a+b}{2}) + f(b)\right]$$

This is known as *Simpson's Rule* for approximating the value of an integral.

In assessing the error involved in using Simpson's Rule, an important observation may be made. There is *no error* if the function $f(x)$ is a *polynomial* of degree three or less (see Exercise 8.5). Phrased in another way, this method gives the actual area under the polynomial function which has the same value as $f(x)$ at $x = a$, $x = (a+b)/2$, and $x = b$.

For functions which are not polynomials of degree three or less, one may expect to incur some error in applying this formula. Again, to reduce this error, the formula may be applied many times to narrow strips and the results added. The result is referred to as the *Compound Simpson's Rule* and may be obtained by expanding the expression

$$S_n = \frac{4}{3}T_{2n} - \frac{1}{3}T_n$$

and letting $h = (b-a)/2n$. Expanding this expression gives the following formula.

$$S_n = \frac{h}{3}[f(a)+4f(a+h)+2f(a+2h)+4f(a+3h)+2f(a+4h)+\cdots$$

$$+2f(b-2h)+4f(b-h)+f(b)]$$

This compound formula is used in writing the WATFIV-S program for Simpson's Rule presented in Figure 8.10. Notice that its structure is very similar to the previous Trapezoidal Rule program.

Since a single numerical output is not likely to inspire confidence, the program is designed to give the approximation for several different values of N, tabulated in Figure 8.11. The question of what values of N to use is discussed in the next section.

```
C Figure 8.10 -- Program to find areas using Simpson's Rule.
C                 Apply it to 7 - 7x**6 from 0 to 1
C                 using 2, 4, 8, ... , 128 intervals.

C**********************************************************************

C A,B    - endpoints of interval
C N      - number of subintervals for use in Simpson's Rule
C F      - function to be integrated
C H      - interval width
C SUMEVN - sum of F(X) values at even points
C SUMODD - sum of F(X) values at odd points
C AREA   - approximation to the total area

C**********************************************************************

        REAL A, B, F, H, AREA, SUMEVN, SUMODD, X
        INTEGER N, I, N2
C Define the specific problem.
        F(X) = 7.0 - 7.0*X**6
        A = 0.0
        B = 1.0
        PRINT, 'THE INTERVAL IS', A, B
        PRINT, ' '
C Label the output table.
        PRINT, '            N         APPROXIMATION'
        PRINT, ' '
```

```
C Figure 8.10 (continued)
C The variable N controls the accuracy of the solution.
C For this example, several values are used via a while loop.
      N = 2
      WHILE(N .LE. 128) DO
C        Calculate the subinterval width.
      N2 = 2*N
      H = (B - A)/N2
C        Initialize and define parameters.
      I = 2
      SUMEVN = 0.0
      SUMODD = F(A+H)
C        Accumulate sums.
      WHILE(I .LE. N2 - 2) DO
         X = A + I*H
         SUMEVN = SUMEVN + F(X)
         SUMODD = SUMODD + F(X+H)
         I = I + 2
      END WHILE
C        Assemble the terms and record the resultant area.
      AREA = (F(A) + F(B) + 4.0*SUMODD + 2.0*SUMEVN)*H/3.0
      PRINT, N, AREA
      N = N*2
      END WHILE
      STOP
      END
$ENTRY
```

Figure 8.11 Output from the Compound Simpson's Rule program of Figure 8.10.

THE INTERVAL IS	0.00000000	1.00000000
N	APPROXIMATION	
2	5.98258300	
4	5.99887000	
8	5.99992300	
16	5.99998400	
32	5.99998900	
64	5.99994300	
128	5.99991300	

8.7   Error Estimation for Simpson's Rule

When applying the Compound Simpson's Rule, one would expect to see rapid improvement in the quality of the results as n is increased; this is easily seen to be the case for the output of the example program since the actual answer is 6.0. However, notice that for very large values of n, round-off errors lead to an *increase* rather than a *decrease* in the errors as n is increased.

Figure 8.12   Simpson's Rule with errors tabulated.

n	S_n	Actual Error	$S_n-S_{n/2}$
2	5.982583	0.017417	----------
4	5.998870	0.001130	0.016287
8	5.999923	0.000077	0.001053
16	5.999984	0.000016	0.000061
32	5.999989	0.000011	0.000005
64	5.999943	0.000057	-0.000046
128	5.999913	0.000087	-0.000030

A study of the errors tabulated in Figure 8.12 shows that for $n = 2$, 4, and 8 their behavior is governed by the formula:

$$\text{Error} \simeq \frac{c}{n^4}$$

where c is about 0.29 for $n = 2$, 4, and 8. Since this c would not be known for a problem whose answer is sought, it is more useful to observe that the following estimate for the error follows from this formula:

$$\text{Error} \simeq \frac{S_n-S_{n/2}}{15}$$

Figure 8.13   Comparison of error and error estimates for Simpson's Rule.

n	Actual Error	$\dfrac{S_n-S_{n/2}}{15}$
2	0.017417	----------
4	0.001130	0.001086
8	0.000077	0.000070
16	0.000016	0.000004
32	0.000011	0.000000

The validity of this estimate is checked in Figure 8.13. At first glance, these results may look somewhat disappointing. There is a good prediction of the error for $n = 4$ and $n = 8$ but the predictions for $n = 16$ and $n = 32$ are not so useful due to *round-off* error. Such round-off error is a great complication in trying to use sophisticated formulas for error estimation.

If S_n and $S_{n/2}$ agree to k digits , then S_n is correct to $k+1$ digits, unless round-off error has contaminated the result. If so, the computation should be repeated with more precision.[1]

A detailed analysis of the effects of round-off error is difficult to do before a calculation. It depends upon the characteristics of the computer arithmetic, primarily the number of digits used in number representation and the rules regarding the truncation of a longer number to fit into such a representation.

---

[1] Most programming languages, including WATFIV-S, allow for arithmetic to be done using approximately double the precision of ordinary arithmetic. Consult Appendix K for more details.

The IBM 360 and 370 series of computers use a hexadecimal number system (base 16). WATFIV-S on these machines has a standard single-precision word length equivalent to about seven decimal digits. Round-off is achieved by *chopping* or simply ignoring any digits beyond this capacity. Thus, whenever an arithmetic operation generates a positive number which is too large to represent, one should expect the result recorded to be *too small* by about 0.8 units in the last decimal digit. This is an average figure, of course, based on the truncation of the base 16 digit which follows the last one retained.

One may see this effect in Figure 8.13. The estimate of the area for N=32 would theoretically give the correct result of 6.000000. The computed answer is too small because of round-off error.

8.8   Summary

Many books have been written which are wholly or largely devoted to the development of approximate methods for solution of this area finding problem, and research continues on better ways to solve it.

With rare exceptions, Simpson's Rule is a remarkably effective method for solving integration problems, and the suggested method of error appraisal is quite reliable. The authors recommend its general use without reservation.

Some recent work develops the ideas presented here to create an algorithm which enables the computer to "learn" how to best use the Compound Simpson's Rule or a similar integration formula. Such *Adaptive Quadrature* algorithms automatically solve an integration problem to some preassigned error tolerance in the most efficient possible way. Although beyond the scope of this text, some readers might like to investigate these ideas in Forsythe, et al., (1977).

8.9   References

Barrodale, I.; Roberts, F.D.K.; and Ehle, B.L. *Elementary Computer Applications*. New York: John Wiley and Sons, 1971.

Conte, S.D. and DeBoor, C. *Elementary Numerical Analysis*. New York: McGraw-Hill Book Co., 1972.

Forsythe, G.E.; Malcolm, M.A.; and Moler, C.B. *Computer Methods for Mathematical Computations*. Englewood Cliffs, N.J.: Prentice-Hall, 1977.

8.10   Exercises

In most of the following exercises a program is requested to solve a specific problem. For each problem it is recommended that step-wise refinement be used in developing a pseudo-code algorithm to solve the problem. This algorithm should then be translated into WATFIV-S and run on the computer. Where appropriate, the program should be tested with a variety of data sufficient to ensure that the program does what it is supposed to do.

8.1 a) Develop a program to approximate the area under a given function for specified endpoints and number of intervals using the lower rectangle rule. Test the program on a simple example with known area.

b) Develop a program to approximate the area under a given function for specified endpoints and number of intervals using the upper rectangle rule. Test the program on a simple example with known area.

c) Combine the programs of parts a) and b) into a single program. Use this program to produce a table comparing the values produced by both rectangle rules for 2, 4, 8, . . . , 64 intervals. Test the program on each of the following functions.

$$f(x) = x, \ x^2, \ x^3, \ x^4, \ x^5$$

8.2 Develop a program to use the Trapezoidal Rule to approximate the area enclosed by the sine curve and the x axis between $-\pi$ and $+\pi$.

8.3 Develop a program that will find the area under the following curves between the limits $x = 1$ and $x = 2$ using Simpson's Rule.

a) $f(x) = \sqrt{2-\sin x^2}$
b) $f(x) = x\cos \dfrac{x}{2}$
c) $f(x) = (x^3-2x^2+x+5)^{\frac{1}{3}}$

8.4 An approximation to the area under a curve $f(x)$ may be calculated using what could be called a midpoint-rectangle rule. It is similar to the rectangle rules of this chapter in that it sums the areas of n rectangles in the given interval. However, for this rule, the height of a rectangle with sides $x = a$ and $x = b$ is calculated using the height of the midpoint of the rectangle, that is, $f(\dfrac{a+b}{2})$.

a) Develop a general formula that when evaluated will give an approximation to an area using the midpoint-rectangle rule.

b) Develop a program that will use the above equation to calculate the area under $f(x) = x\cos \dfrac{x}{2}$ in the interval $(1,2)$.

8.5 a) Show that Simpson's Rule with a single interval is exact for the functions $f(x) = 1, \ x, \ x^2, \ x^3$ on the interval $[-1,1]$.
Hint: The areas are 2, 0, 2/3, 0 respectively.

b) Deduce that Simpson's Rule with a single interval is exact for any polynomial $f(x) = a_3x^3+a_2x^2+a_1x+a_0$ on any interval $[a,b]$.
Hint: This question requires some calculus.

8.6 A farmer has a very irregularly shaped farm bounded on one side by a winding brook, on a second side by a winding river, and on the third side by a curved road

Figure 8.14 A farmer's irregularly shaped field (Exercise 8.6).

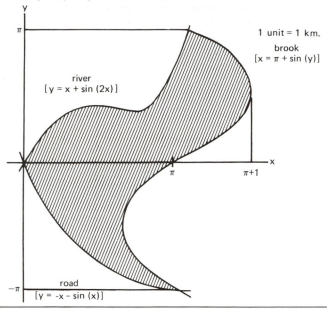

as illustrated in Figure 8.14. After considerable trial and error, he discovers the boundaries of his farm can be described by the equations indicated on the diagram. Develop a program to approximate the area of the farmer's farm.

8.7 On the farm of Exercise 8.6, the owner has observed that crop yields vary with location in direction x, but not in direction y, due to soil quality. For crops c_1 and c_2, the variations are described by

yield c_1 (per acre) $= 1+0.02x$

yield c_2 (per acre) $= 0.95+0.015x^2$

What is the total yield for each crop?

9 Organizing Mathematical Routines into Modules

9.1 Introduction

In the previous chapters, several algorithms and WATFIV-S programs were developed to assist in the accurate determination of some characteristics of mathematical functions. Programs such as those for determining zeros and numerical integrals are often needed in scientific calculations. Because of the wide demand for them, these programs are usually developed only once in the form of what is called a *subprogram*. These subprograms are usually written by someone with considerable expertise in the area and are placed in a subprogram library for general use. Availability of subprogram libraries substantially removes the burden from the programmer since those parts of a program which already exist in the library do not need to be developed. All that is necessary is to understand how to use them, usually a much simpler task. Recall that the plotting routines of Chapter 6 are examples of subprograms which reside in a subprogram library. These routines are examples of quite complicated subprograms which are easy to use.

The above discussion indicates but one advantage of subprograms. The selection and description of such subprograms falls under the more general heading of *modularity*. This chapter discusses the basic ideas of modularity and describes how to design and write a program in modular form. A discussion of how to define modules that are *general* enough for library usage and examples of top-down design using modules is left until Chapter 10.

9.2 Modularity

The term modularity refers to the technique of decomposing large algorithms into several smaller segments. A module is a *small,* relatively *self-contained* section of algorithm which performs a specific function. It has a well-defined interface to its environment (other modules), which means that the input required by the module from other modules and the output supplied for those modules is clearly specified.

A modular algorithm may contain many such modules and a typical structure is illustrated by Figure 9.1. The boxes indicate the modules and the lines between modules imply intermodule references, with the arrow indicating the direction of the reference. For example, module 1 is the *main* module and it references or *invokes* modules 2, 3 and 6; modules 2 and 3 in turn invoke the other modules as shown. A module performs some specific task for the module that invokes it and usually returns some result to that referencing module.

Figure 9.1 A typically structured modular algorithm.

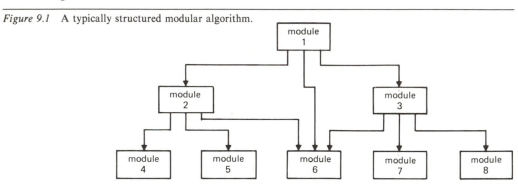

Many benefits accrue from the use of modular design of algorithms and programs. All of them result from the fact that the modules are small, perform a readily identifiable task, and have a well-defined interface. Individual modules may be written independently of other modules. They may be proven correct, tested, or modified separately. Algorithms are much easier to understand in modular form because the level of detail in each module is so much reduced. In fact, some modules may consist primarily of invocations of other modules.

Usually a modular algorithm will be shorter than a *monolithic* (nonmodular) one. For example, if a set of operations is to be performed in many different places within the same algorithm then this set may be defined just once as a module. This module may then be simply referenced at each occurrence rather than rewritten. By having only one *instance* of that algorithmic segment, one is assured that exactly the same operations are being performed each time the module is referenced.

Though modularity has many advantages, there is a penalty to be paid in terms of computation time. There is a time overhead associated with the execution of modular programs because of the need to transfer information between modules. However, with rare exceptions, the benefits outweigh the time penalty and important programs are written and maintained in modular form.

9.3   Modularity as Part of Top-Down Design

As the reader may have already recognized, the concept of modularity is a natural extension of the step-wise refinement process. Recall that in step-wise refinement the idea is to decompose problems into smaller and simpler subproblems. At each stage of the decompositon an attempt is made to make each subproblem as independent as possible of others. Furthermore, every subproblem is represented as an action sequence (one entrance and one exit). Thus, in order to introduce modularity into the step-wise refinement process, it is only necessary to select a *suitable* (sub)problem and designate it as a module.

Once it has been decided that a problem is to form a module, then that module will either have been previously developed (it could be in a library already) or will need further decomposition before it is complete. If further decomposition is performed it could result in the definition of even more modules. The extent to which each module is dependent on the remaining modules determines the interface parameters between them.

9.3.1   Selection of Modules

One of the best ways of performing modularization is to assign modules on the basis of functionality such that the amount of data they require and the number of results they produce is relatively small. That is, each module should perform a single, logically distinct algorithmic function. If one considers the functionality of a module to be its *strength* and the amount of information to be communicated as its *coupling,* then high strength and low coupling are desired (see Meyers (1973)). For instance, a prime number calculation, a zero-finding technique, and an area-finding algorithm are suitable candidates for modules.

As a further restriction, a rule of thumb specifies that a module should be one page or so in length. That is, if the module requires more than one page, it is too large and should be broken down further.

9.4   Modules in Pseudo Code

There are two types of modules, a subroutine module and a function module. The difference between these types results from the different ways in which they are used. The exact details of these differences will be discussed below. The main objective in choosing the pseudo-code form for these modules is to obtain a form that is simple and precise and which lends itself naturally to writing correct algorithms.

There are two basic things that both module types must have, a unique name and a well-defined interface. The unique name distinguishes a module from other modules. The interface specifies the data, called **imports**, which the module needs for its operation, as well as the results, called **exports**, which it produces. Once a module is defined, it may be used or *invoked* by simply giving its name and the values for the interface. A module may be invoked from within any other module. In terms of the algorithms developed thus far, it is usually expedient to think of them as special modules which are exceptions to this format and have the default name main. Each algorithm must have one, but only one, such main module.

9.5   Subroutine Modules

A subroutine module is the simpler of the two module types and is defined as indicated by the general form of Figure 9.2. The actual name of the module is inserted following the keyword **smodule** and the interface contains the **imports** and **exports**. The import and export parameter lists consist of pseudo-code variables which are separated by commas and referred to simply as *parameters*. The import parameters receive values from, and the export parameters return values to, the invoking module. Thus, the import parameters are defined when they receive these values; the export parameters are considered to be undefined until they have been assigned values within the module.

Figure 9.2   Defining a subroutine module in pseudo code.

smodule name (**imports**: import parameter list; **exports**: export parameter list)
⋮
* Pseudo code to perform required calculations
⋮
end module

A subroutine module is invoked by simply **call**ing the name of the module and giving two argument lists. The general form of the **call** statement for subroutine modules is shown in Figure 9.3. The individual items of the argument lists are referred to as *arguments* and are separated by commas. The import arguments may be variables, constants, or expressions, the values of which are to be used by the subroutine module. The export arguments may only be variables and will receive the results from the subroutine module. The number of import and export arguments must agree exactly with the corresponding number of import and export parameters of the module. When a **call** statement is executed, the values of the import arguments are copied into the corresponding import parameters. Then the referenced module is performed starting at the first statement following the **smodule** statement. When the **end** of the module is reached, the values of the export parameters are copied into the corresponding export arguments and a return is made to the calling module.

Figure 9.3   Using a subroutine module in pseudo code.

call name (import argument list; export argument list)

Since these modules are completely self-contained all pseudo-code variables are *local* to each module. Thus, the only way for modules to communicate is through the arguments and parameters. The variable names used as arguments need bear no relationship to the variable names chosen for the parameters. Indeed, the actual names of the parameters are often unknown to the users of a library module. Note that it is possible for a subroutine module to be defined without any import parameters, without any export parameters, or even without any parameters at all.

9.5.1   A Prime Number Subroutine Module

As an example of subroutine module definition and use, the prime number algorithm of Figure 5.13 will be used. In this case the pseudo code which performs the actual prime number calculation will be placed in a module.

This module is quite simple to define since most of it has already been written. It is only necessary to decide upon a module name, its parameters, and to add an **end module** statement. Figure 9.4 defines such a subroutine module named primetest which has one import parameter, n, the number to be tested, and one export parameter, prime, which indicates whether the number is prime (1) or composite (0).

9.5.2   Using the Prime Number Subroutine Module

The main module which calls the primetest module is given in Figure 9.5. This part of the algorithm obtains the number to be tested, calls the module primetest, and then checks its response. When primetest is invoked the value of num is copied into n and the module is executed from the beginning. When the **end module** is reached the value of prime is copied into answer and a return is made to the main module. Execution resumes in the main module with the statement following the reference to primetest.

Figure 9.4 A subroutine module to test a number for primeness.

smodule primetest (**imports**: n; **exports**: prime)

* Subroutine module to test a given number **n** to determine if it is prime
* (set **prime** to **1**) or composite (set **prime** to **0**).

* Variables used:
* n - number tested
* prime - indicator (1 if **n** is prime, 0 if **n** is composite)
* m - possible divisors (3, 5, 7, 9, . . . , k)
* k - square root of n

* Assume the number is a prime.

prime ← 1

* Test whether n is even.

if n(mod 2) = 0 **and** n ≠ 2 **then**

$\left[\vphantom{X}\right.$ prime ← 0

* Otherwise test odd values of **m** from 3 to the square root of n.

else

$\left[\vphantom{X}\right.$
   m ← 3
   k ← $\sqrt{n}$
   while m ≤ k **and** prime ≠ 0 **do**

     $\left[\vphantom{X}\right.$ **if** n(mod m) = 0 **then**

       $\left[\vphantom{X}\right.$ prime ← 0

       else

         $\left[\vphantom{X}\right.$ m ← m + 2

end module

9.6 Function Modules

Function modules are intended for use in a slightly different manner than subroutine modules. A function module is *not* invoked by a **call** statement but rather by using a reference to the function as an operand. Since such references actually take part in arithmetic operations, the function reference must have a value, and it must be up to the function module to decide what that value is. This operation is performed very easily by using the function module name as a variable in the module and having it assigned the appropriate value. What this means then is that function modules have, through this method, a means of returning one additional result.

Figure 9.5 Use of the prime number subroutine module.

* Determine if a number is prime or composite by using the **primetest** subroutine module.
* Variables used:
* **num** - number to be tested
* **answer** - result from module (1 if **num** is prime)
* **primetest** - subroutine module to determine if a number is prime or composite

* Acquire the number to be tested.

get num

* Perform the test for prime or composite.

call primetest(num; answer)

* Test the flag to record the result.

if answer = 1 **then**
    ⌈ **put** num, 'is prime'
  else
    ⌈ **put** num, 'is composite'
stop

The general form of a function module is shown in Figure 9.6. The name of the module follows the keyword **fmodule**. The import and export parameters for function modules serve the same purpose as they do for subroutines modules. The assignment statement shown within the module indicates the assignment of a value to the function name for use in the part of the algorithm that invokes this module.

Figure 9.6 Defining a function module in pseudo code.

fmodule name (**imports**: import parameter list; **exports**: export parameter list)
⋮
name ← expression
⋮
end module

The general form for invoking a function module is shown in Figure 9.7. It is this whole reference that receives the value that was assigned to the function name in the **fmodule**.

9.6.1 A Prime Number Function Module

To illustrate the use of function modules and their difference from subroutine modules, the same prime number algorithm of Figure 5.13 will be converted into a function module. The prime number function module is shown in Figure 9.8.

Figure 9.7   Using a function module in pseudo code.

name (import argument list; export argument list)

Figure 9.8   Function module to test a number for primeness.

fmodule primetest (**imports**: n)

* Function module to test a given number **n** to determine if it is prime
* (set **prime** to **1**) or composite (set **prime** to **0**).

* Variables used:
* n - number tested
* **prime** - indicator(1 if **n** is prime, 0 if **n** is composite)
* m - possible divisors (3, 5, 7, 9, . . . , k)
* k - square root of **n**

* Assume the number is a prime.

prime ← 1

* Test whether **n** is even.

if n(mod 2) = 0 **and** n ≠ 2 **then**
$$\left[\text{prime} \leftarrow 0 \right.$$

* Otherwise test odd values of **m** from 3 to the square root of **n**.

   else
$$\left[\begin{array}{l} m \leftarrow 3 \\ k \leftarrow \sqrt{n} \\ \textbf{while } m \le k \textbf{ and } \text{prime} \ne 0 \textbf{ do} \\ \quad \left[\begin{array}{l} \textbf{if } n(mod\ m) = 0 \textbf{ then} \\ \quad \left[\text{prime} \leftarrow 0 \right. \\ \textbf{else} \\ \quad \left[m \leftarrow m + 2 \right. \end{array}\right. \end{array}\right.$$

primetest ← prime
end module

This function module has only one value to return and this is done by means of the function name. As a result, there are no export parameters in this module. The algorithm performs its calculation and sets the variable prime to indicate the result. Then just before the end of the module, this value is assigned to the module name in order that the module reference will have the correct value when it returns. Note that it would also be possible to replace the variable prime by the module name primetest in all instances of this algorithm and thereby save this assignment operation.

A main module to use this function module in shown in Figure 9.9. Since the reference to a function module may be placed in an expression, the reference was used directly in the **if-then-else** condition. Note that the main module essentially requires only the condition to determine the primeness question. This is a new feature that would have been handy in the step-wise refinement of the original version of the prime number algorithm in Chapter 4, Section 4.6.

Figure 9.9   Use of the prime number function module.

```
* Determine if a number is prime or composite by using the primetest function module.
* Variables used:
* num - number to be tested
* primetest - name of function module (value 1 if num is prime)

* Acquire the number to be tested.

get num

* Perform the test for prime or composite, and record the result.

if primetest(num) = 1 then
    [ put num, 'is prime'
  else
    [ put num, 'is composite'
stop
```

As demonstrated, subroutine and function modules are quite similar. In many problems either module type could be used. However, the subroutine module is more general and thus has wider appeal. The authors usually reserve the function module for the specific instances when there is *one and only one* result to be returned from a module. This usage restriction is adhered to in this text.

9.7   Modules in WATFIV-S

In WATFIV-S modules are referred to as *subprograms*. As with pseudo code, there are two types of subprograms, called *subroutine* subprograms and *function* subprograms respectively. Although the similarities are great, one important difference between pseudo-code modules and WATFIV-S subprograms is that WATFIV-S does not distinguish explicitly between import and export parameters. Nonetheless, distinguishing between these parameters is an important consideration in developing good algorithms. In WATFIV-S the value of each argument is copied into the corresponding parameter on invocation and on return the value of every parameter is copied into its corresponding argument.[1] Furthermore, since in WATFIV-S all variables have a type (so far either REAL or INTEGER) associated with them, the type of an argument must agree with the type of

---

[1] Exceptions to this rule will be discussed at a later stage.

its corresponding parameter. The method for declaring the type of variables in subprograms is the same as for a main program. At compilation time, each subprogram is compiled completely separate from both the main program and other subprograms.

To illustrate how WATFIV-S subprograms are defined and used the following sections will first show how to convert modular pseudo-code algorithms into subprograms in general and then will use the prime number algorithms as more concrete examples.

9.7.1 Subroutine Subprograms

A subroutine module is converted into a subroutine subprogram as shown in Figure 9.10. A module named sample and a reference to it are converted into WATFIV-S.

Figure 9.10 Translation of pseudo-code subroutine modules into WATFIV-S subroutines.

a) Reference

```
                                    REAL A,B,C
                                    INTEGER D
  .                                 .
  .                                 .
call sample (a,b; c,d)              CALL SAMPLE(A,B,C,D)
  .                                 .
  .                                 .
```

b) Definition

```
smodule sample (imports: r,s; exports: x,y)   SUBROUTINE SAMPLE (R,S,X,Y)
                                              REAL R,S,X
                                              INTEGER Y
  .                                           .
  .                                           .
body of sample                                body of SAMPLE
  .                                           .
  .                                           .
end module                                    RETURN
                                              END
```

In this case, the conversion actually needs only slight changes. The word SUBROUTINE replaces the word **smodule** in the first line and the parameter list specifies all of the parameters, both import and export. The distinction between import and export parameters is not explicit but is implied by the action of the program. Although this means that a single WATFIV-S parameter can assume both roles, parameters should be restricted to a single role, if at all possible. The second line of the subroutine subprogram declares the types of the parameters. Here the assumption is made that variables R, S, and X are to be of type REAL and Y of type INTEGER. The other change in converting the module is that the WATFIV-S statements RETURN and END are used to specify a return to the calling program and to indicate the end of the subprogram respectively.

The module reference is converted almost directly with the change being the replacement of the argument list semicolon with a comma. Also, the types of the arguments must be the same as the corresponding parameters, so the variables A, B, and C are declared REAL and D is declared INTEGER.

Using the above transformations as a guide, the complete prime number algorithm (Figures 9.4 and 9.5) would be converted into a WATFIV-S subroutine subprogram and a main program as shown in Figure 9.11. Other than the fact that the subroutine name has been shortened to the WATFIV-S limit of six characters the translation follows the example given previously. The statements of a subroutine subprogram are usually placed immediately following the END statement of the main program. The $ENTRY control card follows the subprogram. If many subprograms are used, they are simply placed one after the other before the $ENTRY.

	SUBROUTINES	FUNCTIONS
def'n	SUBROUTINE name (p1,p2...pN)	FUNCTION name (p1,p2,p3...pN) REAL FUNCT INTEGER
activated by	CALL name (a1,a2...an)	appearance of name (a1,a2,a3...an)
Return point	statement following the call statement	Point in the statement following the appearance of the function
permitted type of arguments	set names, simple or subscripted variables, constants, expression	
permitted type of parameters	set names, simple variables	

```
C Figure 9.11 -- Program to test a given number for primeness
C                using a subroutine subprogram PRIMET
C******************************************************************
C NUM     - number to be tested
C ANSWER - indicator from PRIMET (0 - composite, 1 - prime)
C PRIMET - subroutine subprogram to determine if a number is
C          prime or composite
C******************************************************************
      INTEGER NUM, ANSWER
C Input a number, test it, and output the appropriate message.
      READ, NUM
      CALL PRIMET(NUM,ANSWER)
      IF(ANSWER .EQ. 1) THEN DO
          PRINT, NUM, 'IS PRIME'
        ELSE DO
          PRINT, NUM, 'IS COMPOSITE'
      END IF
      STOP
      END
C******************************************************************
C Subroutine PRIMET -- Given a value for N, determine if N is
C                      prime (set PRIME to 1) or composite
C                      (set PRIME to 0).
C******************************************************************
C N       - number tested
C PRIME  - indicator (1 if N is prime, 0 if N is composite)
C M       - possible divisors (3, 5, 7, 9, ..., K)
C K       - largest integer < square root of N
C******************************************************************
      SUBROUTINE PRIMET(N,PRIME)

      INTEGER N, PRIME, M, K, MOD
      REAL FLOAT, SQRT
C Assume the number is a prime.
      PRIME = 1
C Test whether the number is even.
      IF(MOD(N,2) .EQ. 0 .AND. N .NE. 2) THEN DO
          PRIME = 0
C       Otherwise test odd values of M
C       from 3 to the square root of N.
        ELSE DO
          M = 3
          K = SQRT(FLOAT(N))
          WHILE(M .LE. K .AND. PRIME .NE. 0) DO
             IF(MOD(N,M) .EQ. 0) THEN DO
                 PRIME = 0
               ELSE DO
                 M = M + 2
             END IF
          END WHILE
      END IF
      RETURN
      END
$ENTRY
13
```

9.7.2   Function Subprograms

A WATFIV-S function subprogram is also very similar to the pseudo-code function module definition. However, since WATFIV-S distinguishes between real and integer values, the type of value that the function subprogram returns must be specified. Thus, a function subprogram also has a type of REAL or INTEGER. This type should be declared in both the definition of the subprogram and the referencing program.

To illustrate this conversion the pseudo-code module named test shown in Figure 9.12 will be used.

Figure 9.12   Translation of pseudo-code function modules into WATFIV-S functions.

a) Reference

```
                                        REAL A,B
                                        INTEGER C,TEST
 ⋮                                       ⋮
 c ← test(a,b;)                          C = TEST(A,B)
 ⋮                                       ⋮
```

b) Definition

```
fmodule test (imports: t,u; exports: )    INTEGER FUNCTION TEST(T,U)
                                          REAL T,U
 ⋮                                         ⋮
 body of test                             body of TEST
 ⋮                                         ⋮
 end module                               RETURN
                                          END
```

This module has two import parameters (assumed to be REAL) and returns one result (assumed to be INTEGER) in the function name. Because of the type of the result, the function should be converted into an INTEGER-valued function program. Such a function subprogram begins with the words INTEGER FUNCTION followed by only the import parameters. The second statement of the program declares the type of each parameter. At the end of the function subprogram is the standard RETURN, END sequence and somewhere in the body of test there must be a statement which assigns the function name the value to be returned. In fact, it is possible to use TEST as a variable throughout the body of the function subprogram. The pseudo-code reference to the module is converted into WATFIV-S by simply omitting the semicolon. (If a function has any export parameters, the semicolon would be converted into a comma.) Declarations for the import arguments *and* the function name are provided at the start of the referencing program.

Using the above techniques on the prime number algorithm (Figures 9.8 and 9.9) gives the program of Figure 9.13. Function subprograms are also placed following the END statement of the main program. If many function and subroutine subprograms exist, they may be placed in any order before the $ENTRY control card.

```
C Figure 9.13 -- Program to test a given number for primeness
C                  using a function subprogram PRIMET.
C****************************************************************
C NUM     - number to be tested
C PRIMET - function subprogram to determine if a number is prime
C****************************************************************
      INTEGER NUM, PRIMET
C Input a number, test it, and output the appropriate message.
      READ, NUM
      IF(PRIMET(NUM) .EQ. 1) THEN DO
          PRINT, NUM, 'IS PRIME'
        ELSE DO
          PRINT, NUM, 'IS COMPOSITE'
      END IF
      STOP
      END
C****************************************************************
C Function PRIMET -- Given a value for N, determine if it is
C                    prime (return a value of 1) or
C                    composite (return a value of 0)
C****************************************************************
C N       - number to be tested
C PRIME  - temporary indicator for primeness
C M       - possible divisors (3, 5, 7, 9, ..., K)
C K       - largest integer < square root of N
C****************************************************************
      INTEGER FUNCTION PRIMET(N)

      INTEGER N, PRIME, M, K, MOD
      REAL FLOAT, SQRT
C Assume the number is a prime.
      PRIME = 1
C Test whether the number is even.
      IF(MOD(N,2) .EQ. 0 .AND. N .NE. 2) THEN DO
          PRIME = 0
C       Otherwise test odd values of M
C       from 3 to the square root of N.
        ELSE DO
          M = 3
          K = SQRT(FLOAT(N))
          WHILE(M .LE. K .AND. PRIME .NE. 0) DO
            IF(MOD(N,M) .EQ. 0) THEN DO
                PRIME = 0
              ELSE DO
                M = M + 2
            END IF
          END WHILE
      END IF
      PRIMET = PRIME
      RETURN
      END
$ENTRY
13
```

9.8   Summary

The ability to define and use modules has contributed greatly to the current sophisticated state of software. Modularization is a natural extension of step-wise refinement, and it aids both the algorithm development process and improves the quality of the final product. *Development time* on large projects can be shortened considerably since once module interfaces have been designed the different modules may be developed concurrently by different people. The *final product* of modular development will often be shorter (less duplication), easier to test (well-defined interfaces between modules), less prone to errors, and easier to modify should specifications change (as they always do).

9.9   References

Freeman, P. "Software Reliability and Design: A Survey." *13th Design Automation Conference* (1976), pp. 484-494.

Leavenworth, K. "Modular Design of Computer Programs." *Data Management,* July 1974, pp. 14-19.

Maynard, J. *Modular Programming.* Philadelphia: Auerbach Publishers, 1972.

Meyers, G.J. "Characteristics of Composite Design." *Datamation,* September 1973, pp. 100-102.

9.10   Exercises

In most of the following exercises a program is requested to solve a specific problem. For each problem it is recommended that step-wise refinement be used in developing a pseudo-code algorithm to solve the problem. This algorithm should then be translated into WATFIV-S and run on the computer. Where appropriate, the program should be tested with a variety of data sufficient to ensure that the program does what it is supposed to do.

9.1 a)   Develop a subroutine, named QUAD, to solve an equation of the form $ax^2+bx+c = 0$ for its roots (refer to the final version of the algorithm in Figure 4.12). The subroutine should receive the a, b, c coefficients and return all results through the parameter list. Also, the subroutine itself should not print out any messages.

   b)   Develop a main program that will use QUAD for many different a, b, c values.

9.2 The Fibonacci numbers may be defined as

$$f_1 = 1, f_2 = 1, f_3 = f_2+f_1, f_4 = f_3+f_2, \cdots, f_i = f_{i-1}+f_{i-2}$$

where i is the index of the Fibonacci number.

a) Develop a subprogram, named FIB1, that when given an index will return the value of the corresponding Fibonacci number.

b) An *approximation* to the *i*-th Fibonacci number is given by the formula

$$f_i = 0.447264 \times (1.61803)^{i-1}.$$

Develop a subprogram, named FIB2, that when given an index will return an approximation to the corresponding Fibonacci number.

c) Develop a main program that will plot the percentage error

(difference×100/exact value)

between the values calculated by FIB1 and FIB2 for indices of i = 1, 5, 10, 15, $\cdots$, 50.

9.3 For the following program determine what values will be printed and describe *in detail* the actions performed by the computer when it executes the program. Pay particular attention to the transfer of data to and from the function subprograms.

```
REAL A,B,C        INTEGER FUNCTION FN(X,Y)     REAL FUNCTION AB(Z)
INTEGER FN        REAL X,Y,AB                  REAL Z
A = 5.0           FN = X + Y + 0.2             AB  = Z**2
B = 6.0           X = Y * 2.0                  RETURN
C = FN(A,B)       Y = AB(Y)                    END
PRINT,A,B,C       RETURN
STOP              END
END
```

9.4 The following series

$$-\frac{x^1}{1^1}+\frac{x^2}{2^2}-\frac{x^3}{3^3}+\frac{x^4}{4^4}-\cdots$$

has the property that each term is of the form

$$\left[-\frac{x}{i}\right]^i$$

One way to evaluate this series (although not an efficient way) is to use two subprograms as described below.

a) Develop a function subprogram called TERM which has two parameters x and I. When referenced, this subprogram will calculate the value of the *i*-th term of the series and return this value for the function name.

b) Develop a function subprogram called SERIES which has one parameter x. When referenced, this subprogram will use the function subprogram TERM (part a) in computing the value of 5 terms of the series for the given value of x. The value of the series should be returned as the value of the function.

c) Develop a main program which will use the function subprogram SERIES (part b) in calculating the value of the above series for the range of x = 0.0, 0.5, 1.0, . . . , 10.0. Output the value of x and the value of the series with appropriate identification.

9.5   A particular series is defined by:

$$p_1(x) = x$$

$$p_2(x) = \frac{3x^2-1}{2}$$

$$\vdots$$

$$p_i(x) = \frac{(2i-1)\times x \times p_{i-1}(x)-(i-1)\times p_{i-2}(x)}{i}, \text{ for } i\geq 3.$$

Develop a program that will evaluate the first 10 terms of the series. Since all terms for $i\geq 3$ have the same formula use a function subprogram TERM(P1,P2,I,X) which, when referenced in the main program, will calculate the general formula for the given parameters and return its value as the value of the function. Run your program for x = 1.0 and print out, with suitable identification, the value of each term.

9.6   a)   Develop a subroutine subprogram with the following first statement

          SUBROUTINE CIRCLE(XPOS,YPOS,RADIUS)

that will use the printer-plot routines of Chapter 6 to fill with characters, a circle of radius RADIUS at location (XPOS,YPOS).

   b)   Develop a main program that will use CIRCLE to shade two circles, one at (4.0,2.0) with radius 2.0 and the other at (10.0,8.0) with radius 3.0.

   c)   Develop a program similar to that of parts a) and b) that will shade any ellipse.

9.7   The Euclidean Algorithm is commonly used to determine the greatest common divisor of any two positive integers. The algorithm begins by dividing the first number by the second and retaining the remainder. At each successive stage the previous divisor is divided by the previous remainder. The algorithm continues until the remainder is zero. The greatest common divisor is the last nonzero remainder (or the last divisor). Consider a numerical example.

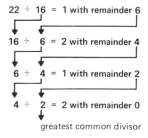

greatest common divisor

a) Show by example that the algorithm still works if the second number is larger than the first.
b) Develop a subprogram to use the Euclidean Algorithm to determine the greatest common divisor of any two positive integers.
c) Develop a main program to find the greatest common divisor for each of several pairs of numbers. Pairs that are relatively prime (that is, their GCD is 1) should be highlighted by an appropriate message.

9.8 a) Develop a subprogram which accepts a three-digit integer and produces a second three-digit integer with the digits of the first integer in reverse order.
b) Develop a subprogram which accepts any integer and produces a second integer with the digits of the first integer in reverse order.
c) A series of digits is said to be a palindrome if the digits read the same backwards and forwards. Develop a main program to use the subprogram of part b) to determine if each of a series of integers is a palindrome. Each integer should have an appropriate message printed beside it.

9.9 The factorial of a positive integer n is defined as:

$$n! = n[(n-1)!] \quad \text{where} \quad 0! = 1$$

(that is, the product of the integers from 1 to n)

or $n! = n(n-1)(n-2) \cdots (3)(2)(1)$

(for example, $5! = 5(4!) = 5(4)(3!) = \cdots = 5(4)(3)(2)(1) = 120$).
$_nP_r$ is the number of permutations (arrangements) of n objects taken r at a time and is given by:

$$_nP_r = \frac{n!}{(n-r)!}.$$

For example, consider the number of permutations of the 3 letters A, B, and C taken 2 at a time, AB, BA, AC, CA, BC, and CB. The number of these permuations can be calculated by:

$$_3P_2 = \frac{3!}{(3-2)!} = \frac{6}{1} = 6.$$

$_nC_r$ is the number of combinations of n distinct objects taken r at a time without repetition and can be evaluated using the following formula.

$$_nC_r = \frac{_nP_r}{r!} = \frac{n!}{r!(n-r)!}$$

For example, consider the number of combinations of the 3 letters A, B, and C taken 2 at a time without repetitions. These combinations are AB, AC, and BC and their number can be predicted by the following calculation.

$$_3C_2 = \frac{3!}{2!(3-2)!} = \frac{6}{(2)(1)} = 3$$

a) Develop a subprogram to compute $n!$ for any integer greater than zero.
b) Develop a subprogram to use the subprogram of part a) to calculate $_nP_r$ for given n and r.
c) Develop a subprogram to use the subprograms of parts a) and b) to compute $_nC_r$ for given n and r.
d) Develop a main program to produce a table of combinations $_nC_1$, $_nC_2$, $_nC_3$, $\cdots$, $_nC_n$ for any given n.
e) Develop a main program to solve the following problem. A person has 6 friends. In how many distinct ways can *one or more* of these friends be invited to dinner?

9.10 a) Develop a subprogram to solve any 2×2 system of linear equations of the following form.

$$ax+by = c$$

$$dx+ey = f$$

If it is impossible for the subprogram to solve for x and y, it should print an appropriate message.
b) Develop a general main program to solve several systems of 2×2 linear equations.

10
Use of Modules in Applications

10.1 Introduction

In most real-life applications the problems encountered are not necessarily of a type which have an immediately obvious solution. Rather, they require an analysis in terms of what is already known. In some circumstances one may be able to take advantage of modules which are predefined. To assure that such modules are general enough for all potential users, care must be exercised when they are originally written. This chapter first discusses how modules may be defined in a general manner and then gives examples of two problems which are analyzed and solved in terms of known techniques.

10.2 Preparing Subprograms for General Use

If a program is going to have wide applicability then it will usually be written in the form of a subprogram and placed in a library. If such a program is to be at all useful in the library it must be in a form that allows a large number of programmers to use it conveniently. Because of this, the subprogram should not unilaterally make decisions better left to the user program. Also, a library subprogram should not stop or print out messages on irregular conditions. It should return this exception information to the calling program to allow a decision regarding appropriate action to be taken there. To illustrate how this may be done the bisection and Simpson's Rule programs of Chapters 7 and 8 will be converted into subprograms.

10.2.1 A Bisection Subroutine

To estimate a zero of a function the bisection program requires four items of information for its operation. It needs an initial interval $[x_l, x_r]$, the tolerance ϵ, and the function $f(x)$ for which the zero is sought. As output, the bisection program either identifies an approximation to the zero, if one exists, or generates a message that there is no zero in the given interval. In keeping with the philosophy of generality in a subprogram all of the above information should be passed back and forth in an argument/parameter list. Thus, the bisection subprogram will have four import parameters and two export parameters. Figure 10.1 shows a subroutine subprogram named BISECT which meets these requirements.

When the subroutine BISECT is called, the parameters PL and PR receive the values of the interval endpoints, EPS receives the value of the tolerance; and F receives the name of the function. The parameter FLAG is used to signify whether or not the initial interval contained a zero, and the parameter XMID sends back the zero approximation. Of course, this approximation is valid only when the value of FLAG is zero.

The body of the subroutine BISECT is quite similar to the previous bisection program. The major difference is that instead of printing a message when FL * FR > 0 (considered to be no zero in the interval), the program merely sets FLAG to 1 and returns. This eliminates the need for printing a message from within BISECT. It is now up to the calling program to check the argument corresponding to FLAG and to take the appropriate action.

Figure 10.2 shows a program that uses the subroutine BISECT to look for a zero of the curve $x^3-4x^2-4x+15$. The main program reads in the interval to be tested, calls BISECT, and then, after checking FLAG, prints out an appropriate message regarding the zero. (Note that in order for both the main program and BISECT to be able to reference F(X), it must be defined in a function subprogram, in this case, FUNC.)

```
C Figure 10.1 -- Subroutine BISECT
C                 Subprogram to use bisection to find a zero for a
C                 given function F in the initial interval (PL,PR)
C                 to accuracy EPS indicating no zero in the
C                 interval by setting FLAG to 1.
C******************************************************************
C PL,PR   - endpoints of initial interval
C XL,XR   - endpoints of successive intervals
C FL,FR   - function values at the endpoints
C XMID    - midpoint of the interval and resulting zero
C FMID    - function value at the midpoint
C EPS     - desired tolerance
C F       - function to be evaluated
C FLAG    - error flag set to 1 if no zero in the interval
C******************************************************************
      SUBROUTINE BISECT(PL,PR,EPS,F,FLAG,XMID)

      REAL PL, PR, XL, XR, FL, FR, XMID, FMID, F, EPS, ABS
      INTEGER FLAG
C Set up the initial interval.
C Compute F at the initial endpoints.
      XL = PL
      XR = PR
      FL = F(XL)
      FR = F(XR)
C Provided a zero exists in the given interval,
C bisect the interval and choose the subinterval
C with a sign change until the tolerance is reached.
      IF(FL*FR .GT. 0.0) THEN DO
          FLAG = 1
        ELSE DO
          FLAG = 0
          XMID = (XL + XR)/2.0
          WHILE(ABS(XL - XMID) .GT. EPS) DO
             FMID = F(XMID)
             IF(FL*FMID .LE. 0.0) THEN DO
                   XR = XMID
                 ELSE DO
                   XL = XMID
                   FL = FMID
             END IF
             XMID = (XL + XR)/2.0
          END WHILE
      END IF
      RETURN
      END
```

Program Notes

- Since the values of XL and XR are changed in the course of bisecting the interval, variables PL and PR are provided to prevent the corresponding import arguments from being changed on return to the calling program.

```
C Figure 10.2 -- Main program to use subroutine BISECT to find
C                a zero of the function x**3 - 4x**2 - 4x + 15.

C**************************************************************

C A,B    - endpoints of the initial interval
C EPS    - desired tolerance
C ZERO   - resulting approximation to the zero
C FLAG   - exception flag from BISECT

C**************************************************************

      EXTERNAL FUNC
      REAL A, B, EPS, ZERO, FUNC
      INTEGER FLAG

C Obtain the initial interval and tolerance.

      READ, A, B, EPS
      PRINT, 'INITIAL INTERVAL, A =',A,' B =',B
      PRINT, 'TOLERANCE =', EPS
      PRINT, ' '

C Find a zero if possible and output an appropriate message.

      CALL BISECT(A,B,EPS,FUNC,FLAG,ZERO)

      IF(FLAG .EQ. 1) THEN DO
          PRINT, 'NO ZERO IN THIS INTERVAL.'
        ELSE DO
          PRINT, 'THE ZERO IN THIS INTERVAL =', ZERO
          PRINT, 'THE FUNCTION VALUE THERE  =', FUNC(ZERO)
      END IF

      STOP
      END

C**************************************************************

C Function FUNC -- Given a value for X, evaluate the function
C                  x**3 - 4x**2 - 4x + 15

C**************************************************************

      REAL FUNCTION FUNC(X)
      REAL X
      FUNC = X**3 - 4.0*X**2 - 4.0*X + 15.0
      RETURN
      END

C Subroutine BISECT would be placed here.

$ENTRY
-2.5 -1.5 1.0E-05
```

Program Notes

- The statement EXTERNAL FUNC is necessary so that the compiler will know that the argument FUNC is the name of a FUNCTION subprogram and not just a variable name.

10.2.2   A Subprogram for Simpson's Rule

The Simpson's Rule program of Figure 8.10 requires values for the initial interval $[a,b]$, the number of subintervals n, and the function $f(x)$ under which the area is sought. The output from that program is either the value of the area or a message indicating an illegal value for n. The subroutine SIMP of Figure 10.3 obtains and returns all of this information through its parameters. The first four parameters A, B, N, and F are imports whose use should be obvious. Note that the variable names A and B may themselves be used in the parameter list since the subroutine does not change them. The export

```
C Figure 10.3 -- Subroutine SIMP
C                 Subprogram to use Simpson's Rule to find
C                 the AREA under the curve F between the
C                 endpoints A and B using N subintervals.
C******************************************************************
C A,B    - endpoints of interval
C N      - number of subintervals
C F      - function to be integrated
C H      - interval width
C SUMEVN - sum of F(X) values at even points
C SUMODD - sum of F(X) values at odd points
C AREA   - approximation to the total area
C FLAG   - error flag set to 1 if N is invalid
C******************************************************************
      SUBROUTINE SIMP(A,B,N,F,FLAG,AREA)

      REAL A, B, F, H, AREA, SUMEVN, SUMODD, X
      INTEGER N, I, N2, FLAG
C Check if N is a valid number (must > 0).
      IF(N .LT. 1) THEN DO
            FLAG = 1
        ELSE DO
            FLAG = 0
C         Calculate the subinterval width.
            N2 = 2*N
            H = (B - A)/N2
C         Initialize and define parameters.
            I = 2
            SUMEVN = 0.0
            SUMODD = F(A+H)
C         Accumulate sums.
            WHILE(I .LE. N2 - 2) DO
               X = A + I*H
               SUMEVN = SUMEVN + F(X)
               SUMODD = SUMODD + F(X+H)
               I = I + 2
            END WHILE
C         Assemble the terms.
            AREA = (F(A) + F(B) + 4.0*SUMODD + 2.0*SUMEVN)*H/3.0
      END IF

      RETURN
      END
```

parameters are FLAG and AREA. On return, AREA contains either the required area
(FLAG = 0) or an illegal value for the area (FLAG = 1). The body of SIMP has been
changed from the previous Simpson's Rule program in that it no longer prints any
messages.

The program of Figure 10.4 shows a main program that uses the SIMP subroutine to
find the area under the curve defined in the function subprogram FUNC.

```
C Figure 10.4 -- Main program to use subroutine SIMP to find
C                 the area under the curve  defined by FUNC
C                 between A and B.
C*****************************************************************
C A,B    - endpoints of the interval
C N      - numbers of subintervals for SIMP
C AREA   - resulting approximation to the area
C FLAG   - exception flag from SIMP
C*****************************************************************
      EXTERNAL FUNC
      REAL A, B, AREA, FUNC
      INTEGER N, FLAG
C Obtain the interval and number of subintervals.
      READ, A, B, N
      PRINT, 'INTERVAL, A =', A,' B =', B
      PRINT, 'NUMBER OF SUBINTERVALS =', N
      PRINT, ' '
C Find the area if possible and output an appropriate message.
      CALL SIMP(A,B,N,FUNC,FLAG,AREA)

      IF(FLAG .EQ. 1) THEN DO
          PRINT, 'VALUE OF N INCORRECTLY SPECIFIED'
      ELSE DO
          PRINT, 'THE AREA IN THIS INTERVAL =', AREA
      END IF

      STOP
      END
C*****************************************************************
C Function FUNC -- Given a value for X, evaluate the function
C                  7 - 7*x**6
C*****************************************************************
      REAL FUNCTION FUNC(X)
      REAL X
      FUNC = 7.0 - 7.0*X**6
      RETURN
      END
C Subroutine SIMP would be placed here.
$ENTRY
0.0 1.0 128
```

10.3   Use of Modules in Applications

In many applications the solutions to the problems posed are not achieved by simply applying known techniques in a straightforward manner. As a rule these techniques provide only basic tools, and the major task is to formulate or reduce the current problem to one or more problems which themselves are solvable by the known techniques. Often there will be many different ways of approaching the problem, some better than others.

The following sections give examples of two problems, each of which may be solved using techniques discussed in earlier sections and chapters. Each problem will be examined and reduced to problems that can be solved by these techniques.

10.3.1   Area Between Two Curves

The first problem involves finding the area between two arbitrary intersecting curves, $f(x)$ and $g(x)$, as illustrated by the shaded area in Figure 10.5.

Figure 10.5   Graph of two intersecting curves.

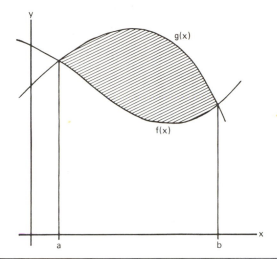

a) Problem Discussion   From previous sections and chapters it is known that numerical integration may be used to calculate areas. However, the previous examples of numerical integration involved finding only the area between one curve and the x axis. Perhaps then the current problem could be reduced to operations similar to these. In fact it can be since the shaded area is really just the area under g minus the area under f. Thus, a start on a solution has been made.

The remaining problem is to determine the limits $[a,b]$ for the integration, which means the intersection points of the two curves must be found. Finding such intersections is also something that has not been discussed previously. The closest related problem is that of finding the intersection of a curve with the x axis, that is, a zero of the function. Again a way is sought to reduce this latest problem to a known one. The question is, how can the intersection of two arbitrary curves be formulated as a zero-finding problem? Or stated another way, can an equation be derived that would have zeroes corresponding to the intersection points of the two curves? A little reflection indicates that the intersections of f and g correspond to zeroes of the function $h = g - f$. That is, h is zero at the intersection points. Thus, by performing a zero-finding operation on h, it is possible to find an intersection point. Illustrating this graphically, Figure 10.6 shows this *difference curve h* in relation to f and g. Looking at this diagram, an added benefit can be seen. Since the y value of each point on the difference curve corresponds to the separation between f and g, the area under h will be exactly the same as the required area. Thus, as a final bonus to this discussion, the area may be found by simply integrating h between the points of intersection, a fact that can be verified by calculus.

Figure 10.6   The difference curve for two arbitrary curves.

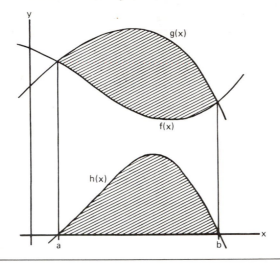

$$\int\limits_a^b gdx - \int\limits_a^b fdx \; = \; \int\limits_a^b (g-f)dx \; = \; \int\limits_a^b hdx$$

b) Selection of an Initial Decomposition   Since this problem requires the finding of only one area initial decomposition #1 should be used. Assuming that the functions *f*, *g*, and thus *h* are defined, the values required for the algorithm are the initial approximations for the points of intersection. These approximations would probably be obtained from a plot of the curves. A first version of the algorithm follows as Figure 10.7.

Figure 10.7   First version of a pseudo-code algorithm for the area between curves.

1.   Acquire initial approximations for intersections.

2.   Find the intersection points, compute the area, and record the results.

stop

c) Refining Step **1.**   Before this refinement may proceed a decision must be made about the zero-finding technique to be used. Since a bisection subprogram was developed in the previous section it is convenient to use it here. For bisection an interval is needed for both intersection points (zeroes), and a bisection tolerance is also required. To find the area, the number of intervals must be supplied. Thus, the refinement will be:

* Obtain initial approximations for the intersections.

get x1, x2, x3, x4, eps, n

d) Refining Step **2.**   This step consists of several distinct operations which are to be performed sequentially. However, the computation of either intersection point may result in an error (that is, if a bad interval is chosen). Thus, the area calculation should not proceed if this condition occurs. This consideration gives the refinement below.

2.1 Find and record the points of intersection.

2.2 Provided that there was no error on the intersection calculations, compute and record the area.

e) Refining Step **2.1**   The intersection calculations are independent of each other, and thus it is best to attempt both calculations even if one is in error. (If both intervals are in error, both errors will be caught on the initial run of the program instead of requiring two runs.) To find the points of intersection requires the application of bisection to the intervals [x1,x2] and [x3,x4] on the function h. A pseudo-code reference will be used that reflects how BISECT was defined in the previous section. This gives the following steps.

```
* Find and record intersection points, if possible.
* If not, record an error message.
call bisect(x1,x2,eps,h;lflag,a)
if lflag = 0 then
    [ put 'The left intersection point is', a
  else
    [ put 'The interval on the left is invalid.'
call bisect(x3,x4,eps,h;rflag,b)
if rflag = 0 then
    [ put 'The right intersection point is', b
  else
    [ put 'The interval on the right is invalid.'
```

f) Refining Step **2.2**   The flags lflag and rflag indicate the presence or absence of errors in the interval computation. Thus, these flags should be checked before performing the area calculation.

```
* Provided that there was no error on the intersection
* calculations, compute and record the area.
if lflag = 1 or rflag = 1 then
    ⌈ put 'No area calculated.'
else
    ⌈ 2.2.1 Compute and record the area.
```

g) Refining Step **2.2.1**   To find the area requires only the application of, say, Simpson's Rule. Using a pseudo-code reference based on the Simpson's Rule subprogram of the previous section gives the following pseudo code.

```
call simp(a,b,n,h;sflag,area)
if sflag = 0 then
    ⌈ put 'The area between the curves is', area
else
    ⌈ put 'The number of subintervals for simp is invalid.'
```

h) Final Version of Algorithm   Combining all of the refinement steps gives the final version of the algorithm shown in Figure 10.8.

i) Program for Final Version of Algorithm   The above algorithm was developed in a general way without reference to any specific mathematical functions. Consider applying the algorithm to finding the area between the parabola $y = 16-x^2$ and the straight line $7x+4y = 36$. Figure 10.9 illustrates two graphs, the top graph giving a plot of both the parabola and the straight line and the bottom graph plotting the difference curve. These graphs are used to supply the input values for the program of Figure 10.10. It is assumed that the subroutines BISECT and SIMP are available in the library. The output from this program is given in Figure 10.11.

Figure 10.8   Final version of the pseudo-code algorithm for the area between curves.

* Calculate the area between two intersecting curves using **bisect** and **simp**.

* Variables used:
* h - difference function g(x) - f(x)
* x1,x2 - starting values to find left intersection
* x3,x4 - starting values to find right intersection
* eps - error tolerance for intersections
* a,b - left and right intersections
* n - number of intervals for **simp** area calculation
* lflag,rflag,sflag - error flags for left, right, and area
* **area** - area enclosed between **f** and **g**

* Obtain and record initial approximations for intersections.

get x1, x2, x3, x4, eps, n
put 'The initial interval on the left is', x1, x2
put 'The initial interval on the right is', x3 , x4
put 'The desired tolerance is', eps
put 'The number of intervals is', n

* Find and record intersection points, if possible.
* If not, record an error message.

call bisect(x1,x2,eps,h;lflag,a)
if lflag = 0 **then**

⌐ put 'The left intersection point is', a

else

⌐ **put** 'The interval on the left is invalid.'

call bisect(x3,x4,eps,h;rflag,b)
if rflag = 0 **then**

⌐ **put** 'The right intersection point is', b

else

⌐ **put** 'The interval on the right is invalid.'

* Provided that there was no error on the intersection
* calculations, compute and record the area.

if lflag = 1 **or** rflag = 1 **then**

⌐ **put** 'No area calculated.'

else

⌐ **call** simp(a,b,n,h;sflag,area)
  if sflag = 0 **then**

  ⌐ **put** 'The area between the curves is', area

  else

  ⌐ **put** 'The number of subintervals for simp is invalid.'

stop

Figure 10.9   The graphs for the parabola $y = 16 - x^2$ and the straight line $7x + 4y = 36$.

a) The two curves on one graph.

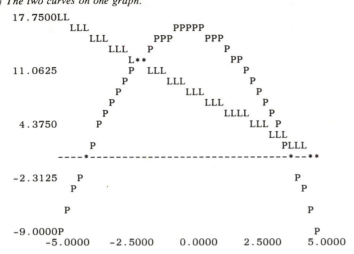

```
 17.7500LL
            LLL              PPPPP
              LLL        PPP      PPP
                LLL    P            P
                  L**                PP
 11.0625            P  LLL            P
                    P      LLL        P
                  P          LLL       P
                 P             LLL     P
                P                LLLL    P
  4.3750       P                  LLL  P
                                     LLL
                 P                    PLLL
        ----*-------------------------------*--**

 -2.3125    P                              P
             P                            P

           P                             P

 -9.0000P                                 P
       -5.0000    -2.5000    0.0000    2.5000    5.0000
```

b) The difference curve.

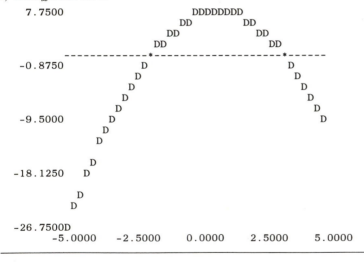

```
  7.7500                    DDDDDDDD
                          DD        DD
                        DD            DD
                      DD                DD
        --------------*--------------------*------
 -0.8750             D                     D
                    D                       D
                   D                         D
                  D                           D
                 D                             D
 -9.5000         D                             D
                D
               D

             D
 -18.1250   D

          D
         D

 -26.7500D
       -5.0000    -2.5000    0.0000    2.5000    5.0000
```

```
C Figure 10.10 -- Using functions BISECT and SIMP, find the
C                 area between y=16-x**2 and 7x+4y=36.
C******************************************************************
C H       - difference function g(x) - f(x)
C X1,X2   - starting values to find left intersection
C X3,X4   - starting values to find right intersection
C EPS     - error tolerance for intersections
C A,B     - left and right intersections
C N       - number of intervals for SIMP area calculation
C LFLAG, RFLAG, SFLAG - error flags for left, right, and area
C AREA    - area enclosed between f and g
C******************************************************************

      REAL X1, X2, X3, X4, A, B, H, EPS, AREA
      INTEGER N, LFLAG, RFLAG, SFLAG
      EXTERNAL H

C Obtain and record initial approximations for the intersections.

      READ, X1, X2, X3, X4, EPS, N
      PRINT, 'THE INITIAL INTERVAL ON THE LEFT IS ', X1, X2
      PRINT, 'THE INITIAL INTERVAL ON THE RIGHT IS', X3, X4
      PRINT, 'THE DESIRED TOLERANCE IS', EPS
      PRINT, 'THE NUMBER OF INTERVALS IS ', N
      PRINT, ' '

C Find and record intersection points, if possible.
C If not, record an error message.

      CALL BISECT(X1,X2,EPS,H,LFLAG,A)
      IF(LFLAG .EQ. 0) THEN DO
           PRINT, 'THE LEFT INTERSECTION POINT IS ', A
         ELSE DO
           PRINT, 'THE INTERVAL ON THE LEFT IS INVALID'
      END IF
      CALL BISECT(X3,X4,EPS,H,RFLAG,B)
      IF(RFLAG .EQ. 0) THEN DO
           PRINT, 'THE RIGHT INTERSECTION POINT IS', B
         ELSE DO
           PRINT, 'THE INTERVAL ON THE RIGHT IS INVALID'
      END IF

C Provided that there was no error on the intersection
C calculations, compute and record the area.

      IF(LFLAG .EQ. 1 .OR. RFLAG .EQ. 1) THEN DO
         PRINT, 'NO AREA CALCULATED'
        ELSE DO
         CALL SIMP(A,B,N,H,SFLAG,AREA)
         IF(SFLAG .EQ. 0) THEN DO
              PRINT, 'THE AREA BETWEEN THE CURVES IS', AREA
            ELSE DO
              PRINT, 'THE NUMBER OF SUBINTERVALS FOR SIMP',
     +               'IS INVALID'
         END IF
      END IF
      STOP
      END
```

```
C Figure 10.10 (continued)
C Function H -- Given a value for X, evaluate the difference
C                function G(X) - F(X).
C****************************************************************
      REAL FUNCTION H(X)
      REAL X, F, G
      F(X) = (36.0 - 7.0*X)/4.0
      G(X) = 16.0 - X*X
      H = G(X) - F(X)
      RETURN
      END
$ENTRY
-3.0, -1.0, 3.0, 4.0, 0.00005, 2
```

Program Notes

- If for some reason the main program needed values of F(X) and G(X), they could be defined in two function subprograms F and G rather than as statement functions in subprogram H.
- The EXTERNAL H statement must be provided since the name H appears as a subprogram argument.
- Note that N=2 suffices to exactly compute this area as discussed in Chapter 8.

Figure 10.11   Output from the area finding program of Figure 10.10.

```
THE INITIAL INTERVAL ON THE LEFT IS          -3.00000000        -1.00000000
THE INITIAL INTERVAL ON THE RIGHT IS          3.00000000         4.00000000
THE DESIRED TOLERANCE IS            0.00005000
THE NUMBER OF INTERVALS IS                 2

THE LEFT INTERSECTION POINT IS            -1.91171200
THE RIGHT INTERSECTION POINT IS            3.66171200
THE AREA BETWEEN THE CURVES IS           28.85380000
```

10.3.2   The Volume at Various Levels in a Tank

This problem requires that the volume of oil in a storage tank be measured by inserting a ruled stick through the top opening. The oil tank has an elliptical cross section, 8 meters wide and 4 meters high, and is 7 meters in length. The ruled stick is marked every 5 centimeters, and one is required to know the volume of the tank at each mark. The situation is illustrated in Figure 10.12.

a) Problem Discussion   Since the volume of the oil at any level is just the length times the cross-sectional area of the oil at that stage, this problem also reduces to one of finding an area. In this case, the area is bounded by the tank sides and the surface of the oil, both of which may be represented by simple equations in an appropriate coordinate system. The diagrams in Figure 10.13 indicate the equations and the two conditions which must be considered. The equation of the ellipse is $x^2/160000 + y^2/40000 = 1$. All values have been converted to centimeters and the origin is taken to be at the center of the tank.

Figure 10.12   Geometry for the tank problem.

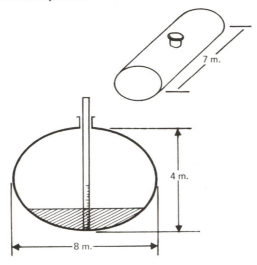

Figure 10.13   Two different level conditions for the tank problem.

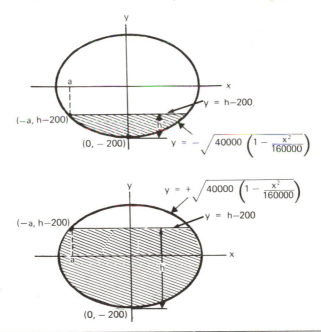

The two diagrams illustrate that the equation of the tank is different above and below the x axis and this must be taken into account. Because of symmetry the areas for only half the tank need to be found and then used for the top half volumes. This problem now seems very similar to the problem of Section 10.3.1. The area to be found is bounded by two curves in the y direction and by $[a,0]$ in the x direction. Again, an intersection point of two curves must be found. Applying these calculations to the area computation when the oil is below the x axis, diagram a) in Figure 10.13 is straightforward. However, when the oil surface is above the x axis, diagram b), it is more involved. In this case, the shaded area is given by:

2×(area below x axis)−(area between the two curves) .

On the basis of the above discussion the area could be calculated, but it would be necessary to calculate the areas under both curves and subtract them instead of using the difference function approach. This restriction is caused by the fact that the curve $y = h-200$ changes with h and the function subprograms as used in the zero-finding and numerical integration subprograms allow only the one argument x. Therefore this area would have to be calculated in the main program. Thus, a complicated but feasible approach has now been found. Is there possibly a simpler way?

If one steps back for a moment and takes a closer look at the above diagrams, it seems that the proposed solution is really just a crude way of performing a numerical integration along the y axis. By turning the diagram on its side this fact is made clearer, as shown in Figure 10.14. From this diagram it can be seen that the area may actually be found by performing a regular numerical integration as a function of y instead of x.

Figure 10.14 Transforming the elliptical tank.

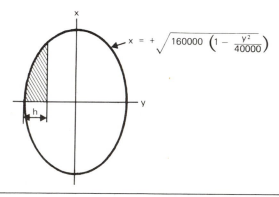

$$x = +\sqrt{160000 \left(1 - \frac{y^2}{40000}\right)}$$

The equation for x is found by rearranging the equation for the ellipse. The limits for this integration are $[-200,-200+h]$, and there is no problem crossing the x axis. This latter approach will be developed below.

b) Selection of an Initial Decomposition This problem requires the calculation of many volumes, one for each marking on the stick. Thus, initial decomposition #2 should be used. A first version of the algorithm is given in Figure 10.15.

Figure 10.15   First version of a pseudo-code algorithm for the tank problem.

1. **while** oil levels still remain **do**

⌈ Calculate the volume for the current oil level and record it.

stop

---

c) Refining Step **1.**   The volume of oil in the tank is to be calculated at intervals of 5 centimeters between −200 and +200 centimeters. This means that the height of oil in the tank will vary from 5 to 400 centimeters in steps of 5 centimeters.

* Keep calibrating volumes as long as the level is < 200 cm.
* Add 5 cm. to the depth each time.

h ← 5
while h ≤ 400 **do**

⌈ **1.1** Calculate the volume for the current oil level and record it.

⌊ h ← h + 5

d) Refining Step **1.1**   The volume in cubic meters is simply seven times the cross-sectional area divided by 10000. The area is calculated by integrating the curve

$$f(y) = \sqrt{160000\,(1-y^2/40000)}$$

between $[-200, -200+h]$ and doubling the result. This gives the formula for the volume of $2 \times 7 \times area/10000$ which reduces to $7 \times area/5000$. The number of intervals for numerical integration is also needed. The resulting refinement is given below.

* Calculate the volume for the current oil level and record it.

get n
call simp(−200,−200+h,n,f;flag,area)
volume ← 7*area/5000
put 'The volume at level', h, 'is', volume

e) Final Version   Combining the refinements together gives the algorithm shown in Figure 10.16. Note that the **get** n has been moved outside the **while** loop, since a single value of n should suffice for all calls of the simp module.

As a further refinement, one may increase the efficiency of the program by computing only the *change* in volume as the depth is increased by 5 centimeters. This change in volume would then be added to the previous volume. The increased efficiency results since a smaller value of n may be used on the change in volume. To do this, Simpson's Rule is invoked to compute the area between $y = h-205$ and $y = h-200$. This is shown in Figure 10.17.

Figure 10.16   Final version of the pseudo-code algorithm for the tank problem.

* Find the volume of oil in an elliptical tank at depth intervals of 5 centimeters.

* Variables used:
* **h** - the x coordinate of the current oil level
* **area** - the area of half of the end cross section
* **volume** - the volume at the current depth
* **n** - number of intervals for area finding
* **flag** - error flag from **simp** (ignored)

* Initialize the depth and x coordinate of that depth
* and volume. Also input the number of intervals for **simp**.

get n
put 'The number of subintervals for simp is', n
h ← 5

* Keep calibrating volumes as long as the level is < 200 cm. Add 5 cm.
* to the depth and calculate the area and volume each time through the loop.

while h ≤ 400 **do**

$$\begin{array}{l} \textbf{call } simp(-200,-200+h,n,f;\ flag,area) \\ volume \leftarrow 7*area/5000 \\ \textbf{put } \text{'The volume at level'}, h, \text{'is'}, volume \\ h \leftarrow h + 5 \end{array}$$

stop

32

---

f) Program for Final Version of Algorithm   The program given in Figure 10.18 is an implementation of the more efficient algorithm. The output from this program is shown in Figure 10.19.

Figure 10.17   More efficient version of the pseudo-code algorithm for the tank problem.

```
* Find the volume of oil in an elliptical tank at depth intervals of 5 centimeters.

* Variables used:
* h - the x coordinate of the current oil level
* area - the area of half of the end cross section
* volume - the volume at the current depth
* n - number of intervals for area finding
* flag - error flag from simp (ignored)

* Initialize the depth and x coordinate of that depth
* and volume.  Also input the number of intervals for simp.
get n
put 'Number of intervals is', n
h ← 5
volume ← 0

* Keep calibrating volumes as long as the level is < 200 cm. Add 5 cm.
* to the depth and calculate the increment in area and volume each time
* through the loop.
while h ≤ 400 do
    call simp(h−205,h−200,n,f;flag,area)
    volume ← volume + 7*area/5000
    put 'The volume at level', h, 'is', volume
    h ← h + 5

stop
32
```

```
C Figure 10.18 -- Find the volume of oil in an elliptical tank
C                   at depth intervals of 5 centimeters.

C******************************************************************
C H       - the x coordinate of the current oil level
C AREA    - the area of half of the end cross section
C VOLUME  - the volume at the current depth
C N       - number of intervals for area finding
C FLAG    - error flag from SIMP (ignored)

C******************************************************************
        REAL H, AREA, VOLUME, F
        INTEGER N, FLAG
        EXTERNAL F

C Initialize the depth and x coordinate of that depth and volume.
C Also input the number of intervals for SIMP.

        READ, N
        PRINT, 'THE NUMBER OF SUBINTERVALS FOR SIMP IS', N
        PRINT, ' '
        H = 5.0
        VOLUME = 0.0

C Keep calibrating volumes as long as the level is < 200 cm.
C Add 5 cm. to the depth & calculate the increment in area and
C volume each time through the loop.

        WHILE(H .LE. 400.0) DO
            CALL SIMP(H-205.0,H-200.0,N,F,FLAG,AREA)
            VOLUME = VOLUME + 7.0*AREA/5000.0
            PRINT, 'THE VOLUME AT LEVEL', H, ' IS', VOLUME
            H = H + 5.0
        END WHILE

        STOP
        END


C******************************************************************

C Function F -- Given a value for X, evaluate equation of tank.

C******************************************************************
        REAL FUNCTION F(X)
        REAL X, SQRT
        F = SQRT(160000.0*(1.0 - X*X/40000.0))
        RETURN
        END
$ENTRY
32
```

Figure 10.19   Output from the tank problem program of Figure 10.18.

```
THE NUMBER OF SUBINTERVALS FOR SIMP IS              32

THE VOLUME AT LEVEL         5.00000000  IS         0.41573090
THE VOLUME AT LEVEL        10.00000000  IS         1.17158700
THE VOLUME AT LEVEL        15.00000000  IS         2.14420100
        :                       :                       :
THE VOLUME AT LEVEL       390.00000000  IS       174.75610000
THE VOLUME AT LEVEL       395.00000000  IS       175.51190000
THE VOLUME AT LEVEL       400.00000000  IS       175.92770000
```

10.4   Summary

The use of predefined modules (subprograms) in applications can simplify the development task tremendously. To achieve the fullest benefit from these modules they must be defined in a manner which allows maximum flexibility in their use. However, even with an extensive subprogram library, the solution of large problems is still a formidable task. The reason for this is that the large problems are not always stated in terms that allow immediate application of known techniques. Thus, the problems have to be carefully examined, decomposed, and refined until they can be solved with existing tools.

10.5   References

Freeman, P. "Software Reliability and Design: A Survey." *13th Design Automation Conference,* New York: IEEE Computer Society and Association for Computing Machinery, 1976.

Leavenworth, K. "Modular Design of Computer Programs." *Data Management,* July 1974, pp. 14-19.

Maynard, J. *Modular Programming.* Philadelphia: Auerbach Publishers, 1972.

Meyers, G.J. "Characteristics of Composite Design." *Datamation,* September, 1973, pp. 100-102.

10.6   Exercises

In most of the following exercises a program is requested to solve a specific problem. For each problem it is recommended that step-wise refinement be used in developing a pseudo-code algorithm to solve the problem. This algorithm should then be translated into WATFIV-S and run on the computer. Where appropriate, the program should be tested with a variety of data sufficient to ensure that the program does what it is supposed to do.

10.1 Convert the Trapezoidal main program of Chapter 7 into a generalized subroutine subprogram named TRAP.
Develop a main program that will use TRAP to determine the area under the curve $f(x) = \sin x$ between 0 and π radians.

10.2 The following curves cross the x axis in two places. Develop a program that will compute the area between the curve and the x axis. Your program should be general enough to compute the area under any of the curves by merely changing the function definition and the initial parameters.

a) $f(x) = -x^2 + 10.9x - 20.4$
b) $f(x) = x^2 - x - 15.75$
c) $f(x) = -x^2 + 14.31x - 33.4$

10.3 The following function pairs completely enclose an area or areas by their curves. Develop a program that will compute the enclosed area or areas. Your program should be general enough that it may be used for any function pair by changing only the function definitions and the initial parameters.

a) $f(x) = \sqrt{6.25-(x+1.5)^2}$, $g(x) = \sqrt{9-(x-1)^2}$
b) $f(x) = x^4-5$, $g(x) = -2x+6$
c) $f(x) = \sin x$, $g(x) = 0.1+0.2x$
    (Find the enclosed area within the range 0 to π)
d) $f(x) = \cos x$, $g(x) = -.5$
    (Find the enclosed area within the range 0 to π)
e) $f(x) = 1+x^2$, $g(x) = \sqrt{4-x^2}$

10.4 The following function pairs completely enclose two separate areas. Develop a program that will determine the total enclosed area.

a) $f(x) = x^3-2x^2-5x+6$, $g(x) = -x$
b) $f(x) = 2.0\sin(x-\pi)$, $g(x) = 0.2-0.2x$

10.5 The following sets of three curves enclose at least one area. Develop a program that will compute the enclosed area.

a) $f(x) = x^2-10x+9$, $g(x) = .5x+4$, $h(x) = -.25x-7$
b) $f(x) = -0.2-0.2x$, $g(x) = 2-x^2$, $h(x) = 2.0\sin(x-\pi)$
    (Compute the enclosed area within the range -0.5 to -4)

10.6 The following two curves intersect in two places.

a) $f(x) = 2x^2-20x+55$
b) $g(x) = -4x^2+20x-5$

Develop a program that will use the printer-plot routines to plot the curves in the range $(-1.5,+1.5)$ and then fill in the enclosed area with the character A.

10.7 Increasing the number of intervals in the Trapezoidal and Simpson's rule calculations will, within limits, increase the accuracy of the result.

a) Develop a main program that will plot the error (difference between the exact and calculated value) versus the values of N = 2, 4, 8, 16, . . . , 1024. Test your program on the curve $f(x) = 7-7x^6$ whose exact area between 0 and 1 is 6. Because of the range of N and the error, a $\log_{10}$-$\log_{10}$ scale should be used for the plot.
    (Hint: use a built-in function to take the $\log_{10}$ of the argument to be plotted.)
b) Explain the resulting curves in the graph of part a).

10.8 a)   Develop a subroutine subprogram with the following first statement

SUBROUTINE PLOTFX(XL,XR,NPTS,FX,XSIZE,YSIZE,MODE)

that on each call will plot the curve FX between XL and XR with NPTS. The parameters XSIZE and YSIZE determine the size of the plot, and MODE determines whether or not a grid is plotted. Make use of the printer-plot subroutines of Chapter 6 to solve this problem.

b)   Develop a WATFIV-S main program that will use PLOTFX to plot both of the following curves.

$g(x) = 2sin(x-\pi)$, between $[-\pi,+\pi]$ with 257 points.

$h(x) = 2x^2$, between $[-1.75,+1.75]$ with 129 points.

10.9 A car manufacturer is about to install a new type of gas tank having a slightly irregular cross-sectional shape, as illustrated in Figure 10.20. The tank will be 1.5 meters across and have the same odd shape from end to end. The company would like to calibrate the volume (in litres) of the tank at 1 centimeter depth intervals. Develop a program to determine these volumes and list them in table form.

Figure 10.20   Cross section of an irregularly shaped gas tank (Exercise 10.9).

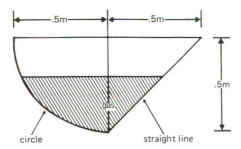

10.10 An architect has designed an asymmetric storage shed having the cross-sectional shape as shown in Figure 10.21. The shed is to be 50 meters in length. It is designed such that both roof/side structures, y_1 and y_2, are curves from parts of two circles. The radii of the circles are 20 meters and 30 meters, respectively. The centers of the circles are 30 meters apart and are located at ground level. The architect needs to compute the volume of air contained by the storage building in order to determine the heating requirements. Develop a program, using zero-finding and numerical integeration techniques, to help the architect in this computation. *Note:* The equation of a circle with center (h,k) and radius r is $(x-h)^2+(y-k)^2 = r^2$.

Figure 10.21   Cross section of a storage shed (Exercise 10.10).

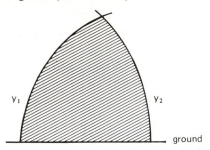

11
Handling Large Masses of Data

11.1 Introduction

In previous chapters the problems being solved did not require the retention of very much information to achieve the desired result. However, many mathematical problems, such as analyzing experimental results, gathering statistical information, plotting graphs, and solving systems of equations, do involve the manipulation of large quantities of data. Fortunately, computers are useful not only for their computational speed but also for their facility in handling data in such volumes.

A variety of techniques are available for handling masses of data. In terms of storage the options include internal computer memory and external devices such as magnetic tapes and discs. The differing speeds, capacities, and other attributes of these devices have considerable influence on the choice of a best method for dealing with the data for a particular problem. In terms of manipulating data the choice of algorithm varies according to the storage medium used.

The entire topic of storage techniques is very important. With most real-life applications the amount of data is quite large, and as a result the processing of such data on even the largest computers may take several hours. Consequently, much research has been done on devising techniques for storing and manipulating this data to minimize this processing time. One way of improving processing time is to arrange the data in storage to reflect any inherent structure in the data itself or to reflect any obvious order in the way the data will be accessed. A more thorough discussion of this topic falls under the heading of *data* or *file structures*.

This chapter is concerned with only a small portion of this entire field, that is, the use of internal storage as applied to simple one- and two-dimensional sets. For more information on other aspects of this topic, the reader is directed to some of the references supplied at the end of this chapter.

11.2   One-Dimensional Sets in Pseudo Code

In many applications it is necessary to deal with each element of a set of numbers in a similar way or to deal with the entire set as a unit. Such sets are often ordered and then may also be thought of as lists or one-dimensional arrays.

In problems involving sets it is sometimes possible to process one element of the set completely before continuing with another. Thus, as the algorithm obtains a new value, the old one can be destroyed. Frequently, however, the original value is required at a later stage; in such cases the entire set should be retained throughout the process. Thus, methods are required for retaining and accessing simple sets of numbers.

11.2.1   Representation

The representation of a simple ordered set is similar to the commonly used mathematical notation. A complete set is referenced by writing its name in upper case letters. To refer to individual elements of a set, the set name is written in lower case letters while the position of the element in the set is indicated by a subscript. Consider representing a set of daily temperature readings for one week.

Sun.	Mon.	Tues.	Wed.	Thurs.	Fri.	Sat.
12	15	16	14	21	25	30

If the complete set is called T, the temperature on Sunday is t_1, on Monday t_2, . . . , and on Saturday t_7. In general, the i-th element of the set is referenced by t_i. Notice that the natural order of days of the week is retained in this representation of the set as summarized below.

t_1	t_2	t_3	t_4	t_5	t_6	t_7
12	15	16	14	21	25	30

11.2.2   Input and Output

The pseudo code to input the elements of a set X could be written quite simply as:

get X

Though this statement may be useful for early refinements of an algorithm, it is deceptive in that no information is given about the size of the set. Assuming that the set X has 10 elements, reading the 10 values for X is expressed more clearly by a **while** loop using a counter or index for the position of the element in the set.

```
i ← 1
while i ≤ 10 do
  ⎡ get x_i
  ⎣ i ← i + 1
```

For convenience, it may be desirable to write this loop in an abbreviated form such as:

get $(x_i, \; i \leftarrow 1 \; \text{to} \; 10)$

where the **while** action is implied but not written explicitly.

The above three methods of expressing input for a set may also be used for describing the **put** action. Again, it is preferable to refer to each element individually in the final refinement of an algorithm.

11.2.3   Processing

The manipulation of elements of a set may take on many forms. In early refinements of an algorithm it may again be useful to simply refer to the entire set by name. For example, finding the sum of the 25 entries in a set called LIST might be written as

$$\text{sum} \leftarrow \sum \text{LIST}$$

However, the actions inherent in the above statement are more clearly expressed by the following pseudo-code expansion.

```
sum ← 0
index ← 1
while index ≤ 25 do
    ⎡ sum ← sum + list_index
    ⎣ index ← index + 1
```

11.2.4   Applications of Simple Sets

Ordered sets or lists are useful in solving a variety of mathematical problems. This section investigates one simple example, which is developed using step-wise refinement. Later chapters will study arrays used in statistics as well as in sorting and searching.

Example 11.1

Given a set of temperature readings for the seven days of a week, for each day find the number of degrees above or below the average temperature for the week.

a) Problem Discussion   In order to find the difference between the temperature on each day and the average for the week, it is necessary to find the average first and then subtract the temperature each day from the average. Thus, the daily temperature readings are required twice, and it is useful to store them in a set.

b) Selection of Initial Decomposition   Since the entries of the set must be available before processing can begin, initial decomposition #1 is a good way to start. A first version is given as Figure 11.1.

Figure 11.1 First version of a pseudo-code algorithm for Example 11.1.

1. Acquire the daily temperature readings.

2. For each day, find and record the number of degrees above or below the average.

stop

---

c) Refining Step **1.** Let the name of the set for the temperatures be T. Then reading the entries may be written as follows.

> * Acquire the daily temperature readings.
>
> **get** T

No further refinement is necessary in this example since the size of the set must clearly be 7. In other cases, where the set size is not predictable, the statement would be refined as a **while** loop.

d) Refining Step **2.** As stated previously, finding the number of degrees above or below the average requires finding the average first and then computing the difference for each day.

> **2.1** Find and record the average temperature for the week.
>
> **2.2** Find the difference for each day and record the results.

e) Refining Step **2.1** Finding the average temperature involves adding the temperature for each day to a sum and dividing by the number of days.

> * Find and record the average temperature for the week.
> ```
> sum ← 0
> i ← 1
> while i ≤ 7 do
>     ⌈ sum ← sum + tᵢ
>     ⌊ i ← i + 1
> average ← sum/7
> put 'The average temperature is', average
> ```

f) Refining Step **2.2** To compute the number of degrees above or below the average, it is necessary to create a **while** loop to subtract the average from the temperature for each day. These differences could be written out directly. Though this would be the most efficient method, here the differences are stored in a set called HILO instead. This serves to isolate the output as a logical unit and to illustrate the creation of a set as part of processing data.

* Find the difference for each day.

i ← 1
while i ≤ 7 **do**
$$\left[\begin{array}{l} \text{hilo}_i \leftarrow t_i - \text{average} \\ i \leftarrow i + 1 \end{array}\right.$$

2.2.1 Record the difference for each day.

g) Refining Step **2.2.1**   Recording the results can best be accomplished by listing the number of degrees above or below the average beside the temperature for each day. Column titles should also be included to identify the output.

* Record the difference for each day.

put 'Temperature Difference'
i ← 1
while i ≤ 7 **do**
$$\left[\begin{array}{l} \textbf{put } t_i, \text{hilo}_i \\ i \leftarrow i + 1 \end{array}\right.$$

h) Final Version of the Algorithm   The refinements for the various steps of the algorithm can now be collected and are presented in Figure 11.2.

11.3   One-Dimensional Arrays in WATFIV-S

11.3.1   Representation

Just as the use of ordinary or scalar variables is more formal in WATFIV-S, so is the definition and use of arrays. Recall that the type of each variable should be declared in a REAL or INTEGER statement. The type of number to be stored in the elements of an array must be similarly declared. In fact, only values of this type may be stored in the array. In addition, it is necessary to specify the number of elements in the array. Thus, for example, if the array T is to have 7 integral entries the declaration would be:

```
INTEGER T(7)
```

This statement instructs the compiler to reserve 7 consecutive locations for the array called T and that all 7 values stored there will be integers. Subscripts are also used to reference individual entries in the array. However, in WATFIV-S, the subscript or index is placed in parentheses following the name. The subscript must be either an integer or an integer-valued expression with a value between 1 and the size of the array, inclusive. The diagram which follows illustrates this naming convention for the array of 7 temperatures encountered in the previous section.

Figure 11.2   Final version of the pseudo-code algorithm for Example 11.1.

* Given a set of temperature readings for each day of a week find
* the number of degrees above or below the average for each day.

* Variables used:
* T - set of daily temperatures
* **HILO** - set of temperature differences
* **sum** - sum of readings for averaging
* **average** - average temperature for the week

* Acquire the daily temperature readings.

get T

* Find and record the average temperature for the week.

sum ← 0
i ← 1
while i ≤ 7 **do**
$$\left[\begin{array}{l} \text{sum} \leftarrow \text{sum} + t_i \\ i \leftarrow i + 1 \end{array}\right.$$
average ← sum/7
put 'The average temperature is', average

* Find the difference for each day.

i ← 1
while i ≤ 7 **do**
$$\left[\begin{array}{l} \text{hilo}_i \leftarrow t_i - \text{average} \\ i \leftarrow i + 1 \end{array}\right.$$

* Record the difference for each day.

put 'Temperature   Difference'
i ← 1
while i ≤ 7 **do**
$$\left[\begin{array}{l} \textbf{put } t_i, \text{hilo}_i \\ i \leftarrow i + 1 \end{array}\right.$$
stop

12, 15, 16, 14, 21, 35, 30

			T			
T(1)	T(2)	T(3)	T(4)	T(5)	T(6)	T(7)
12	15	16	14	21	25	30

As with the pseudo code, T(I) is used to reference the temperature on the *i*-th day.

11.3.2 Input and Output

There are a variety of ways of expressing input and output of array elements in WATFIV-s. To begin with, <mark>the READ and PRINT statements are two of the few instances in which it is legal to use the name of an array by itself.</mark> Consider the following brief example which reads and prints the first 10 prime numbers.

```
      INTEGER PRIME(10)
      READ, PRIME
      PRINT, PRIME
      STOP
      END
$ENTRY
2, 3, 5, 7, 11, 13, 17, 19, 23, 29
```

The read statement causes ten values to be read into the array PRIME while the PRINT statement causes these same ten values to be printed. In each case the number of entries is specified by the declared size of the array.

Though the above convention is easy to use, frequently the exact number of entries in an array is supplied as data. In cases like this it is necessary to guess at an upper bound for the size of the array (using information supplied in the statement of the problem if possible) and to use a **while** loop to read in the values. The following example performs a similar function as the previous example but in a more general fashion. It allows for a variable number of primes (up to 100) and expects a data count to precede the actual values.

```
      INTEGER PRIME(100), I, N
      READ, N
      I = 1
      WHILE(I .LE. N) DO
         READ, PRIME(I)
         I = I + 1
      END WHILE
      :
$ENTRY
4
2
3
5
7
```

In this example the READ statements are encountered N+1 times and, therefore, there must be at least N+1 data lines.

As with pseudo code, the **while** loop in this example can be written in an abbreviated form such as the following.

```
   READ, (PRIME(I), I=1,N)
```

In fact, it may be convenient to include the input of N in the same statement.

```
   READ, N, (PRIME(I), I=1,N)
```

Here a value of N is read before it is needed to control the reading of values for the array PRIME. This implied loop has the advantage that, since the READ statement is encountered only once, several data values may be placed on one line.

When the values of an array are to be printed, using an explicit **while** loop will cause each value to be printed on a separate line. An implied loop will print the values across the page, continuing on subsequent lines as necessary.

11.3.3   Applications of Simple Arrays

To illustrate the application of arrays, the algorithm of Figure 11.2 will be translated to WATFIV–S. Translation of this algorithm requires a little care. Though the daily temperature readings are probably integral, it is quite likely that the average and, therefore, the differences are not. Thus, the set T could be INTEGER while the set HILO should be REAL. The complete program is listed in Figure 11.3, while the corresponding output is presented in Figure 11.4.

```
C Figure 11.3 -- Program to take a set of temperature readings
C                for each day of a week and find the number of
C                degrees above or below the average each day.
C*****************************************************************
C T      - set of daily temperatures
C HILO   - set of temperature differences
C SUM    - sum of readings for averaging
C AVER   - average temperature for the week
C*****************************************************************
      INTEGER T(7), SUM, I
      REAL HILO(7), AVER
C Acquire the daily temperature readings.
      READ, T
C Find and record the average temperature for the week.
      SUM = 0
      I = 1
      WHILE(I .LE. 7) DO
         SUM = SUM + T(I)
         I = I + 1
      END WHILE
      AVER = SUM/7.0
      PRINT, 'THE AVERAGE TEMPERATURE IS', AVER
C Find the difference for each day.
      I = 1
      WHILE(I .LE. 7) DO
         HILO(I) = T(I) - AVER
         I = I + 1
      END WHILE
C Record the difference for each day.
      PRINT, ' '
      PRINT, ' TEMPERATURE            DIFFERENCE'
      PRINT, ' '
      I = 1
      WHILE(I .LE. 7) DO
         PRINT, T(I), HILO(I)
         I = I + 1
      END WHILE
      STOP
      END
$ENTRY
12 15 16 14 21 25 30
```

Figure 11.4   Output from the temperature analysis program of Figure 11.3.

THE AVERAGE TEMPERATURE IS   19.00000000

TEMPERATURE	DIFFERENCE
12	-7.00000000
15	-4.00000000
16	-3.00000000
14	-5.00000000
21	2.00000000
25	6.00000000
30	11.00000000

This first example has illustrated but a few of the operations commonly applied to ordered sets or lists. Further examples are suggested in the exercises.

11.4 Multidimensional Sets

Simple ordered sets are useful in solving many mathematical problems. However, not all data is inherently one-dimensional in structure. Consider the data presented in

Figure 11.5   Precipitation for one year at 4 locations.

Month		Location		
	North	East	South	West
January	12.4	13.5	12.1	12.6
February	8.2	9.5	8.0	7.5
March	14.9	13.5	12.9	15.3
April	30.0	35.5	40.2	37.7
May	24.5	26.1	23.4	24.0
June	10.0	9.0	8.5	7.9
July	4.0	.5	2.3	3.2
August	3.4	0.0	4.5	6.1
September	7.8	7.9	7.6	7.8
October	10.1	10.6	10.9	12.0
November	12.3	12.5	12.1	12.6
December	14.1	15.2	12.8	9.5

Figure 11.6   Nicotine levels in 5 brands of cigarettes by 4 measurements in 3 tests.

	Test 1	Test 2	Test 3
A	2.1, 2.3, 1.9, 2.0	2.3, 2.4, 2.3, 2.5	2.0, 1.9, 2.0, 2.1
B	4.5, 4.6, 4.7, 4.8	4.0, 3.9, 4.1, 4.3	4.4, 4.4, 4.5, 4.4
C	0.5, 0.5, 0.5, 0.5	0.4, 0.6, 0.5, 0.5	0.6, 0.6, 0.4, 0.5
D	6.1, 6.5, 6.7, 6.3	6.5, 6.5, 6.7, 6.9	5.9, 6.0, 6.2, 6.0
E	3.7, 3.8, 3.7, 3.6	3.8, 3.6, 3.7, 3.7	3.6, 3.7, 3.5, 3.8

Figures 11.5 and 11.6. The table in Figure 11.5 lists the precipitation readings taken over each of the 12 months of the year at 4 locations in the same region. To retain the relationship between region and month it would be desirable to organize the set as a two-dimensional array having 12 rows, one for each month, and 4 columns, one for each region. The second table of Figure 11.6 gives 4 nicotine measurements for each of 3 tests

applied to each of 5 brands of cigarettes. To represent this data adequately would require a three-dimensional array.

11.5   Multidimensional Sets in Pseudo Code

The basic techniques required to handle multidimensional sets in pseudo code are illustrated in this section by using sets with only two dimensions. Extension of these ideas to sets with three or more dimensions is straightforward and is not done explicitly in this chapter.

11.5.1   Representation

The representation of multidimensional sets in pseudo code can be handled in a manner similar to ordinary sets. A name written in upper case will refer to the entire set, whereas individual elements in the set will be referenced by using a lower case letter with a subscript for each dimension. For example, the data given in Figure 11.5 could be labeled P, and the elements can be referenced as illustrated by the following diagram.

$$p_{1,1} \qquad p_{1,2} \qquad p_{1,3} \qquad p_{1,4}$$
$$p_{2,1} \qquad p_{2,2} \qquad p_{2,3} \qquad p_{2,4}$$
$$\vdots \qquad\qquad \vdots \qquad\qquad \vdots \qquad\qquad \vdots$$
$$p_{12,1} \qquad p_{12,2} \qquad p_{12,3} \qquad p_{12,4}$$

11.5.2   Input and Output

There is much flexibility in expressing the getting and recording of array elements. The order of the data plays an important role in the structuring of the **while** loops necessary to input or output the set. In all likelihood the data is not organized at random but rather in either *row-major* or *column-major* order. If the data is in row-major order, the column entries for row 1 are followed by the column entries for row 2, and so on. On the other hand, if the data is in column-major order, the row entries for column 1 are followed by the row entries for column 2, and so on. Most algorithmic segments can easily be changed from row to column order by rearranging the loop structure. For simplicity the illustrations for input will only use row-major order for the data.

The most straightforward method of expressing array input is to use nested **while** loops, that is, an outer loop and an inner loop. The outer **while** loop controls the row number while the inner **while** loop controls the reading of column entries for that row. Consider reading the 12×4 values for the table in Figure 11.5.

```
* P is the array name
* r is the row index
* c is the column index

r ← 1
while r ≤ 12 do
    ⌈ c ← 1
    | while c ≤ 4 do
    |     ⌈ get p_r,c
    |     ⌊ c ← c + 1
    ⌊ r ← r + 1
```

Because of the length of such an organization it may again be appealing to abbreviate the looping structure as:

```
while r ≤ 12 do
    ⌈ get (p_r,c, c ← 1 to 4)
    ⌊ r ← r + 1
```

or even as two implied loops.

```
    get ((p_r,c, c ← 1 to 4), r ← 1 to 12)
```

In this latter arrangement, the inner loop involving the column counter c is repeated for each value of r in the outer loop, which varies the row number. Of course, the same structures can be applied to recording the elements of an array by changing the word **get** to **put**.

11.5.3 Processing
The manipulations applied to the entries of a two-dimensional set can vary considerably. In most cases it is necessary to use a double loop structure similar to that used for reading the entries of the array. Examples will be given in the following section.

11.5.4 Applications
This example will involve analyzing the weather data given in Figure 11.5.

Example 11.2
    For the table of precipitation levels for four locations over a 12-month period find the average rainfall per month over the entire region as well as the wettest location over the year.

a) Problem Discussion   Since the problem involves several analyses of the data it is appropriate to retain the table in storage. As mentioned in the previous section, the most natural arrangement is a two-dimensional array.

b) Selection of Initial Decomposition   Initial decomposition #1 will be used to first input the entire array and then analyze the data as required, as shown in Figure 11.7.

Figure 11.7   First version of a pseudo-code algorithm for Example 11.2.

1.   Acquire the precipitation measurements.

2.   Find the average rainfall for each month and the wettest location over the year.

stop

c) Refining Step **1.**   Assume that the data is to be entered on 12 lines with the 4 readings for each month on the same line. It is, therefore, convenient to use an outer **while** loop to process each line. Within this loop, an implied loop is used to input the 4 readings for each month. Finally, these values should also be recorded and it is easiest to do so as the values are obtained.

```
*  Acquire and record the precipitation measurements.
put 'Month  North  East  South  West'
r ← 1
while r ≤ 12 do
    ┌  get (p_{r,c}, c ← 1 to 4)
    │  put r, (p_{r,c}, c ← 1 to 4)
    └  r ← r + 1
```

d) Refining Step **2.**   There are two distinct analyses required as part of step **2.** It is most convenient to record each as it is found. This is reflected in the next expansion.

2.1 Find and record the average rainfall for each month.

2.2 Find and record the wettest location over the year.

e) Refining Step **2.1**   To find the average rainfall for each month the averaging process must be repeated 12 times, once for each month. This is done using a **while** loop as shown below.

```
*  Find and record the average rainfall for each month.
r ← 1
while r ≤ 12 do
    ┌  2.1.1 Find and record the average for the r-th month.
    └  r ← r + 1
```

f) Refining Step **2.1.1**   The averaging process involves summing the elements along each row of the array. This, in turn, requires a loop to advance along the 4 column entries for the row.

```
sum ← 0
c ← 1
while c ≤ 4 do
    ⎡ sum ← sum + p_{r,c}
    ⎣ c ← c + 1
average ← sum/4
put 'The average rainfall for month', r, 'is', average
```

g) Refining Step **2.2**   Finding the wettest location over the year first requires finding the total rainfall at each location then searching for the largest total and recording the result.

2.2.1 Find the total rainfall for each location.

2.2.2 Search for the largest total and record the wettest location.

h) Refining Step **2.2.1**   Finding the total rainfall for each location can be done very easily by observing that it involves a simple rearrangement of the summing used in the previous averaging process. However, it will be necessary to retain these values in order to find the wettest location later. They are stored in a simple set called LT for location totals. These totals are recorded as a check that the largest total found later is indeed correct.

```
*  Find the total rainfall for each location.
c ← 1
while c ≤ 4 do
    ⎡ lt_c ← 0
    ⎢ r ← 1
    ⎢ while r ≤ 12 do
    ⎢     ⎡ lt_c ← lt_c + p_{r,c}
    ⎢     ⎣ r ← r + 1
    ⎢ put 'The total rainfall for location', c, 'is', lt_c
    ⎣ c ← c + 1
```

i) Refining Step **2.2.2**   There are several ways to approach the problem of finding the location with the most rainfall. Since all the rainfalls must be non-negative, initialize the maximum rainfall at a negative number and the location at 0, and then check each of the totals for a better estimate.

```
* Search for the largest total.
rain ← -1
where ← 0
c ← 1
while c ≤ 4 do
    ⎡ if lt_c ≥ rain then
    ⎢     ⎡ rain ← lt_c
    ⎢     ⎣ where ← c
    ⎣ c ← c + 1
```

```
* Record the wettest location.
```

put 'The wettest location is', where

Notice that this code will determine the last location with the largest total if several should have the same value.

j) Final Version of the Algorithm   The various sections of the algorithm are presented together in Figure 11.8.

Figure 11.8   Final version of the pseudo-code algorithm for Example 11.2.

```
* Given a table of rainfall readings for 4 locations over a 1 year period,
* find the average rainfall per month and the wettest location over the year.

* Variables used:
* P - set of monthly rainfall measurements
* r - a row index
* c - a column index
* sum - sum of location readings for monthly averaging
* aver - monthly averages
* LT - locations totals array
* rain - current largest rainfall total
* where - position of wettest location

* Acquire and record the precipitation measurements.
put 'Month   North   East   South   West'
r ← 1
while r ≤ 12 do
    ⎡ get (p_{r,c}, c ← 1 to 4)
    ⎢ put r, (p_{r,c}, c ← 1 to 4)
    ⎣ r ← r + 1
```

Figure 11.8   (continued)

* Find and record the average rainfall for each month.

r ← 1
while r ≤ 12 **do**

>   sum ← 0
>   c ← 1
>   **while** c ≤ 4 **do**
>
> >   sum ← sum + $p_{r,c}$
> >   c ← c + 1
>
>   average ← sum/4
>   **put** 'The average for month', r, 'is', average
>   r ← r + 1

* Find the total rainfall for each location.

c ← 1
while c ≤ 4 **do**

> lt_c ← 0
>   r ← 1
>   **while** r ≤ 12 **do**
>
> > lt_c ← lt_c + $p_{r,c}$
> >   r ← r + 1
>
>   **put** 'The total rainfall for location', c, 'is', lt_c
>   c ← c + 1

* Search for the largest total.

rain ← −1
where ← 0
c ← 1
while c ≤ 4 **do**

>   **if** lt_c ≥ rain **then**
>
> >   rain ← lt_c
> >   where ← c
>
>   c ← c + 1

* Record the wettest location.

put 'The wettest location is', where
stop

11.6   Multidimensional Arrays in WATFIV-S

11.6.1   Representation

Implementing multidimensional sets in WATFIV-S is similar to the way simple sets were defined and used. Multidimensional sets are referred to by name with a subscript for each dimension placed in brackets after it. The first subscript refers to the row number, the second to the column number, and so on. The type of value to be stored in an array and the maximum size for each dimension must be declared before the set is used, preferably at the outset of the program. Thus, the storage for the precipitation table of Figure 11.5 could be declared by the following statement.

```
REAL P(12,4)
```

This causes the compiler to set aside 12×4 or 48 consecutive spaces for the values of the array and to treat them as floating point numbers. WATFIV-S will store the values in column-major order. However, this does vary in other languages.

11.6.2   Input and Output

WATFIV-S has features for reading and writing set entries that correspond to those discussed for pseudo code. Again, this is one of the few places where an array name can be used by itself. Thus, the entire 48 entry array of precipitations can be read in by the following statement.

```
READ, P
```

All 48 data values for P must be arranged in *column-major* order. This form always requires enough data values (that is, 48) to fill each element in the array.

To provide for more generality in a program an array is usually declared with a maximum size of rows and columns sufficiently large to handle all expected cases. When working with such a general program, whether reading or manipulating elements of the array, it is necessary to specify the limits on the rows and columns appropriate for the smaller problem. On input, for example, the number of rows and columns actually desired might constitute two additional data items preceding the array entries themselves. In the following program segment the initial READ statement obtains the limits for the data (NR and NC) from the first data line and proceeds to read NR*NC values for the array, each from a separate line, in row-major order.

```
READ, NR, NC
R = 1
WHILE(R .LE. NR) DO
   C = 1
   WHILE(C .LE. NC) DO
      READ, P(R,C)
      C = C + 1
   END WHILE
   R = R + 1
END WHILE
```

For this program segment, the arrangement of data is dictated by the need to insure that data appears on a new line each time a READ statement is re-entered. This awkwardness can be circumvented by using an implied loop for each row as illustrated below.

```
READ, NR, NC
R = 1
WHILE(R .LE. NR) DO
    READ, (P(R,C), C=1,NC)
    R = R + 1
END WHILE
```

This arrangement only requires a new line for the start of each new row of data. One may also use the following form which allows for the most flexibility.

```
READ, NR, NC, ((P(R,C), C=1,NC), R=1,NR)
```

11.6.3   Processing

When processing entries of multidimensional sets it is always necessary to specify a subscript for each dimension. Examples of how to express these manipulations will be given in the next section.

11.6.4   Applications

To illustrate the use of arrays, consider translating the algorithm for Example 11.2. The WATFIV-S version of the algorithm is presented in Figure 11.9. The output produced by the program is listed in Figure 11.10.

```
C Figure 11.9 -- Program to take a set of rainfall readings
C                for 4 locations over a 1 year period,
C                find the average rainfall per month and
C                the wettest location over the year.

C****************************************************************

C P       - set of monthly rainfall measurements
C R       - a row index
C C       - a column index
C SUM     - sum of location readings for monthly averaging
C AVER    - monthly averages
C LT      - location totals array
C RAIN    - current largest rainfall total
C WHERE   - position of wettest location

C****************************************************************

      INTEGER R, C, WHERE
      REAL P(12,4), SUM, AVER, LT(4), RAIN
C Acquire and record the precipitation measurements.
      PRINT, '        MONTH                NORTH
     +' EAST                SOUTH                WEST'
      PRINT, ' '
      R = 1
      WHILE(R .LE. 12) DO
          READ, (P(R,C), C=1,4)
          PRINT, R, (P(R,C), C=1,4)
          R = R + 1
      END WHILE
```

```
C Figure 11.9 (continued)
C Find and record the average rainfall for each month.
      PRINT, ' '
      R = 1
      WHILE(R .LE. 12) DO
         SUM = 0.0
         C = 1
         WHILE(C .LE. 4) DO
            SUM = SUM + P(R,C)
            C = C + 1
         END WHILE
         AVER = SUM/4.0
         PRINT, 'THE AVERAGE FOR MONTH', R,' IS', AVER
         R = R + 1
      END WHILE
C Find the total rainfall for each location.
      PRINT, ' '
      C = 1
      WHILE(C .LE. 4) DO
         LT(C) = 0.0
         R = 1
         WHILE(R .LE. 12) DO
            LT(C) = LT(C) + P(R,C)
            R = R + 1
         END WHILE
         PRINT, 'THE TOTAL RAINFALL FOR LOCATION', C,' IS', LT(C)
         C = C + 1
      END WHILE
C Search for the largest total.
      PRINT, ' '
      RAIN = -1.0
      WHERE = 0
      C = 1
      WHILE(C .LE. 4) DO
         IF(LT(C) .GE. RAIN) THEN DO
               RAIN = LT(C)
               WHERE = C
         END IF
         C = C + 1
      END WHILE
C Record the wettest location.
      PRINT, 'THE WETTEST LOCATION IS', WHERE
      STOP
      END
$ENTRY
12.4 13.5 12.1 12.6
 8.2  9.5  8.0  7.5
14.9 13.5 12.9 15.3
30.0 35.5 40.2 37.7
24.5 26.1 23.4 24.0
10.0  9.0  8.5  7.9
 4.0   .5  2.3  3.2
 3.4  0.0  4.5  6.1
 7.8  7.9  7.6  7.8
10.1 10.6 10.9 12.0
12.3 12.5 12.1 12.6
14.1 15.2 12.8  9.5
```

Figure 11.10   Output from the rainfall analysis program of Figure 11.9. (Spacing edited)

MONTH	NORTH	EAST	SOUTH	WEST
1	12.39999000	13.50000000	12.10000000	12.60000000
2	8.19999900	9.50000000	8.00000000	7.50000000
3	14.89999000	13.50000000	12.89999000	15.30000000
4	30.00000000	35.50000000	40.19999000	37.69999000
5	24.50000000	26.10000000	23.39999000	24.00000000
6	10.00000000	9.00000000	8.50000000	7.89999900
7	4.00000000	0.50000000	2.30000000	3.19999900
8	3.39999900	0.00000000	4.50000000	6.10000000
9	7.80000000	7.89999900	7.60000000	7.80000000
10	10.10000000	10.60000000	10.89999000	12.00000000
11	12.30000000	12.50000000	12.10000000	12.60000000
12	14.10000000	15.19999000	12.80000000	9.50000000

```
THE AVERAGE FOR MONTH        1  IS        12.64999000
THE AVERAGE FOR MONTH        2  IS         8.29999900
THE AVERAGE FOR MONTH        3  IS        14.14999000
THE AVERAGE FOR MONTH        4  IS        35.84999000
THE AVERAGE FOR MONTH        5  IS        24.50000000
THE AVERAGE FOR MONTH        6  IS         8.84999800
THE AVERAGE FOR MONTH        7  IS         2.50000000
THE AVERAGE FOR MONTH        8  IS         3.50000000
THE AVERAGE FOR MONTH        9  IS         7.77499300
THE AVERAGE FOR MONTH       10  IS        10.89999000
THE AVERAGE FOR MONTH       11  IS        12.37499000
THE AVERAGE FOR MONTH       12  IS        12.89999000

THE TOTAL RAINFALL FOR LOCATION      1  IS      151.69990000
THE TOTAL RAINFALL FOR LOCATION      2  IS      153.79990000
THE TOTAL RAINFALL FOR LOCATION      3  IS      155.29990000
THE TOTAL RAINFALL FOR LOCATION      4  IS      156.19990000

THE WETTEST LOCATION IS          4
```

11.7   Sets and Modules

The idea of organizing commonly used routines as modules was first presented in Chapter 9. It is, of course, often desirable to write modules which make use of sets of data.

The use of sets in pseudo-code modules does not require any special attention. Set names may appear in argument or parameter lists just as any other type of variable.

However, using sets in WATFIV-S subprograms may require extra care when these sets form part of the argument/parameter list. Naturally, the type (that is, REAL or INTEGER) of a set used in an argument list must be the same as the type declared in the subprogram. Furthermore, it is important that the declared size and number of dimensions of the set be the same in both the calling program and the subprogram[1]. At compile time the translated version of the subprogram is designed to handle sets of the declared size. However, no space is set aside to contain the set entries. Rather, at execution time, the subprogram uses the space for the set in the calling program. Note that this is different from the way in which ordinary or scalar variables are handled. However, the effect is the same; any change made to a parameter in a subprogram affects the value of the corresponding argument in the calling program. All of this activity is hidden from the WATFIV-S user and is, therefore, of minimal concern provided

[1]There are exceptions to this rule which will not be discussed in this introduction.

the set is properly declared.

Consider an example of both a pseudo-code module and its equivalent WATFIV-S subprogram.

Example 11.3

Develop a module to find the largest and smallest entries in a given set of numbers. Test this module on the following three sets.

1) 12, 15, 18
2) 25, 25, 25
3) 10, 20, 0, 50

a) Problem Discussion   Since very few guidelines are specified, the problem solver is given a lot of flexibility. In such circumstances, it is tempting to be guided by the sample data. Assuming that the routine might be useful elsewhere it is best to be as general as possible. The module will be designed to find the largest and smallest number in any set of given length while the main module will handle an arbitrary number of sets.

b) A Minimum/Maximum Module   In order to perform its task the module will need to be given the set of numbers as well as the number of entries in the set. The module should supply the smallest and largest values as export parameters. In order to find these values it will be necessary to scan all of the entries in the list. To begin with, some assumption must be made about these entries. One possibility is to use an arbitrary large guess for the smallest and an equivalent small guess for the largest (as was done in the previous example). Alternatively, it is possible to assume that the first number in the set is both the smallest and largest and then search for contradictions in the remainder of the list. The second option is preferable since it removes any uncertainty about the range of numbers in the set. The pseudo-code module minmax in Figure 11.11 will perform these tasks.

Figure 11.11   A pseudo-code module to find the minimum and maximum elements in a set.

module minmax (**imports**: SET, num; **exports**: small, large)

* Module to find the smallest and largest entries in a given **SET** of length **num**.

* Variables used:
* **SET** - the given set of numbers
* **num** - length of the set
* **small** - smallest entry in the set
* **large** - largest entry in the set

* Initialize the smallest and largest as the first entry.

small $\leftarrow$ set$_1$
large $\leftarrow$ set$_1$

* Search the rest of the set for better values.

i $\leftarrow$ 2
while i $\leq$ num **do**
    if set$_i$ < small **then**
        small $\leftarrow$ set$_i$
    else
        if set$_i$ > large **then**
            large $\leftarrow$ set$_i$
    i $\leftarrow$ i + 1
end module

c) Main Module to Test the Three Sets of Numbers   Since the main module must handle several sets of numbers, initial decomposition #2 can be applied. Each set is preceded by a data count, and an end-of-data flag will be supplied to terminate the process, as shown in Figure 11.12.

Figure 11.12   A pseudo-code algorithm to test module minimax of Figure 11.11

* Main module to find the largest and smallest number in several sets of data lists.

* Variables used:
* **LIST** - the current list
* **n** - the number of entries in the current list
* **small** - the smallest entry in the current list
* **large** - the largest entry in the current list

* Continue processing sets as long as **n** is positive.

get n
while n > 0 **do**

> **get** (list$_i$, i ← 1 to n)
> **put** 'The list of', n, 'numbers is:'
> **put** (list$_i$, i ← 1 to n)
> **call** minmax(LIST, n; small, large)
> **put** 'The smallest entry is', small
> **put** 'The largest entry is ', large
> **get** n

stop

3, 12, 15, 18
3, 25, 25, 25
4, 10, 20, 0, 50
−1

---

d) A Subprogram for Minmax   Translation of the module minmax to WATFIV-S requires a little forethought about the maximum size of the set. Since no specifications are given a limit of 1000 is arbitrarily chosen. It will also be assumed that the entries are integral. The WATFIV-S version follows as Figure 11.13.

```
C Figure 11.13 -- Subroutine MINMAX
C                   Subprogram to find the smallest and largest
C                   entries in a given SET of length NUM.
C******************************************************************
C SET     - the given set of numbers
C NUM     - length of the set
C SMALL   - smallest entry in the set
C LARGE   - largest entry in the set
C******************************************************************
      SUBROUTINE MINMAX(SET,NUM,SMALL,LARGE)

      INTEGER SET(1000), NUM, SMALL, LARGE, I
C Initialize the smallest and largest as the first entry.
      SMALL = SET(1)
      LARGE = SET(1)
C Search the rest of the set for better values.
      I = 2
      WHILE(I .LE. NUM) DO
         IF(SET(I) .LT. SMALL) THEN DO
              SMALL = SET(I)
         ELSE DO
            IF(SET(I) .GT. LARGE) THEN DO
                 LARGE = SET(I)
            END IF
         END IF
         I = I + 1
      END WHILE
      RETURN
      END
```

e) A Mainline Program to Use Subprogram MINMAX   Translation of the main pseudo-code module to WATFIV-S again requires introducing the type declarations for each variable. Since the subprogram is designed to handle sets of maximum size 1000 the mainline should use the same size for the array. Organizing the input data also requires some care. The length of each array to follow should be typed on a separate line since it is read separately. This program is shown as Figure 11.14. As a check that the program functions properly the output for the sample data is given in Figure 11.15.

```
C Figure 11.14 -- Program to find the largest and smallest
C                     number in several sets of data lists.
C****************************************************************
C LIST    - the current list
C N       - the number of entries in the current list
C SMALL   - the smallest entry in the current list
C LARGE   - the largest entry in the current list
C****************************************************************
        INTEGER LIST(1000), N, SMALL, LARGE, I
C Continue processing sets as long as N is positive.
        READ, N
        WHILE(N .GT. 0) DO
           READ, (LIST(I), I=1,N)
           PRINT, 'THE LIST OF', N, ' NUMBERS IS:'
           PRINT, (LIST(I), I=1,N)
           CALL MINMAX(LIST,N,SMALL,LARGE)
           PRINT, 'THE SMALLEST ENTRY IS', SMALL
           PRINT, 'THE LARGEST  ENTRY IS', LARGE
           PRINT, ' '
           READ, N
        END WHILE
        STOP
        END
C Subroutine MINMAX is placed here.
$ENTRY
3
12 15 18
3
25 25 25
4
10 20 0 50
-1
```

Figure 11.15   Output from the minimum/maximum program of Figure 11.14.

```
THE LIST OF          3  NUMBERS IS:
         12         15            18
THE SMALLEST ENTRY IS            12
THE LARGEST   ENTRY IS           18

THE LIST OF          3  NUMBERS IS:
         25         25            25
THE SMALLEST ENTRY IS            25
THE LARGEST   ENTRY IS           25

THE LIST OF          4  NUMBERS IS:
         10         20             0            50
THE SMALLEST ENTRY IS             0
THE LARGEST   ENTRY IS           50
```

11.8   Summary

This chapter has introduced the idea of structuring data in storage to facilitate the manipulation of that data and to retain as much of any natural relationships as possible. The chapters to follow will exercise this ability as several major application areas are examined in more detail.

11.9   References

Cress, P.; Dirksen, P.H.; and Graham, J.W. *FORTRAN IV with WATFOR and WATFIV*. Englewood Cliffs, N.J.: Prentice-Hall, 1970.

Holt, R.C. and Hume, J.N.P. *Fundamentals of Structured Programming using FORTRAN with SF/k and WATFIV-S*. Reston, Va: Reston Publishing Co., 1977.

Moore, J.B. and Makela, L.J. *Structured FORTRAN with WATFIV*. Reston, Va: Reston Publishing Co., 1978.

Tremblay, J.P. and Sorenson, P.G. *An Introduction to Data Structures with Applications*. New York: McGraw-Hill Book Co., 1976.

Wirth, N. *Algorithms + Data Structures = Programs*. Englewood Cliffs, N.J.: Prentice-Hall, 1976.

11.10   Exercises

In most of the following exercises a program is requested to solve a specific problem. For each problem it is recommended that step-wise refinement be used in developing a pseudo-code algorithm to solve the problem. This algorithm should then be translated into WATFIV-S and run on the computer. Where appropriate, the program should be tested with a variety of data sufficient to ensure that the program does what it is supposed to do. In some cases, this will involve writing a main program to test the required subprogram.

11.1 Chapters 4 and 5 included examples involving the testing of numbers to determine whether thay were prime or composite. The most efficient algorithm presented in Chapter 5 (see Figure 5.13) tested for divisibility by 2 and then all odd numbers from 3 to the square root of the number. Ideally, it is only necessary to check for divisibility by the prime numbers less than the square root. This can only be accomplished if the necessary primes are stored in a list. Develop a program to generate a list of the first 100 prime numbers by taking advantage of numbers already in the list.

11.2 A popular exercise in generating primes was suggested by the Greek mathematician, Eratosthenes, and is called the Sieve of Eratosthenes. As an illustration of how the method works, consider confining the search to the integers from 1 to 200. The algorithm begins with an ordered list of the integers. Starting with the first prime (2), all further multiples of this prime are eliminated from consideration (perhaps by setting these list entries to zero). The next prime will be the first integer following the current prime that has not been eliminated. Multiples of this prime are then eliminated, and again the remaining integers are searched for the next prime. The algorithm continues until the current prime is greater than $\sqrt{200}$. Develop a program to simulate this method of generating primes.

11.3 In the physical sciences the term *vector* is often used to denote a quantity such as force or velocity, which has both a magnitude and direction. Geometrically, vectors can be represented by directed line segments. With every such vector **v** can be associated a triplet of numbers, (v_x, v_y, v_z) called the components of the vector. The length of the vector, **v**, denoted by $|v|$, is defined as:

$$|v| = \sqrt{v_x^2 + v_y^2 + v_z^2}$$

The inner product of two vectors, **u** and **v**, denoted **u**·**v**, is defined as:

$$\mathbf{u} \cdot \mathbf{v} = u_x \times v_x + u_y \times v_y + u_z \times v_z$$

The angle between any two vectors **u** and **v** is given by:

$$\cos^{-1} \left[\frac{\mathbf{u} \cdot \mathbf{v}}{|u|\,|v|} \right]$$

a)   Write a program to find the angle between two 3-dimensional vectors. The program should handle an arbitrary number of such pairs.

b)   Generalize the program of part a) to find the angle between two *n*-dimensional vectors.

11.4 Given *n* points on the Euclidean plane with coordinates (x_i, y_i), $i = 1, 2, \cdots, n$, then the perimeter of the enclosed area is given by the following formula.

$$\sum_{i=1}^{n-1} \sqrt{(x_{i+1} - x_i)^2 + (y_{i+1} - y_i)^2} + \sqrt{(x_1 - x_n)^2 + (y_1 - y_n)^2}$$

Develop a program to compute the perimeter of the area enclosed by a given set of *n* coordinate pairs.

11.5 Given *n* points on the Euclidean plane with coordinates (x_i, y_i), $i = 1, 2, \cdots, n$, then an approximation to the enclosed area is given by the following formula.

$$\frac{1}{2} \sum_{i=1}^{n-1} \left[(x_{i+1} - x_i) \times (y_{i+1} + y_i) \right] + \frac{1}{2} \left[(x_1 - x_n) \times (y_1 + y_n) \right]$$

Develop a program to compute this approximation to the area enclosed by a given set of *n* coordinate pairs.

11.6 A magic square is a square array such that each of the following quantities has the same value:

- the sum of the elements in each row
- the sum of the elements in each column
- the sum of the elements along each diagonal.

The following 3×3 array is an example since all of the above quantities have the sum 15.

$$\begin{bmatrix} 4 & 3 & 2 \\ 3 & 5 & 7 \\ 8 & 1 & 6 \end{bmatrix}$$

Develop a subprogram to determine if a given array is a magic square.

11.7 a) Develop a subprogram to produce a list of the divisors (including 1 and itself) for any given integer.

   b) It has been conjectured that for any integer the sum of the cubes of its divisors is equal to the square of the sum of its divisors. Write a program to test this conjecture on the integers from 1 to 100.

11.8 a) Develop a subprogram to remove all of the negative entries from a given list. Do not make use of a second list in this process.

   b) Develop a program to test the subprogram of part a) on the following lists.

   1) 12, 14.5, 5.4, 9.56
   2) −3.4, 4.5, 5.6, −4.2,−7.8, 6.7, −8.9
   3) −1,−2,−3,−4,−5

11.9 a) Develop a subprogram to take a given list and produce a second list with the entries of the first list in reverse order.

   b) Modify the subprogram of part a) to return the reversed entries in the same list. Do not use a second list to reverse the entries. It should only be necessary to use one other variable for storage.

11.10 When considering investments it is useful to have access to tables listing the compounded amount over a number of years for a variety of interest rates. Develop a program to produce such a table for an initial investment of one dollar at rates of 5%, 6%, 7%, 8%, 9%, and 10% invested for 1, 2, 3, . . . , and 20 years.

11.11 One method of normalizing a set of data consists of reducing the range of data to between 0 and 1. Thus, the smallest value becomes 0, the largest becomes 1, and all other values are between the two. Develop a subprogram to normalize a given set of data.

11.12 The greatest common divisor (GCD) of a group of numbers is the largest integer that will divide evenly into each number, for example,

   a) the GCD of 45, 295, 75, and 1900 is 5,
   b) the GCD of 42, 63, and 84 is 21, and
   c) the GCD of 7, 13, 17, and 25 is 1.

Develop a subprogram to find the GCD for an arbitrary group of numbers.

11.13 Develop a function subprogram called REPEAT to perform a repeated operation on successive elements of a list and return the result as the value of the function. The function is given A, the list of entries, N, the number of entries in A, and OPER, the name of a function subprogram designed to take two arguments and perform the required operation on them. For example, if the elements of the list are:

$$a_1, a_2, a_3, \cdots, a_n$$

then the function will calculate:

$$a_1 \oplus a_2 \oplus a_3 \oplus \cdots \oplus a_n$$

where $\oplus$ represents the operation to be performed. For instance, to calculate the product of the elements of a list it would be necessary to write a function subprogram such as the one given below and then use it in the call to function REPEAT.

```
REAL FUNCTION MULT(X,Y)
REAL X,Y
MULT = X*Y
RETURN
END
```

11.14 In some mathematical problems it is desirable to perform arithmetic to higher accuracy than is possible using available computing machinery. In cases like this the individual digits of a number are stored in a list and arithmetic operations are performed using the list entries. Develop a series of subprograms to add, subtract, multiply, and divide n-digit integers. The subprograms should be able to handle at least 25-digit integers.

11.15 A real polynomial of degree n is an expression of the form:

$$p(x) = a_1 + a_2 x + a_3 x^2 + \cdots + a_i x^{i-1} + \cdots + a_{n+1} x^n,$$

where the a_i are real numbers called coefficients. The x's are merely symbols used as "place-holders" and in themselves have no meaning. For computer implementation, it is convenient to think of polynomials as just a finite sequence of real numbers

$$(a_1, a_2, a_3, \cdots, a_{n+1})$$

which can be stored as entries of a set A of length $n+1$

a) In Chapter 6, Horner's rule was introduced as an efficient way to evaluate polynomials. Develop a subprogram which uses Horner's rule to evaluate a given n-th degree polynomial for a specific given value of x.

b) The derivative of an *n*-th degree polynomial is given by the following expression.

$$p'(x) = a_2 + 2a_3x + 3a_4x^2 + \cdots + (i-1)a_ix^{i-2} + \cdots + na_{n+1}x^{n-1}$$

Develop a subprogram which uses Horner's rule to evaluate the derivative of a given *n*-th degree polynomial for a specific value of *x*.

c) Chapter 7 includes a discussion of Newton's method for approximating the zero of a function. Develop a subprogram to use Newton's method to approximate a zero of a given *n*-th degree polynomial function for a given starting value.

d) Develop a program to use the subprograms of parts a), b), and c) to approximate as many zeros as possible for any *n*-th degree polynomial of size $n \leq 25$. Test the program on the following polynomials.

  1) $p(x) = -25.25 - 17.75x + 17.25x^2 + 9.75x^3 + x^4$
  2) $p(x) = -254 + 5078x - 40x^2 - 242x^3 + 2x^5$

e) There is a rule in algebra called the "Descartes Rule of Signs" which states that:

  1) the maximum number of positive real zeros of a polynomial is given by the number of sign changes in the coefficents
  2) the maximum number of negative real zeros of a polynomial is given by the number of sign changes in the coefficents when *x* is replaced by $-x$.

Develop a program to use this rule to determine the maximum number of positive and negative real zeros for an *n*-th degree polynomial.

f) Develop a subprogram to find the sum polynomial, $C = A + B$, of two polynomials *A* (of degree *m*) and *B* (of degree *n*).

g) Develop a subprogram to find the product polynomial, $C = A \times B$, of two polynomials *A* (of degree *m*) and *B* (of degree *n*). The *i*th term of the product polynomial will be the sum of all terms of the form $a_q b_r$ with $q + r = i + 1$, that is,

$$c_i = a_ib_1 + a_2b_{i-1} + a_3b_{i-2} + \cdots + a_ib_1$$

h) If *A* is a polynomial of degree *m*, *B* is a polynomial of degree *m*, and *C* is a polynomial of degree *p*, then develop a program which uses the subprograms of parts f) and g) to compute the polynomial $A^2 + B \times C$.

11.16 In mathematics, the term matrix is often used to describe a rectangular array of numbers. An $m \times n$ matrix A is a rectangular array having *m* rows and *n* columns

$$
A \;=\; \begin{bmatrix} a_{1,1} & a_{1,2} & \cdots & a_{1,n} \\ a_{2,1} & a_{2,2} & \cdots & a_{2,n} \\ . & . & & . \\ . & . & & . \\ . & . & & . \\ a_{m,1} & a_{m,2} & \cdots & a_{m,n} \end{bmatrix}
$$

Develop subprograms to perform each of the following tasks.

a) Create an $n \times n$ identity matrix.
b) Find the sum of two $m \times n$ matrices.
c) Find the product of an $m \times n$ and an $n \times p$ matrix.
d) Determine if a given $n \times n$ matrix is upper triangular.
e) Find the transpose of a given $n \times n$ matrix.
f) Determine if a given $n \times n$ matrix is symmetric.
g) Interchange the two diagonals of a given $n \times n$ matrix.
h) Exchange two rows of a given $m \times n$ matrix.
i) Exchange two columns of a given $m \times n$ matrix.

12
Searching and Sorting Techniques

12.1 Introduction

The topic of organizing and manipulating collections of data was first introduced in Chapter 11. This chapter will discuss two types of operations frequently applied to a list of data, namely, searching and sorting.

Naturally, the idea of a search is to find something. Each day a person spends time looking for things, whether it be for a matching sock in a drawer, a particular car in a parking lot, or a word in a dictionary. With computer applications the item sought is usually a value such as a specific entry in a list of numbers, or the largest number in a list. Computers can be quite useful because they can deal with very large lists. For example, a request by the police to identify the owner of a particular vehicle with a given licence number requires the search of potentially several million items on file.

Ordering information according to a predetermined criterion is also common in everyday life and provides the motivation for sorting. For example, playing cards are organized by rank within suit for convenience in playing such games as hearts or bridge. Names in a telephone directory must be listed in alphabetical order within towns or cities for easy reference. Of course, the telephone company also maintains lists ordered by telephone number as well as by street. The large size of these telephone lists necessitates the use of a computer in their production and maintenance.

The two topics of searching and sorting are usually discussed together since some searching techniques require a presorted list, and most sorting methods involve searching for values. Since searching and sorting are such common operations in computer processing, many different algorithms and approaches have been developed. Although searching and sorting techniques exist for both internally and externally stored data, the discussion here will be limited to internal sorting techniques. Algorithms for externally stored data are included in the texts referenced at the end of the chapter.

12.2 Searching Techniques

The problem of searching a list may take many forms. The purpose of the search may be to determine the absence or presence of an entry, to locate its position in the list, or to find the frequency of occurrence.

The choice of a searching technique depends on several factors such as the order and size of the list and whether or not the search must be repeated. If the order of the list entries is random, items must be examined one at a time until the desired item is found (a linear search). However, if the list is ordered (such as an alphabetical listing of words in a dictionary), it may be possible to use a more sophisticated approach such as a binary search. Intuitively, for short lists and infrequent searches, one would expect a simple method to be sufficient. However, for long lists and frequent references, a more elaborate method involving a prior ordering of the list may be appropriate.

This section examines two approaches to locating the position of a particular item in a list of numbers. Each technique is discussed and implemented as a module to allow for inclusion in a library. The label of the item being sought is usually referred to as a *key*. Hence, these modules are all designed to locate a value called key in a list labeled LIST having n unique entries. The position of key will be returned in a variable called place.

12.2.1 Simple Linear Searches

The most straightforward method of finding the position of a specific value in a list of numbers is simply to compare the value with each entry in the list, checking for equality. A first approach is illustrated by the following pseudo code. This segment compares key with each of the n elements in LIST. If a match is found, place is given the value of the location, loc.

```
loc ← 1
while loc ≤ n do
    if key = list_loc then
        place ← loc
    loc ← loc + 1
```

Several observations can be made about this approach. Firstly, should the key not appear at all, the variable place will remain undefined. Secondly, if a match is found, the searching continues to the end of the list, an obvious inefficiency.

The module of Figure 12.1 illustrates a solution to both of these problems. This module, called linear, accepts as imports LIST, n, and key and returns, as exports, place and flag. The variable flag has been introduced to reflect whether or not the key has been located. flag is initialized to 0 prior to the search, then changed to 1 when the position of key is found. The **while** loop uses flag to terminate the search if a match is found before the list is exhausted.

This module will determine the correct position of a value regardless of the order of the entries in the list. Thus, for an *unordered* list, the algorithm will require an average of n/2 iterations through the loop and, therefore, n/2 comparisons between the key and LIST entries. If the value is not located, exactly n comparisons will be made.

Figure 12.1   A pseudo-code module for a linear search.

smodule linear (**imports**: LIST, n, key; **exports**: place, flag)

```
*  Module to use a linear search to find the place of a given key value
*  in a given LIST of length n.
*  A value of 0 is returned in flag if key is not in the list whereas a 1 is returned if it is.

*  Variables used:
*  LIST - given list of numbers
*  n - given number of entries in the list
*  key - given value to be found in the list
*  place - position of key in the list
*  flag - set to 1 if key is in the list, 0 otherwise
*  loc - location of current entry in the list

flag ← 0
loc ← 1
while loc ≤ n and flag = 0 do
    ⎡  if key = list_loc then
    ⎢      ⎡  place ← loc
    ⎢      ⎣  flag ← 1
    ⎢  else
    ⎣      ⎡  loc ← loc + 1

end module
```

If the list is *ordered,* then improvements to the module are possible. The condition used to terminate the **while** loop can be expanded to take advantage of the ordering for items not found in the list. For instance, if the list is sorted in ascending order, the search can be terminated as soon as a list value is greater than key. Likewise, if the list is in descending order the search ends when a list value is less than key. Thus, for an *ordered* list, the average number of comparisons is always $n/2$ regardless of whether the item is found or not.

12.2.2   A Binary Search

The linear searching techniques presented in the previous section, while simple to understand and easy to write, are very time consuming for long lists of numbers, particularly if the search operation is to be applied frequently. In such situations it is usually expedient to maintain the list sorted in ascending or descending order. Then an improved searching technique can be modeled on the way a person looks for a name in a telephone directory and the way in which bisection approached the problem of zero-finding, as discussed in Chapter 7.

The technique is called a *binary search* and starts by comparing the key with the middle entry in the current sorted list. (Note that there may be two middle entries for lists of even length but nothing is lost by choosing either arbitrarily.) If a match is found, the search is over. Otherwise, if the key is less than the middle entry, the search can be confined to the first half of the list. Similarly, if the key is greater than the middle entry, the search is confined to the second half of the list. In either case, the same logic is then applied to the middle entry in the new list. (This new list will be approximately half the size of the previous list.) The process continues until either a match is found or the length of the sublist becomes zero. In the latter case the key is not in the original list.

Consider the list of 15 numbers

5, 6, 9, 12, 13, 20, 23, 29, 30, 41, 45, 49, 60, 65, 78

which have been sorted into ascending order. Suppose that it is necessary to determine the locations of several values in the list. The diagram in Figure 12.2 shows the actions involved in performing a binary search on the list for the key value 20. The complete list is indexed as it would be for computer processing. The key is compared to the middle or eighth entry and is found to be less than the value 29. Thus, the first half of the list becomes the subject of the next search. This time the middle entry is in position four, and since the key is greater than 12, the second half of this list, that is, positions five through seven, form the subsequent list. After 3 comparisons, the key is found to be equal to the value of the middle entry (position six).

Figure 12.2   A binary search for the value 20 in a sorted list.

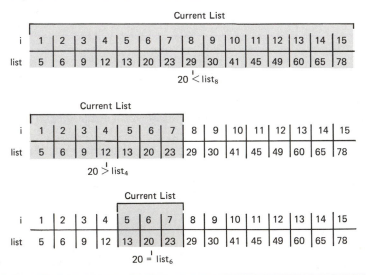

As a second example, Figure 12.3 demonstrates an attempt to find the key value 40 in the same list of 15 numbers. In this case, however, the value does not appear in the list and the search terminates when the key value is greater than the only entry remaining in the sublist.

Figure 12.3   A binary search for the (absent) value 40 in a sorted list.

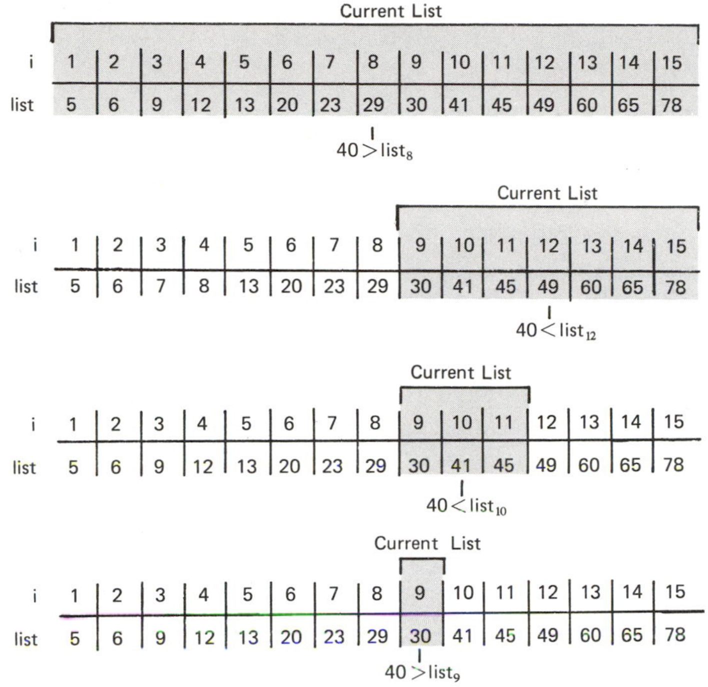

a) Developing the Algorithm   With the understanding gained from the previous numerical examples, an algorithm for the binary search can now be developed. The binary search algorithm will also be developed as a module and will thus have the same parameters as module linear, namely LIST, n, and key as imports and place and flag for exports. The initial description follows as Figure 12.4.

Figure 12.4   First version of a pseudo-code module for a binary search.

smodule binary (**imports**: LIST, n, key; **exports**: place, flag)

1.   Find the place of **key** in the list LIST of **n** entries using a binary search technique.

end module

b) Refining Step **1.**   While considering the previous numerical examples it was clear that the portion of the list being considered at any stage of the search kept changing. It is therefore necessary to retain some means of referring to each end of the current list. These references are called *pointers* and are simply variables whose values indicate a position in a list. In this case two pointers will be used, called low and high. The search for the key will continue as long as a list exists, that is, as long as low ≤ high. However, the search should stop if the key is found. As with the linear search, a variable called flag will be used to terminate the search when the key has been found. It will be set to 0 prior to the search to indicate that the key has not been located and changed to 1 if the location is found. The resulting refinement of step **1**. follows.

> * Initialize the pointers to the endpoints of the entire LIST.

low ← 1
high ← n
flag ← 0
while flag = 0 **and** low ≤ high **do**

> **1.1** Perform a binary search for **key** on the sublist bounded by **low** and **high** setting **flag** and **place** if **key** is found.

c) Refining Step **1.1**   At each stage it is necessary to determine the middle entry of the current list and compare the middle entry of LIST with key. Either key will be equal to the middle entry or it will be necessary to choose the left or right sublist for further consideration. The appropriate refinement follows.

> * Compute the position of the middle entry.

middle ← int [(low + high)/2]
if key = list$_{middle}$ **then**

> **1.1.1** Remember the position of the key and indicate that it has been found.

else

> **1.1.2** Refine the list for the subsequent search.

d) Refining Step **1.1.1**   The position of key is given by the current value of middle. To indicate that key has been found, flag is set to 1.

> * Remember the position of the key and indicate that it has been found.

place ← middle
flag ← 1

e) Refining Step **1.1.2**   For the subsequent search, the list is refined to the first or second half of the current list. If the key is less than the current middle entry, move the high pointer to the left of the middle entry, that is to middle−1. Otherwise the key must be greater than the middle entry and the low pointer is moved to the right of the middle entry, that is to middle+1.

* Refine the list for the subsequent search.

if key $<$ list$_{middle}$ **then**

$\quad\Big[$ high $\leftarrow$ middle $-$ 1

else

$\quad\Big[$ low $\leftarrow$ middle $+$ 1

f) The Final Algorithm   The algorithm is now complete and is presented in Figure 12.5.

g) Program for the Final Version of the Algorithm   Whereas a linear search is relatively easy to write, a binary search is somewhat longer and would be a valuable addition to a personal library of programs if not available elsewhere. Presented in Figure 12.6 is a WATFIV-S implementation of module binary.

Figure 12.5 Final version of the pseudo-code module for a binary search.

smodule binary (**imports**: LIST, n, key; **exports**: place, flag)

* Module to use a binary search to find the **place** of a given **key** value
* in a given **LIST** of length n.
* A value of **0** is returned in **flag** if **key** is not in the list whereas a **1** is returned if it is.

* Variables used:
* **LIST** - given list of numbers
* **n** - given number of entries in the list
* **key** - given value to be found in the list
* **place** - position of **key** in the list
* **flag** - set to **1** if **key** is in the list, **0** otherwise
* **low** - pointer to the first entry in the current sublist
* **high** - pointer to the last entry in the current sublist
* **middle** - pointer to the middle entry in the current sublist

* Initialize the pointers to the endpoints of the entire list.

low $\leftarrow$ 1
high $\leftarrow$ n
flag $\leftarrow$ 0

* Continue the search as long as **key** has not been found
* or as long as a list exists to search.

while flag $=$ 0 **and** low $\leq$ high **do**

    * Compute the position of the middle entry.

    middle $\leftarrow$ int [(low + high)/2]
    if key $=$ list$_{middle}$ **then**

        * Remember the position of the key and indicate that it has been found.

        place $\leftarrow$ middle
        flag $\leftarrow$ 1

    else

        * Refine the list for the subsequent search.

        if key $<$ list$_{middle}$ **then**

            high $\leftarrow$ middle $-$ 1

        else

            low $\leftarrow$ middle $+$ 1

end module

```
C Figure 12.6 -- Subroutine BINARY
C                 Subprogram to use a binary search to find the
C                 PLACE of a given KEY value in a given LIST of
C                 length N.  A value of 0 is returned in FLAG if
C                 KEY is not in the list whereas a 1 is returned
C                 if it is.
C**************************************************************
C LIST    - given list of numbers
C N       - given number of entries in the list
C NMAX    - given maximum value for N
C KEY     - given value to be found in the list
C PLACE   - position of key in the list
C FLAG    - set to 1 if key is in the list, 0 otherwise
C LOW     - pointer to the first entry in the current sublist
C HIGH    - pointer to the last entry in the current sublist
C MIDDLE  - pointer to the middle entry in the current sublist
C**************************************************************
      SUBROUTINE BINARY(LIST, NMAX, N, KEY, PLACE, FLAG)

      INTEGER NMAX, LIST(NMAX), N, KEY, PLACE, FLAG
      INTEGER LOW, HIGH, MIDDLE
C Initialize the pointers to the endpoints of the entire list.
      LOW = 1
      HIGH = N
      FLAG = 0
C Continue the search as long as KEY has not been found
C or as long as a list exists to search.
      WHILE(FLAG .EQ. 0 .AND. LOW .LE. HIGH) DO
C        Compute the position of the middle entry.
         MIDDLE = (LOW + HIGH)/2
         IF(KEY .EQ. LIST(MIDDLE)) THEN DO
C            Remember the position of the KEY
C            and indicate that it has been found.
             PLACE = MIDDLE
             FLAG = 1
         ELSE DO
C            Refine the list for the subsequent search.
             IF(KEY .LT. LIST(MIDDLE)) THEN DO
                 HIGH = MIDDLE - 1
               ELSE DO
                 LOW = MIDDLE + 1
             END IF
         END IF
      END WHILE
      RETURN
      END
```

Program Notes

- An additional import parameter, NMAX, has been added to represent the maximum size of LIST as declared in the calling program. This allows the subroutine to specify a variable size for LIST and yet agree with the calling program. This feature of WATFIV-S is called *variable dimensioning*. A variable dimension can only be used in a subprogram. The dimension must be an import parameter, and its value must be less than or equal to the declared size of the list in the calling program.

12.2.3 Linear Versus Binary Searches

The principle of the binary search is repeated division of the list by 2. The maximum number of comparisons needed to find an entry or to determine that the key is not in the list is, therefore, the number of times the length of the list can be divided by 2. Mathematically this can be expressed as

$$\lfloor \log_2 n \rfloor + 1$$

This formula gives the maximum number of comparisons required. While it is possible to derive an expression for the average number of comparisons necessary, the formula is complex and gives little added information.

The table below contrasts the *average* number of comparisons required by the linear search with the *maximum* number of comparisons needed for a binary search for several values of *n*. In each case it is assumed that the list is presorted.

n	*4*	*8*	*16*	*32*	*64*	*128*	*256*	*512*	*1024*	
linear	2	4	8	16	32	64	128	256	512	*average*
binary	3	4	5	6	7	8	9	10	11	*maximum*

Notice how much better the binary search is for larger values of *n*. It should be remembered, however, that a binary search can only be used with an ordered list.

12.3   Sorting Techniques

Since sorting is such a common and necessary activity in computer applications there are literally dozens of sorting techniques described in the literature. There are two overall classes of techniques, those involving only internal storage and those that also use external storage devices. The discussion to follow will investigate an example in each of three groups of algorithms which use only internal storage. These are a selection method, an exchange method, and an insertion method. A combination of these techniques is the basis for a relatively modern method called Quicksort which is also discussed. In all cases, the sorting method will be developed to sort the numbers in ascending order.

12.3.1   A Simple Selection Sort

A simple selection sort most closely approximates how a list of numbers might be sorted by hand using pencil and paper. The given list of numbers is scanned from beginning to end to find the smallest value. This number is copied to a new list while its entry in the old list is destroyed (by hand the entry might be crossed out; by computer the entry might be replaced by a very large number) to remove it from further consideration. Then the modified old list is searched again to find the new smallest number. When found, this number is placed at the end of the new list and its original in the old list is destroyed. The selection process continues until the old list is depleted.

This technique is illustrated for a sample list of numbers in Figure 12.7. During the first pass the smallest value of 3 is found in position four. Thus 3 becomes the first entry in the new list, and the fourth entry in the old list is removed from consideration. On the second pass the number 4 in position five is smallest. It is appended to the new list, and its entry in the old list is destroyed. In this way the algorithm continues selecting 7, 7, 8, and 9 to form the sorted new list.

Figure 12.7   Example of a simple selection sort.

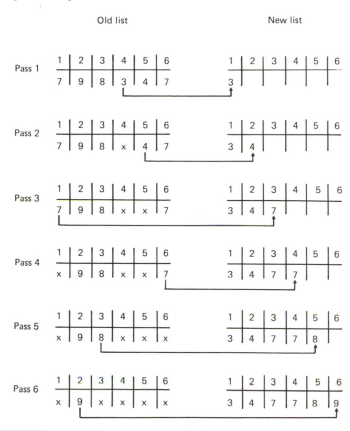

a) Developing the Algorithm   Since this algorithm has potential value for a library, it will be developed as a module designed to accept an unsorted list, OLD, of n numbers and produce a second list, NEW, sorted in increasing order. A first version is given in Figure 12.8.

Figure 12.8   First version of a pseudo-code module for a selection sort.

smodule select (**imports**: OLD, n; **exports**: NEW)

1.   Sort the entries of list **OLD** into list **NEW** using a simple selection sort.

end module

b) Refining Step **1.**   The selection process is repeated once for each number in the original list. For each pass through the original list it is necessary to find the smallest number in the old list, copy it to the new list, and remove it from the old list. In the refinement below, these three steps are imbedded in a **while** loop controlled by a counter variable, pass, that will control the passes from 1 to n.

```
* During each pass, find the smallest entry in OLD,
* copy it to list NEW, and destroy it in list OLD.

pass ← 1
while pass ≤ n do
    ┌  1.1 Find the smallest value in OLD.
    │
    │  1.2 Copy this smallest value to NEW.
    │
    │  1.3 Destroy the original in OLD.
    │
    └  pass ← pass + 1
```

c) Refining Step **1.1**   Finding the smallest value in a list was described as part of the module minmax in Chapter 11. Unfortunately, this module does not return its position. However, such a modification is easy to incorporate. As well, the code to find the largest entry can be deleted from the module. A modified module called min is presented in Figure 12.9.

With this module available, step **1.1** of the algorithm can be expressed by the following module reference:

call min(OLD, n; small, place)

d) Refining Step **1.2**   During each pass, another number will be appended to list NEW. Its position is given quite simply by the pass value. Thus the refinement of step **1.2** becomes

$$new_{pass} \leftarrow small$$

e) Refining Step **1.3**   Destroying the smallest value in the old list can be accomplished by changing it to a very large number, for example,

$$old_{place} \leftarrow \infty$$

f) The Final Algorithm   Collecting the pieces of the algorithm together results in the description given in Figure 12.10.

Figure 12.9 Pseudo-code module for finding the smallest value in a list.

smodule min (**imports**: LIST, n; **exports**: small, place)

* Module finds the smallest entry **small** and its position **place** in a given **LIST** of length **n**.

* Variables used:
* **LIST** - given list of numbers
* **n** - given number of entries in the list
* **small** - smallest entry in the list
* **place** - position of the smallest
* **i** - current location being examined

* Initialize the smallest as the first entry.

small ← list$_1$
place ← 1

* Search the rest of the list for a better value updating
* **small** and **place** each time a better estimate is found.

i ← 2
while i ≤ n **do**

$\quad$ **if** list$_i$ < small **then**

$\qquad$ small ← list$_i$
$\qquad$ place ← i

$\quad$ i ← i + 1

end module

---

g) *Final Discussion*   The selection sort will always require *n* passes over the list being sorted. During each pass the first entry in the old list is assumed to be the smallest and is then compared to each of the remaining entries in the old list. The number of comparisons is therefore *n*−1 for each of the *n* passes for a total of *n*(*n*−1). These comparisons will be necessary regardless of how the entries are initially ordered. Some improvement in the number of comparisons needed can be realized by using a single list and storing the partially sorted entries at the beginning of the same list (see Exercise 12.3 c). With such a strategy, the number of entries to scan for the smallest decreases by one after each pass resulting in an algorithm that requires approximately half the number of comparisons.

12.3.2   An Exchange Sort

Techniques involving exchanges form the second group of internal sorting methods. In an exchange sort, pairs of entries in the list are compared, and if the entries are out of order, they are interchanged. The comparison process is repeated systematically until no more exchanges are necessary. The order in which pairs are examined varies from algorithm to algorithm, but all methods make several passes over all or part of the list in some systematic fashion.

Figure 12.10 Final version of the pseudo-code module for a selection sort.

smodule select (**imports**: OLD, n; **exports**: NEW)

* Module to use a simple selection process to sort the **n** entries of list **OLD**
* into list **NEW** in increasing order.

* Variables used:
* **OLD** - original list of numbers
* **n** - number of entries in the list
* **NEW** - resulting sorted list
* **pass** - current pass number
* **small** - current smallest entry in **OLD**
* **place** - position of the smallest in **OLD**

* During each pass, find the smallest entry in **OLD**, copy it to list **NEW**,
* and destroy it in list **OLD**.

pass ← 1
while pass ≤ n **do**

> **call** min(OLD, n; small, place)
> new$_{pass}$ ← small
> old$_{place}$ ← ∞
> pass ← pass + 1

end module

```
Integer Old(30), NEW(30), N,
READ, P
R=1
WHILE (R.LE.P) DO
   READ, N, (OLD(I),
   PRINT, 'Old List is'
   PRINT, (OLD(I), I=1, N
   PASS = 1
   WHILE (PASS.LE.N) D
      I= 1
      SMALL = OLD(1)
      PLACE = I
      WHILE (I.LE.N) D
         IF OLD(I).LE. SMALL
            SMALL = OLD(I)
            PLACE = I
         END IF
         I = I + 1
      END WHILE
      NEW(PASS) = SMALL
      OLD(PLACE) = 100
      PASS = PASS + 1
   ENDWHILE
```

The most common exchange method is known as the bubble sort. It employs the obvious pairing of consecutive entries in the list. During the first pass through the list, the comparison begins with the items in locations one and two. If out of order, these two items are interchanged. This process is then repeated for the items in locations two and three, three and four, . . . , up to $n-1$ and n. After this pass, the largest entry will have "bubbled" to position n, even if it started at position one. Thus, pass two need only examine the first $n-1$ entries in the list as the same sequence of comparisons is carried out. The algorithm continues passing through the list, reducing the size of the list each time, until all of the entries are in order.

Figure 12.11 illustrates the bubble technique as it is applied to the list of numbers

7, 9, 8, 3, 4, 7

At each stage of the algorithm the pair of numbers being examined or exchanged is highlighted. From this diagram, note that five comparisons and four exchanges are made during the first pass as the algorithm examines all 6 numbers. Pass two requires only 4 comparisons, and 3 exchanges are made in moving the number 8 into position. Three comparisons are made in pass three and 2 interchanges occur. Finally, pass four makes 2 comparisons but no exchanges and thus the numbers have been sorted.

Figure 12.11   Example of a bubble sort.

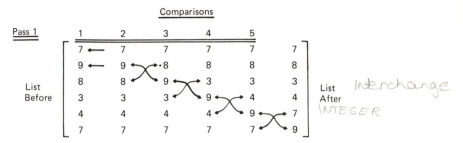

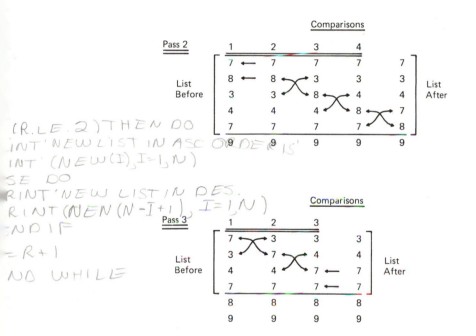

(Handwritten notes on the page:)

Interchange
INTEGER

(R.LE.2)THEN DO
INT'NEW LIST IN ASC ORDER IS'
INT'(NEW(I),I=1,N)
SE DO
RINT'NEW LIST IN DES.
RINT(NEW(N-I+1),I=1,N)
ND IF
=R+1
NO WHILE

a) Developing the Algorithm   The bubble sort algorithm will also be designed as a module. Module bubble will accept as import parameters, an unsorted list called LIST and n, the number of entries in LIST. The sole export parameter will be LIST sorted in ascending order. A first version is given as Figure 12.12.

Figure 12.12   First version of a pseudo-code module for a bubble sort.

smodule bubble (**imports**: LIST, n; **exports**: LIST)

1.   Sort the entries of LIST into ascending order using the Bubble Sort.

end module

b) Refining Step **1.**   The bubble sort algorithm makes a series of passes over the list of numbers until no more exchanges are necessary. Thus, a loop is required to repeat the comparison/exchange sequence for each pair of entries. During the first pass, n−1 pairs must be examined. Since each pass succeeds in moving the next largest entry into position near the end of the list, the maximum number of pairs for each subsequent pass can be reduced by one. The loop continues as long as there are pairs to examine. Thus, the refinement of step **1.** follows.

```
    * Initialize the number of comparisons.
maxpairs ← n − 1
while maxpairs > 0 do
    1.1 Compare entries in pairs exchanging the pair if the values are out of order.
    maxpairs ← maxpairs − 1
```

c) Refining Step **1.1**   The number of pairs to be examined is determined by variable maxpairs. A loop must be constructed to control the comparison of these pairs.

```
    * For each pass, compare the LIST entries in pairs.
    * Exchange entries that are out of order.
    * After each pass, reduce the comparisons by 1.
pair ← 1
while pair ≤ maxpairs do
    1.1.1 Compare entries pair and pair + 1 and if necessary, exchange them.
    pair ← pair + 1
```

d) Refining Step **1.1.1**   The simplest way to exchange two values involves a three-step process, illustrated by the following picture.

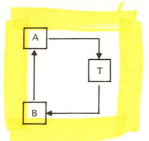

To exchange two items A and B, first copy A to a temporary location T, second, copy B to A, and third, move the copy of A from T to B. Thus, in the refinement of step **1.1.1**, if the list entry in position pair is greater than the entry in position pair+1, these two entries are exchanged.

if $list_{pair} > list_{pair+1}$ **then**

$$\begin{bmatrix} temp \leftarrow list_{pair} \\ list_{pair} \leftarrow list_{pair+1} \\ list_{pair+1} \leftarrow temp \end{bmatrix}$$

e) Improving the Efficiency of Step **1.**   The outer loop controls the number of passes over the list. These passes are designed to continue until the number of pairs to examine is reduced to zero. Frequently, the list becomes sorted before all passes have been made. Such was the case in the previous numerical example. This condition can be detected by remembering whether or not any exchanges took place during any given pass. This can be accomplished by using an exchange flag (called xflag) that starts each pass with the value 0 and is changed to 1 whenever an exchange takes place. The loop is redesigned to continue as long as the previous pass required at least one exchange (xflag = 1). These improvements are incorporated in the final algorithm.

f) The Final Algorithm   The complete module to accomplish the bubble sort is presented in Figure 12.13.

g) Final Discussion   The bubble sort algorithm requires one less comparison for each subsequent pass through the list. Thus, for a list of *n* numbers, the maximum number of comparisons is

$$(n-1)+(n-2)+ \cdots +2+1 = \frac{n(n-1)}{2}$$

Though this maximum number would only be required if the smallest number appeared last in the original list, it can be shown that even for random lists of numbers, the average does not deviate much from this formula. The one distinct advantage, however, is that if the list is already in increasing order, only one pass entailing $n-1$ comparisons is necessary.

Figure 12.13 Final version of the pseudo-code module for a bubble sort.

smodule bubble (**imports**: LIST, n; **exports**: LIST)

* Module to sort the entries of **LIST** into ascending order using the bubble sort technique.

* Variables used:
* **LIST** - list of numbers before and after sorting
* **n** - number of entries in the list
* **maxpairs** - maximum number of pairs for current pass
* **pair** - comparison pair counter
* **xflag** - exchange flag, **0** if none, **1** if some

* Initialize the number of comparisons and exchange flag.

maxpairs ← n − 1
xflag ← 1

* Continue passing over the list until there are no exchanges.

while xflag = 1 **do**

    * For each pass, compare the **LIST** entries in pairs.
    * Exchange entries that are out of order and set **xflag**.
    * After each pass, reduce the comparisons by 1.

    xflag ← 0
    pair ← 1
    while pair ≤ maxpairs **do**

        if list$_{pair}$ > list$_{pair+1}$ **then**

            temp ← list$_{pair}$
            list$_{pair}$ ← list$_{pair+1}$
            list$_{pair+1}$ ← temp
            xflag ← 1

        pair ← pair + 1

    maxpairs ← maxpairs − 1

end module

(handwritten annotations:)
READ, N, (LIST(I), I=1,N)
PRINT, 'The unordered list is
PRINT, (LIST(I) I=1,N)
MAX = N-1
WHILE (MAX .GT.0) DO
    I = 1
    WHILE (I LE MAX) DO
        IF (LIST (I) .GT. LIST(I+
            TEMP = LIST (I)
            LIST (I) = LIST (I+1)
            LIST(I+1) = TEMP
        END IF
        I = I + 1
    END WHILE
    MAX = MAX - 1
END WHILE

12.3.3   An Insertion Sort

The third family of sorting techniques involves taking elements sequentially from a given list and inserting them in their correct relative positions in a new list.

The diagram in Figure 12.14 illustrates the building of a sorted list from the list of numbers 7, 9, 8, 3, 4, 7. The new list is initially given its first entry, 7, from the old list. To insert the second entry, 9, no shifting is necessary since 9 is greater than the last entry of the new list. Thus, 9 is simply added to the end. For the third entry, the 9 in the new list is shifted to make room for the 8 from the old list. The insertion continues for the entries 3, 4, and 7. Figure 12.15 gives a more detailed look at the movement of data to make room for the insertion of the last entry, 7.

Figure 12.14   An example of an insertion sort.

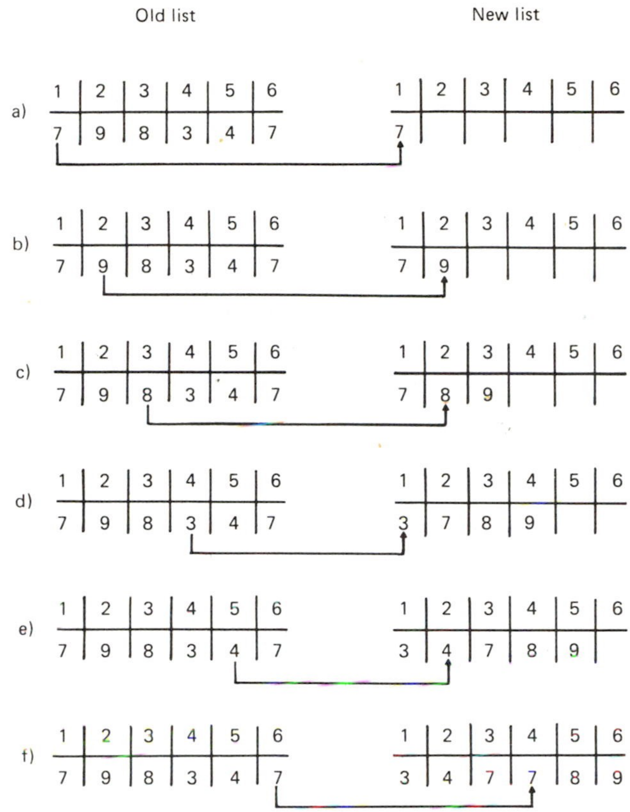

Figure 12.15   Inserting the second 7 in the previous example.

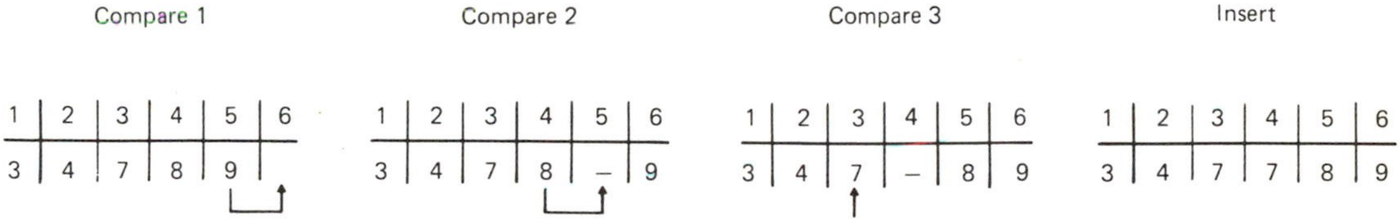

a) Developing the Algorithm   The algorithm for linear insertion will be written as a module called **insert** and will have import parameters OLD, the unsorted list, and n, the number of entries in this list. The export parameter will be the list NEW containing the values sorted in ascending order. A first version of the algorithm is shown as Figure 12.16.

Figure 12.16   First version of a pseudo-code module for a linear insertion sort.

smodule insert (**imports**: OLD, n; **exports**: NEW)

1. Sort the entries of list **OLD** into ascending order in list **NEW** using a linear insertion sort.

end module

---

b) *Refining Step* **1.**   The insertion process is repeated once for each of the n entries in the list OLD. This is controlled by an outer loop using the index i. Each time through the loop the i-th entry in the list will be correctly positioned in the current list NEW.

* Repeat the insertion for each entry in **OLD**.

i ← 1
while i ≤ n **do**

> **1.1** Insert the ith entry of the old list into the correct position of the new list using a linear search from the end of the list.
>
> i ← i + 1

c) *Refining Step* **1.1**   To find the correct position for the current entry, it is necessary to adapt the linear search, written earlier in this chapter, to proceed backwards through list NEW. The current length of the new list is given by the number of entries already inserted, one less than the position of the current key (i−1). Using variable j as the index in the new list, the search will start at position i−1 and continue backwards until either the correct position is found (set flag to 1) or until the list is exhausted (j=0). The correct position for the current key is preceding all entries that are larger. Thus, each larger entry is advanced one location to eventually make room for the key. When a smaller entry is found or if all entries are larger, the key can be placed in location j+1, already vacated by previous shifting. These refinements are given in the correct sequence below.

```
READ N, (OLD(I), I=1,N)
PRINT, the original list is
PRINT, (OLD(I), I=1,N)
I=1
WHILE (I.LE.N) DO
  FLAG = 0
  J = I - 1
  WHILE ((J.GT.0) and FLAG =0) DO
    IF ((NEW(J).GT.OLD(I)) THEN
      K = J + 1
      NEW (K) = NEW(J)
      J = J - 1
    ELSE DO
      FLAG = 1
    ENDIF
  END WHILE
  K = J + 1
  NEW(K) = OLD(I)
  I = I + 1
END WHILE
```

```
* Search NEW backwards for position of OLD entry
* until the position is found or the list exhausted.
flag ← 0
j ← i − 1
while j > 0 and flag = 0 do
    if newj > oldi then
            * OLD entry must appear before NEW entry.
            * Advance the NEW entry and move on to the next.
            newj+1 ← newj
            j ← j − 1
    else
            * Correct position found, set the flag.
            flag ← 1
newj+1 ← oldi
```

d) The Final Algorithm   Now that all the refinements are complete, the final algorithm can be presented in Figure 12.17.

e) Final Discussion   The number of comparisons needed to locate the position for each entry changes as the length of the new list changes. Each time one would expect, on the average, to search halfway through the new list. Thus, to insert the i-th entry, $(i-1)/2$ comparisons would be expected. For a list of n entries the average number of comparisons would be

$$\frac{1}{2}(0+1+2+\cdots+n-1) = \frac{1}{2}\left[\frac{n(n-1)}{2}\right] = \frac{n(n-1)}{4}$$

The maximum number of comparisons would be required if the list were in exactly reverse order. In this case twice the above number would be required since each old entry would always be inserted at the first of the new list. Conversely, if the list were already sorted, each old entry would be added to the end of the new list and only $n-1$ comparisons would be needed. In general, some improvement in efficiency can be made by using a binary search rather than a linear search. This suggestion is left as an exercise (see Exercise 12.5d).

12.3.4   Quicksort
Quicksort is a relatively modern and fast sorting algorithm devised by C.A.R. Hoare. It is essentially an insertion/exchange scheme that at each stage succeeds in correctly positioning at least one number in the list. The knowledge that this element is so positioned is used to reduce the number of comparisons needed to position subsequent entries.

Figure 12.17 Final version of the pseudo-code module for a linear insertion sort.

smodule insert (**imports**: OLD, n; **exports**: NEW)

* Module to sort the entries of list **OLD** into ascending order in list **NEW**
* using a linear insertion sort.

* Variables used:
* **OLD** - original list of numbers
* **n** - number of entries in the list
* **NEW** - resulting sorted list
* **i** - position of **OLD** entry being inserted
* **j** - current entry being compared in **NEW**
* **flag** - flag set to **0** before, **1** after entry found

* Repeat the insertion for each entry in OLD.

$i \leftarrow 1$
while $i \leq n$ **do**

    * Search **NEW** backwards for position of **OLD** entry until the position is found
    * or the list exhausted.

    flag $\leftarrow$ 0
    $j \leftarrow i - 1$
    while $j > 0$ **and** flag $= 0$ **do**

        if $new_j > old_i$ **then**

            * **OLD** entry must appear before **NEW** entry.
            * Advance the **NEW** entry and move on to the next.

            $new_{j+1} \leftarrow new_j$
            $j \leftarrow j - 1$

        else

            * Correct position found, set the flag.

            flag $\leftarrow$ 1

    * Place the entry in the last vacated slot.

    $new_{j+1} \leftarrow old_i$
    $i \leftarrow i + 1$

end module

The object of Quicksort is to rearrange or *partition* the list of numbers relative to a specific entry called the *pivot* so that in the resulting partitioned list, all entries preceding the pivot are less than or equal the pivot and all entries following the pivot are greater than or equal the pivot.

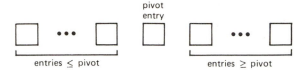

As a result of the partitioning, the pivot entry has its correct final position. The same partitioning process is then applied to the two sublists on either side of the pivot entry. In this way the original list is gradually reduced to a number of sublists of length one that are sorted relative to each other.

Consider the same list of numbers used earlier and choose the first entry as the pivot.

pivot
↓
7, 9, 8, 3, 4, 7

One possible partitioning relative to this entry is:

pivot
↓
3 4 7 8 9 7
  <7   ≥7

The two elements preceding 7 are less in magnitude while the three elements following 7 are greater or equal. Furthermore, when this list is finally sorted, 7 should be in this position. The partitioning process would now be applied to the two sublists, 3, 4 and 8, 9, 7.

The most important feature of the algorithm is the partitioning. The entry selected as the pivot entry is usually the first entry, but other selections are also possible (see Exercise 12.6). Having chosen the pivot entry, the algorithm scans the list from each end, exchanging larger entries near the left with smaller entries near the right.

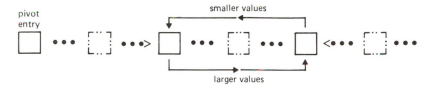

When the two scans meet, the pivot entry is positioned at the intersection to maintain the relative ordering.

To illustrate the partitioning process the following larger list of numbers will be used.

54, 13, 56, 95, 21, 94, 31, 69, 46, 19, 55, 65, 72, 81, 74

Figure 12.18 illustrates the partitioning relative to the first entry, 54. The list is scanned from each end, from the right to find an entry less than or equal to the pivot, and from

Figure 12.18 Partitioning a set relative to the first entry.

Stage

i)

1	2	3	4	5	6	7	8	9	10	11	12	13	14	15
54	13	56	95	21	94	31	69	46	19	55	65	72	81	74

left scan⟶   ⟵right scan

ii)

1	2	3	4	5	6	7	8	9	10	11	12	13	14	15
54	13	19	95	21	94	31	69	46	56	55	65	72	81	74

left scan⟶   ⟵right scan

iii)

1	2	3	4	5	6	7	8	9	10	11	12	13	14	15
54	13	19	46	21	94	31	69	95	56	55	65	72	81	74

left scan⟶   ⟵right scan

iv)

1	2	3	4	5	6	7	8	9	10	11	12	13	14	15
54	13	19	46	21	31	94	69	95	56	55	65	72	81	74

left scan⟶   ⟵right scan

v)

1	2	3	4	5	6	7	8	9	10	11	12	13	14	15
54	13	19	46	21	31	94	69	95	56	55	65	72	81	74

position the pivot entry

vi)

1	2	3	4	5	6	7	8	9	10	11	12	13	14	15
31	13	19	46	21	54	94	69	95	56	55	65	72	81	74

left sublist   right sublist

the left to find an entry greater than or equal to the pivot. The left scan starts in position two and stops at position three locating the value 56. The right scan starts in position fifteen and stops at position ten locating the value 19 as shown in stage i) of the diagram. Notice that the entries in the positions before three are all ≤54 and that those in positions after ten are all ≥54. To extend the patterns, the 19 and 56 exchange positions. Then the two scanning procedures move on. Advancing from the left locates 95 ≥ 54 in position four and from the right finds 46 in position nine (see stage ii). These two entries are also exchanged. The next scans stop at 94 in position six and 31 in position seven (see stage iii). Following their exchange, 31 will be in position six and 94 in position seven. If the scanning is allowed to continue, the left scan for larger values stops at position seven, the rightmost entry greater than or equal to the pivot, while the right scan stops at position six, the leftmost entry less than or equal to the pivot (see stage iv). Since the pivot is in position one, among the entries less or equal, it is exchanged with the entry in position six, where the right scan ended (see stage v). This places the pivot in its correct ultimate position thus providing the required partitioning (see stage vi). The resulting two sublists, [31, 13, 19, 46, 21] and [94, 69, 95, 56, 65, 72, 81, 74] can now be partitioned in the same way. The partitioning at any stage terminates when a sublist is of length one or less.

a) Developing the Algorithm   The Quicksort algorithm will be designed as a module called quick. Recall that the algorithm begins by partitioning the complete list to form two sublists. The partitioning is then applied to these sublists, a process which presumably leads to further sublists to partition. It is, therefore, desirable to design the module to be flexible enough to handle a portion of a list as well as the entire list. Thus, the import parameter list for module quick includes the LIST entries as well as ll and rl, the left and right limits of the current portion of LIST to be considered. The resulting list will be the sole export parameter. A first version of the module appears in Figure 12.19.

Figure 12.19   Version 1 of a pseudo-code module for Quicksort.

smodule quick (**imports**: LIST, ll, rl; **exports**: LIST)

1.   Sort the entries of LIST into ascending order using the Quicksort technique.

end module

b) Refining quick *Step* **1.**   The essential step in the Quicksort algorithm is the partitioning of the list so that:

$$list_{ll} \ldots list_{p-1} \leq list_p \leq list_{p+1} \ldots list_{rl}$$

After this partitioning is complete, the same process must then be applied to list entries ll, ll+1, . . . , p−1 and to entries p+1, p+2, . . . , rl Of course this process should only continue if there is a list to partition, that is, if ll < rl. These steps can be described by the following lines.

if ll < rl **then**
> Partition the entries of $list_{ll} \ldots list_{rl}$ so that:
> $list_{ll} \ldots list_{p-1} \leq list_p \leq list_{p+1} \ldots list_{rl}$
> **call** quick(LIST, ll, p−1; LIST)
> **call** quick(LIST, p+1, rl; LIST)

This refinement attempt suggests something new, the use of a module reference to itself. Such a reference is called *recursive*. It involves remembering the current status of the module, including the statement being executed within the module and the current values of all variable names, while the module is invoked with a different list of argument values. Though recursive module references are supported by some programming languages, such is not the case with WATFIV-S. It is, therefore, necessary to program such references explicitly.

Module quick begins by partitioning the original list. Then this same partitioning must be applied to the two partitions. This process must be repeated until all partitions are of length one or less and thus are sorted. To remember which sublists require further partitioning, it is expedient to introduce an algorithmic tool called a *stack*. A stack is essentially a list in which the last or top entry is always the current entry. All additions to or deletions from the stack are made only at the top.

In module quick, therefore, it is necessary to maintain two stacks, one for each endpoint of the sublist, as well as a variable pointing to the current top of the stacks. The current list being partitioned will appear at the top of the stacks. At the end of each partitioning process, the current list is deleted from the stacks and the two sublists are added. The partitioning will continue as long as there are lists on the stacks. Lists of length one or less are completely partitioned and so are immediately removed from the stacks.

Module quick can now be restated as described in Figure 12.20. Notice that import parameters ll and rl are no longer appropriate and that n, the length of the original list, has taken their place.

Figure 12.20   Version 2 of a pseudo-code module for a non-recursive Quicksort.

smodule quick (**imports**: LIST, n; **exports**: LIST)

1.1 Stack the original LIST.

1.2 while there are more lists on the stacks **do**

  1.3 if length of current stacked list is 0 or 1 **then**

    The current list is partitioned; remove it from the stacks.

  else

    1.4 Partition the list currently on top of the stacks.

    1.5 Delete the current list from the stacks and add the left and right sublists to the stacks.

end module

---

c) Refining quick *Step* **1.1**   The essential things to remember about each list or sublist are the two endpoints. Consequently two stacks called lstack and rstack will be maintained for the left and right endpoints respectively. Variable nstack will be the number of lists currently on the stacks and, therefore, represents a pointer to the top of the stacks. Thus, stacking the original list in step **1.1** requires that:

* Stack the original list.

nstack ← 1

lstack$_{nstack}$ ← 1

rstack$_{nstack}$ ← n

d) Refining quick *Step* **1.2**   Deciding whether or not there are more lists on the stacks simply involves checking the value of nstack. Consequently step **1.2** can be written as:

* Keep partitioning as long as stacked lists remain.

while nstack > 0 **do**

e) Refining quick *Step* **1.3**   The length of the current list can be calculated from the two endpoints. To remove the list from the top of the stacks, decrement the stack pointer. In pseudo code these steps can be described by:

* If the length of the current list is 0 or 1, remove it from the stacks; it is partitioned.

if lstack$_{nstack}$ ≥ rstack$_{nstack}$ **then**

$\quad$ ⌈ nstack ← nstack − 1

f) Refining quick *Step* **1.4**   Step **1.4** is the all important partitioning process. Since it has a logically distinct role in the algorithm, it is appropriate to define a module called partition which will take the portion of a list from a left limit, ll, to a right limit, rl, and partition it as required. The necessary import parameters are therefore LIST, ll, and rl. The exports from the module partition are the positions of the two sublists created by the partitioning process. This information will be conveyed by specifying the endpoints of the sublists, llleft and rlleft for the left sublist and llright and rlright for the right sublist.

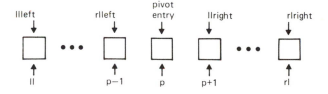

The definition of module partition is listed in Figure 12.21. The step-wise refinement is presented following the completion of module quick. With the aid of module partition, step **1.5** in module quick is easy to refine. The left endpoint of the current list is given by the top of lstack and the right endpoint is on top of rstack. The appropriate reference to module partition is:

Figure 12.21   First version of a pseudo-code module for partitoning a list.

smodule partition (**imports**: LIST, ll, rl; **exports**: LIST, llleft, rlleft, llright, rlright)

1. Partition the portion of LIST from ll to rl so that:
$list_{ll} \ldots list_{p-1} \leq list_p \leq list_{p+1} \ldots list_{rl}$

end module

---

   * Employ the partitioning process.

   call partition (LIST, $lstack_{nstack}$, $rstack_{nstack}$; LIST, llleft, rlleft, llright, rlright)

g) Refining quick *Step* **1.5**   Now that the current list has been partitioned it can be removed from the stacks and the two sublists added. To remove the current list from the stacks, the pointer to the top of the stacks is decremented by one. Finally, the two sublists created by the partitioning must be added to the stacks. The operation of adding to a stack is called *pushing* the stack. In contrast, the operation of deleting the top entry of a stack is called *popping* the stack. To minimize the number of lists that are stacked waiting to be partitioned, the shortest list will always be stacked last so that it is attacked first. Thus, the stacking process is refined as follows.

   * Remove the current list from the stack.

   nstack ← nstack − 1

   * Add the left and right sublists to the stack adding the shortest list last.

llength ← rlleft − llleft + 1
rlength ← rlright − llright + 1
if llength ≤ rlength **then**
    ⎡ nstack ← nstack + 1
    ⎢ $lstack_{nstack}$ ← llright
    ⎢ $rstack_{nstack}$ ← rlright
    ⎢ nstack ← nstack + 1
    ⎢ $lstack_{nstack}$ ← llleft
    ⎣ $rstack_{nstack}$ ← rlleft

  else
    ⎡ nstack ← nstack + 1
    ⎢ $lstack_{nstack}$ ← llleft
    ⎢ $rstack_{nstack}$ ← rlleft
    ⎢ nstack ← nstack + 1
    ⎢ $lstack_{nstack}$ ← llright
    ⎣ $rstack_{nstack}$ ← rlright

FORMAT (b, /, the new list in ascending order is, 30 I

h) The Final Algorithm   The complete algorithm to implement Quicksort is presented in Figure 12.22.

Figure 12.22   A Quicksort module.

smodule quick (**imports**: LIST, n; **exports**: LIST)

* Module to sort the entries of **LIST** into ascending order using the Quicksort algorithm.

* Variables used:
* **LIST** - given list of numbers to sort
* **n** - given number of entries in the list
* **lstack/rstack** - stack of pointers to the left/right end of a list
* **nstack** - number of entries on each stack; pointer to current top of each stack
* **llleft/rlleft** - left/right limit of the left sublist
* **llright/rlright** - left/right limit of the right sublist
* **llength/rlength** - length of left/right sublist

```
Interchange Sorting Method
Integer LIST(30), Pass, small, place, store(30)
Check = 1
while(Check.LE.3) DO
     READ, N(LIST(I), I=1,N)
     I=1
     WHILE(I.LE.N) DO
             STORE (I)= LIST(I)
             I = I+1
     END WHILE
     PASS=1
     WHILE (PASS.LE.N) DO
             SMALL= LIST(PASS)
             PLACE = PASS
             I= PASS+1
             WHILE(I.LE.N) DO
                 IF (LIST(I).LE.SMALL) THEN DO
                     SMALL = LIST(I)
                     PLACE = I
                     I = I+1
                 ELSE DO
                     I=I+1
                 END IF
             END WHILE
             TEMP= LIST(PASS)
             LIST (PASS)=LIST(PLACE)
             LIST (PLACE) =TEMP
             PASS = PASS+1
     END WHILE
         PRINT 4, (STORE(I), I=1,N)
         CHECK= CHECK+1
     END WHILE
```

Figure 12.22 A Quicksort module (continued)

* Stack the original list.

nstack ← 1
lstack$_{nstack}$ ← 1
rstack$_{nstack}$ ← n

* Keep partitioning as long as stacked lists remain.

while nstack > 0 **do**

    * If the length of the current list is 0 or 1,
    * remove it from the stacks; it is partitioned.

    if lstack$_{nstack}$ ≥ rstack$_{nstack}$ **then**

        nstack ← nstack − 1

    else

        * Otherwise, employ the partitioning process.

        call partition (LIST, lstack$_{nstack}$, rstack$_{nstack}$; LIST, llleft, rlleft, llright, rlright)

        * Remove the current list from the stacks.

        nstack ← nstack − 1

        * Add the left and right sublists to the stacks, adding the shortest list last.

        llength ← rlleft − llleft + 1
        rlength ← rlright − llright + 1
        if llength ≤ rlength **then**

            nstack ← nstack + 1
            lstack$_{nstack}$ ← llright
            rstack$_{nstack}$ ← rlright
            nstack ← nstack + 1
            lstack$_{nstack}$ ← llleft
            rstack$_{nstack}$ ← rlleft

        else

            nstack ← nstack + 1
            lstack$_{nstack}$ ← llleft
            rstack$_{nstack}$ ← rlleft
            nstack ← nstack + 1
            lstack$_{nstack}$ ← llright
            rstack$_{nstack}$ ← rlright

end module

---

i) Refining partition *Step* **1.**   The partitioning process revolves around the pivot element, arbitrarily chosen as the first in the list. The remainder of the list is scanned relative to this value. The scanning proceeds from each end exchanging entries from left to right as required until the scans overlap. At this point it is possible to correctly position the pivot element. These essential steps can be phrased in the following way.

    1.1 Choose the pivot element.

    1.2 while the scans don't overlap **do**

        ⎡ Scan the list from both ends exchanging values as needed to partition the list.

    1.3 Position the pivot element.

    1.4 Compute the sublist endpoints.

j) Refining partition *Step* **1.1**   For this version of Quicksort the first or leftmost entry of the current list is selected as the pivot element.

    * Choose the pivot element.

    pivot ← list$_{ll}$

k) Refining partition *Step* **1.2**   To scan the list from each end, two indices or pointers, appropriately called left and right, are used to maintain the current scanning position in each case. The two scans do not overlap as long as left is less than right. The first question to ask is where should these two scanning processes start. In order to make this decision, consider the following schematic diagram depicting the list at some arbitrary stage in the process.

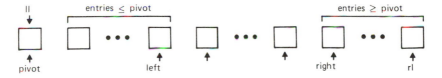

The entries in positions left and right have just been exchanged, and the scanning is about to continue. Since the entries at left and at right are correctly positioned, the left scan should continue at position left+1 and the right scan should continue with the entry in position right−1. In order for the first left scan to start at position ll+1, left must be initialized at ll. Similarly, for the first right scan to begin at position rl, right must be initialized at rl+1.

    The next question becomes, when should the two scanning processes terminate. The left scan stops when an entry greater than or equal to the pivot entry is found. What if all entries are less than pivot? In this isolated case, the left scan must be stopped when it reaches position rl, before it tries to access entries beyond the end of the list. However, if the left scan is performed first, it could conceivably still reach rl+1 (the initial value of right) and try to examine this nonexistent entry. A simple solution to avoid this potential problem is to perform the right scan prior to the left scan.

The right scan is halted when an entry less than or equal to pivot is located. Since pivot is chosen as the leftmost entry in the list, even if all other entries are greater than pivot, the right scan will terminate before it goes beyond the left end of the list.

The final question concerns the exchange of entries. As long as the scan pointers have not overlapped, the entries they point to should be exchanged. Though either or both entries may be equal to pivot and would not have to be moved, little is gained by avoiding such instances. However, once the scans overlap, no interchange should take place. The mechanism to exchange entries was already discussed as part of the bubble sort technique. The refinement for step **1.1** can now be written in detail.

```
* Set the scan pointers.
left ← ll
right ← rl + 1
* Proceed as long as the endpoints do not overlap.
while left < right do
    * Scan from the right looking for entries ≤ pivot.
    right ← right − 1
    while list_right > pivot do
        [ right ← right − 1

    * Scan from the left looking for entries ≥ pivot.
    left ← left + 1
    while list_left < pivot and left < right do
        [ left ← left + 1

    * Exchange the current entry on the left with the current entry on the right
    * provided the scans have not overlapped.
    if left < right then
        [ temp ← list_left
          list_left ← list_right
          list_right ← list_left
```

l) Refining partition *Step* **1.3**   This final step concerns the positioning of the element pivot. Following the scanning process, the list is described by the following diagram.

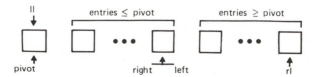

Thus, the entry pivot and the entry in position right must be exchanged to produce the final partitioning. The final position of the pivot entry, p, is given by the value of right.

The pseudo-code description is therefore:

> * Exchange the pivot entry with the one at right.
>
> $list_{ll} \leftarrow list_{right}$
> $list_{right} \leftarrow pivot$
> $p \leftarrow right$

Notice that **pivot** serves as the temporary location for the entry in position ll during the exchange.

m) Refining partition *Step* **1.4**   Computing the sublist endpoints is straightforward and is given by the following refinement.

> * Compute the sublist endpoints.
>
> $llleft \leftarrow ll$
> $rlleft \leftarrow p - 1$
> $llright \leftarrow p + 1$
> $rlright \leftarrow rl$

n) The Complete Partitioning Algorithm   The complete module for partitioning the list is presented in Figure 12.23.

o) Program for the Final Version of the Algorithm   The WATFIV-S translations of modules **quick** and **partition** are given as subroutines QUICK and PARTIT in Figures 12.24 and 12.25.

Figure 12.23   Final version of the pseudo-code module for partitioning a list.

smodule partition (**imports**: LIST, ll, rl; **exports**: LIST, llleft, rlleft, llright, rlright)

```
* Partition the portion of LIST from ll to rl so that:
* list_ll . . . list_p−1 ≤ list_p ≤ list_p+1 . . . list_rl

* Variables used:
* LIST - given list of numbers to partition
* n - given number of entries in the list
* ll/rl - left/right limit of sublist to be partitioned
* left/right - current scan position from the left/right
* pivot - first element in the list to be partitioned
* p - final position of pivot in partitioned list
* llleft/rlleft - left/right limit of the left sublist
* llright/rlright - left/right limit of the right sublist
```

Figure 12.23 Final version of the pseudo-code module for partitioning a list. (continued)

* Choose the pivot element and set the scan pointers.

pivot ← list$_{ll}$
left ← ll
right ← rl + 1

* Proceed as long as the endpoints do not overlap.

while left < right **do**

    * Scan from the right looking for entries ≤ **pivot**.

    right ← right − 1
    while list$_{right}$ > pivot **do**

        right ← right − 1

    * Scan from the left looking for entries ≥ **pivot**.

    left ← left + 1
    while list$_{left}$ < pivot **and** left < right **do**

        left ← left + 1

    * Exchange current left entry with right entry provided scans have not overlapped.

    if left < right **then**

        temp ← list$_{left}$
        list$_{left}$ ← list$_{right}$
        list$_{right}$ ← temp

* Exchange the pivot entry with the one at right.

list$_{ll}$ ← list$_{right}$
list$_{right}$ ← pivot
p ← right

* Compute the sublist endpoints.

llleft ← ll
rlleft ← p − 1
llright ← p + 1
rlright ← rl
end module

```
C Figure 12.24 -- Subroutine QUICK
C                 Subprogram to sort the N entries of LIST into
C                 ascending order using Quicksort.
C******************************************************************
C LIST          - given list of numbers to sort
C N             - given number of entries in the list
C NMAX          - maximum value for N
C LSTACK/RSTACK - stack of pointers to left/right end of list
C NSTACK        - number of entries on each stack
C               - pointer to the current top of each stack
C LLLEFT/RLLEFT - left/right limit of the left sublist
C LLRITE/RLRITE - left/right limit of the right sublist
C LLEN/RLEN     - length of the left/right sublist
C******************************************************************
      SUBROUTINE QUICK(LIST,N,NMAX)
      INTEGER NMAX, LIST(NMAX), N, LSTACK(20), RSTACK(20), NSTACK
      INTEGER LLLEFT, RLLEFT, LLRITE, RLRITE, LLEN, RLEN
C Stack the original list.
      NSTACK = 1
      LSTACK(NSTACK) = 1
      RSTACK(NSTACK) = N
C Keep partitioning as long as stacked lists remain.
      WHILE(NSTACK.GT.0) DO
C        If the length of the current list is 0 or 1,
C        remove it from the stack - it is partitioned.
         IF(LSTACK(NSTACK).GE.RSTACK(NSTACK)) THEN DO
              NSTACK = NSTACK - 1
            ELSE DO
C           Otherwise, employ the partitioning process.
            CALL PARTIT(LIST,NMAX,LSTACK(NSTACK),RSTACK(NSTACK),
     +                  LLLEFT,RLLEFT,LLRITE,RLRITE)
C           Remove the current list from the stack.
            NSTACK = NSTACK - 1
C           Add the left and right sublists to the stack,
C           adding the shortest list last.
            LLEN = RLLEFT - LLLEFT + 1
            RLEN = RLRITE - LLRITE + 1
            IF(LLEN.LE.RLEN) THEN DO
                 NSTACK = NSTACK + 1
                 LSTACK(NSTACK) = LLRITE
                 RSTACK(NSTACK) = RLRITE
                 NSTACK = NSTACK + 1
                 LSTACK(NSTACK) = LLLEFT
                 RSTACK(NSTACK) = RLLEFT
               ELSE DO
                 NSTACK = NSTACK + 1
                 LSTACK(NSTACK) = LLLEFT
                 RSTACK(NSTACK) = RLLEFT
                 NSTACK = NSTACK + 1
                 LSTACK(NSTACK) = LLRITE
                 RSTACK(NSTACK) = RLRITE
            END IF
         END IF
      END WHILE
      RETURN
      END
```

```
C Figure 12.25 -- Subroutine PARTIT
C                 Subprogram to partition the portion of LIST
C                 from LL to RL relative to the LLth entry,
C                 called PIVOT.  All entries before position P
C                 in LIST are less than or equal to PIVOT and
C                 all entries after P are greater than or equal
C                 to PIVOT.
C*****************************************************************
C LIST          - given list of numbers to partition
C N             - given number of entries in the list
C NMAX          - maximum value for N
C LL/RL         - left/right limit of sublist to be partitioned
C LEFT/RIGHT    - current scan position from the left/right
C PIVOT         - first element in the list to be partitioned
C P             - final position of pivot element in partitioned list
C LLLEFT/RLLEFT - left/right limit of the left sublist
C LLRITE/RLRITE - left/right limit of the right sublist
C*****************************************************************
      SUBROUTINE PARTIT(LIST,NMAX,LL,RL,LLLEFT,RLLEFT,LLRITE,RLRITE)

      INTEGER NMAX, LIST(NMAX), LL, RL, LLLEFT, RLLEFT, LLRITE, RLRITE
      INTEGER LEFT, RIGHT, PIVOT, P, TEMP
C Choose the pivot element and set the scan pointers.
      PIVOT = LIST(LL)
      LEFT = LL
      RIGHT = RL + 1
C Proceed as long as the endpoints do not overlap.
      WHILE(LEFT .LT. RIGHT) DO
C        Scan from the right looking for entries greater than or
C        equal to PIVOT.
         RIGHT = RIGHT - 1
         WHILE(LIST(RIGHT) .GT. PIVOT) DO
            RIGHT = RIGHT - 1
         END WHILE
C        Scan from the left looking for entries less than or
C        equal to PIVOT.
         LEFT = LEFT + 1
         WHILE(LIST(LEFT) .LT. PIVOT .AND. LEFT .LT. RIGHT) DO
            LEFT = LEFT + 1
         END WHILE
C        Exchange current left entry with right entry
C        provided the scans have not overlapped.
         IF(LEFT .LT. RIGHT) THEN DO
               TEMP = LIST(LEFT)
               LIST(LEFT) = LIST(RIGHT)
               LIST(RIGHT) = TEMP
         END IF
      END WHILE
C Exchange the pivot entry with the one at RIGHT.
      LIST(LL) = LIST(RIGHT)
      LIST(RIGHT) = PIVOT
      P = RIGHT
C Compute the sublist endpoints.
      LLLEFT = LL
      RLLEFT = P - 1
      LLRITE = P + 1
      RLRITE = RL
      RETURN
      END
```

Figure 12.25   Subroutine PARTIT (continued)

Program Notes

- Variable dimensions have been used for the list in both subroutines. Recall that the value of NMAX must agree with the declared size of the list in the calling program.
- The maximum size for the stacks has been chosen as 20 in QUICK. This size is large enough to handle lists of size one million or less. For proof of this fact, see Exercise 12.6 g).

p) Final Discussion   A thorough and detailed discussion of the efficiency of Quicksort is relatively complicated. It can be shown that the average number of comparisons required is approximately

$$2n\log_e n \quad \text{or about} \quad 1.4n\log_2 n$$

Thus, Quicksort is theoretically much faster than any of the methods discussed previously. The maximum number of comparisons required is $n(n-1)/2$. Unfortunately, this occurs for lists that are already sorted. Finally, it can also be shown that the minimum number of comparisons is about

$$0.5\log_2 n$$

12.3.5   Comparison of Sorting Methods

The discussion of each sorting method included calculation of the number of comparisons required to sort a list of length n. Counting the number of comparisons required is one of the standard methods of comparing the efficency of various sorting techniques (other criteria include a measure of the data movement involved). The table in Figure 12.26 presents the average, maximum, and minimum number of comparisons required by each of the four methods discussed in this chapter. Since such formulas are sometimes difficult to grasp, the average number of comparisons is tabulated for several values of n in Figure 12.27. For relatively short lists $(n < 30)$ the insertion sort exhibits the best characteristics. Thereafter, Quicksort is clearly the fastest method to use.

Figure 12.26   Comparison of sorting techniques.

Method	Average	Number of Comparisons Maximum	Minimum
Selection	$n(n-1)$	$n(n-1)$	$n(n-1)$
Exchange	$< \dfrac{n(n-1)}{2}$	$\dfrac{n(n-1)}{2}$	$n-1$
Insertion	$\dfrac{n(n-1)}{4}$	$\dfrac{n(n-1)}{2}$	$n-1$
Quicksort	$1.4n\log_2 n$	$\dfrac{n(n-1)}{2}$	$.5\log_2 n$

Figure 12.27   Tabulation of average number of comparisons.

				Length of the List			
Method	*16*	*32*	*64*	*128*	*256*	*512*	*1024*
Selection	240	992	4032	16256	65280	261632	1047552
Exchange	120	486	2016	8128	37640	130816	523776
Insertion	60	243	1008	4064	18820	65408	261888
Quicksort	90	224	538	1255	2868	6452	14336

12.4   Using Sorts in Applications

The previous sorting section presented an idealized approach to the task of sorting. In each case the algorithm was applied to a single list of integers. Since the algorithms are fundamentally sound they can be applied to floating point numbers or alphabetic information equally well with only minor changes to the WATFIV-S declarations. Similarly, to change the sort sequence from ascending to descending order would only require a few changes to the comparisons made in each algorithm. However, when performing sorts of real life data, more substantial changes may be needed.

Consider the tables of data listed in Appendix N. When such collections are presented as data for a program, they are usually referred to as files. Each line in a table is called a *record* in the file. Furthermore, each piece of information in a record is called a *field* of that record. Finally, the field or piece of information that forms the basis for sorting the file is called the *key* or *sort key*. For instance, the table of hockey statistics recorded in Appendix N could be labeled the NHL file since it represents the performance of hockey players in the National Hockey League. Each line in the table is appropriately a record in the file and coincidentally represents the record of a player during the 1977/1978 hockey season. The fields for each record or player include the player's name, team, position, games played, goals, assists, total points, penalty minutes, and salary.

The problems encountered in working with such a file are twofold. A sort usually requires that additional information be presented to identify the field chosen as the sort key. For example, a list sorted by salary is more meaningful if it includes the players' names. The second problem is that the sort often involves more than one field in each record thus requiring a *compound sort key*. It is not unreasonable, for example, to desire a list of players sorted by total points with players having an equal number of points being ranked by goals scored. The following discussion will present solutions to both of these problems.

12.4.1   Sorting With Added Information

There are several ways to manage the additional information during a sort. One possibility is to manipulate the entire record in the sorting process. However, this suggestion can be discarded quickly since it involves a great deal of data movement each time it is necessary to rearrange entries in the sorting process. A second option involves maintaining a list of pointers or indices to the actual data. Then, during the sorting process these pointers are moved rather than the actual data. For instance, Figure 12.28 shows a series of records to be sorted. Each record has a key and additional information.

Shown to the left of the records is the pointer list before sorting. On the right is the pointer list after sorting is completed. The pointer list after sorting indicates where the records may be found in the original file for the file to be ordered. Thus, the first item can be found in position four (the key 3 and its fields), the second in position five (the key 4 and its fields), and so on. The file itself does not change; only the pointers are manipulated.

Figure 12.28   An example of a pointer sort.

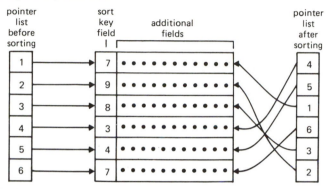

All of the sorting modules developed earlier in this chapter can be changed to manipulate pointers rather than the actual data. As an example, consider making such modifications to module bubble. The module still accepts LIST and n as import parameters but now returns PTR, the resulting list of pointers, as the export parameter.

smodule bubble (**imports**: LIST, n; **exports**: PTR)

Before the sorting process starts, the module bubble must create the initial PTR list from the integers 1 through n as follows.

$$p \leftarrow 1$$
while $p \le n$ **do**
$$\begin{bmatrix} ptr_p \leftarrow p \\ p \leftarrow p + 1 \end{bmatrix}$$

As the list is sorted, all references to LIST are done through the PTR list, for example,

if $list_{ptr_{pair}} > list_{ptr_{pair+1}}$ **then**

Whenever successive entries are out of order, their pointers are exchanged,

$$temp \leftarrow ptr_{pair}$$
$$ptr_{pair} \leftarrow ptr_{pair+1}$$
$$ptr_{pair+1} \leftarrow temp$$

rather than the entries themselves. These modifications will be presented later in this section when discussing an example.

12.4.2   Sorting With a Compound Sort Key

The second problem of a compound key is relatively easy to solve. It involves modifying the sort algorithm to accept more than one import list. Whenever a decision must be made and the first pair of keys is equal, the comparison process continues with successive pairs of keys, until the tie is broken or the compound keys are found to be identical.

Consider making further modifications to module bubble to accomodate a record consisting of two fields contained in the lists FA and FB. The corresponding elements of FA and FB form the compound sort key. Naturally, LIST is replaced in the parameter list by the lists FA and FB. The decision about when to exchange pointers is expanded to include instances when the FA entries are equal. The revised test can be written as:

$$\textbf{if } fa_{ptr_{pair}} > fa_{ptr_{pair+1}} \textbf{ or}$$
$$(fa_{ptr_{pair}} = fa_{ptr_{pair+1}} \textbf{ and } fb_{ptr_{pair}} > fb_{ptr_{pair+1}}) \textbf{ then}$$

The next example will require the use of such modifications.

12.4.3   Application to a Specific Example

Sorting many of the files in Appendix N would require the use of the modifications suggested in this section. Consider the following example.

Example 12.1

Given the file of information for players in the NHL as contained in Appendix N, produce a listing of players ranked by total points. Players with the same number of total points should be ranked by goals scored.

a) Problem Discussion   In order to solve this problem it will be advantageous to use a pointer sort that can handle a compound sort key. In addition, it will be necessary to process alphabetic information. WATFIV-S allows for the definition of a CHARACTER data type to make such processing easier. The succeeding discussion will first develop modifications to module bubble, now called PTRBUB, and then outline the mainline program to use PTRBUB to produce the desired sorted list.

b) A Modified Bubble Sort   This example obviously requires a sort that can handle additional information as well as a compound sort key. In addition, the ranking requested is in decreasing order. Listed in Figure 12.29 is a subroutine PTRBUB which combines all of these requirements. The fields FA and FB have replaced LIST in the import parameter list. A pointer list, PTR, is used to refer to the data fields, and these pointers are manipulated rather than the actual data. Successive pointers are exchanged if the FA entries are out of order or if the FA entries are equal but the FB entries are out of order. The result is a list of pointers to the data indicating the required order.

c) A Mainline to Produce the Listing   A mainline program to input the file, sort it according to the specified criteria, and output the resulting sorted list is presented in Figure 12.30. In order to handle the character information in the file, the CHARACTER data type has been introduced. The variable lists to represent a player's name, team, and position of play are declared to be of type CHARACTER. Each entry in these lists is given a specific length to correspond to the maximum length for that field. In order to prepare the file for input to the program, quotes are used to delimit the character fields. For more details on the character data type, read Appendix I.

A portion of the output generated by this sort program is presented in Figure 12.31. The horizontal spacing has been altered slightly to fit the information on the page of text.

```
C Figure 12.29 -- Subroutine PTRBUB
C                    Subprogram to use a combination pointer and
C                    bubble sort to sort a file with a compound
C                    sort key having two fields, FA and FB.
C**************************************************************
C FA      - first part of the compound sort key
C FB      - second part of the compound sort key
C N       - number of records in the file
C NMAX    - maximum value of N
C PTR     - resulting list of pointers to sort the file
C MAXPAR  - number of comparisons for current pass
C PAIR    - comparison pair counter
C XFLAG   - exchange flag, 0 if none, 1 if some in current pass
C TEMP    - temporary used to exchange out-of-order pointers
C**************************************************************
        SUBROUTINE PTRBUB(FA,FB,N,NMAX,PTR)

        INTEGER N, NMAX, P, MAXPAR, PAIR, XFLAG, TEMP
        INTEGER FA(NMAX), FB(NMAX), PTR(NMAX)
C Set up the pointer list to point to the initial positions
C of the records in the file, that is, 1, 2, 3, ..., N.

        P = 1
        WHILE(P .LE. N) DO
           PTR(P) = P
           P = P + 1
        END WHILE
C Initialize the number of comparisons & exchange flag.

        MAXPAR = N - 1
        XFLAG = 1
C Continue passing over the list until there are no exchanges.

        WHILE(XFLAG .EQ. 1) DO
C          For each pass, compare the records in pairs.
C          If the records are out of order, exchange the pointers
C          to the records and set the exchange flag.
C          After each pass, reduce the comparisons by 1.

           XFLAG = 0
           PAIR = 1
           WHILE(PAIR .LE. MAXPAR) DO
              IF(FA(PTR(PAIR)) .LT. FA(PTR(PAIR+1)) .OR.
       +         (FA(PTR(PAIR)) .EQ. FA(PTR(PAIR+1)) .AND.
       +          FB(PTR(PAIR)) .LT. FB(PTR(PAIR+1)))) THEN DO
                 TEMP = PTR(PAIR)
                 PTR(PAIR) = PTR(PAIR+1)
                 PTR(PAIR+1) = TEMP
                 XFLAG = 1
              END IF
              PAIR = PAIR + 1
           END WHILE
           MAXPAR = MAXPAR - 1
        END WHILE
        RETURN
        END
```

```
C Figure 12.30 -- Program to produce a listing of the NHL file
C                 sorted by goals within total points.
C                 Use a bubble sort which returns a list of
C                 pointers to the records in the correct order.

C**************************************************************

C PLAYER - the player's name (CHARACTER*19)
C TEAM   - the player's team (CHARACTER*12)
C PLACE  - the player's playing position (CHARACTER*1)
C GAMES  - the number of games played
C GOALS  - the number of goals scored
C ASISTS - the number of assists scored
C TOTAL  - the total number of points scored
C SALARY - the player's salary
C PIM    - the number of penalties in minutes
C PTR    - the pointer list to position the records in order
C N      - the number of players in the file
C NMAX   - the maximum number of players planned for
C I, P   - miscellaneous indices and pointers

C**************************************************************

      CHARACTER PLAYER*19(400), TEAM*12(400), PLACE*1(400)
      INTEGER GAMES(400), GOALS(400), ASISTS(400), TOTAL(400)
      INTEGER PIM(400), SALARY(400), PTR(400), N, NMAX, I, P
C Allow for a maximum of 400 players on file.
C Input the actual number of players and their records.
      NMAX = 400
      READ, N
      I = 1
      WHILE( I .LE. N) DO
          READ, PLAYER(I), TEAM(I), PLACE(I), GAMES(I),
     +          GOALS(I), ASISTS(I), TOTAL(I), PIM(I), SALARY(I)
          I = I + 1
      END WHILE
C Invoke the sorting routine to sort the file.
      CALL PTRBUB(TOTAL,GOALS,N,NMAX,PTR)
C Output the file in order using the pointer list
C to access the records in the correct order.
      PRINT, 'NAME              ','TEAM         ','P',
     +       '           GP',' 	          G','          A',
     +       '           TP','          PIM','      SALARY'
      PRINT, ' '
      I = 1
      WHILE( I .LE. N) DO
          P = PTR(I)
          PRINT, PLAYER(P), TEAM(P), PLACE(P), GAMES(P),
     +          GOALS(P), ASISTS(P), TOTAL(P), PIM(P), SALARY(P)
          I = I + 1
      END WHILE

      STOP
      END
C Subroutine PTRBUB is placed here.
$ENTRY
371
'MacMillan, Bob     ' 'Atlanta      ' 'W' 80 38 33  71  49  85000
'Lysiak, Tom        ' 'Atlanta      ' 'C' 80 27 42  69  54 130000
   :                        :          :   :  :  :   :   :      :
```

Figure 12.31 Partial output from the program of Figure 12.30. (Spacing edited)

NAME	TEAM	P	GP	G	A	TP	PIM	SALARY
Lafleur, Guy	Montreal	W	78	60	72	132	26	180000
Trottier, Bryan	NY Islanders	C	77	46	77	123	46	90000
Sittler, Darryl	Toronto	C	80	45	72	117	100	165000
Lemaire, Jacques	Montreal	C	76	36	61	97	14	135000
Potvin, Denis	NY Islanders	D	80	30	64	94	81	150000
Bossy, Mike	NY Islanders	W	73	53	38	91	6	50000
O Reilly, Terry	Boston	W	77	29	61	90	211	70000
Perreault, Gilbert	Buffalo	C	79	41	48	89	20	200000
Clarke, Bobby	Philadelphia	C	71	21	68	89	83	160000
McDonald, Lanny	Toronto	W	74	47	40	87	54	145000
⋮	⋮	⋮	⋮	⋮	⋮	⋮	⋮	⋮

12.5   Summary

This chapter has investigated several methods of searching and sorting. In each case both elementary and sophisticated methods have been presented. The binary search technique is one of the best available and should be used whenever a list is presorted or the searches are sufficiently frequent to warrant sorting the file.

Several approaches to sorting were presented to provide an insight into the many methods available. There is no best method of sorting - it usually depends on the characteristics of the data presented. Often existing methods can be modified to work well for the specific data at hand. Except for isolated cases, the Quicksort algorithm provides excellent characteristics as a general purpose sorting technique.

12.6   References

The amount of literature on sorting and searching techniques is too voluminous to list exhaustively. The references listed below are some of the better sources of additional information. Each reference in turn includes listings of appropriate articles in the journals.

Aho, A.V.; Hopcroft, J.E.; and Ullman, J.D. *The Design and Analysis of Computer Algorithms.* Reading Mass: Addison-Wesley Publishing Co., 1974, pp. 76-105.

Kernighan, B.W. and Plauger, P.J. *Software Tools.* Reading Mass: Addison-Wesley Publishing Co., 1976, pp. 105-116.

Knuth, D.E. *The Art of Computer Programming - Volume 3 - Sorting and Searching.* Reading Mass: Addison-Wesley Publishing Co., 1973.

Page, E.S. and Wilson, L.B. *Information Representation and Manipulation in a Computer.* Cambridge: Cambridge University Press, 1973, pp. 152-216.

12.7 Exercises

In most of the following exercises a program is requested to solve a specific problem. For each problem it is recommended that step-wise refinement be used in developing a pseudo-code algorithm to solve the problem. This algorithm should then be translated into WATFIV-S and run on the computer. Where appropriate, the program should be tested with a variety of data sufficient to ensure that the program does what it is supposed to do.

12.1 a) Translate module linear into a WATFIV-S subroutine subprogram.

b) Write a WATFIV-S mainline program to test subroutine LINEAR by trying to find the positions of

   1, 2, 7, 8, 23, 29

in the following list of numbers.

   2, 3, 5, 7, 11, 13, 17, 19, 21, 23

c) Modify subroutine LINEAR of part a) to take advantage of the ordering in the given list of numbers and then rerun the program of part b).

d) Another approach to searching involves a linear search from both ends of a list. Such a search would alternately compare the key to entries at the beginning and the end of the list until either the position of the key is found or the two searches intersect. Again modify subroutine LINEAR of part a) and rerun the program of part b).

12.2 a) If subroutine BINARY is not available in an accessible library of subprograms, prepare it in machine readable form.

b) Create a list of the first 100 prime numbers and write a WATFIV-S mainline program to find various entries in this list using subroutine BINARY of part a).

c) Modify subroutine LINEAR of Exercise 12.1 c) and subroutine BINARY of part a) to include an export parameter for the number of comparisons needed to either find an entry or determine that it does not appear in the list. Modify the program of part b) to compare the performance of these two subroutines.

12.3 a) Translate modules min and select into WATFIV-S subroutine subprograms.

b) Write a WATFIV-S mainline program to test these subroutines on several lists of randomly chosen numbers.

c) Module select was designed to sort the entries of a list OLD into a second list NEW. By exchanging the smallest entry with the first entry, the second smallest with the second entry, . . . , the list can be sorted in place without the need for a second list. Furthermore, less effort is required to find the current smallest since the initial portion of the list will already be sorted.

Make the necessary changes to subroutines MIN and SELECT and test them with the program of part b).

d) An alternate selection sort is based on choosing the largest entry at each stage rather than the smallest. These larger entries are placed towards the end of the list in such a fashion that it is constructed backwards.

Write a MAX subroutine to find the largest, then modify SELECT, and test it with the program of part b).

12.4 a) Translate module bubble into a WATFIV-S subroutine subprogram.

   b) Write a WATFIV-S mainline program to test subroutine BUBBLE on several lists of randomly chosen numbers.

   c) Module bubble is designed to make one less comparison with each subsequent pass, on the premise that at least the current largest entry has moved into the correct position. Depending on the specific entries in the list, more than one entry may have "bubbled" into position. In fact, all entries from the point of the last interchange to the end of the list will be in the proper order.

   Modify subroutine BUBBLE to remember the position of the last interchange and to use this information to reduce the number of comparisons. Rerun the program of part b) with this subroutine as a test of your revisions.

   d) Module bubble is designed to start at the beginning of a list and "bubble" the larger entries to the end of the list. It is also feasible to take the reverse approach and start the comparisons at the end of the list and therefore "bubble" the smaller entries to the beginning of the list. Redevelop module bubble to take this bottom-up approach. Translate the revised module into a WATFIV-S subroutine subprogram and test it with an appropriate mainline program.

   e) Redesign module bubble to perform odd numbered passes top-down and even numbered passes bottom-up. Translate the revised module into a WATFIV-S subroutine subprogram and test it with an appropriate mainline program.

   f) Assess the relative merits of each version of subroutine BUBBLE. Modify each version to compute the number of comparisons involved. Then write a single mainline program to test each version on

   1) a list already sorted in ascending order.
   2) a list sorted in descending order.
   3) several partially order lists.
   4) several randomly ordered lists.

   State your conclusions.

12.5 a) Translate module insert into a WATFIV-S subroutine subprogram.

   b) Write a WATFIV-S mainline program to test subroutine INSERT on several appropriate lists of numbers.

c) Module insert was designed to sort the entries of a list OLD into a second list NEW. By removing the current entry to be inserted, it is possible to retain the sorted portion of the list in the initial section of the list without using a second list. Make the necessary changes to subroutine INSERT so that it sorts the entries using only the given list. Test the resulting subroutine with the program of part b).

d) Redesign module insert to use a binary rather than a linear search to find the correct position for each entry. Note that this will require some slight modifications to module binary. Translate the revised module into a WATFIV-S subroutine subprogram and again test the subroutine with the program of part b).

12.6 a) If subroutines QUICK and PARTIT are not available in an accessible library of subprograms, prepare them in machine readable form.

b) Write a WATFIV-S program to test subroutines QUICK and PARTIT on several appropriate lists of numbers.

c) An alternate pivoting strategy for the partitioning in Quicksort involves choosing the last entry rather than the first. Rewrite subroutine PARTIT to pivot about the last entry. Rerun the program of part b) to test the revisions.

d) Still another pivoting strategy for the partitioning in Quicksort chooses the median of three of the entries in the list, for example, the first, the middle, and the last. Again rewrite subroutine PARTIT and rerun the program of part b).

e) Though Quicksort is very fast for longer lists of numbers, it does not perform as well for short lists. Redesign the module quick to use an insertion sort whenever the length of the current sublist ≤ 30. Test the revisions by rerunning the program of part b).

f) As presented, module quick does not take advantage of the fact that at any stage of the partitioning process, there may be several list elements equal to the pivot. Ideally these elements should be grouped together so that:

$$list_{ll} \leq \ldots \leq list_{m-1} < list_m$$
$$list_m = \ldots = list_p = \ldots = list_q$$
$$list_q < list_{q+1} \leq \ldots \leq list_{rl}$$

Successive partitioning is then carried out on entries ll through $m-1$ and $q+1$ through rl. Make the necessary changes to the quick algorithm, then translate the resulting module to WATFIV-S, and compare its performance with the original version.

g) Prove that the maximum number of stack entries in the Quicksort technique is given by

$$\lfloor \log_2 n \rfloor + 1$$

12.7 Consider an array which contains only numbers ≥ 0. It is necessary to move all nonzero entries to the start of the array. Develop an appropriate pseudo-code algorithm and translate the algorithm to a WATFIV-S program. Demonstrate the program for several examples including the following.

0, 2, 0, 3, 6, 9, 3, 9, 3, 9, 0, 15, 0, 0, 1

Output the number of nonzero entries as well as the resulting list.

Hint: Although this problem can be handled by using sorting techniques, it is a special case which can be handled in order n.

12.8 Suppose A and B are two lists of integral entries. It is necessary to know which entries are in:

1) both A and B
2) A but not B
3) B but not A

Develop a pseudo-code algorithm to get the two lists, A and B, and produce three lists of entries satisifying each of the three criteria. Translate the algorithm into WATFIV-S and test the program on the following two lists of entries.

A = (2, −5, 8, 4, −7, 1, −6, 10)
B = (9, 8, 4, −10, 3, −5, 12, 11, −3)

12.9 Given two lists of numbers,

$$X = (x_1, x_2, \cdots, x_n)$$

and

$$Y = (y_1, y_2, \cdots, y_m)$$

develop a pseudo-code algorithm to create a single list

$$Z = (z_1, z_2, \cdots, z_k)$$

which contains each distinct element of X and Y, with no repetitions, and arranged in ascending order, that is,

$$z_1 < z_2 < \cdots < z_k$$

For example, if $X = (5, 2, 6, 2, 6)$ and $Y = (1, 5, 2, 5, 3, 5)$, then the resulting list should be $Z = (1, 2, 3, 5, 6)$.

12.10 Given a sorted list with possible duplicates, develop a pseudo-code algorithm to produce a list of the entries with duplicates removed.

12.11 Modify each sorting subroutine to produce an additional export parameter representing the number of comparisons needed to sort the given list. Next, write a single mainline program to use these methods for

• a list of about 100 entries already sorted in ascending order
• a list of about 100 entries sorted in descending order
• several lists of random entries, choosing lengths from 10 to 100.

13
Statistics

13.1 Introduction

The collection and analysis of information is a pervasive activity in today's society, and is performed by a variety of individuals, agencies, and institutions. Scientists collect data from their experiments, financial firms collect data about credit ratings and profit margin, and governments collect data about food prices and unemployment. However, for these data to be meaningful, they must be analyzed, condensed, and summarized in order to understand them. The results of such analyses are often used to develop and support hypotheses, to make policy decisions, and to predict trends. Such analyses and predictions are called *descriptive* and *inductive* statistics, respectively.

When information is collected, the set of possible measurements is called the *population*. Since in many cases the entire population may not be tested, a representative subset or *sample* of the population must be used. Assuring that the sample is indeed representative is a challenging and important task since far-reaching decisions are based on the results. For instance, the results of samplings performed for political polls and television ratings can affect government actions and program scheduling respectively.

Almost everyone is familiar with statistical measures in one form or another. Statistics are kept in sports such as hockey, baseball, and football, to describe team or individual performances. Statistical measures are used in the actuarial mathematics of insurance companies to determine life insurance premiums. Pharmaceutical houses use statistical techniques to compute the effectiveness of new drugs. Closer to home, everybody has received, perhaps too frequently, a statistical measure of scholastic performance; that is, he or she has received an average grade on his or her courses. That the study of statistics is broadly based is evidenced by the diversity of disciplines which include an introductory statistics course as part of their basic curriculum.

Statistics is a very important topic. Unfortunately, it is very easy to misinterpret or misuse statistical results. Many television advertisements quote statistics to imply that their product is superior. The fact that some of the given statistics are incomplete and have other interpretations is often missed by an uninformed viewer. Campbell (1974) gives an interesting discussion of this topic.

The limited space available in this chapter allows only an introduction to some of the standard statistical techniques and terminology such as collection of data, computation of descriptive measures, and the use of tools for analysis. In many cases computer programs will be developed to facilitate these calculations.

13.2 Tables and Graphs

The data that are collected, called the *raw data,* are often presented in the form of a table. For instance, consider the typical table of data given in Figure 13.1. Such data are very difficult to analyze visually since humans usually have a limited ability to remember numbers. (Without looking at the table again, how many of the numbers in Figure 13.1 can you remember? For that matter, how many of them would you really want to remember?) When the data are arranged in a table, the first piece of information one usually knows about is the total number of data values (33 in this case).

Figure 13.1 Typical table of raw data.

4.90	1.75	5.01	6.30	3.01	8.50
6.19	5.02	2.37	7.90	5.64	9.77
9.63	7.41	5.32	3.35	6.10	10.28
10.11	6.91	8.61	9.14	10.42	6.05
2.10	6.89	9.45	9.63	12.51	11.34
12.17	15.99	11.89			

The next thing that can be determined about the data is the maximum and minimum values. In this case, they are 15.99 and 1.75 respectively. (The module minmax of Chapter 11 can be used to determine these attributes.) From the values of the maximum and minimum, one may obtain the *range* of the data which is simply the difference between the maximum and minimum values, $15.99 - 1.75 = 14.24$.

To obtain more insight into the data requires a little more effort. A common technique is to count the number of data values which fall into several predetermined, consecutive intervals or *classes* which cover the range of the numbers. The number of values in each class is called the *class frequency.* The collection of class frequencies is called a *frequency distribution.* Data summarized in such a manner are called *grouped data.* Conversely, raw data are often referred to as *ungrouped data.* Grouped data may be presented in several ways, and these are discussed in the following sections.

13.2.1 Frequency Tables
When a frequency distribution is presented in tabular form it is called a *frequency table.* A frequency table for the data of Figure 13.1 is shown in Figure 13.2. In this case, the *class width* is 2.0 for each of the 8 classes.

Figure 13.2   A frequency table for the data of Figure 13.1.

class boundaries	class frequency
0.0–2.0	1
2.0–4.0	4
4.0–6.0	5
6.0–8.0	8
8.0–10.0	7
10.0–12.0	5
12.0–14.0	2
14.0–16.0	1

The number of classes used is somewhat arbitrary and may require several attempts to achieve reasonable values. The number of classes is commonly between 8 and 25. Some people make use of Sturges' formula

$$k = 1 + 3.3\log_{10} n \tag{13.1}$$

where k is the number of classes and n is the total number of data values. The class widths are usually, but not necessarily, uniform and are determined by the number of classes and the range. It is important to assign data values to classes in a unique way. This requires a decision as to whether a data value which occurs on a boundary will be assigned consistently to the next higher or next lower class.

13.2.2   Histograms

Another method of presenting data which has been grouped into classes is to use a *histogram.* A histogram presents the same information as a frequency table but is somewhat more visual in its presentation. A histogram is essentially a graph which uses rectangles to present the class and frequency information. The width of the rectangle is equal to the class width and the height of the rectangle corresponds to the class frequency. Figure 13.3 shows a histogram corresponding to the frequency table of Figure 13.2. As may be seen from the diagram, a histogram provides a summary of the data which allows relative class frequencies to be better appreciated.

Alternate ways of determining the height of a bar are to divide the class frequency by n or to divide the class frequency by the class width. The latter is the only correct way when the classes have unequal widths.

.With respect to the choice of the classes themselves, there is some flexibility. For the sample data, a different number of classes could be chosen, different class widths are possible, and different class boundaries may be used. It is conceivable that a change in the choice of these parameters will produce a histogram that conveys an entirely different impression of the data. For instance, Figure 13.4 shows a histogram for the same data with only the class boundaries changed.

Figure 13.3   A histogram for the data of Figure 13.1.

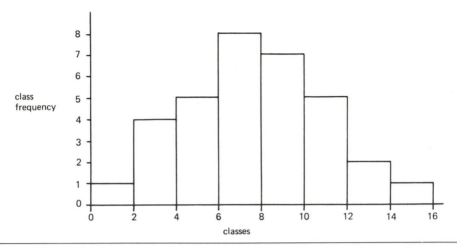

Figure 13.4   An alternate histogram for the data of Figure 13.1.

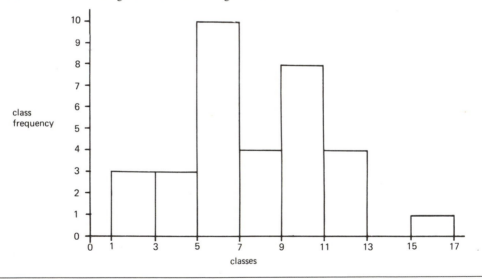

Although this histogram does not present as pleasing a diagram as the previous one, it is nevertheless an equally valid summary of the data.

13.2.3   Frequency Polygons and Curves

A third way of presenting the frequency information is through the use of line graphs. In the simplest case, a *frequency polygon* is obtained by joining the center points on the top of each histogram rectangle. Such a graph is shown in Figure 13.5 for the histogram of Figure 13.3.

Figure 13.5   A frequency polygon for the data of Figure 13.1.

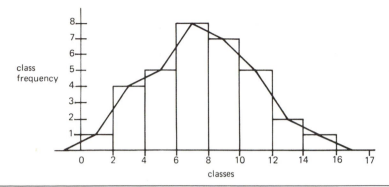

In the case of a very large mass of continuous data, it is possible to make the class widths very small and still have a representable frequency in each class. This reduction in class width will have the effect of smoothing out the frequency polygon into a *frequency curve*. Figure 13.6 shows three such frequency curves exhibiting properties often found in data. Frequency curves such as these are quite important and a lot of analysis has been expended in determining their properties.

Figure 13.6   Examples of frequency curves.

13.3   Measures of Central Tendency

Statistical measures which tend to predict where the central region of the data lies are called *measures of central tendency*. The mean, median, and the mode all fall into this category.

13.3.1   The Mean

There are several different types of means, the most common of which is the *arithmetic mean* or simply the *mean*. The mean or *average* is computed by summing all data values and dividing the total sum by the number of data values in the sum. Thus, for a set of data values X, the arithmetic mean $\bar{x}$ (called *xbar*) is computed by:

$$\bar{x} = \frac{x_1 + x_2 + x_3 + \cdots + x_n}{n} = \frac{1}{n} \sum_{i=1}^{n} x_i \tag{13.2}$$

As an example, for the data 1, 7, 4, 6, 9, 5, 4, the arithmetic mean is

$$\bar{x} = (1+7+4+6+9+5+4)/7 = 5.14.$$

Two less commonly used means are called the *geometric mean GM*

$$GM = (x_1 x_2 x_3 x_4 \cdots x_n)^{1/n} \tag{13.3}$$

and the *harmonic mean HM*.

$$HM = \cfrac{1}{\cfrac{1}{n}\left[\cfrac{1}{x_1}+\cfrac{1}{x_2}+\cfrac{1}{x_3}+\cdots+\cfrac{1}{x_n}\right]}$$

$$= \cfrac{1}{\cfrac{1}{n}\sum_{i=1}^{n}\cfrac{1}{x_i}} \tag{13.4}$$

These latter means are used in special circumstances and are presented here only to inform the reader as to their existence and how they are calculated.

13.3.2   The Median
The *median* of a set of data values is the data value which occupies the middle position when the data have been sorted into either ascending or descending order. In the case when there are two middle values (*n* even) the median is the average of these two middle values.

$$\text{Median} = \begin{cases} x_{(n+1)/2} & n \text{ is odd} \\ \dfrac{x_{n/2}+x_{(n+2)/2}}{2} & n \text{ is even} \end{cases} \tag{13.5}$$

The seven data values 1, 7, 4, 6, 9, 5, 4 would have to be sorted into the order 1, 4, 4, 5, 6, 7, 9 (or 9, 7, 6, 5, 4, 4, 1) from which the median is in the $(7+1)/2$-th $=$ 4-th position. Thus, the median is the value 5.

13.3.3   The Mode
The *mode* of a set of data values is the data value(s) which occur(s) the most number of times. The mode is not necessarily a unique value and, in fact, may not even exist. The numbers 1, 7, 4, 6, 9, 5, 4 have a mode of 4 since that value occurs most often. The numbers 1, 7, 4, 6, 9, 5 do not have a mode. For a frequency curve, the mode is the value of x corresponding to the maximum point on the curve. Curves with two maxima are called *bimodal* and those with more than two maxima are called *multimodal*.

13.4   Measures of Dispersion

The measures of the above section described where the central region of the data was but they did not tell anything else about the distribution. For example, the curves of Figure 13.7 have the same arithmetic mean, median, and mode (all falling at the same place in this case) but still have vastly different distributions. Looking at the curves one could say that one curve is more spreadout or *dispersed* than the other. Thus, some measures to describe this dispersion are also desired. Note that the range is in fact one measure of dispersion but even it is the same for the above curves. However, what does distinguish the above curves from each other is the frequency of data values at different distances or *deviations* from the mean. Many measures of dispersion compute some average of these deviations.

Figure 13.7   Two distributions with the same mean, median, and mode.

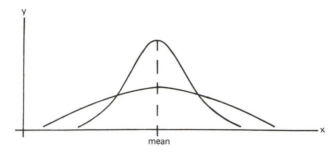

13.4.1 Mean Deviation

The first dispersion measure is the *mean deviation* which simply computes the average of the magnitude of the deviation. This calculation is indicated by the equation below.

$$MD = \frac{|x_1-\bar{x}|+|x_2-\bar{x}|+|x_3-\bar{x}|+ \cdots +|x_n-\bar{x}|}{n}$$

$$= \frac{1}{n}\sum_{i=1}^{n}|x_i-\bar{x}| \tag{13.6}$$

Notice that this equation takes the absolute value (magnitude) of the deviation in order that all summed terms are positive. If this were not done both positive and negative values would be summed, and the mean deviation would be zero, which is useless.

13.4.2 The Standard Deviation

The standard deviation also computes the deviation from the mean, but in this case the square root of the average of the squares of the deviations is used as given by the following formula.

$$S = \left(\frac{(x_1-\bar{x})^2+(x_2-\bar{x})^2+(x_3-\bar{x})^2+ \cdots +(x_n-\bar{x})^2}{n-1} \right)^{\frac{1}{2}}$$

$$= \left(\frac{1}{n-1}\sum_{i=1}^{n}(x_i-\bar{x})^2 \right)^{\frac{1}{2}} \tag{13.7}$$

The motivation for this measure is similar to the previous mean deviation in that the summed terms should all be positive. The squaring operation accomplishes this, and although it is not obvious from the formulas, the standard deviation is much easier to work with in mathematical analysis. The use of $n-1$ instead of n as the divisor is also motivated by advanced mathematical considerations, and there is little numerical difference in the final result when n is large (say, $n > 10$).

There is another version of the standard deviation formula which may also be used. It is derived from the above equation as shown below.

$$S = \left(\frac{1}{n-1} \sum_{i=1}^{n} (x_i - \bar{x})^2 \right)^{1/2}$$

$$= \left(\frac{1}{n-1} \sum (x_i^2 - 2x_i\bar{x} + \bar{x}^2) \right)^{1/2}$$

$$= \left(\frac{1}{n-1} \left[\sum x_i^2 - \sum 2x_i\bar{x} + \sum \bar{x}^2 \right] \right)^{1/2}$$

$$= \left(\frac{1}{n-1} \left[\sum x_i^2 - 2n\bar{x} \left(\frac{\sum x_i}{n} \right) + n\bar{x}^2 \right] \right)^{1/2}$$

$$= \left(\frac{1}{n-1} \left[\sum x_i^2 - 2n\bar{x}\,\bar{x} + n\bar{x}^2 \right] \right)^{1/2}$$

$$= \left(\frac{1}{n-1} \left[\sum x_i^2 - n\bar{x}^2 \right] \right)^{1/2} \tag{13.8}$$

$$= \left(\frac{1}{n-1} \left[\sum x_i^2 - \frac{1}{n} \left(\sum x_i \right)^2 \right] \right)^{1/2} \tag{13.9}$$

Although formulas (13.7) and (13.9) are algebraically equivalent there is, as often happens, quite a difference when they are used in computations. For instance, formula (13.7) requires processing the data values twice, once to compute $\bar{x}$ and once more to compute the n values of $(x_i - \bar{x})^2$. Formula (13.9) requires only one processing of the data since $\sum x_i^2$ and $(\sum x_i)^2$ may be calculated at the same time. Thus, formula (13.9) would require approximately half the data handling of formula (13.7).

On the other hand, notice that formula (13.7) has potential for better accuracy. If the standard deviation is small relative to the data values, both sums in equation (13.9) may be so large that any difference between them is lost due to the limited number of digits in computer and calculator arithmetic. Equation (13.7) does not suffer from this difficulty as long as the x_i's may be distinguished from $\bar{x}$. For example, consider computing the standard deviation of the following numbers on an IBM 370 computer (7 digits and truncated arithmetic).

1000.00, 1000.01, 1000.02, 1000.03, . . . , 1000.50

There are 51 data values in total, and their mean is 1000.25. The first formula computes the standard deviation as follows.

$$s_1 = \left(\frac{1}{50} [(-.25)^2 + (-.24)^2 + (-.23)^2 + \cdots + (.25)^2] \right)^{\frac{1}{2}}$$

$$= \sqrt{.02211243}$$

$$= .1487024$$

The second formula computes

$$s_2 = \left(\frac{1}{50} \left[(1000.00)^2 + (1000.01)^2 + \cdots + (1000.50)^2 - \frac{1}{51} (51012.75)^2 \right] \right)^{\frac{1}{2}}$$

$$= \sqrt{-2.240000}$$

Thus, the second formula gives a completely erroneous result in a case such as this when the standard deviation is small with respect to the mean.

In all fairness to the second formula, however, this difficulty may be negated if one can reduce the value of each data value by a constant amount Δx before the calculations. This magnitude reduction does not affect the dispersion of the curve; rather it just shifts the curve towards the y axis such that the new mean is much smaller. Both the standard deviation and the mean will now be small, and there should be no difficulty

Figure 13.8 Shifting a curve by a constant value.

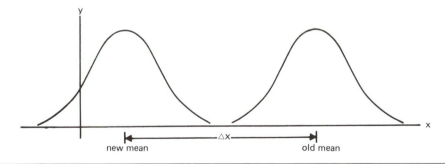

with the calculation. This situation is shown in Figure 13.8. The formula for this calculation is as follows.

$$s = \left(\frac{1}{n-1} \left[\sum_{i=1}^{n} (x_i - \Delta x)^2 - \frac{1}{n} \left(\sum_{i=1}^{n} (x_i - \Delta x)^2 \right) \right] \right)^{\frac{1}{2}} \tag{13.10}$$

The ideal amount to shift the curve would, of course, be $\Delta x = \bar{x}$, but $\bar{x}$ is unknown before the one pass computation. In fact, if it was known, the first standard deviation formula would be used instead. An informed guess about a good value for Δx could be made from previous knowledge about the data values or by analyzing the first few data values and assuming they are representative of the remaining values. The fact that the introduction of the Δx term does not change the value of the standard deviation may be proven algebraically (see Exercises 13.3 and 13.4).

13.4.3   The Variance
The variance of a set of data values is defined as the square of the standard deviation.

$$variance = s^2 \tag{13.11}$$

Notice that both formulas for the standard deviation compute the variance first and then take its square root to get the standard deviation.

13.5   Computing the Statistical Measures

The computation of the most common statistical measures of mean, variance, and standard deviation on computers is a relatively simple task. As a result, a step-wise refinement and presentation of an algorithm have not been included. Figures 13.9 and 13.10 present two subroutines, called STATS1 and STATS2 respectively, which compute these statistics. STATS1 uses the standard deviation formula of equation (13.7) and STATS2 uses equation (13.9).

```
C Figure 13.9 -- Subroutine STATS1
C                 Subprogram to calculate the mean, variance, and
C                 standard deviation of the values in an array.
C******************************************************************
C X      - one-dimensional array containing raw data
C N      - number of data values in the array X
C XBAR   - mean
C VAR    - variance
C STDEV  - standard deviation
C SUMX   - variable to sum the x values
C SUMDIF - variable to sum the squares of the differences
C******************************************************************
      SUBROUTINE STATS1(X, N, XBAR, VAR, STDEV)
      INTEGER I, N
      REAL X(N), XBAR, VAR, STDEV, SUMX, SUMDIF, SQRT
C Calculate the sum of the X values and the mean.
      SUMX = 0.0
      I = 1
      WHILE(I .LE. N) DO
         SUMX = SUMX + X(I)
         I = I + 1
      END WHILE
      XBAR = SUMX/N
C Calculate the sum of the differences squared, the variance,
C and the standard deviation.
      SUMDIF = 0.0
      I = 1
      WHILE(I .LE. N) DO
         SUMDIF = SUMDIF + (X(I) - XBAR)**2
         I = I + 1
      END WHILE
      VAR = SUMDIF/(N-1)
      STDEV = SQRT(VAR)
      RETURN
      END
```

Program Notes

- The variable dimension feature has been used in the subprogram to declare the size of the X array.
- If N is smaller than the maximum size of the array in the calling program, only the first N locations of the array are used.

13.5.1 Analyzing Some Real-Life Data

To illustrate the use of the above subroutines in actual calculations, the National Hockey League file of Appendix N will be used as data. Suppose that one wishes to determine salary statistics on a team basis. If one is content to have a program that will calculate the statistics for one team at a time, then the program of Figure 13.11 may be used. This program first reads in the name of the team to be analyzed and then reads in the entire player file. A data count is used to indicate the number of players in the file. Since the statistics are required for just one team at a time, only the salaries for that team are stored by the program.

```
C Figure 13.10 -- Subroutine STATS2
C                    Subprogram to calculate the mean, variance, and
C                    standard deviation of the values in an array.

C***************************************************************
C X      - one-dimensional array containing raw data
C N      - number of data values in the array X
C XBAR   - mean
C VAR    - variance
C STDEV  - standard deviation
C SUMX   - variable to sum the x values
C SUMXSQ - variable to sum the squares of the x values

C***************************************************************
       SUBROUTINE STATS2(X, N, XBAR, VAR, STDEV)

       INTEGER I, N
       REAL X(N), XBAR, VAR, STDEV, SUMX, SUMXSQ, SQRT
C Calculate the summations.
       SUMX = 0.0
       SUMXSQ = 0.0
       I = 1
       WHILE(I .LE. N) DO
          SUMX = SUMX + X(I)
          SUMXSQ = SUMXSQ + X(I)*X(I)
          I = I + 1
       ENDWHILE
C Compute the actual statistics.
       XBAR = SUMX/N
       VAR = (SUMXSQ - SUMX*SUMX/N)/(N-1)
       STDEV = SQRT(VAR)
       RETURN
       END
```

Program Notes

• The variable dimension feature has been used in the subprogram to declare the size of the X array.
• If N is smaller than the maximum size of the array in the calling program, only the first N locations of the array are used.

The output from the program in Figure 13.11 is shown in Figure 13.12. The average salary for Montreal turns out to be $103,695 with a standard deviation of $41,264.

```
C Figure 13.11 -- Program to compute statistics about the
C                  salaries of the players on a hockey team.
C******************************************************************
C NAME    - name of hockey player
C POSITN - position of hockey player
C TEAM    - team of hockey player
C GAMES   - games played by hockey player
C GOALS   - goals scored by hockey player
C ASSIST - assists obtained by hockey player
C POINTS - total points earned by hockey player
C PENALT - penalty minutes incurred by hockey player
C WAGE    - salary earned by hockey player
C RTEAM   - team for which statistic are to be calculated
C SALARY - storage for salaries of selected team
C AVE     - average (mean) salary of selected team
C VAR     - variance in salary of selected team
C STDEV  - standard deviation in salary of selected team
C MANY    - total number of hockey players in the data list
C NUM     - count of number of players on selected team
C******************************************************************
        CHARACTER NAME*19, TEAM*12, RTEAM*12, POSITN
        INTEGER GAMES, GOALS, ASSIST, POINTS, PENALT, WAGE
        INTEGER MANY, NUM, I
        REAL SALARY(100), AVE, VAR, STDEV
C Read in the name of the team to be analysed.
        READ, RTEAM
        PRINT, 'THE TEAM TO BE ANALYSED IS', RTEAM
        PRINT, ' '
C Read in the hockey file and store the salaries for
C the requested team.
        PRINT, 'THE MEMBERS OF THE TEAM AND THEIR SALARIES ARE:'
        PRINT, ' '
        READ, MANY
        NUM = 0
        I = 0
        WHILE(I .LT. MANY) DO
            READ, NAME, TEAM, POSITN, GAMES, GOALS, ASSIST, POINTS,
     +          PENALT, WAGE
            IF(TEAM .EQ. RTEAM) THEN DO
                NUM = NUM + 1
                SALARY(NUM) = WAGE
                PRINT, NAME, TEAM, POSITN, WAGE
            END IF
            I = I + 1
        END WHILE
C Calculate the salary statistics.
        CALL STATS1(SALARY,NUM,AVE,VAR,STDEV)
        PRINT, ' '
        PRINT, 'THE SALARY STATISTICS FOR ', RTEAM, ' ARE:'
        PRINT, 'THE AVERAGE SALARY IS =', AVE
        PRINT, 'THE STANDARD DEVIATION =', STDEV
        STOP
        END
$ENTRY
'Montreal'
  371
```

Program Notes

• Character variables have been used to store the character information. See Appendix I for more information.

Figure 13.12   Salary statistics for a National Hockey League team, output from the program of Figure 13.11.

```
THE TEAM TO BE ANALYSED IS Montreal
THE MEMBERS OF THE TEAM AND THEIR SALARIES ARE:
Lafleur, Guy         Montreal     W       180000
Lemaire, Jacques     Montreal     C       135000
Shutt, Steve         Montreal     W       120000
Robinson, Larry      Montreal     D       125000
Larouche, Pierre     Montreal     C       100000
Houle, Rejean,       Montreal     W        80000
Cournoyer, Yvan      Montreal     W       160000
Mondou, Pierre       Montreal     C        70000
Savard, Serge        Montreal     D       155000
Risebrough, Doug     Montreal     W        80000
Lapointe, Guy        Montreal     D       175000
Lambert, Yvon        Montreal     W        85000
Jarvis, Doug         Montreal     C        70000
Gainey, Bob          Montreal     W        80000
Nyrop, Bill          Montreal     D        70000
Tremblay, Mario      Montreal     W        75000
Chartraw, Rick       Montreal     W        75000
Bouchard, Pierre     Montreal     D        80000
Lupien, Gilles       Montreal     D        55000
Larocque, Michel     Montreal     G       105000
Engblom, Brian       Montreal     D        55000
Dryden, Ken          Montreal     G       180000
Wilson, Murray       Montreal     W        75000
THE SALARY STATISTICS FOR   Montreal      ARE:
THE AVERAGE SALARY IS =        103695.60000000
THE STANDARD DEVIATION =        41264.56000000
```

13.6   The Normal Distribution

There are several frequency distributions that are used in statistical computations. These distributions have been developed because they bear a close resemblance to distributions which occur naturally. The most important of these is a bell-shaped distribution called the *normal* or *Gaussian distribution*. The normal distribution has the general shape shown in Figure 13.13.

Figure 13.13   The general shape of the normal distribution.

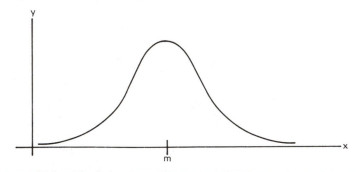

The equation for the general normal curve is

$$y = \frac{e^{-\frac{(x-m)^2}{2s^2}}}{s\sqrt{2\pi}}$$
(13.12)

where $e \simeq 2.718283$, $\pi \simeq 3.141593$, m = mean, s = standard deviation, and $-\infty < x < +\infty$. From this formula it should be obvious that there is not just one normal curve. If the mean is varied, the curve is just displaced along the x axis (an effect that was mentioned earlier). If the standard deviation is increased, the curve will flatten out but still retain its bell shape and contain the same area. Figure 13.14 indicates the effect of changing these parameters of the equation. However, regardless of the changes, the area under the curve remains at 1. All normal distributions have the property that 68.26% of the area lies within one standard deviation of the mean; 95.44% of the area lies within two standard deviations of the mean; and 99.74% of the area lies within three standard deviations of the mean. This property is illustrated in Figure 13.15 and can easily be verified through numerical integration (see Exercise 13.6).

Figure 13.14   Changes in the normal distribution formula.

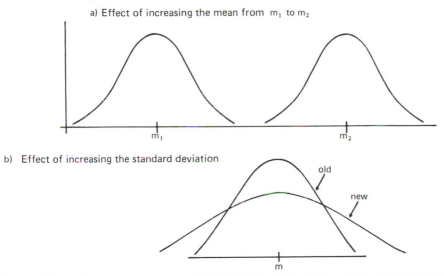

a) Effect of increasing the mean from m_1 to m_2

b)   Effect of increasing the standard deviation

The above properties of the normal distribution may be quite useful. If a frequency distribution of raw data is known to be normally shaped then one may use these percentages to make statements about the data. For instance, assume that a class of 150 students writes an exam, which when graded results in marks which are approximately normally distributed. If the mean mark is 65 and the standard deviation is 15, then one can say that approximately 102 students (68% of 150) have marks between 50 (65−15) and 80 (65+15) and that approximately 143 students (95% of 150) have marks between 35 (65−2×15) and 95 (65+2×15).

Figure 13.15 Distribution of areas for a normal distribution.

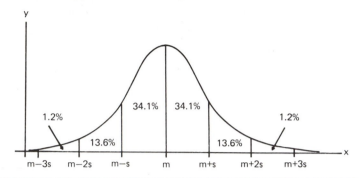

By looking at the above areas from a different perpective one can determine the relative position of a data value in its set. For instance, one could say that a student who obtained a mark of 80 performed better than approximately 84% of the class (the area under the curve less than the mean plus 1 standard deviation). This calculation is straightforward since the mark of 80 occurs at the 1 standard deviation position. However, if one chooses a mark which is not quite so conveniently placed, a bit more work is required. Since a computer is not always available (or appropriate) statisticans have traditionally used tables to obtain the percentage area information. However, since one can not describe tables for all possible distributions, statisticans provide a table for just one normal distribution and describe how to convert other normal distributions to it. Currently, good numerical approximations for normal calculations are available on most computers and even on some hand-held calculators.

13.6.1 Standard Form of the Normal Distribution
The normal distribution usually tabulated by statisticians has a mean of zero and a standard deviation of one. The formula of this *standardized normal distribution* or *z-distribution* is given by

$$y = \frac{e^{-\frac{z^2}{2}}}{\sqrt{2\pi}}$$
(13.13)

Ordinary normal distributions may be converted to this standard form by the formula

$$z = \frac{(x-m)}{s}$$
(13.14)

which gives what is called a *z-score*. (This conversion holds when m and s have been computed for a fairly large sample, that is, 20 or 30 measurements.) The standard normal curve is shown in Figure 13.16. z-scores of ± 1, ± 2, and ± 3 correspond to positions which are ± 1, ± 2, and ± 3 standard deviations away from the mean. With respect to ordinary normal distributions one can see from equation (13.14) that a value of $x = m$ will map onto $z = 0$, $x = m+s$ will map onto $z = 1$, and so on. The majority of the area under a normal curve (99.74%) lies between $-3 \leq z \leq +3$, and thus, z-scores outside this range are not often encountered.

Figure 13.16 Standardized normal curve.

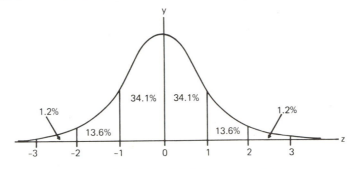

The *z*-score is thus a nondimensional description of where a data value lies with respect to the mean of its set. Since all normally distributed measurements may be converted into a *z*-score, only the standard distribution needs to be tabulated. Appendix O contains such a table.

13.7 Relationships Between Sets of Measurements

From a given sample of a population, it is possible to measure several different attributes. For instance, one could measure the height and weight of university students, the weight and gas mileage of cars, or the size and cost of textbooks in the bookstore. When one measure accompanies another measure as in the above examples, one may wish to determine whether there is any relationship between the two. The degree to which measurements are linearly related is called their *correlation*. If two measurements are correlated then it may be possible to determine an equation to describe this relationship and thereby one may use one measure to predict the other. This process is called *simple linear regression*.

Correlation and regression calculations are relatively easy to perform with the use of a computer. Unfortunately, this is exactly what causes some problems. The fact that one can perform these calculations for almost any set of data does not guarantee that the results are useful.

One of the simpler ways to gain insight into this problem is to generate an *x*–*y* graph, called a *scatter plot,* of the data points. Such a plot may reveal characteristics of the data which will suggest whether a correlation or regression calculation would be appropriate.

13.7.1 Scatter Plots and Correlation

The simplest way to determine if two measurements are related is to plot the measurements on an *x*–*y* graph. One measurement is taken as the *x* value (abscissa) and the other measurement is taken as the *y* value (ordinate). The graph so obtained is the scatter plot. If the points on a scatter plot seem to form a straight line then they are *correlated*. Figure 13.17 shows three scatter plots in which graph a) shows a negative correlation (as *x* gets larger *y* gets smaller), graph b) shows no correlation, and graph c) shows a positive correlation (as *x* gets larger *y* gets larger). If all points should happen to lie exactly on a straight line then measurements are said to be *perfectly correlated*.

Figure 13.17   Scatter plots showing different data possibilities.

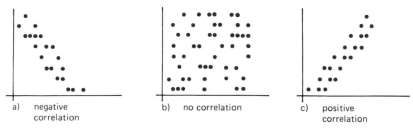

a)   negative   b)   no correlation   c)   positive
     correlation   correlation

The measure of correlation is called the *correlation coefficient* which takes on values of −1.0 (perfect negative correlation) to +1.0 (perfect positive correlation). Values of the correlation coefficient near 0.0 imply no correlation at all. The correlation coefficient for Figure 13.17 a) would be near −1, for Figure 13.17 b) it would be near 0, and for Figure 13.17 c) it would be near +1. It should be pointed out that a correlation between two measurements does not imply a causative effect. That is, one does not necessarily cause the other to happen.

To be able to compute the correlation coefficient between two sets of measurements, it is necessary to determine if there is a consistent relationship between corresponding individual measurements. The way this can be done is to compare each measurement with respect to its mean. The three scatter plots of Figure 13.18 show data points which have a perfect negative correlation, no correlation, and a perfect positive correlation respectively. On each plot the deviation from the mean and the sign of the deviation are indicated for each point. For graph a), when the *x* deviation is small, the *y* deviation is also. When the *x* deviation is large, the *y* deviation is large. In both cases, the *x* and *y* deviations have opposite signs. A similar situation exists in graph c) except that the signs are the same. In graph b) there is no such consistent relationship between the signs of

Figure 13.18   Relationship between data points and their mean for correlation.

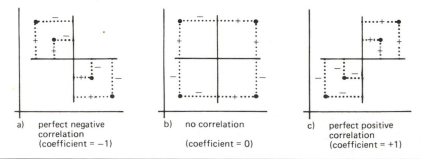

a)   perfect negative   b)   no correlation   c)   perfect positive
     correlation   correlation
     (coefficient = −1)   (coefficient = 0)   (coefficient = +1)

deviations. Thus, when a correlation does exist there is a consistent relationship between the *x* and *y* deviations and their means. A method is now needed to quantify this relationship and to take into account that correlations may have to be performed on measurements which vary greatly in scale relative to each other. It turns out that the z-score serves this purpose exactly since it is a nondimensional indication of where a data value lies with respect to its mean.

The correlation coefficient r is computed by determining the average of the products of the z-scores according to the following formula.

$$r = \frac{\sum_{i=1}^{n} \left(z_{x_i} z_{y_i} \right)}{n-1} \tag{13.15}$$

where the z_x are z-scores for abscissa measurements, and the z_y are z-scores for ordinate measurements.

As an example, consider the values in Figure 13.19 which give two measurements,

Figure 13.19 Number of pages and prices for some softcover textbooks.

Book	Pages	Price	Book	Pages	Price
1	166	6.75	6	335	13.50
2	195	10.25	7	370	11.75
3	200	9.00	8	450	14.75
4	260	9.00	9	517	19.00
5	265	11.25	10	552	16.50

the number of pages and the price for some softcover textbooks. A scatter plot of these measurements shown in Figure 13.20 implies that there is some positive correlation between the price and number of pages for the books. Therefore, it seems reasonable to compute the correlation coefficient.

Figure 13.20 Scatter plot of prices and pages for some softcover textbooks.

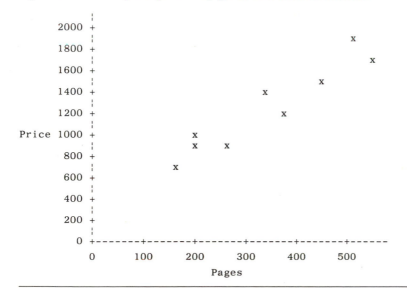

To determine the correlation coefficient between the prices and pages, it is necessary to determine the z-scores and then use equation (13.15). (For illustrative purposes, the z-score calculations are being allowed here with only 10 measurements instead of demanding the 20 or more that are usually required.) The z-scores for these

Figure 13.21   z-scores for pages and prices for some softcover textbooks.

Measurement	*Pages(x)*	z_x	*Price(y)*	z_y	$z_x z_y$
1	166.	−1.20	6.75	−1.44	1.72
2	195.	−0.99	10.25	−0.51	0.50
3	200.	−0.95	9.00	−0.84	0.80
4	260.	−0.51	9.00	−0.84	0.43
5	265.	−0.48	11.25	−0.25	0.12
6	335.	0.03	13.50	0.35	0.01
7	370.	0.28	11.75	−0.11	−0.03
8	450.	0.86	14.75	0.68	0.59
9	517.	1.35	19.00	1.81	2.44
10	552.	1.60	16.50	1.15	1.84

					8.41

$\bar{x} = 331.0, \bar{y} = 12.0, s_x = 138.01, s_y = 3.77$

measurements are calculated in Figure 13.21 along with the product of the z-scores. The correlation coefficient may now be calculated as follows.

$$r = \frac{\sum\limits_{i=1}^{n} z_{x_i} z_{y_i}}{n-1} = \frac{8.41}{9} = .93$$

Thus, there is a large positive correlation of .93 between the price and number of pages in the softcover books that were sampled. However, to emphasize again, this high correlation value does not necessarily mean that the number of pages is the only factor in the price of the books. There are other factors that can contribute greatly to the price such as the number of copies printed per run, the market demand, and competition.

The more common forms of the equation for the correlation coefficient may be obtained by first substituting equation (13.14) into equation (13.15).

$$r = \frac{1}{n-1} \sum_{i=1}^{n} \left[\frac{(x_i - \bar{x})}{s_x} \times \frac{(y_i - \bar{y})}{s_y} \right]$$

$$= \frac{\sum (x_i - \bar{x})(y_i - \bar{y})}{(n-1)s_x s_y}$$

Then by substituting equation (13.7) for s_x and s_y gives

$$r = \frac{\sum (x_i - \bar{x})(y_i - \bar{y})}{\left(\sum (x_i - \bar{x})^2 \sum (y_i - \bar{y})^2 \right)^{1/2}} \tag{13.16}$$

while substituting equation (13.8) gives

$$r = \frac{\sum x_i y_i - \frac{1}{n} \sum x_i \sum y_i}{\left(\left[\sum x_i^2 - \frac{1}{n} (\sum x_i)^2 \right] \left[\sum y_i^2 - \frac{1}{n} (\sum y_i)^2 \right] \right)^{\frac{1}{2}}}$$

(13.17)

This latter equation of course is prone to round-off error as is equation (13.8).

13.7.2   Regression

In many circumstances it is not enough to know that two measurements are correlated. What is needed is a description of the actual functional relationship between the variables. A technique for obtaining such an function is called regression.

Simple linear regression is used when the underlying relationship between the variables seems to be truly linear and when the data is of roughly constant variance. This may be interpreted visually to mean that the data points should lie in a band of approximately constant width as is the case in Figures 13.17a) and 13.17c). In Figure 13.17b) a regression is useless since r is 0 (that is, one can not use x to predict y). The graphs of Figure 13.22 show two scatter plots of data for which computation of a regression line would be meaningless. In Figure 13.22 a), the two data points which are remote from the others can have a large effect on the line. When data like this occurs, the first inclination is to go back and check these points to see if they are correct. Another alternative is to collect more data because there may indeed be a relationship between the points, but it may be a nonlinear one. In the case of Figure 13.22 b), if there really are no data values between the two groups, the data are not correlated even though a computed correlation coefficient would be near -1. There are merely two distinct pairs of observations with some clustering around them.

Figure 13.22   Scatter plots for which linear correlation is questionable.

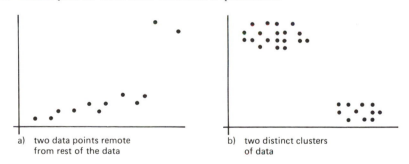

a) two data points remote
    from rest of the data

b) two distinct clusters
    of data

The curve that is fitted to a set of data values may be a straight line, a quadratic, or some higher order curve. The scatter plot can give some indication as to which type of curve (if any) should be fitted. Regardless of which curve is being used, the objective is to determine the best one. The curve which best fits the data values is usually taken to be the one which minimizes the sum of squared vertical distances between the data points and the curve itself. The individual vertical deviations are referred to as the *residuals*. The diagram of Figure 13.23 illustrates the residual values for an arbitrary curve. Minimization of the sum of squares of the residuals is called the *least squares method*.

Figure 13.23   Residuals of a curve fitted to a set of data points.

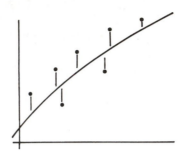

a) Least-Squares Lines   If a straight line is being fitted to the data points, the equation of the line will be of the following form.

$$y = a+bx$$

The *y residual* for the *i*-th data point is then given by the following.

$$y \; residual \; = \; y_i-(a+bx_i)$$

According to the least-squares criterion, the values of *a* and *b* are those for which the sum of squared residuals is minimized. That is, minimize

$$ls_1 \; = \; (y_1-(a+bx_1))^2+(y_2-(a+bx_2))^2+ \cdots +(y_n-(a+bx_n))^2 \qquad (13.18)$$

$$= \; \sum_{i=1}^{n} (y_i-(a+bx_i))^2$$

It can be shown using calculus that a minimum value of ls_1 results when the following equations are solved for *a* and *b*. (Note that *a* and *b* are the unknowns in these equations.)

$$na+b\sum x_i \; = \; \sum y_i \qquad (13.19)$$

$$a\sum x_i+b\sum x_i^2 \; = \; \sum x_i y_i$$

These equations may be solved through elimination techniques (see Chapter 14) and transformed to give the following expressions for *a* and *b*.

$$b \; = \; \frac{\sum (x_i-\bar{x})(y_i-\bar{y})}{\sum (x_i-\bar{x})^2} \qquad (13.20)$$

$$a \; = \; \bar{y}-b\bar{x}$$

The equations of (13.20) can easily be evaluated by a computer program. Figure 13.24 gives a program that does exactly this. In addition, the program generates a scatter plot and also plots the regression line so that one can see if it is a good fit. The program assumes that the data pairs are preceded by a data count.

```
C Figure 13.24 - This program generates a scatter plot of the
C                input data pairs, calculates a least squares
C                line for the points, and then plots this line.

C*******************************************************************

C X,Y      - storage for the location of the data points
C N        - number of data points to be processed
C SUMX, SUMY - variables for summation of X and Y values
C SUMXY    - variable for summation of X*Y terms
C SUMXDS   - variable for summation of (X-XBAR)*(Y-YBAR) terms
C XMIN, XMAX - variables to store min and max values of X
C A, B     - coefficients of the regression line
C XINCR    - size of increment for plot of regression line
C XP, YP - X and Y points for plotting the regression line
C XBAR, YBAR - X and Y means

C*******************************************************************

      INTEGER I, N
      REAL X(1000), Y(1000)
      REAL XBAR, YBAR, SUMX, SUMY, XDIFF, SUMXY, SUMXDS
      REAL A, B, XMIN, XMAX, XINCR, XP, YP, AMIN1, AMAX1
C Initialize the plotting routines and read in the data.
      CALL SETPLT
      CALL SETSIZ(31,41)
      READ, N
      I = 1
      WHILE(I .LE. N) DO
         READ, X(I), Y(I)
         CALL STOPNT(X(I),Y(I),'X')
         I = I + 1
      END WHILE
C Calculate the terms of the least-squares line and the
C  maximum and minimum data point in the x direction.
      SUMX = 0.0
      SUMY = 0.0
      XMIN = X(1)
      XMAX = X(1)
      I = 1
      WHILE(I .LE. N) DO
         SUMX = SUMX + X(I)
         SUMY = SUMY + Y(I)
         XMIN = AMIN1(XMIN,X(I))
         XMAX = AMAX1(XMAX,X(I))
         I = I + 1
      END WHILE
      XBAR = SUMX/N
      YBAR = SUMY/N
C Calculate the sum of the product of the X and Y differences
C and the sum of the X differences squared.
      SUMXY = 0.0
      SUMXDS = 0.0
      I = 1
      WHILE(I .LE. N) DO
         XDIFF = X(I) - XBAR
         SUMXY = SUMXY + XDIFF*(Y(I) - YBAR)
         SUMXDS = SUMXDS + XDIFF**2
         I = I + 1
      END WHILE
C Compute the actual coefficients.
      B = SUMXY/SUMXDS
      A = YBAR - B*XBAR
      PRINT, 'THE LEAST-SQUARES LINE IS:'
      PRINT, ' '
      PRINT, 'Y =', A, '+', B, 'X'
```

```
C Figure 13.24 (continued)
C Add the least-squares line to the plot.
      XINCR = (XMAX - XMIN)/16
      XP = XMIN
      WHILE(XP .LE. XMAX) DO
         YP = A + B*XP
         CALL STOPNT(XP, YP, '.')
         XP = XP + XINCR
      END WHILE
      CALL PLOTC(0)

      RETURN
      END
$ENTRY
```

The output from the program for the textbook data of Figure 13.19 is shown in Figure 13.25. The equation of the line is also given there preceding the actual plot. From the plot it appears that the least-squares line is a reasonable fit for the given data.

Figure 13.25 Computer-generated scatter plot and regression line, output from the program of Figure 13.24.

```
THE LEAST-SQUARES LINE IS:
Y =              3.71772100 +           0.02555069 X
 - NUMBER OF POINTS: SUBMITTED    27, PLOTTED     27

       19.0000                                    X


                                              .
       16.9583
                                          .   X
                                        .
       14.9167
                                  .X
                        X    .
       12.8750
                       .
                          X
                    X  .
       10.8333
              X       .
                    .
            X.    X
        8.7917
            .

            .
        6.7500X
              166.0000   262.4998   358.9998   455.4998   551.9998
       - SCALE FACTORS: ORDINATE 10** 0, ABSCISSA 10** 0
```

b) Least-Squares Quadratic Curves   To compute a least squares quadratic curve for a set of data points, similar reasoning may be used. In this case, one wishes to use a quadratic equation of the form

$$y = a+bx+cx^2 \qquad (13.21)$$

and to minimize

$$ls_2 = \sum_{i=1}^{n} (y_i - (a+bx_i+cx_i^2)) \qquad (13.22)$$

which requires solving the equations

$$
\begin{aligned}
na &+ b\sum x_i &+ c\sum x_i^2 &= \sum y_i \\
a\sum x_i &+ b\sum x_i^2 &+ c\sum x_i^3 &= \sum x_i y_i \\
a\sum x_i^2 &+ b\sum x_i^3 &+ c\sum x_i^4 &= \sum x_i^2 y_i
\end{aligned}
\qquad (13.23)
$$

The solution of these equations in a general form is certainly not recommended. Even if the coefficients are computed and the equations then solved, it is still a tedious task. Chapter 14 presents a subprogram which when given the coefficients of such equations will perform the solution for the unkowns.

c) General Least-Squares Curves   This technique of formulating linear equations for the coefficients does extend to making higher degree polynomial curve fits. However, special numerical techniques are needed to solve these problems accurately. If desired, one may also fit more complicated functions than polynomials. Programs for these techniques exist in many program libraries.

13.8   Special Languages for Statistical Analysis

Since many people who use statistical analysis in their work are not necessarily computer programmers, special languages have been developed to allow them to still use the computer but with a minimum of effort. Perhaps the best known of these is the SPSS (Statistical Package for the Social Sciences) language, Klecka et al. (1975) and Nie (1970), developed during the late 1960's.

This language allows users to specify, in more-or-less statistical terms and English phrases, the actions and analyses that are to be performed on their data. SPSS language statements consist of single word commands which are accompanied by some parameters. These commands are simple but quite powerful. For instance, only one command is needed to specify each of the following actions.

- Production of frequency tables.
- Generation of scatter plots.
- Calculation of the standard statistical measures of mean, median, mode, standard deviation, variance, range, maximum, and minimum.

In addition, many other options exist including basic data and file manipulation commands. Figure 13.26 shows a simple SPSS program which processes the book data of Figure 13.19. These statements are all that are necessary to generate a scatter plot, calculate the statistical measures listed above, and perform a regression calculation.

```
COMMENT              Figure 13.26 SPSS program to process the book data.

RUN NAME             BOOKDATA

COMMENT              Provide the data for the program.

DATA LIST            FIXED/ 1 PAGES 1-3, PRICE 5-9
INPUT MEDIUM         CARD
N OF CASES           10
READ INPUT DATA
166   6.75
195  10.25
200   9.00
260   9.00
265  11.25
335  13.50
370  11.75
450  14.75
517  19.00
552  16.50

COMMENT              Perform the plots and statistical computations.

SCATTERGRAM          PRICE WITH PAGES
STATISTICS           ALL
REGRESSION           VARIABLES = PRICE,PAGES/
                     REGRESSION=PRICE WITH PAGES(2) RESID=0 /
STATISTICS           6
FINISH
```

Thus, this language has some very attractive features and is heavily used. However, the same caution must again be issued with the interpretation and use of the statistical results. In fact, the cautions may be even more important here since so much information may be generated so easily. The ability to perform all kinds of statistical analysis does not guarantee that the results generated are meaningful.

13.9 Summary

Statistical analysis is very important and widely used. It allows one to summarize data to gain insight into its characteristics. As well, it is used to detect relationships between measurements and to predict other results on the basis of these relationships.

It is relatively easy to perform statistical calculations. One may either write one's own programs, use a special language such as SPSS, or use library subroutines. However, interpretation of statistical results and the making of inferences from them can be difficult. Consultation with a statistician is often advisable before setting out to acquire the data. Such expert advice can ensure that the proper quantity and quality of data is collected to provide the information sought. Statisticians will also be aware of the most accurate and efficient computational procedures to use in the analysis of the data.

13.10   References

Anscombe, F.J. "Graphs in Statistical Analysis." *The American Statistician* 29, no.1 (1973).

Campbell, S.K. *Flaws and Fallacies in Statistical Thinking.* Englewood Cliffs, N.J.: Prentice-Hall, 1974.

Ehrenberg, A.S.C. *Data Reduction - Analysing and Interpreting Statistical Data.* New York: John Wiley and Sons, 1971.

Kalbfleisch, J.G. *Probability and Statistical Inference.* Waterloo, Ont.: Faculty of Mathematics, University of Waterloo, 1975.

Klecka, W.R.; Nie, N.H.; and Hull, C.H. *SPSS Primer.* New York: McGraw-Hill Book Co., 1975.

Nie, N.H. *SPSS - Statistical Package for the Social Sciences.* New York: McGraw-Hill Book Co., 1970.

Spiegal, M.R. *Theory and Problems of Statistics.* New York: Schaum Publishing Co., 1961.

13.11   Exercises

In most of the following exercises a program is requested to solve a specific problem. For each problem it is recommended that step-wise refinement be used in developing a pseudo-code algorithm to solve the problem. This algorithm should then be translated into WATFIV-S and run on the computer. Where appropriate, the program should be tested with a variety of data sufficient to ensure that the program does what it is supposed to do.

13.1 The following data represent the heights (in centimeters) of a number of university professors.

```
157   158   160   161   161   161   165   166   166
116   167   168   169   171   171   171   171   171
171   171   172   172   172   172   172   172   172
172   173   173   173   174   174   174   174   174
175   175   175   177   177   177   177   178   178
179   179   180   183   184   187   189   190   190
191   191   193
```

a) Develop a program that will generate a frequency table for the above data.

b) A histogram may be printed easily on a computer if the histogram is turned on its side. The following statements will print N lines with the character * occurring M times on each line.

```
I = 1
WHILE(I .LE. N) DO
   PRINT, ('*', J=1,M)
   I = I + 1
END WHILE
```

Thus, these statements may be used to print a bar of a histogram.

1) Develop a subroutine subprogram with first statement SUBROUTINE HIST(FREQ,NUM,N) in which FREQ is a one-dimensional array containing frequency counts, NUM is the number of entries in FREQ, and N is the number of print lines per bar. This subroutine should print a histogram of the frequency distribution contained in the array FREQ.

2) Develop a main program which will use the above subprogram to draw a histogram for the data of part a).

13.2 The following data values represent the term-work averages (out of 50) of a class of 18 students.

```
29.7   29.9   26.9   29.2   33.0   31.1   27.1   24.0
28.9   29.0   27.2   28.0   32.5   33.0   24.5   29.7
27.0   26.7
```

Develop a program that will perform the following tasks.

a) Compute the mean and standard deviation of the class averages using the subroutine STATS1 of Figure 13.9.

b) Determine the median mark of the class.

13.3 Prove algebraically that the standard deviation of equation (13.10) is equivalent to the standard deviation formula of equation (13.9).

13.4 Develop a program that will compute the standard deviation using the formula of equation (13.10). The program should assume that the first data value is representative of the remaining data. Test your program on suitable data to be sure that it works. Compare the results of this program with the results from the other standard deviation formulas on the same data.

13.5 Some statisticians believe that the extreme values in a sample of data should not be used in the calculation of the sample mean and variance. Assuming that an array X contains data values in ascending order, then the data values from x_1 to x_{k-1} and from x_{l+1} to x_n ($1 \le k < l \le n$) are the extreme values and hence are ignored. Thus, for an array X, which contains n data values, they would use the following equations

$$\bar{x}_t = \frac{\sum\limits_{i=k}^{l} x_i}{l-k+1} \quad \text{and} \quad s_t^2 = \frac{\sum\limits_{i=k}^{l} (x_i-\bar{x}_t)^2}{l-k}$$

to compute the mean $\bar{x}_t$ and variance s_t^2 from x_k to x_l.

a) Develop a subroutine subprogram with first statement

    SUBROUTINE SAMPT(X,K,L,N,XBART,SSQT)

    which when given the one-dimensional array x (the data values have already
    been sorted in ascending order) and the index values K and L will compute
    XBART $=\bar{x}_l$ and SSQT $=s_l^2$ as defined above.

b) Develop a main program that will use the above subroutine to compute the
    sample mean and standard deviation of the data of Exercise 13.2.

13.6 Develop a program that will perform numerical integration on the normal curve,
      equation (13.12), to determine the area within 1, 2, and 3 standard deviations of the
      mean. Assume different values for the mean and standard deviation including a
      mean of 0 and standard deviation of 1.

13.7 Develop a program that will plot the following normal distributions. There should
      be one graph for part a) and a different one for part b).

a) $m = 10.0, s = 0.5; m = 10.0, s = 2.5; m = 10.0, s = 5.0$
b) $m = 10.0, s = 1.0; m = 8.0, s = 1.0; m = 6.0, s = 1.0$

Plot the curves in the range of ±3 standard deviations.

13.8 The following list contains 15 student identification numbers together with 4 course
      grades for each.

77000001	82	63	92	43
77000002	83	73	77	58
77000003	72	51	64	24
77000004	45	80	67	29
77000005	59	35	74	54
77000006	97	84	94	89
77000007	85	41	86	63
77000008	74	74	72	59
77000009	83	94	97	92
77000010	93	78	88	60
77000011	76	84	63	89
77000012	100	78	100	82
77000013	80	92	91	81
77000014	74	84	91	68
77000015	71	58	63	68

Develop a program that will process this data to produce the two tables shown
below.

I.D number	Average Mark	Standard Deviation
77000001	----	----
77000002	----	----
77000003	----	----
⋮	⋮	⋮
77000015	----	----

Course Number	Average Mark	Standard Deviation
1	----	----
2	----	----
3	----	----
4	----	----

13.9 Develop a program that will process the student data file of Appendix N and determine the average and standard deviation marks for each student and for each assignment.

13.10 a) Show algebraically that the use of the z-scores in the correlation calculation of equation (13.15) will give it a value of ± 1 for points which lie on a nonhorizontal straight line. What happens if the line is horizontal?

   b) Compute by hand the correlation coefficient for the data points $(1,1)$, $(3,2)$, and $(5,3)$.

13.11 Develop a program that will process the Indianapolis 500 race data of Appendix N and plot the least-squares linear regression line for the data. The largest departures of the data from the regression line tend to occur after the resumption of the races in 1945. Can you suggest a change in application of the linear regression technqiue to fit the data more closely?

13.12 Develop a program that will calculate the least-squares quadratic polynomial for the following data values. Plot both the data values and the quadratic polynomial to compare the fit.

   a) $(x_i, y_i) = (0,6)$, $(1,9)$, $(2,12)$, $(3,13)$, $(4,10)$, $(5,6)$, $(6,5)$, $(7,0)$

   b) $(x_i, y_i) = (-6,6)$, $(-5,4)$, $(-4,2)$, $(-3,-1)$, $(-2,-3)$, $(-1,-3)$, $(0,-2)$, $(1,-1)$, $(2,1)$, $(3,2)$, $(4,3)$, $(5,5)$, $(6,5)$

14
Vectors, Matrices, and Linear Equations

14.1 Introduction

In this chapter, some problems will be considered which can be handled by the use of matrix and vector notation. A simple marketing example will be developed, and aspects of problems arising from this example will be used as a theme for the entire chapter. The main mathematical ideas involve matrix-vector multiplication, matrix multiplication, and the solution of linear systems of equations. Simple modules will be constructed, which will enable the reader to perform the computations associated with the problems simply and elegantly.

14.2 A Marketing Example

As an introduction to the use of vectors and matrices, consider the following competetive marketing problem. Assume that two bakeries A and B compete for the bread market in a particular city. A certain exchange of customers occurs between the two firms: each month 90% of bakery A's customers stay and 10% switch to B; at the same time, 80% of B's customers stay and 20% switch to A.

If the objective of the study is a determination of the way in which the market shares evolve with time, then the first step should be the construction of a model. Bakery A's fraction of the market will be represented by x and B's share by y, so that $x+y = 1$, assuming that A and B share the entire market between them.

Letting x' and y' be the shares after one month, it is seen that

$$x' = 0.9x + 0.2y \tag{14.1}$$

$$y' = 0.1x + 0.8y$$

In matrix notation, this could be written as

$$Z' = T \times Z,$$

where

$$T = \begin{bmatrix} 0.9 & 0.2 \\ 0.1 & 0.8 \end{bmatrix} , \quad Z' = \begin{bmatrix} x' \\ y' \end{bmatrix} , \quad Z = \begin{bmatrix} x \\ y \end{bmatrix} \tag{14.2}$$

Matrix T is the representation of the *transformation* which changes Z to Z'. The *vector* of market shares Z with elements x and y is changed to Z' by multiplying Z by the *matrix* T.

The rule for this multiplication is that the elements in the first row of matrix T are multiplied, element by element, with the corresponding elements of vector Z. The first element of Z' is the sum of these products. Similarly, the second element of Z' is the sum of products of elements of the second row of T with the corresponding elements of vector Z.

For example, if the initial shares are $x = 0.4$ and $y = 0.6$ then the shares after one month will be

$$Z' = \begin{bmatrix} 0.9 & 0.2 \\ 0.1 & 0.8 \end{bmatrix} \times \begin{bmatrix} 0.4 \\ 0.6 \end{bmatrix} = \begin{bmatrix} 0.9 \times 0.4 + 0.2 \times 0.6 \\ 0.1 \times 0.4 + 0.8 \times 0.6 \end{bmatrix} = \begin{bmatrix} 0.48 \\ 0.52 \end{bmatrix}$$

That is, $x' = 0.48$ and $y' = 0.52$.

14.3 Matrix-Vector Multiplication

The rule for performing the multiplication in the previous section may be generalized for matrices and vectors of any size. Suppose that the multiplication is to be done for a matrix of size $n \times n$ and a vector of size n, represented by

$$T = \begin{bmatrix} t_{11} & t_{12} & t_{13} & \cdots & t_{1n} \\ t_{21} & t_{22} & t_{23} & \cdots & t_{2n} \\ t_{31} & t_{32} & t_{33} & \cdots & t_{3n} \\ \cdot & \cdot & \cdot & & \cdot \\ \cdot & \cdot & \cdot & & \cdot \\ \cdot & \cdot & \cdot & & \cdot \\ t_{n1} & t_{n2} & t_{n3} & \cdots & t_{nn} \end{bmatrix} \quad \text{and} \quad Z' = \begin{bmatrix} z_1 \\ z_2 \\ z_3 \\ \cdot \\ \cdot \\ \cdot \\ z_n \end{bmatrix} \tag{14.3}$$

The rule for multiplication of $T \times Z$ to give Z' is that the corresponding elements in row r of matrix T and in vector Z are multiplied in pairs and these n products are summed to give element r of Z'. This is done for $r = 1, 2, \cdots, n$. A formula for the operation is

$$z'_r = t_{r1} \times z_1 + t_{r2} \times z_2 + t_{r3} \times z_3 + \cdots + t_{rn} \times z_n, \quad r = 1, 2, \cdots, n.$$

It is convenient to represent such sums by a summation symbol and an equivalent form is then

$$z'_r = \sum_{i=1}^{n} t_{ri} \times z_i, \quad r = 1, 2, \cdots, n. \tag{14.4}$$

14.3.1 A Module for Matrix-Vector Multiplication

This matrix-vector multiplication is a good candidate for the construction of a module, since the operation is an important tool in solving many problems. The form of the module will be

smodule matvec (**imports**: n, T, Z; **exports**: V)

This module accepts as import an integer n, a matrix T of dimension n*n, and a vector Z of dimension n. Its export is a vector V, the matrix-vector product of T with Z. A first version of this module follows as Figure 14.1.

Figure 14.1   First version of a pseudo-code module for matrix-vector multiplication.

smodule matvec (**imports**: n, T, Z; **exports**: V)

1. For each element of V, $v_r \leftarrow$ sum of products of elements of row r of T with elements of Z.

end module

---

a) Refining Step **1.**   To account for all elements of vector V, a **while** loop is used to vary the row r from 1 to n and to compute the elements of V as follows:

```
    * For each row r, form the sum of products of elements of row r of T
    * with vector Z.

    r ← 1
    while r ≤ n do
    ┌
    │  1.1  vᵣ ← Σⁿᵢ₌₁ tᵣᵢ * zᵢ
    │
    │  r ← r + 1
    └
```

b) Refining Step **1.1**   To compute the elements of V, another **while** loop is used to accumulate the sums of the products of corresponding elements in row r of matrix T and vector Z.

* Accumulate the products.

sum ← 0
i ← 1
while i ≤ n **do**
$$\left[\begin{array}{l} \text{sum} \leftarrow \text{sum} + t_{ri} * z_i \\ i \leftarrow i + 1 \end{array}\right.$$
v_r ← sum

c) Final Version of the Algorithm   The complete algorithm may now be assembled, and is shown as Figure 14.2.

Figure 14.2   Final version of the pseudo-code module for matrix-vector multiplication.

smodule matvec (**imports**: n, T, Z; **exports**: V)

* Module to form the matrix-vector product, V = T×Z.

* Variables used:
* n - import dimension of arrays
* T - import matrix (n×n)
* Z - import vector (n×1)
* V - export vector (n×1)

* For each row r, form the sum of products of the elements of row r of T with vector Z.

r ← 1
while r ≤ n **do**
$$\left[\begin{array}{l} \text{* Accumulate the products.} \\ \text{sum} \leftarrow 0 \\ i \leftarrow 1 \\ \textbf{while } i \leq n \textbf{ do} \\ \quad \left[\begin{array}{l} \text{sum} \leftarrow \text{sum} + t_{ri} * z_i \\ i \leftarrow i + 1 \end{array}\right. \\ v_r \leftarrow \text{sum} \\ r \leftarrow r + 1 \end{array}\right.$$
end module

d) Conversion to WATFIV-S   A WATFIV-S version of the module is given as a subroutine in Figure 14.3.

e) Testing the Subroutine   The use of this subroutine is illustrated by using the numerical data of the example at the end of Section 14.2, in the program of Figure 14.4. Its output appears in Figure 14.5.

```
C Figure 14.3 -- Subroutine MATVEC
C                Subprogram to multiply matrix T by vector Z to
C                produce vector V.
C******************************************************************
C N - dimension of all arrays
C T - import matrix (NxN)
C Z - import vector (Nx1)
C V - export vector (Nx1)
C******************************************************************
      SUBROUTINE MATVEC(N,T,Z,V)

      INTEGER N, R, I
      REAL T(N,N), Z(N), V(N), SUM

C For each row R, sum the products of the elements of row R of T
C with vector Z.
      R = 1
      WHILE(R .LE. N) DO
         SUM = 0.
         I = 1
         WHILE(I .LE. N) DO
            SUM = SUM + T(R,I)*Z(I)
            I = I + 1
         END WHILE
         V(R) = SUM
         R = R + 1
      END WHILE
      RETURN
      END
```

```
C Figure 14.4 -- Program to illustrate the use of
C                 subroutine MATVEC.
C******************************************************************
C T  - transformation matrix
C Z  - vector to be transformed
C ZP - transformed vector
C******************************************************************
       INTEGER I, J, N
       REAL T(2,2), Z(2), ZP(2)
C Input and echo matrix T and vector Z.
       N = 2
       READ, ((T(I,J), J=1,N), I=1,N)
       READ, (Z(I), I=1,N)
       PRINT, 'MATRIX T'
       I = 1
       WHILE (I .LE. N) DO
          PRINT, (T(I,J), J=1,N)
          I = I + 1
       END WHILE
       PRINT, ' '
       PRINT, 'VECTOR Z'
       PRINT, (Z(I), I=1,N)
C Form the matrix-vector product ZP = T*Z.
       CALL MATVEC(N,T,Z,ZP)
C Print out the transformed vector.
       PRINT, ' '
       PRINT, 'VECTOR ZP'
       PRINT, (ZP(I), I=1,N)
       STOP
       END
C Subroutine MATVEC is placed here.
$ENTRY
   0.9, 0.2
   0.1, 0.8
   0.4, 0.6
```

Handwritten annotation:

```
R = 1
WHILE(R.LE.N) DO
   SUM = 0.0
   J = 1
   WHILE(J.LE N)
      SUM = SUM + T(R,J) * Z(J)
      J = J+1
   END WHILE
   ZP() = SUM
   R = R+1
END WHILE
```

Figure 14.5   Output from the test program of Figure 14.4.

MATRIX T
0.89999990	0.19999990
0.10000000	0.80000000

VECTOR Z
0.39999990	0.60000000

VECTOR ZP
0.47999980	0.51999990

14.3.2 Applications of Matrix-Vector Multiplication

The matrix-vector multiplication module may be used to answer a number of questions about the behavior of the bread marketing model. For example, it may be used to determine the market shares after two years, given the transition rules for each month. Alternately, the effects of an advertising campaign designed to alter the brand-switching behavior could be studied as could the effects of a third competitor in the market.

Determination of the market shares after two years may be addressed by a simple modification to the program of Figure 14.4. Solution of this problem requires that the monthly tranformation be applied 24 times to the initial vector. To do this requires that the line CALL MATVEC(N,T,Z,ZP) of Figure 14.4 be replaced by the **while** loops of the following code.

```
I = 1
WHILE(I .LE. 24) DO
   CALL MATVEC(N,T,Z,ZP)
   J = 1
   WHILE(J .LE. N) DO
      Z(J) = ZP(J)
      J = J + 1
   END WHILE
   I = I + 1
END WHILE
```

Notice that the outer loop invokes the matrix-vector multiplication 24 times. The inner loop copies the output from one transformation, ZP, to Z, where it may be used as input for the next transformation.

The second problem, which deals with the effects of an advertising campaign, could be dealt with using this model by simply altering the definition of the transformation matrix at the point in the program which corresponds to the time of the campaign. This problem is left as an exercise (see Exercise 14.6).

The effect of a third competitor is a bit more complicated and will now be examined in detail. Suppose that bakeries A and B compete with brand-switching occurring each month according to the transformation T of Section 14.2. Suppose further that a new bakery C starts operations after a market survey which indicates that it could attract the business of half of all switching customers, and 10% of all other customers of A and B. The survey also suggests that bakery C could retain 80% of its customers each month and lose 10% to each of A and B.

Assuming that A and B each have half of the market when C starts operations, what will be the distribution of market shares after 1, 2, and 3 years?

a) Problem Analysis   If the market shares of A, B, and C are represented by x, y, z and x', y', z' at the beginning and end of a month, respectively, then the information given produces the following equation for the new value of x:

$$x' = 0.81x+0.10y+0.10z$$

The terms in this equation are found by observing that A previously retained 90% of its market but now 10% of the 90% or 9% switches to C, leaving A with 81%. This gives the term $0.81x$. A previously gained 20% of B's customers each month but now half go to C, producing the term $0.10y$. C loses 10% of its market to A, producing the term $0.10z$.

Similar arguments are applied to deduce the system of equations:

$$x' = 0.81x+0.10y+0.10z \tag{14.5}$$

$$y' = 0.05x+0.72y+0.10z$$

$$z' = 0.14x + 0.18y + 0.80z$$

As before, this may be represented as a matrix-vector multiplication $Z' = T \times Z$, where

$$T = \begin{bmatrix} 0.81 & 0.10 & 0.10 \\ 0.05 & 0.72 & 0.10 \\ 0.14 & 0.18 & 0.80 \end{bmatrix}, \quad Z' = \begin{bmatrix} x' \\ y' \\ z' \end{bmatrix}, \quad \text{and} \quad Z = \begin{bmatrix} x \\ y \\ z \end{bmatrix} \tag{14.6}$$

b) Developing the Algorithm The general structure of an algorithm for the solution of the problem should now be clear. A first version is shown as Figure 14.6.

Figure 14.6 First version of a pseudo-code algorithm for the Three Bakery Problem.

```
* Algorithm to compute the market shares of the Three Bakery Problem.

* Variables used:
* n - size of arrays
* T - transformation matrix (n×n)
* Z - vector of market shares
* ZP - transformed vector of shares at the end of a month

* Input and echo-print the elements of the transformation matrix
* and the vector of initial shares.
get n, T, Z
put 'The array size is', n
put 'The transformation matrix T is', T
put 'The initial vector of market shares Z is', Z

* Compute the market shares for 1, 2, and 3 years.
years ← 1
while years ≤ 3 do
    1.  For each of the 12 months, transform the old vector of market shares Z to the
        new vector ZP using matvec, then copy ZP to Z.
    2.  Record the year-end market position.
    years ← years + 1
end
```

---

c) Refining Step **1.** This step corresponds closely to the WATFIV-S code added to solve the first problem. In pseudo code:

* For each of the 12 months, transform Z to ZP and copy ZP to Z.

months ← 1
while months ≤ 12 **do**

> **call** matvec (n, T, Z; ZP)
>
> **1.1** Z ← ZP
>
> months ← months + 1

d) Refining Step **1.1**   Step **1.1** requires refinement since the replacement of *vector* Z by *vector* ZP cannot be done directly in WATFIV-S. The pseudo-code expansion of this step is:

* Copy ZP to Z.

i ← 1
while i ≤ n **do**

> $z_i ← zp_i$
> i ← i + 1

e) Refining Step **2.**   This refinement is straightforward.

* Record the year-end market position.

put 'After year', years
put 'Market shares are'
put (z_i, i ← 1 to 3)

f) Final Program   The complete algorithm may now be assembled and converted to WATFIV-S as shown in Figure 14.7. Output from the WATFIV-S program follows as Figure 14.8.

```
C Figure 14.7 -- Program to compute market shares of the
C               Three Bakery Problem.

C****************************************************************

C T  - transformation matrix
C Z  - vector of market shares at the start of a month
C ZP - transformed vector of shares at the end of a month

C****************************************************************
        INTEGER I, J, MONTHS, YEARS, N
        REAL T(3,3), Z(3), ZP(3)

C Input and echo-print the elements of the transformation
C matrix and vector of initial shares.
        READ, N
        READ, ((T(I,J), J=1,N), I=1,N)
        READ, (Z(I), I=1,N)
        PRINT, 'MATRIX T'
        I = 1
        WHILE(I .LE. N) DO
            PRINT, (T(I,J), J=1,N)
            I = I + 1
        END WHILE
        PRINT, ' '
        PRINT, 'VECTOR Z'
        PRINT, (Z(I), I=1,N)

C Compute the market shares for 1, 2, and 3 years.
        YEARS = 1
        WHILE(YEARS .LE. 3) DO

C           Transform the monthly market shares 12 times.
            MONTHS = 1
            WHILE(MONTHS .LE. 12) DO
                CALL MATVEC(N,T,Z,ZP)

C               Copy ZP to Z.
                I = 1
                WHILE(I .LE. N) DO
                    Z(I) = ZP(I)
                    I = I + 1
                END WHILE
                MONTHS = MONTHS + 1
            END WHILE

C           Print the year-end market position.
            PRINT, ' '
            PRINT, 'AFTER YEAR',YEARS
            PRINT, 'MARKET SHARES ARE'
            PRINT, (ZP(I), I=1,N)
            YEARS = YEARS + 1
        END WHILE
        STOP
        END

C Subroutine MATVEC is placed here.
$ENTRY
 3
 0.81, 0.1,  0.1
 0.05, 0.72, 0.1
 0.14, 0.18, 0.8
 0.5,  0.5,  0.0
```

Figure 14.8   Output from the Three Bakery Problem program of Figure 14.7.

```
MATRIX  T
              0.81000000              0.10000000              0.10000000
              0.05000000              0.72000000              0.10000000
              0.13999990              0.18000000              0.80000000
VECTOR  Z
              0.50000000              0.50000000              0.00000000
AFTER  YEAR            1
MARKET  SHARES  ARE
              0.34737300              0.21755930              0.43506530
AFTER  YEAR            2
MARKET  SHARES  ARE
              0.34486760              0.21776530              0.43736210
AFTER  YEAR            3
MARKET  SHARES  ARE
              0.34482570              0.21778380              0.43738310
```

g) Discussion of Results   After 3 years, indeed after 1 year, bakery A has about 34% of the market, bakery B has about 22%, and bakery C about 44%. One might conclude that bakery C has been very successful in moving into this market. Alternately, one may conclude that A and B must be more aggressive in their sales efforts.

14.4   Multiplication of Matrices.

In the previous section, the transformation of a vector Z to another vector Z′ was represented by Z′ = T×Z. T was called the transformation matrix and the formation of T×Z was called a matrix-vector multiplication. In many circumstances, there will be more than one transformation involved, say Z″ = U×Z′, where U is another matrix. This could be written in two ways:

Z″ = U×(T×Z), or Z″ = (U×T)×Z.

Although very similar in appearance, the brackets radically alter the interpretation of the equations. In the first equation the *matrix* U multiplies the *vector* T×Z. In the second equation the *matrix* U×T multiplies the *vector* Z. However, the results should be the same, and this fact will be used to decide what is meant by matrix U×T. The notation suggests that U×T be called the *product* of U and T, but the rules for its computation must be deduced.

Returning to the simple marketing example (see equation 14.2) it might be desired to form Z″ = T×Z′ = (T×T)×Z. Using the rules for matrix-vector multiplication gives

Z″ = T×Z′

$$= \begin{bmatrix} 0.9 & 0.2 \\ 0.1 & 0.8 \end{bmatrix} \times \begin{bmatrix} 0.9x+0.2y \\ 0.1x+0.8y \end{bmatrix}$$

$$= \begin{bmatrix} 0.9\,(0.9x+0.2y\,)+0.2\,(0.1x+0.8y\,) \\ 0.1\,(0.9x+0.2y\,)+0.8\,(0.1x+0.8y\,) \end{bmatrix}$$

The x and y terms in this vector may be separated and the result expressed as $Z'' = R \times Z$.

$$Z'' = \begin{bmatrix} 0.9 \times 0.9 + 0.2 \times 0.1 & 0.9 \times 0.2 + 0.2 \times 0.8 \\ 0.1 \times 0.9 + 0.8 \times 0.1 & 0.1 \times 0.2 + 0.8 \times 0.8 \end{bmatrix} \times \begin{bmatrix} x \\ y \end{bmatrix}$$

Closer inspection reveals that the *first column* of R is simply the matrix-vector product of matrix T with the vector consisting of the *first column* of T. Similarly, the *second column* of R is the matrix-vector product of T with the *second column* of T. R would be referred to as T^2.

Matrix multiplication makes sense in some applications even when the matrices have different dimensions; it is necessary that the number of columns of the matrix on the left should match the number of rows of the matrix on the right. The general formula for the product of a matrix A having m rows and n columns with a matrix B having n rows and k columns is

$$c_{rs} = \sum_{i=1}^{n} a_{ri} \times b_{is} \; ; \quad r = 1,2, \cdots ,m; \; s = 1,2, \cdots ,k. \tag{14.7}$$

Note that the product $C = A \times B$ has m rows and k columns.

14.4.1   A Matrix Multiplication Module

Conversion of the formula for matrix multiplication to a module is desirable, since such a module may be useful in many applications. The module will have the form

smodule matmpy (**imports**: m, n, k, A, B; **exports**: C)

The module accepts as imports the integers m, n, and k, a matrix A (dimension m×n), and a matrix B (dimension n×k), and produces for export the matrix C (dimension m×k). A first version is shown as Figure 14.9.

Figure 14.9   First version of a pseudo-code module for matrix multiplication.

smodule matmpy (**imports**: m, n, k, A, B; **exports**: C)

1.   For each element c_{rs} of matrix **C**, compute $c_{rs} \leftarrow$ sum of products of elements of row r of **A** with column s of **B**.

end module

---

a) Refining Step **1.**   Matrix C will have m rows and k columns. An outer loop is needed to produce each of the m rows. Within this outer loop, an inner loop is used to compute each of the k column entries for the current row.

* Compute c_{rs}, for all r, s.

r ← 1
while r ≤ m **do**

$\quad$ s ← 1
$\quad$ **while** s ≤ k **do**

$\qquad$ **1.1** $c_{rs} \leftarrow \sum_{i=1}^{n} a_{ri} * b_{is}$

$\qquad$ s ← s + 1

$\quad$ r ← r + 1

b) Refining Step **1.1**   Formation of this sum is quite straightforward.

* Sum the products of elements of row **r** of **A** and column **s** of **B**.

sum ← 0
i ← 1
while i ≤ n **do**

$\quad$ sum ← sum + a_{ri} * b_{is}
$\quad$ i ← i + 1

c_{rs} ← sum

c) Final Version of the Matrix Multiplication Algorithm   This algorithm is assembled in Figure 14.10.

d) A WATFIV-S *Matrix Multiplication Subroutine*   A WATFIV-S version follows as Figure 14.11.

Handwritten notes (rotated in margin):

```
* N - no. rows in first Matrix
* Y - no. columns in first matrix
* P - no. rows in second matrix
* L - no. columns in the second matrix

Integer
Real T(10,10), Z(10,10), ZP(10,10), Sum
READ, N, Y, P, L
READ, ((T(I,J),J=1,Y),I=1,N)
READ, ((Z(I,J),J=1,L),I=1,P)
PRINT, 'MATRIX T IS'
I=1
WHILE(I.LE.N)DO
  PRINT, (T(I,J),J=1,Y)
  I=I+1
END WHILE
PRINT, 'MATRIX Z IS'
I=1
WHILE(I.LE.P)DO
  PRINT, (Z(I,J),J=1,L)
  I=I+1
END WHILE
IF(V.NE.P)THEN DO
  PRINT, 'Matrix T & Z are not comp'
ELSE DO
  R=1
  WHILE(R.LE.N)DO
    S=1
    WHILE(S.LE.L)DO
      I=1
      SUM=0.0
      WHILE(I.LE.P)DO
        SUM=SUM+T(R,I)*Z(I,S)
        I=I+1
      ENDWHILE
      S=S+1
    ENDWHILE
    R=R+1
  END WHILE
```

Figure 14.10   Final version of the pseudo-code module for matrix multiplication.

smodule matmpy (**imports**: m, n, k, A, B; **exports**: C)

* Module for matrix multiplication

* Variables used:
* A - import matrix (m×n)
* B - import matrix (n×k)
* C - export matrix (m×k)
* sum - temporary storage for sum of products

* Compute c_{rs}, for all r, s.

r ← 1
while r ≤ m **do**

    s ← 1
    while s ≤ k **do**

        * Sum the products of elements of row r of A and column s of B.
        sum ← 0
        i ← 1
        while i ≤ n **do**

            sum ← sum + a_{ri} * b_{is}
            i ← i + 1

        c_{rs} ← sum
        s ← s + 1

    r ← r + 1

end module

14.4.2   Applications of Matrix Multiplication

Matrix multiplication provides the tool needed to construct a single transformation which corresponds to a sequence of other transformations.

In the three bakery model of Section 14.3.2, a matrix was constructed which represented the transformation of market shares in a one-month period. It might be desirable to know the representation of the single transformation which corresponds to an entire year's evolution of the market. The matrix which represents this transformation is T^{12}, or the twelfth power of the matrix T. An algorithm to do this calculation will now be developed.

a) Developing an Algorithm for T^{12}   In the pseudo code given in Figure 14.12, note that some of the operations previously done on simple variables are now done on matrices. For example, B ← C means "assign the values in C to the corresponding places in B.' Indeed, it is just this freedom to work with matrices in this way which gives matrix notation such great power.

```
C Figure 14.11 -- Subroutine MATMPY
C                   Subprogram to form the matrix product C = A*B.
C******************************************************************
C A   - import matrix (MxN)
C B   - import matrix (NxK)
C C   - export matrix (MxK)
C SUM - temporary storage for sum of products
C******************************************************************
        SUBROUTINE MATMPY(M,N,K,A,B,C)

        INTEGER M, N, K, R, S, I
        REAL A(M,N), B(N,K), C(M,K), SUM
C For each R and S, sum the products of the elements of row R of A
C with elements of column S of B.
        R = 1
        WHILE (R .LE. M) DO
          S = 1
          WHILE (S .LE. K) DO
             SUM = 0.0
             I = 1
             WHILE (I .LE. N) DO
                SUM = SUM + A(R,I)*B(I,S)
                I = I + 1
             END WHILE
             C(R,S) = SUM
             S = S + 1
          END WHILE
          R = R + 1
        END WHILE
        RETURN
        END
```

b) A WATFIV-S *Final Version*   This algorithm is given as a WATFIV-S program in
Figure 14.13. A short segment is added at the end of the program to confirm that the
one-year transformation, T^{12}, produces the same results as T applied twelve times. The
output follows as Figure 14.14.

```
PRINT, 'The new matrix 2P is'
R = 1
[WHILE (R .LE. N) DO
    PRINT 6 (2P(R,S), S=1,C)
    R = R+1
[END WHILE
[END IF

4 Format (' ', >10 (F5.2,2X))
5 Format (' ', >10 (F5.2,2X))
6 Format (' ', >10 (F7.2,2X))

    4  5  6
```

Figure 14.12   Pseudo-code algorithm to compute T^{12}.

* Algorithm to compute T^{12} using the module **matmpy**.

* Variables used:
* n - size of arrays
* T - import matrix (n×n)
* B - matrix in which powers of T are developed
* C - temporary matrix storage

* Define the original matrix T and its size, n.

get n, T
put 'The original matrix T is'
put T

* Form T**2 in B initially.

call matmpy (n, n, n, T, T; B)

* Form the twelfth power of T in B.

powers ← 2
while powers < 12 **do**
```
    call matmpy (n, n, n, T, B; C)
    B ← C
    powers ← powers + 1
```
put 'One year transformation or T**12 is'
put B
stop

```
C Figure 14.13 - Program to compute T**12 using the subroutine
C                MATMPY and to verify the result.
C****************************************************************
C T  - transformation matrix
C B  - matrix in which powers of T are developed
C C  - temporary matrix storage
C Z  - Input vector of initial market shares
C ZP - Output vector of year-end shares
C****************************************************************
      INTEGER N, I, J, POWERS
      REAL T(3,3), B(3,3), C(3,3), Z(3), ZP(3)
C Input and echo the data.
      READ, N
      READ, ((T(I,J), J=1,N), I=1,N)
      PRINT, 'MATRIX T'
      I = 1
      WHILE(I .LE. N) DO
         PRINT, (T(I,J), J=1,N)
         I = I + 1
      END WHILE
```

```
C Figure 14.13 (continued)
C Form T**2 in B.
      CALL MATMPY(N,N,N,T,T,B)
C Form successive powers of T in B.
      POWERS = 2
      WHILE(POWERS .LT. 12) DO
          CALL MATMPY(N,N,N,T,B,C)
C         Copy C to B for the next step.
          I = 1
          WHILE(I .LE. N) DO
             J = 1
             WHILE(J .LE. N) DO
                B(I,J) = C(I,J)
                J = J + 1
             END WHILE
             I = I + 1
          END WHILE
          POWERS = POWERS + 1
      END WHILE
C Output results.
      PRINT, ' '
      PRINT, 'ONE YEAR TRANSFORMATION'
      I = 1
      WHILE(I .LE. N) DO
          PRINT, (B(I,J), J=1,N)
          I = I + 1
      END WHILE
C Test on market share data of Figure 14.8.
      READ, (Z(I), I=1,N)
      PRINT, ' '
      PRINT, 'INITIAL VECTOR OF MARKET SHARES'
      PRINT, (Z(I), I=1,N)

      CALL MATVEC(N,B,Z,ZP)

      PRINT, ' '
      PRINT, 'MARKET SHARES AFTER ONE YEAR'
      PRINT, (ZP(I), I=1,N)

      STOP
      END
C Subroutines MATMPY and MATVEC are placed here.
$ENTRY
  3
  0.81, 0.1,  0.1
  0.05, 0.72, 0.1
  0.14, 0.18, 0.8
  0.5,  0.5,  0.0
```

Figure 14.14   Output from the program from Figure 14.13.

```
MATRIX T
          0.81000000          0.10000000          0.10000000
          0.05000000          0.72000000          0.10000000
          0.13999990          0.18000000          0.80000000
ONE YEAR TRANSFORMATION
          0.35557800          0.33916810          0.33916830
          0.21228410          0.22283440          0.21960820
          0.43213560          0.43799480          0.44122130
INITIAL VECTOR OF MARKET SHARES
          0.50000000          0.50000000          0.00000000
MARKET SHARES AFTER ONE YEAR
          0.34737300          0.21755920          0.43506520
```

c) Notes on the Program   When the matrix T^{12} is used to multiply the vector
$(0.5,0.5,0.0)$, then the results agree quite closely with the one-year shares of
Figure 14.8, as they should. Roundoff errors differ slightly for the two computations. It
should also be observed that the program could be shortened if additional utility
programs were available. Some useful subroutines would provide for reading or printing
of the elements of a matrix by rows or the copying of the elements of one matrix to
another. Restructuring of the preceding program in this way is suggested as an exercise
(see Exercise 14.1). Other programming languages, notably *APL*, incorporate matrix
operations in a very concise way. In WATFIV-S, however, the programmer must rely on a
library of programs, which may be provided by the computing center or by the
programmer.

14.5   Undoing a Transformation or Solving Equations.

The previous problems have been concerned with predicting the future evolution of a
market. Sometimes it is also necessary to use similar information about the present state
of a system to deduce its previous state.

Suppose, for instance, that you are a tax investigator with the assignment of
deducing the market shares of the three bakeries one month ago, given the present
distribution of the market and the matrix T governing the monthly change in market
shares. Such information might be necessary to determine if reported incomes are
unreasonable.

In this problem, the notation of the previous sections will be used. Z will represent
the vector of market shares one month ago, and Z' will represent the present vector of
shares. As before, $T \times Z = Z'$, but now it is Z' which is known, and Z which is to be
found. Looking first at the two bakery model of Section 14.2, it is seen that
$(x',y') = (0.48,0.52)$ with (x,y) to be determined from

$$\begin{bmatrix} 0.9 & 0.2 \\ 0.1 & 0.8 \end{bmatrix} \times \begin{bmatrix} x \\ y \end{bmatrix} = \begin{bmatrix} 0.48 \\ 0.52 \end{bmatrix}. \tag{14.8}$$

Doing the matrix-vector multiplication gives

$$0.9x+0.2y = 0.48 \tag{14.9}$$

$$0.1x+0.8y = 0.52.$$

Written in this way, the two equations in two unknowns present a problem familiar to all readers from high school mathematics courses. The solution, also familiar, involves the elimination of one unknown from one equation. For example, *both sides* of the second equation of (14.9) might be multiplied by 9 to give

$$0.9x+7.2y = 4.68.$$

Subtracting the first equation (left side from left side and right side from right side) gives

$$(0.9-0.9)x+ (7.2-0.2)y = 4.68-0.48, \quad \text{or} \quad 7.0y = 4.2.$$

Now it is clear that $y = 0.6$, and substituting this into the first equation of (14.9) gives

$$0.9x+0.2 \times 0.6 = 0.48 \quad \text{or} \quad x = 0.4.$$

14.5.1 Solving Triangular Systems of Equations

Reflecting upon what was done to solve the system of equations, it is seen that the system was transformed to the *triangular form* shown below.

$$0.9x+0.2y = 0.48 \tag{14.10}$$

$$7.0y = 4.20$$

The solution was then easy to deduce from this form of the equations.

The general form of n equations in n unknowns is

$$
\begin{bmatrix}
a_{11} & a_{12} & a_{13} & \cdots & a_{1n} \\
a_{21} & a_{22} & a_{23} & \cdots & a_{2n} \\
a_{31} & a_{32} & a_{33} & \cdots & a_{3n} \\
\cdot & \cdot & \cdot & & \cdot \\
\cdot & \cdot & \cdot & & \cdot \\
\cdot & \cdot & \cdot & & \cdot \\
a_{n1} & a_{n2} & a_{n3} & \cdots & a_{nn}
\end{bmatrix}
\times
\begin{bmatrix}
z_1 \\
z_2 \\
z_3 \\
\cdot \\
\cdot \\
\cdot \\
z_n
\end{bmatrix}
=
\begin{bmatrix}
c_1 \\
c_2 \\
c_3 \\
\cdot \\
\cdot \\
\cdot \\
c_n
\end{bmatrix}. \tag{14.11}
$$

Observe that the solution to the system will be easy if it has the triangular form

$$
\begin{bmatrix}
t_{11} & t_{12} & t_{13} & \cdots & t_{1n} \\
0 & t_{22} & t_{23} & \cdots & t_{2n} \\
0 & 0 & t_{33} & \cdots & t_{3n} \\
\cdot & \cdot & \cdot & & \cdot \\
\cdot & \cdot & \cdot & & \cdot \\
\cdot & \cdot & \cdot & & \cdot \\
0 & 0 & 0 & \cdots & t_{nn}
\end{bmatrix}
\times
\begin{bmatrix}
z_1 \\ z_2 \\ z_3 \\ \cdot \\ \cdot \\ \cdot \\ z_n
\end{bmatrix}
=
\begin{bmatrix}
c_1 \\ c_2 \\ c_3 \\ \cdot \\ \cdot \\ \cdot \\ c_n
\end{bmatrix}. \tag{14.12}
$$

The solution proceeds by observing that

$$ z_n = \frac{c_n}{t_{nn}}. $$

Knowing this value permits solution for

$$ z_{n-1} = \frac{(c_{n-1} - t_{n-1,n} \times z_n)}{t_{n-1,n-1}}. $$

Knowing z_n and z_{n-1} then permits solution for $z_{n-2}, z_{n-3}, \cdots, z_1$. This process of *back-substitution* continues until all unknowns have been determined. Note, however, that the process fails if any one of the diagonal elements of T is zero, since a division by each diagonal element occurs once.

14.5.2   A Module for Solving Triangular Systems of Equations
Using the notation of the previous section, a module will be developed to solve the linear system of equations

   $T \times Z = C,$

where T is a triangular transformation matrix. A first version of the module is presented in Figure 14.15.

Figure 14.15   First version of a pseudo-code module for triangular linear equation solution.

smodule backsolve (**imports**: n, T, C; **exports**: Z)

1.   For each element of Z, starting at z_n, compute

$$ z_i \leftarrow (c_i - \sum_{j=i+1}^{n} t_{ij} * z_j) / t_{ii} $$

end module

---

*a) Refining Step **1.**   It is necessary to solve for the elements of Z in reverse order, starting with n and going to 1. Therefore, a **while** loop is constructed which reduces index i from n to 1. The solution for each of the Z entries is left as a summation formula for expansion at the next step.

* Starting with $z_n = c_n/t_{nn}$, solve for $z_{n-1}, z_{n-2}, \ldots, z_1$.

i ← n
while i ≥ 1 **do**

$$\quad \textbf{1.1} \quad z_i \leftarrow (c_i - \sum_{j=i+1}^{n} t_{ij} * z_j)/t_{ii}$$

$\quad$ i ← i − 1

b) Refining Step **1.1**   The operations involved in this computation may now be expanded. The portion of the formula in parentheses is called sum. sum is initalized at the i-th component of C. Then, a second **while** loop controls the substitution of "known" Z entries from i+1 to n in calculating sum.

sum ← c_i
j ← i + 1
while j ≤ n **do**

$\quad$ sum ← sum − t_{ij} * z_j
$\quad$ j ← j + 1

z_i ← sum/t_{ii}

c) Final Version of the Algorithm   The complete algorithm may now be assembled and is shown as Figure 14. 16. A WATFIV-S version follows as Figure 14.17. Output from tests of this module will be presented in a later section.

Figure 14.16   Final version of the pseudo-code module to solve triangular linear systems.

smodule backsolve (**imports**: n, T, C; **exports**: Z)

* Module to solve triangular linear systems.
* This module assumes that there is a unique solution.

* Variables used:
* n - import dimension of all arrays
* T - upper triangular coefficient matrix
* C - right-hand side of the linear system
* Z - solution of the system of equations
* sum - temporary storage for sum of products

* Starting with $z_n = c_n/t_{nn}$, solve for z_{n-1}, z_{n-2}, . . . , z_1.

```
i ← n
while i ≥ 1 do
      sum ← cᵢ
      j ← i + 1
      while j ≤ n do
            sum ← sum − tᵢⱼ * zⱼ
            j ← j + 1
      zᵢ ← sum/tᵢᵢ
      i ← i − 1
end module
```

14.5.3   Solving General Systems of Linear Equations.

In the previous section it was shown that the solution of triangular systems of linear equations was quite easy using the back-substitution algorithm. Therefore, the first step in solving a general linear system is to transform the system to an equivalent triangular system having the same solution.

To do this, it is necessary to examine some possible changes which could be made to a system of equations without changing its solution. Each equation in the system represents a valid statement about a relationship among the unknowns. If enough equations are given, then a solution may be found. In general, if there are n unknowns, n equations are needed. However, none of the equations is permitted to contradict the others, nor should any equation be a consequence of the others, if a unique solution is expected.

There are really only two valid operations which may be applied to a single equation. Both sides may be *multiplied* by the same nonzero constant or the same quantity may be *added* to both sides.

If there are *two* equations, one of them may be replaced by a new equation formed by adding a constant multiple of one equation to another. This was the process which lead to the conclusion earlier that

```
C Figure 14.17 -- Subroutine BSOLVE

C                        Subprogram to solve a triangular system of
C                        N equations in N unknowns.
C******************************************************************
C N    - the actual size of all arrays
C NDIM - the variable dimension of all arrays
C T    - upper triangular coefficient matrix of size NxN
C        (assumed to be non-singular)
C C    - right hand side of the system
C Z    - solution of the system of equations
C SUM  - temporary storage for sum of products
C******************************************************************
       SUBROUTINE BSOLVE(NDIM,N,T,Z,C)

       INTEGER NDIM, N, I, J
       REAL T(NDIM,NDIM), Z(NDIM), C(NDIM), SUM
C Starting with Z(N) = C(N)/T(N,N),
C solve for Z(N-1), Z(N-2), ... , Z(1).
       I = N
       WHILE(I .GE. 1) DO
          SUM = C(I)
          J = I + 1
          WHILE(J .LE. N) DO
             SUM = SUM - T(I,J)*Z(J)
             J = J + 1
          END WHILE
          Z(I) = SUM/T(I,I)
          I = I - 1
       END WHILE
       RETURN
       END
```

$$0.9x + 0.2y = 0.48$$

$$0.1x + 0.8y = 0.52$$

had the same solution as

$$0.9x + 0.2y = 0.48$$

$$7.0y = 4.20$$

For the general linear system

$$
\begin{bmatrix}
a_{11} & a_{12} & a_{13} & \cdots & a_{1n} \\
a_{21} & a_{22} & a_{23} & \cdots & a_{2n} \\
a_{31} & a_{32} & a_{33} & \cdots & a_{3n} \\
\cdot & \cdot & \cdot & & \cdot \\
\cdot & \cdot & \cdot & & \cdot \\
\cdot & \cdot & \cdot & & \cdot \\
a_{n1} & a_{n2} & a_{n3} & \cdots & a_{nn}
\end{bmatrix}
\times
\begin{bmatrix}
z_1 \\
z_2 \\
z_3 \\
\cdot \\
\cdot \\
\cdot \\
z_n
\end{bmatrix}
=
\begin{bmatrix}
c_1 \\
c_2 \\
c_3 \\
\cdot \\
\cdot \\
\cdot \\
c_n
\end{bmatrix} .
\tag{14.13}
$$

the reduction to triangular form may be carried out systematically. Any equation may be altered by adding to it a multiple of any other equation. Notice that this corresponds to adding a multiple of one row of the coefficient matrix, A, to another row, with the same operations done on the right hand side, C.

Provided that the first element of the first row is not zero, multiples of this row may be added to subsequent rows to produce zeros in the first position of the subsequent rows. The elements of these rows are changed, and this is denoted by the use of primes.

$$
\begin{bmatrix}
a_{11} & a_{12} & a_{13} & \cdots & a_{1n} \\
0 & a'_{22} & a'_{23} & \cdots & a'_{2n} \\
0 & a'_{32} & a'_{33} & \cdots & a'_{3n} \\
\cdot & \cdot & \cdot & & \cdot \\
\cdot & \cdot & \cdot & & \cdot \\
0 & \cdot & \cdot & & \cdot \\
0 & a'_{n2} & a'_{n3} & \cdots & a'_{nn}
\end{bmatrix}
\times
\begin{bmatrix}
z_1 \\ z_2 \\ z_3 \\ \cdot \\ \cdot \\ \cdot \\ z_n
\end{bmatrix}
=
\begin{bmatrix}
c_1 \\ c'_2 \\ c'_3 \\ \cdot \\ \cdot \\ \cdot \\ c'_n
\end{bmatrix} .
\qquad (14.14)
$$

Similarly, if the second element of row two is not zero, multiples of row two may be added to subsequent rows to produce

$$
\begin{bmatrix}
a_{11} & a_{12} & a_{13} & \cdots & a_{1n} \\
0 & a'_{22} & a'_{23} & \cdots & a'_{2n} \\
0 & 0 & a''_{33} & \cdots & a''_{3n} \\
\cdot & \cdot & \cdot & & \cdot \\
\cdot & \cdot & \cdot & & \cdot \\
0 & 0 & \cdot & & \cdot \\
0 & 0 & a''_{n3} & \cdots & a''_{nn}
\end{bmatrix}
\times
\begin{bmatrix}
z_1 \\ z_2 \\ z_3 \\ \cdot \\ \cdot \\ \cdot \\ z_n
\end{bmatrix}
=
\begin{bmatrix}
c_1 \\ c'_2 \\ c''_3 \\ \cdot \\ \cdot \\ \cdot \\ c''_n
\end{bmatrix} .
\qquad (14.15)
$$

This process may be continued to give a triangular system, provided that the diagonal elements remain nonzero at each step.

If a diagonal element should happen to be zero, it is a simple matter to exchange that row with a subsequent row whose first entry is not zero. If no subsequent row has a nonzero initial entry, then the equations do not have a unique solution. It is acceptable to interchange rows of the coefficient matrix since this corresponds to writing down the original equations in a different order, which should not affect the solution.

The process of creating a triangular coefficient matrix is called *Gaussian Elimination.* It will now be developed more formally as a pseudo-code algorithm.

a) Developing a Gaussian Elimination Algorithm The previous discussion permits the first version of the algorithm to be outlined directly as a module, as shown in Figure 14.18.

Figure 14.18   First version of a pseudo-code module for Gaussian Elimination.

smodule gauss (**imports**: n, T, C; **exports**: T, C, flag)

* Module to convert the linear system T*Z = C to triangular form.

* Variables used:
* n - import dimension of all arrays
* T - import (general) and export (triangular) matrix
* C - import and export vector
* flag - error condition (no solution) if **flag** = 1

1.   For each diagonal element t_{ii}, transform the elements $t_{i+1,i}$, $t_{i+2,i}$, . . . , $t_{n,i}$ to zero by row operations.
end module

---

b) Refining Step **1.**   This first refinement will incorporate the doublé loop structure required to step along the diagonal and to create zeros in subdiagonal positions.

> * Create zeros below t_{ii}, for i ← 1, 2, . . . , n−1.
>
> i ← 1
> **while** i ≤ n−1 **do**
> >   j ← i + 1
> >   **while** j ≤ n **do**
> > >   **1.1** Create a zero in position (j,i) by a row operation.
> > >   j ← j + 1
> >
> >   i ← i + 1

c) Refining Step **1.1**   A zero may be created in position i of row j if row j is replaced by

$$(\text{row } j) - (\text{row } i)*t_{ji}/t_{ii}$$

This requires another loop to step along all elements of row j.

> * Do the row operation (first attempt).
> k ← i + 1
> **while** k ≤ n **do**
> > t_{jk} ← t_{jk} − $t_{ik}*(t_{ji}/t_{ii})$
> >   k ← k + 1
> c_j ← c_j − $c_i*(t_{ji}/t_{ii})$

Since the ratio in parentheses is independent of k, it should be computed only once for each entry to this loop. This is a level two efficiency optimization, as described in Chapter 5. The refinement follows:

* Do the row operation (second attempt).

$k \leftarrow i + 1$
ratio $\leftarrow t_{ji}/t_{ii}$
while $k \le n$ **do**

> $t_{jk} \leftarrow t_{jk} - t_{ik}*\text{ratio}$
> $k \leftarrow k + 1$

$c_j \leftarrow c_j - c_i*\text{ratio}$

d) Further Refinements   The algorithm as refined to this point will fail if the diagonal or *pivot* element is zero. For reasons beyond the scope of this text, the algorithm may also produce inaccurate results if the pivot element is small.

For these reasons, a good Gaussian Elimination algorithm incorporates row interchanges so that the row with the largest possible element in position *i* (at the *i*-th stage) is moved to row *i*. This may be accomplished by adding an additional step, say **1.2**, in the refinement of Step **1.**, as follows

$i \leftarrow 1$
while $i \le n{-}1$ **do**

> **1.2** Search for the row with maximum i-th element and exchange with row i.
>
> $j \leftarrow i + 1$
> **while** $j \le n$ **do**
>
> > * Do the row operation.
> >
> > $k \leftarrow i + 1$
> > ratio $\leftarrow t_{ji}/t_{ii}$
> > **while** $k \le n$ **do**
> >
> > > $t_{jk} \leftarrow t_{jk} - t_{ik}*\text{ratio}$
> > > $k \leftarrow k + 1$
> >
> > $c_j \leftarrow c_j - c_i*\text{ratio}$
> > $j \leftarrow j + 1$
>
> $i \leftarrow i + 1$

e) Refining Step **1.2**   This pseudo-code segment will be presented directly in Figure 14.19, since such search algorithms were fully described in Chapter 12.

f) Final Version of the Gaussian Elimination Algorithm   The preceding refinements may now be assembled and the complete module is presented in Figure 14.20.

Figure 14.19   Search and row interchange pseudo code.

* Find the maximum $t_{index,i}$ of t_{ii}, $t_{i+1,i}$, . . . , t_{ni}.

```
j ← i + 1
index ← i
max ← abs(t_ii)
while j ≤ n do
        if abs(t_ji) > max then
                max ← abs(t_ji)
                index ← j
        j ← j + 1
```

* If **index** > i, exchange rows i and **index**.

```
if index > i then
        k ← i
        while k ≤ n do
                temp ← t_ik
                t_ik ← t_index,k
                t_index,k ← temp
                k ← k + 1
        temp ← c_i
        c_i ← c_index
        c_index ← temp
```

* Set **flag** = 1 if the pivot will be zero.

```
if max = 0 then
        flag ← 1
```

Handwritten notes:

```
• multiplies matrix by a scalar
SUBROUTINE MBYS(P,T,Q,N)
REAL P(5,5), Q(5,5)
DO 31  I=1,N
  DO 30 J=1,N
    Q(J,I)=T*P(J,I)
```

```
• program to square a matrix
Subroutine MBYM(P,R,N)
REAL P(5,5), R(5,5)
DO 12 K=1,N
  DO 12 I=1,N
    R(K,I)=0
    DO 12 I=1,N
      R(K,I)=R(K,I)+ P(K,I)*P(I,I)
12 RETURN
   END
```

```
multiplies a vector by a matrix
SUBROUTINE MBYV(TM,Y,C,N)
REAL TM(5,5), Y(5), C(5)
DO 21 J=1,N
  SUM=0.0
  DO 20 I=1,N
    SUM=SUM+TM(J,I)*Y(I)
20 CONTINUE
   C(J)=SUM
21 CONTINUE
```

Figure 14.20   Final version of the pseudo-code module for Gaussian Elimination.

smodule gauss (**imports**: n, T, C; **exports**: T, C, flag)

* Module to convert the linear system T*Z = C to triangular form.

* Variables used:
* **n** - import dimension of all arrays
* **T** - import matrix (general) and export (triangular)
* **C** - import and export vector
* **flag** - error condition (no solution) if **flag** = 1
* **max** - largest (in magnitude) subdiagonal element
* **index** - row in which max is found
* **ratio** - ratio of subdiagonal to diagonal elements

flag ← 0
i ← 1

```
        DIMENSION  A(10,0), W(10,) IR(10), IC(6)
        READ (5,1) ((A(I,J)) J=1,10), I=1,10)
        READ (5,1) (W(I), I=1,10)
  1     FORMAT (5F12.8)
        CALL LNEQN (A, 10, 10, 10, W, IR, IC, IER)
        PRINT , IER
        PRINT , (W(I), I=1,10)
        CALL EXIT
        END
```

$$\begin{bmatrix} & \\ & \end{bmatrix}\begin{bmatrix} x_1 \\ x_2 \\ x_3 \end{bmatrix} = \begin{bmatrix} \\ \\ \end{bmatrix}$$

CALL LNEQN (A, IA, JA, MA, W, IR, IC,

name of matrix   # rows   # columns   # N

if no solution   error parameter is 1

Figure 14.20   Final version of the pseudo-code module for Gaussian Elimination. (continued)

while $i \leq n-1$ **do**

   * Find the maximum $t_{index,i}$ of t_{ii}, $t_{i+1,i}$, . . . , t_{ni}.

   $j \leftarrow i + 1$
   $index \leftarrow i$
   $max \leftarrow abs(t_{ii})$
   while $j \leq n$ **do**

      if $abs(t_{ji}) > max$ **then**

         $max \leftarrow abs(t_{ji})$
         $index \leftarrow j$

      $j \leftarrow j + 1$

   * If $index > i$, exchange rows i and $index$.

   if $index > i$ **then**

      $k \leftarrow i$
      while $k \leq n$ **do**

         $temp \leftarrow t_{ik}$
         $t_{ik} \leftarrow t_{index,k}$
         $t_{index,k} \leftarrow temp$
         $k \leftarrow k + 1$

      $temp \leftarrow c_i$
      $c_i \leftarrow c_{index}$
      $c_{index} \leftarrow temp$

   * If maximum pivot is zero, set **flag** $\leftarrow 1$ and
   * bypass the row operations at stage i.

   if $max = 0$ **then**

      $flag \leftarrow 1$

   else

      $j \leftarrow i + 1$
      while $j \leq n$ **do**

         * Create a zero in position (j,i) by a row operation.

         $k \leftarrow i + 1$
         $ratio \leftarrow t_{ji}/t_{ii}$
         while $k \leq n$ **do**

            $t_{jk} \leftarrow t_{jk} - t_{ik} * ratio$
            $k \leftarrow k + 1$

         $c_j \leftarrow c_j - c_i * ratio$
         $j \leftarrow j + 1$

   $i \leftarrow i + 1$

end module

g) A WATFIV-S *Gaussian Elimination Module*   The final version of the module is presented as a WATFIV-S subroutine in Figure 14.21. The translation is quite direct, but it may be worth noting the use of both NDIM as the potential dimension of the arrays and N as the actual(smaller) dimension of all arrays. Both the pseudo-code and WATFIV-S versions use the arrays T and C for both import and export. This means that the original information in the arrays is destroyed by the module, so copies must be made if the original values will be needed at a later point in a program which calls GAUSS.

h) A Test of GAUSS *and* BSOLVE   To test the subroutines GAUSS and BSOLVE a WATFIV-S program was written and is shown as Figure 14.22. Note the great similarity to the program in Figure 14.4. This would be expected, since the previous program finds C from $C=T*Z$, whereas this one finds Z given T and C.

To emphasize that solving equations may be regarded as undoing a transformation the coefficient matrix was taken as the one-year transformation T^{12} computed in Figure 14.14. The vector C was taken as the one-year distribution of market shares of Figure 14.8. If the program works correctly, it should reproduce the input vector of Figure 14.8, namely $(0.5, 0.5, 0.0)$. The results given in Figure 14.23 are as close to this as one might expect, given the limited accuracy of computer arithmetic.

```
C Figure 14.21 -- Subroutine GAUSS
C                    Subprogram to reduce a system of N equations
C                    in N unknowns, T*X = C, to triangular form.

C*****************************************************************

C NDIM   - dimensioned(available) size of all arrays
C N      - array size(actual) for problem to be solved
C T      - import matrix(general) and export matrix(triangular)
C C      - import and export form of right-hand-side vector
C FLAG   - FLAG = 1 if a diagonal element of (triangular) T is 0
C MAX    - largest (in magnitude) subdiagonal element
C INDEX  - row containing the largest subdiagonal element
C RATIO  - ratio of subdiagonal to diagonal element

C*****************************************************************

      SUBROUTINE GAUSS(NDIM,N,T,C,FLAG)

      INTEGER NDIM, N, I, J, K, INDEX, FLAG
      REAL T(NDIM,NDIM), C(NDIM), MAX, TEMP, RATIO, ABS
```

```
C Figure 14.21 -- Subroutine GAUSS (continued)
C Create zeros in subdiagonal positions of columns 1 to N-1.
C Check for zero diagonal elements in the reduction.
      FLAG = 0
      I = 1
      WHILE(I .LE. N-1) DO
C        Find the maximum subdiagonal element in column I.
         INDEX = I
         MAX = ABS(T(I,I))
         J = I + 1
         WHILE(J .LE. N) DO
            IF(ABS(T(J,I)) .GT. MAX) THEN DO
               MAX = ABS(T(J,I))
               INDEX = J
            END IF
            J = J + 1
         END WHILE
C        If INDEX exceeds I, exchange rows INDEX and I.
         IF(INDEX .GT. I) THEN DO
            K = I
            WHILE(K .LE. N) DO
               TEMP = T(I,K)
               T(I,K) = T(INDEX,K)
               T(INDEX,K) = TEMP
               K = K + 1
            END WHILE
            TEMP = C(I)
            C(I) = C(INDEX)
            C(INDEX) = TEMP
         END IF
C        If the maximum pivot element is zero, set FLAG = 1 and
C        bypass the row operations at stage I.
         IF(MAX .EQ. 0) THEN DO
            FLAG = 1
            I = I + 1
         ELSE DO
C           For nonzero pivot, create zeros in subdiagonal
C           positions of column I by row operations.
            J = I + 1
            WHILE(J .LE. N) DO
               K = I + 1
               RATIO = T(J,I)/T(I,I)
               WHILE(K .LE. N) DO
                  T(J,K) = T(J,K) - T(I,K)*RATIO
                  K = K + 1
               END WHILE
               C(J) = C(J) - C(I)*RATIO
               J = J + 1
            END WHILE
            I = I + 1
         END IF
      END WHILE
      RETURN
      END
```

```
C Figure 14.22 -- Program to illustrate the use of subroutines
C                 GAUSS and BSOLVE in linear equation solution.

C****************************************************************
C T    - coefficient matrix
C Z    - solution vector
C C    - given right-hand-side
C N    - number of equations and number of unknowns
C FLAG - returned by subroutine GAUSS

C****************************************************************
      INTEGER I, J, FLAG, N
      REAL T(5,5), C(5), Z(5)
C Input and echo the data.
      READ, N
      READ, ((T(I,J), J=1,N), I=1,N)
      READ, (C(I), I=1,N)
      PRINT, 'MATRIX T'
      I = 1
      WHILE(I .LE. N) DO
         PRINT, (T(I,J), J=1,N)
         I = I + 1
      END WHILE
      PRINT, ' '
      PRINT, 'VECTOR C'
      PRINT, (C(I), I=1,N)
C Reduce the system to triangular form.
      CALL GAUSS(5,3,T,C,FLAG)
C If no solution, print an error message.
      IF(FLAG .EQ. 1) THEN DO
            PRINT, ' '
            PRINT, 'NO SOLUTION, SINCE THE MATRIX IS SINGULAR'
      ELSE DO
C        Find the solution by back-substitution.
            CALL BSOLVE(5,3,T,Z,C)

            PRINT, ' '
            PRINT, 'SOLUTION VECTOR Z'
            PRINT, (Z(I), I=1,N)
      END IF
      STOP
      END
C Subroutines GAUSS and BSOLVE are placed here.
$ENTRY
  3
  0.3555780, 0.3391681, 0.3391684
  0.2122841, 0.2228344, 0.2196082
  0.4321356, 0.4379949, 0.4412214
  0.3473730, 0.2175593, 0.4350653
```

14.6 Summary

This chapter has given a brief introduction to the use of a few subroutines which facilitate matrix computations. The program libraries of typical computing centers contain dozens of subroutines, which enable the programmer to produce efficient

Figure 14.23   Output from linear equations solution test program of Figure 14.22.

```
MATRIX T
          0.35557800          0.33916800          0.33916840
          0.21228400          0.22283440          0.21960810
          0.43213550          0.43799480          0.44122140
VECTOR C
          0.34737300          0.21755920          0.43506530
SOLUTION VECTOR Z
          0.49999730          0.50000430         -0.00000149
```

solutions to a wide variety of problems which arise in practical applications.

It is hoped that the reader of this chapter will be starting to feel comfortable with the idea of manipulating matrices and vectors as freely as simple variables in pseudo-code algorithm development. Translation of the algorithm to WATFIV-S may then proceed, making full use of the subroutine library.

It should be noted that matrix notation is merely a powerful shorthand for mathematical ideas which can be discussed without it. However, many such ideas would be completely lost in a morass of technical details without this tool. In a sense, the use of matrices shares many ideas with stuctured program design and fits in nicely with pseudo-code algorithm development. In mathematical analysis, matrices shield the user from the need to cope with large numbers of mathematical relationships. In developing pseudo-code algorithms, one is shielded from immediate worries about detailed conventions required in the final programming language.

14.7   References

There is a vast amount of literature on matrix computations and the solution of linear systems of equations. A small selection is listed here, with much more extensive lists appearing in the bibliographies of some of these references.

Dahlquist, G. and Bjorck, A. *Numerical Methods*. Translated by N. Anderson. Englewood Cliffs, N.J.: Prentice-Hall, 1974.

Barrodale, I.; Roberts, F.D.K.; and Ehle, B.L. *Elementary Computer Applications*. New York: John Wiley and Sons, 1971.

Forsythe, G.E.; Malcolm, M.A.; and Moler, C.B. *Computer Methods for Mathematical Computations*. Englewood Cliffs, N.J.: Prentice-Hall, 1977.

Forsythe, G.E. and Moler, C.B. *Computer Solution of Linear Algebraic Systems*. Englewood Cliffs, N.J.: Prentice-Hall, 1967.

Noble, B. *Applied Linear Algebra*. Englewood Cliffs, N.J.: Prentice-Hall, 1969.

14.8   Exercises

In most of the following exercises a program is needed to solve a specific problem. For each problem it is recommended that step-wise refinement be used in developing a pseudo-code algorithm to solve the problem. This algorithm should then be translated into WATFIV-S and run on the computer. Where appropriate, the program should be tested with a variety of data sufficient to ensure that the program does what it is supposed to do.

It is suggested that the reader become familiar with the matrix manipulation programs available in the local computing center. It may be useful to compare them to the programs presented in this chapter. These programs are often in the form of subroutines which may be used to make the program development task much easier.

14.1 a)   Develop WATFIV-S subroutines to do the following matrix operations:

1) Read in the elements of an N*N matrix by rows, into an array of dimension NDIM*NDIM;
2) Print out the elements of the matrix in 1);
3) Copy matrix A to B, where both matrices are of size N*N and are stored in arrays of dimension NDIM*NDIM.

b)   Rewrite the program in Figure 14.13. using these subroutines.

14.2 Compute and plot the monthly market shares for each bakery over a two-year period for the matrix T and initial vector of Figure 14.8.

14.3 Construct a transformation matrix which corresponds to the Three Bakery Model of Section 14.3.2 with the additional assumption that the total market starts to grow by 3% per month when C starts operations, with 2% of the new customers going to C and 1% to A. Follow the market for 3 years, tabulating the output for each month.

14.4 Assume that 5 countries, A, B, C, D, and E, share the world newsprint market with present shares 0.15, 0.18, 0.35, 0.25, and 0.07 respectively. Assume that each one retains 96% of its market each year and loses 1% to each of its competitors.

a)   Formulate a model and use it to compute and plot the market shares over a 25-year period.
b)   Repeat the calculation starting with an initial state in which A has 10% of the market, C has 87%, and the others have 1% each. What do you conclude about the relative importance of the initial state and the transformation in the ultimate behavior of the market?

14.5 Find the transformation which corresponds to a five-year period in the newsprint marketing example of the previous problem. Test the supposition that five applications of this transformation give the same results as 25 applications of the one-year transformation.

14.6 In Section 14.3.2, it was observed that the effects of an advertising campaign could be accounted for by a change in the transformation matrix. If one examines the output of Figure 14.8, it is reasonable to assume that bakery B would not sit idly by while its market share drops from 50% to 22%. Construct a transformation matrix under the assumption that bakery B succeeds in an advertising campaign to the extent that it subsequently retains 83% of its customers and loses 7% to A and 10% to C each month.

Write a program which computes and tabulates the market shares using the same T and initial state as in Figure 14.8 for a six-month period. Assume that bakery B's advertising campaign starts then and continues for the next 18 months. Plot the shares for the entire two-year period.

14.7 Use the programs developed in the text to solve the following linear systems:

a)
$$
\begin{aligned}
4x_1 &-x_2 & &-x_4 &= 0 \\
-x_1 &+4x_2 &-x_3 & &= 5 \\
&-x_2 &+4x_3 &-x_4 &= 5 \\
-x_1 & &-x_3 &+4x_4 &= 0
\end{aligned}
$$

b)
$$
\begin{aligned}
2.713x+8.356y+3.259z &= 5.222 \\
1.997x+4.347y+7.558z &= 4.386 \\
9.854x+3.656y+4.775z &= 7.547
\end{aligned}
$$

c)
$$
\begin{aligned}
1.000x_1+0.500x_2+0.333x_3+0.250x_4 &= 2.083 \\
0.500x_1+0.333x_2+0.250x_3+0.200x_4 &= 1.283 \\
0.333x_1+0.250x_2+0.200x_3+0.167x_4 &= 0.950 \\
0.250x_1+0.200x_2+0.167x_3+0.143x_4 &= 0.760
\end{aligned}
$$

14.8 a) Solve the following system of linear equations for $t = 0, 0.5, 1.0, 1.5, 2.0$.
$$
\begin{aligned}
25.5x_1 &-1.50x_2 &+2.00x_3 & &= 30(1+t) \\
1.50x_1 &+30.5x_2 & &+2.00x_4 &= 35(1+t) \\
-10.0x_1 &+2.00x_2 &+20.5x_3 &+3.50x_4 &= 15(1+t) \\
1.00x_1 &-3.50x_2 &-3.00x_3 &+40.0x_4 &= 30(1+t)
\end{aligned}
$$

b) How would you modify the elimination program so that all five problems are solved at once? (Hint: Think about how you might replace vector C by five vectors in the elimination phase of the solution.)

14.9 Solve the system of linear equations:

$$
\begin{aligned}
-2x_1 \; +x_2 & = 0.01 \\
x_1 \; -2x_2 \; +x_3 & = 0 \\
x_2 \; -2x_3 \; +x_4 & = 0 \\
& \;\; \vdots \\
x_{98} \; -2x_{99} \; +x_{100} & = 0 \\
x_{99} \; -2x_{100} & = 0.05
\end{aligned}
$$

You will probably find that your computer system will not permit you to store the 10,000 coefficients of a system of 100 linear equations. Observing that only 298 of the coefficients are nonzero, devise a suitable storage scheme for this system and modify the elimination and back-substitution algorithms appropriately. (Pivoting is not necessary.)

How large a system of the above structure could be solved using the computing facilities available to you?

14.10 Suppose that you wish to find the polynomial

$$a_0 + a_1 x + a_2 x^2 + \cdots + a_k x^k$$

which is the best least-squares approximation to data given in the form of coordinate pairs

$$(x_j, y_j), \; j = 1, 2, 3, \cdots, m$$

It can be shown that the vector A of values of the coefficients satisfies the equation

$$\mathsf{T} \times \mathsf{T}' \times \mathsf{A} = \mathsf{T} \times \mathsf{Y}, \quad \text{where}$$

$$
\mathsf{T} =
\begin{bmatrix}
1 & 1 & 1 & \cdots & 1 \\
x_1 & x_2 & x_3 & \cdots & x_m \\
x_1^2 & x_2^2 & x_3^2 & \cdots & x_m^2 \\
\cdot & \cdot & \cdot & & \cdot \\
\cdot & \cdot & \cdot & & \cdot \\
\cdot & \cdot & \cdot & & \cdot \\
x_1^k & x_2^k & x_3^k & \cdots & x_m^k
\end{bmatrix},
\quad
\mathsf{A} =
\begin{bmatrix}
a_0 \\
a_1 \\
a_2 \\
\cdot \\
\cdot \\
\cdot \\
a_k
\end{bmatrix}
\quad \text{and} \quad
\mathsf{Y} =
\begin{bmatrix}
y_1 \\
y_2 \\
y_3 \\
\cdot \\
\cdot \\
y_k \\
\cdot \\
\cdot \\
\cdot \\
y_m
\end{bmatrix}
$$

T' is the transpose of T; that is, the matrix whose first row is the first column of T, second row is the second column of T, etc.

Write a program which uses the subroutines MATMPY, MATVEC, GAUSS, and BSOLVE of this chapter (or alternatives) to find the best least-squares approximation of degree 2 ($k = 2$) to the data:

$$(x_j, y_j) = (0,1.00), (30,0.75), (45,0.50), (60,0.27), (90,0.00)$$

14.11 The temperature distribution over a rectangular plate, with given temperature prescribed at its edges is known to satisfy Laplace's equation.

If a uniform grid is drawn over the plate, giving nodes at a number of interior points, an approximation to the solution may be found by determining the temperature only at the node points. The solution is determined from the rule that the temperature at any interior point must be the average of the temperatures at the four adjacent points - up, down, left, and right. (This is a discrete version of Laplace's equation.)

a)   Formulate the equations to be solved for the temperatures at the 12 interior points of the following diagram.

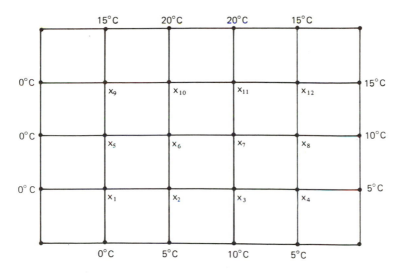

b)   Calculate the approximate temperature distribution over the plate by solving the 12 equations.

15
Deterministic
Simulation

15.1 Introduction

Simulation is the process of making a model of a real system and then performing experiments on the model. The purpose of simulation is to understand the behavior of the system; one may wish simply to predict its future behavior or to evaluate alternate means of operating or controlling the system.

An important example of the first objective is the prediction of weather. Today, there exist mathematical models of the atmosphere which may be solved on large-scale computers to give weather forecasts valid for a few days. An example of the second kind would be a model of an economy which is sensitive to many different factors. A government may gain some insight into appropriate policy actions by observing the effects of such actions on a simulation model. Experimenting with the real system in this case can be (and sometimes is!) catastrophically expensive.

In these two examples, the corresponding models may be very sophisticated and very expensive to develop and run. Even so, the importance of the insight gained through the simulation may make such an investment worthwhile. In the next two chapters, elementary models of simpler systems will be developed which should give the reader some feeling for the way in which simulation models are designed and used.

15.2 Simulation Models

A simulation involves a description of the way in which a system changes over some period of time. A quantitative *representation* of the system at some instant of time is called the *state* of the system. Thus, the heart of any simulation model is a description of the way in which states of the system change with time. *Continuous* models examine the rate of change of state variables with time. *Discrete* models give rules for the way in which the state variables change over a specified time increment. One usually needs to examine the state of the system only at a sequence of discrete time intervals, so that continuous models are usually approximated by discrete models. For this reason, such discrete time models will be the only kind dealt with here.

The rules governing the change of state may be either *deterministic* or *probabilistic*. In a deterministic model, the new state may be completely deduced from the old state by applying well-defined rules. In a probabilistic model, a variety of new states are all possible, but the one which actually occurs is subject to some predefined laws of chance. Deterministic models are discussed in the remainder of this chapter and probabilistic models in Chapter 16.

15.3 Structure of Simulation Model Programs

All programs which are examined in this chapter and the next have a general structure similar to that shown in Figure 15.1.

Figure 15.1 General structure of a simulation algorithm.

Obtain simulation parameters and initial states.

while termination criterion is not met **do**

⎡ time ← time + time step

⎣ Change the state variables and record the state of the system.

Summarize the system behavior.

stop

In the case of the weather example alluded to in the introduction, the initial conditions would be the observed state of the weather at the time when the forecast is made. The innocent looking line change the state variables and record the state of the system would correspond to the use of a massive program module which involves the solution of literally thousands of equations. The same structure applies to simple programs. For example, a program is developed in Section 15.6 which plots the path of a bouncing ball. In this case, the initial state is the initial location and velocity of the ball. The line change the state variables and record the state of the system represents an application of simple physical laws to deduce the changes in the location and velocity of the ball after a short time step. The summary involves recording the computed points and subsequently plotting the trajectory.

A second basic structure is appropriate for those problems in which one wishes to study the effect of various combinations of parameters on the system, with a view to optimizing it in some way. Then, the algorithm structure of Figure 15.1 is more appropriately described as a module which may be invoked for many combinations of import parameters. Alternately, the simulation module may be used adaptively to seek out a "best" combination of parameters. In these cases the module structure would be as shown in Figure 15.2.

Figure 15.2   General structure of a simulation module.

module simulation (**imports**: parameters, initial state; **exports**: final state, summary data)

Initialize the system.

while termination criterion is not met **do**

    time ← time + time step

    Change state variables and record data.

Compute the final state and summary.

end module

15.4   An Investment Example

To illustrate the steps involved in the construction of a simulation model and program, a simple investment problem is examined.

Example 15.1

A person who has a present annual salary of 13,000 dollars wishes to plan an investment program. If the salary increases by 8% at the end of each year, and 10% of the old salary is invested then at an interest rate of 6% compounded annually, what is the status of the investment at the end of 5, 10, 15, . . . , 30 years?

a) Problem Discussion   In this example, the output desired is a simple table showing the amount of money saved at the end of each 5 year period. The state variables are the current salary and the savings. The simulation parameters are the salary increase, the fraction of salary invested, and the interest rate. Although fixed values of these quantities are given in the statement of the problem, it is useful to regard them as parameters which may be varied, so that the effect of changes to them may be studied.

For the specific 8% increase in the example, the new salary at the end of each year is easily computed as

$salary\,(t+1) = salary\,(t)+0.08{\times}salary\,(t).$

The new savings may be found by adding together the old savings, interest on the old savings, and the current amount of salary saved.

$savings\,(t+1) = savings\,(t)+0.06{\times}savings\,(t)+0.10{\times}salary\,(t).$

b) Initial Decomposition   The general algorithm structure of Figure 15.1 is appropriate
for this problem. This gives the initial version of the algorithm shown as Figure 15.3,
with the steps labeled for subsequent refinement.

Figure 15.3   First version of a pseudo-code algorithm for the investment problem.

1. Obtain investment parameters and initial states.

2. **while** termination criterion is not met **do**

> time ← time + timestep
> Change the investment variables and record the state of the system.

3. Summarize the investment behavior.

stop

c) Refining Step **1.**   The simulation parameters are the salary increase, perinc, the
fraction of salary invested, persav, and the interest rate, perint, all expressed as
percentages. The refinement is as follows:

> **get** perinc, persav, perint

Initial conditions must be given for the salary and savings. This is expressed as:

> **get** salary, savings

Good programming practice dictates that these quantities be labeled and listed
along with the program output, so that a final refinement of step **1.** is given below. Note
that the variable year has also been added to identify the salary and savings information.

> * Obtain and record the simulation parameters.
>
> **get** perinc, persav, perint
> **put** '% salary increase is', perinc
> **put** '% of salary saved is', persav
> **put** '% interest on savings', perint
>
> * Obtain and record the initial conditions.
>
> **get** salary, savings
> year ← 0
> **put** 'year', 'salary', 'savings'
> **put** year, salary, savings

d) Refining Step **2.**   For this example, the simulation ends when the elapsed time is 30
years. Thus, a **while** loop will be used with control variable year, which was initialized to
0 in step **1.**

* Simulate the system for 30 years, tabulating the state at 5 year intervals.

while year < 30 **do**

> year ← year + 1
>
> **2.1** Compute new salary and savings.
>
> **2.2** Record the salary and savings if the year is a multiple of 5.

e) Refining Step **2.1**   Using the formulas given in a), but generalized to use the simulation parameters, the refinement of **2.1** is:

* Compute new salary and savings.

savings ← savings + (perint*savings + persav*salary)/100
salary ← salary + perinc*salary/100

Note that the new values of salary and savings replace the old values. Observe that it would be wrong to reverse the order of these two statements. Why?

f) Refining Step **2.2**   An appropriate way to express step **2.2** is:

* Record the salary and savings if the year is a multiple of 5.

if year(mod 5) = 0 **then**

> **put** year, salary, savings

g) Refining Step **3.**   No summary is needed in this example since the generated table will contain all of the necessary information, so this step may be omitted.

h) The Final Algorithm   The various refinements may now be combined to give the final version of the algorithm as shown in Figure 15.4.

i) Program for Final Version of Algorithm   The translation of this algorithm into WATFIV-S is straightforward and is presented in Figure 15.5.

Figure 15.4   Final version of the pseudo-code algorithm for the investment problem.

```
* Simulate a simple investment problem involving the saving of a fixed percentage of
* salary at a fixed interest rate while the salary increases by a fixed percent each year.

* Variables used:
* salary - the current salary
* savings - the current savings
* year - the current year of the simulation
* perinc - the percentage increase in salary
* perint - the percentage interest earned on savings

* Obtain and record the simulation parameters.

get perinc, persav, perint
put '% salary increase is', perinc
put '% of salary saved is', persav
put '% interest on savings', perint

* Obtain and record the initial conditions.

get salary, savings
year ← 0
put 'year', 'salary', 'savings'
put year, salary, savings

* Simulate the system for 30 years, tabulating the state at 5 year intervals.

while year < 30 do
      year ← year + 1
      savings ← savings + (perint*savings + persav*salary)/100
      salary ← salary + perinc*salary/100
      if year(mod 5) = 0 then
            put year, salary, savings

stop
8, 10, 6, 13000, 0
```

The output for the program is listed in Figure 15.6. Though the accumulated investment is more than 280 thousand dollars, the salary has also increased, to more than 130 thousand dollars. Thus, the savings amount to little more than double the final salary. It is possible, therefore, that a more aggressive savings program is needed. It is easy to modify the simulation parameters and run the simulation again to study other alternatives. The next chapter will also investigate this problem to study variable increases in salary.

```
C Figure 15.5 - Program to simulate a simple investment problem
C                involving the saving of a fixed percentage of
C                salary at a fixed interest rate while the
C                salary increases by a fixed percent each year.

C****************************************************************

C SALARY - the current salary
C SAVING - the current savings
C YEAR   - the current year of the simulation
C PERINC - the percentage increase in salary
C PERSAV - the percent of salary put into savings
C PERINT - the percentage interest earned on savings

C****************************************************************

       REAL SALARY, SAVING, PERINC, PERSAV, PERINT
       INTEGER YEAR, MOD
C Obtain and record the simulation parameters.

       READ, PERINC, PERSAV, PERINT
       PRINT, '% SALARY INCREASE IS ', PERINC
       PRINT, '% OF SALARY SAVED IS ', PERSAV
       PRINT, '% INTEREST ON SAVINGS', PERINT
       PRINT, ' '
C Obtain and record the initial conditions.

       READ, SALARY, SAVING
       YEAR = 0
       PRINT, '        YEAR         SALARY              SAVINGS'
       PRINT, ' '
       PRINT, YEAR, SALARY, SAVING
C Simulate the system for 30 years, tabulating
C the state at 5 year intervals.

       WHILE(YEAR .LT. 30) DO
          YEAR = YEAR + 1
          SAVING = SAVING + (PERINT*SAVING + PERSAV*SALARY)/100.0
          SALARY = SALARY + PERINC*SALARY/100.0
          IF(MOD(YEAR,5) .EQ. 0) THEN DO
               PRINT, YEAR, SALARY, SAVING
          END IF
       END WHILE
       STOP
       END
$ENTRY
8. 10. 6.
13000. 0.
```

Figure 15.6   Output from the investment program of Figure 15.5.

% SALARY INCREASE IS	8.00000000
% OF SALARY SAVED IS	10.00000000
% INTEREST ON SAVINGS	6.00000000

YEAR	SALARY	SAVINGS
0	13000.00000000	0.00000000
5	19101.25000000	8521.65200000
10	28066.00000000	23924.98000000
15	41238.15000000	50414.63000000
20	60592.35000000	94498.12000000
25	89029.81000000	166178.50000000
30	130813.80000000	280744.30000000

15.5 Pursuit Problems

In a pursuit problem one body is chasing or pursuing another. The objective of simulation in such a problem is the computation of the paths followed, with a view to determining the outcome. One may also wish to study the effects of various strategies of pursuit or evasion.

The example developed in detail is that of a bull chasing a hiker, but with different parameter values and variable names it could equally well be a missile pursuing an aircraft or the coast guard trying to intercept a rumrunner. The main tool needed to develop the algorithms is elementary geometry.

15.5.1 The Bull-Hiker Problem

Example 15.2

While a hiker is walking in an open area towards some trees 400m distant, an angry bull starts to pursue him. The bull is initially at a point 100m directly opposite a point on the path 50m ahead of the hiker. The bull's pursuit strategy is rather simple-minded. It moves directly towards the hiker, rather than trying to intercept him. The bad news is that the bull has a speed advantage. The bull can run at 8.5m/sec, whereas the hiker can only manage 8.0m/sec over this distance. Does the story have a happy ending?

a) Problem Discussion   A simple mathematical model of the pursuit process can be developed to model this situation. The objective will be to compute and plot the paths of both the bull and the hiker and to check if they remain safely separated until the hiker gets to the trees.

The first stage in such a process is to make a diagram, including some reference coordinate system. The system is chosen to be as simple as possible. For instance, the hiker's path will be taken as the *x* axis, with his initial location as the origin. This is shown in Figure 15.7.

Figure 15.7   Diagram for the bull-hiker pursuit problem.

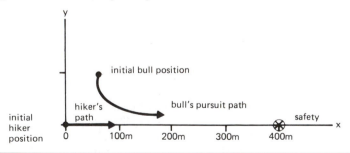

The second step is to make a detailed description of the way in which the bull and hiker positions change with time. These positions will be denoted $(x_b(t), y_b(t))$ and $(x_h(t), y_h(t))$ respectively, with initial values (in meters):

$$x_b(0) = 50, \quad y_b(0) = 100, \quad x_h(0) = 0, \quad y_h(0) = 0.$$

Note that subscripts b and h refer to the bull and hiker, respectively. The argument t specifies the time. These coordinates are *state variables* and represent the *state* of the *system* at any time t. The hiker's change of position over a short time step δt may be described quite simply as

new position ← old position+distance traveled.

Symbolically, the x and y components are isolated and written in the following way:

$$x_h(t+\delta t) \leftarrow x_h(t) + velocity \times time\ step$$

$$\leftarrow x_h(t) + v_h \times \delta t$$

$$y_h(t+\delta t) \leftarrow y_h(t) \leftarrow 0.$$

The bull's motion is dependent upon the hiker's position, since the bull always moves directly towards the hiker. It will be assumed that the bull's change in position over a *short* time step δt will be adequately described by motion in a straight line. The direction of this line is determined at the start of the time interval δt. At this point, reference to the diagram of Figure 15.8 may help to clarify the relative positions of the bull and hiker at an arbitrary time t. This diagram illustrates the situation at the beginning of the chase when the bull is located to the *right* of the hiker (larger x coordinate). The reader should confirm that the same equations may be derived from a diagram showing the bull to the *left* of the hiker (smaller x coordinate) (see

Figure 15.8   Diagram of the relative bull and hiker positions.

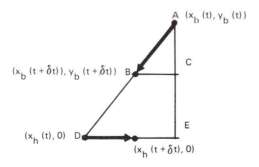

Exercise 15.4). The distance **AB** from $(x_b(t), y_b(t))$ to $(x_b(t+\delta t), y_b(t+\delta t))$ is the distance traveled by the bull in the time step δt and is known to be $8.5 \times \delta t$. The distance between the bull and hiker at time t may be computed from the Pythagorean relation (triangle **ADE**) as:

$$s(t) = \sqrt{(x_b(t)-x_h(t))^2 + (y_b(t)-y_h(t))^2}$$

In the diagram, it will be observed that triangle ABC is similar to triangle ADE. This fact may be used to compute CB and AC, the changes in the x and y coordinates of the bull. Since

$$\frac{CB}{AB} = \frac{ED}{AD} \text{ and } \frac{AC}{AB} = \frac{AE}{AD}$$

it follows that

$$\frac{x_b(t+\delta t)-x_b(t)}{x_h(t)-x_b(t)} = \frac{v_b \times \delta t}{s(t)} \text{ and}$$

$$\frac{y_b(t+\delta t)-y_b(t)}{y_h(t)-y_b(t)} = \frac{v_b \times \delta t}{s(t)}.$$

Rearranging these equations for the motion of the bull gives

$$x_b(t+\delta t) = x_b(t) + \frac{x_h(t)-x_b(t)}{s(t)} \times v_b \times \delta t \text{ and}$$

$$y_b(t+\delta t) = y_b(t) + \frac{y_h(t)-y_b(t)}{s(t)} \times v_b \times \delta t.$$

Recall that the equations for the motion of the hiker are

$$x_h(t+\delta t) = x_h(t) + v_h \times \delta t \quad \text{and} \quad y_h(t+\delta t) = 0.$$

Together, these equations for the bull and hiker give a complete description of the change of state which occurs from time t to time $t+\delta t$, and form the basis for the simulation model. It is conventional to eliminate the arguments t and $t+\delta t$ in developing algorithms using these formulas; it is then understood that new coordinate values replace old values as they are computed.

b) Initial Decomposition   For this simulation problem the general algorithm structure of Figure 15.1 may be used. It gives the initial version of the algorithm shown in Figure 15.9, with the steps labeled for subsequent refinement.

Figure 15.9   First version of a pseudo-code algorithm for the bull-hiker pursuit problem.

1.   Obtain the pursuit parameters and initial states.

2.   **while** termination criterion is not met **do**

> time ← time + timestep
>
> Change the pursuit variables and record the state of the system.

3.   Summarize the results of the pursuit.

stop

---

c) Refining Step **1.**   The simulation parameters in this case are: the time step, the speeds of the bull, the hiker, and the distance to safety in the trees. The initial states are the initial coordinates of the bull and hiker. Thus, the refinement is as follows.

```
* Obtain and record the simulation parameters and initial states.
get tstep, xb, yb, xh, yh, vb, vh, xmax
put 'The bull coordinates are', xb, yb
put 'The hiker coordinates are', xh, yh
put 'The velocity of the bull is', vb
put 'The velocity of the hiker is', vh
put 'The time increment is', tstep
put 'The distance to safety is', xmax
```

Notice that the subscripts used in the problem discussion have been changed to constitute part of the variable.

In addition to defining these variables, it is also necessary to initialize the plotting process and to record the initial positions for plotting. These steps are written as:

```
call setplt
call stopnt(xb,yb,'b')
call stopnt(xh,yh,'h')
```

d) Refining Step **2.**   The simulation comes to an end if either the hiker reaches safety or the bull overtakes him. An appropriate elaboration of this **while** loop and its termination criterion is:

```
* Simulate the motion of the bull and hiker until the hiker is overtaken
* or reaches safety.
```
$$s \leftarrow sqrt((xh-xb)^2 + (yh-yb)^2)$$
$$t \leftarrow 0$$
while xh < xmax **and** s > 1 **do**
> $t \leftarrow t + tstep$
>
> **2.1** Change state variables.
>
> **2.2** Record the state of the system.

This means that the bull is assumed to have overtaken the hiker if the distance between them, s, becomes one meter or less. Note that both xh and s change with time t, and that both must be initialized before the **while** statement

e) Refining Step **2.1**   The change in the state variables is accomplished by using the formulas developed earlier.

$$s \leftarrow \mathrm{sqrt}((xh-xb)^2 + (yh-yb)^2)$$
$$xb \leftarrow xb + (xh-xb)*vb*tstep/s$$
$$yb \leftarrow yb + (yh-yb)*vb*tstep/s$$
$$xh \leftarrow xh + vh*tstep$$

Notice that these statements simply replace the old coordinates by their new values.

f) Refining Step **2.2**   For this problem, the state of the system at the end of each time step may be recorded using the plotting routines.

  * Record the current coordinates.

call stopnt(xb,yb,'b')
call stopnt(xh,yh,'h')

g) Refining Step **3.**   The final summary for this problem can be restricted to a message as to whether the hiker made it to the trees or not, and the generation of a plot.

  * Record the final outcome and plot the paths.

put 'At time =', t
if xh ≥ xmax **then**
    ⎡ **put** 'The hiker reached safety'
    ⎣ **put** 'The distance between the bull and hiker is', s
  else
    ⎡ **put** 'The hiker was overtaken at x =', xh
call plotc(0)

h) Final Version of the Algorithm   The final algorithm may now be assembled and appears as Figure 15.10.

i) Program for Final Version of Algorithm   A WATFIV-S version of the algorithm is given as Figure 15.11.

Figure 15.10   Final version of the pseudo-code algorithm for the bull-hiker pursuit problem.

```
* Algorithm to simulate the bull-hiker pursuit problem.

* Variables used:
* t - the time
* xb,yb - the coordinates of the bull's position
* xh,yh - the coordinates of the hiker's position
* vb - the velocity of the bull
* vh - the velocity of the hiker
* s - the distance of the bull from the hiker
* tstep - the time increment
* xmax - the x coordinate of safety

* Obtain and record the simulation parameters and initial states.

get tstep, xb, yb, xh, yh, vb, vh, xmax
put 'The bull coordinates are', xb, yb
put 'The hiker coordinates are', xh, yh
put 'The velocity of the bull is', vb
put 'The velocity of the hiker is', vh
put 'The time increment is', tstep
put 'The distance to safety is', xmax

* Initialize plotting and store the initial coordinates.

call setplt
call stopnt(xb,yb,'b')
call stopnt(xh,yh,'h')

* Simulate the motion of the bull and hiker until the hiker is overtaken or reaches safety.

s ← sqrt((xh−xb)² + (yh−yb)²)
t ← 0
while xh < xmax and s > 1 do
        t ← t + tstep
        s ← sqrt((xh−xb)² + (yh−yb)²)
        xb ← xb + (xh−xb)*vb*tstep/s
        yb ← yb + (yh−yb)*vb*tstep/s
        xh ← xh + vh*tstep

        * Record the current coordinates.

        call stopnt(xb,yb,'b')
        call stopnt(xh,yh,'h')


* Record the final outcome and plot the paths.

put 'At time =', t
if xh ≥ xmax then
        put 'The hiker reached safety'
        put 'The distance between the bull and hiker is', s
    else
        put 'The hiker was overtaken at x =', xh
call plotc(0)
stop

0.125, 50, 100, 0, 0, 8.5, 8.0, 400
```

```
C Figure 15.11 - Program to simulate the bull-hiker pursuit
C                  problem.
C****************************************************************
C T       - the time
C XB,YB   - the coordinates of the bull's position
C XH,YH   - the coordinates of the hiker's position
C VB      - the velocity of the bull
C VH      - the velocity of the hiker
C S       - the distance of the bull from the hiker
C TSTEP   - the time increment
C XMAX    - the x coordinate of safety
C****************************************************************
        REAL T, TSTEP, XB, YB, XH, YH, VB, VH, XMAX, S, SQRT
C Obtain and record the simulation parameters and initial states.
        READ, TSTEP, XB, YB, XH, YH, VB, VH, XMAX
        PRINT, 'THE BULL COORDINATES ARE', XB, YB
        PRINT, 'THE HIKER COORDINATES ARE', XH, YH
        PRINT, 'THE VELOCITY OF THE BULL IS', VB
        PRINT, 'THE VELOCITY OF THE HIKER IS', VH
        PRINT, 'THE TIME INCREMENT IS', TSTEP
        PRINT, 'THE DISTANCE TO SAFETY IS', XMAX
C Initialize plotting and store the initial coordinates.
        CALL SETPLT
        CALL SETSIZ(21,41)
        CALL STOPNT(XB,YB,'B')
        CALL STOPNT(XH,YH,'H')
C Simulate the motion of the bull and hiker until
C the hiker is overtaken or reaches safety.
        S = SQRT((XH-XB)**2 + (YH-YB)**2)
        T = 0.0
        WHILE(XH.LT.XMAX .AND. S.GT.1.0) DO
            T = T + TSTEP
            S = SQRT((XH-XB)**2 + (YH-YB)**2)
            XB = XB + (XH-XB)*VB*TSTEP/S
            YB = YB + (YH-YB)*VB*TSTEP/S
            XH = XH + VH*TSTEP
C           Record the current coordinates.
            CALL STOPNT(XB,YB,'B')
            CALL STOPNT(XH,YH,'H')
        END WHILE
C Record the final outcome and plot the paths.
        PRINT, ' '
        PRINT, 'AT TIME =',T
        IF(XH .GE. XMAX) THEN DO
            PRINT, 'THE HIKER REACHED SAFETY'
            PRINT, 'THE DISTANCE BETWEEN THE BULL AND HIKER IS', S
        ELSE DO
            PRINT, 'THE HIKER WAS OVERTAKEN AT X =', XH
        END IF
        CALL PLOTC(0)
        STOP
        END
$ENTRY
0.125, 50.0, 100.0, 0.0, 0.0, 8.5, 8.0, 400.0
```

The output from the program is shown in Figure 15.12. For the given parameters, the hiker did manage to beat the bull to the safety of the trees. Notice that the paths of the bull and the hiker overlap for a portion of the chase, as indicated by the asterisks along a portion of the hiker's path. not actually mean that the bull caught the hiker.

Figure 15.12   Ouput from the bull-hiker pursuit program of Figure 15.11.

```
THE  BULL  COORDINATES  ARE            50.00000000        100.00000000
THE  HIKER  COORDINATES  ARE            0.00000000          0.00000000
THE  VELOCITY  OF  THE  BULL  IS        8.50000000
THE  VELOCITY  OF  THE  HIKER  IS       8.00000000
THE  TIME  INCREMENT  IS           0.12500000
THE  DISTANCE  TO  SAFETY  IS      400.00000000

AT  TIME  =        50.00000000
THE  HIKER  REACHED  SAFETY
THE  DISTANCE  BETWEEN  THE  BULL  AND  HIKER  IS          8.79150200

 -  NUMBER  OF  POINTS:  SUBMITTED    802,  PLOTTED    802


      100.0000        B
                      B
                      BB
                      B
                      B
       75.0000        B
                      B
                      B
                      B
                      B
       50.0000        B
                      B
                      B
                      BB
                      B
       25.0000        B
                      BB
                        BB
                        BB
                        BBBB
        0.0000OHHHHHHHHHHH*****************************H
              0.0000   100.0000   200.0000   300.0000   400.0000
```

Exercises 15.5 and 15.6 suggest some variations on this example that may be of interest.

15.6   Problems in Dynamics

Simulation problems in dynamics are concerned with the motion of physical objects under the action of external forces. There is a standard approach to all such problems. A coordinate system is chosen, and a diagram is drawn which shows the object and all forces acting upon it. The forces are decomposed into components in the coordinate directions, and converted to accelerations. Finally, the knowledge of accelerations is used to calculate changes in velocity components over a short time step, and these in turn are used to calculate changes in coordinates. The basic rules, which are applied in each coordinate direction, are:

1) *force = mass × acceleration* or *acceleration = force / mass*;
2) *change in velocity = average acceleration × time step*;
3) *change in coordinate = average velocity × time step.*

15.6.1 The Bouncing Ball

As an example of a dynamics simulation, consider the following problem involving a bouncing ball.

Example 15.3

  Calculate and plot the path of a ball for *n* bounces along a level floor, given its initial location and velocity. Assume that the only external force is gravity and that the acceleration due to gravity is 9.8 m/sec². The bouncing characteristics of the ball may be assumed to follow the rule that 10% of the vertical velocity is lost when the ball bounces, but no loss in horizontal velocity occurs.

a) Problem Discussion   A natural choice of coordinate system in this case is the direction along the floor as the *x* coordinate and the vertical height as the *y* coordinate. The "free-body diagram" is very simple in this case, and is shown in Figure 15.13.

Figure 15.13   Free-body diagram for the bouncing ball problem.

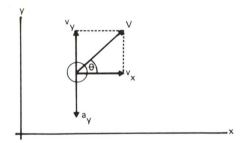

  The state variables in this example will be the *x* and *y* coordinates of the ball and its velocity components in the *x* and *y* directions. The initial state of the simulation will be the initial coordinates and velocity components.

  The change of state of the system is described by using the simple physical laws governing motion under acceleration. Since no forces act to alter the motion in the *x* direction, the velocity will remain constant at its initial value. If the ball is projected at *v* m/sec at an angle θ to the horizontal, this initial velocity in the *x* direction is $v_x = v \cos \theta$. Similarly, the motion in the *y* direction is initially $v_y = v \sin \theta$ but this velocity changes as the ball is accelerated under the force of gravity.

  Since acceleration is the rate of change of velocity, the new velocity component will be

$$v_y (t + \delta t) = v_y (t) + a_y \times \delta t$$

In this case, the acceleration a_y is due to gravity in the negative y direction, so
$a_y = -9.8$

This velocity may be used to calculate the new y coordinate. For motion under constant acceleration, an elementary physics text will provide the formula

$$y(t+\delta t) = y(t)+\frac{1}{2}\Big[v_y(t+\delta t)+v_y(t)\Big] \times \delta t$$

The new x coordinate follows simply from

$$x(t+\delta t) = x(t)+v_x \times \delta t$$

There remains the problem of what to do when the ball hits the floor. The assumption that 10% of the velocity is lost when the bounce occurs is implemented as:

if y(t+dt) < 0 **then**
$\quad\Big[\ $ v_y(t+dt) ← |0.9 * v_y(t+dt)|

This assumption is obviously not quite correct, since it allows the ball to move slightly below floor level before its direction is changed. The error caused by this assumption will be negligible if δt is small enough. Alternatively, one could use a zero finding program such as the bisection routine of Chapter 7 to find that fraction of δt which will produce a zero value of y exactly.

b) Development of the Algorithm   Working from an initial decomposition such as Figure 15.1, the various steps of the algorithm may be refined to give the pseudo-code algorithm of Figure 15.14 for the bouncing ball problem. For brevity the intermediate steps are omitted. Notice that the subscripts used to indicate direction have been incorporated into the variable names and that the times have been dropped except for the velocities in the y direction. In this case, vyold and vynew have been used.

c) Program for Final Version of the Algorithm   The details of the WATFIV-S program in Figure 15.15 should now be clear. Notice that the angle must be changed from degrees to radians in order to use the built-in SIN and COS functions. The graphical output of the program follows as Figure 15.16.

Figure 15.14   Final version of the pseudo-code algorithm for the bouncing ball problem.

```
* Simulate the motion of a ball for a given number of bounces.
* Assume that gravity is the only external force.

* Variables used:
* t - the time
* tstep - the time increment
* nbounces - the number of bounces to be simulated
* bounce - the current number of bounces
* x,y - the x and y coordinates of the ball
* v - the initial velocity of the ball
* vx - the x component of the velocity
* vyold/vynew - the y component of the velocity at the start/end of tstep
* ay - the y component of the acceleration
* angle - the angle at which the ball is thrown

* Initialize and calculate the simulation parameters and states.

get v, angle, nbounces, tstep
put 'The initial velocity of the ball is', v
put 'The angle at which the ball is thrown is', angle
put 'The number of bounces is', nbounces
put 'The time increment is', tstep
x ← 0
y ← 0
ay ← −9.8
vx ← v * cos (angle)
vyold ← v * sin (angle)

* Initialize the plot routines and plot the ball's initial position.

call setplt
call stopnt(x,y,'b')

* Perform the simulation for nbounces bounces.
* When the ball hits the floor, it changes direction and loses 10% of its velocity.

bounce ← 0
t ← 0
while bounce < nbounces do
    ┌ t ← t + tstep
    │ x ← x + vx * tstep
    │ vynew ← vyold + ay * tstep
    │ y ← y + (vyold + vynew) * tstep/2
    │ vyold ← vynew
    │ call stopnt(x,y,'b')
    │ if y ≤ 0 then
    │     ┌ vyold ← | 0.9 * vyold |
    │     │ y ← 0
    └     └ bounce ← bounce + 1

* The simulation is complete.  Plot the path.

call plotc(0)
stop

10, 45, 5, .01
```

```
C Figure 15.15 - Simulate the motion of a ball for a given
C                number of bounces.  Assume that gravity is
C                the only external force.
C*****************************************************************
C T      - the time
C TSTEP  - the time increment
C NBOUNC - the number of bounces to be simulated
C BOUNCE - the current number of bounces
C X,Y    - the x and y coordinates of the ball
C V      - the initial velocity of the ball
C VX     - the x component of the velocity
C VYOLD  - the y component of the velocity at the start of TSTEP
C VYNEW  - the y component of the velocity at the end of TSTEP
C AY     - the y component of the acceleration
C ANGLE  - the angle at which the ball is thrown (in degrees)
C THETA  - the angle at which the ball is thrown (in radians)
C*****************************************************************
      REAL T, TSTEP, X, Y, V, VX, VYOLD, VYNEW, AY
      REAL ANGLE, PI, THETA, SIN, COS, ABS
      INTEGER BOUNCE, NBOUNC
C Initialize and calculate the simulation parameters and states.
      READ, V, ANGLE, NBOUNC, TSTEP
      PRINT, 'THE INITIAL VELOCITY OF THE BALL IS', V
      PRINT, 'THE ANGLE AT WHICH THE BALL IS THROWN IS', ANGLE
      PRINT, 'THE NUMBER OF BOUNCES IS', NBOUNC
      PRINT, 'THE TIME INCREMENT IS', TSTEP

      X = 0.0
      Y = 0.0
      PI = 3.1415926
      AY = -9.8
      THETA = ANGLE*PI/180.0
      VX = V*COS(THETA)
      VYOLD = V*SIN(THETA)
C Initialize the plot routines and
C plot the ball's initial position.
      CALL SETPLT
      CALL SETSIZ(41,41)
      CALL STOPNT(X,Y,'B')
C Perform the simulation for NBOUNC bounces.
C When the ball hits the floor, it changes direction
C and loses 10% of its velocity.
      BOUNCE = 0
      T = 0.0
      WHILE(BOUNCE .LT. NBOUNC) DO
         T = T + TSTEP
         X = X + VX*TSTEP
         VYNEW = VYOLD + AY*TSTEP
         Y = Y + (VYOLD+VYNEW)*TSTEP/2.0
         VYOLD = VYNEW
         CALL STOPNT(X,Y,'B')
         IF(Y .LE. 0.0) THEN DO
               VYOLD = ABS(0.9*VYOLD)
               Y = 0.0
               BOUNCE = BOUNCE + 1
         END IF
      END WHILE
C The simulation is complete.  Plot the path.
      CALL PLOTC(0)
      STOP
      END
$ENTRY
10.0  45.0  5  0.01
```

Figure 15.15 (continued)

Program Notes

- In order to convert from the pseudo code to WATFIV-S, it is necessary to convert the angle from degrees to radians. The angle in radians has the variable name THETA.

Figure 15.16 Output from the bouncing ball program of Figure 15.15.

```
THE INITIAL VELOCITY OF THE BALL IS          10.00000000
THE ANGLE AT WHICH THE BALL IS THROWN IS       45.00000000
THE NUMBER OF BOUNCES IS            5
THE TIME INCREMENT IS          0.01000000
 - NUMBER OF POINTS: SUBMITTED   606, PLOTTED    606


      2.5510      BB
                  BBB
                  B B
                 BB B
                 B  B
      2.2250     B  BB
                 B   B
                 B   B    BBB
                 B   B    B B
                BB   B    B B
      1.8990    B    B   BB B
               B     B   B BB
               B     B   B  B    BB
               B     BB  B  B   BBB
               B     B   B  B   B B
      1.5731   B     B   B  B   B BB
              B      B   B  B   B  B
              B      B  BB  B   B  B   BB
              B      B   B  B   B  B   BBB
             B       B   B   B  B   B  B B
      1.2471 B       B   B   B  B   B BB B
             B       B   B   B  B  BB  B  B    BB
             B       B   B   B  B   B  B  BB   BBB
             B       B   B   B  B   B  B   B  B B
             B        B B    B  B   B  B   B B B
      0.9211 B        B B    B  B   B  B   B B B
             B        B B    B B    B  B   B B B
             B        B B    B B    B  B   B  B  B
             B        BB     B B    B  B   B  B  B
             B        BB     BB     B  B   B  B  B
      0.5952 B        BB     BB     BBB    BB    B
             B        BB     BB     BB     BB    B
              B       BB     BB     BB     BB    B
              B       BB     BB     BB     BB    B
              B       BB     BB     BB     BB    B
      0.2692B         BB     BB     BB     BB     B
             B        BB     BB     BB     BB     B
             B        BB     BB     B      BB     B
             B        BB     B      B      BB     B
             B         B     B      B      B      B
     -0.0568           B     B      B      B
          0.0000    10.6948   21.3896   32.0844   42.7793
```

15.7   Population Dynamics

An interesting class of simulation problems arises when the variations in the numbers of members of interdependent populations are studied as they vary with time. In this section, some simple population models will be developed and programmed. Although very simple, the models demonstrate some of the essential features of the complex models of world economies, which have received so much publicity in recent years.

15.7.1   A Model for Single Species Populations

In this section, a model will be developed which may be used to predict the future numbers of members of a single species population. Naturally, such predictions depend upon the assumptions made, such as the rate at which members of the population reproduce or die and whether or not these rates depend on the presence of other members of the population.

The purpose of this section is to show how verbal statements of these assumptions may be converted to simple mathematical models, suitable for use in simulation programs.

a) Development of the Mathematical Model   The number of members of a single population at time t will be represented by $P(t)$. A simple birth (or death) process means that a certain fraction of the population reproduces (or dies) in a particular time interval, say δt. Such a process may be modeled by an equation of the form

$$P(t+\delta t) = P(t)+c\times P(t)\delta t$$

In this case, c is called the relative growth rate. The words relative and rate imply that c must be multiplied by the actual population $P(t)$ and by the time increment δt to produce the actual growth during δt of $P(t+\delta t)-P(t)$. If c is negative, the population is, of course, decreasing.

One may rearrange this equation to produce

$$P(t+\delta t) = (1+c\times\delta t)\times P(t)$$

and, by induction, obtain the solution

$$P(t) = P(0)\times(1+c\times\delta t)^n, \text{ where } t = n\times\delta t.$$

Solutions to this equation are shown in Figure 15.17.

This equation would be a poor description of a large population which is competing for a limited food supply, sufficient to support a population P_{max}, but not adequate to allow reproduction at this level. How might this be modeled?

The solution is to arrange that the relative growth rate c should decrease to 0 as $P(t)$ increases to P_{max}. A simple formula which achieves this is

$$c' = c\times\left[\frac{P_{max}-P(t)}{P_{max}}\right]\times P(t)\times\delta t$$

which has the value c for the limiting case $P(t) \rightarrow 0$ and vanishes for $P(t) = P_{max}$. Thus, the single species model with competition is

Figure 15.17   Solutions to the simple growth equation.

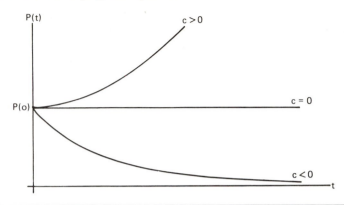

$$P(t+\delta t) \;=\; P(t)+c\times\left[\frac{P_{max}-P(t)}{P_{max}}\right]\times P(t)\times\delta t.$$

A simplification of this equation results if both sides of the equation are divided by P_{max} and if the ratio $P(t)/P_{max}$ is denoted by $p(t)$. This process of *normalization* is a useful tool in making mathematical models; here it results in the elimination of one parameter, P_{max}, from the model, thereby simplifying any simulation study. The normalized equation is

$$p(t+\delta t) \;=\; p(t)+c\times[1-p(t)]\times p(t)\times\delta t$$

When rewritten in the form of a differential equation, this equation is sometimes called the fundamental equation of ecology.

b) Development of the Algorithm   An algorithm will now be developed to test the model. The general structure of the simulation algorithm will follow the outline of Figure 15.1, and is given in pseudo code as Figure 15.18.

c) Program for Final Version of the Algorithm   A WATFIV-S program for the population growth simulation is given as Figure 15.19. The output from this program follows as Figure 15.20.

Figure 15.18   Pseudo-code algorithm for simulation of population growth with competition.

* Simulate a single species population.

* Variables used:
* **p** - the normalized population ratio P/Pmax
* **t** - the time
* **dt** - the time increment
* **c** - the relative growth rate
* **pinit** - the initial population (normalized)
* **tlimit** - the time limit for the simulation

* Obtain and record the simulation parameters and initial states.

get c, dt, pinit, tlimit
put 'The relative growth rate is', c
put 'The time increment is', dt
put 'The initial population ratio is', pinit
put 'The time limit is', tlimit

* Initialize the system.

t ← 0
p ← pinit
call setplt
call stopnt(t,p,'*')

* Compute and plot population values at time-steps **dt**.

while t ≤ tlimit **do**
    ⎡ t ← t + dt
    ⎢ p ← p + c*(1−p)*p*dt
    ⎣ **call** stopnt(t,p,'*')
call plotc(0)
stop

1, .25, .05, 9.99

```
C Figure 15.19 - Simulate a single species population.
C***************************************************************
C P      - the normalized population ratio P/Pmax
C T      - the time
C DT     - the time increment
C C      - the relative growth rate
C PINIT  - the initial population (normalized)
C TLIMIT - the time limit for the simulation
C***************************************************************
      REAL P, T, DT, C, PINIT, TLIMIT
C Obtain and record the simulation parameters and initial states.
      READ,   C, DT, PINIT, TLIMIT
      PRINT, 'THE RELATIVE GROWTH RATE IS     ', C
      PRINT, 'THE TIME INCREMENT IS           ', DT
      PRINT, 'THE INITIAL POPULATION RATIO IS', PINIT
      PRINT, 'THE TIME LIMIT IS               ', TLIMIT
C Initialize the system.
      T = 0.0
      P = PINIT
      CALL SETPLT
      CALL SETSIZ(21,41)
      CALL STOPNT(T,P,'*')
      CALL STOPNT(0.0,0.0,'-')
      CALL STOPNT(0.0,1.0,'-')
C Compute and plot population values at time-steps DT.
      WHILE(T.LE.TLIMIT) DO
         T = T + DT
         P = P + C*(1.0 - P)*P*DT
         CALL STOPNT(T,P,'*')
      END WHILE
      CALL PLOTC(0)
      STOP
      END
$ENTRY
  1.0, 0.25, 0.05, 9.99
```

Program Notes

• Two additional calls to STOPNT are included to place a dash at the 0 and 1 ratio levels. This ensures that the scale runs from 0 to 1 in the *y* direction.

It is clear that the model has the behavior which is desired. The population rises quickly but stabilizes as $p(t)$ approaches 1. Recall that this corresponds to $P(t)$ approaching P_{max}. Additional experiments with the model would reveal that this same limiting behavior is observed for all starting values, including those for which the initial population values are slightly larger than P_{max}. The reader is invited to try a number of such starting values and various growth rates to see the effect on the solutions (see Exercise 15.16).

Figure 15.20 Simulation of population growth with competition, output from the program of Figure 15.19.

```
THE RELATIVE GROWTH RATE IS            1.00000000
THE TIME INCREMENT IS                  0.25000000
THE INITIAL POPULATION RATIO IS        0.05000000
THE TIME LIMIT IS                      9.98999900
 - NUMBER OF POINTS: SUBMITTED    43, PLOTTED    43


       1.0000-                        * * * * * * * * * * * * *
                                    * * * *
                                  * * *
                                *
                               *
       0.7500                  *
                              *
                             *
                            *
       0.5000               *
                           *
                          *
                         *
       0.2500           *
                       *
                      * *
                    * * *
                  * *
       0.0000-
            0.0000    2.5000    5.0000    7.5000    10.0000
```

15.7.2 A Prey-Predator System

A more complex simulation problem is the study of the interactions between two (or more) species, one of which (the predator) depends upon another (the prey) as a primary food source. Such a system is called a prey-predator ecological system, and the one which will be examined here is a hypothetical fox-rabbit system.

a) Development of the Mathematical Model   It will be assumed that the rabbits exist in an environment in which vegetable food sources suffice to support a maximum population of R_{max} rabbits. The model developed in the last section may be applied to this problem to give a "rabbit" equation:

$$R(t+\delta t) = R(t)+c\times\delta t\times\left[\frac{R_{max}-R(t)}{R_{max}}\right]\times R(t)$$

The fractional growth rate c for the rabbit population would have to be found by experimental observation in an actual environment. For the hypothetical situation discussed here, it will be assumed that the increase, with no competition, is four/month for each pair, corresponding to $c = 2$ when δt is measured in months.

It is also assumed that, in the presence of R_{max} rabbits and few foxes, the foxes will reproduce at the rate of four cubs per year per pair. However, if the foxes grow or the rabbits decline in numbers, the model must allow for the reproduction rate of the foxes to slow down. At the level of 15 rabbits/fox, it is assumed that the foxes will no longer reproduce at all, and will die off if the rabbit supply is even lower. A possible equation which incorporates these assumptions to model the number of foxes, $F(t)$, at time t is:

$$F(t+\delta t) = F(t)+0.167\times\delta t\times\left[\frac{R(t)-15\times F(t)}{R_{max}}\right]\times F(t)$$

Note that the growth rate for the foxes is 2/year or 2/12 = 0.167 (approximately) per month. All rates have to be related to the same time scale, of course, which is months for this model.

The model still needs to allow for the decrease in rabbits due to consumption by the foxes. The first model will assume that the foxes will consume 15 rabbits/month when there are R_{max} rabbits, but that the foxes will ration themselves to a consumption proportional to the number of rabbits when there are fewer rabbits. The modification to the rabbit equation which accomplishes this is

$$R(t+\delta t) = R(t)+2\times\delta t\times R(t)\times\left[\frac{R_{max}-R(t)}{R_{max}}\right]-15\times\delta t\times\left[\frac{R(t)}{R_{max}}\right]\times F(t)$$

Rather than deal with absolute numbers of rabbits and foxes it is convenient to deal with them as fractions of R_{max}. Letting $r(t) = R(t)/R_{max}$ and $f(t) = F(t)/R_{max}$ leads to the equations

$$r(t+\delta t) = r(t)+2\times\delta t\times r(t)\times(1-r(t))-15\times\delta t\times r(t)\times f(t)$$

$$f(t+\delta t) = f(t)+0.167\times\delta t\times f(t)\times(r(t)-15\times f(t))$$

A simulation program may now be produced for the rabbit-fox system using these latter two equations to change the state of the system, namely the values of $r(t)$ and $f(t)$, over the time-step δt. In this case, the initial states are $r(0)$ and $f(0)$ and the simulation parameters are δt and *timelimit*. One could also regard the growth rates and consumption rates as parameters, rather than fixing their values and imbedding them in the equations.

b) Development of the Program   The initial decomposition of Figure 15.1 is a useful starting point for the construction of this simulation program. The structure is so similar to that of the bull-hiker pursuit program that a step-wise refinement will not be repeated. It will be assumed that a study is to be carried out over a five-year period, and that the state of the system is to be recorded each month for plotting. A time step of one month does not prove to be satisfactory, however, due to the large changes which could occur in the rabbit population in one month (see Exercise 15.17). Ten time steps are used between calls on the plotting subroutine, with each step of size (1/10) month or 3 days (approximately). A WATFIV-S program follows as Figure 15.21.

The reader is invited to try the program with a variety of plausible initial data. Two examples are given in the output listed in Figures 15.22 and 15.23.

```
C Figure 15.21 - Study of rabbit-fox populations (version 1)
C****************************************************************
C R      - the normalized rabbit population ratio R(t)/Rmax
C F      - the normalized fox population ratio F(t)/Rmax
C T      - the time
C DT     - the time increment
C TMAX   - the number of months to run the simulation
C NSTEPS - the number of time steps per month
C****************************************************************
       REAL R, F, T, DT, RNEW
       INTEGER TMAX, MONTHS, NSTEPS, ISTEP
C Obtain and record the simulation parameters and initial states.
       TMAX = 60
       NSTEPS = 10
       T = 0.0
       DT = 1.0/NSTEPS
       READ, R, F
       PRINT, 'THE INITIAL RABBIT RATIO IS', R
       PRINT, 'THE INITIAL FOX RATIO IS   ', F
C Initialize plotting.
       CALL SETPLT
       CALL SETSIZ(31,41)
       CALL STOPNT(T,R,'R')
       CALL STOPNT(T,10.0*F,'F')
       CALL STOPNT(0.0,0.0,'-')
       CALL STOPNT(0.0,1.0,'-')
C Compute and plot population values.
C Compute the populations at tenth of a month intervals.
C Plot the population at the end of each month.
       MONTHS = 0
       WHILE(MONTHS.LT.TMAX) DO
          ISTEP = 0
          WHILE(ISTEP.LT.NSTEPS) DO
             ISTEP = ISTEP + 1
             T = T + DT
             RNEW = R + 2.0*DT*R*(1.0 - R) - 15.0*DT*R*F
             F = F + 0.167*DT*F*(R - 15.0*F)
             R = RNEW
             IF(R.LE.0.0) THEN DO
                  R = 0.0
             END IF
          END WHILE
          MONTHS = MONTHS + 1
          CALL STOPNT(T,R,'R')
          CALL STOPNT(T,10.0*F,'F')
       END WHILE
       CALL PLOTC(0)
       STOP
       END
$ENTRY
0.1, 0.002
```

Figure 15.22 First example of a rabbit/fox simulation, output from the program of Figure 15.21.

```
THE INITIAL RABBIT RATIO IS            0.10000000
THE INITIAL FOX RATIO IS               0.00200000
 - NUMBER OF POINTS: SUBMITTED    124, PLOTTED      124


     1.0000-
           RRRRR
               RRR
                RRR
                 RR
     0.8333 R        RR
                      R
                     RR
                    RRR
                   RRRRR
     0.6667                RRRRRRRRRRRRRRRR

     0.5000
           R                FFFFFFFFFFFFFFFFFF
                          FFF
                        FF
     0.3333            FF
                     FF
                    F
                  FF
                 FF
     0.1667      F
                FF
           R    FFF
              FFF
        FFFFFF
     0.0000-
        0.0000    14.9990    29.9979    44.9969    59.9959
```

It is apparent that both of these populations stabilize after a few years at $r = 0.67$ and $f = 0.045$ approximately. The actual values are $r = 2/3$ and $f = 2/45$, since substitution of these values in the equations produces no change in the state of the system.

This model is said to be stable, in the sense that the same final population values are reached regardless of the starting values. A mathematician could predict this property of the model using advanced techniques, but simulation allows the same result to be seen in an elementary way.

15.7.3 An Alternate Prey-Predator Model

Another version of the rabbit-fox model will now be developed to demonstrate that the behavior of such models may be a bit more subtle than the previous output would suggest. This version will be called the greedy fox model since it incorporates the assumption that a fox continues to consume rabbits at the rate of fifteen per month, as long as any rabbits remain. Another assumption is that the foxes may survive in small numbers, by consuming chipmunks, if all the rabbits disappear.

The first feature is incorporated by altering the term $-15 \times r(t) \times f(t) \times \delta t$ to $-15 \times f(t) \times \delta t$ in the first equation. The second assumption is modeled by changing $0.167 \times f \times (r - 15 \times f) \times \delta t$ to $0.167 \times f \times (c + r - 15 \times f) \times \delta t$ where c is a small constant. For

Figure 15.23 Second example of a rabbit/fox simulation, output from the program of Figure 15.21.

```
THE INITIAL RABBIT RATIO IS         0.10000000
THE INITIAL FOX RATIO IS            0.10000000
 - NUMBER OF POINTS: SUBMITTED   124, PLOTTED    124


         1.0000*


         0.8333
               F

               F
         0.6667          RRRRRRRRRRRRRRRRRRRRRRRRRRRRRRRRR
                    RRRR
             F  RR
              F
              *F
         0.5000     FF
              R    FFFFFF
                        FFFFFFFFFFFFFFFFFFFFFFFFFFFFFFFF

              R
         0.3333

              R

         0.1667
              R
             R

         0.0000-
            0.0000    14.9990   29.9979   44.9969    59.9959
```

example, $c = 0.01$ and $r = 0$ implies that the fox population would eventually become $R_{max}/1500$.

These changes are made in the WATFIV-S program which follows as Figure 15.24.

The output for three different sets of data is presented in Figures 15.25, 15.26, and 15.27. In Figure 15.25, for the initial values $r = 0.1$, $f = 0.002$, and $c = 0$, the study indicates that the rabbits and foxes may coexist indefinitely in this greedy fox model. Note, however, that the limiting values of the rabbit and fox populations are $R_{max}/2$ and $R_{max}/30$, somewhat lower than for the previous model.

```
C Figure 15.24 - Study of rabbit-fox populations (version 2)
C****************************************************************
C R      - the normalized rabbit population ratio R(t)/Rmax
C F      - the normalized fox population ratio F(t)/Rmax
C T      - the time
C C      - the chipmunk parameter
C DT     - the time increment
C TMAX   - the number of months to run the simulation
C NSTEPS - the number of time steps per month
C****************************************************************
        REAL R, F, T, DT, RNEW, C
        INTEGER TMAX, MONTHS, NSTEPS, ISTEP
C Obtain and record the simulation parameters and initial states.
        TMAX = 60
        NSTEPS = 10
        T = 0.0
        DT = 1.0/NSTEPS
        READ, R, F, C
        PRINT, 'THE INITIAL RABBIT RATIO IS', R
        PRINT, 'THE INITIAL FOX RATIO IS   ', F
        PRINT, 'THE CHIPMUNK PARAMETER IS  ', C
C Initialize plotting.
        CALL SETPLT
        CALL SETSIZ(31,41)
        CALL STOPNT(T,R,'R')
        CALL STOPNT(T,10.0*F,'F')
        CALL STOPNT(0.0,0.0,'-')
        CALL STOPNT(0.0,1.0,'-')
C Compute and plot population values.
C Compute the populations at tenth of a month intervals.
C Plot the population at the end of each month.
        MONTHS = 0
        WHILE(MONTHS.LT.TMAX) DO
            ISTEP = 0
            WHILE(ISTEP.LT.NSTEPS) DO
                ISTEP = ISTEP + 1
                T = T + DT
                RNEW = R + 2.0*DT*R*(1.0 - R) - 15.0*DT*F
                F = F + 0.167*DT*F*(C + R - 15.0*F)
                R = RNEW
                IF(R.LE.0.0) THEN DO
                    R = 0.0
                END IF
            END WHILE
            MONTHS = MONTHS + 1
            CALL STOPNT(T,R,'R')
            CALL STOPNT(T,10.0*F,'F')
        END WHILE
        CALL PLOTC(0)
        STOP
        END
$ENTRY
 0.1, 0.002, 0.0
```

Figure 15.25 First example of a greedy-fox/rabbit/chipmunk simulation, output from the program of Figure 15.24.

```
THE INITIAL RABBIT RATIO IS          0.10000000
THE INITIAL FOX RATIO IS             0.00200000
THE CHIPMUNK PARAMETER IS            0.00000000
 - NUMBER OF POINTS: SUBMITTED    124, PLOTTED     124


       1.0000-
                RRRRR
                    RRR
                    RR
                     R
       0.8333        RR
              R        R
                     RR
                      R
                    RR
       0.6667        R
                      RR
                       R
                      RR
                       R          RRRRR
       0.5000            RR      RR       RRR
                       RRR    R           RR
                       RRRR
              R
       0.3333            FFFFFFFFFFFFFFFFFFFFFFFF
                     FF
                    F
                   FF
                   FF
       0.1667      F
                  FF
              R     FFF
                 FFF
              FFFFFF
       0.0000-
            0.0000    14.9990   29.9979   44.9969   59.9959
```

In Figure 15.26, the results are given for the same initial values of r and f but with a small c value of 0.01. It may surprise the reader to observe that this apparently minor change results in the collapse of the system. The rabbit population rises to roughly R_{max} as before, but as the foxes become established, the rabbit population is completely destroyed. Then, the fox population dwindles away to the small residual value $R_{max}/1500$. This effect is perhaps more dramatic in Figure 15.27. Here the initial values $r = 0.49$, $f = 0.033$, with $c = 0.03$ represent values at which the system should be nearly in equilibrium, with very little change of state in any one time-step.

Figure 15.26 Second example of a greedy-fox/rabbit/chipmunk simulation, output from the program in Figure 15.24.

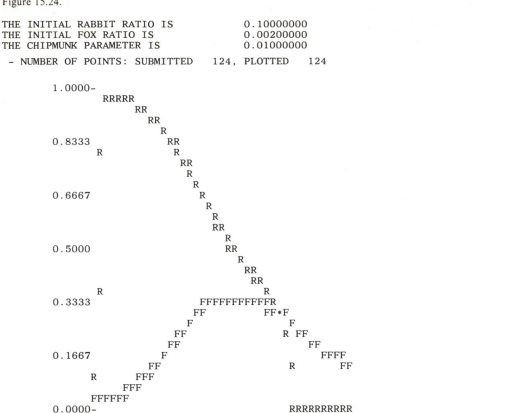

```
THE  INITIAL  RABBIT  RATIO  IS              0.10000000
THE  INITIAL  FOX  RATIO  IS                 0.00200000
THE  CHIPMUNK  PARAMETER  IS                 0.01000000
 - NUMBER  OF  POINTS:  SUBMITTED    124,  PLOTTED     124

        1.0000-
                RRRRR
                    RR
                    RR
                    R
        0.8333          RR
            R           R
                        RR
                        R
                        R
        0.6667          R
                        R
                        R
                        RR
                        R
        0.5000          RR
                        R
                        RR
                        RR
            R           R
        0.3333        FFFFFFFFFFFFR
                    FF          FF*F
                    F               F
                    FF          R FF
                    FF              FF
        0.1667      F                 FFFF
                    FF          R       FF
            R     FFF
                FFF
              FFFFF
        0.0000-                     RRRRRRRRRR
            0.0000    14.9990    29.9979    44.9969    59.9959
```

Note how the rabbit population oscillates with the small initial fluctuation increasing until the rabbit population shows a precipitate disappearance at about four years. The fox population then dwindles to about $R_{max}/500$.

There are many ways in which these models may be varied or improved. One possibility would be the incorporation of the assumption that the populations may reproduce only after a certain age has been reached. This will not be pursued here, but the reader is invited to think about ways in which this might be done.

15.8   Summary

This chapter presented a few simple simulation problems, and developed models and programs to investigate them. The principles used are valid, however, for the much more complex problems encountered in the real world.

Figure 15.27   Third example of a greedy-fox/rabbit/chipmunk simulation, output from the program of Figure 15.24.

```
THE  INITIAL  RABBIT  RATIO  IS          0.49000000
THE  INITIAL  FOX  RATIO  IS             0.03300000
THE  CHIPMUNK  PARAMETER  IS             0.03000000
 - NUMBER OF POINTS: SUBMITTED    124, PLOTTED    124


      1.0000-


      0.8333


      0.6667

                                   RR
      0.5000RRRR             RR   RRR
              RRRR       RR       RR
                RRRRRRR           R
                                  RR
                                  RR
      0.3333FFFFFFFFFFFFFFFFFFFFFFFFFFFFFFFFR
                                     *FF
                                      FF
                                  R   FF
                                        FF
      0.1667                             FFFF
                                            FF
                                  R

      0.0000-                    RRRRRRRRRRRR
           0.0000    14.9990    29.9979   44.9969    59.9959
```

An important aspect which was only addressed briefly was that of testing the models and programs for a range of parameters and initial conditions to gain insight into some real system. The variety and unpredictability of the results from the prey-predator model should make the reader cautious about accepting the results of any simulation study without extensive investigation.

15.9   References

The following references provide greater elaboration of the ideas of this chapter. Barrodale et al. (1971) provides additional elementary material and Braun (1975, 1978) is a good source for a variety of interesting problems. Forrester (1971) and Meadows (1972) extend the ideas of simulation to predictions about the evolution of the world.

Barrodale, I.; Roberts, F.D.K.; and Ehle, B.L. *Elementary Computer Applications*. New York: John Wiley and Sons, 1971.

Braun, M. *Differential Equations and Their Applications*. New York: Springer-Verlag, 1975 and 1978.

Forrester, J.W. *World Dynamics*. Cambridge, Mass.: Wright-Allen Press, 1971.

Gordon, G. *System Simulation*. Englewood Cliffs, N.J.: Prentice-Hall, 1969.

Meadows, D., et al. *The Limits to Growth.* New York: Universe Books, 1972.

15.10 Exercises

In most of the following exercises a program is requested to solve a specific problem. For each problem it is recommended that step-wise refinement be used in developing a pseudo-code algorithm to solve the problem. This algorithm should then be translated into WATFIV-S and run on the computer. Where appropriate, the program should be tested with a variety of data sufficient to ensure that the program does what it is supposed to do.

15.1 a) Generalize the investment example of Section 15.4 to allow for interest on the investment to be compounded semiannually.

  b) Generalize the investment example of Section 15.4 to allow for interest on the investment to be compounded quarterly.

15.2 Modify the investment example of Section 15.4 to determine, to the nearest tenth of a percent, the minimum interest rate required to have an accumulated investment of at least three times the final salary.

15.3 Modify the investment example of Section 15.4 to determine, to the nearest tenth of a percent, the minimum percentage of the income that must be saved in order to have the final investment be double the final salary.

15.4 Derive the equations for the motion of the bull and hiker in the example of Section 15.5 with the bull located to the left of the hiker.

15.5 For the bull-hiker problem of Section 15.5, what is the minimum speed for the hiker so that he may reach the trees safely, if the bull can run at 9m/sec?

15.6 Derive the equations for the motion of the bull and hiker under the assumption that the hiker initially runs at right angles to the line joining the bull and hiker. When the hiker's direction is straight towards the trees, he continues in this direction. Does this strategy improve the hiker's chances?

15.7 A hawk perches at the peak of a 30m tree, watching for field mice in a nearby pasture to move far enough from their burrows to be caught. The mice can run at 2m/sec and the hawk flies at a constant 20m/sec directly towards any mouse which is a potential meal.

  a) If a mouse is initially at a point 35m from the base of the tree and his burrow is 5m further away in a direct line, does the mouse reach safety?

  b) If the mouse is not caught, how much closer to the tree could he forage and remain safe?

  c) What if the burrow is 5m away but perpendicular to the line between the mouse and tree? (This is harder, since you must work in three dimensions.)

15.8 A short sighted owl makes its home at the peak of a 35m tree. When it dimly perceives any flying object passing within 30m, the owl pursues it at a speed of 20m/sec. The pursuit is stopped and the owl returns home if the object passes out of range. Some children enjoy teasing the owl by throwing a ball from the base of the tree at various angles to the horizontal at a speed of 25m/sec.

Develop a WATFIV-S program to determine and plot the path of the ball and of the owl (if he pursues the ball). The owl takes the ball home if he catches it and abandons the pursuit if he has not caught it before it returns to ground after bouncing once (losing 20% of its vertical velocity). Do the simulation for angles of 30, 45, 60, and 75 degrees.

15.9 Four cockroaches are initially placed at the corners of a square room with sides of length 3m. At a given time, each roach starts to pursue the one adjacent to it in a counter-clockwise direction, at a speed of 0.3m/sec. Plot the four trajectories, terminating when the separation between the roaches is less than 0.05m.

15.10 Generalize the previous problem to n (≤ 10) roaches placed uniformly about the periphery of a circle of radius 2m.

15.11 A stock car demolition derby is to be organized according to the following weird rules.

a) Seven cars are to be placed at 45 degree intervals (clockwise) around the perimeter of a circular field of radius 150m, in order of increasing maximum speed. The speeds are 10, 11, 13, 14, 14, 15, and 17m/sec.

b) Each car attempts to overtake the car adjacent to it in a clockwise direction (that is, the next faster car except for #7 which attacks #1).

c) Upon impact (separation < 2m), the overtaken car is knocked out. The overtaking car is somewhat damaged, however, and is assumed to suffer a 2.5m/sec reduction in maximum speed. It continues and attacks the next car in a clockwise direction.

d) When there are only two cars left, the faster one is declared to be the winner.

Develop a WATFIV-S program to simulate the derby. Modify the program to allow a rerun of the derby with car #4 scratched at the start, and the remaining cars fixed.

15.12 In 1943, London was attacked by V-1 "buzz-bombs" which flew over the English Channel at a constant altitude of 2,500m at a speed of 195 m/sec. In defense, the R.A.F patrolled at this altitude in their fastest aircraft, the Tempest, which could do 175m/sec indefinitely, and 200m/sec for a period of 20 seconds without overheating. Assuming that the Tempests patrol at right angles to the missiles' anticipated path, can sight an incoming missile at a range of 1,500m, and can turn at a maximum rate of 15°/sec, how closely must the Tempests be spaced so as to be able to intercept any V-1? (A Tempest pilot is deadly at 150m.)

15.13 Simulate the motion of a ball bouncing down a 25m corridor with a 3m ceiling. Assume that the ball is thrown at a speed of 15m/sec at an angle of −45 degrees (downwards). Follow the motion for a distance of 10m beyond the end of the corridor, where the floor but not the ceiling is assumed to continue. Assume that the acceleration due to gravity is −9.8 m/sec/sec and that the ball retains 85 percent of its vertical velocity when it bounces from the floor or ceiling.

15.14 A ball of mass 0.1kg is tethered to the ground by a light elastic cord of length 1m when unstretched. The force required to stretch the elastic is proportional to the distance stretched and is given by the formula

$$f = 0.75 \times elongation(kg\text{-}m/sec/sec).$$

Develop a program to simulate the motion of the ball if the ball is initially at rest at a point 3m above a point on the ground which is 1m away from the tether point. Assume that the acceleration due to gravity is −9.8 m/sec/sec, and that the ball loses 5 percent of its vertical velocity when it bounces. Follow the motion for 6 bounces.

15.15 A baseball team is considering a move from Oakland to Denver. The commissioner agrees, subject, among other things, to the fences being located far enough away that home run hitters do not gain any advantage due to Denver's thin air. Assuming that the Oakland fence is 135m from home plate, how far away should the Denver fence be? It is known that the force due to air resistance (drag) is proportional to the cross-sectional area and to the square of the velocity. That is,

$$f = k \times a \times v^2$$

At sea level, $k = 0.080$ and in Denver, $k = 0.065$ (approximately), when a is in m^2 and v is in m/sec. Assume that the mass of the ball is 0.1kg and that its diameter is 0.07m.

a)   First, find the initial velocity required for a ball to travel 135m, when hit at an angle of 45 degrees at sea level.
b)   Then, find the distance the same initial conditions will produce in Denver.

15.16 a)   Modify the single species population program of Figure 15.19 to simulate several populations with different initial populations but with the same growth rate. The program should produce a single graph.
b)   Modify the single species population program of Figure 15.19 to simulate several populations with different growth rates but with the same initial populations. The program should only produce a single graph.

15.17 It was suggested in Section 15.7.2 that a time step of one month would not be appropriate. Try running the program in Figure 15.24 with NSTEPS = 1 and observe what happens.

15.18 A river system contains two distinct fish populations - a species of large fish and another of small fish. The current population of small fish, which eat other small marine life, is 0.2p, where the environment could support p small fish. The small fish would double in numbers each month with unlimited food resources.

The large fish currently number $0.01p$ and consume 3 small fish per day each. The large fish would double each year with abundant small fish, but their reproduction falls to 0 if the ratio of small fish to large fish falls to 100 or less.

a) Construct a model of this system.
b) Construct a program to simulate the system for ten years with a variety of initial conditions.

15.19 An isolated lake could support a maximum population of 500,000 whitefish, which feed on various vegetable and marine life. With no competition, the whitefish would triple each year.

A government agency decides to promote a sport fishing industry by introducing a species of salmon to the lake. The salmon prey on whitefish and would increase at the rate of 50% per year in the presence of abundant whitefish. The salmon growth rate shrinks to 0 as their numbers grow to exceed 10% of the whitefish population. Salmon consume 10 whitefish per month.

a) Develop a program to simulate the growth of the whitefish from an initial level of 5,000, with no salmon predation.
b) Three years after the start of the simulation of a), introduce 2,000 salmon to the lake and follow the system for 20 years.

15.20 In the previous whitefish-salmon system, assume that each of the populations is reduced at a relative rate of 0.2% per day for a six-month fishing season each year. That is, 2 fish per 1000 of each species are caught each day. Start the fishing season 2 years after the introduction of the salmon and follow the system behavior for 18 years. How do the numbers compare to the previous problem? If the numbers surprise you, investigate the question in, for example, Braun (1975, 1978).

16
Probabilistic Simulation

16.1 Introduction

Probabilistic or *stochastic* models are used in the simulation of systems whose change in state is affected by chance. Although analytical techniques do exist for analyzing such systems, stochastic processes are often quite complex and thus simulation is an attractive tool.

The simulation of stochastic processes had its origin in the 1940's when it was used to solve nuclear reaction and shielding problems. The term *Monte Carlo* was coined at that time to describe some of the analysis techniques by analogy to games of chance. Since then, the use of simulation techniques has spread to almost all fields of science. Currently, probabilistic simulation techniques are used in the analysis and solution of problems in transportation, industrial production, business economics, marketing strategy, physical and chemical processes, performance of computer systems, and many other fields. In addition, these simulation techniques are also used in the playing of games which range from simple coin and dice tossing to extremely complex military games played by governments.

Although most of the above systems are too complex to be considered in detail at this time, this chapter introduces the basic terminology and concepts of probabilistic simulation. For further information, the reader may consult the references at the end of the chapter.

16.2   Simulating Stochastic Processes — Random Numbers

A stochastic process is characterized by the fact that the state of the system changes in response to random stimuli. This element of randomness is introduced through the use of a random number generator and some distribution function. The random numbers, usually generated over a fixed range, provide the randomness; the distribution functions describe the relative frequencies of possible outcomes; that is, how the random numbers should be interpreted for each specific problem.

Consider the simulation of a simple coin toss. If the coin does not land on its edge, there are only two possible outcomes of a toss, either heads or tails. Over many tosses, the order of occurrence of heads and tails would be random but, if the coin is fair, one would expect approximately the same total number of heads and tails to be produced. In this case the distribution of heads and tails is said to be uniform.

In the simulation of a gas station, the arrival times of cars would be random according to some distribution which described the overall arrival process. The service times would also show some pattern with a few cars requiring either very long or very short periods of service. The distributions of service times and arrivals are mathematical descriptions of these variations.

There are many ways in which random numbers may be generated. Manual techniques such as spinning a roulette wheel or drawing numbers from a hat are possible generation techniques, but they are not suitable for use in a computer simulation. Another possibility is to have library tables of random numbers such as those produced by the RAND Corporation, see RAND Corporation (1955). However the use of such tables is limited by either the storage requirements or the time required to access them. Furthermore, there is always the chance of requiring more numbers than are contained in the tables. Thus, for simulation purposes the random numbers are usually generated internally in the computer.

When generating random numbers for simulation there is a requirement that the numbers be *reproducible* (for comparision and testing purposes) but not *predictable,* and that the sequence of random numbers so produced should be as long as possible before it repeats itself (all such random number generators eventually repeat the sequence). Further requirements are that the random numbers be statistically independent of each other and that they be produced quickly with minimal storage requirements.

To achieve reproducibility, the random numbers must be generated by some deterministic method and as a result are called *pseudo-random* numbers. The "goodness" of such pseudo-random numbers is determined by whether or not they pass a series of statistical tests of randomness (see Exercise 16.3). In all subsequent discussions it will be assumed that a reference to random numbers in fact refers to such pseudo-random numbers.

Random numbers may be produced in many different distributions for a variety of possible applications. The following sections describe several different types of random numbers, their generation, and their use.

16.3   Uniformly Distributed Random Numbers

The simplest and most basic random number distribution is the uniform distribution. These random numbers may be used in the generation of all other distributions using suitable transformations. The property of uniformly distributed random numbers is that all numbers are equally likely to occur. A WATFIV-S subroutine called RANDOM, shown in Figure 16.2, will generate such random numbers. For the reader who is interested in finding out more about how they are generated see the remaining parts of this section. *Other readers should go to Section 16.4 directly.*

16.3.1   Generation of Uniformly Distributed Random Numbers

The most common ways of generating random numbers are the *congruential* methods. The three basic methods of this type are the *additive, multiplicative,* and *mixed congruential* techniques. The first two use only addition and multiplication, respectively, in the calculation of the random numbers while the mixed method uses a combination of both. Each of these method generates a sequence $\{n_i\}$ of nonnegative integers each less than some positive value m. In the mixed congruential method each random number n_{i+1} is derived (deterministically) from the previous random number by the relationship

$$n_{i+1} \leftarrow [a \times n_i + c] \ (\text{mod } m)$$

where a and c are non-negative integers and m is a large positive integer closely related to the word size of the machine. Thus, to generate a sequence of random numbers, one needs a starting value or *seed* n_0 and values for the constants a, c, and m. The values chosen for these quantities are quite important since they affect the *period* or length of the sequence before it repeats and the statistical properties of the random number sequence. For a given m, the values of a and c should be selected such that n_0 may be chosen arbitrarily.

As an example to illustrate what is happening, consider the generation of single digit numbers using decimal arithmetic ($m = 10$). It should be obvious that $a = 0$ and $c = 0$ are not good choices and that $a = 1$ would probably not introduce the desired randomness. It also turns out that $a = 5$ is a disastrous choice. Ignoring these possibilities for the constants, sequences of period 1, 2, 4, and 5 may be generated. The table of Figure 16.1 illustrates the sequences for several $a,c,$ and n_0 choices. As may be seen from the table, some values of a and c are better than others. The best sequences are those generated when $a = 6$ as they have the longest period. As an added bonus, which is not obvious from the few examples in the table, the choice of $a = 6$ and $c \neq 0$ or 5 allows *any* value to be chosen for the seed, and the sequence of random numbers will still have a period of 5. This characteristic does not hold for any other a and c combination as in those cases the choice of n_0 does affect the period.

As a result of their importance, the a and c values are usually predetermined for a particular random number generator. Even from this very simple example it may be seen that the choice of multiplier and addend must be made carefully.

For binary computers, m is usually chosen to give the maximum possible range, that is, from 0 to the largest positive number that can be represented. This usually means that $m = 2^{(b-1)}$ where b is the number of binary digits (bits) in the computer word. The maximum possible period, given suitable values for a and c, is $2^{(b-3)}$ or $m/4$. To

---

Figure 16.1 One-digit random number sequences for different choices of a, c and n_0.

a	c	n_0	next 6 digits of sequence	period
2	3	3	9, 1, 5, 3, 9, 1	4
2	3	5	3, 9, 1, 5, 3, 9	4
2	3	7	7, 7, 7, 7, 7, 7	1
3	7	1	0, 7, 8, 1, 0, 7	4
3	7	2	3, 6, 5, 2, 3, 6	4
3	7	4	9, 4, 9, 4, 9, 4	2
6	3	2	5, 3, 1, 9, 7, 5	5
6	3	3	1, 9, 7, 5, 3, 1	5
6	3	4	7, 5, 3, 1, 9, 7	5
6	6	3	4, 0, 2, 8, 4, 0	5
7	9	3	0, 9, 2, 3, 0, 9	5

---

obtain the maximum periodicity and the minimum amount of correlation between the numbers, a and c should be chosen such that:

1) $a = 8t \pm 5$ (t a positive integer);
2) $m/100 < a < m - \sqrt{m}$;
3) the binary digits of a have no obvious pattern;
4) c should be an odd integer with $c/m \simeq 0.21132$.

n_0 may be chosen arbitrarily. For more discussion, see Forsythe et al. (1977), page 242.

16.3.2   Uniformly Distributed Random Numbers in the Range [0,1)

The integer valued random numbers generated by the mixed congruential technique described above will have a range determined by the word size of the computer. In order to provide a measure of standardization over different computers, these random numbers are usually mapped into the range [0,1).[1] This mapping is performed by dividing each integer random number by m. The pseudo-code statements below indicate the calculations necessary to generate the next random number r in a sequence in the range [0,1).

```
n ← [ n * a + c ] (mod m)

r ← n / m
```

When implementing this algorithm on a computer one can take advantage of the fact that (mod 2^b) calculations are performed automatically in integer arithmetic. Because of the internal representation of integer numbers (an intrinsic property of computers) the (mod 2^b) calculation may generate either a positive or negative number. If the number is positive then it is in fact a (mod $2^{(b-1)}$) value which is desired. If the number is negative it may be converted to a (mod $2^{(b-1)}$) positive value by simply adding to it the *magnitude* of the largest negative number ($2^{(b-1)}$).

---

[1] The notation [0,1) means that 0 is included in the range but 1 is not.

A WATFIV-S subroutine to generate uniformly distributed random numbers is given in Figure 16.2. The constants in the subroutine are for the IBM 360/370 series computers, which have a 32-bit word length. Thus, the values are derived from

$$m = 2^{b-1} = 2^{31} = 2147483648$$

$$1/m = .4656612E-9 \quad \text{(value truncated)}$$

$$\text{range of integers} = -2147483648 \text{ to } +2147483647$$

and appropriate choices for the multiplier and addend are

$$a = 843314861$$

$$c = 453816693$$

The maximum possible period is $2^{29} = 536,870,912$ random numbers, many more than could be stored in a table of random numbers.

```
C Figure 16.2 -- Subroutine RANDOM
C               Subprogram to generate uniformly distributed
C               random numbers over the range 0.0 to 1.0 on a
C               32-bit word computer.  It will generate 2**29
C               random numbers before repeating.
C******************************************************************
C N       - previous integer valued random number (initially the
C            seed)
C U       - real valued random number where U is in [0,1)
C******************************************************************
        SUBROUTINE RANDOM(N,U)
        REAL U
        INTEGER N
        N = N * 843314861 + 453816693
        IF(N .LT. 0) THEN DO
            N = N + 2147483647 + 1
        END IF
        U = N * .4656612E-9
        RETURN
        END
```

Program Notes

• The addition of the magnitude of the largest negative number must be done by adding the value of the largest positive number and then adding one.

The random numbers produced by the mixed congruential method are statistically reasonable, reproducible, and generated quickly. Also, the method requires little storage. Thus, the technique is quite suitable for the majority of applications.

16.4   Using Uniformly Distributed Random Numbers

In most simulation problems it is not sufficient to just generate uniformly distributed random numbers (variates) in the standardized range [0,1). The specific requirements of each problem must be taken into consideration. Usually this means that the generated variates will be transformed through either a continuous or discrete mapping function onto a range of possible outcomes. The specification of the possible outcomes is given by a distribution curve such as those described in Chapter 13. Stating this in another way, one is given a distribution function and one wants to generate random variates with that distribution. The following sections describe two mapping operations for the uniform distribution.

16.4.1   Continuous Mappings of Standard Uniform Variates
Consider the situation in which a simulation problem requires random variates to be distributed uniformly in the range [a,b). The distribution function for these numbers is

Figure 16.3   Uniform distribution function.

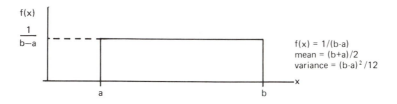

given in Figure 16.3. The required mapping operation is performed by the following expression.

$$x = u \times (b-a) + a$$

Thus, the mapping function needs only a standard uniform variate u and the limits of the required range [a,b). For instance, if it is desired to have random numbers which are uniformly distributed over the range [5,8), then the equation would be as follows.

$$x = u \times 3 + 5$$

The table of Figure 16.4 shows the mapping performed by this equation for selected values of u.

Figure 16.4   Examples of a continuous mapping of uniform variates.

u	x
0.0	5.0
0.25	5.75
0.5	6.5
0.75	7.25
0.999999	7.99999

16.4.2   Discrete Mappings of Standard Uniform Variates

Suppose that a simulation process is controlled by an event which has only 4 possible outcomes and that they occur randomly with the following probabilities.

$$\left. \begin{array}{l} \text{probability of outcome } 1 = p_1 \\ \text{probability of outcome } 2 = p_2 \\ \text{probability of outcome } 3 = p_3 \\ \text{probability of outcome } 4 = p_4 \end{array} \right\} \text{ where } p_1 + p_2 + p_3 + p_4 = 1.0$$

What these probabilities mean is that outcome 1 should occur $p_1 \times 100\%$ of the time; outcome 2 should occur $p_2 \times 100\%$ of the time; outcome 3 should occur $p_3 \times 100\%$ of the time; and outcome 4 should occur $p_4 \times 100\%$ of the time.

The diagrams in Figure 16.5 show possible histograms for two different probability weightings for the four outcomes. The weightings are indicated below each diagram.

Figure 16.5   Frequency histograms for two hypothetical processes.

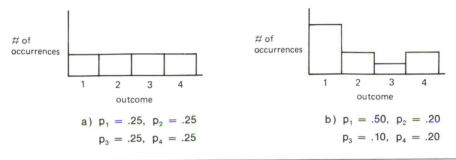

a) $p_1 = .25$, $p_2 = .25$
   $p_3 = .25$, $p_4 = .25$

b) $p_1 = .50$, $p_2 = .20$
   $p_3 = .10$, $p_4 = .20$

To obtain a mapping of standard uniform variates such that the above distributions occur is relatively simple. All that is necessary is to divide up the range of the uniform variate into classes, one for each outcome. The width of each class corresponds to the probability that that outcome will occur. The rationale behind this scheme is that since the random variates are uniformly distributed over the entire range, then the number of times a random variate falls in a given class is determined by the width of the class.

The diagrams in Figure 16.6 illustrate classifications for the probabilities given above, and an interpretation is provided below each diagram. These classifications will result in each outcome occurring the required percentage of the time.

To perform these mappings it is only necessary to check the value of the random variate. The following pseudo-code segment shows how to do this mapping for distribution b) in Figure 16.6.

Figure 16.6   Subdivision of the range [0,1) for the processes of Figure 16.5.

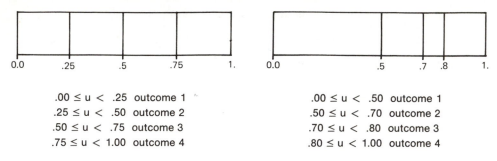

.00 ≤ u < .25 outcome 1
.25 ≤ u < .50 outcome 2
.50 ≤ u < .75 outcome 3
.75 ≤ u < 1.00 outcome 4

.00 ≤ u < .50 outcome 1
.50 ≤ u < .70 outcome 2
.70 ≤ u < .80 outcome 3
.80 ≤ u < 1.00 outcome 4

if 0.0 ≤ u < .50 **then**
  outcome 1
else
  if .50 ≤ u < .70 **then**
    outcome 2
  else
    if .70 ≤ u < .80 **then**
      outcome 3
    else
      outcome 4

If the mapping was to be done for distribution a) in Figure 16.6, the pseudo code would have an identical structure with only the probabilities changed. Of course, if the number of outcomes was changed the pseudo code could be modified to accommodate it.

Up to now, there has been no qualification on exactly what an outcome is. In fact, an outcome may just determine a specific value for a variable, or an outcome may be that an entire set of actions is performed. The technique described above is suitable for all such possibilities. However, a more specific mapping is possible for a restricted class of outcomes. For instance, when the set of outcomes is a set of consecutive integer values, $(a, a+1, a+2, \ldots, b)$, then the mapping of the standard uniform variate onto this range may be performed by the following equation.

$$x = int (u * (b-a+1)) + a$$

For example, if the set of possible outcomes is the integers (5, 6, 7, 8), then the following equation will perform the mapping.

$$x = int (u * 4) + 5$$

This mapping will give the same result as when the previous technique is used with each outcome having a probability of .25. The table of Figure 16.7 demonstrates this mapping on what would be the class limits in the previous method. Remember that the random variate 1.0 is never generated.

Figure 16.7   Examples of mapping uniform variates onto integer sequences.

class #	u	u*4	int(u*4)	int(u*4)+5
1	.00	0.0	0	5
	.2499999	.9999996	0	5
2	.25	1.0	1	6
	.4999999	1.999999	1	6
3	.50	2.0	2	7
	.7499999	2.999999	2	7
4	.75	3.0	3	8
	.9999999	3.999999	3	8

16.5   The Investment Problem Revisited

The investment problem of Chapter 15 was made quite simple by assuming that the simulation parameters were constant. Perhaps the most unrealistic assumption was that the increase in salary would be a constant percentage. It would be more likely that this figure would vary with the performance of the individual and with inflation. One could accept a constant value for the percentage of the salary put into savings since this is more-or-less under the direct control of the individual. A constant value for the percentage interest earned on savings could be rationalized on the grounds that it represents an average investment objective.

This section examines the investment problem when the percentage salary increase is not a constant, but is subject to random perturbations.

Example 16.1
Develop a program to simulate the investment problem of Example 15.1 when the percentage salary increase varies, from year to year, uniformly over the range 6.5 to 12%.

a) Problem Discussion   Since the percentage salary increase varies uniformly over the continuous range of 6.5% to 12%, a probabilistic simulation and the mapping technique of Section 16.4.1 can be used.

b) Development of a Program   Since this problem is very similar to Example 15.1, the program of Figure 15.5 may be used in this example with small modifications.

Since the percentage salary increase is no longer constant, it is not possible to obtain a value for PERINC from the data list. Instead, it must be computed for each year from the upper and lower bounds for the percentage increase. Letting the variables PERHIG and PERLOW represent these values respectively, the program statements to obtain and record the simulation parameters become as shown below.

```
READ, PERLOW, PERHIG, PERSAV, PERINT, SEED
PRINT, '% SALARY INCREASE RANGE IS', PERLOW, PERHIG
PRINT, '% OF SALARY SAVED IS ', PERSAV
PRINT, '% INTEREST ON SAVINGS', PERINT
PRINT, 'RANDOM NUMBER SEED', SEED
```

With respect to the percentage salary increase, PERINC, the following statements will perform the required calculation.

```
CALL RANDOM(SEED,U)
PERINC = U*(PERHIG - PERLOW) + PERLOW
```

These changes are incorporated into the program of Figure 16.8. The output of this program is shown in Figure 16.9. Notice that for the data given, the salary increase varies from 6.5% to 12%. However, despite this difference from the example in Chapter 15, the final amount saved is still only about double the final salary.

Call Rands (NSTART, R, N)

NSTART - defines the initial starting value
   (it must be an integer variable which contains
   a large odd positive value)

R - is a vector dimensioned to at least the value N

N - is the number of random numbers required

you want between A & B

(B-A) U + A

```
C Figure 16.8 - Program to simulate the investment problem
C                involving the saving of a fixed percentage of
C                salary at a fixed interest rate while the salary
C                increases vary uniformly over a given range.

C*****************************************************************

C SALARY - the current salary
C SAVING - the current savings
C YEAR   - the current year of the simulation
C PERLOW - the lower bound for the percentage salary increase
C PERHIG - the upper bound for the percentage salary increase
C PERINC - the percentage increase in salary
C PERSAV - the percent of salary put into savings
C PERINT - the percentage interest earned on savings
C SEED   - the seed for the random number generator
C U      - uniformly distributed random number

C*****************************************************************

      REAL SALARY, SAVING, PERLOW, PERHIG, PERINC, PERSAV, PERINT
      REAL U
      INTEGER YEAR, MOD, SEED
C Obtain and record the simulation parameters.
      READ, PERLOW, PERHIG, PERSAV, PERINT, SEED
      PRINT, '% SALARY INCREASE RANGE IS', PERLOW, PERHIG
      PRINT, '% OF SALARY SAVED IS ', PERSAV
      PRINT, '% INTEREST ON SAVINGS', PERINT
      PRINT, 'RANDOM NUMBER SEED', SEED
      PRINT, ' '
C Obtain and record the initial conditions.
      READ, SALARY, SAVING
      YEAR = 0
      PRINT, '           YEAR      % SALARY INCREASE        SALARY',
     +       '              SAVINGS'
      PRINT, ' '
      PRINT, YEAR, 0.0, SALARY, SAVING
C Simulate the system for 30 years, tabulating
C the state at 5 year intervals.
      WHILE(YEAR .LT. 30) DO
         YEAR = YEAR + 1
         SAVING = SAVING + (PERINT*SAVING + PERSAV*SALARY)/100.0
C        Calculate the percentage increase in salary.
         CALL RANDOM(SEED,U)
         PERINC = U*(PERHIG - PERLOW) + PERLOW

         SALARY = SALARY + PERINC*SALARY/100.0
         IF(MOD(YEAR,5) .EQ. 0) THEN DO
              PRINT, YEAR, PERINC, SALARY, SAVING
         END IF
      END WHILE
      STOP
      END
$ENTRY
6.5 12.0 10. 6. 9418537
13000. 0.
```

Figure 16.9   Output from the investment program of Figure 16.8.

% SALARY INCREASE RANGE IS	6.50000000	12.00000000
% OF SALARY SAVED IS	10.00000000	
% INTEREST ON SAVINGS	6.00000000	
RANDOM NUMBER SEED	9418537	

YEAR	% SALARY INCREASE	SALARY	SAVINGS
0	0.00000000	13000.00000000	0.00000000
5	8.41973500	18947.21000000	8412.34700000
10	8.61585500	30243.48000000	24128.33000000
15	10.14108000	48371.04000000	52882.97000000
20	7.00603700	73690.18000000	102871.70000000
25	10.97596000	116605.00000000	186598.60000000
30	7.70633800	169880.00000000	325153.00000000

16.6   Rolling a Die

As another simple example of probabilistic simulation consider the roll of a die.

Example 16.2

Develop a program to simulate rolls of a die. Count the number of occurrences of each side.

a) Problem Discussion   For this problem the system being simulated is a six-sided die, and the state of the system is determined by which side of the die is facing upwards. The system has six possible states, one state for each side of the die, and a change in state depends upon the event of rolling the die. Of course, this event also has six possible outcomes. In particular, the outcomes are that the die may show the numbers 1, 2, 3, 4, 5, or 6 on any roll. Assuming that the die is fair, each of these six outcomes has a probability 1/6 of occurring. Note the similarity to the example of Section 16.4.2. In order to keep track of the occurrences of each side, six counters must exist, the correct one being incremented after each roll.

b) Initial Decomposition   For this simulation, the general simulation model of Figure 15.1 can be used as a starting point. For this particular problem, however, it is somewhat artifical to associate a time step with the intervals between rolls of the die. Thus, the statement which increments the time will be omitted from the general form. The result is shown in Figure 16.10.

Figure 16.10 Initial version of a pseudo-code algorithm for rolling a single die.

1. Obtain simulation parameters and initial states for rolling the die.

2. **while** termination criterion is not met **do**

⌈ Change the state variables by rolling the die and record the state of the system.

3. Summarize the system behaviour.

stop

---

c) Refining Step **1.**   For maximum generality, the number of rolls of the die and the seed are made simulation parameters and obtained from a data list.

    * Obtain the number of rolls and the random number seed.

    get nrolls, seed
    put 'Number of rolls to be simulated =', nrolls
    put 'Random number seed =', seed

d) Refining Step **2.**   The criterion for termination is that all the rolls of the die must have been completed. Rolling the die involves determining the side that is facing up and keeping track of the number of occurrences of each side. Counting the occurrences of each side may be done using a six-element array with the side numbers as the index of the array. This counter array must be initialized before the simulation starts.

    * Initialize the counters.
    $i \leftarrow 1$
    while $i \leq 6$ **do**
        ⌈ $count_i \leftarrow 0$
        ⌊ $i \leftarrow i + 1$

    * Roll the die and collect statistics.
    $i \leftarrow 0$
    while $i <$ nrolls **do**
        ⌈ **2.1** Roll the die and count the result.
        ⌊ $i \leftarrow i + 1$

e) Refining Step **2.1**   The rolling of the die is simulated using the techniques of Section 16.4. A standard uniform variate is mapped onto the set of face numbers (1, 2, 3, 4, 5, 6) to determine which side is showing. This face number is then used as the index into the array COUNT.

```
call random(seed;u)
side ← int(u * 6) + 1
count_side ← count_side + 1
```

f) Refining Step **3.** The array COUNT contains the total occurrences for each face so it must be recorded. In order to make these statistics more readable, they are recorded on separate lines using a **while** loop.

```
* Record the number of times each side occurred.
put 'The statistics on rolling the die are:'
i ← 1
while i ≤ 6 do
  ⌈ put 'side', i, 'occurred', count_i , 'times'
  ⌊ i ← i + 1
```

f) Final Version Collecting all the refinements together gives the algorithm shown in Figure 16.11.

h) Program for the Final Version of the Algorithm A WATFIV-S program for the above algorithm is given in Figure 16.12.

Figure 16.11   Final version of the pseudo-code algorithm for rolling a single die.

* Simulate the rolling of a single die and count the occurrences of each side.

* Variables used:
* **nrolls** - number of rolls of the die to be simulated
* **seed** - seed for the random number generator
* **COUNT** - table of 6 elements to keep track of the number of times each side occurs
* **side** - side of the die which turns up after each roll
* **u** - uniformly distributed random number

* Obtain the number of rolls and the random number seed.

get nrolls, seed
put 'Number of rolls to be simulated =', nrolls
put 'Random number seed =', seed

* Initialize the counters.

i ← 1
while i ≤ 6 **do**
  count$_i$ ← 0
  i ← i + 1

* Roll the die and collect statistics.

i ← 0
while i < nrolls **do**
  call random(seed;u)
  side ← int(u * 6) + 1
  count$_{side}$ ← count$_{side}$ + 1
  i ← i + 1

* Record the number of times each side occurred.

put 'The statistics on rolling the die are:'
i ← 1
while i ≤ 6 **do**
  put 'side', i, 'occurred', count$_i$, 'times'
  i ← i + 1
stop

3000, 7498631

The output from the program is shown in Figure 16.13. As is expected the number of occurrences of each side is approximately the same. Note that one should never expect that these occurrences would be exactly the same. In fact, one would be suspicious if they had.

```
C Figure 16.12 - Program to simulate the rolling of a single die
C                    and count the occurrences of each side.
C****************************************************************
C NROLLS - number of rolls of the die to be simulated
C SEED   - seed for the random number generator
C COUNT  - table of 6 elements to keep track of the number
C            of times each side occurs
C SIDE   - side of the die which turns up after each roll
C U      - uniformly distributed random number
C****************************************************************
        INTEGER NROLLS, SEED, I, COUNT(6), SIDE, IFIX
        REAL U
C Obtain the number of rolls and the random number seed.
        READ, NROLLS, SEED
        PRINT, 'NUMBER OF ROLLS TO BE SIMULATED =', NROLLS
        PRINT, 'RANDOM NUMBER SEED =', SEED
C Initialize the counters.
        I = 1
        WHILE(I .LE. 6) DO
            COUNT(I) = 0
            I = I + 1
        END WHILE
C Roll the die and collect statistics.
        I = 0
        WHILE(I .LT. NROLLS) DO
            CALL RANDOM(SEED,U)
            SIDE = IFIX(U * 6) + 1
            COUNT(SIDE) = COUNT(SIDE) + 1
            I = I + 1
        END WHILE
C Record the number of times each side occurred.
        PRINT, 'THE STATISTICS ON ROLLING THE DIE ARE:'
        PRINT, ' '
        I = 1
        WHILE(I .LE. 6) DO
            PRINT, 'SIDE', I, 'OCCURRED', COUNT(I), 'TIMES'
            I = I + 1
        END WHILE
        STOP
        END
$ENTRY
3000    7498631
```

Figure 16.13 Results of rolling a die, output from the program of Figure 16.12.

```
NUMBER OF ROLLS TO BE SIMULATED =            3000
RANDOM NUMBER SEED =        7498631
THE STATISTICS ON ROLLING THE DIE ARE:

SIDE            1 OCCURRED        501 TIMES
SIDE            2 OCCURRED        488 TIMES
SIDE            3 OCCURRED        501 TIMES
SIDE            4 OCCURRED        489 TIMES
SIDE            5 OCCURRED        514 TIMES
SIDE            6 OCCURRED        507 TIMES
```

16.7   Other Distributions

In the investigation of real-life phenomena it has been observed that not all systems may be modeled using the uniform variates. There are several other distributions which have been found necessary. The following sections describe some of these.

16.7.1   Generating Normally Distributed Variates

The normal or Gaussian distribution is one of the more commonly used distributions in stochastic modeling. The normal distribution has the shape illustrated in Figure 16.14.

Figure 16.14   The normal distribution.

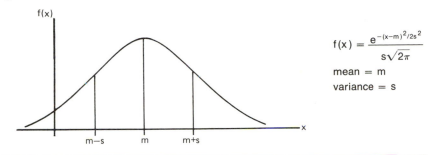

$$f(x) = \frac{e^{-(x-m)^2/2s^2}}{s\sqrt{2\pi}}$$

mean = m

variance = s

The generation of normally distributed random variates is given by the following equation. Note that it is necessary to generate twelve standard uniform variates to obtain one normally distributed variate.

$$x = \left[\sum_{i=1}^{12} u_i - 6 \right] \times s + m$$

Thus, it is necessary to supply a mean and standard deviation for use in the generation of the normal variates. A WATFIV-S subprogram to generate normally distributed variates using the above technique is shown in Figure 16.15.

16.7.2   Generating Exponentially Distributed Variates

If in a stochastic process the probability that an event will occur in a small time interval is quite small and if the occurrence of an event is statistically independent of other events, then the time interval between occurrences of these events is said to be exponentially distributed. Thus, in order to simulate these processes, it is necessary to generate random variates with an exponential distribution. Figure 16.16 shows a graph of the exponential distribution and the position of its mean.

```
C Figure 16.15 -- Subroutine NORMAL
C                    Subprogram to generate normally distributed
C                    random numbers.
C*****************************************************************
C N       - seed for the uniformly distributed random number
C             generator
C U       - uniformly distributed random number
C MEAN    - desired mean for the normally distributed random
C             numbers
C STDEV   - desired standard deviation for the normally
C             distributed random numbers
C XN      - normally distributed random number
C R       - uniformly distributed random number
C I       - counter
C*****************************************************************
        SUBROUTINE NORMAL(N,MEAN,STDEV,XN)
        REAL MEAN, STDEV, XN, U, SUM
        INTEGER I, N
        SUM = 0.0
        I = 1
        WHILE(I .LE. 12) DO
            CALL RANDOM(N,U)
            SUM = SUM + U
            I = I + 1
        END WHILE
        XN = MEAN + (SUM - 6.0)*STDEV
        RETURN
        END
```

Figure 16.16   The Exponential distribution.

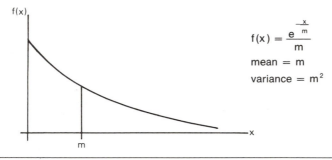

$$f(x) = \frac{e^{-\frac{x}{m}}}{m}$$

$$\text{mean} = m$$

$$\text{variance} = m^2$$

The mapping of the standard uniform variates into the exponential distribution is given by

$$x = -m \times \log_e (u_i)$$

Thus, for this distribution it is necessary to supply a mean before generation of the exponentially distributed random numbers. The WATFIV-S subprogram of Figure 16.17 performs the above computation.

```
C Figure 16.17 -- Subroutine EXPON

C                    Subprogram to generate exponentially
C                    distributed random numbers.

C*******************************************************************
C N       - seed for the uniformly distributed random number
C           generator
C U       - uniformly distributed random number
C MEAN    - desired mean for the exponentially distributed
C           random numbers
C E       - the exponentially distributed random number

C*******************************************************************
       SUBROUTINE EXPON(N,MEAN,E)

       REAL MEAN, E, ALOG, U
       INTEGER N

       CALL RANDOM(N,U)
       E = -MEAN * ALOG(U)
       RETURN
       END
```

16.7.3   Generating Poisson Distributed Variates

The Poisson distribution is a discrete distribution related to the exponential distribution and is concerned with predicting the total number of events that will occur in a given time interval if the time between arrivals is exponentially distributed. The Poisson

Figure 16.18   Two Poisson distributions with different mean values.

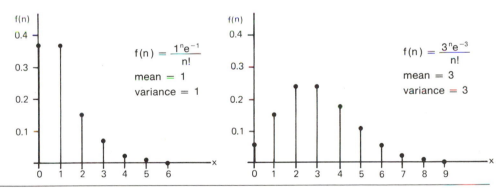

distribution function is shown in Figure 16.18. Note that the ordinate $f(n)$ gives the probability that a particular integer variate n occurs. The generation of a Poisson variate n is done by forming the products of successive standard uniform variates until the following relationship holds.

$$\prod_{i=0}^{n} u_i > e^{-m} > \prod_{i=0}^{n+1} u_i$$

In this case, just the mean must be provided for the calculation. The WATFIV-S subprogram of Figure 16.19 calculates Poisson variates.

```
C Figure 16.19 -- Subroutine POISSN
C                    Subprogram to generate random numbers which
C                    have a Poisson Distribution.
C******************************************************************
C N        - seed for the uniformly distributed random number
C            generator
C MEAN     - desired mean for the Poisson variates
C P        - Poisson distributed random number
C PROD     - product of uniformly distributed random numbers
C U        - uniformly distributed random number
C******************************************************************
      SUBROUTINE POISSN(N,MEAN,P)
      REAL MEAN, PROD, U, B, EXP
      INTEGER N, P

      P = 0.0
      B = EXP(-MEAN)
      PROD = 1.0
      CALL RANDOM(N,U)
      PROD = PROD * U
      WHILE(PROD .GE. B) DO
         CALL RANDOM(N,U)
         PROD = PROD * U
         P = P + 1.0
      END WHILE
      RETURN
      END
```

16.8   Queuing Systems

Waiting in a line or queue has become almost a daily experience for everybody. One waits in line for the teller's window in a bank, for the gas pumps in a filling station, for the cashiers in a grocery store, for food and the cashiers in a cafeteria, and especially at student registration time. In industry, one may have queues of items awaiting assembly, or a queue may exist for the services of a forklift truck or an overhead crane. Queues also exist in computer systems where many programs are waiting to be read in, waiting for execution, or waiting to be printed. These are but a few examples.

The motivation for waiting in a queue is that a common service or action is required by many persons or things. Thus, the basic elements of queuing systems are *servers* and *queues*. The server performs some service and the queue provides an ordering for those things awaiting service. A queuing system will usually have *arrivals* and *departures*. Arrivals enter the queuing system for service and departures leave the queuing system hopefully, but not necessarily, having been serviced.

There are many possible organizations for queuing systems. It is possible for queuing systems to have one or more servers and one or more queues. The diagram of Figure 16.20 illustrates several simple possibilities. In examples a) and b) the arrivals to the system enter into the single queue. Queuing systems often consist of many single-server single-queue systems in which case an arrival must make a decision as to which queue is to be entered. The organization and rules governing the operation of such queuing systems is called the *queuing strategy*.

Figure 16.20   Simple examples of possible queuing organizations.

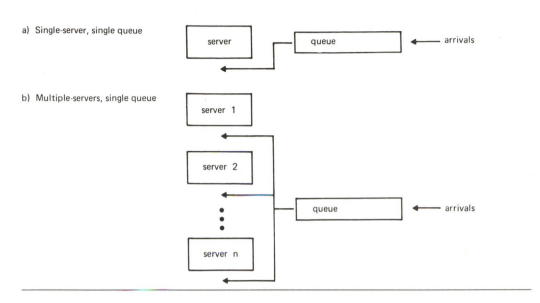

a) Single-server, single queue

b) Multiple-servers, single queue

In most queuing systems there is a desire to obtain a cost effective means of service. The objectives in providing the actual service are somewhat contradictory. It is desired that:

1)   the server(s) be as highly utilized as possible and the number of servers be kept to a minimum,
2)   the average waiting time be kept within a reasonable limit.

The utilization of the servers has a direct influence on the cost of providing the service. An acceptable average waiting time is sometimes determined by potential customer irritation (indeed a difficult thing to predict) and in other systems, such as in industry, may be determined by the fact that some processes need service within a specified time to prevent production losses.

To simulate such systems one needs to determine which of the numerous possible parameters have an influence on the operation of the system, specifically at the level on which it is to be simulated. The minimum information needed is the number of servers and queues, the number of events and how they affect the system, and the distributions of arrival times and expected service times. The following section gives an example of a simple queuing system.

16.8.1   Simulation of a Single-Pump Gas Station
As a first example of a queuing system consider the gas station problem stated below.

Example 16.3

Simulate a gasoline filling station which has one gas pump and one queue. Assume that from observations, the arrivals to the system are uniformly distributed with an average of 20 cars arriving per hour and that the service time is constant at 5 minutes. Statistics are to be gathered about the average queue length.

a) Problem Discussion   Although this problem as stated represents a simplification of a real filling station both in terms of the queuing strategies and the statistics requested, it can illustrate some important concepts.

Since the arrivals to the system are uniformly distributed at a rate of 20 cars per hour, this means that one car will arrive approximately every 3 minutes. Thus, in a one-minute time period, there is a 1/3 probability of a car arriving, and the techniques of the section on mapping of uniform variates may be used. The generation of service times in this problem is easy since it is a fixed value. The statistics concerning the queue length must be gathered by summing the queue lengths at every time step.

b) Selection of an Initial Decomposition   Since in this problem there is just one simulation to be performed on the filling station, the general simulation model of Figure 15.1 may be used, as shown in Figure 16.21.

Figure 16.21   Initial version of a pseudo-code algorithm for the gas station problem.

1.   Obtain simulation parameters and initial states for the filling station.

2.   **while** termination criterion is not met **do**

⌐ time ← time + tstep

⌊ Change the state variables of the filling station and record the state of the system.

3.   Summarize the system behaviour.

stop

---

c) Refining Step **1.**   The simulation parameters necessary for this problem include information regarding the simulation time step, time limit, service time, the seed for the random number generator, and the arrival probability. These values may be obtained from a data list.

```
* Obtain the simulation parameters for the filling station.

get tstep, tlimit, prarr, stime, seed
put 'The time step =', tstep
put 'The time limit =', tlimit
put 'The probability of arrival =', prarr
put 'The service time =', stime
put 'The random number seed =', seed
```

d) Refining Step **2.**   During each time interval it is necessary to check arrivals to the system, to check the pumps, and to collect the required measurements. The system should terminate when the time limit is exceeded. The following refinement does this.

```
queue ← 0
totque ← 0
tpump ← 0
time ← 0
while time < tlimit do
    ┌ time ← time + tstep
    │ 2.1 Check arrivals to the system.
    │ 2.2 Check the status of the pump.
    └ 2.3 Sum the queue length.
```

e) Refining Step **2.1**   If one knows the probability of a car arriving in one minute is some value prarr, then as long as the simulation time step is fixed at one minute, this probability may be checked against a standard uniform variate. However, if the simulation time step were to be reduced to a fraction of a minute, then the probability must be similarly adjusted. This may be done by generating a standard uniform variate and considering an arrival to occur if the random number is less than prarr*tstep. The queue may be maintained as a counter since no information is kept with the cars on their arrival.

```
* Check if a car arrives and if so, add it to the queue.
arrive ← 0
call random(seed;u)
if u < prarr*tstep then
    ┌ arrive ← 1
    └ queue ← queue + 1
```

f) Refining Step **2.2**   On each time step the pump must be checked to see whether it is busy or free. If it is busy, then the remaining service time required for the car should be computed, and a check performed as to whether the car has finished service. Since the pump may become free during a time step, a separate check must be made again as to whether it is free or not. If the pump is free and the queue is not empty, a car is taken from the queue and placed at the pump.

```
2.2.1 if pump is busy then
    [ Decrement the time the car has left in its service time and check if it is finished.
2.2.2 if pump is free and the queue is not empty then
    [ Take a car out of the queue, assign it a service time, and place it at the pump.
```

g) Refining Step **2.2.1**   If the pump is not free then it is still occupied by a car getting service. The car's service time must now be decremented to account for the time step just past. If the car's service time is finished, the car may be removed from the pump by marking the pump as free.

```
* If pump is busy, decrement the time the car has left
* in its service time, and check if it is finished.
if tpump > 0 then
    ┌  tpump ← tpump − tstep
    │  if tpump < 0 then
    │      ┌  tpump ← 0
    └
```

h) Refining Step **2.2.2**   When the pump is free and there are cars in the queue, it is necessary to take a car from the queue (just decrement the count), assign it the service time, and place the car at the pump. This may be done as follows.

```
* If pump is free and the queue is not empty, take a car out of the queue,
* assign it a service time, and place it at the pump.
if tpump = 0 and queue ≠ 0 then
    ┌  queue ← queue − 1
    └  tpump ← stime
```

i) Refining Step **2.3**   In order to determine the average queue length, it is necessary to sum the queue lengths at the end of each time interval.

```
* Sum the queue length.
totque ← totque + queue
```

j) Refining Step **3.**   The calculation of the average queue length is accomplished by dividing the sum of the queue lengths in each time interval by the total number of time intervals

```
* Calculate the average queue length and record it.
aveque ← totque / (tlimit/tstep)
put 'The average queue length was', aveque
```

k) Final Version   Putting all the refinements together gives the algorithm of Figure 16.22.

l) Program for the Final Version of the Algorithm A WATFIV-S program for the above algorithm is given in Figure 16.23. It is a direct translation of the algorithm with the addition of a statement which prints out the state of the system on every time step. This information allows some insight into the operation of the gas station.

The output of the program given in Figure 16.24 shows a simulation of the gas station over a 60-minute time period with a 1-minute time step. The arrival rate of 20 cars per hour was used, giving the probability of arrival as 1/3. As may be seen from the queue length, the gas station was unable to keep up with the number of cars arriving. The average queue length was four and steadily increasing. For this particular problem and the data given, such a result could have been predicted. In a given hour, an average of 20 cars should arrive. Since each car requires 5 minutes of service time, a total of 100 minutes would be required for their service.

In a real-life situation the length of the queue would probably deter many customers from arriving. Thus, the effective arrival rate of cars to the system would drop, and the queue would probably stabilize at some reasonable length. This sort of situation could actually be simulated by making the model more sophisticated.

Figure 16.22   Final version of the pseudo-code algorithm for the gas station problem.

```
* Simulate a single-queue, single-pump gas station

* Variables used:
* time - the time expressed in minutes
* tstep - the time increment expressed in minutes
* tlimit - the time limit expressed in minutes
* tpump - the service time in minutes that a car has left
* queue - the number of cars in the queue
* totque - the totals of the queue lengths
* aveque - the average queue length
* u - uniformly distributed random number
* prarr - the probability of a car arriving in any minute
* arrive - 0 = no car arrived, 1 = a car has arrived
* stime - the service time
* seed - starting value for the random number generator

* Obtain the simulation parameters for the filling station.

get tstep, tlimit, prarr, stime, seed
put 'The time step =', tstep
put 'The time limit =', tlimit
put 'The probability of arrival =', prarr
put 'The service time =', stime
put 'The random number seed =', seed
queue ← 0
totque ← 0
tpump ← 0
time ← 0
```

Figure 16.22   Final version of the pseudo-code algorithm for the gas station problem. (continued)

* Continue the simulation for **tlimit** minutes.

while time < tlimit **do**

> time ← time + tstep
>
> * Check if a car arrives and if so, add it to the queue.
>
> arrive ← 0
> **call** random(seed;u)
> **if** u < prarr*tstep **then**
>
> > arrive ← 1
> > queue ← queue + 1
>
> * If pump is busy, decrement the time the car has left
> * in its service time, and check if it is finished.
>
> **if** tpump > 0 **then**
>
> > tpump ← tpump − tstep
> > **if** tpump < 0 **then**
> >
> > > tpump ← 0
>
> * If pump is free and the queue is not empty, take a car out of the queue,
> * assign it a service time, and place it at the pump.
>
> **if** tpump = 0 **and** queue ≠ 0 **then**
>
> > queue ← queue − 1
> > tpump ← stime
>
> * Sum the queue length.
>
> totque ← totque + queue

* Calculate the average queue length and record it.

aveque ← totque / (tlimit/tstep)
put 'The aveque queue length was', aveque
stop

1, 60, .3333333, 5, 7948317

```
C Figure 16.23 -- Simulate a single-queue, single-pump gas
C               filling station.
C TIME     - the time expressed in minutes
C TSTEP    - the time increment expressed in minutes
C TLIMIT   - the time limit expressed in minutes
C TPUMP    - the service time in minutes that a car has left
C QUEUE    - the number of cars in the queue
C TOTQUE   - the totals of the queue lengths
C AVEQUE   - the average queue length
C U        - uniformly distributed random number
C PRARR    - the probability of a car arriving in any minute
C ARRIVE   - 0 - no car arrived, 1 - a car has arrived
C STIME    - the service time
C SEED     - starting value for the random number generator
```

```
C Figure 16.23 (continued)
      INTEGER QUEUE, TOTQUE, ARRIVE, SEED
      REAL TIME, TSTEP, TLIMIT, TPUMP, AVEQUE, PRARR, STIME, U
C Obtain the simulation parameters for the filling station.
      READ, TSTEP, TLIMIT, PRARR, STIME, SEED
      PRINT, 'THE TIME STEP            =', TSTEP
      PRINT, 'THE TIME LIMIT           =', TLIMIT
      PRINT, 'THE PROBABILITY OF ARRIVAL =', PRARR
      PRINT, 'THE SERVICE TIME         =', STIME
      PRINT, 'THE RANDOM NUMBER SEED   =', SEED
      PRINT, ' '
      PRINT, '            TIME            ARRIVALS       QUEUE',
     +      '        TIME LEFT'
      PRINT, ' '

      QUEUE = 0.0
      TOTQUE = 0.0
      TPUMP = 0.0
      TIME = 0.0
C Continue the simulation for TLIMIT minutes.
      WHILE(TIME .LT. TLIMIT) DO
         TIME = TIME + TSTEP
C Check if a car arrives and if so, add it to the queue.
         ARRIVE = 0
         CALL RANDOM(SEED,U)
         IF(U .LT. PRARR*TSTEP) THEN DO
            ARRIVE = 1
            QUEUE = QUEUE + 1
         ENDIF
C If pump is busy, decrement the time the car has left
C in its service time, and check if it is finished.
         IF(TPUMP .GT. 0.0) THEN DO
            TPUMP = TPUMP - TSTEP
            IF(TPUMP .LT. 0.0) THEN DO
               TPUMP = 0.0
            END IF
         END IF
C If a pump is free and the queue is not empty, take a car out of
C the queue, assign it a service time, and place it at the pump.
         IF(TPUMP .EQ. 0.0 .AND. QUEUE .NE. 0) THEN DO
            QUEUE = QUEUE - 1
            TPUMP = STIME
         END IF
C Sum the queue length.
         TOTQUE = TOTQUE + QUEUE
         PRINT, TIME, ARRIVE, QUEUE, TPUMP
      END WHILE
C Calculate the average queue length and record it.
      AVEQUE = TOTQUE / (TLIMIT/TSTEP)
      PRINT, ' '
      PRINT, 'THE AVERAGE QUEUE LENGTH WAS ', AVEQUE
      STOP
      END
$ENTRY
1.0 60.0 .3333333 5.0 7948317
```

Figure 16.24   Output from the gas station program of Figure 16.23.

```
THE TIME STEP              =              1.00000000
THE TIME LIMIT             =             60.00000000
THE PROBABILITY OF ARRIVAL =              0.33333330
THE SERVICE TIME           =              5.00000000
THE RANDOM NUMBER SEED     =        7948317
```

TIME	ARRIVALS	QUEUE	TIME LEFT
1.00000000	1	0	5.00000000
2.00000000	1	1	4.00000000
3.00000000	0	1	3.00000000
4.00000000	0	1	2.00000000
5.00000000	1	2	1.00000000
6.00000000	0	1	5.00000000
7.00000000	1	2	4.00000000
8.00000000	0	2	3.00000000
9.00000000	1	3	2.00000000
10.00000000	0	3	1.00000000
11.00000000	0	2	5.00000000
12.00000000	0	2	4.00000000
⋮	⋮	⋮	⋮
48.00000000	1	6	3.00000000
49.00000000	1	7	2.00000000
50.00000000	0	7	1.00000000
51.00000000	0	6	5.00000000
52.00000000	0	6	4.00000000
53.00000000	0	6	3.00000000
54.00000000	0	6	2.00000000
55.00000000	0	6	1.00000000
56.00000000	0	5	5.00000000
57.00000000	1	6	4.00000000
58.00000000	1	7	3.00000000
59.00000000	0	7	2.00000000
60.00000000	0	7	1.00000000

```
THE AVERAGE QUEUE LENGTH WAS              3.96666600
```

16.9   Simulation of a Multiple Pump Gas Station

The previous gas station model contained many simplifications concerning the number of pumps (1), the distribution of arrivals (uniform), and the service time (constant). In spite of these, the model does illustrate the concepts and general structure of a queuing problem. Extensions to that model may be incorporated relatively easily in the simulation program. Consider the following extension to that problem

Example 16.4

Develop a program to simulate a multiple pump, single queue gas station in which the arrivals have a Poisson distribution and the service time depends upon the number of gallons required by a car. The number of gallons required is normally distributed.

a) Problem Discussion   If the multiple pumps are to be incorporated, the actions on each pump will be identical to that of the single pump example. The program would probably best simulate multiple pumps with an array for the service time remaining on each pump. The changes required for the new arrivals and service time distributions will just replace the previous calculations.

b) Changes to the Single Pump Gas Station Program   In order to generate Poisson arrivals, it is necessary to have a seed and a mean. Note that the mean is the expected number of arrivals in the chosen time interval. The number of gallons calculation requires another seed and the mean and standard deviation of that distribution. Variables for these quantities must be declared and values obtained for them. To handle multiple pumps, it is necessary to be able to store the service time left for the car at each pump. For this problem it has been assumed that the number of pumps is a simulation parameter and may have a maximum value of 10. The following WATFIV-S program segment shows the changes, to the program of Figure 16.23, necessary to declare and obtain the simulation parameters.

```
      INTEGER NPUMPS, QUEUE, TOTQUE, ARRIVE, I
      REAL TIME, TSTEP, TLIMIT, TPUMP(10), AVEQUE
      REAL PMEAN, NMEAN, NSTDEV, RNUM, GALONS
      INTEGER PSEED, NSEED
C
C Initialize the various parameters.
C
      READ, TSTEP, TLIMIT, NPUMPS
      READ, PSEED, PMEAN, NSEED, NMEAN, NSTDEV
      PRINT, 'THE TIME STEP                     =', TSTEP
      PRINT, 'THE TIME LIMIT                    =', TLIMIT
      PRINT, 'THE NUMBER OF PUMPS               =', NPUMPS
      PRINT, 'THE EXPECTED ARRIVAL RATE         =', PMEAN
      PRINT, 'THE POISSON SEED                  =', PSEED
      PRINT, 'THE NORMAL SEED                   =', NSEED
      PRINT, 'THE AVERAGE GALLONS               =', NMEAN
      PRINT, 'THE STANDARD DEVIATION IN GALLONS =', NSTDEV
```

To initialize the system now requires a loop for each pump and may be done as follows.

```
      I = 0
      WHILE(I .LT. NPUMPS) DO
         I = I + 1
         TPUMP(I) = 0.0
      END WHILE
```

The arrivals to the system are generated using the Poisson random number generator POISSN described earlier. It is only necessary to supply the expected value to the subroutine and add the generated number to the queue.

```
      CALL POISSN(PSEED, PMEAN*TSTEP, ARRIVE)
      QUEUE = QUEUE + ARRIVE
```

The number of gallons required by each car is generated by supplying the normal random number generator NORMAL with the mean and standard deviation for the desired gallon distribution. It is assumed that the service time is composed of a constant term of 1 minute and a term of 1/2 minute per gallon pumped.

```
        CALL NORMAL(NSEED, NMEAN, NSTDEV, GALONS)
        TPUMP(I) = 1.0 + 0.5*GALONS
```

In order to check the status of each pump, the statements which perform this checking must be placed in a loop. This change and all of the changes above are shown together in the complete program of Figure 16.25.

The output from this program is given in Figure 16.26 for a 3-gas-pump station. Again the simulation was over a 60-minute period with the same probability of arrival. The normally distributed gallon requirements have a mean of 10 gallons and a standard deviation of 2.5 gallons. Thus, the service time would have a mean of 6 minutes in this case. As may be seen from the output, the 3 pumps are more than able to handle this number of cars.

```
C Figure 16.25 -- The gas pump simulation expanded.
C                    Simulate a single queue, variable number of
C                    pumps gas station queuing model at given
C                    time increments and for a given time limit.
C                    Allow for a variable arrival probability
C                    with Poisson distribution and allow for gas
C                    requirements that are normalized.
C******************************************************************
C TIME       - the time expressed in minutes
C TSTEP      - the time increment expressed in minutes
C TLIMIT     - the time limit expressed in minutes
C TPUMP(I)   - the service time in minutes that a car has left
C                at pump I
C NPUMPS     - the number of pumps
C QUEUE      - the number of cars in the queue
C TOTQUE     - the totals of the queue lengths
C AVEQUE     - the average queue length
C ARRIVE     - number of cars arriving in a time step
C PSEED      - seed for the Poisson distribution
C PMEAN      - expected number of arrivals per minute
C NSEED      - seed for the normal distribution
C NMEAN      - mean or average number of gallons required
C NVAR       - variance for the number of gallons required
C NSTDEV     - standard deviation for the number of gallons
C RNUM       - normalized random number
C GALONS     - number of gallons required
C******************************************************************
        INTEGER NPUMPS, QUEUE, TOTQUE, ARRIVE, I
        REAL TIME, TSTEP, TLIMIT, TPUMP(10), AVEQUE
        REAL PMEAN, NMEAN, NVAR, NSTDEV, RNUM, GALONS
        INTEGER PSEED, NSEED
```

```
C Figure 16.25 (continued)
C Obtain the simulation parameters for the filling station.
      READ, TSTEP, TLIMIT, NPUMPS
      READ, PSEED, PMEAN, NSEED, NMEAN, NSTDEV
      PRINT, 'THE TIME STEP              =', TSTEP
      PRINT, 'THE TIME LIMIT             =', TLIMIT
      PRINT, 'THE NUMBER OF PUMPS        =', NPUMPS
      PRINT, 'THE EXPECTED ARRIVAL RATE  =', PMEAN
      PRINT, 'THE POISSON SEED           =', PSEED
      PRINT, 'THE NORMAL SEED            =', NSEED
      PRINT, 'THE AVERAGE GALLONS        =', NMEAN
      PRINT, 'THE STANDARD DEVIATION IN GALLONS =', NSTDEV
      PRINT, ' '
      PRINT, '                TIME            ARRIVE          QUEUE'
      PRINT, ' '

      TIME = 0
      QUEUE = 0
      TOTQUE = 0
C Initialize the pump time parameters.
      I = 0
      WHILE(I .LT. NPUMPS) DO
         I = I + 1
         TPUMP(I) = 0.0
      END WHILE
C Continue the simulation for TLIMIT minutes.
      WHILE(TIME .LT. TLIMIT) DO
         TIME = TIME + TSTEP
C How many cars if any arrived?
         CALL POISSN(PSEED,PMEAN*TSTEP,ARRIVE)
         QUEUE = QUEUE + ARRIVE
C Process the various pumps.
         I = 0
         WHILE(I .LT. NPUMPS) DO
            I = I + 1
            IF(TPUMP(I) .GT. 0.0) THEN DO
                  TPUMP(I) = TPUMP(I) - TSTEP
                  IF(TPUMP(I) .LT. 0.0) THEN DO
                     TPUMP(I) = 0.0
                  END IF
            END IF
            IF(TPUMP(I) .EQ. 0.0 .AND. QUEUE .NE. 0) THEN DO
                  QUEUE = QUEUE - 1
                  CALL NORMAL(NSEED,NMEAN,NSTDEV,GALONS)
                  TPUMP(I) = 1.0 + .5*GALONS
            END IF
         END WHILE
C Sum and record the queue length.
         TOTQUE = TOTQUE + QUEUE
         PRINT, TIME, ARRIVE, QUEUE
      END WHILE
C Calculate the average queue length and record it.
      AVEQUE = TOTQUE / (TLIMIT/TSTEP)
      PRINT, ' '
      PRINT, 'THE AVERAGE QUEUE LENGTH WAS ', AVEQUE
      STOP
      END
$ENTRY
1.0,60.0,3
1073741827,0.3333333,1073741827,10.0,2.5
```

Figure 16.26 Output from the expanded gas station program of Figure 16.25.

```
THE TIME STEP                    =            1.00000000
THE TIME LIMIT                   =           60.00000000
THE NUMBER OF PUMPS              =            3
THE EXPECTED ARRIVAL RATE        =            0.33333330
THE POISSON SEED                 =   1073741827
THE NORMAL SEED                  =   1073741827
THE AVERAGE GALLONS              =           10.00000000
THE STANDARD DEVIATION IN GALLONS =           2.50000000
```

TIME	ARRIVE	QUEUE
1.00000000	1	0
2.00000000	0	0
3.00000000	1	0
4.00000000	0	0
5.00000000	0	0
6.00000000	0	0
7.00000000	0	0
8.00000000	0	0
9.00000000	0	0
10.00000000	0	0
11.00000000	1	0
12.00000000	0	0
. . .		
48.00000000	0	0
49.00000000	0	0
50.00000000	0	0
51.00000000	0	0
52.00000000	1	0
53.00000000	0	0
54.00000000	0	0
55.00000000	0	0
56.00000000	0	0
57.00000000	2	0
58.00000000	1	1
59.00000000	0	0
60.00000000	1	1

```
THE AVERAGE QUEUE LENGTH WAS                  0.05000000
```

16.10 Summary

A simulation of a probabilistic system has many similarities with a deterministic simulation, the major difference being that a probabilistic system selects which of its next possible states to enter in a random manner. This randomness is controlled according to the characteristics of the individual systems.

16.11 References

Forsythe, G.E.; Malcolm, M.A.; and Moler, C.B. *Computer Methods for Mathematical Computations.* Englewood Cliffs, N.J.: Prentice-Hall, 1977.

Knuth, D.E. *The Art of Computer Programming,* Vol.2: *Semi-Numerical Algorithms.* Reading, Mass.: Addison-Wesley Publishing Co., 1969.

Naylor, T.H.; Balintfy, J.L.; Burdick, D.S; and Chu, K., *Computer Simulation Techniques*. New York: John Wiley and Sons, 1966.

RAND Corporation. *A Million Random Digits with 100,000 Normal Deviates*. Glencoe, Ill.: The Free Press, 1955.

Shannon, R.E. *Systems Simulation*. Englewood Cliffs, N.J.: Prentice-Hall, 1975.

16.12   Exercises

In most of the following exercises a program is requested to solve a specific problem. For each problem it is recommended that step-wise refinement be used in developing a pseudo-code algorithm to solve the problem. This algorithm should then be translated into WATFIV-S and run on the computer. Where appropriate, the program should be tested with a variety of data sufficient to ensure that the program does what it is supposed to do.

16.1 The random number generator RANDOM generates random numbers which are uniformly distributed in the range 0.0 to 1.0. The expected mean of these numbers is 0.5 with a standard deviation of 0.289.

  a) Develop a WATFIV-S program which will plot the mean versus N, the number of random numbers being tested, for N = 1, 11, 21, . . . , 1001.

  b) Develop a WATFIV-S program that, for a given seed, will calculate the mean and standard deviation for 5 consecutive groups of random numbers, each group containing 200 random numbers.

16.2 Develop a WATFIV-S program to compute the mean and standard deviation for random numbers generated according to the normal, exponential, and Poisson distributions. Compute the percentage difference between the calculated values and the expected values.

16.3 There are many ways available to test the "goodness" of a uniformly distributed, random number generator. Two of the simplest tests are described below.

  a) Divide the range [0,1] into *l* equal classes. Generate *n* random numbers and count how many fall into each class. The class frequencies should be approximately the same and equal to *n/l*.

  b) Count the number of upward runs (that is, sequential runs of random numbers in ascending order) of length *k* and count the number of downward runs (that is, sequential runs of random numbers in descending order) of length *k*. For each value of *k* the counts should be approximately the same.

Develop and test WATFIV-S subroutines, one for each of a) and b), that will test the random numbers produced by the random number generator RANDOM.

16.4 The probability density function illustrates the shape of the curve for each random number distribution. Develop a WATFIV-S program that will draw a curve corresponding to the histogram of the values generated by the uniform, normal, exponential, and Poisson distributed random numbers.

16.5 The game of ODDS and EVENS involves tossing 2 coins. The result of each toss may be either ODDS (that is, one HEAD and one TAIL) or EVENS (that is, two HEADS or two TAILS). Develop a WATFIV-S program to simulate this game for 1000 tosses and determine the number of ODDS and EVENS that occur.

16.6 The following game is played by two people using coins. In each play of the game, each person *shows* one side of a coin (that is, either HEADS or TAILS). The payoff on each play is determined by the following rules.

Person 1	*Person 2*	*result*
HEADS	HEADS	person 2 pays person 1 $20
HEADS	TAILS	person 1 pays person 2 $30
TAILS	HEADS	person 1 pays person 2 $10
TAILS	TAILS	person 2 pays person 1 $20

a) Assuming that there is an equal chance of each person choosing HEADS or TAILS the amount of money lost by either player should be approximately zero. Develop a WATFIV-S program to simulate this game over 1000 plays.

b) Assume that person 1 is a crafty individual who recognizes that if he can show TAILS more often than HEADS (without alerting person 2), he can minimize the amount of money he gives away (that is, he will give away $10 more often than $30 when he loses). Person 1 decides to show TAILS 5/8 of the time and HEADS 3/8 of the time. Develop a WATFIV-S program to simulate 1000 plays of this game and determine the wins and losses. Compare these results to those of part a).

16.7 Assume that you are a passenger in a car driving down a highway. The driver of the car suggests a friendly wager which involves keeping track of the last two digits of the license plates of passing cars. He will bet you $10 that within the next twenty cars that pass, the same two digit number (00-99) will occur more than once. Develop a WATFIV-S program that will simulate this game to determine whether or not you should have taken the bet. Perform the simulation 100 times and determine the amount of money you would have won or lost.

16.8 Jack Spratt's wife has introduced the following domestic procedure to reduce the amount of money they spend on meat. If Jack is served meat today, his wife randomly selects one ball from a box containing 3 black balls and one white ball. If the selected ball is white, he is served meat tomorrow; if the ball is black, he goes vegetarian. On the other hand, if Jack is a vegetarian today, she randomly chooses one ball from another box containing 3 black and 2 white balls. Again, a white ball signifies meat tomorrow and a black ball signifies no meat tomorrow. The rules are suspended on Fridays, when fish is served (and counted as meat).

Develop a WATFIV-S program to simulate Jack's diet for one year, recording the number of vegetable and meat days. Start your simulation on a Friday.

16.9 The weather in a region is somewhat peculiar. According to the local weather office, the winter weather has the property that if it snows on one day, then the probability is 0.7 that it will snow the next day. If it does not snow on a certain day, then the probability is 0.2 that it will snow the next day.

Develop a WATFIV-S program that will simulate the weather in this region over 150 days of winter and count the number of snowy days. Assume that the probability is 0.5 that it will snow on the first day of the simulation.

16.10 One of the authors has been coerced into reducing his smoking habits according to the following scheme. Sixteen times a day, his wife will break one of his 100mm filterless cigarettes into 3 distinct pieces. If the author can form a triangle from the three pieces, he then smokes the pieces; otherwise he throws them away.

The author believes that his wife is deliberately attempting to break each cigarette in such a way as to prevent him from smoking the pieces. Develop a WATFIV-S program to check the validity of his suspicion. The program should determine the number of cigarettes the author would be able to smoke if the cigarettes were broken in a random manner with the breaks distributed uniformly over the length of the cigarette. Perform the simulation for a 100-day period.

16.11 Assume that the following diagram represents the street layout of a section of a city.

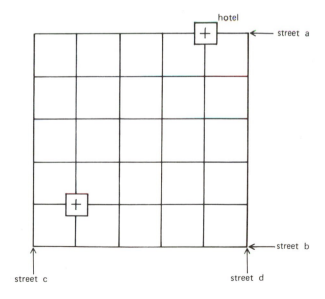

One evening two groups of students were out drinking at the hotel. At closing time, both groups left the hotel to walk back to the university and realized that they had forgotten the way. Thus, each group decided that in order to get back, they would adopt the following strategy. To start they would choose a street at random and walk to the next intersection. There they would again decide at random which street to choose next and walk one more block, and so on. Fortunately, both groups were able to remember the main streets indicated and thus did not go beyond them.

Each group started off by itself, and immediately a difference in their strategy became apparent. When group 1 reached an intersection, they could not remember which street they used to get there and thus had to choose their next direction from all streets leading into the intersection. Group 2, however, was in a little better shape and could remember the street they just took and thus always took a different street from the intersection.

Develop a WATFIV-S program that will simulate the above problem and determine which group gets to the university first. Perform several simulations varying the random number seed.

16.12 Consider a gas station which has only one pump. Cars arrive at an average rate of 20 per hour. The service time for a car is either 1 minute or 10 minutes, with probabilities of 4/5 and 1/5 respectively. In order to optimize the service, the gas station owner has two queues for the single pump. A car requiring 1 minute of service enters the first queue, and other cars enter the second queue. The first queue is a priority queue, and whenever the pump becomes free a car from this queue has priority.

Develop a WATFIV-S program which will simulate the operation of this gas station over a period of 3 hours. Determine the average number of cars in the queues.

16.13 A university has a computer on which student jobs are run. Students arrive at an average rate of 200 per hour, and queue if necessary. When they reach the front of the queue, they hand their program to the operator. Student jobs are of two types. Type 1 jobs fail to run and these take 10 seconds. Type 2 jobs are jobs which run successfully, and these take 20 seconds. On average, half the student jobs fail and half run successfully.

Develop a WATFIV-S program to simulate this process for 1 hour using a 5-second time step. Your program should print out the status of the system at the end of each time step and determine the time at which the computer is next free. Determine the average queue length over the complete simulation.

16.14 A local supermarket is considering setting up a single cash register express checkout for all customers with 8 items or less. By observation it has been determined that in any 1-minute time period the probability is 0.3 that such a customer will arrive at the checkout. The service time for a customer is observed to be 1 minute half the time, 2 minutes a quarter of the time, and 3 minutes one quarter of the time.

Develop a WATFIV-S program which will simulate the operation of this express checkout lane for an 8-hour period with a one-minute time increment. Determine the maximum number of people in the queue.

Appendices

A
A Summary of Pseudo-Code Algorithms

An algorithm describes a sequence of operations which may be followed to solve a particular problem. Pseudo code is a language used to describe the individual steps of the algorithms in this text. This appendix briefly summarizes the pseudo-code statements and their rules.

A.1 Constants

A constant is just a decimal number. For instance, the numbers 10, -5, 0, 846.94, -7.12, $.56 \times 10^{-3}$ are all constants.

A.2 Variables

A variable is simply a name which is used to represent or remember an integer or real value. The value represented by a variable may change, but a variable may have only one value at any given time. Variable names are written in lower-case characters. A variable is considered to be undefined until it has been given a value. A variable may not be used in a calculation until it has been assigned some value, that is, until it has been defined. As examples, the names sum, i, j, count, and price are all valid pseudo-code variable names.

A.3 Sets

A set is a collection of numeric values. The name of the entire set is referenced by an upper-case name. Individual values or elements of the set are referenced by using the set name in lower-case followed by a subscript to indicate the position of the particular element in the set. Examples are given in Figure A.1.

Figure A.1   Examples of references to a set and set elements.

X   - refers to an entire set of values which has the name X
X_1 - refers to the 1st element of the set X
X_2 - refers to the 2nd element of the set X
X_j - refers to the jth element of the set X

A.4   Expressions

There are two types of expressions: arithmetic and logical.

a) Arithmetic Expressions   An *arithmetic* expression describes required arithmetic calculations. The result of such an expression is a single numeric value. The arithmetic operations have a priority to describe the order in which these operations are performed. If adjacent operations have the same priority, they are performed from left to right. A summary and some examples appear in Figure A.2.

Figure A.2   Arithmetic operators and arithmetic expressions.

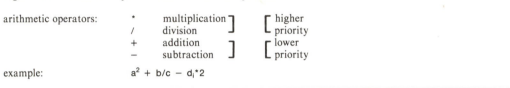

arithmetic operators:

*	multiplication ⎤	⎡ higher	
/	division ⎦	⎣ priority	
+	addition ⎤	⎡ lower	
−	subtraction ⎦	⎣ priority	

example: $a^2 + b/c - d_i*2$

---

b) Logical Expressions   A *logical* expression or *condition* is used for testing purposes and contains relational and logical operators. The result of a logical expression is either **true** or **false**. A relational operator tests the relationship between two arithmetic expressions. If the relation holds, then that relation has the logical value **true**; otherwise it has the logical value **false**. A logical operator performs Boolean logic on logical values. The relational and logical operators, Boolean logic, and operator priority are all listed in Figure A.3 along with several examples. The **and** and **or** logical operators are binary in that they require two operands, one on either side. The **not** logical operator is unary because it needs only one operand placed to the right of it.

A.5   Assignment Statements

Assignment statements are used to assign the value of an expression to a variable or a set element. The general form and an example are given in Figure A.4. The expression to the right of the assignment operator (←) is evaluated completely before the resultant value is assigned to the variable on the left-hand side (LHS).

Figure A.3   Operators and Boolean logic for logical expressions.

relational operators:

$=$	equal
$\neq$	not equal
$<$	less than
$\leq$	less than or equal
$>$	greater than
$\geq$	greater than or equal

logical operators:

not	not	highest priority
and	and	
or	or	lowest priority

Boolean logic:

not false → true
not true → false

false and false → false
false and true → false
true and false → false
true and true → true

false or false → false
false or true → true
true or false → true
true or true → true

Priority between types of operations:
1. arithmetic operations (highest priority)
2. relational operations
3. logical operations (lowest priority)

examples:

$x \neq y$
$r < s$ **or** $r > t$
$a+b \leq c^2-7$ **and not** $(d \geq 5)$

Figure A.4   Assignment statements.

general form: variable ← arithmetic expression

example: $r \leftarrow a^2 + b/c - d_i * 2$

A.6   The **stop** Statement

The **stop** statement is used to specify that execution of the algorithm is to terminate. Examples of this statement are shown in the following sections.

A.7   Comment Statements

Comment statements are used to provide an English description of a pseudo-code algorithm. Each such line starts with an * to distinguish it from the regular pseudo-code statements (see Figure A.5). A good algorithm includes comment lines to describe:

1) A brief English description of what the algorithm does.
2) A list of variables and their purpose in the algorithm.
3) A running commentary about important aspects in the algorithm itself.

Figure A.5   Comment statements.

general form: * Comment information.

example: * Algorithm to calculate a simple expression

$x \leftarrow 5$
$y \leftarrow x^3 + 5x^2 - 3.7x + 11$
put x, y
stop

A.8   The **get** Statement

These statements are used to obtain data values from a data list and to assign these values to the variables in the input list of the **get** statement. The data list is usually shown following the last statement of the algorithm. When executed, the **get** statement implies that the next data values in the data list are assigned to the values in the input list. Values on the data list are not reused. In the Figure A.6, x and y obtain the values 1 and 5.7 respectively. Variable z receives the value 4, while d_1 and d_2 receive the values 3 and 6.

Figure A.6   The **get** statement.

general form: **get** input list

example: * Algorithm to illustrate the **get** statement

get x, y
get z
get (d_i, i $\leftarrow$ 1 to 2)
stop
1, 5.7, 4, 3, 6

A.9   The **put** Statement

A **put** statement is used to indicate when messages and values are to be recorded by the algorithm (see Figure A.7). When executed, the **put** statement implies that the values of the variables and the messages in the output list are to be recorded.

Figure A.7   The **put** statement.

general form: **put** output list

example: **put** 'The values are:', x, y

A.10   The **while-do** Statement

These statements are used to indicate that a group of statements is to be executed repeatedly while some condition is **true**. All statements enclosed by the large left bracket are repeated while the condition (logical expression) in the **while-do** statement has a value of **true**. When the condition is **false** the statement following the body of the **while** loop is executed. The general form and an example appear in Figure A.8.

Figure A.8   The **while-do** statement.

general form:

```
while condition do
    ⎡ S - a sequence of statements to be repeated
```

example:

```
* This algorithm calculates the squares
* of the numbers from 1 to 10.
i ← 1
while i ≤ 10 do
    ⎡ j ← i * i
    ⎢ put i, j
    ⎣ i ← i + 1
stop
```

A.11   The **if-then-else** Statement

These statements are used to select alternate statements for execution depending on whether a condition is **true** or **false** (see Figure A.9). Only one of the sequences S_1 or S_2 is executed. After one of them is executed, the statement following the **if-then-else** is executed. The **if-then-else** does not imply repetition.

Figure A.9   The **if-then-else** statement.

general form:

```
if condition then
    ⎡ S₁ - statements executed if "condition" is true
else
    ⎡ S₂ - statements executed if "condition" is false
```

example:

```
if x ≤ 0.0 then
    ⎡ z ← x + y
else
    ⎡ z ← x − y
```

Note: If S_2 is null, the **else** clause is left off, resulting in an **if-then** statement.

A.12   Modules

A module is used to contain a segment of pseudo code which is logically distinct in the task that it performs. This allows for clean design of algorithms and allows a module to be executed from many different places. There are two types of modules, a subroutine module and a function module.

a) Subroutine Modules   Subroutine modules are the more common type of module. The general form of definition and usage is shown in Figure A.10. An example involving the definition and use of a subroutine module is presented in Figure A.11.

Figure A.10   General form of a subroutine module.

definition:
                                    smodule name (**imports**: import parameters; **exports**: export parameters)
                                    : S - statements executed when this module is referenced
                                    end module

use:
                                      call name (import arguments; export arguments)

Figure A.11   Example of a subroutine module.

```
* Use a subroutine module to square the numbers from 1 to 10.

i ← 1
while i ≤ 10 do
    ⎡ call square (i;j)
    ⎢ put i, j
    ⎣ i ← i + 1
stop
```

* Subroutine module to calculate m ← k*k

```
smodule square (imports: k; exports: m)
m ← k * k
end module
```

b) Function Modules   Function modules are used when the result of the module is to be part of an arithmetic expression. The general form of definition and usage is shown in Figure A.12. An example involving the definition and use of a function module is presented in Figure A.13.

Figure A.12   General form of a function module.

definition:
                                      fmodule name (**imports:** import parameters; **exports:** export parameters)
                                    : S - statements executed when this module is referenced
                                    name ← expression
                                      end module

use:
                                      name (import arguments; export arguments)

Figure A.13   Example of a function module.

```
* Use a function module to square the numbers from 1 to 10.
i ← 1
while i ≤ 10 do
    ⎡ j ← square (i;)
    ⎢ put i, j
    ⎣ i ← i + 1
stop

* Function module to calculate k*k

fmodule square (imports: k;)
square ← k * k
end module
```

B
Algorithms Expressed in Flowcharts

B.1 Introduction

A flowchart, sometimes called a block diagram or flow diagram, is simply a pictorial representation of an algorithm. Boxes of different shapes are used to depict the various actions. Lines with arrows are used to connect the boxes and to indicate the sequence of operations.

Flowcharts were one of the first ways of describing algorithms and still have many supporters. Although international standards have been established, numerous flowcharting symbols and conventions are used in practice. In addition, new flowcharting techniques are continually being developed in an attempt to keep them current with structured programming practices. The discussion of flowcharts in this appendix is neither extensive nor rigorous, presenting only one set of basic concepts and symbols.

B.2 Basic Flowchart Symbols

In flowcharting, the shape of each box is used to indicate a particular type of operation. The basic shapes used in this discussion are summarized in Figure B.1. Typically, each box will have lines leading to it (called *entries*) and lines leading from it (called *exits*) to indicate the sequence of operations or *flow of control*.

B.3 Terminal Elements

In a pseudo-code algorithm, the problem solver always begins with the topmost action and proceeds sequentially, unless otherwise instructed, until the **stop** action is encountered. Though a flowchart algorithm normally flows from top to bottom, this is not a strict requirement. Thus a flowchart normally includes both a start and stop symbol. Both are depicted in an oval box as shown in Figure B.2.

Figure B.1   The basic flowchart symbols.

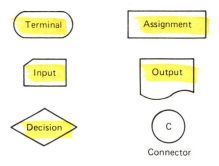

Figure B.2   The start and stop elements.

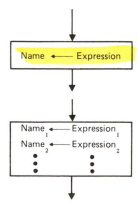

Naturally, each flowchart must have only one start symbol, located at the top of the diagram, but may include several stop symbols. Again, good practice should limit the algorithm to one **stop** symbol, preferably located at the bottom of the diagram.

B.4   Assignment Operations

Expressing calculations and assignment of values in a flowchart is very similar to pseudo code. The same notation is used inside a rectangle, as illustrated in Figure B.3. It is conventional to express several related calculations and corresponding assignments within the same rectangle where appropriate.

Figure B.3   The assignment element.

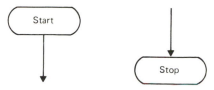

B.5   The get Element

To express the **get** action in a flowchart, the list of names requiring values is written inside a rectangle with the top left corner cut off — presumably to approximate the appearance of a punched card on which data historically has been recorded. Thus, the shape of the input box replaces the word **get** in pseudo code. The **get** element is illustrated in Figure B.4.

Figure B.4   The get element.

B.6   The put Element

Since the most common output medium is the printer, the flowchart output symbol is designed to resemble the end of a long piece of paper. The names of the quantities to be recorded are listed inside the box. The word **put** used in pseudo code is implied by the shape of the output box, illustrated in Figure B.5.

Figure B.5   The **put** element.

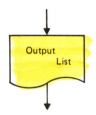

B.7   The while-do Element

Unlike the basic Elements expressed so far, the **while-do** action requires several flowchart symbols, as described in Figure B.6.

The condition, placed in a diamond-shaped box, is evaluated when the symbol is encountered. If the condition is **true**, the path labeled T is followed and the sequence of symbols S is performed. Then the flow returns to test the condition. When the condition becomes **false**, the flow jumps around the action sequence S along the line labeled F, to continue with the actions following the **while-do**. Notice that the S placed in the square box indicates any sequence of flowchart elements.

As with the pseudo-code version of the **while-do**, the same three conditions must be satisfied for the flowchart version of the **while-do** to function properly. Specifically, it is necessary to initialize the **while-do** control variables before entering the **while-do**, the condition must be properly phrased, and the action sequence S must at some point change the parameters.

Figure B.6   The **while-do** element.

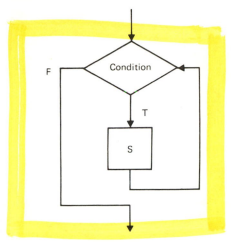

B.8   The **if-then-else** Element

The **if-then-else** action is also expressed using several flowchart symbols as illustrated in Figure B.7. Again the diamond box contains the condition to be evaluated. If the condition is **true**, the path labeled T is followed, and action sequence S_1 is performed. Otherwise, the condition must be **false** and the path labeled F is followed to action sequence S_2. In both cases, the procedure continues with the operations which follow the **if-then-else**.

Figure B.7   The **if-then-else** element.

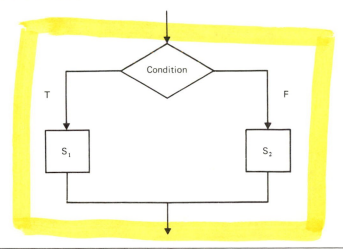

B.8.1 The if-then Element

In cases when the **else** action of an **if-then-else** is null, the flowchart description would be drawn as demonstrated in Figure B.8.

Figure B.8   The **if-then** element.

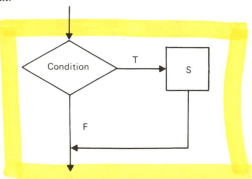

Notice that, for each diamond box, there are two "exit" arrows, one labeled T indicating the flow if the condition is **true**, the other labeled F specifying the flow for a **false** condition.

B.9   Drawing a Complete Flowchart

In the preceding sections, the flowchart elements for each of the six basic actions have been presented. It is now appropriate to combine these elements into a complete diagram. Consider the composite Example 2.5 discussed in Chapter 2.

Example B.1
   Draw a flowchart for an algorithm which will list the winning speeds at the Indianapolis 500 race and will indicate the amount that each speed is up or down from the previous race.

   Since this example has already been presented in pseudo-code form, the correspondence between the pseudo-code constructs and the flowchart elements is easy to see. The complete flowchart is presented in Figure B.9.

Figure B.9   Flowchart for Example 2.5 — the Indianapolis 500 problem.

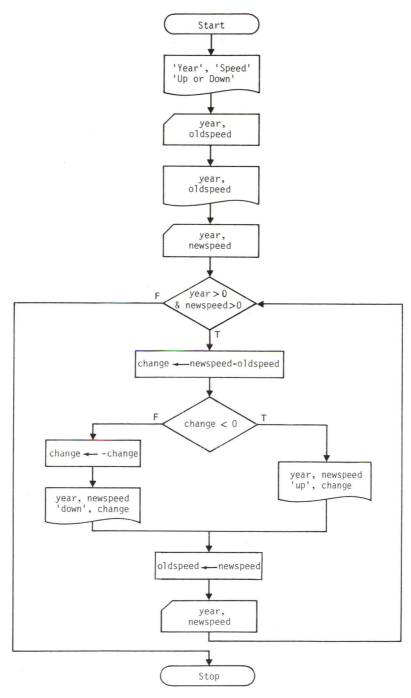

C
Translation of Pseudo Code to
WATFIV-S

The development of algorithms in this text is done independently of a programming language. In the place of a real programming language, a simple hypothetical language, called pseudo code, is used to describe algorithms. When it comes time to run the algorithms on the computer, the pseudo code may be translated very simply into a WATFIV-S program.

Because a programming language runs on a computer, there are always more details to be considered. For instance, a computer imposes restrictions on the size of values that may be used. It often needs additional information, such as specification statements and control cards, and has rules regarding where statements may be placed. The diagram in Figure C.1 illustrates some of the general considerations in the translation. The WATFIV-S statements which begin with a $ are control cards and are discussed in more detail in Appendix E. The END statement in WATFIV-S defines the end of a program segment.

Figure C.1   General form of pseudo code to WATFIV-S translation.

```
                                    $JOB    WATFIV
                                      :     specification statements

 :  statements of a                   :     WATFIV-S statements which
    pseudo-code                              correspond to statements
    algorithm                                of the algorithm
 stop                               STOP
                                    END
 :  data                            $ENTRY
                                     :  data
```

To run a WATFIV-S program on the computer, the program must be prepared in a machine readable form, traditionally punched cards. A computer card is 80 columns wide; each column may hold one character. The WATFIV-S statements must be in upper-case (a limitation imposed by keypunches), and rules exist to describe in which columns of a card the statements may be placed. For instance, the control cards and comment statements begin in column 1, while the regular WATFIV-S statements begin at or to the right of column 7. WATFIV-S statements may not extend past column 72.

This appendix describes the conversion process for each type of pseudo-code statement. Since Appendix A gives a summary of the pseudo code, the same order of discussion has been followed here. This appendix does not give an exhaustive set of rules for WATFIV-S since these are given in Appendix F. For more details on the WATFIV-S features, please refer to the appropriate sections of that appendix. Note: Conversion of pseudo code to standard WATFIV and FORTRAN IV is discussed in Appendix D.

C.1 Constants

The constants in WATFIV-S are similar to those in pseudo code except that WATFIV-S makes a distinction between integer- and real-valued constants.

a) Integer Constants An integer-valued constant is a constant which does not contain a decimal point. The numbers 10, -5, 0, and 76319 are all integer constants. Integer constants are also called *fixed-point* numbers since the decimal point is assumed to be fixed immediately to the right of the number.

b) Real Constants A real constant is a number which does contain a decimal point and thus may have fractional decimal values. The numbers 846.94, 0.0, -7.12, and .56E-3 are all real constants. Real constants are also called *floating-point* constants since the decimal point may appear anywhere in the number.

The distinction between integer and real numbers originated because it is easier for a computer to perform integer arithmetic than arithmetic on real values. In fact, in the early days of computing, integer arithmetic was performed by special electronic circuits (hardware), and real arithmetic was performed by programs (software). This situation still exists today but only in very small computers.

In WATFIV-S there is a physical limit (determined by the computer) to the size of both types of constants, and there are some alternate ways of specifying real constants.

C.2 Variables

WATFIV-S also has variables, but it distinguishes between those variables that may store integer values and those that may store real values. There are rules to determine which type of value a variable may store as well as rules on what constitutes a valid variable name. A valid variable name is composed of up to six characters. The first character must be an alphabetic character (A-Z), while the remaining characters may be alphanumeric (A-Z, 0, 1, 2, 3, 4, 5, 6, 7, 8, 9). The type of variable is specified in a special declaration statement. For example, the following statements declare that the variables COUNT and INDEX are to store integer values and that the variables ITEM and JOE are to store real values:

```
INTEGER COUNT, INDEX
REAL ITEM, JOE
```

C.3 Sets

In WATFIV-S, a set is usually called an array. Arrays are just variables which have been declared to contain a certain number of elements. The maximum size of arrays must be predefined in WATFIV-S using a specification statement. The entire array may be referred to by just using the name of the array by itself (allowed only in a limited number of places) and elements of the array have the subscript enclosed in parentheses.

Figure C.2   Referencing elements of a set in pseudo code and WATFIV-S.

x_1	X(1)
x_2	X(2)
x_j	X(J)
$y_{1,5}$	Y(1,5)
$y_{i,j}$	Y(I,J)

C.4   Expressions

As with pseudo code, WATFIV-S contains arithmetic and logical expressions. The differences are very few and are detailed below.

a) Arithmetic Expressions   An arithmetic expression in WATFIV-S has all the arithmetic operators of pseudo code and one additional operator to explicitly define the exponentiation operation. The priorities of these operators are identical to those of pseudo code, with exponentiation being the highest of all. Like pseudo code, adjacent operators of equal priority are normally executed from left to right. Exponentiation is an exception since adjacent exponentiation operators are executed right to left. These operators are shown in Figure C.3.

Figure C.3   Translation of arithmetic expressions from pseudo code to WATFIV-S.

a) Operators

x^2	exponentiation	X**2
*	multiplication	*
/	division	/
+	addition	+
−	subtraction	−

b) Example

$a^2 + b/c + 7 \cdot c^2 - d_i^2$	A**2 + B/C + 7.0*C**2 - D(I)**2

---

b) Logical Expressions   A logical expression in WATFIV-S differs from that in pseudo code only in that the symbols for the operators are different. WATFIV-S requires the symbols shown in Figure C.4.

C.5   Assignment Statements

The most visible difference between the assignment statements of pseudo code and WATFIV-S is that in WATFIV-S the assignment operator is the = symbol. A less obvious, but very important, difference results from the distinction WATFIV-S makes between integer and real values. This results when the LHS and RHS of an assignment statement are of different types, that is, REAL = INTEGER or INTEGER = REAL. In these cases, after the RHS has been completely evaluated, the result is converted into the type of the variable on the LHS.

Figure C.4   Translation of logical expressions from pseudo code to WATFIV-S

a) Relational Operators

$=$	equal	.EQ.
$\neq$	not equal	.NE.
$<$	less than	.LT.
$\leq$	less than or equal	.LE.
$>$	greater than	.GT.
$\geq$	greater than or equal	.GE.

b) Logical Operators

not	not	.NOT.
and	and	.AND.
or	or	.OR.

c) Examples

$x \neq y$	X .NE. Y
$r < s$ **or** $r > t$	R .LT. S .OR. R .GT. T
$a+b \leq c^2 - 7$ **and** $d \geq 5$	A+B .LE. C**2-7 .AND. D .GE. 5

Figure C.5   Translation of assignment statements from pseudo code to WATFIV-S

$r \leftarrow a^2 + b/c - d_i^2$	R = A**2 + B/C - D(I)**2

C.6   The **stop** and STOP Statements

The **stop** statement converts directly into the STOP statement of WATFIV-S. Both statements have the same role of halting the algorithm or program.

Figure C.6   Translation of the **stop** statement from pseudo code to WATFIV-S

stop	STOP

C.7   Comment Statements

In WATFIV-S, a comment statement is any statement which begins with a C in column 1. Such statements are ignored by WATFIV-S and are simply printed with the program listing. Exceptions to this rule are described in Appendix E.

Figure C.7   Translation of comment statements from pseudo code to WATFIV-S

* These are pseudo code	C THESE ARE WATFIV-S
* comments	C COMMENTS

C.8 The get and READ Statements

The input statement in WATFIV-S is the READ statement. There are many forms of the READ statement, but the simplest version is almost identical in form to the pseudo code get statement and is called the *free-format* READ statement. The actions of the get and READ statements, however, are slightly different. In pseudo code, the data is considered to be in one big list, and when a new get statement is encountered, the data for it is taken from the next values on the list. In WATFIV-S, the data is punched on cards (all 80 columns may be used). Each time a new READ statement is encountered, a new data card is read. When the computer reads a new data card, it starts scanning the card in column 1 looking for the data. The individual items of data are separated from each other by one or more blanks, a comma, or both. The computer assigns the first data value to the first variable in the input list, the second data value to the second variable in the input list, and so on. If there are not enough data values on the first data card, the computer automatically reads the next one and continues by scanning it. If the number of data values on a data card exceeds the number of variables in the input list, then the extra data values are ignored and lost.

Figure C.8 Translation of the get statement from pseudo code to WATFIV-S

a) General Form

get input list

READ, input list

b) Example

get x, y, z, (d$_i$, i←1 to 2)

READ, X, Y, Z, (D(I), I=1,2)

C.9 The put and PRINT Statement

The PRINT statement in WATFIV-S corresponds to the put statement. The form of the PRINT statement illustrated in Figure C.9 is called the *free-format* PRINT statement. Each time a PRINT statement is encountered, the computer starts printing on a new line. If the output list contains too many values to be printed on that line, the computer automatically advances to the next line and continues printing there.

Figure C.9 Translation of the put statement from pseudo code to WATFIV-S

a) General Form

put output list

PRINT, output list

b) Example

put 'The values are', x, y

PRINT, 'THE VALUES ARE', X, Y

C.10 The while-do and WHILE-DO Statements

The while loop structure exists in WATFIV-S with only minor differences in syntax. The pseudo-code condition is just a logical expression which is transformed according to the rules given in Section C.4. However, it must be placed within parentheses in the WHILE-DO statement. The range of the while loop in WATFIV-S is indicated by a special END WHILE statement.

Figure C.10   Translation of the **while-do** statement from pseudo code to WATFIV-S

a) *General Form*

while condition **do**	`WHILE(condition)DO`
⌐ S	`    :  WATFIV-S statements for S`
	`END WHILE`

b) *Example*

```
* This algorithm calculates          C This program calculates
* the squares of the                 C the squares of the
* numbers from 1 to 10.              C numbers from 1 to 10.
                                          INTEGER I, J
i ← 1                                     I = 1
while i ≤ 10 do                           WHILE(I .LE. 10)DO
    ⌐ j ← i * i                              J = I * I
    | put i, j                               PRINT, I, J
    ⌐ i ← i + 1                              I = I + 1

                                          END WHILE
stop                                      STOP
                                          END
```

C.11   The **if-then-else** and IF-THEN-ELSE **Statements**

The **if-then-else** statement of pseudo code may be translated directly into the IF-THEN-ELSE statement of WATFIV-S. The WATFIV-S statement has a slightly different syntax in that it uses a THEN DO and an ELSE DO in place of the **then** and **else**. The only other difference is that an END IF statement must be used to indicate the end of the IF statement. As with pseudo code, the ELSE DO clause of WATFIV-S may be omitted. In this case, the END IF statement is used to terminate the THEN DO clause.

Figure C.11   Translation of the **if-then-else** statement from pseudo code to WATFIV-S

a) *General Form*

if condition **then**	`IF(condition) THEN DO`
⌐ S₁	`        :   WATFIV-S statements for S₁`
else	`    ELSE DO`
⌐ S₂	`        :   WATFIV-S statements for S₂`
	`    END IF`

b) *Example*

if a ≤ b **then**	`IF(A .LE. B) THEN DO`
⌐ r ← a + s	`        R = A + S`
else	`    ELSE DO`
⌐ r ← a + t	`        R = A + T`
	`    END IF`

C.12 Modules and Subprograms

In pseudo code there are two ways to define a module and two ways in which modules can be used. The two module types are subroutine modules and function modules. In WATFIV-S, these modules are called subprograms, and there are the same two ways of defining and referencing a subprogram. Thus, there is a subroutine subprogram and a function subprogram.

The WATFIV-S action of transferring the data values between the arguments and parameters is similar to that in pseudo code. However, WATFIV-S does not make any distinction between **import** and **export** arguments or parameters. The values of all WATFIV-S arguments are copied into the corresponding subprogram parameters when the subprogram is invoked. On return from a subprogram, the values of all parameters are copied back into the corresponding argument. The exception to this rule is that arrays are not copied down and back. Because of their potential size, the invoking program and invoked subprogram share the same memory locations for arrays.

Figure C.12 Translation of pseudo-code subroutine modules into WATFIV-S

a) General Form

smodule name (**imports**: import list;	SUBROUTINE name(parameter list)
exports: export list)	
⋮ S	⋮ WATFIV-S statements for S
end module	RETURN
	END

b) Example

```
* Use a subroutine module          C Use a subroutine subprogram
* to square the numbers            C to square the numbers
* from 1 to 10.                    C from 1 to 10.
                                          INTEGER I,J
i ← 1                                     I = 1
while i ≤ 10 do                           WHILE(I .LE. 10) DO
    call square (i;j)                         CALL SQUARE(I,J)
    put i, j                                   PRINT, I, J
    i ← i + 1                                  I = I + 1

                                          END WHILE
stop                                      STOP
                                          END

* Subroutine module to            C Subroutine subprogram to
* calculate m ← k*k.              C calculate M = K*K.
smodule square (imports: k; exports: m)   SUBROUTINE SQUARE(K,M)
                                          INTEGER M, K
m ← k * k                                 M = K*K
                                          RETURN
end module                                END
```

Figure C.13   Translation of pseudo-code function modules into WATFIV-S

a) General Form

fmodule name (**imports**: import list; **exports**: export list) : S name ← "results" **end module**	```FUNCTION name(parameter list)``` : WATFIV-S statements for S NAME = "results" RETURN END

b) Example

```
* Use a function module            C Use a function subprogram
* to square the numbers            C to square the numbers
* from 1 to 10.                    C from 1 to 10.
                                          INTEGER I, J, SQUARE
i ← 1                                     I = 1
while i ≤ 10 do                           WHILE(I .LE. 10) DO

      ┌ j ← square (i;)                       J = SQUARE(I)
      │ put i, j                              PRINT, I, J
      └ i ← i + 1                             I = I + 1

stop                                      END WHILE
                                          STOP
                                          END

*Function module to                C Function subprogram to
*calculate m ← k*k.                C calculate M = K*K.
fmodule square (imports: k; )             INTEGER FUNCTION SQUARE(K)
                                          INTEGER K
m ← k * k                                 M = K*K
square ← m                                SQUARE = M
                                          RETURN
end module                                END
```

D
Pseudo Code to Standard WATFIV and FORTRAN IV

The standard WATFIV language and the FORTRAN IV language do not contain the structured statements of WATFIV-S. Thus, the translation of the **while-do** and the **if-then-else** as described in Appendix C are not possible, and these statements must be translated in a different way. A further consideration is that FORTRAN IV does not have the free-format statements of WATFIV and WATFIV-S. Thus, when translations into FORTRAN IV are performed, the **get** and **put** statements must be translated differently. This appendix is concerned with only these four statements since the other translations in Appendix C still hold. It should be noted that WATFIV-S does have all the statements of standard WATFIV and FORTRAN IV, but its added statements allow easier conversions.

There are several ways the translation can be done. The ways described here are simple methods which allow for an almost mechanical translation without having to be concerned with the details of the statements themselves. The translations use statement numbers, logical IF statements, GO TO statements, CONTINUE statements, DO loops, and FORMAT statements. Detailed information on these features is available in Appendix F.

D.1 Translation of the **while-do** Statement

The **while-do** may be translated into standard WATFIV or FORTRAN IV by using a logical IF and two GO TO statements. The translation is shown in Figure D.1. The **while** statement is replaced by a logical IF statement. Since the statements S are to be executed when the pseudo-code condition is **true**, the IF statement should branch around the statements S when the WATFIV-S or FORTRAN IV condition is not **true**. Thus, the .NOT. operator is used to negate the condition. The end of the loop requires a GO TO statement to start the loop over again, and the CONTINUE statement (which is a do-nothing statement) provides a destination for branching over the loop when execution of the loop is finished.

Under certain circumstances, it is possible to translate the **while-do** by using a DO loop. For instance, if the **while-do** uses a counter which starts at some value j, is incremented by some positive value l to a final value k, and j, k, and l are all greater than zero, then the translation may use a DO loop as shown in Figure D.2.

Figure D.1 Translation of the **while-do** statement from pseudo code to standard FORTRAN

a) General Form

```
while condition do                    mmmmm  IF(.NOT.(condition))GO TO nnnnn
     ┌ S                                   :    FORTRAN statements for S

                                           GO TO mmmmm
                                      nnnnn CONTINUE
```

b) Example

```
sum ← 0                                    SUM = 0.0
x ← 1                                      X = 1.0
while x ≠ 0 do                        1000 IF(.NOT. (X .NE. 0.0))GO TO 1001

     ┌ get x                                    READ, X
     │ sum ← sum + x                            SUM = SUM + X
                                                GO TO 1000
                                      1001 CONTINUE
```

Note: in this program the statement
1000 IF(.NOT. (X .NE. 0.0))GO TO 1001
can be replaced by
1000 IF(X .EQ. 0.0) GO TO 1001

Figure D.2 Translation of the **while-do** statement from pseudo code to standard FORTRAN

a) General Form

```
i ← j
while i ≤ k do                            DO mmmmm I=J,K,L
     ┌ S                                       :    FORTRAN statements for S
     │ i ← i + l
                                          mmmmm CONTINUE
```

Note: for this translation to be equivalent, K and L
must be unsigned integer constants or variables
which are non-zero. J must be an integer variable with
$0 < J \leq K$.

b) Example

```
i ← 1
while i ≤ 10 do                           DO 2000 I=1,10,1
     ┌ j ← i * i                               J = I*I
     │ put i, j                                PRINT, I, J
     │ i ← i + 1
                                          2000 CONTINUE
```

D.2 Translation of the if-then-else Statement

There are three different cases that may be considered here: the complete **if-then-else** statement, the **if-then**, and the **if-then** when the sequence block consists of just one simple statement.

For the **if-then-else** and the **if-then** translations, the logical IF is used, and the pseudo-code condition is again negated by the .NOT. logical operator. Figures D.3 and D.4 show the translations for these statements respectively. Figure D.5 shows how an **if-then** statement may be translated when S is a single statement.

Figure D.3   Translation of the **if-then-else** statement from pseudo code to standard FORTRAN

a) General Form

if condition **then**
```
    ⎡ S₁
```
else
```
    ⎡ S₂
```

```
                              IF(.NOT.(condition))GO TO mmmmm
                                :    FORTRAN statements for S₁
                                GO TO nnnnn
              mmmmm CONTINUE
                                :    FORTRAN statements for S₂
              nnnnn CONTINUE
```

b) Example

if a ≤ b **then**
```
    ⎡ r ← a + s
```
else
```
    ⎡ r ← a + t
```

```
                              IF(.NOT. (A .LE. B))GO TO 2000
                                     R = A + S
                                GO TO 2001
              2000       R = A + T
              2001 CONTINUE
```

Figure D.4   Translation of the **if-then** statement from pseudo code to standard FORTRAN

a) General Form

if condition **then**
```
    ⎡ S
```

```
                              IF(.NOT.(condition))GO TO nnnnn
                                :    FORTRAN statements for S
              nnnnn CONTINUE
```

b) Example

if r ≥ s **then**
```
    ⎡ t ← r
    ⎢ r ← s
    ⎣ s ← t
```

```
                              IF(.NOT. (R .GE. S))GO TO 100
                                     T = R
                                     R = S
                                     S = T
              100 CONTINUE
```

```
read (5,100)              write (6,100)
100  format          100  format
```

Figure D.5   Translation of **if-then** from pseudo code to standard FORTRAN when S_1 is a single statement.

a) General Form

if condition **then**   IF(condition) FORTRAN statement for S

$\quad\Big[$ S (a single statement)

b) Example

if x=0 **then**   IF(X .EQ. 0.0) Z = Y**2 + 6.0

$\quad\Big[$ z ← y^2 + 6.0

D.3   Translation of the **get** and **put** Statements.

Since FORTRAN IV does not have free-format input/output statements, formatted input/output must be performed. The use of formatted input/output allows the programmer much more control over this process, but it also requires more work on the part of the programmer. Through the use of FORMAT statements, the programmer indicates where data is placed on the data cards and where results are to be printed on the printer paper. FORMAT statements also control how the individual values are printed. Integer and real values must be handled differently. More information on FORMAT statements is available in Appendix H.

Figure D.6   Translation of **get** and **put** statements from pseudo code to standard FORTRAN

a) General Form

get input list

READ(5, mmmmm) input list
mmmmm FORMAT(format codes)

put output list

WRITE(6, nnnnnn) output list
nnnnn FORMAT(format codes)

b) Example

get x, y, i, j

READ(5,8000) X, Y, I, J
8000 FORMAT(F10.5,F10.5,I5,I5)

put 'The result is', r

WRITE(6,9000) R
9000 FORMAT(' THE RESULT IS',F10.5)

E
WATFIV-S Control Cards and Options

The WATFIV-S language has two special control cards which must be placed in a WATFIV-S program before it may be run on the computer. These control cards are the $JOB card and the $ENTRY card. The $JOB card identifies the start of the WATFIV-S program and allows specification of accounting information and compiler options. The $ENTRY card separates the program from the data. The complete program, including control cards, is called a *job*.

A typical WATFIV-S job will have the following format. The placement of these two cards and their formats is shown by the column numbers.

```
col. 1 col. 8  col. 16
   |     |       |
$JOB    WATFIV  acct#,optionsɒcomment
        ⋮   WATFIV-S program statements
$ENTRY
⋮    data for the program
```

With respect to the $JOB card, the account number format will depend upon the computer center or installation. The options (described below) are separated from the account number and each other by commas. A blank character (ɒ) terminates the options list and, thus, the options list may not contain a blank. All information following the blank character is assumed to be a comment. The information on the $JOB card may extend up to column 71. In some instances, the information may extend to column 79 at the discretion of the computer installation. However, it is preferable to use a C$OPTIONS card as described later in this appendix.

E.1 WATFIV-S Basic Options

The WATFIV-S compiler is rich with options. The options are commands to the compiler which allow users to tailor some of the compiler features to suit themselves. For instance, one can increase or decrease the error checking and reporting of the compiler as well as obtaining some control over its output format. Options exist which affect both compile time and/or execution time. All of the options have default

settings, so a novice programmer need not be concerned with these details initially.
There are two ways in which the options may be specified by the programmer:

1) Options may be placed on the $JOB card as described above. This means that the
    options specified will be in effect over the entire program unless changed in
    another manner.
2) Options may be placed on a C$OPTIONS card. This card has the following format
    and may be placed anywhere in a program:

        C$OPTIONS options list

Thus, options may be set and changed for selected portions of a program. The C$
notation allows a program containing such statements to be run under other
FORTRAN compilers where such statements are treated as comments.

a) Program Accounting, Input, and Output Options   The notation used in some of the
following options specifies alternate choices by separating them by the slash (/)
character and specifies the default setting of an option by underlining.

TIME=s / (m) / (m,s)
Specifies the maximum amount of execution time to be allowed for this program.
Numeric values are specified in seconds, or minutes, or minutes and seconds. The
default value is installation dependent.

PAGES=n
Specifies the maximum number of pages of output to be allowed for this program at
execution time. The default value is installation dependent.

LINES=n
Specifies the number of lines that are to be printed on each page for both the program
listing (compile time) and the output of the program (execution time). The default
value is 60. A value of 0 implies a continuous listing.

S=n
Specifies the maximum number of statements that may be executed by the WATFIV-S
compiler. The default value is installation dependent but is usually unlimited.

KP=29 / 26
Specifies the type of keypunch that was used to punch the program. The 029 keypunch
uses an EBCDIC code, and the 026 keypunch uses a BCD code.

PGM=mname
Allows a mainline program of a specified name to be compiled from the WATFIV-S
program library.

DECIMAL
This option forces the free-format output of REAL*4 values to be printed in a normal
decimal notation (F20.8) as opposed to the default scientific notation (E16.7). Note
that if values are too large, asterisks will be printed, and values that are too small will
be printed as zero.

LIST / NOLIST
Allows a programmer to print or suppress respectively, the program listing. (See also
Section E.2.)

LIBLIST / NOLIBLIST
Allows a programmer to print or suppress respectively, the listing of a library program.
Note that the LIST/NOLIST and LIBLIST/NOLIBLIST options are independent. (See
also Section E.2.)

b) Warnings and Extensions   In addition to extensive error diagnostics, the WATFIV-S compiler also issues the following types of messages:

1) Warnings   These messages are for conditions which, although not errors, are things the programmer may not have intended.
2) Extensions   These messages are issued when the WATFIV-S compiler detects something in the program, which, although it allows, may not be permitted by other compilers.

These messages do not affect program execution. The messages are controlled by the following options. (See also Section E.2.)

WARN / NOWARN
The WARN option causes the compiler to print the warning messages, and NOWARN suppresses these messages. Independent of this option, a count of the number of warning conditions is provided in the program summary at the end of the program listing.

EXT / NOEXT
The EXT option causes the compiler to print the extension messages, and NOEXT suppresses these messages. Independent of this option, a count of the number of extension conditions is provided in the program summary on the program listing.

c) Undefined Variable Checking   A common error in programming is attempting to use a variable before it has been assigned a value. The WATFIV-S compiler checks for this condition and issues an error message when it happens. However, this check does require extra storage and execution time. As a result, provision is made to turn off the checking when the program is known to be correct.

CHECK / NOCHECK / FREE
Allows control of undefined variable checking. The CHECK option turns on undefined variable checking, while NOCHECK turns it off. The FREE option is the same as CHECK except that it allows execution of the program to proceed as far as possible when compile time errors exist. (See also Section E.2.)

d) Miscellaneous Options   The following options allow the user some flexibility in the definition of parameter arrays and conditional compilation:

SUB / NOSUB
Relates to subscript checking on parameter arrays in subprograms. WATFIV-S contains a feature called pseudo-variable dimensioning (PVD), which allows a parameter array in a subprogram to be defined with a last dimension of size 1. When this is done, the actual size allocated for that dimension is such that as much as possible of the corresponding argument array is used. The NOSUB option allows a parameter array reference to have its last subscript larger than 1 and up to the actual size allocated for that dimension. The SUB option restricts the last subscript to the defined size.

CCOMP=nnnn / CCOFF=nnnn
Allows a user to specify that certain comment statements are to be compiled. The string nnnn represents a series of one or more digits 0 to 9. If a statement in the program begins with Cn in columns 1 and 2, then that statement is compiled as a regular WATFIV-S statement. The compiler blanks out the Cn. The option CCOMP=nnnn turns on the option; CCOFF=nnnn turns it off.

E.2   Miscellaneous Control Cards

There are many other control cards allowed by WATFIV-S. The following table shows the control cards which provide an alternate way of specifying the options indicated previously:

Options	Corresponding Control Cards	
CHECK / NOCHECK	C$CHECK	C$NOCHECK
EXT / NOEXT	C$EXT	C$NOEXT
LIST / NOLIST	C$LIST	C$NOLIST
WARN / NOWARN	C$WARN	C$NOWARN

Several more control cards are shown below.

C$EJECT
Force the compiler to skip to the top of the next page and continue printing the program listing. This control card is not printed and has no effect if NOLIST is in effect.

C$SPACE n
Forces the compiler to leave n blank lines in the listing. This control card is not printed and has no effect if NOLIST is in effect.

C$COPY membername
Allows a program segment of the specified name to be copied from the WATFIV-S library into this spot in the program. (In some installations the membername may refer to an OS data set.)

E.3   Cross Reference of Variables

As another debugging tool, a cross-reference table may be requested from WATFIV-S. These tables are produced on a subprogram basis and indicate the occurrence, by line number, of each variable, statement number, and function name. The tables also tell whether or not a variable has been declared in a specification statement.

a) Options (allowed on $JOB card only)

XREF / XREFP / NOXREF / NOXREFP
The XREF and XREFP options invoke the cross-reference options, whereas NOXREF and NOXREFP turn it off. The XREF option causes the cross-reference output to be printed one item per line. The XREFP option provides the same information but in a condensed format to reduce the number of lines printed. If a variable has not been declared in a specification statement, a # is printed following that variable name in the table.

b) Control Cards

C$XREFON / C$XREFOFF
Allows the cross referencing to be turned on and off for individual program segments. These control cards have no effect unless the XREF option was specified on the $JOB card. An example of the cross-referencing feature is shown in Figure E.1.

E.4   Tracing A Program

The trace feature of the WATFIV-S compiler provides a way to trace a program as it is executing. The output of the trace provides a message for each statement that is executed.

Control Cards

C$ISNON / C$ISNOFF
These control cards turn the tracing on and off to allow selective tracing of parts of a program. An example of the trace feature is provided in Figure E.2.

Figure E.1   Program listing showing the WATFIV-S cross-referencing feature.

```
        $JOB    WATFIV  ********,XREF
        C Sample Program to demonstrate the use
        C of the cross-referencing option.
  1             INTEGER SUM
  2             SUM = 0
  3             N = 50
  4             I = 1
  5             WHILE(I .LE. N) DO
  6                 SUM = SUM + I
  7                 I = I + 1
  8             END WHILE
  9             PRINT,'THE SUM OF THE FIRST',N,'NUMBERS IS',SUM
 10             STOP
 11             END
                    *** WATFIV CROSS REFERENCE ***
*** '#' INDICATES VARIABLE DID NOT APPEAR IN A TYPE STATEMENT
    VARIABLE       - REFERENCES
    *I      *#      4       5       6       7
    *N      *#      3       5       9
    *SUM    *       1       2       6       9
                *** END OF WATFIV CROSS REFERENCE ***
        $ENTRY
THE SUM OF THE FIRST            50 NUMBERS IS            1275
STATEMENTS EXECUTED=       155
```

E.5   Profiling a Program

The WATFIV-S compiler allows an execution time profile to be generated for a program. The profiler output provides frequency counts and histograms for the specified statements. This information may then be used to improve the efficiency of a program and to determine if any parts of the program are not used. The output of the profiler is printed upon termination of the program.

Both options and control cards exist for the profiler. The options describe which profile statistics are to be kept, and the control cards describe which statements are to be profiled.

a) Options

PROFC / NOPROFC
Controls the generation of the profiler's frequency counts.

PROFP / NOPROFP
Controls the generation of the profiler's percentage histogram.

PROFA / NOPROFA
Controls the generation of the profiler's absolute histogram.

PROF / NOPROF
Controls the above three options simultaneously.

NARROW / NONARROW
Allows the profile information to be compressed to fit within an 80-column width.

Figure E.2   Program listing showing the WATFIV–S trace feature.

```
        $JOB    WATFIV  ************
        C Sample program to demonstrate the
        C use of the trace feature.
    1           INTEGER SUM, I
        C$ISNON
    2           SUM = 0
    3           N = 3
    4           I = 0
    5           WHILE(I .LE. N) DO
    6               SUM = SUM + I
    7               I = I + 1
    8           END WHILE
    9           PRINT,'THE SUM OF THE FIRST',N,'NUMBERS IS',SUM
   10           STOP
   11           END
        $ENTRY
*** ISN =      2   IN ROUTINE M/PROG ***
*** ISN =      3   IN ROUTINE M/PROG ***
*** ISN =      4   IN ROUTINE M/PROG ***
*** ISN =      5   IN ROUTINE M/PROG ***
*** ISN =      6   IN ROUTINE M/PROG ***
*** ISN =      7   IN ROUTINE M/PROG ***
*** ISN =      5   IN ROUTINE M/PROG ***
*** ISN =      6   IN ROUTINE M/PROG ***
*** ISN =      7   IN ROUTINE M/PROG ***
*** ISN =      5   IN ROUTINE M/PROG ***
*** ISN =      6   IN ROUTINE M/PROG ***
*** ISN =      7   IN ROUTINE M/PROG ***
*** ISN =      5   IN ROUTINE M/PROG ***
*** ISN =      6   IN ROUTINE M/PROG ***
*** ISN =      7   IN ROUTINE M/PROG ***
*** ISN =      5   IN ROUTINE M/PROG ***
*** ISN =      9   IN ROUTINE M/PROG ***
THE SUM OF THE FIRST            3 NUMBERS IS            6
STATEMENTS EXECUTED=      17
```

---

b) Control Cards

C$PROFON / C$PROFOFF
These cards control turning the profiler on and off around desired program segments.
When used without any option, they result in just a brief profiler summary. An
example of the profiler in action is shown in Figure E.3.

Figure E.3   Program listing showing the WATFIV-S profiler feature.

```
       $JOB    WATFIV  ********,PROF,NARROW
       C Sample program to demonstrate the
       C use of the profiler.
       C$PROFON
  1            INTEGER SUM, I, N
  2            SUM = 0
  3            N = 50
  4            I = 0
  5            WHILE(I .LE. N) DO
  6               SUM = SUM + I
  7               I = I + 1
  8            END WHILE
  9            PRINT,'THE SUM OF THE FIRST',N,'NUMBERS IS',SUM
 10            STOP
 11            END
       $ENTRY
THE SUM OF THE FIRST          50 NUMBERS IS          1275
```

WATFIV PROGRAM PROFILE

```
     158   STATEMENT(S) EXECUTED
       0   SECONDARY STATEMENT(S) EXECUTED
       0   STATEMENT(S) NOT EXECUTED
```

TABLE OF FREQUENCY COUNT

FROM	TO	COUNT	FROM	TO	COUNT
2	4	1	5	5	52
5	ENDWHILE	1	6	7	51
9	9	1			

HISTOGRAM OF PERCENTAGE FREQUENCY COUNT

STMT	COUNT	0%	20%	40%	60%	80%	100%
2	1	*	.	.	.	.	.
3	1	*	.	.	.	.	.
4	1	*	.	.	.	.	.
5	52	*****************	.	.	.	.
6	51	****************	.	.	.	.
7	51	****************	.	.	.	.
9	1	*	.	.	.	.	.

```
     158 TOTAL STATEMENT(S) EXECUTED
```

HISTOGRAM OF ABSOLUTE FREQUENCY COUNT

STMT	COUNT	1	12	23	34	45	56
2	1	*	.	.	.	.	.
3	1	*	.	.	.	.	.
4	1	*	.	.	.	.	.
5	52	***	.
6	51	**	.
7	51	**	.
9	1	*	.	.	.	.	.

```
     158 TOTAL STATEMENT(S) EXECUTED
STATEMENTS EXECUTED=      158
```

F
Summary of
WATFIV-S
Statements and
Rules

This appendix provides a summary of WATFIV-S. The name WATFIV is an acronym for WATerloo Fortran IV, which is a fast, debugging compiler for the FORTRAN IV programming language. WATFIV-S is a superset of WATFIV with the addition of the special structured statements of IF-THEN-ELSE, WHILE-DO, AT END DO, DO CASE, REMOTE BLOCK and EXECUTE. Only the first two of these are discussed in the main body of the text. All recent releases of the WATFIV compiler automatically include the WATFIV-S features. However, not all installations implement the newer versions of the compiler.

The WATFIV language itself is a superset of FORTRAN IV having among its extensions the CHARACTER data type. The relationship among WATFIV-S, WATFIV, and FORTRAN IV can best be illustrated by the diagram in Figure F.1. Thus, WATFIV-S includes the features of WATFIV, and WATFIV includes the features of FORTRAN IV.

Figure F.1   Relationship of WATFIV-S, WATFIV, and FORTRAN IV.

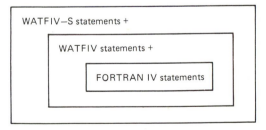

The following pages describe most features of WATFIV and the special structured statements added for WATFIV-S. Many of these statements have not been mentioned elsewhere in the text because they are not necessary at the introductory level. However, for each statement a description is now given along with an example of its use. The more important features are given a more detailed discussion in a later appendix.

F.1   Arithmetic Expressions

1) They are composed of constants and/or variables separated by arithmetic operators. The general form of an arithmetic expression is

    A op B op C . . .

    where op refers to an arithmetic operator and A, B, and C are called *operands* and may be variables, constants, or function references.

2) Valid operators are **, *, /, +, and –. These operators are called *binary* because they require two operands, one on each side. The + and – may also be used as *unary* operators, in which case only one operand is used and is placed to the right of the operator.

3) Expressions may also contain parentheses to remove ambiguity or improve readability.

4) Expressions are evaluated according to a priority scheme. The priority means that, whenever an operand has an arithmetic operator on both sides, the one with the highest priority is done first.

    a) Expressions in parentheses are evaluated first. If parentheses are nested, evaluation of the innermost level precedes the others.

    b) Exponentiation has the highest priority of the operators. Consecutive exponentiation operators are performed starting from the right.

    c) Multiplication and division are the next highest and are of equal priority. They are performed in the order they are encountered going from left to right in the expression.

    d) Addition and subtraction are the lowest priority and are of equal priority. They are performed in the order in which they are encountered going from left to right in the expression.

5) The result of an integer division (integer by integer) is always an integer. Any fractional part is truncated (that is, ignored).

6) Division by zero is an error.

7) If an expression contains both integer and real values, it is called a mixed-mode expression.

    a) In all mixed-mode calculations other than exponentiation, the integer value is converted to real immediately before each individual calculation takes place.

    b) In exponentiation, a value which is raised to an integer exponent is calculated by performing repetitive multiplication. If a value is raised to a real exponent, logarithms are used to compute the result.

Examples

1) $5 + 3*4 \rightarrow 5 + 12 \rightarrow 17$
2) $5 + 2**3*7 \rightarrow 5 + 8*7 \rightarrow 5 + 56 \rightarrow 61$
3) $-4**2 \rightarrow -16$ (unary operator –)
4) $(- 4)**2 \rightarrow +16$ (unary operator –)
5) $5/2 \rightarrow 2$
6) $5/-2 \rightarrow$ error   (two operators together)
7) $2**3**2 \rightarrow 2**9 \rightarrow 512$
8) $3*5/4*2 \rightarrow 15/4*2 \rightarrow 3*2 \rightarrow 6$
9) $2.0**3 \rightarrow 2.0*2.0*2.0 \rightarrow 8.0$
10) $2.0**3.0 \rightarrow$ antilog$(3.0*\log(2.0)) \rightarrow 8.0$
11) $(-2.0)**3 \rightarrow (-2.0)*(-2.0)*(-2.0) \rightarrow -8.0$
12) $(-2.0)**3.0 \rightarrow$ antilog$(3.0*\log(-2.0)) \rightarrow$ error $(\log(-2.0))$
13) $2 + 3.0 \rightarrow 2.0 + 3.0 \rightarrow 5.0$
14) $7/3*4.0 \rightarrow 2*4.0 \rightarrow 2.0*4.0 \rightarrow 8.0$

15) $4.0*7/3 \rightarrow 4.0*7.0/3 \rightarrow 28.0/3 \rightarrow 28.0/3.0 \rightarrow 9.333333$

F.2   Arithmetic IF

Purpose
This statement branches to one of three executable statements, depending on the value of an arithmetic expression.

General Form

    IF(arithmetic expression) stnol, stno2, stno3

The next statement executed will be one of the statements labeled stnol, stno2, or stno3 depending on the value of the arithmetic expression. If the arithmetic expression has the value:

    < 0 transfer to stnol
    = 0 transfer to stno2
    > 0 transfer to stno3.

Rules

1) stnol, stno2, and stno3 are statement numbers on executable statements.
2) Any or all of the statement numbers may be similar. If they are all the same, the statement is an unconditional transfer statement, that is, it always branches to the same place regardless of the value of the arithmetic expression.

Examples

1) IF(I) 21,51,42
    The next statement executed will be the statement labeled 21 if the value of I is less than 0, the statement labeled 51 if the value of I is equal to 0, or the statement labeled 42 if the value of I is greater than 0.
2) IF(A+5.0) 100,100,200
    The next statement executed will be the statement labeled 100 if the value of A+5.0 is less than or equal 0.0 or the statement labeled 200 if the value of A+5.0 is greater than 0.0.

F.3   ASSIGN Statement

Purpose
This statement assigns a statement number to an integer variable for use with the assigned GO TO statement.

General Form

    ASSIGN stno TO name

This statement is used only in conjunction with the assigned GO TO statement. The rules and example of its use are given with that statement.

F.4   **Assigned** GO TO **Statement**

Purpose

This statement branches to one of several statements depending on the statement number that was assigned to a variable in an ASSIGN statement. (The authors view this statement as of little use in the language and include it only for completeness.)

General Form

```
ASSIGN stno TO name
⋮
GO TO name,(stno1,stno2, . . . ,stnok)
```

The name in the ASSIGN and the assigned GO TO statement is an INTEGER variable.

Rules

1) Variable name may not be used in arithmetic operations.
2) The value of name may be changed only in an ASSIGN statement.
3) The statement number stno must be one of stno1, stno2, . . . , stnok; otherwise, an error is issued.

Example

```
C This program sums the first 10 integers.
      INTEGER BACK, I, N, SUM

      N = 10
      SUM = 0.0
      I = 1
      ASSIGN 100 TO BACK
100   SUM = SUM + I
      I = I + 1
      IF(I .GT. N)ASSIGN 300 TO BACK
      GO TO BACK,(100,300)
300 PRINT, 'THE SUM OF THE FIRST', N, 'INTEGERS IS', SUM
      STOP
      END
```

F.5   **Assignment Statements**

Purpose

Assignment statements are used to assign the value of an arithmetic expression to a variable.

General Form

```
variable name = arithmetic expression
```

The arithmetic expression on the right-hand side (RHS) is completely evaluated and then the result is assigned to the variable on the left-hand side (LHS). The = symbol is referred to as the assignment operator.

Rules

1) If the types of the LHS and the RHS do not agree, then the value of the RHS is converted automatically to that of the LHS before assignment is done. This is called mixed-mode assignment. For example, if B is REAL and K is INTEGER,

    B = 9   → B is assigned the value 9.0, and
    K = 4.9   → K is assigned the value 4

2) Special conventions are needed if either side of the assignment operator involves a complex quantity. See Appendix L.
3) Blanks may be used to improve readability. The authors have a convention of placing blanks around the assignment operator and around the lower priority operators.

Examples

```
1)   R = S*T + 5.0*Y
2)   A = 0.0
3)   I = J + 17
```

F.6   AT END DO **Statement**

Purpose

This feature allows the user to recover from an end-of-file condition on a READ statement.

General Form

```
READ, input list
   AT END DO
   :    statements
   END AT END
```

If a READ statement is executed when there are no more data cards, an end-of-file condition is generated. The standard READ statement recognizes this condition by issuing an error message and halting execution. This AT END DO facility, called the AT END DO block, allows the user to intercept this condition to take some appropriate action. If an AT END DO block follows a READ statement, which causes an end-of-file condition, the statements inside the AT END DO block are executed. If an end-of-file does not occur on the READ, the AT END DO block is skipped over, and execution proceeds with the statement following the END AT END statement.

Rules

1) The AT END DO block must immediately follow the READ statement.
2) If the END AT END statement is reached when executing the AT END DO block, it is ignored and execution continues with the statement following it.

Example

```
C Read in and sum an unknown number of data values
C which are arranged one data value per card.
      INTEGER N, FLAG, SUM

      FLAG = 0
      N = 0
      SUM = 0
      READ, X
         AT END DO
            FLAG = 1
         END AT END
      WHILE(FLAG .EQ. 0) DO
         SUM = SUM + X
         N = N + 1
         READ, X
            AT END DO
               FLAG = 1
            END AT END
      END WHILE
      PRINT, 'THE NUMBER OF DATA VALUES IS', N
      IF(N .NE. 0) THEN DO
            PRINT, 'THE AVERAGE IS', FLOAT(SUM)/N
      END IF
      STOP
      END
```

F.7   BLOCK DATA **Subprogram**

Purpose

This feature provides a means of initializing named and unnamed COMMON blocks.

General Form

```
BLOCK DATA
COMMON/common name/ common list
:    initialization and specification statements only
END
```

Rules

1) BLOCK DATA subprograms may not contain any executable statements. They may only contain IMPLICIT, COMMON, DATA, DIMENSION, and the type declaration statements (INTEGER, REAL, etc.).
2) If the BLOCK DATA subprogram contains an IMPLICIT statement, that statement must directly follow the BLOCK DATA statement.
3) All initialization must be performed following the COMMON declaration.

Example

```
C This program segment has a named COMMON which
C is initialized by a BLOCK DATA subprogram.
      INTEGER I, J, K
      REAL X, Y
      COMMON/CHARLY/ I, J, X(10), K(7), Y
      ⋮
      STOP
      END
      BLOCK DATA
      COMMON/CHARLY/ I, J, X(10), K(7), Y
      INTEGER I/0/, J/1/
      REAL X/10*0.0/
      DATA K/7*0/, Y/2.0/
      END
```

F.8   Built-in Functions

Purpose
Built-in functions provide a simple way for the user to perform common calculations.

General Form of Usage

```
name(argument list)
```

This reference may appear anywhere an arithmetic expression is allowed. The argument list consists of one or more arguments separated by commas. An argument may be a constant, an arithmetic expression or a variable. All built-in functions are predefined and a table of those available is given in Appendix P. The type of the function and the type and number of arguments must agree with the function definition specified in that table.

Rule

1)   The first-letter rule for variables applies to built-in function names. However, the authors recommend that such function names be explicitly declared.

Examples

```
1)   A = SQRT(FLOAT(I))
2)   R = AMIN0(A+5,S,X)
3)   C = SIN(ANGLE)
4)   PRINT, ABS(T)+5.462
```

F.9   CALL **Statement**

Purpose
The CALL statement allows a user to invoke a subroutine subprogram from another program.

General Form

```
CALL name (argument list)
```

A detailed description and examples of this statement accompany the discussion of the SUBROUTINE statement.

F.10   CASE **Statement**

Purpose
This statement may be used to select one of many sets of statements to be executed depending on the value of an integer variable.

General Form

```
DO CASE i
   CASE
       statements 1
   CASE
       statements 2
   CASE
     ⋮
   CASE
       statements n
   IF NONE DO
       statements
END CASE
```

The DO CASE index i is an integer variable. Its value determines which CASE statements are executed. If $1 \leq i \leq n$, then the i-th CASE statements are executed. If $i < 1$ or $i > n$, then statements of the IF NONE DO are executed. In either situation, execution then continues with the statement following the END CASE statement.

Rules

1)   The first CASE statement is optional.
2)   The IF NONE DO block is optional.

Example

```
C This program reads in 10 cards.  Each card contains 1
C integer and 2 real values. It performs arithmetic on the
C real numbers as determined by the integer value.
C If the integer is: 1 - add A+B
C                    2 - subtract A-B
C                    3 - multiply A*B
C                    4 - divide A/B
C         anything else - print a warning message
      INTEGER I, NUM
      REAL A, B

      I = 0
      WHILE( I .LT. 10) DO
          READ, NUM, A, B
          DO CASE NUM
              CASE
                  PRINT, 'THE SUM OF', A, B, 'IS', A+B
              CASE
                  PRINT, 'THE DIFFERENCE OF', A, B, 'IS', A-B
              CASE
                  PRINT, 'THE PRODUCT OF', A, B, 'IS', A*B
              CASE
                  PRINT, 'THE QUOTIENT OF', A, B, 'IS', A/B
              IF NONE DO
                  PRINT, 'BAD CODE', NUM
          END CASE
          I = I + 1
      END WHILE
      STOP
      END
```

F.11   CHARACTER **Statement**

Purpose

This statement allows a user to define specific variable or array names to be of type
CHARACTER.

General Form

```
CHARACTER*n list
```

The list contains variable or array names separated by commas. The *n, $1 \leq n \leq 255$,
indicates the number of characters each item in the list may store. If omitted the
default number of characters is 1. This statement and the entire topic of character
data types are discussed in Appendix I.

F.12   COMMON **Statement**

Purpose

This statement provides an alternate communication method between main programs
and subprograms, other than through the argument/parameter lists.

General Form

```
COMMON/common name/ common list
```

The common list is composed of variable and array names. A COMMON statement reserves a block of memory large enough to contain all the common list variables in order of appearance in the list. When a COMMON statement of the same name appears in another subprogram, the exact same area of memory is used for both. Thus the subprograms have access to a 'common' area of memory.

Rules

1) The common name may be up to six symbols in length and must begin with an alphabetic character.
2) A common name and a variable name may not be the same.
3) If many COMMON statements with the same common name appear in the same program segment, then the common lists are appended. Of the following statements, those on the left are equivalent to the one on the right, for example:

```
COMMON/SAM/ A,B,C          COMMON/SAM/ A,B,C,D,E
COMMON/SAM/ D,E
```

4) If the /common name/ is omitted, then the resulting area is called an unnamed or blank common. (Consider it to be a named common with an internal name defined by the compiler.) For example:

```
COMMON R,S,T
```

5) COMMON is a compile-time feature. It is completely established before execution begins.
6) Variables may not be initialized in the COMMON statement nor may a variable that has been previously initialized through compile-time initialization be placed in a common list.
7) Variable and array names may appear in type specification statements as well as COMMON. Also, the size of an array may be declared in a COMMON statement, but an array must not be given a size twice. For example:

```
INTEGER A, B(10)
REAL X
COMMON/ARNOLD/ A(15),B,X
```

8) An array name in the common list may not have variable dimensions.
9) A variable or array name may not be both a subprogram parameter and in COMMON.
10) The common list acts as a template which tells how the associated common area is to be accessed. Thus a particular common area may be accessed in different ways by different program segments. For example, if the following COMMON statements appear in different program segments,

```
COMMON/HARRY/ I(10),J(3),K
COMMON/HARRY/ L(6),M(8)
```

then they both refer to the same 14 words of memory. Array L and I(1) ... I(6) use the same 6 locations, while array M uses the same locations as I(7) ... I(10), J(1), ... ,J(3), and K.
11) The size of a particular common area may be declared differently in different program segments, and the largest size is used.

F.13   Compile-time Initialization of Variables

Purpose
This feature allows the user to assign values to variables at compile time.

General Form
Compile-time initialization of variables is performed in the type specification statements. The following shows its use in the INTEGER and REAL specification statements. (See also the DATA statement, and for other data types, see Appendices I, J, K, and L.)

```
REAL rname/real constant/
INTEGER iname/integer constant/
```

The first statement implies that the real variable rname is to be assigned the value of the real constant. In the second statement, the integer variable iname is to be assigned the value of the integer constant.

Rules

1) The type of the variable and the value must usually be the same. One exception to this rule is that a constant may be a character string (see Appendix I).
2) Many variable initializations may be performed at the same time.

```
REAL X/5.0/, Y/10.0/, Z/123.54/
```

3) Arrays may be declared and initialized at the same time.

```
REAL A(3)/0.0,0.0,0.0/, B(2)/5.0,27.0/
```

4) A shorthand notation of n* may be used to indicate that a constant is to be repeated n times. The repetition factor n must be a nonnegative, nonzero integer constant.

```
INTEGER I(1000)/1000*0/, J(128)/100*1,28*2/
```

5) Initialization of multidimensional arrays is performed in column order. For instance, the following statement will initialize all elements in the first column of A to 1.0, the second column of A to 2.0, and the third column to 3.0.

```
REAL A(10,3)/10*1.0,10*2.0,10*3.0/
```

6) This initialization takes place once only at compile time.

F.14   COMPLEX Statement

Purpose
This statement allows the user to declare a specific variable, array, or function name to be of type COMPLEX.

General Forms

```
COMPLEX list
COMPLEX*8 list
COMPLEX*16 list
```

The lists contain variable, array, or function names separated by commas. The first two statements perform the same operation of declaring the items in the list to be single-precision complex (that is, two single-precision values). The last statement declares the items in its list to be extended-precision complex (that is, two extended-precision values). This statement and the entire topic of complex data types are discussed in Appendix L.

F.15 Computed GO TO

Purpose

The computed GO TO statement is used to branch to one of several statements depending on the value of an INTEGER variable.

General Form

```
GO TO(stno1,stno2, . . . ,stnok),i
```

The stno1, stno2, ..., stnok are statement numbers on executable statements, and i is an INTEGER variable. When executed the statement has the following action:

a) If: i has the value 1, branch to stno1
        i has the value 2, branch to stno2
        ⋮
        i has the value k, branch to stnok

b) If: i is outside the range i<1 or i>k, then control is passed to the statement following the computed GO TO.

Example

```
C This program reads in 10 cards.  Each card contains 1
C integer and 2 real values. It performs arithmetic on the
C real numbers as determined by the integer value.
C If the integer is: 1 - add A+B
C                    2 - subtract A-B
C                    3 - multiply A*B
C                    4 - divide A/B
C         anything else - print a warning message
      INTEGER I, NUM
      REAL A, B

      I = 0
      WHILE( I .LT. 10) DO
         READ, NUM, A, B
         GO TO(100,200,300,400),NUM
         PRINT, 'BAD CODE', NUM
            GO TO 500
  100    PRINT, 'THE SUM OF', A, B, 'IS', A+B
            GO TO 500
  200    PRINT, 'THE DIFFERENCE OF', A, B, 'IS', A-B
            GO TO 500
  300    PRINT, 'THE PRODUCT OF', A, B, 'IS', A*B
            GO TO 500
  400    PRINT, 'THE QUOTIENT OF', A, B, 'IS', A/B
            GO TO 500
  500    I = I + 1
      END WHILE
      STOP
      END
```

F.16   Constants

Integer Constants

1) Integer constants are numbers written without a decimal point.
2) They may take on only integer values. For example:

     17, -5, 0, +25, 94786

3) They are stored internally in the computer as 32-bit binary numbers and thus are limited in range from -2147483648 to +2147483647. (See Appendix G for more information.)

Real Constants

1) Real constants are numbers written with a decimal point and may have many forms. All of the following numbers have the same value:

     by hand: $12.74, .0001274 \times 10^5, 12740 \times 10^{-3}$
     WATFIV-S: 12.74, .0001274E5, 12740E-3

2) They are stored internally as 32-bit binary numbers in an exponent form and contain up to 7 decimal digits. The range is from $0.5397605 \times 10^{-78}$ to 0.7237005×10^{76}. (See Appendix G for more information.)

F.17   CONTINUE **Statement**

Purpose
This is a do-nothing statement which is often used as the object of a DO loop and in conversion from pseudo code into standard WATFIV.

General Form

     nnnnn CONTINUE

The nnnnn is a statement number and is optional, but the statement has no use without one.

Rules

1) This statement by itself causes no action.
2) In all cases other than when a CONTINUE is the object of a DO loop, a branch to a CONTINUE statement causes the computer to proceed immediately to the statement following it.

Examples

1) See the section on the DO statement in this appendix for more information concerning the CONTINUE as the object of a DO loop.
2) See Appendix D for use of the CONTINUE in translation of pseudo code into standard WATFIV.

F.18   DATA **Statement**

Purpose
This statement allows variables and arrays to be initialized at compile time. (See also the section in this appendix on the compile-time initialization of variables.)

General Form

```
DATA vlist1/clist1/, vlist2/clist2/, . . .
```

The vlist1 and vlist2 are variable lists and clist1 and clist2 are constant lists. The variable lists contain one or more variables, array names, or array elements which are to be initialized. The constant list contains the initialization values. The type of the variable and its corresponding constant must be the same.

Rules

1) This statement is nonexecutable, and the initializations are performed only once before any execution begins.
2) The operation of the DATA statement is similar to that of initialization in the INTEGER and REAL statements. For example:

```
REAL X, A
INTEGER I, J
DATA X/5.0/, A/3,0/, I,J/7,10/
```

   is equivalent to

```
REAL X/5.0/, A/3.0/
INTEGER I/7/, J/10/
```

3) The variable list may contain more than one name for initialization. The constant list must contain the correct number of constants to initialize all of the variables in the variable list.

```
REAL X, A
INTEGER I, J
DATA X,A,I,J/5.0,3.0,7,10/
```

4) When arrays are initialized, the size of the array must have been declared previously. The following DATA statement initializes the three elements of A to 0.0 and only the third element of B to 7.9.

```
DIMENSION A(3),B(5)
DATA A/0.0,0.0,0.0/, B(3)/7.9/
```

5) To help in the initialization, a replication factor of the form n* may be used as well as an implied DO structure. The following statements initialize all elements of X to 0.0, the odd elements of Y to 0.0, and the even elements of Y to 1.0. The variables R, S, and T are all initialized to 5.0.

```
REAL X(1000), Y(2000), R, S, T
DATA X/1000*0.0/,(Y(I),I=1,1999,2)/1000*0.0/
DATA (Y(I),I=2,2000,2)/1000*1.0/,R,S,T/3*5.0/
```

   The implied DO loops may be nested.
6) If a variable is initialized twice, the last value is used.

F.19 DIMENSION **Statement**

Purpose

This statement provides an alternate way to define the size of arrays. (For most uses this statement may be replaced by REAL and/or INTEGER statements.)

General Form

    DIMENSION array list

The array list contains the names of arrays and their sizes.

Rules

1) An array may only have its size defined once.
2) If the size of an array is declared in a DIMENSION statement, it may also have its type defined in a specification statement. The following statements are equivalent:

    REAL IRVING   REAL IRVING(10)
    DIMENSION IRVING(10)

F.20 **Disk File Commands**

A disk file is used to maintain frequently needed information such that programs may access the information quickly. Program libraries are also maintained in disk files as are system programs like the compilers. A disk file is located on a magnetic coated 'disc' which rotates continuously.

For extensive use of disk files, one usually needs to supply extra information outside the WATFIV-S program. However, many computer centers provide special disk files (often called scratch files), which are predefined and may be used for storing information temporarily while the program is executing. The computer consultants at each computer center can provide more information on both of these features.

Information is written on and read from disk files using the WRITE and READ statements. In addition to these, there are other commands available. They are described below, and the i refers to the unit number allocated to the disk file. (See Appendix H for more details on unit numbers with the READ and WRITE statements.)

The following two commands are used with data which are stored sequentially and in a direct-access manner respectively. If a file contains information stored sequentially, a program must start at the beginning of the file and read each record in turn. In a direct-access file, numbers are assigned to each record, thus allowing a program to read any record in any order by merely specifying its record number.

1) REWIND i instructs the computer to reposition to the beginning of the sequential disk file. This feature allows the file to be read many times.

2) `DEFINE FILE i (# of records,length of records,code,variable)`
provides information to the computer about the size of the direct-access file. A
record can be thought of as a line of information. The first argument specifies the
total number of records in the file. The second argument describes the number of
characters that can be put in each record. The code specifies information about
the type of input and output that is to be done, that is, formatted, unformatted,
and so on. The variable is of type `INTEGER` and is set to the number of the record
following the one last accessed.

The `READ` and `WRITE` statements for direct-access use have a form as shown
below.

```
READ(unit # ' record #, . . . ) input list
WRITE(unit # ' record #, . . . ) output list
```

The `record #` is either an integer variable, constant, or expression which
indicates the record to be read or written.

F.21   DO **Statement and** DO **Loop**

Purpose
This feature is used to provide a convenient way to perform looping with automatic
incrementing of the index.

General Form

```
DO nnnnn i = j,k,1
    :    statements
nnnnn CONTINUE
```

In the DO statement, i is an integer variable and is called the index of the loop. As
well, j, k, and 1 are called the parameters of the DO loop and must be unsigned integer
constants or variables with values greater than 0.

```
        j - is the initial value
        k - is the test value
        1 - is the increment
nnnnn CONTINUE - is the object of the DO loop
```

The statements which follow the DO statement up to and including the object of the DO
loop are said to be within the *range* of the DO loop. The DO loop operates in the
following way:

1)   Set the index to the initial value;
2)   Execute all statements up to and including the object of the DO, that is, the
     statements in the range of the DO loop;
3)   Add the increment to the index;
4)   Compare the index with the test value

 a)   If index ≤ test value, go back to step 2;
 b)   If index > test value, start executing statements following the object of the
      DO.

Rules

1) If the increment is omitted, it is assumed to be 1.
2) The values of the index and the DO-loop parameters may not be changed inside the DO loop.
3) A DO loop may only be entered by way of the DO statement. A branch into the range of a DO loop may not be made from outside the range of that loop.
4) A branch may be made from inside the range of a DO loop to outside the range of that DO, and the value of the index is the last value assigned to it.
5) If an exit is made from a DO loop by way of the object of the DO, (that is, all repetitions are done) the value of the index is uncertain.
6) A DO loop is executed

   a) once, if initial value $>$ test value;
   b) 1 + (test − initial)/increment times, otherwise.

Points

1) It is good programming practice to always use a CONTINUE statement as the object of the DO loop.
2) Indentation of the statements inside a DO loop makes the program easier to read.

Example

```
C This program uses a DO loop to sum
C the first 10 integers.
      INTEGER I, N, SUM

      N = 10
      SUM = 0
      DO 100 I=1,N,1
          SUM = SUM + I
  100 CONTINUE
      PRINT, 'THE SUM OF THE FIRST', N, 'INTEGERS IS', SUM
      STOP
      END
```

F.22 DOUBLE PRECISION Statement

Purpose
This statement allows a user to declare specific variable, array, or function names to be of type double precision.

General Form

```
DOUBLE PRECISION list
```

The list contains variable, array, or function names separated by commas. This statement and the entire topic of double precision arithmetic (also called extended precision) are discussed in Appendix K.

F.23   DUMPLIST **Statement**

Purpose
This statement allows automatic print-out of specified variables when an execution-time error occurs.

General Form

    DUMPLIST/name/ list

This statement causes the list variables and their values to be printed when an execution-time error occurs. The form of the statement and its output is the same as for the NAMELIST statement.

F.24   END **Statement**

Purpose
The END statement indicates the end of a main program or the end of a subprogram to the compiler.

General Form

    END

When this statement is encountered by the compiler, the compiler ends compilation of the current program segment.

Rule

1)   Since it is a compile-time statement only, the END statement does not have any effect at execution time.

Example
See any WATFIV-S program example.

F.25   ENTRY **Statement**

Purpose
This statement allows a user to define additional entry points to a subroutine or function subprogram. (Do not confuse this statement with the $ENTRY control card.)

General Form

    ENTRY name(parameter list)

The name, is any valid WATFIV-S name, and the parameter list consists of variable, array, or function names.

Rules

1)   The ENTRY statement defines an alternate entry point to a subprogram and an alternate parameter list. The type of entry point, that is, a SUBROUTINE or FUNCTION which determines how it is referenced, is decided by the subprogram type.

2) The ENTRY statement is placed within the body of the subprogram but is not an executable statement in the normal sense. An ENTRY statement is ignored if it occurs in a sequence of statements being executed.
3) The ENTRY statement may not be placed in the range of a DO or WHILE loop.
4) Any variable in the subprogram not in the ENTRY parameter list has the last value it was assigned.

Example

```
C This program reads N integer values into the array
C VALUES.  It uses the subroutine SETUP to setup the
C argument and parameter correspondences for the array
C and its size.  Then it uses the subroutine entry SUM
C to sum the numbers in the array.
      INTEGER I, N, VALUES(1000), ANSWER

      READ, N, (VALUES(I), I=1,N)
      CALL SETUP(VALUES, N)

      CALL SUM(ANSWER)
      PRINT, 'THE SUM OF THE', N, 'NUMBERS IS =', ANSWER
      STOP
      END
      SUBROUTINE SETUP(ARRAY, N)
      INTEGER N, ARRAY(N), I, RESULT
      RETURN
      ENTRY SUM(RESULT)
      RESULT = 0
      I = 1
      WHILE(I .LE. N) DO
         RESULT = RESULT + ARRAY(I)
         I = I + 1
      END WHILE
      RETURN
      END
```

F.26   EQUIVALENCE **Statement**

Purpose
This statement allows a user to declare that variables and arrays in the same program segment may be forced to occupy the same storage locations.

General Form

```
EQUIVALENCE (equivalence group1), (equivalence group2), . . .
```

The equivalence groups contain variable and array names separated by commas. The effect of the statement is that all those items within a group will be forced to overlap their storage locations.

Rules

1) The EQUIVALENCE statement is not executable. It should be placed before all executable statements.

2) Since the items in an equivalence group share the same locations, they share the same values. For example, in the following program:

```
EQUIVALENCE (A,B)
A = 1.0
PRINT, B
STOP
END
```

when A is assigned the value 1.0, B also takes on this value and the value printed will be 1.0.

3) Variables of different types may be equivalenced together. However, since the internal representations for different types are not the same, the results are somewhat unpredictable. For instance, in the following program the value printed for I is 1091567616. The internal representations for this number and 1.0 are the same.

```
EQUIVALENCE (I,X)
X = 1.0
PRINT, I
STOP
END
```

4) Arrays may be equivalenced to simple variables or other arrays. For instance, as a result of the following EQUIVALENCE, the arrays A and Y overlap completely, array B overlaps the last 5 locations of C, and R is in the same place as C(2).

```
REAL A(15), Y(15), B(5), C(10), R
EQUIVALENCE (A,Y), (B,C(6)), (R,C(2))
```

5) If compile-time initialization is to be performed on items to be equivalenced, it must be done after equivalence.

6) An EQUIVALENCE statement must not cause any item to be in two different positions. The following equivalence is illegal.

```
REAL R(10)
EQUIVALENCE (S,R(5)), (S,R(4))
```

7) Items in COMMON may be equivalenced provided that the result does not try to extend past the beginning of the COMMON storage area. It is, however, legal to extend the length of the COMMON storage in the other direction. These situations are illustrated below.

a) The following equivalencing is legal:

```
REAL C(5), D(6)
COMMON/JOE/ C
EQUIVALENCE (C(3),D(1))
```

b) The following equivalencing is illegal because it tries to extend back past the start of the COMMON area.

```
REAL C(5), D(6)
COMMON/JOE/ C
EQUIVALENCE (C(1),D(3))
```

8) Subprogram parameters may not be equivalenced.

F.27   EXECUTE **Statement**

Purpose
This statement is used to invoke execution of a REMOTE BLOCK.

General Form

    EXECUTE name

The name is the name of the REMOTE BLOCK to be executed. For more details see the
section in this appendix on the REMOTE BLOCK statement.

F.28   **Execution-Time Dimensioning of Arrays**

Purpose
This feature allows a calling program to specify the size of an argument array to a
subprogram.

Rules

1) Execution-time dimensioning may be used only in a subprogram.
2) Execution-time dimensioning is indicated by placing integer variables in place of
   constants for the array size in the array declaration in a subprogram.
3) The array must be in the subprogram parameter list. The variable dimensions
   must also be in the parameter list.
4) A parameter array may have more than one variable dimension or may have
   constant and variable dimensions.

        SUBROUTINE DOUG(X,L,M,Y,N)
        INTEGER X(L,M), Y(2,N)

5) The size of the argument array in the calling program is the maximum size
   allowed for the corresponding parameter arrays in the subprogram.

Example

```
C This program uses a subroutine to sum the elements of two
C arrays of different sizes. The name of the array to be summed
C and its size are included as arguments to the subroutine.
C The subroutine uses these to assign the corresponding
C parameter array the correct size.
      REAL X(10), Y(5), XSUM, YSUM

      READ, X, Y
      CALL SUM(X,10,XSUM)
      CALL SUM(Y,5,YSUM)
      PRINT, 'X AND Y SUMS ARE', XSUM, YSUM
      STOP
      END

      SUBROUTINE SUM(A,N,RESULT)
      INTEGER I, N
      REAL A(N), RESULT

      RESULT = 0.0
      I = 1
      WHILE(I .LE. N) DO
         RESULT = RESULT + A(I)
         I = I + 1
      END WHILE
      RETURN
      END
```

F.29   EXTERNAL **Statement**

Purpose

The EXTERNAL statement indicates to the compiler that specific names are those of functions which are external to the current program.

General Form

```
EXTERNAL external list
```

The external list contains function or subroutine names separated by commas. These names need only be in the external list when the function or subroutine name is being passed as an argument.

Rule

1)   Statement function names may not be passed as an argument and, thus, need not appear in an external list.

Example

```
C Use the bisection program to determine a zero
C of the functions x**2+5x-204 and x**2-4x-77.
C The bisection program is assumed to be in the library
C as defined in the main body of the text.
      EXTERNAL SAM,GEORGE
      INTEGER FLAG1, FLAG2
      REAL A, B, C, D, EPS, SAM, GEORGE, ROOT1, ROOT2

      READ, A, B, C, D, EPS
      CALL BISECT(A,B,EPS,SAM,FLAG1,ROOT1)
      CALL BISECT(C,D,EPS,GEORGE,FLAG2,ROOT2)
      PRINT, 'THE ROOTS ARE', ROOT1, ROOT2
      STOP
      END

      REAL FUNCTION SAM(X)
      SAM = X**2 + 5.0*X - 204.0
      RETURN
      END

      REAL FUNCTION GEORGE(X)
      GEORGE = X**2 - 4.0*X - 77.0
      RETURN
      END
```

F.30   FORMAT **Statement**

Purpose

This statement provides the user with complete control over how data is input to and output from a program.

General Form

```
nnnnn FORMAT(format codes)
```

The nnnnn is the statement number of the FORMAT statement. The FORMAT statement is not an executable statement as such but is used in conjunction with the READ, PRINT, and WRITE statements. Refer to Appendix H for a discussion of the FORMAT statement and its use.

F.31   FUNCTION **Subprograms**

Purpose

These subprograms allow the user to define multi-line functions.

General Form of Definition

```
FUNCTION name(parameter list)
:    statements
RETURN
END
```

The function name obeys the rules for WATFIV-S names. The parameter list contains variable, array, or function names separated by commas.

General Form of Usage

```
name(argument list)
```

This reference may appear anywhere an arithmetic expression is allowed. The argument list contains one or more arguments separated by commas. An argument may be a constant, an arithmetic expression, variable, array, function, or subroutine name. The number of arguments must be the same as the number of parameters, and each argument must be of the same type as its corresponding parameter.

When the reference is executed, the following happens:

1) The computer transfers to the first statement of the subprogram.
2) The values of the arguments are copied into the corresponding parameters. For arrays, only their location is passed, and the subroutine uses the same data area.
3) Execution of the subprogram begins at the first executable statement.
4) When a RETURN statement is executed

  a) the values of the parameters are copied back into the corresponding argument.
  b) the computer returns to the calling program and resumes execution in the same statement from which it came. The function reference is given the value that was last assigned to the function name in the subprogram.

Rules

1) The function name may be used as a variable in the subprogram and must be assigned a value before returning.
2) Function parameters may not be initialized at compile time.
3) Function references may not form a loop.
4) If an argument is a DO-loop index or a DO-loop parameter, the value of the corresponding parameter may not be changed in the function.
5) Variables and statement numbers are local to a subprogram. If the same names and numbers are used in another program segment, they are not considered the same by the compiler.
6) A function subprogram has a data type. The type of a function is determined implicitly by the first letter rule of variables or by explicit declaration in the function statement.

```
REAL FUNCTION name (parameter list)
INTEGER FUNCTION name (parameter list)
```

  (See Appendices I, J, K, and L for information on the function subprograms associated with the other data types.)
7) The type of a function in the calling program must be the same as in the definition.

Example

```
C Calculate L!/(M!*K!) using function subprograms.
      INTEGER L, M, K, FACT, ANSWER

      READ, L, M, K
      ANSWER = FACT(L)/(FACT(M)*FACT(K))
      PRINT, 'THE ANSWER IS', ANSWER
      STOP
      END

      INTEGER FUNCTION FACT(I)
      INTEGER I

      FACT = 1.0
      WHILE(I .GE. 2) DO
         FACT = FACT*I
         I = I - 1
      END WHILE
      RETURN
      END
```

F.32   GO TO **Statement**

Purpose

The GO TO statement is used to branch unconditionally to an executable statement.

General Form

    GO TO nnnnn

The nnnnn is the statement number on an executable statement.

Rule

1)   It may be used by itself or may appear after a logical IF statement.

Example

```
C This program sums the first 10 integers.
      INTEGER I, N, SUM

      N = 10
      SUM = 0
      I = 1
   50 IF(I .GT. N) GO TO 1000
         SUM = SUM + I
         I = I + 1
         GO TO 50
 1000 PRINT, 'THE SUM OF THE FIRST', N, 'INTEGERS IS', SUM
      STOP
      END
```

F.33   IF-THEN-ELSE **Statement**

Purpose
This statement allows the selection of alternate statements for execution.

General Form

```
IF(logical expression) THEN DO
:    statements S1
ELSE DO
:    statements S2
END IF
```

The logical expression is evaluated, and if it has the value .TRUE., then the statements
S1 are executed. If the logical expression has a value .FALSE., the statements S2 are
executed. Following execution of either S1 or S2, execution continues with the
statement following the END IF.

Rules

1) Only one of the statement groups, S1 or S2 is executed.
2) The THEN DO words must be on the same line (or a continuation thereof) as the
   IF(logical expression).
3) The END IF must always be included.
4) The ELSE DO and its statements S2 may be omitted to give the IF-THEN
   statement. The END IF is still necessary.

Example

```
C This program reads in 10 cards.  Each card contains 1
C integer and 2 real values. It performs arithmetic on the
C real numbers as determined by the integer value.
C If the integer is: 1 - add A+B
C                    2 - subtract A-B
C          anything else - print a warning message
      INTEGER I, NUM
      REAL A, B

      I = 0
      WHILE(I .LT. 10) DO
         READ, NUM, A, B
         IF(NUM .EQ. 1) THEN DO
             PRINT, 'THE SUM OF', A, B, 'IS', A+B
           ELSE DO
             IF(NUM .EQ. 2) THEN DO
                 PRINT, 'THE DIFFERENCE OF', A, B, 'IS', A-B
               ELSE DO
                 PRINT, 'BAD CODE', NUM
             END IF
         END IF
         I = I + 1
      END WHILE
      STOP
      END
```

F.34   IMPLICIT **Statement**

Purpose

This statement allows a user to change the settings which are used to determine the default type of variable names. (See the variables section of this appendix for information on the default settings.)

General Form

```
IMPLICIT type1(character list 1), type2(character list 2), . . .
```

The character lists contain alphabetic characters separated by commas. Each character list gives the characters that are to make a variable a specific type by the first letter rule.

Rules

1) An IMPLICIT statement may contain only one list specification for any specific data type.
2) Those characters which are not changed in an IMPLICIT statement retain their previous settings. For example, the statement

```
IMPLICIT INTEGER(O,P,Q,R,S,T)
```

would result in the characters from I through T as defining integer variables by the first letter rule.
3) A character list may specify the range of characters instead of the characters individually. For example, the actions of the statements in a) and b) directly below are equivalent. They make all variables beginning with I, J, K, L, M, and N of type REAL and those beginning with A through H and O through Z of type INTEGER.

```
a)   IMPLICIT INTEGER(A-H,O-Z), REAL(I-N)
b)   IMPLICIT REAL(I,J,K-M,N)
     IMPLICIT INTEGER(A-H,O-P,Q-Z)
c)   IMPLICIT LOGICAL(L)
     IMPLICIT CHARACTER(C)
```

F.35   INTEGER **Statement**

Purpose

This statement is used to declare specific variable, array, or function names to be of type INTEGER.

General Forms

```
INTEGER list
INTEGER*4 list
INTEGER*2 list
```

The lists may contain variable names, function names, and array names. The first two statements are equivalent and declare the items in their lists to be full-word INTEGERs. The *4 notation refers to the fact that such integer values occupy 4 bytes of memory (a full word). The INTEGER*2 statement declares the items in its list to be half-word INTEGERs. The *2 notation refers to the fact that such integer values occupy 2 bytes of memory (a half word). (See also the section in this appendix on the compile-time initialization of variables.)

Rules

1) This statement should be placed before all executable statements.
2) This statement may be used to declare individual names to be of type INTEGER.

        INTEGER A, B, ISUM, COUNT

3) The size of arrays may be declared in this statement:

        INTEGER I(10), C(10,2)

4) Variables declared to be of type INTEGER*2 have a much reduced range of numbers that they may store (-32168 to +32167) and, thus, must be used carefully. In addition, there are some restrictions on their use.

F.36 LOGICAL **Statement**

Purpose
This statement is used to declare specific variable, array, or function names to be of type LOGICAL.

General Forms

        LOGICAL list
        LOGICAL*4 list
        LOGICAL*1 list

The lists may contain variable, array, or function names separated by commas. The first two statements are equivalent and declare items in their list to be of type LOGICAL which occupies 4 bytes (*4) of memory. The last statement declares items which occupy 1 byte (*1) of memory. Refer to Appendix J for a discussion of these statements and the logical data types.

F.37 **Logical** IF

Purpose
This statement allows some action to be taken as a result of some test or comparison.

General Form

        IF(logical expression) executable statement

If the logical expression has the value .TRUE. then the statement following the IF is executed. Otherwise the statement on the next line is executed.

Rule

1) The executable statement may not be a DO statement, a WHILE-DO statement, a SUBROUTINE or FUNCTION statement, a computed GO TO, or assigned GO TO statement.

Examples

```
1)  IF(I .LT. 10) PRINT, A, B
2)  IF(A+B .GT. C+D) GO TO 25
```

F.38   Logical Expressions

Purpose

Logical expressions permit the expression of complicated logical relationships.

Rules

1) Logical expressions are composed of relational expressions and logical operators. The logical operators in order of their priority are: .NOT., .AND., and .OR..
2) The priority of the logical operators as a group is less than that of the relational expressions and thus, is also less than arithmetic expressions.
3) In a logical expression with operators of equal priority, the evaluation is performed left to right.

Examples

In the following, Example 1) is equivalent to Example 2), and Example 3) is equivalent to Example 4). Note that the parentheses in Example 5) are necessary to preserve the intended meaning.

```
1)  A.LT.0.0 .AND. A.GT.10.0
2)  (A.LT.0.0) .AND. (A.GT.10.0)
3)  A**2+5.0+B+C.LT.25.0 .OR. D.GE.17.0
4)  (A**2+5.0+B+C.LT.25.0) .OR. (D.GE.17.0)
5)  .NOT.(X.GE.4 .AND. Y.LE.6)
```

F.39   Magnetic Tape Unit Commands

Magnetic tape is used on computers to store information which is either large in amount or infrequently needed. The magnetic tape is wound on removable reels. These magnetic tape reels are mounted on a magnetic tape unit by the computer operator.

The use of magnetic tapes can be quite complicated, and a detailed discussion is beyond the scope of this text. As a rule, extra information outside the WATFIV-S program must be supplied to allow for their use. The computer consultants at each computer center can provide more information on the use of magnetic tapes.

Information is written on and read from these tapes using the WRITE and READ statements. In addition, there are three other commands to control the tape. They are described below. In each case, the i refers to the unit number allocated to the magnetic tape unit. (See Appendix H for more details on unit numbers with the READ and WRITE statements.)

1) BACKSPACE i instructs the magnetic tape unit to move the tape back to the beginning of the previous record. This feature allows records to be re-read.
2) ENDFILE i instructs the magnetic tape unit to write out an end-of-file record on the tape to indicate the end of the file.
3) REWIND i instructs the magnetic tape unit to rewind the tape back to the beginning. This statement allows the program to start over at the beginning of the file.

F.40   NAMELIST **Statement**

Purpose
This statement is used to supply a named list of variables which may be used in input and output statements.

General Form

```
NAMELIST/name/ list
```

The name represents the name of the list and may be any valid WATFIV-S name. The list contains variable or array names separated by commas.

Rules

1) The name of the list is used in PRINT and READ statements.
2) When a PRINT statement uses a NAMELIST, the variable and array names in the list as well as their values are printed as shown in Example 1).
3) When a READ statement is used, the names of the variables or arrays and their values are both supplied on the data cards as illustrated in Example 2).

   a) The &name must begin in column 2.
   b) The order of the variables does not matter.
   c) Not all variables in the list need be assigned values.
   d) A repetition factor n* may be used to imply that the constant that follows is to be repeated n times.

Examples

1)

```
C Program to illustrate NAMELIST output
      INTEGER I(2), J
      REAL SUM
      NAMELIST/OUTPUT/ I, J, SUM

      I(1) = 1
      I(2) = 2
      J = 3
      SUM = 15.5
      PRINT OUTPUT
      STOP
      END
```

output of the above program is:

```
 &OUTPUT
 I=          1,          2,J=          3,SUM= 0.1550000E 02,&END
```

2)

```
C Program to illustrate NAMELIST input
      INTEGER I(2), J
      REAL SUM
      NAMELIST/INFO/ I, J, SUM
      READ INFO
      STOP
      END
$ENTRY
 &INFO SUM=1547.045, I=2*0,&END
```

F.41   PAUSE **Statement**

Purpose

This statement is used to allow a temporary halt in the execution of a program to allow the computer operator to perform some task.

General Forms

```
PAUSE
PAUSE n
PAUSE 'message'
```

The number n or the message are printed on the operator's console when the PAUSE statement is executed. In most computer installations, the PAUSE statement is ignored. WATFIV-S gives a warning message as well.

F.42   PRINT **Statement**

Purpose

This statement allows a program to print messages and the values of variables, constants, and expressions.

General Form

```
PRINT, output list
```

When executed, this statement will cause the computer to advance to a new line and print the messages and values in the output list. Other forms of this statement exist and are discussed in Appendix H.

Rules

1) Each PRINT statement starts printing on a new line.
2) The output list may contain variables, messages inside quotes, constants, and expressions.
3) No expression in the output list may begin with a left parenthesis, for example:

```
PRINT, (A+B)      - is illegal
PRINT, A+B        - is legal
PRINT, +(A+B)     - is legal
```

4) If the output list contains too many values for all of them to be printed on one line, the computer automatically advances to the next line. A print line usually contains from 120 to 133 characters, depending on the type of line printer installed.
5) If an array name is contained in the output list, then all elements of that array will be printed out in column order.
6) Implied DO loops are allowed to provide a shorthand notation for the output list. The following examples illustrate their use:

```
PRINT, A(1),A(2),A(3),A(4)          PRINT, (A(I), I=1,4)
PRINT, B(1,1),B(1,2),B(2,1),B(2,2)  PRINT, ((B(I,J), J=1,2), I=1,2)
PRINT, 1, 3, 5, 7                   PRINT, (I, I=1,7,2)
```

F.43   PUNCH **Statement**

Purpose
This statement provides an alternate way to output data to the card punch. (A WRITE statement may also be used.)

General Form

```
PUNCH, output list
```

When executed this statement will cause the computer to start punching the messages and values in the output list.

Rules

1) Each PUNCH statement starts punching on a new card.
2) The output list may contain variables, messages inside quotes, constants, and expressions.
3) No expression may begin with a left parenthesis.
4) If the output list contains too many values for all of them to be punched on a card, the computer automatically advances to the next line. A card contains 80 character positions.
5) If an array name is contained in the output list, then all elements of that array will be punched out in column order.
6) Implied DO loops are allowed to provide a shorthand notation for the output list. The following examples illustrate their use:

```
PUNCH, A(1),A(2),A(3),A(4)          PUNCH, (A(I), I=1,4)
PUNCH, B(1,1),B(1,2),B(2,1),B(2,2)  PUNCH, ((B(I,J), J=1,2), I=1,2)
```

F.44   READ **Statement**

Purpose
This statement allows a program to obtain data from data cards.

General Form

```
READ, input list
```

When executed, this statement will cause the computer to read the next data card and assign the numbers or values on it to the variables in the input list. Other forms of this statement exist and are discussed in Appendix H.

Rules

1) The data cards are placed following the $ENTRY control card.
2) Values on the data cards must be separated by a comma and/or one or more blanks.
3) All 80 columns of the card may be used for the data values.
4) The input list may contain only variable names. It may not contain constants or expressions.
5) The values on the data card should agree in type (REAL or INTEGER) with the corresponding variables in the input list. Data values may not be expressions.
6) Each READ statement encountered causes a new data card to be read. Thus, if there are more values per card than variables in the input list, the remaining values are ignored.
7) If there are insufficient data values on a card, another card is read automatically. If there are not enough data cards, an error message is issued.
8) If an array name is contained in the input list, the computer will try to read in enough data for every element of the array and will assign them in column order.
9) Implied DO loops are allowed to provide a shorthand notation for the input list. The following examples illustrate their use:

```
READ, A(1),A(2),A(3),A(4)        READ, (A(I), I=1,4)
READ, B(1,1),B(1,2),B(2,1),B(2,2) READ, ((B(I,J), J=1,2), I=1,2)
```

Examples

1) In the following program segment, two data cards are read, and I is given the value 100, X is given the value 2.0, and Y is given the value 5.0.

```
        READ, I, X, Y
        ⋮
$ENTRY
    100
2.0 5.0
```

2) In this program segment, an error will be issued since there are not enough data values. However, before the error is issued, X is assigned the value 2.0, A receives 3.0, and I is assigned 25. The value 4.0 is not used.

```
        READ, X, A
        READ, I, Z
        ⋮
$ENTRY
    2.0 3.0 4.0
    25
```

F.45   REAL **Statement**

Purpose

This statement is used to declare specific variable, array, or function names to be of type REAL.

General Forms

```
REAL list
REAL*4 list
REAL*8 list
```

The lists contain variable, array, or function names separated by commas. The first two statements are equivalent and declare all items in their lists to be of type single-precision REAL. The *4 notation refers to the fact that a single-precision real number occupies 4 bytes of memory. The last statement declares the items in its list to be of type extended-precision REAL. Refer to Appendix K for more information on this data type. (See also the section in this appendix on the compile-time initialization of variables.)

Rules

1) This statement should be placed before all executable statements.
2) This statement may be used to declare individual names to be of type REAL.

```
REAL ISUM, J, COUNT, JOE
```

3) The size of an array may be declared in this statement.

```
REAL R(10), JOE(20,5)
```

F.46 Relational Expressions

Purpose
Relational expressions are used to compare the values of arithmetic expressions.

General Form

```
arithmetic expression REOP arithmetic expression
```

where REOP stands for one of the six relational operators, .EQ., .NE., .LT., .LE., GT., and .GE..

Rules

1) The priority of the relational operators is less than that of the arithmetic operators.
2) The result of a relational expression is either .TRUE. or .FALSE..

Examples

1) X .LT. 5.0
2) Y .GE. X**2 + 3*X + 1.5

F.47 REMOTE BLOCK **Statement**

Purpose
This feature allows a user to group statements of a program together under a name and execute them by name.

General Form of Definition

```
REMOTE BLOCK name
:    statements
END BLOCK
```

The remote block is defined within a main program or subprogram and used only from within that same program. The REMOTE BLOCK name obeys the rules for WATFIV-S names.

General Form of Usage

```
EXECUTE name
```

When this statement is executed, the computer transfers to the first executable statement of the REMOTE BLOCK and begins execution there. When the END BLOCK is reached, the computer returns to the statement following the EXECUTE statement. There are no arguments or parameters to be passed back and forth.

Rules

1) REMOTE BLOCKs may only be executed by means of an EXECUTE statement.
2) A REMOTE BLOCK may contain any regular WATFIV-S statements except another REMOTE BLOCK statement.

Example

```
C This program reads in 10 cards.  Each card contains 1
C integer and 2 real values. It performs arithmetic on the
C real numbers as determined by the integer value.
C If the integer is: 1 - add A+B
C                    2 - subtract A-B
C                    3 - multiply A*B
C                    4 - divide A/B
C        anything else - print a warning message
      INTEGER I, NUM
      REAL A, B

      I = 0
      WHILE(I .LT. 10) DO
         READ, NUM, A, B
         DO CASE NUM
            CASE
               EXECUTE ADD
            CASE
               EXECUTE SUB
            CASE
               EXECUTE MULT
            CASE
               EXECUTE DIVIDE
            IF NONE DO
               EXECUTE NONE
         END CASE
         I = I + 1
      END WHILE
      STOP
      REMOTE BLOCK ADD
         PRINT, 'THE SUM OF', A, B, 'IS', A+B
      END BLOCK

      REMOTE BLOCK SUB
         PRINT, 'THE DIFFERENCE OF', A, B, 'IS', A-B
      END BLOCK

      REMOTE BLOCK MULT
         PRINT, 'THE PRODUCT OF', A, B, 'IS', A*B
      END BLOCK

      REMOTE BLOCK DIVIDE
         PRINT, 'THE QUOTIENT OF', A, B, 'IS', A/B
      END BLOCK

      REMOTE BLOCK NONE
         PRINT, 'BAD CODE', NUM
      END BLOCK

      END
```

F.48   RETURN **Statement**

Purpose

This statement is used to return from a subprogram to the program that called it.

General Form

```
RETURN
```

The operation of the RETURN varies slightly depending on whether the return is being made from a subroutine subprogram or a function subprogram. See the discussion of the SUBROUTINE and FUNCTION statements for details.

Rules

1) A subprogram may have several RETURN statements.
2) A RETURN statement is an unconditional transfer statement.

Example
See the examples in this appendix for the SUBROUTINE and FUNCTION statements.

F.49 Statement Format

1) Columns 1-5 are reserved for statement numbers. Statement numbers are not necessary when using the structured statements and free format of WATFIV-S. Otherwise, a statement number is a number from 1 to 99999 used to identify and refer to statements. Only those statements which need to be referenced require a statement number. The statement numbers need not be in ascending order, but it aids the readability of the program if they are. A statement number may go anywhere within these five columns.
2) Column 6 is reserved for a continuation indicator. Any nonzero or nonblank character in column 6 indicates that this statement is a continuation of the previous statement. For instance, the following two statements are identical in operation.

```
col. 6                              col. 6
   ¦                                   ¦
   ¦ X = A+B+C                         ¦ X = A+B+C+D
   *+D
```

3) Program statements are punched in columns 7 to 72.
4) Columns 73 to 80 are reserved for sequence numbers. These columns are not checked by WATFIV-S.

F.50 Statement FUNCTIONS

Purpose
These subprograms allow users to write their own one-line functions.

General Form of Definition

```
name(parameter list) = arithmetic expression
```

The parameter list contains one or more variable names, called parameters, separated by commas. The arithmetic expression includes these parameters in the calculations.

General Form of Usage

```
name(argument list)
```

This reference may appear anywhere an arithmetic expression is allowed. The argument list contains one or more arguments separated by commas. An argument may be a constant, an arithmetic expression, or a variable. The number of arguments must be the same as the number of parameters, and each argument value must be of the same type (INTEGER or REAL) as its corresponding parameter.

When a statement function reference is executed the following actions occur:

1) The values of the arguments are transferred into their corresponding parameters.
2) The arithmetic expression of the statement function is evaluated, and the resultant value is assigned to the function name on the LHS of the statement function.
3) The statement function reference is given the value of the statement function, and execution continues in the statement which contained the reference.

Rules

1) Statement functions may appear in main programs and subprograms. However, a statement function may only be used from within the program segment in which it is defined.
2) Statement function names follow the same rules as variable names.
3) Statement functions may be of type INTEGER, REAL, COMPLEX, LOGICAL, or DOUBLE PRECISION.
4) Statement functions should be placed before all executable statements but after the declaration statements.
5) Statement functions may be evaluated only by referencing their name in some other statement. Thus, statement functions are not executable statements in the usual sense of the word.

Example

```
C This program uses a statement function to generate a table
C of Fahrenheit degrees versus Celsius degrees over the range
C of 0.0 to 212.0 degrees Fahrenheit.
      REAL FDEG, CEL, FAHREN
C     Define the statement function CEL.               .
      CEL(FAHREN) = (FAHREN - 32.0)*5.0/9.0

      PRINT, 'TABLE OF FAHRENHEIT VERSUS CELSIUS DEGREES'
      FDEG = 0.0
      WHILE(FDEG .LE. 212.0) DO
          PRINT, FDEG, CEL(FDEG)
          FDEG = FDEG + 1.0
      END WHILE
      STOP
      END
```

F.51   STOP **Statement**

Purpose
The STOP statement is used to terminate execution of the program.

General Form

```
    STOP nnnnn
```

When this statement is executed by the computer, it causes the computer to terminate the current program. The nnnnn is an integer number which is printed to identify which STOP statement halted the program.

Rules

1) The nnnnn is optional and may be omitted.
2) Some installations may disable the nnnnn message.

Example
See any WATFIV-S program in this text.

F.52   SUBROUTINE **Subprograms**

Purpose
These subprograms allow a user to define a group of statements to be a separate program segment which may be invoked from within other program segments using the CALL statement.

General Form of Definition

```
SUBROUTINE name(parameter list)
:    statements
RETURN
END
```

The subroutine name obeys the rules for WATFIV-S names. The parameter list contains variable, array, or function names separated by commas.

General Form of Usage

```
CALL name(argument list)
```

The argument list contains one or more arguments separated by commas. An argument may be a constant, arithmetic expression, variable, array, or function name. The number of arguments must be the same as the number of parameters, and each argument must be of the same type as its corresponding parameter.

When, the CALL statement is executed, the following actions occur:

1) The computer transfers to the first statement of the SUBROUTINE.
2) The values of the arguments are copied into the corresponding parameters. For arrays, only their location is passed, and the subroutine uses the same data area.
3) Execution of the subroutine begins at the first executable statement.
4) When a RETURN statement is executed

   a) the values of the parameters are copied back into the corresponding arguments.
   b) the computer returns to the calling program and resumes execution at the statement following the CALL statement.

Rules

1) A Subroutine name may not be used as a variable in the subprogram.
2) Subroutine parameters may not be initialized at compile time.
3) Subroutine calls may not form a loop.
4) If an argument is a DO loop index or a DO loop parameter, the value of the corresponding parameter may not be changed in the subroutine.

5) Variables and statement numbers are local to a subroutine. If the same names and numbers are used in another program segment, they are not considered the same by the compiler.

Example

```
C Calculate L!/(M!*K!) using subroutine subprograms
      INTEGER L, M, K, LFACT, MFACT, KFACT, ANSWER

      READ, L, M, K
      CALL FACT(L,LFACT)
      CALL FACT(M,MFACT)
      CALL FACT(K,KFACT)
      ANSWER = LFACT/(MFACT*KFACT)
      PRINT, 'THE ANSWER IS', ANSWER
      RETURN
      END

      SUBROUTINE FACT(I,IFACT)
      INTEGER I, IFACT

      IFACT = 1.0
      WHILE(I .GE. 2) DO
         IFACT = IFACT*I
         I = I - 1
      END WHILE
      RETURN
      END
```

F.53   Variables

1) A variable name may have up to 6 symbols. The first symbol must be alphabetic A-Z, for example:

    A, X, COUNT, GEORGE, A1234

2) Operators and delimiters may not appear in a variable name. Thus the following characters are illegal:

    * / + -) (. ' , & =

3) Blanks may appear in a variable name but are ignored by the compiler and not counted as one of the six symbols.

    WO MAN   is equivalent to   WOMAN

4) A variable name is undefined until it has been assigned a value, and an error message is issued if an undefined variable is used in a calculation.

5)   Both integer and real variables exist for storing integer and real values. There are two ways of determining the type of a given variable name.

a)   *Implicit Typing (first letter rule):* Variable names beginning with the symbols A-H, O-Z are REAL while those beginning with I, J, K, L, M, and N are INTEGER. If only these default rules are used, then the variable names JIM, MOE, and LESTER are of type INTEGER, and SAM, GEORGE, FRED, and X are of type REAL.

b)   *Explicit Typing:* This feature is used to override the default rules for individual variable names. The REAL and INTEGER specification statements are used.

```
REAL X, Y, FRED, JIM, JOE
INTEGER ABLE, GEORGE, JOKER
```

F.54   WHILE-DO **Loop**

Purpose

This feature is used to repeatedly execute a group of statements while some condition is true.

General Form

```
WHILE(logical expression) DO
   statements
END WHILE
```

The statements within the WHILE loop are executed repeatedly while the logical expression has the value .TRUE.. When the END-WHILE statement is encountered, execution starts over again at the WHILE statement, and the logical expression is reevaluated. When the logical expression is evaluated and has the value .FALSE., the computer starts executing the first statement following the END-WHILE statement.

Rules

1)   A WHILE-DO loop must be terminated by an END-WHILE statement.
2)   The DO portion of the statement must be on the same line as the WHILE(logical expression).
3)   A WHILE loop may contain other WHILE loops.
4)   A special form, namely the WHILE-EXECUTE statement, exists for use with REMOTE BLOCKs. For instance, the following are equivalent:

```
WHILE(condition) DO
    EXECUTE JOE          WHILE(condition) EXECUTE JOE
END WHILE
```

Example

```
C This program calculates the sum of the
C first 10 integers.
      INTEGER I, N, SUM

      N = 10
      SUM = 0
      I = 1
      WHILE(I .LE. N) DO
         SUM = SUM + I
         I = I + 1
      END WHILE
      PRINT, 'THE SUM OF THE FIRST', N, 'INTEGERS IS', SUM
      STOP
      END
```

F.55 WRITE **Statement**

Purpose

This statement allows a user more control over the output of data.

General Form

```
WRITE(unit #,fmt stno)
```

The unit # is used to select the output device of the WRITE statement. This unit # allows selection of a line printer, card punch, disks, and even magnetic tape units. The exact unit # used depends on the individual computer installation. The fmt stno refers to the statement number of the FORMAT statement which is to control the output. Refer to Appendix H for more information on the use of this statement.

G
Internal Representation of Numbers in
WATFIV-S

The decimal number system (base 10) used by humans has 10 different states (the decimal digits 0 to 9) and is not very convenient for computers. The technological properties of electronic components are much better suited to representing the two electrical states of 'on' and 'off'. As a result, most computers make use of a two-state number system called a base 2 or *binary* representation which has only the binary digits of 0 and 1. A binary digit is also called a *bit* and binary numbers consist of one or more bits. All data to be stored on a computer is converted into or represented by such numbers. The following are base 2 numbers of 8 bits each with their corresponding base 10 values. To prevent confusion, subscripts are given to indicate the base of the numbers.

$$00000000_2 = 0_{10} \qquad 01101111_2 = 111_{10}$$
$$11111111_2 = 255_{10} \qquad 11011110_2 = 222_{10}$$

The conversion between base 2 numbers and base 10 numbers may be accomplished in a straightforward manner. Conversion of a decimal number into binary may be done by repeatedly dividing the decimal number by 2, taking the remainder (0 or 1) at each stage to form the binary number. This is illustrated below for the decimal number 119.

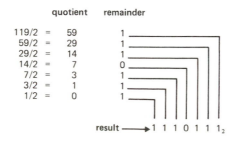

To convert a binary number into a decimal number, it is first necessary to realize that the following equation holds for decimal numbers:

$$d_4 d_3 d_2 d_1 d_0 = d_4 \times 10^4_{10} + d_3 \times 10^3_{10} + d_2 \times 10^2_{10} + d_1 \times 10^1_{10} + d_0 \times 10^0_{10},$$

where d_i represents a decimal digit. A simple example follows:

$$58764_{10} = 5 \times 10^4_{10} + 8 \times 10^3_{10} + 7 \times 10^2_{10} + 6 \times 10^1_{10} + 4 \times 10^0_{10}.$$

A similar equation holds for binary numbers,

$$b_4 b_3 b_2 b_1 b_0 = b_4 \times 2^4_2 + b_3 \times 2^3_2 + b_2 \times 2^2_2 + b_1 \times 2^1_2 + b_0 \times 2^0_2,$$

where b_i represents a binary digit. Of course, in base 2 arithmetic, multiplication by 2 means shifting the digit one place to the left, that is, $b_4 \times 2^4 = b_4 0000$. For example:

$$10101_2 = 1 \times 2^4_2 + 0 \times 2^3_2 + 1 \times 2^2_2 + 0 \times 2^1_2 + 1 \times 2^0_2$$

$$= 1000 + 0000 + 100 + 00 + 1.$$

Having established the above, it is only necessary to perform the evaluation of the binary digits using base 10 arithmetic.

$$10101_2 = 1 \times 2^4_2 + 0 \times 2^3_2 + 1 \times 2^2_2 + 0 \times 2^1_2 + 1 \times 2^0_2$$

$$= 1 \times 16_{10} + 0 \times 8_{10} + 1 \times 4_{10} + 0 \times 2_{10} + 1 \times 1_{10}$$

$$= 16_{10} + 4_{10} + 1_{10}$$

$$= 21_{10}$$

Since binary numbers are very difficult to remember, the individual binary digits are usually grouped together. The bit combinations in each group are represented by a different character. It is possible to take the bits in groups of 2,3,4, and so on. A group of 3 bits has $2^3 = 8$ different digits and is called the base 8 or *octal* representation. A group of 4 bits has $2^4 = 16$ different digits and is called the base 16 or *hexadecimal* representation. These are the two most common representation systems. It should be emphasized that grouping the bits together does not change how the computer stores the information but just allows a human to remember the numbers more easily.

The IBM 360/370 uses the hexadecimal representation. The binary-hexadecimal-decimal relationships are described in Figure G.1.

Figure G.1   Relationship between binary, hexadecimal, and decimal values.

binary group	hexadecimal digit	decimal value
0000	0	0
0001	1	1
0010	2	2
0011	3	3
0100	4	4
0101	5	5
0110	6	6
0111	7	7
1000	8	8
1001	9	9
1010	A	10
1011	B	11
1100	C	12
1101	D	13
1110	E	14
1111	F	15

Thus, by using the hexadecimal representation, the following binary numbers may be written as indicated below.

$$100101111_2 = 97_{16} \qquad 000100111111 = 13F_{16}$$

$$10100101_2 = A5_{16}$$

In the IBM 360/370 computers, the basic unit of memory is the byte, which contains 8 bits and thus can store 2 hexadecimal digits. Since different data types have different memory requirements, several consecutive bytes are necessary to store some values. When 2 bytes are used, they form a unit of memory called a half word, when 4 bytes are used they are called a full word, and 8 bytes form a double word. The following table illustrates the relationship between these units of memory.

1 bit	= 0 or 1	
1 byte	= 8 bits	
1 half word	= 2 bytes	= 16 bits
1 word	= 4 bytes	= 32 bits
1 double word	= 8 bytes	= 64 bits

The following table describes the storage requirements for the various data types available in WATFIV-S.

1 integer value	- 4 bytes
1 real value	- 4 bytes
1 character value	- 1 byte (see Appendix I)
1 logical value	- 1 or 4 bytes (see Appendix J)
1 half word integer	- 2 bytes (see INTEGERs in Appendix F)
1 extended precision value	- 8 bytes (see Appendix K)

G.1   Integer Numbers

An integer number may be either negative, zero, or positive. Representing zero and positive numbers is not difficult. It is the representation of negative numbers that is somewhat unusual. Of the many ways of storing negative numbers, the IBM 360/370 uses what is called a 2's complement notation. In this notation, a positive number is converted into a negative number of the same magnitude by complementing all of the bits (change 0 to 1 and 1 to 0) and adding 1. This is illustrated below for the decimal number 119.

$+119_{10}$	0	0	0	0	0	0	7	7_{16}	positive hex number
	0000	0000	0000	0000	0000	0000	0111	0111	binary form
	1111	1111	1111	1111	1111	1111	1000	1000	complement it
								+1	add 1
	1111	1111	1111	1111	1111	1111	1000	1001	negative binary form
-119_{10}	F	F	F	F	F	F	8	9_{16}	negative hex number

As it turns out, the left most bit of an integer number gives the sign (0 means positive, 1 means negative) of the integer value.

G.2   Real Numbers

The real number system requires not only negative, zero, and positive numbers but must also allow for a floating decimal point. If the general form of a decimal floating-point number can be said to be $0.d_{-1}d_{-2}d_{-3}d_{-4} \cdots \times 10^{dexp}$ then a hexadecimal representation of a number could have a general form of $0.h_{-1}h_{-2}h_{-3}h_{-4} \cdots \times 16^{hexp}$. Conversion between these two representations is not straightforward and, thus, will not be discussed here. The storage of the hexadecimal representation is done by reserving a portion (7 bits) of a word to represent the exponent. The remainder of the word is reserved for the mantissa or fractional part of the real number. The internal representation of a floating-point number has the following format.

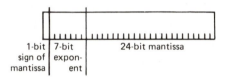

1-bit   7-bit   24-bit mantissa
sign of   expon-
mantissa   ent

The exponent is stored in what is called an *excess-64* notation which simply means that the value of the actual hexadecimal exponent is represented by adding it to 64. The mantissa is stored in what is called a normalized form. This normalization means that the mantissa is stored as a number between $.100000_{16}$ and $.FFFFFF_{16}$ with the exponent adjusted appropriately. For example, the decimal number 119.0 (which is hexadecimal 77) would be represented as 0.77×16^2. In terms of the internal format, this number would be stored as follows.

119.0_{10} = 0|100 0010 |0111 0111 0000 0000 0000 0000$_2$ binary

119.0_{10} =   4   2   7   7   0   0   0   0$_{16}$ hexadecimal

H
Formatted Input and Output

H.1 Introduction

All of the programs in the main body of this text used simple READ and PRINT statements to handle the input and output of information in an algorithm. Little control over the appearance or precision of information was exercised. Though the programs were easy to write, the results may not always be adequate. It is often desirable to present the output from a program in a more readable form or to squeeze more information on each line or to decide exactly what information should appear on each page.

In order to specify the layout of input data or the appearance of output lines, it is necessary to introduce the WATFIV-S FORMAT statement. By associating an input or output statement with a FORMAT statement, it is possible to control the operation of these statements and the associated spacing of information. This appendix describes the basic details of formatted input and output.

H.2 Alternate Input and Output Statements

The card reader and printer are but two of many possible input/output devices. To allow for the flexibility of using other media, there are standard general input/output statements, namely:

```
READ (u, f, END=stno1, ERR=stno2) list
WRITE (u, f) list
```

u   is an integer variable or constant called the unit number which refers, by installation convention, to a specific type of device. The card reader is usually numbered 5 and the printer is normally 6. Thus, this portion of each statement specifies *where* the information is coming from or going to.

f   is the statement number (appearing in columns 1-5) of a FORMAT statement. This specifies *how* the information is to be transferred. The use of an asterisk implies that free format is to be used. More than one input/output statement may refer to the same FORMAT statement if desired.

stno1   is the statement number of the first statement to be executed if an end-of-file condition is encountered on the input device. The END=stno1 portion of the statement may be omitted if desired. However, if it is omitted, and an end-of-file does occur, the compiler will issue an error message and terminate execution of the program.

stno2   is the statement number of the first statement to be executed should a hardware error be discovered during an attempt to input information. The ERR=stno2 portion of the statement may be omitted if desired. However, if it is omitted, and a hardware error does occur, the compiler will issue an error message and terminate execution of the program.

list   is the list of variables to be supplied values on input or supplying values for output, thus specifying *what* information is to be transmitted.

Statements of these types can be used to replace the READ and PRINT statements used in the text.

H.3   The FORMAT **Statement**

FORMAT statements provide instructions on how information is to be read or printed. The general form of the FORMAT statement is:

    nnnnn FORMAT(codes)

The nnnnn is a 1-5 digit statement number appearing in columns 1-5 of the line. The codes represent instructions about how the information in an input or output statement is to be transmitted. This includes information on horizontal as well as vertical spacing and information about the column layout of constant values. Normally, several codes appear together and are separated by commas.

The following sections describe the individual FORMAT codes in detail. Examples of how to use these codes are given in Section H.19.

H.4   FORMAT **Codes and** FORMAT **Masks**

A wide variety of FORMAT codes or *masks* are provided for use in WATFIV-S. These are summarized in Figure H.1 and described in detail on succeeding pages. The term mask is used to describe the codes designed to handle numeric, character, and logical values. It describes the appearance of such values. The portion of the input or output record containing the value is called the *field*, and the number of columns is called the *field width*.

H.5   The A-Mask

Purpose
The A-mask is used to control the input and output of character information. The information may be stored in variables of any data type including the WATFIV-S CHARACTER type.

General Form

Aw   w is an unsigned integer constant specifying the total field width or number of characters to be transmitted.

Input Rules

1)   If the field width is shorter than the number of characters that can be stored in the receiving variable, blank characters are added on the right to fill the variable.

Figure H.1   The WATFIV-S FORMAT codes.

Code	General Form	Purpose		Meaning
A	Aw	Character strings	w =	total field width
D	Dw.d	Double- or extended-precision	w =	total field width
		floating-point values	d =	number of significant digits
E	Ew.d	Single-precision	w =	total field width
		floating-point values	d =	number of significant digits
F	Fw.d	Single- or extended-precision	w =	total field width
		floating-point values	d =	number of digits to the right of the decimal
G	Gw.d	General purpose	w =	total field width
		for D, E, F, I, or L	d =	see D, E, F-codes
H	nHs	Literal strings	n =	number of characters after H included in s
			s =	string following H to be included
I	Iw	Integer or fixed-point values	w =	total field width
L	Lw	Logical values	w =	total field width
P	sPf	Scaling factor	s =	power of 10
		by powers of 10	f =	one of E, F, or G-codes
T	Tp	Tabbing to specific columns	p =	tab column position
X	nX	Horizontal spacing	n =	number of columns to skip
Z	Zw	Hexadecimal strings	w =	total field width (number of hex digits)
/	/	Vertical skipping		
'	's'	Enclosed literal string	s =	literal string

2) If the field width is longer than the number of characters that can be stored in the receiving variable, characters are truncated on the left.

Input Examples

Assume that the maximum number of characters to be stored in the variable is 4.

Characters in Input Field	Mask	Resulting Value Assigned
ABCD	A4	'ABCD'
ABC	A3	'ABCb'
ABCDE	A5	'BCDE'

Output Rules

1) If the field width is shorter than the number of characters stored in the variable, characters are truncated on the right.
2) If the field width is longer than the number of characters stored in the variable, the field is padded on the left with blank characters.

Output Examples

Assume that the maximum number of characters stored in the variable is 8.

Value to be Characters in Output	Mask	Characters in Output Field
'ZYXWVUTS'	A8	ZYXWVUTS
'ZYXWVUTS'	A6	ZYXWVU
'ZYXWVUTS'	A10	bbZYXWVUTS

Further examples may be found in the sample programs in Appendix I.

H.6   The D-Mask

Purpose
The D-mask is used to control the input and output of extended-precision (double-precision) values in exponent notation.

General Form

Dw.d   w is an unsigned integer constant specifying the total field width.
       d is an unsigned integer constant specifying the number of significant digits.

Rule
The D-mask functions in the same fashion as the E-mask except that up to 16 significant digits can be handled, and the letter D rather than E is used for the exponent.

Examples
The programs in Appendix K include examples of the D-mask.

H.7   The E-Mask

Purpose
The E-mask is used to control the input and output of single precision (REAL) floating-point values in exponent notation.

General Form

Ew.d   w is an unsigned integer constant specifying the total field width.
       d is an unsigned integer constant specifying the number of significant digits and/or the number of digits appearing between the decimal point and the exponent.

Input Rules
Considerable freedom is allowed in specifying the value in the field.

1) Any blank columns are treated as zeros.
2) If no exponent is specified, an exponent of zero is assumed.
3) The exponent may be expressed in several ways so that 10^5 may be written as E+05, E05, E5, E+5, +05, or +5, and 10^{-4} may be written as E-04, E-4, -04, or -4.
4) If the exponent is out of range (about -75 to $+75$), an error message is issued and execution halted.
5) If a decimal point is specified, the value of d is ignored.
6) If no decimal point is given, a decimal point is inserted d positions to the left of the exponent.
7) If more than 7 significant digits are specified, the resulting value may or may not be rounded.

Input Examples

Characters in Input Field	Mask	Resulting Value Assigned
ƀƀƀ0.98765	E10.5	.98765
.98765E+05	E10.5	98765.
.98765Eƀƀƀ	E10.5	.98765
.98765E5ƀƀ	E10.5	error message
98.765E2	E8.2	9876.5
-98765+03	E9.4	-9876.5
-ƀ987ƀ5	E7.2	-987.05

Output Rules

1) The value is placed right justified in the w columns as illustrated below.

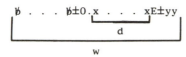

2) The rightmost 4 columns are always used for the exponent, including the letter E, a sign column, and two columns for the numeric exponent.
3) The two-digit exponent includes a leading zero if necessary.
4) If the exponent is positive, the column reserved for the sign of the exponent is left blank. Similarly, if the value is positive, no sign is specified.
5) The d columns immediately to the left of the exponent are used to represent the fractional portion of the number.
6) A zero and decimal point always precede the fractional portion on the left.
7) Any additional columns to the left are set to blanks.
8) The number is represented as a normalized fraction with the exponent adjusted accordingly.
9) The value of w must be at least d+6 for positive values and at least d+7 for negative values to provide for the leading sign (if any), leading zero, decimal point and exponent.
10) If the value of w is too small to allow for all of the components of the number, the field is filled with asterisks.
11) If the value of d is less than 7, the fraction will be rounded.

Output Examples

Value to be Output	Mask	Characters in Output Field
123456.	E12.6	0.123456Eƀ06
-123.456	E12.5	-0.12346Eƀ03
-123.456	E12.6	************
-123.000	E12.4	ƀ-0.1230Eƀ00
-.000123	E12.4	ƀ-0.1230E-03

H.8   The F-Mask

Purpose

The F-mask is used to control the input and output of single- (REAL) or extended-precision (DOUBLE PRECISION) floating-point values without the exponent notation.

General Form

Fw.d w is an unsigned integer constant specifying the total field width.
d is an unsigned integer constant specifying the number of digits to the right of the decimal point.

Input Rules

1) Only the digits 0 to 9, a sign, + or -, a decimal point ., or a blank may appear in the w columns. If an invalid character is found in the w columns, an appropriate error message is printed, and the program is halted.
2) Blank columns are treated as zeros.
3) If a decimal point appears anywhere in the w columns, the value of d is ignored.
4) If no decimal point appears, the value of d is used to insert a decimal point d+1 columns from the right end of the field.
5) If too many significant figures are specified - more than 7 for single precision or more than 17 for extended-precision — the result may or may not be correctly rounded. Unfortunately, the compiler is not consistent in this respect.

Input Examples

Characters in Input Field	Mask	Resulting Value Assigned
ƀƀ1234	F6.2	12.34
ƀ12.34	F6.2	12.34
12.34ƀ	F6.2	12.34
ƀ12.34	F6.0	12.34
1ƀ2.34	F6.2	102.34
1234.5	F6.3	1234.5

Output Rules

1) The value is printed right justified in the w columns with the decimal point d+1 columns from the right.
2) If w is larger than necessary, blanks are placed to the left to fill the w columns.
3) Positive values are printed unsigned. Negative values have the minus sign placed immediately to the left of the most significant digit.
4) At least one digit appears to the left of the decimal, including a leading zero if the magnitude of the value is less than 1.
5) If necessary, zeros are supplied to fill the d columns to the right of the decimal.
6) The value is rounded to fit the columns specified.
7) If w is not sufficiently large, the w columns are filled with asterisks.

Output Examples

Value to be Output	Mask	Characters in Output Field
12.34	F5.2	12.34
-12.34	F6.2	-12.34
12.34	F8.4	ƀ12.3400
-12.34	F8.3	ƀ-12.340
12.34	F4.0	ƀ12.
12345.6	F7.0	ƀ12346.
12.34	F4.2	****
-12.34	F5.2	*****

H.9   The G-Mask

Purpose

The G-mask is used to control the input and output of a variety of data types including COMPLEX, DOUBLE PRECISION, INTEGER, LOGICAL, and REAL. This generalized mask is designing to save time in designing FORMAT masks, especially for beginning programmers.

General Form

Gw.d   w is an unsigned integer constant specifying the total field width.
         d is an unsigned integer constant specifying the number of digits to the right of the decimal point (if appropriate for the data type).

Input Rules

1) The rules that apply are determined by the variable type and the form of the input data.
2) For integer and logical values, the G-mask functions like the I- and L-masks, respectively. The d is ignored and may be omitted.
3) For real or complex values, the G-mask functions like the F- or E-mask, depending on whether or not an exponent is included in the input field.
4) For extended-precision values, the G-mask functions like the F- or D-mask, depending on whether or not an exponent is included in the input field.

Input Examples

Characters in Input Field	Mask	Variable Type	Resulting Value Assigned
⌀⌀⌀12345	G8.3	I	12345
1⌀2⌀3⌀4⌀	G8	I	10203040
GARBAGE	G7.7	L	error message
WHAT⌀LUCK	G9	L	.TRUE.
0.1234E4	G8.4	R	1234.
12345678	G8.0	R	12345670.
12345678	G8.0	D	12345678.

Output Rules

1) For integer and logical values, the G-mask performs like the I- or L-mask, respectively. The d may be omitted since it is ignored.
2) For floating-point values (real, complex, or extended-precision), the G-mask operates as a D-, E-, or F-mask depending on the value to be printed. For values outside the range $.1 \leq x < 10^d$ the value is printed in exponent notation with d significant digits. For values within the specified range, the value is printed with d digits to the right of the decimal. The rightmost 4 columns used for the exponent are left blank.

Output Examples

Value to be Output	Variable Type	Mask	Characters in Output Field
98765	I	G6	ƀ98765
.TRUE.	L	G6	ƀƀƀƀƀT
.098765	R	G10.4	0.9877E-01
.98765	R	G10.4	0.9876ƀƀƀƀ
98765.	R	G10.4	0.9877Eƀ05
9876.5	R	G10.4	ƀ9877.ƀƀƀƀ
.098765	D	G10.4	0.9876D-01
.98765	D	G10.4	0.9876ƀƀƀƀ
98765.	D	G10.4	0.9877Dƀ05

H.10   The H-Code

Purpose

The H-code is used to provide an alternate way of handling literal information on output (characteristic of early versions of FORTRAN). See also the '-code.

General Form

nHs   n is an unsigned integer constant specifying the number of characters after H
      that form the literal string.
      s is the literal character string of length n.

Output Rules

1) The value of n must be an exact count of the number of characters in the literal string.
2) Any character may appear in the literal string including single quotes.

Output Examples

Code	Characters in Output Field
4HXƀ=ƀ	Xƀ=ƀ
7HIT'Sƀ0K	IT'Sƀ0K

H.11   The I-Mask

Purpose

The I-mask is used to control the input and output of fixed-point (INTEGER) values.

General Form

Iw   w is an unsigned integer constant specifying the total field width.

Input Rules

1) Only the numeric digits 0-9, a sign, + or -, or blanks are permitted in the w columns. If, an invalid symbol appears, an error message is printed and execution halted.
2) Blank columns are treated as zeros.

3) The sign may appear anywhere to the left of the value. A plus sign is optional and may be omitted.
4) If the value is outside the range for an integer, an error message is printed and execution halted.

Input Examples

Characters in Input Field	*Mask*	*Resulting Value Assigned*
123456	I6	123456
ƀƀ1ƀ2ƀ	I6	1020
ƀ-ƀ123	I6	-123
123.45	I6	error message
9999999999	I10	error message

Output Rules

1) The value is printed right justified in the w columns.
2) Any extra columns to the left of the value are set to blanks.
3) If the value is positive, the sign is omitted.
4) If the value is negative, the sign is placed immediately to the left of the most significant digit.
5) If the value is too large to fit into the w columns, the w columns are filled with asterisks. No error message is printed, and execution continues.

Output Examples

Value to be Output	*Mask*	*Characters in Output Field*
123456	I9	ƀƀƀ123456
-123456	I9	ƀƀ-123456
123456	I3	***

H.12   The L-Mask

Purpose
The L-mask is used to control the input and output of logical values.

General Form

Lw   w is an unsigned integer constant specifying the total field width.

Input Rules

1) The w columns are scanned from left to right looking for the first occurrence of a T or F.
2) If the letter T is encountered first, the value .TRUE. is assigned. If the letter F is found first, a value of .FALSE. is assigned.
3) If the w columns are entirely blank, a value of .FALSE. is assumed. Otherwise, if neither a T nor an F is found, an error message is issued, and execution is terminated.

Input Examples

Characters in Input Field	Mask	Resulting Value Assigned
T	L1	.TRUE.
ƀƀFƀ	L4	.FALSE.
WHATƀLUCK	L9	.TRUE.
BLANK	L5	error message
ƀ	L1	.FALSE.

Output Rule

1) A single letter T or F corresponding to the values .TRUE. and .FALSE., is placed in the rightmost column, and the remaining columns are filled with blanks.

Output Examples

Value to be Output	Mask	Characters in Output Field
.TRUE.	L1	T
.FALSE.	L3	ƀƀF

H.13   The P-Mask

Purpose

The P-mask is used to provide a scaling factor by powers of 10 for very large or very small values or to overcome accuracy problems caused by difficulties in expressing fractional values exactly. The authors have found little use for this mask.

General Form

sPf   s is an unsigned or negatively signed integer constant specifying the scaling factor (power of 10).
f is one of the FORMAT masks Ew.d, Fw.d, or Gw.d.

Input Rules

1) The external value received is divided by 10 to the power s (equivalently, multiplied by 10 to the power -s) before it is assigned internally to the receiving variable.

$$\text{External} = 10^s * \text{Internal}$$

2) The P-code only affects an F-mask on input. It has no effect on an E-mask.
3) If a field count (see the Section H.19) is to be used, it is inserted after the letter P but before the mask.
4) Once a P-code is encountered in a group of FORMAT masks, it remains in effect for all subsequent masks of the same type in the FORMAT string unless changed by another P-code.

Input Examples

Characters in Input Field	*Mask*	*Resulting Value Assigned*
98765	F5.3	98.765
98765	0PF5.3	98.765
98765	1PF5.3	9.8765
98765	-2PF5.3	9876.5
98765432	-2P2F4.1	98760. & 54320.
98765432	-2PF4.1,F4.1	98760. & 54320.
98765432	-2PF4.1,0PF4.1	98760. & 543.2

Output Rules

The effect of a P-code depends on whether the mask is an E- or F-mask. For an E-mask the following rules apply:

1) The P-code is used to change the appearance of the value on output, namely to shift the position of the decimal point relative to the most significant digit by s positions.
2) The d specifies the number of digits to appear between the decimal point, and the exponent (rather than the number of significant digits).
3) If s is negative, s zeros are inserted to the right of the decimal point, and the exponent is modified accordingly.
4) If s is zero, it is ignored.
5) If s is positive, s significant digits appear to the left of the decimal point, and the exponent is adjusted accordingly.

The next rule applies only to an F-mask.

6) The internal value is multiplied by 10^s before it is transmitted for external presentation.

The following rules apply for both E- and F-masks:

7) If a field count (see the Section H.19) is to be used, it is inserted after the letter P but before the mask.
8) Once a P-code is encountered in a group of FORMAT masks, it remains in effect for all subsequent masks of the same type in the FORMAT string unless followed by another P-code.

The rules which apply for a G-mask depend on whether the value would include an exponent. See the description of the G-mask for details.

Output Examples

Value to be Output	*Mask*	*Characters in Output Field*
12.34	E13.5	ƀƀ0.12340Eƀ02
12.34	0PE13.5	ƀƀ0.12340Eƀ02
12.34	2PE13.5	ƀ12.34000Eƀ00
12.34	-2PE13.5	ƀƀ0.00123Eƀ04
12.34	F13.5	ƀƀƀƀƀ12.34000
12.34	3PF13.5	ƀƀ12340.00000
12.34	-2PF13.5	ƀƀƀƀƀƀ0.12340

H.14   The T-Code

Purpose
The T-code is used to position the next field in a specific column in a fashion similar to tabs on a typewriter.

General Form

Tp   p is an unsigned integer constant representing the tab column position.

Rules

1)   For all input devices and most output devices, the tab causes the next field to start in column position p.
2)   For the line printer, the first character is used to control the line spacing and is not printed. Thus the field will start in column p-1.

H.15   The X-Code

Purpose
The X-code is used insert blanks between masked fields and, thus, provide horizontal spacing.

General Form

nX   n is an unsigned integer constant specifying the number of columns to skip.

Rule
This code is very easy to use, and no specific rules are required. Note that the n precedes the letter X contrary to positioning for the FORMAT masks.

Examples
Examples of the X-code appear in Section H.19.

H.16   The Z-Mask

Purpose
The Z-mask is used to control the input and output of data in the internal hexadecimal form.

General Form

Zw   w is an unsigned integer constant specifying the total field width (number of hex digits).

Input Rules

1)   Only the hexadecimal digits 0-9 or A-F or blank characters may appear in the w columns.
2)   Any blanks in the w columns are treated as zeros.
3)   If the field width w is greater than the number of hex digits in the representation of the variable, the extra columns on the left are ignored.
4)   If the field width w is less than the number of hex digits in the representation of the variable, additional hex zeros are padded on the left.

Input Examples

Characters in Input Field	Mask	Variable Type	Resulting Value Assigned
0000001E	Z8	I	30
ƀƀFF	Z4	I	255
ƀƀFƀF	Z5	I	3855
421A4000	Z8	R	26.25
FC21A4000	Z9	R	-26.25

Output Rules

1) · If the number of hex digits (twice the number of bytes) used for the data type of the variable is less than w, the field is padded on the left with blanks.
2) If the number of hex digits used for the data type of the variable is greater than w, the value is truncated on the left.

Output Examples

Value to be Output	Variable Type	Mask	Characters in Output Field
65536	I	Z8	00010000
65536	I	Z5	10000
-65536	I	Z10	ƀƀFFFF0000
65536.	R	Z8	45100000
-65536.	R	Z8	C5100000
'ABCD'	C	Z8	C1C2C3C4

H.17   The /-Code

Purpose

The /-code is used to cause a skip to a new card, line, or record within a single string of FORMAT codes.

General Form

/   This indicates that the end of the relevant information on a card, printer line, or record has been reached and that processing should continue with the next.

Rules

1) No special caution is necessary except for the line printer. In this case, it must be remembered that the first character of each line to be printed is used as the line spacing character and is not printed.
2) Slashes may be placed side by side to skip several records. If the consecutive slashes appear in the middle of a string of FORMAT codes, n slashes will cause n-1 records to be skipped. At the end of a FORMAT string, n records will be skipped.

H.18   The '-Code

Purpose

The '-code is used to output literal information, such as messages and identifying information. Though this code can technically be used for input as well, this usage is rather obscure and will not be described.

General Form

'ѕ' s the literal string to be transmitted.

Output Rule

To include a single quote within the string, two single quotes in adjacent columns are used.

Output Examples

Code	*Characters in Output Field*
'Xb̸=b̸'	Xb̸=b̸
'IT''Sb̸OK'	IT'Sb̸OK

H.19 Using FORMAT **Codes and Masks**

The previous sections presented the various FORMAT masks and codes in isolation. A single FORMAT statement usually includes a combination of codes and masks to produce the desired effect. Such a list is applied sequentially to the variables or values in the input or output list. The FORMAT codes and masks are usually separated by commas to remove ambiguity and may also be separated by blanks to improve readability. In the examples which follow, those variables beginning with the letter I are assumed to be INTEGER, those beginning with R are REAL, those with L are LOGICAL, those with DP are DOUBLE PRECISION, and those with CX are COMPLEX.

H.19.1 **Considerations for Printer Output**

Information on a line printer may be displayed in many different ways, depending on the physical characteristics of the printer. The details of what is available should be checked with the individual computer center. The most common width of a printer page is 133 characters.

When a PRINT statement is being processed, a string of characters equal in length to the printer page is set up by the compiler. This string of characters, called a *buffer*, is initialized to blanks, and a pointer is set to the first position. As each FORMAT code and mask is processed, the pointer is advanced along the character string, and the characters produced by the FORMAT masks are placed in the buffer. When all values have been converted and placed in the buffer, if a slash code is encountered, or if there are more values but not FORMAT masks, as discussed in Section H.19.5, the buffer is transmitted to the printer. Of course, an attempt to place more than 133 characters in the buffer will result in an error message and termination of the program.

When applying FORMAT control for printed output, horizontal spacing is determined by the successive masks and codes used. In addition, it is necessary to specify vertical spacing information. By convention, the first character of each line is *not* printed but is used to determine how to vertically space the current line. This first character is called the *carriage control character* (CCC). Alternate names include printer or vertical control character. The effect of specific characters is shown in table form below. If none of these characters appear as the first to be printed, single spacing is assumed.

CCC	*Effect*	
+	no spacing	print the current line without advancing, that is, over the previous line of output
b̸	single spacing	advance to the next line before printing the current line
0	double spacing	advance two lines before printing, thus leaving one blank line between
-	triple spacing	advance three lines before printing, thus leaving two blank lines between
1	new page	advance to the top of a new page before printing the current line

It should be emphasized that the first character on a line is used for this purpose, regardless of how it is produced. Thus, it is feasible to generate the character as the first character of a masked field. This is a dangerous practice, however, since the value placed in the masked field may produce unexpected results. It is best to explicitly specify the carriage control character by one of the following methods (illustrated for single spacing):

```
1X       1Hb̸       'b̸'
```

Examples

1) The following statements:

```
        I = 12345
        PRINT 9000, I
   9000 FORMAT(1X,I8)
```

will produce the following output:[1]

```
b̸b̸b̸12345b̸ . . .
```

2) The following statements:

```
        R = 1234.5
        PRINT 9010, R
   9010 FORMAT('b̸',F10.5)
```

will produce the following output:

```
1234.50000b̸ . . .
```

3) The following statements:

```
        WRITE (6, 9020)
   9020 FORMAT(18H-ENDb̸OFb̸PROCESSING)
```

will produce the following output:

```
b̸ . . .          ←    two blank
b̸ . . .          ←        lines
ENDb̸OFb̸PROCESSINGb̸ . . .
```

The first character in the literal string, -, is used to achieve triple spacing and, thus, does not appear as part of the message.

---

[1] The use of an ellipsis indicates that the preceeding character, normally a blank (b̸) is repeated for the remainder of the line.

4)   The following statements:

```
        PRINT 9030, 1, 2, 3
   9030 FORMAT('1','LINE',I2,/'0LINE',I2/1X,'LINE',I2)
```

will produce the following output:

```
   LINE␢1␢ . . .        ←   first line on a new page
   ␢ . . .          ←   blank line
   LINE␢2␢ . . .
   LINE␢3␢ . . .
```

5)   The following statements:

```
        CX = (1., 2.)
        WRITE (6, 9040) 1234.5, 987, CX, 12345678.9
   9040 FORMAT(F6.1, 5X, I3 / '0', F5.1, F5.1 / '0', D20.12)
```

will produce the following output:

```
   234.5␢␢␢␢␢987␢ . . .     ←   first line on a new page
   ␢ . . .        ←   blank line
   ␢␢1.0␢␢2.0␢ . . .
   ␢ . . .        ←   blank line
   ␢␢0.123456789000D␢08␢ . . .
```

Since no control character was specified for the first line, the first character produced under the F-mask, the 1, was used as the carriage control character. Note that 5X,I3 is equivalent to I8 in this example.

H.19.2   Considerations for Card Input

The use of FORMAT control for input from cards means that data values are no longer separated by commas or blanks. Since the standard punched card contains 80 columns, an attempt to read information beyond column 80 results in an error message and program termination. Unlike the printer, no vertical control is exercised. Each execution of a READ statement from the card reader automatically accesses the information on the next card.

Examples

1)   Consider the effect of the following program segment:

```
        READ 8000, R
   8000 FORMAT(F8.1)
        ⋮
   $ENTRY
   ␢␢␢12345␢ . . .
```

```
        1234.5
```

```
        R
```

2) Consider the effect of the following program segment:

```
        READ (5, 8010), I, RONE, RTWO, L, CX
   8010 FORMAT(I5, E10.4, F5.2, L5, F4.0, F4.0)
        ⋮
   $ENTRY
   987650.1234Eϸ04-1.23ϸϸϸϸTϸϸϸ3ϸϸϸ4ϸ . . .
```

```
   98765   1234.   -1.23   T   (3.,4.)

     I     RONE    RTWO    L     CX
```

H.19.3 Field Counts

Frequently, the same FORMAT mask is to be used for a number of consecutive values. Rather than repeating the same mask several times, it is possible to precede the mask by an unsigned integer constant called a *field count* or *repeat factor*.

Examples

1) Consider the following program segment:

```
        READ (5, 8000) (R(I), I = 1, 6)
   8000 FORMAT(3F6.2, 3F6.3)
        ⋮
   $ENTRY
   ϸϸϸ111ϸϸϸ222ϸϸϸ333ϸϸ4444ϸϸ5555ϸϸ6666ϸ . . .
```

```
   1.11   2.22   3.33   4.444  5.555  6.666

   R(1)   R(2)   R(3)   R(4)   R(5)   R(6)
```

2) The following statements:

```
        WRITE (6, 9000) (I, I = 1, 5)
   9000 FORMAT('ϸ', 5I4)
```

will produce the following output:

```
   ϸϸϸ1ϸϸϸ2ϸϸϸ3ϸϸϸ4ϸϸϸ5ϸ . . .
```

H.19.4 Group Counts

As well as repeating individual masks, it is often desirable to repeat groups of masks and/or codes. This can be accomplished by surrounding the group with parentheses and placing an unsigned integer constant called a *group count* or *group factor* before the left parenthesis. Such groups may be nested to a maximum depth of two, that is, a group within a group but not a group within a group within a group. If the constant is missing, a group factor of one is assumed.

Examples

1) Consider the effect of the following program segment:

```
      READ (5,8000) (R(I), I = 1, 6)
 8000 FORMAT(3(2F6.2,F6.3))
      ⋮
$ENTRY
```

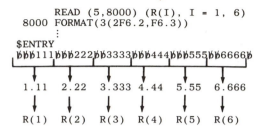

2) The following statements assume the values from the previous example:

```
      WRITE (6, 9000) (R(I), I = 1, 6)
 9000 FORMAT(' b', 3('R(', I1, ')b=', F6.3, 2X),
     +        /'b', 3('R(', I1, ')b=', F6.3, 2X) )
```

will produce the following output:

```
R(1)b=b1.110bbR(2)b=b2.220bbR(3)b=3.333b . . .
R(4)b=b4.440bbR(5)b=b5.550bbR(6)b=6.666b . . .
```

A continuation card is used to specify the FORMAT for the second line of output.

H.19.5 When the Number of Values and Masks Do Not Match
In a general program, it is not always feasible to design FORMAT statements that suit all possible situations. Consequently, the number of FORMAT masks does not always match the number of items in the input or output list. As a result, the following two problems arise:

a) more masks than items
b) more items than masks

a) More Masks than Items In order to handle this situation, it is helpful to know how a list of FORMAT codes and masks is processed. Processing proceeds from left to right in the FORMAT list. Codes are processed as they are encountered. Each time a mask is found, the next entry in the input/output list is considered. If the mask is not appropriate for the item, an error message is issued, and the program is terminated. Assuming the type is legal, the value is transmitted under control of the mask. In this way, the processing continues until no variable is found for the current mask. All codes and masks up to, but not including, this mask are processed. This is summarized in a general form below, while the appropriate results are illustrated for several examples thereafter.

```
variable list        var₁            var₂       . . .        varₙ
                       ↓               ↓                       ↓
format list  (code₁, mask₁, code₂, mask₂, . . . codeₙ, maskₙ, codeₙ₊₁, maskₙ₊₁, . . . )
                        └──────────────────────────────────────────┘
                                        processed
```

where var_i is a variable name, $code_i$ is zero, one, or more FORMAT codes, and $mask_i$ is one of the FORMAT masks.

Examples

1) Consider the effect of the following program segment:

```
      READ 8000, I, R
 8000 FORMAT(I5,F5.0,I10,F10.5)
      ⋮
$ENTRY
```

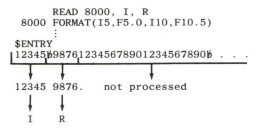

12345 9876.   not processed

I   R

2) The following statements assume the values from the previous example:

```
      PRINT 9000, I, R
 9000 FORMAT(' b', 'Ib=', I5, 2X, 'Rb=', F6.0,2X,'GARBAGE', I3)
```

These statements produce the following output:

Ib=b12345bbRb=b9876.bbGARBAGEb . . .

b) More Items than Masks   The answer to this problem depends on whether the FORMAT list contains any group counts.

Consider first the absence of group counts. Recall that in processing a FORMAT list, each mask is associated with the next item in the input/output list. When the last right parenthesis is encountered, a check is made for additional items in the list. Should there be additional items, the process will advance to a new card or line and continue processing with the left end of the FORMAT list, thus recycling the codes and masks.

If the FORMAT list contains group counts, the answer is not quite as straightforward. In such cases, processing also advances to the next card or line. However, it continues with the group count corresponding to the group whose rightmost parenthesis is nearest to the closing parenthesis of the FORMAT statement. Several possible situations are illustrated below.

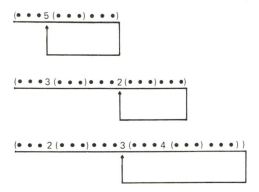

Examples

1)   The following statements:

```
        R(1) = 1.
        R(2) = 2.
        R(3) = 3.
        PRINT 9000, (I, R(I), I = 1, 3)
   9000 FORMAT('0', 'R(', I1, ')ƀ=', F3.0)
```

will produce the output below:

```
ƀ . . .          ←    blank line
R(1)ƀ=ƀ1.ƀ . . .
ƀ . . .          ←    blank line
R(2)ƀ=ƀ2.ƀ . . .
ƀ . . .          ←    blank line
R(3)ƀ=ƀ3.ƀ . . .
```

2)   The following statements:

```
        R(1) = 1.
        R(2) = 2.
        R(3) = 3.
        PRINT 9010, (I, R(I), I = 1, 3)
   9010 FORMAT('0', 'OUTPUT', 2(2x,'R(', I1, ')ƀ=', F3.0))
```

will produce the output below:

```
ƀ . . .            ←    blank line
OUTPUTƀƀR(1)ƀ=ƀ1.ƀƀR(2)ƀ=ƀ2.ƀ . . .
ƀR(3)ƀ=ƀ3.ƀƀR(ƀ . . .
```

When the recycling starts, the first of the two blanks inside the group is used as the carriage control character.

H.19.6   General Considerations

1)   Since FORMAT statements are non-executable statements, only input and output statements may refer to them.
2)   More than one input and/or output statement may refer to a single FORMAT statement.
3)   FORMAT statements may be placed anywhere in the program or subprogram that uses them. Some programmers group them together at the beginning or at the end of the program segment. Others prefer to place each FORMAT statement with the input or output statement that uses it. The authors' preference is to place all FORMAT statements for a program between the declarations and the body of a program.
4)   Good programming practice dictates that easily identifiable statement numbers be used for FORMAT statements. The authors' choice is to number FORMAT statements used for input as 8000, 8010, . . . and those for output as 9000, 9010, ... See the plotting programs in Appendix M for examples.

I
Character
Manipulation

I.1 Introduction

Though scientific and engineering problems primarily involve numerical computations, it is often desirable to include character information to supplement the numeric quantities. This has been evident in the programs throughout the text where titles and messages are used to identify the numeric output. It is also useful to maintain portions of scientific data in character form when sorting files or presenting statistical data. In fact, character quantities were necessary to plot the graphs in Chapter 6 and to draw the histograms in Chapter 13.

Computers were originally designed and built to perform numerical computations. Gradually, the storage and manipulation of character quantities were included in their repertoire, and, today, probably more computer processing involves character information than numerical quantities. However, since FORTRAN was devised during the infancy of this transition, and since FORTRAN was originally designed to solve primarily numerical problems, the storage and handling of characters in standard FORTRAN are somewhat cumbersome. More modern hybrids of FORTRAN, such as WATFIV-S, enhance these facilities by providing for a CHARACTER data type.

This appendix introduces the basic notions of storing and manipulating character information in WATFIV-S as well as pointing out the equivalent methods for standard FORTRAN.

I.2 Character Strings

A character string is simply an ordered set of alphanumeric characters. The basic units of such a string are the individual characters or symbols. The allowable symbols may vary depending on the computer, the programming language, the input medium, or the output medium. The basic FORTRAN character set usually includes the symbols:

```
A B C D E F G H I J K L M N O P Q R S T U V W X Y Z
0 1 2 3 4 5 6 7 8 9
0 - * / = ( ) . , $ % ' " @ blank
```

though lower-case letters and additional special symbols are often added.

Since character strings may contain blank characters as well as various special symbols, a character string is usually delimited by single quote marks. Listed below are several examples of character strings. Notice that two single quotes, side by side, are used to represent a single apostrophe or quote within a string.

```
'ABC'    '1 PLUS 2 = 3'
'HE SAID, '' #% (EXPLETIVE DELETED)'''
'CARTER''S PEANUTS'
```

I.3   Character Representation

The internal representation of characters in computer memory is highly machine dependent. Each individual character is normally represented by a numeric code. The two most common codes are EBCDIC (Extended Binary Coded Decimal Interchange Code) and ASCII (American Standard Code for Information Interchange). The explanation to follow will be based on the IBM 370 use of EBCDIC.

The memory of a computer is usually organized into what are called *words* of memory. Each word of memory is composed of a set of binary digits called *bits*. The number of bits is called the *word-length* which typically varies from 16 to 64. A word of memory is normally used to store a single number in binary form. Since this is the case, character information is also represented by a binary number.

The basic unit of memory on a 370 is the *byte,* capable of storing a single character. Groups of 4 bytes are organized into words which may be used to store either numbers or characters. Each byte is further subdivided into 8 bits. Since each bit can be either 0 or 1, a byte can represent 2^8 or 256 different characters. The codes for the characters are often written in base 16 or *hexadecimal*. In hexadecimal the letters A-F are used to extend the digits 0-9 in order to represent the digits from 0-15 by a single symbol. Figure I.1 lists the internal codes for some of the commonly used symbols in both hexadecimal and decimal notation. These EBCDIC codes have been chosen carefully so that they maintain alphabetic and numeric order. This ordering is called a *collating sequence.*

I.4   Character Manipulation in WATFIV-S

I.4.1   Character Storage

The manipulation of character strings in WATFIV and WATFIV-S is facilitated by the CHARACTER data type. Since character strings can be of various lengths, the declaration of variables specifies not only the type as character but also the maximum number of characters that can be represented. By default, the length is 1 but may range to a maximum of 255. The length for each variable in a list can be specified after the keyword CHARACTER with an asterisk and the numeric length. Alternately, each variable declared can be followed by an asterisk and its individual numeric length. Of course, variables of type CHARACTER may also be arrays. Listed below are several examples of character declarations.

```
CHARACTER A, ALPHA(26), CHKBRD(8,8)
CHARACTER*1 A, ALPHA(26), CHKBRD(8,8)
CHARACTER A*1, ALPHA*1(26), CHKBRD*1(8,8)
CHARACTER SINGLE, NAME*20, BRAND*30(100)
```

Though different in form, the first three statements all produce the same result. A is defined as a simple character variable of length 1, ALPHA is a one-dimensional array having 26 entries each of length 1, and CHKBRD is a two-dimensional array having 8 rows and 8 columns for character length 1 entries. The last declaration defines SINGLE as a character variable of length 1, NAME as a character variable of length 20, and BRAND as an array of length 100, where each entry can contain a maximum of 30 characters.

Figure I.1   Basic FORTRAN character codes (EBCDIC) for an IBM 370.

	Letters			Digits			Special Symbols	
C	Hex	Dec	C	Hex	Dec	C	Hex	Dec
A	C1	193	0	F0	240	ᵬ	40	064
B	C2	194	1	F1	241	.	4B	075
C	C3	195	2	F2	242	(	4D	077
D	C4	196	3	F3	243	+	4E	078
E	C5	197	4	F4	244	$	5B	091
F	C6	198	5	F5	245	*	5C	092
G	C7	199	6	F6	246	)	5D	093
H	C8	200	7	F7	247	–	60	096
I	C9	201	8	F8	248	/	61	097
J	D1	209	9	F9	249	,	6B	107
K	D2	210				%	6C	108
L	D3	211				@	7C	124
M	D4	212				'	7D	125
N	D5	213				=	7E	126
O	D6	214				"	7F	127
P	D7	215						
Q	D8	216						
R	D9	217						
S	E2	226						
T	E3	227						
U	E4	228						
V	E5	229						
W	E6	230						
X	E7	231						
Y	E8	232						
Z	E9	233						

ᵬ = blank

I.4.2   Assignment of Character Values

a) Execution-Time Assignment   Character values may be assigned to character variables at execution time using an assignment statement of the form

```
character variable = character value
```

The value on the right may be a constant or a variable. When the length of the value does not match the length of the variable, the following actions are taken. If the value is too long, characters are truncated from the right until the value fits into the variable. If the value is too short, blank characters are added on the right to make the value long enough for the variable. The three possibilities are illustrated below for a character variable FIVE of length 5.

Assignment	*Result in* FIVE
FIVE = 'ABCDE'	'ABCDE'
FIVE = 'ABCDEFG'	'ABCDE'
FIVE = 'AB'	'ABᵬᵬᵬ'

b) Compile-Time Assignment   Character constants may also be assigned to character variables at compile time in one of two ways. If the variables have already been declared as type character, it is possible to use the DATA statement to assign values to the variables. General forms of the DATA statement are:

```
DATA name1 / value1 /, name2 / value2 /, . . .
DATA name1, name2, . . . / value1, value2, . . . /
```

An example of a character declaration and an appropriate DATA compile-time initialization is given below:

```
CHARACTER ONE, STARS*6
DATA ONE / '1' /, STARS / '******' /
```

It is also legal to declare and initialize variables in the same statement as follows:

```
CHARACTER ONE / '1' /, STARS*6 / '******' /
```

As with execution time assignments, strings that are too long are truncated on the right, and strings that are too short are padded on the right with blanks.

I.4.3   Input and Output of Character Values

WATFIV-S allows for the input and output of character values with or without FORMAT control. The relevant rules are summarized below. Various examples are used in the problems discussed in the next section.

a) Free-format Input   Character values may be read without a FORMAT. Such data values must be specified with surrounding quotes. Successive values are separated by a comma and/or one or more blanks. Character strings that are too long are truncated on the left, while strings that are too short are padded with blanks on the right.

b) Formatted Input   A special FORMAT code called the A-mask is provided for character values. The general form is Aw where w specifies the width of the field. If the specified width is too short for the character value, the string is truncated on the left. However, if the value is shorter than the specified width, blanks are added on the right to fill the space.

c) Free-format Output   Character values can be printed without specifying a FORMAT. WATFIV-S assigns its own A-mask equal to the length of the value plus one. Thus, one blank will always precede the character value.

d) Formatted Output   The A-mask is also used to control the output of character values. If the value is too long for the mask, characters are truncated from the right. If the value is too short for the mask, blank characters are added on the left to fill the mask.

I.4.4   Using Character Quantities

Character strings are a useful addition to many applications programs. An important initial decision concerns the length of variable to use. Since the length of each variable must be specified at compile time, it is not possible to react dynamically to the specific data encountered at execution time. Typically, there are two choices. If the program will need to examine individual characters in the string, then each character should be stored in a separate entry of a character array where each entry has a length of one. On the other hand, if no such individual manipulation is necessary, it is feasible to choose a maximum length and declare the variables with this length. The examples to follow demonstrate both conventions.

Example I.1

Produce a listing of the roster of players and their current records for any given team in the National Hockey League.

a) Choosing the Variables   The data for this problem is listed in Appendix N. Since only a listing is required, maximum lengths for each field can be chosen. Since the length of the longest player's name is 19, 19 characters should suffice for the name field. The longest team names are NY Islanders and Philadelphia, so 12 is chosen as the length of TEAM. Next, the position played is coded by a single letter and, thus, PLACE is declared as length one. The remaining fields are integral values. The names chosen are GAMES, GOALS, ASISTS, TOTAL, PIM, and SALARY.

b) Designing the Data Layout   In WATFIV-S the choice between formatted and unformatted input of character information must be made. For this example, assume that no FORMAT is to be used. It is, therefore, necessary to surround all character fields by quotes. In order to select the team, it is necessary to input the name of the team. If the name were placed at the end of the player file, it would be necessary to retain the entire file in memory. Thus, it is preferable to place the name preceding the file and to select the records for printing as they are read. Finally, the exact number of players on file may not be known. To recognize the end of the file, an end-of-data record containing blank or zero fields is appended to the file to act as a flag.

c) Designing the Algorithm   The algorithm to produce the desired listing is quite straightforward. After reading the specific team name and printing the column titles, the first record is read in. As long as the end-of-data record has not been read, a **while** loop controls the printing of selected records and the reading of the next.

d) The WATFIV-S *Program*   The simple program with a portion of the data is listed in Figure I.2. A sample of the resulting output is presented in Figure I.3.

```
C Figure I.2 -- Program to produce a listing of players on a
C                specific team in the National Hockey League.
C**************************************************************
C PLAYER - the player's name (CHARACTER*19)
C TEAM   - the player's team (CHARACTER*12)
C PLACE  - the player's playing position (CHARACTER*1)
C GAMES  - the number of games played
C GOALS  - the number of goals scored
C ASISTS - the number of assists scored
C TOTAL  - the total number of points scored
C PIM    - the number of penalties in minutes
C SALARY - the player's salary
C TEAMX  - the specific team selected for the listing
C**************************************************************
      CHARACTER PLAYER*19, TEAM*12, PLACE*1, TEAMX*12
      INTEGER GAMES, GOALS, ASISTS, TOTAL, PIM, SALARY
C Input the specific team for which the listing is required.
      READ, TEAMX
C Output the team and column headings.
      PRINT, 'ROSTER FOR ',TEAMX
      PRINT, ' '
      PRINT, 'NAME                    P        GP           G',
     +       '           A        TP       PIM           S'
      PRINT, ' '
C Keep processing players until a blank is encountered.
      READ,  PLAYER,TEAM,PLACE,GAMES,GOALS,ASISTS,TOTAL,PIM,SALARY
      WHILE(PLAYER .NE. ' ') DO
         IF(TEAM .EQ. TEAMX) THEN DO
            PRINT,  PLAYER,PLACE,GAMES,GOALS,ASISTS,TOTAL,PIM,SALARY
         END IF
         READ,  PLAYER,TEAM,PLACE,GAMES,GOALS,ASISTS,TOTAL,PIM,SALARY
      END WHILE
      STOP
      END
$ENTRY
'Montreal'
'MacMillan, Bob    ' 'Atlanta    ' 'W' 80 38 33 71 49  85000
'Lysiak, Tom       ' 'Atlanta    ' 'C' 80 27 42 69 54 130000
'Chouinard, Guy    ' 'Atlanta    ' 'C' 73 28 30 58  8  65000
'Vall, Eric        ' 'Atlanta    ' 'W' 79 22 36 58 16  65000
      :                   :          :   :  :  :  :  :    :
'Wolfe, Bernie     ' 'Washington ' 'G' 25  0  0  0  0  65000
'                  ' '           ' ' '  0  0  0  0  0      0
```

Program Notes

- Blank fields have been chosen to signal the end of the player file. Though only the player's name is used to terminate the processing, all of the fields are input in the same READ statement. Therefore, dummy values must be given for each field.

Figure I.3   Listing of players for an NHL team, output from the program of Figure I.2. (Spacing edited)

ROSTER FOR   Montreal

NAME	P	GP	G	A	TP	PIM	S
Lafleur, Guy	W	78	60	72	132	26	180000
Lemaire, Jacques	C	76	36	61	97	14	135000
Shutt, Steve	W	80	49	37	86	24	120000
Robinson, Larry	D	80	13	52	65	39	125000
Larouche, Pierre	C	64	23	37	60	11	100000
Houle, Rejean,	W	76	30	28	58	50	80000
Cournoyer, Yvan	W	68	24	29	53	12	160000
Mondou, Pierre	C	71	19	30	49	8	70000
Savard, Serge	D	77	8	34	42	24	155000
Risebrough, Doug	W	72	18	23	41	97	80000
Lapointe, Guy	D	49	13	29	42	19	175000
Lambert, Yvon	W	77	18	22	40	20	85000
Jarvis, Doug	C	80	11	28	39	23	70000
Gainey, Bob	W	66	15	16	31	57	80000
Nyrop, Bill	D	72	5	21	26	37	70000
Tremblay, Mario	W	56	10	14	24	44	75000
Chartraw, Rick	W	68	4	12	16	64	75000
Bouchard, Pierre	D	59	4	6	10	29	80000
Lupien, Gilles	D	46	1	3	4	108	55000
Larocque, Michel	G	30	0	4	4	0	105000
Engblom, Brian	D	28	1	2	3	23	55000
Dryden, Ken	G	52	0	2	2	0	180000
Wilson, Murray	W	12	0	1	1	0	75000

Example I.2

Given a deck of 500 data cards supposedly containing only numeric information in columns 1 - 30, check the data for accuracy, and flag any invalid characters.

a) Problem Discussion   Very few guidelines are given for solving this problem. It is obvious, though, that each character must be analyzed individually. Thus, each character should be stored in a separate entry of a character array. To check each character for numeric validity, all that is necessary is to check for a code between '0' and '9' inclusive. To highlight invalid characters, an asterisk will be printed under the offending character. The structure of the algorithm involves an outer loop to control the input and processing of each of the 500 cards. Within this outer loop is an inner loop to check each character for validity. An array of characters is established to correspond to each character in the data card. If the character is valid, a blank is assigned; if the character is invalid, an asterisk is assigned. Since the data is keyed in successive columns, it is necessary to specify FORMAT masks for the input.

b) The WATFIV-S *Program*   The complete program, including a portion of the data, is listed in Figure I.4, while some sample output appears in Figure I.5.

```
C Figure I.4 -- Process a deck of 500 data cards containing
C                numeric information in columns 1 to 30.
C                Check the cards for obvious typing errors
C                (non-numeric characters).

C*****************************************************************

C INPUT   - current set of input characters
C ERROR   - set of asterisks flagging errors in INPUT
C CARD    - position of current input card in the deck
C CC      - current card column

C*****************************************************************

      CHARACTER INPUT(30), ERROR(30)
      INTEGER CC, CARD
 8000 FORMAT(30A1)
 9000 FORMAT('1',1X,A 8,1X,30A1)
 9010 FORMAT('0',I5,5X,30A1)
 9020 FORMAT(' ',10X,30A1)

C Output titles for the output.

      PRINT 9000, 'POSITION', ('=', CC = 1, 30)

C Process the 500 cards one at a time.

      CARD = 1
      WHILE(CARD .LE. 500) DO
C        Input and echo output the current card.

         READ 8000, (INPUT(CC), CC = 1, 30)
         PRINT 9010, CARD, (INPUT(CC), CC = 1, 30)

C        Examine each character, flagging invalid characters.

         CC = 1
         WHILE(CC .LE. 30) DO
            IF(INPUT(CC).LT.'0' .OR. INPUT(CC).GT.'9') THEN DO
               ERROR(CC) = '*'
             ELSE DO
               ERROR(CC) = ' '
            END IF
            CC = CC + 1
         END WHILE

C        Output the error symbols and proceed to the next card.

         PRINT 9020, (ERROR(CC), CC = 1, 30)
         CARD = CARD + 1
      END WHILE

      STOP
      END
$ENTRY
0123456789012345678901234567890
0123456789012345678901234567890I23456789
QWERTYUIOPASDFGHJKLZXCVBNM<>?
    :       :       :     ,  :       :
```

I.5   Character Manipulation in Standard FORTRAN

I.5.1   Character Storage

Standard FORTRAN does not provide a specific character data type. Rather, character information must be stored in variables of one of the other data types, INTEGER, REAL, DOUBLE PRECISION, COMPLEX, or LOGICAL. The number of characters that a variable of each type can store depends on the word size of the computer being used. On the IBM 370, a word of memory consists of 4 bytes and is, therefore, capable of storing 4

Figure I.5 Checking cards for obvious typing errors, output from the program of Figure I.4.

```
POSITION  ==============================
   1      012345678901234567890123456789

   2      012345678901234567890123456789
          *          *          **
   3      QWERTYUIOPASDFGHJKLZXCVBNM<>?
          *****************************
```

characters. The table in Figure I.6 lists the various data types and the number of characters that can be stored in a variable of each type.

Figure I.6 Number of characters for each data type.

Data Type	Characters
INTEGER	4
REAL	4
DOUBLE PRECISION	8
COMPLEX	8
LOGICAL	4

Though COMPLEX and DOUBLE PRECISION variables are sometimes useful for handling long character strings, the most common data type used is INTEGER. Because of the word length restrictions, it is necessary to divide longer character strings into variable-sized units. For INTEGER variables, this means substrings of length 4 or less must be used.

I.5.2 Assignment of Character Values

a) Execution-Time Assignment   Character constants cannot be used in any execution time statements in standard FORTRAN. However, variables being used to store character information can appear wherever such variables are normally valid, even though many of these uses, such as DO statement parameters, do not make sense. It is, therefore, permissible to use arithmetic means to create or manipulate character information. However, this can be tricky and should be avoided whenever possible.

b) Compile-Time Assignment   A convenient and often necessary way to initialize variables having character values is at compile time. The values may be assigned using a DATA statement or may be assigned in the appropriate declaration statement. In standard FORTRAN, character constants are specified by the H code, sometimes called the Hollerith code, of the form nH where n specifies the number of characters immediately following the H that are part of the constant. Thus the statements:

```
INTEGER SENT(5)
DATA SENT / 4HTHIS, 4HßISß, 4HAßSE, 4HNTEN, 2HCE /
```

are equivalent to

```
INTEGER SENT(5) / 4HTHIS, 4HßISß, 4HAßSE, 4HNTEN, 2HCE /
```

Note that it is necessary to subdivide the character string to fit the size of the variable in use. Many versions of FORTRAN allow the use of quotes to surround the character strings as follows:

```
INTEGER SENT(5) / 'THIS', 'ßISß', 'AßSE', 'NTEN', 'CE' /
```

I.5.3   Input and Output of Character Values

Since standard FORTRAN requires that FORMATs be specified for all input and output, the A-mask must be used. The rules are the same as those described in the previous section. However, care must be exercised to divide the character string into word-size lengths. Examples are given in the next subsection.

I.5.4   Using Character Quantities

Manipulating character quantities in FORTRAN is somewhat cumbersome because of the restrictions imposed by the fixed number of characters that can be stored in each variable. When handling longer strings, it is necessary to store word-size pieces in separate variables or in entries of an array. As with WATFIV-S CHARACTER variables, if the application requires any character-by-character analysis, it is expedient to place each character in a separate entry of an array. These considerations are best illustrated by reprogramming the previous examples in standard FORTRAN.

a) Example I.1 in Standard FORTRAN   The CHARACTER variables used in the WATFIV-S version must be converted to INTEGER variables. Since the player's name field is 20 characters long, an array of 5 elements will be required. The team names are 11 characters long, thus requiring an array of 3 elements. A single variable suffices for the position field. All references to these fields must be replaced by appropriate references to individual entries of the arrays. When checking for the last card in the deck, a variable initialized to blanks must be set up for comparison purposes. Thus, variable BLANK is initialized to blanks at compile time. In the **while** loop, the test for the correct team must ensure that each of the 3 subunits of the team match. The resulting FORTRAN program is given in Figure I.7. Notice that the structure of the WATFIV-S program has been retained according to the conventions suggested in Appendix D. The output from this program is not given since it is similar to that given in Figure I.3.

b) Example I.2 in Standard FORTRAN   Little restructuring of the principle data areas is required to translate this example. However, the various constants used liberally in the WATFIV-S program must all be defined as variables and initialized at compile time. The FORTRAN DO loop has been introduced for the 2 major loops in the program. The translated FORTRAN program is presented in Figure I.8. The output from this program is identical to that listed in Figure I.5.

```
C Figure I.7 -- Program to produce a listing of players on a
C                 specific team in the National Hockey League.
C******************************************************************
C PLAYER - the player's name (19 characters long)
C TEAM   - the player's team (12 characters long)
C PLACE  - the player's playing position (1 character long)
C GAMES  - the number of games played
C GOALS  - the number of goals scored
C ASISTS - the number of assists scored
C TOTAL  - the total number of points scored
C PIM    - the number of penalties in minutes
C SALARY - the player's salary
C TEAMX  - the specific team selected for the listing
C******************************************************************
       INTEGER PLAYER(5), TEAM(3), PLACE, TEAMX(3)
       INTEGER GAMES, GOALS, ASISTS, TOTAL, PIM, SALARY, P
       INTEGER BLANK / ' ' /
 8000 FORMAT(3A4)
 8010 FORMAT(4A4,A3,3A4,A1,5I3,I6)
 9000 FORMAT(12H1ROSTER FOR ,3A4
      +        /5H NAME,15X,1HP,3X,2HGP,4X,1HG,3X,1HA,3X,2HTP,
      +        3X,3HPIM,7X,1HS)
 9010 FORMAT(1H ,4A4,A3,A1,I5,I5,I4,I5,I6,I8)
C Input the specific team for which the listing is required.
       READ(5,8000) (TEAMX(P), P = 1, 3)
C Output the team and column headings.
       WRITE(6,9000) (TEAMX(P), P = 1, 3)
C Keep processing players until a blank is encountered.
       READ(5,8010) (PLAYER(P), P = 1, 5), (TEAM(P), P = 1, 3),
      +             PLACE, GAMES, GOALS, ASISTS, TOTAL, PIM, SALARY
100    IF(PLAYER(1) .EQ. BLANK) GO TO 300
          IF(TEAM(1) .NE. TEAMX(1) .OR.
      +      TEAM(2) .NE. TEAMX(2) .OR.
      +      TEAM(3) .NE. TEAMX(3)) GO TO 200
             WRITE(6,9010) PLAYER, PLACE, GAMES, GOALS, ASISTS, TOTAL,
      +                    PIM, SALARY
200       CONTINUE
          READ(5,8010) PLAYER, TEAM, PLACE, GAMES, GOALS, ASISTS, TOTAL,
      +                PIM, SALARY
          GO TO 100
300    CONTINUE
       STOP
       END
$ENTRY
Montreal
MacMillan, Bob      Atlanta      W 80 38 33 71 49 85000
Lysiak, Tom        Atlanta      C 80 27 42 69 54130000
Chouinard, Guy     Atlanta      C 73 28 30 58  8 65000
Vall, Eric         Atlanta      W 79 22 36 58 16 65000
   :                  :         : :  :  :  :  :     :
Wolfe, Bernie      Washington   G 25  0  0  0  0 65000
                                  0  0  0  0  0     0
```

```
C Figure I.8 -- Process a deck of 500 data cards containing
C                numeric information in columns 1 to 30.
C                Check the cards for obvious typing errors
C                (nonnumeric characters).
C**************************************************************
C INPUT   - current set of input characters
C ERROR   - set of asterisks flagging errors in INPUT
C CARD    - position of current input card in the deck
C CC      - current card column
C POSI    - the letters 'POSI'
C TION    - the letters 'TION'
C TITLE   - the symbol '=' used for a title
C BLANK   - the symbol ' '
C STAR    - the symbol '*' used to flag errors
C ZERO    - the symbol '0'
C NINE    - the symbol '9'
C**************************************************************
        INTEGER INPUT(30), ERROR(30), CC, CARD
        INTEGER POSI, TION, TITLE, BLANK, STAR, ZERO, NINE
        DATA POSI, TION, TITLE, BLANK, STAR, ZERO, NINE
       +   / 4HPOSI,4HTION,1H=, 1H ,   1H*,  1H0,  1H9  /
 8000 FORMAT(30A1)
 9000 FORMAT('1',1X,2A4,1X,30A1)
 9010 FORMAT('0',I5,5X,30A1)
 9020 FORMAT(' ',10X,30A1)
C Output titles for the output.
        WRITE(6,9000) POSI, TION, (TITLE, CC = 1, 30)
C Process the 500 cards one at a time.
        DO 300 CARD = 1, 500
C       Input and echo output the current card.
        READ(5,8000) (INPUT(CC), CC = 1, 30)
        WRITE(6,9010) CARD, (INPUT(CC), CC = 1, 30)
C       Examine each character, flagging invalid characters.
        DO 200 CC = 1, 30
           IF(.NOT.(INPUT(CC).LT.ZERO .OR. INPUT(CC).GT.NINE)) GOTO 100
              ERROR(CC) = STAR
              GO TO 200
  100         ERROR(CC) = BLANK
  200      CONTINUE
C       Output the error symbols and proceed to the next card.
        WRITE(6,9020) (ERROR(CC), CC = 1, 30)
  300 CONTINUE
      STOP
      END
$ENTRY
012345678901234567890123456789
012345678901234567890I23456789
QWERTYUIOPASDFGHJKLZXCVBNM<>?
    ⋮      ⋮      ⋮      ⋮      ⋮
```

J
Manipulation of
Logical Values

J.1 Introduction

Logical-valued expressions are an essential feature in all programming languages. Their use in expressing conditions in the **if-then-else** and **while-do** constructs is essential to making decisions about the flow of operations in an algorithm. A discussion of such expressions was given in Chapter 4 and again in Appendix C.

As an extension to these basic uses of logical expressions, the notion of a logical data type is a formal feature of the WATFIV-S and FORTRAN languages. A logical variable is very convenient to use as a program flag. Such variables are also useful for solving problems in set theory and electrical circuit design. The following sections will investigate the details of this data type.

J.2 Logical Constants

There are only two logical constants:

.TRUE. and .FALSE.

The periods on either side are necessary to distinguish these constants from potential variables with similar names.

J.3 Logical Variables

Like all special data types, any variable that will have logical values must be declared in a LOGICAL declaration statement such as:

LOGICAL FLAG, SCORE(100), TEST(20,25)

Notice that sets or arrays of logical variables can also be established. Each logical variable is stored in one full word of computer memory. On the IBM 370 a word of memory is composed of four equal subunits called *bytes*. An equivalent declaration reflecting this usage is written as:

```
LOGICAL*4 FLAG, SCORE(100), TEST(20,25)
```

Since there are only two possible logical values, use of a full word to represent such values hardly seems necessary. Consequently, WATFIV-S and some FORTRAN compilers allow the declaration and manipulation of LOGICAL*1 variables which use a single byte for each value.

J.4   Logical Operators

Logical values, by their nature, are different from arithmetic values and, thus, require a unique selection of operators. WATFIV-S provides three logical operators:

.NOT.   .AND.   .OR.

for the manipulation of logical entities. The .NOT. operator negates the value of its single operand. The .AND. operator produces a .TRUE. value if and only if both operands are .TRUE. while the .OR. operator gives a .TRUE. result if either or both of its two operands is true. These operators are applied to logical variables P and Q in the table presented in Figure J.1.

Figure J.1   Logical operators and their operation.

P	Q	.NOT. P	.NOT. Q	P .AND. Q	P .OR. Q
.FALSE.	.FALSE.	.TRUE.	.TRUE.	.FALSE.	.FALSE.
.FALSE.	.TRUE.	.TRUE.	.FALSE.	.FALSE.	.TRUE.
.TRUE.	.FALSE.	.FALSE.	.TRUE.	.FALSE.	.TRUE.
.TRUE.	.TRUE.	.FALSE.	.FALSE.	.TRUE.	.TRUE.

J.5   Relational Operators

Logical operators are not the only ones that produce logical-valued results. The six relational operators, introduced in Chapter 4 and summarized in Figure J.2, are used to test the relationship between arithmetic quantities. The result of a relational operation is either .TRUE. or .FALSE.

Figure J.2   The relational operators.

Symbol	Operator
=	.EQ.
≠	.NE.
>	.GT.
≥	.GE.
<	.LT.
≤	.LE.

J.6   Logical Expressions and Assignment Statements

Any expression involving logical variables, logical constants, logical operators, or relational operators is called a *logical expression*. While such expressions are used primarily as conditions in IF-THEN-ELSE and WHILE-DO statements, their values may also be assigned to logical variables.

In evaluating expressions, recall that WATFIV-S employs a priority scheme to remove ambiguity between successive operators. The scheme is extended in Figure J.3 to include logical and relational operators. Of course, parentheses can be used to alter the order of operations. Should two adjacent operators have the same priority, they are performed from left to right. The sole exception to this rule is successive exponentiation, which is performed from right to left. Examples of such expressions are given at the end of this appendix.

Figure J.3   WATFIV-S operator priority scheme.

```
highest        **
   |           *,/
   |           +,-
   |           .EQ., .NE., .GT., .GE., .LT., .LE.
   |           .NOT.
   ↓           .AND.
lowest         .OR.
```

J.7   Input and Output of Logical Values

Logical values may be read or printed with or without FORMAT control in WATFIV-S. As usual, it is necessary to include formatting in standard FORTRAN.

a) Input Without FORMAT   Data values can be expressed in full as .TRUE. or .FALSE. or may be abbreviated to the single letters T or F respectively. Naturally, pairs of values must be separated by a single comma, one or more blanks, or a combination of both.

b) Input With FORMAT   A specific L format code is provided for logical values. The code is of the form Lw where w specifies the number of columns in the input field. A T or F may be placed anywhere in the w columns. In fact, the w columns may contain any characters whatsoever since WATFIV-S scans the columns from left to right looking for the first T or F. If neither T nor F is found in the w columns, a value of .FALSE. is assigned.

c) Output Without FORMAT   In WATFIV-S logical values may be printed without formal control. The single letters T or F are printed for the values.

d) Output with FORMAT   In standard FORTRAN, the L-mask must be used when recording logical values. A single letter T or F is printed in the rightmost of the w columns specified.

J.8   Built-in Functions

Neither WATFIV-S nor FORTRAN provide any built-in functions for use with logical variables.

J.9   Function Subprograms and Statement Functions

Function subprograms that produce a logical-valued result may be defined using any of the following declarations.

```
LOGICAL FUNCTION name    (parameter list)
LOGICAL FUNCTION name*4  (parameter list)
LOGICAL FUNCTION name*1  (parameter list)
```

The name of the function must be declared as a logical value of the same size in the calling program. It is also possible to define logical-valued statement functions as illustrated in the example in the next section.

J.10   An Example Using Logical Variables

The following example involves making decisions about points on the cartesian coordinate plane:

Example J.1
    Consider a circle centered at the origin with a given radius, and a rectangle, also centered at the origin with given width and height. List all points in the first quadrant having integral coordinates that lie either strictly within the circle or strictly within the rectangle but not both.

a) Problem Discussion   A variety of possible situations is illustrated in Figure J.4. The required points are indicated for each of the four cases shown.

Figure J.4   Integral points within a circle or rectangle.

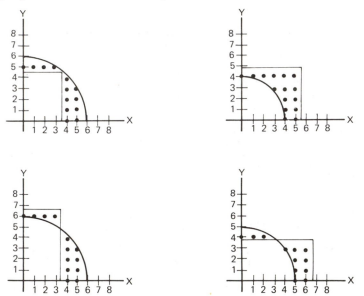

A number of approaches may be taken to find the necessary points. One of the easiest involves checking all x coordinates from zero to the maximum of the radius and half the rectangle width. For each x coordinate, all y coordinates from zero to the maximum of the radius and half the rectangle height must be checked. The program will need to use a nested loop structure to test all integral points given by these computed limits.

c) Testing for Within the Circle and/or Rectangle   To illustrate several features of logical variables, the decision as to whether a point is within the circle can be made by a logical-valued statement function, such as the following:

```
CIRCLE(X,Y,R) = X**2 + Y**2 .LT. R**2
```

The decision relative to the rectangle is written as a logical function subprogram, although it also could be a statement function,

```
LOGICAL FUNCTION RECTGL(X,Y,WIDTH,HEIGHT)
```

which must check that the x coordinate is less than half the width and that the y coordinate is less than half the height. The results of these functions are then used to determine whether the point is within one or the other but not both the circle and the rectangle. This relationship between two logical quantities is called the *exclusive-or* function.

c) The Program   The complete program to accomplish the requested task is presented in Figure J.5. Take particular notice of the detailed notes at the end of the program.

Figure J.6 illustrates the output that is generated for a circle of radius 5 and a rectangle 6 units wide and 12 units high.

```
C Figure J.5 -- Program to list the integral points within
C                a circle or a rectangle but not both.
C****************************************************************
C RADIUS - radius of the circle centered at the origin
C WIDTH  - width of the rectangle centered at the origin
C HEIGHT - height of the rectangle (y-direction)
C X,Y    - coordinate pairs tested
C XL     - maximum value of X to be tested
C YL     - maximum value of Y to be tested
C CIRCLE - logical function for inclusion in the circle
C RECTGL - logical function for inclusion in the rectangle
C INC    - logical flag for inside the circle
C INR    - logical flag for inside the rectangle
C EXORCR - logical exclusive or flag for inside one or other
C****************************************************************
      INTEGER X, XL, Y, YL, WIDTH, HEIGHT, RADIUS, MAX0, R
      LOGICAL CIRCLE, RECTGL, INC, INR, EXORCR
C The statement function for points within the circle.
      CIRCLE(X,Y,R) = X**2 + Y**2 .LT. R**2
C Input the circle radius and rectangle size.
C Echo output these parameters and output titles.
      READ, RADIUS, WIDTH, HEIGHT
      PRINT, 'THE RADIUS OF THE CIRCLE IS', RADIUS
      PRINT, 'THE RECTANGLE SIZE IS', WIDTH, HEIGHT
      PRINT, ' '
      PRINT, '           X              Y'
      PRINT, ' '
```

```
C Figure J.5 (continued)
C Assuming that both the circle and the rectangle are centered
C at the origin, determine the range of (X,Y) pairs to check.
      XL = MAX0(RADIUS, WIDTH/2)
      YL = MAX0(RADIUS, HEIGHT/2)
C Generate and test points in the first quadrant.
      X = 0
      WHILE(X .LE. XL) DO
         Y = 0
         WHILE(Y .LE. YL) DO
            INC = CIRCLE(X,Y,RADIUS)
            INR = RECTGL(X,Y,WIDTH,HEIGHT)
            EXORCR = INC .AND. .NOT.INR .OR. .NOT.INC .AND. INR
            IF(EXORCR) THEN DO
                   PRINT, X, Y
            END IF
            Y = Y + 1
         END WHILE
         X = X + 1
      END WHILE
      STOP
      END
C*****************************************************************
C Function RECTGL -- Logical function to determine if (X,Y)
C                    is within a rectangle WIDTH x HEIGHT
C                    centered at the origin.
C*****************************************************************
      LOGICAL FUNCTION RECTGL(X,Y,WIDTH,HEIGHT)

      INTEGER X, Y, WIDTH, HEIGHT
      REAL XL, YL, FLOAT

      XL = FLOAT(WIDTH)/2.0
      YL = FLOAT(HEIGHT)/2.0
      RECTGL = FLOAT(X) .LT. XL .AND. FLOAT(Y) .LT. YL
      RETURN
      END
$ENTRY
5, 6, 12
```

Program Notes

- Both CIRCLE and RECTGL must be declared as logical values in the main program. Notice that even the dummy argument, R, used in the definition of CIRCLE must be declared as INTEGER.
- The expression for evaluating EXORCR could be written with parentheses to read more clearly. However, the order of operations is correct without these parentheses.
- Since only integral coordinates are requested, INTEGER values are used for most of the numerical quantities. Even though the width and height of the rectangle may not be evenly divisible by 2, the main program need only consider the next lowest integer. However, function RECTGL must include the fractional portion for testing whether a point is within or on the rectangle. The FLOAT function is used to emphasize this conversion.

Figure J.6   List of the integral points within a circle or a rectangle but not both, output from the program of Figure J.5.

```
THE RADIUS OF THE CIRCLE IS               5
THE RECTANGLE SIZE IS               6           12
              X               Y
              0               5
              1               5
              2               5
              3               0
              3               1
              3               2
              3               3
              4               0
              4               1
              4               2
```

K
Manipulation of Extended-Precision Values

K.1 Introduction

The examples in several chapters, notably 7 and 8, have exposed the limitations of computer arithmetic. Though it is theoretically possible to obtain 7-significant-digit accuracy with WATFIV-S REAL arithmetic, such is rarely the case. Because many common decimal fractions are represented by truncating a repeating binary fraction, and because at most 7 significant digits are retained as the result of arithmetic operations, inaccuracies accumulate so that even the fourth or fifth significant digit is often suspect. To improve the accuracy of computation, most machines and the accompanying scientific programming languages include extended-precision capabilities that allow for up to 17-significant-digit accuracy. The sections of this appendix describe the elements of WATFIV-S to use for gaining this additional precision.

K.2 Extended-Precision Constants

Extended-precision constants are distinguished from single-precision or REAL constants by either writing more than 7 significant digits or by writing the number with a D exponent. The following are examples of valid extended-precision constants:

```
2.718281828459045    0.052D 3     0.0D0
-31.0062767          0.3665D-2    25.D+1
```

The maximum precision and limits on the size of extended-precision values vary depending on the computer in use. For an IBM 370, the maximum precision is 17 significant digits, the smallest non-zero value is $0.5397605346934028D-78$, and the largest value is $0.7237005577332261D\ 76$. On most computers, the size of the exponent does not differ between single and extended precision.

K.3   Extended-Precision Variables

All variables and arrays to be used for extended-precision values must be declared in a
DOUBLE PRECISION or REAL*8 declaration statement. The use of the *8 notation
stems from the fact that 8 units of memory called *bytes* are used to represent an
extended-precision value in an IBM 370. (In this sense, single-precision REAL
declarations may alternately be replaced by REAL*4 since 4 bytes are used to represent
such values.) Thus, storing an extended-precision value requires twice the amount of
space as a single-precision value. Hence the label DOUBLE PRECISION is used. In fact,
since the portion of the space used for the exponent remains the same, all of the
additional space is used to represent the fractional portion of the number. Thus, the
improvement in precision from single to extended values is slightly greater than double.
Both of the following declarations specify that SUM is to be a simple extended-precision
variable, that ROWS is to be an array of 10 extended-precision values and that MATRIX
is to be a 3×4 array having 12 extended-precision values.

```
DOUBLE PRECISION SUM, ROWS(10), MATRIX(3,4)
REAL*8 SUM, ROWS(10), MATRIX(3,4)
```

Rather than explicitly declaring variables as extended precision, it is sometimes
advantageous to implicitly define all variables as extended precision using the
IMPLICIT statement discussed in more detail in Appendix F.

K.4   Arithmetic Expressions and Assignment Statements

To achieve greater accuracy in the evaluation of arithmetic expressions, it is only
necessary to declare all names as extended precision and to express all constants in
extended-precision form. The same arithmetic operators and rules of evaluation used
for single-precision quantities apply.
Any operation involving an extended-precision value and a nonextended-precision
value causes the nonextended-precision value to be converted to extended-precision
form before the operation takes place. Thus, the resulting value is always extended
precision. The sole exception is exponentiation to an integer power. As with single
precision, exponentiation to an integer power employs successive multiplication by the
base to achieve the desired result, and, thus, no conversion of the exponent is
necessary. In general, it is best to avoid mixed mode expressions whenever possible.
This is particularly true for fractional values that cannot be represented exactly in
binary notation. For instance, the number 0.1 does not have an exact internal
representation. As a result, the approximations in single and extended precision differ.
If the value of each of the following expressions is assigned to an extended-precision
variable, the results are significantly different.

Expression	*Result*
0.1E0 + 0.1E0	0.2000000476837158
0.1D0 + 0.1E0	0.2000000238418579
0.1D0 + 0.1D0	0.2000000000000000

While the representation of 0.1D0 uses 8 full bytes to represent 0.1, 0.1E0 uses only 4
bytes. When 0.1E0 is converted to extended precision, the additional 4 bytes are set to
0 rather than a more accurate representation of one tenth. This also means that the
value of the following condition:

```
0.1E0 .EQ. 0.1D0
```

is .FALSE. Sufficient inaccuracy is introduced by mixing single-precision and
extended-precision constants to destroy the benefits of using extended precision.
Forgetting to declare even one variable or to express one constant as extended
precision is sufficient to invalidate the results of a program.

K.5   Input and Output of Extended-Precision Values

Very little additional caution is needed to read or print the value of an extended-precision variable. On input, the value may or may not include more than 7 significant digits and may be written with or without the D exponent. On output, extended-precision values are printed to 17 significant digits using the D exponent.

In order to better control the spacing for extended-precision values, two format codes are available. In addition to using the F-mask introduced in Appendix H, a D-mask of the form Dw.d, similar to the E-mask for single precision, can be used. Recall that w is an integer specifying the total number of character spaces to use, that d is the number of significant digits to be included, and that $w \geq d+7$.

K.6   Built-in Functions

A large number of built-in functions is available for use with extended-precision quantities. In most cases, these functions are similar and equivalent to their single-precision counterparts. Thus, DABS computes the extended-precision absolute value of the extended-precision argument. Both DABS and the argument variable must be declared as extended precision. Consult Appendix P for a complete list of such functions. Most extended-precision functions start with the letter D and produce an extended-precision result (labeled r8 in the appendix).

K.7   Function Subprograms

To obtain more accurate results from user-defined function subprograms, it is possible to define the subprogram as an extended-precision function so that the value returned is extended precision. Such a declaration can be accomplished in either of the following two ways:

```
DOUBLE PRECISION FUNCTION name (parameters)
REAL FUNCTION name*8  (parameters)
```

Notice the positioning of the *8 in the second alternative. Of course, in the program that references such a function, the name must also be declared as extended precision.

K.8   Using Extended Precision in a Program

The use of extended-precision variables is best illustrated by translating a known program from single to extended precision. Listed in Figures K.1, K.2, K.4, and K.5 are the translations of subprograms BISECT and SIMP and the accompanying mainline programs from Chapter 10. The translated subroutines are relabeled as DISECT and DSIMP. All single-precision declarations and constants have been changed to extended precision. FORMAT statements have been added to demonstrate the use of F- and D-masks for extended-precision quantities. The output produced by each program is given in Figures K.3 and K.6. The zero-finding program was executed with a much smaller value of the tolerance resulting in a significantly better approximation of the zero. The area-finding program used 128 intervals to approximate the area. The extended-precision answer is 5.999999998913459 compared to the single-precision 5.999913 (see Figure 8.11).

```
C Figure K.1 -- Main program to use subroutine DISECT to find
C                 a zero of the function x**3 - 4x**2 - 4x + 15.
C****************************************************************
C A,B     - endpoints of the initial interval
C EPS     - desired tolerance
C ZERO    - resulting approximation to the zero
C FLAG    - exception flag from DISECT
C****************************************************************
      EXTERNAL FUNC
      DOUBLE PRECISION A, B, EPS, ZERO, FUNC
      INTEGER FLAG
 9000 FORMAT('1INITIAL INTERVAL, A =',F6.2,' B =',F6.2)
 9010 FORMAT('0TOLERANCE =',D25.17)
 9020 FORMAT('0NO ZERO IN THIS INTERVAL.')
 9030 FORMAT('0THE ZERO IN THIS INTERVAL =',F20.16)
 9040 FORMAT(' THE FUNCTION VALUE THERE =',D25.17)
C Obtain the initial interval and tolerance.
      READ, A, B, EPS
      PRINT 9000, A, B
      PRINT 9010, EPS
C Find a zero if possible and output an appropriate message.
      CALL DISECT(A,B,EPS,FUNC,FLAG,ZERO)

      IF(FLAG .EQ. 1) THEN DO
            PRINT 9020
         ELSE DO
            PRINT 9030, ZERO
            PRINT 9040, FUNC(ZERO)
      END IF

      STOP
      END
C****************************************************************
C Function FUNC -- Given a value for X, evaluate the function
C                    x**3 - 4x**2 - 4x + 15
C****************************************************************
      DOUBLE PRECISION FUNCTION FUNC(X)
      DOUBLE PRECISION X
      FUNC = X**3 - 4.0D0*X**2 - 4.0D0*X + 15.0D0
      RETURN
      END
C Subroutine DISECT would be placed here.
$ENTRY
-2.5D0, -1.5D0, 0.1D-14
```

```
C******************************************************************
C Figure K.2 -- Subroutine DISECT
C                Subprogram to use bisection to find a zero for a
C                given function F in the initial interval (PL,PR)
C                to accuracy EPS indicating no zero in the
C                interval by setting FLAG to 1.
C******************************************************************
C PL,PR   - endpoints of initial interval
C XL,XR   - endpoints of successive intervals
C FL,FR   - function values at the endpoints
C XMID    - midpoint of the interval and resulting zero
C FMID    - function value at the midpoint
C EPS     - desired tolerance
C F       - function to be evaluated
C FLAG    - error flag set to 1 if no zero in the interval
C******************************************************************
      SUBROUTINE DISECT(PL,PR,EPS,F,FLAG,XMID)

      REAL*8 PL, PR, XL, XR, FL, FR, XMID, FMID, F, EPS, DABS
      INTEGER FLAG

      XL = PL
      XR = PR
      FL = F(XL)
      FR = F(XR)

C Provided a zero exists in the given interval,
C bisect the interval and choose the subinterval
C with a sign change until the tolerance is reached.

      IF(FL*FR .GT. 0.0D0) THEN DO
            FLAG = 1
         ELSE DO
            FLAG = 0
            XMID = (XL + XR)/2.0D0
            WHILE(DABS(XL - XMID) .GT. EPS) DO
               FMID = F(XMID)
               IF(FL*FMID .LE. 0.0D0) THEN DO
                     XR = XMID
                     FR = FMID
                  ELSE DO
                     XL = XMID
                     FL = FMID
                  END IF
               XMID = (XL + XR)/2.0D0
            END WHILE
      END IF
      RETURN
      END
```

Figure K.3   Finding a zero of a cubic polynomial, output from the program of Figure K.1.

```
INITIAL INTERVAL, A = -2.50 B = -1.50

TOLERANCE =  0.10000000000000000D-14

THE ZERO IN THIS INTERVAL = -1.9575869857265650

THE FUNCTION VALUE THERE  =  0.17763568394002500D-13
```

```
C Figure K.4 -- Main program to use subroutine DSIMP to find
C               the area under the curve  defined by FUNC
C               between A and B.
C**************************************************************
C A,B     - endpoints of the interval
C N       - numbers of subintervals for DSIMP
C AREA    - resulting approximation to the area
C FLAG    - exception flag from DSIMP
C**************************************************************
      EXTERNAL FUNC
      DOUBLE PRECISION A, B, AREA, FUNC
      INTEGER N, FLAG
 9000 FORMAT('1INITIAL INTERVAL, A =',F6.2,' B =',F6.2)
 9010 FORMAT('0NUMBER OF SUBINTERVALS =',I3)
 9020 FORMAT('-VALUE OF N INCORRECTLY SPECIFIED')
 9030 FORMAT('-THE AREA IN THIS INTERVAL =',D25.17)
C Obtain the interval and number of subintervals.
      READ, A, B, N
      PRINT 9000, A, B
      PRINT 9010, N
C Find the area if possible and output an appropriate message.
      CALL DSIMP(A,B,N,FUNC,FLAG,AREA)

      IF(FLAG .EQ. 1) THEN DO
           PRINT 9020
         ELSE DO
           PRINT 9030, AREA
      END IF

      STOP
      END
C**************************************************************
C Function FUNC -- Given a value for X, evaluate the function
C                  7.0 - 7.0*X**6
C**************************************************************
      REAL FUNCTION FUNC*8(X)
      REAL*8 X
      FUNC = 7.0D0 - 7.0D0*X**6
      RETURN
      END
C Subroutine DSIMP would be placed here.
$ENTRY
0.0, 1.0, 128
```

```
C Figure K.5 -- Subroutine DSIMP
C               Subprogram to use Simpson's Rule to find
C               the AREA under the curve F between the
C               endpoints A and B using N subintervals.
C******************************************************************
C A,B    - endpoints of interval
C N      - number of subintervals
C F      - function to be integrated
C H      - interval width
C SUMEVN - sum of F(X) values at even points
C SUMODD - sum of F(X) values at odd points
C AREA   - approximation to the total area
C FLAG   - error flag set to 1 if N is invalid
C******************************************************************
       SUBROUTINE DSIMP(A,B,N,F,FLAG,AREA)

       DOUBLE PRECISION A, B, F, H, AREA, SUMEVN, SUMODD, X
       INTEGER N, I, N2, FLAG
C Check if N is a valid number (must > 0).
       IF(N.LT.1) THEN DO
              FLAG = 1
          ELSE DO
              FLAG = 0
C          Calculate the subinterval width.
           N2 = 2*N
           H = (B - A)/N2
C          Initialize values for the computation.
           I = 2
           SUMEVN = 0.0D0
           SUMODD = F(A+H)
C          Accumulate sums.
           WHILE(I.LE.N2 - 2) DO
              X = A + I*H
              SUMEVN = SUMEVN + F(X)
              SUMODD = SUMODD + F(X+H)
              I = I + 2
           END WHILE
C          Assemble the terms.
           AREA = (F(A) + F(B) + 4.0D0*SUMODD + 2.0D0*SUMEVN)*H/3.0D0
       END IF

       RETURN
       END
```

Figure K.6   Finding the area under a curve, output from the program of Figure K.4.

INITIAL INTERVAL, A = 0.00 B = 1.00

NUMBER OF SUBINTERVALS =128

THE AREA IN THIS INTERVAL =   0.59999999989134590D 01

L
Manipulation of Complex Values

CPD = CMPLX (3.8 * R * S * T, Q * SQRT (ABS (S * T)))

L.1 Introduction

The complex number system is of theoretical interest to mathematicians and of practical importance to scientists and engineers. For these reasons, the FORTRAN family of programming languages, including WATFIV-S, has been endowed with the facilities for handling complex arithmetic.

In mathematics, a complex number consists of a pair of numbers; a real part, called x; an imaginary part y; and is written as $x+yi$, where $i^2 = -1$.

L.2 COMPLEX Constants

In WATFIV-S, a COMPLEX constant is written as two single-precision or two extended-precision constants in parentheses with the two parts separated by a comma. The following are examples of valid COMPLEX constants:

COMPLEX Constant	Meaning
(2.5,-3.7)	$2.5-3.7i$
(0.5E1,2.4E-1)	$5+0.24i$
(-1.25,-9.8E+1)	$-1.25-98i$
(123456789.,1.D0)	$123456789+i$

Notice that either single- or extended-precision constants are legitimate. However, the precision of the two components must agree for the constant to be valid.

L.3 COMPLEX Variables

A variable is of type COMPLEX if it has been declared in a COMPLEX declaration statement. Since a COMPLEX value consists of two REAL constants, it requires 8 bytes of memory for single precision and 16 bytes for extended precision. Thus, the following two declarations are equivalent:

```
COMPLEX Z, PTS(25), TBELL(5,5)
COMPLEX*8 Z, PTS(25), TBELL(5,5)
```

In order to extend the precision, the same variables are declared DOUBLE PRECISION COMPLEX by the following statement:

```
COMPLEX*16 Z, PTS(25), TBELL(5,5)
```

Notice that one and two dimensional sets can also be declared as COMPLEX variables.

L.4   Arithmetic Expressions and Assignment Statements

Any arithmetic expression involving one or more COMPLEX constants or variables is called a *complex expression.* The rules governing COMPLEX arithmetic are summarized below for two constants, (a,b) and (c,d):

$$(a,b)+(c,d) = (a+c,b+d)$$

$$(a,b)-(c,d) = (a-c,b-d)$$

$$(a,b)\times(c,d) = (ac-bd,ad+bc)$$

$$\frac{(a,b)}{(c,d)} = \left[\frac{ac+bd}{c^2+d^2}, \frac{bc-ad}{c^2+d^2} \right]$$

$(a,b)^{(c,d)}$ not defined

Notice that exponentiation of a COMPLEX value by a COMPLEX or even REAL value is not defined. It is, however, possible to take a COMPLEX value to an INTEGER exponent, resulting in a COMPLEX value.

It is also possible to perform operations on COMPLEX values using other data types. The table below summarizes the type of result when any of the operations +, -, *, or / are applied. The first letter of each data type (plus length attribute if necessary) has been used in the table.

	INTEGER	REAL*4	REAL*8	COMPLEX*8	COMPLEX*16
COMPLEX*8	COMPLEX*8	COMPLEX*8	COMPLEX*16	COMPLEX*8	COMPLEX*16
COMPLEX*16	COMPLEX*16	COMPLEX*16	COMPLEX*16	COMPLEX*16	COMPLEX*16

Addition and subtraction by an INTEGER, REAL, or extended-precision quantity only affects the real part of the COMPLEX value, whereas multiplication and division affect both the real and imaginary components.

When COMPLEX values are assigned across an equals sign, the value is converted (if necessary) to the data type of the variable on the left. If variables of type INTEGER, REAL*4, or REAL*8 are being assigned a COMPLEX value, they take on the real component of the COMPLEX value (converted in type if necessary). Conversely, if such values are assigned to a COMPLEX variable, the value is assigned to the real component of the COMPLEX variable, and the imaginary component is set to zero.

L.5   Input and Output of COMPLEX Values

Whenever values for a COMPLEX variable are read, 2 REAL constants must be provided for the real and imaginary components respectively. When a free format read is used, the constant must include the surrounding parentheses and a comma to separate the components. With a formatted read, the brackets and comma are omitted, and appropriate F-, E-, or D-codes are supplied for each component. Thus, two FORMAT masks must be supplied for each COMPLEX value.

COMPLEX values can also be printed with or without a FORMAT specification. On free-format output, the brackets and comma are included. If a FORMAT is specified, then an F-, E-, or D-code must be supplied for each component. If the brackets and comma are desired, then explicit formatting is required.

L.6   Built-in Functions

A variety of built-in functions are supplied for both single- and extended-precision COMPLEX arithmetic. These are listed in Appendix P. Notice that single-precision functions normally begin with the letter C and that extended-precision COMPLEX functions begin with the letters CD. These functions must be declared with the corresponding length in the program segment using them. In fact, failure to do so will cause an error message to be issued.

Of particular note in the list of functions are CMPLX and DCMPLX. In order to combine the value of two REAL variables, X and Y, into the real and imaginary parts of a COMPLEX variable, Z, it is necessary to write

```
Z = CMPLX(X,Y)
```

Expressions such as (X,Y), (0.0,Y), or (X,0.0) are invalid.

Two additional functions listed in Appendix P are useful when processing COMPLEX values. In order to isolate either part of a COMPLEX variable or to compare two COMPLEX numbers for equality, the functions REAL and AIMAG must be used. Both functions produce real-valued results and should be declared appropriately. These functions are commonly used to compare two COMPLEX variables, Z1 and Z2, for equality as follows:

```
REAL(Z1).EQ.REAL(Z2) .AND. AIMAG(Z1).EQ.AIMAG(Z2)
```

It is not permissible to use COMPLEX values with any of the relational operators.

L.7   Function Subprograms and Statement Functions

It is sometimes desirable to define COMPLEX-valued functions. Such functions may be defined in a single statement or may be introduced by one of the following declaration statements:

```
COMPLEX name (parameter list)
COMPLEX name*8 (parameter list)
COMPLEX name*16 (parameter list)
```

The first two alternatives declare a single-precision function, while the third specifies an extended-precision function. Whether a COMPLEX-valued function is defined as a subprogram or in a single statement, the name of the function must be declared in the program segment that uses it.

L.8   An Example Using COMPLEX Variables

Consider the following example involving the tabulation of a complex-valued function.

Example L.1
   Evaluate the complex function:

$$
f(z) = \begin{cases} e^z \times z^3 & \text{if } x > 0,\, y > 0 \\ \dfrac{3z}{(2+3.5i)z-4.2} & \text{otherwise} \end{cases}
$$

for a given value of x and for $y = -5, -4, \cdots, +5$.

Since the subject of function tabulation was discussed in detail in Chapter 6, no development of a solution is necessary. The sample program is presented in Figure L.1, while the resulting output is given in Figure L.2. Take particular note of the use of the built-in functions and the declarations of variable types.

```
C Figure L.1 -- Program to tabulate a complex-valued function.

C****************************************************************

C Z       - a complex number
C X       - the real component of Z
C Y       - the imaginary component of Z
C F       - the complex-valued function
C CMPLX   - built-in function to combine components

C****************************************************************

      COMPLEX Z, F, CMPLX
      REAL X, Y

C Read a value for X and tabulate F for this X and Y from -5 to +5.

      READ, X
      Y = -5.0
      WHILE(Y .LE. 5.0) DO
         Z = CMPLX(X,Y)
         PRINT, Z, F(Z)
         Y = Y + 1.0
      END WHILE

      STOP
      END

C****************************************************************

C Function F -- Complex function defined by:
C                    z    3
C                   e  *  z    if x>0 and y>0
C
C                        3z
C                   ----------------  otherwise.
C                   (2 +3.5i)z - 4.2

C****************************************************************

C Z - value for which to evaluate the function
C CEXP, REAL, AIMAG - built-in functions

C****************************************************************

      COMPLEX FUNCTION F*8(Z)
      COMPLEX Z, CEXP
      REAL REAL, AIMAG

      IF(REAL(Z).GT.0.0 .AND. AIMAG(Z).GT.0.0) THEN DO
         F = CEXP(Z)*Z**3
        ELSE DO
         F = 3.0*Z / ((2.0,3.5)*Z - 4.2)
      END IF

      RETURN
      END
$ENTRY
2.0
```

Figure L.2   Tabulation of a complex-valued function, output from the program in Figures L.1.

```
(   0.2000000E 01,   -0.5000000E 01) (   0.4826632E 00,   -0.7833543E 00)
(   0.2000000E 01,   -0.4000000E 01) (   0.4951943E 00,   -0.8336816E 00)
(   0.2000000E 01,   -0.3000000E 01) (   0.4930433E 00,   -0.9216546E 00)
(   0.2000000E 01,   -0.2000000E 01) (   0.4127445E 00,   -0.1064445E 01)
(   0.2000000E 01,   -0.1000000E 01) (   0.1337420E 00,   -0.1111730E 01)
(   0.2000000E 01,    0.0000000E 00) ( -0.2446980E-01,   -0.8564438E 00)
(   0.2000000E 01,    0.1000000E 01) ( -0.6040977E 02,    0.5635091E 02)
(   0.2000000E 01,    0.2000000E 01) ( -0.5830267E 02,   -0.1567005E 03)
(   0.2000000E 01,    0.3000000E 01) (   0.3271101E 03,   -0.1138021E 03)
(   0.2000000E 01,    0.4000000E 01) (   0.3355503E 03,    0.5693777E 03)
(   0.2000000E 01,    0.5000000E 01) ( -0.7581914E 03,    0.8699075E 03)
```

M
The Plotting
Routines

This appendix describes the plotting routines used in the main body of the text. A WATFIV-S version of the routines is listed on succeeding pages. A machine-readable version of the programs is available through the publisher. (Versions of these programs for standard FORTRAN IV also exist.)

These routines generate a line-printer plot of maximum size 101 by 51 characters. The routines perform an automatic scaling of the data points such that they always fill the entire plot area. As a result, the user need not worry about data points accidentally going off the graph. There are four subroutines in total. A brief description of their use follows, and numerous examples of their use are given in Chapter 6.

M.1 SETPLT

This subroutine initializes (or prepares) the other plotting subroutines. It must be the first of the subroutines called and should be executed only once for each complete graph. The statement to use this subroutine is

```
CALL SETPLT
```

There are no arguments associated with this subroutine.

M.2 SETSIZ

This subroutine is used to change the default size of the plotting surface. The statement to use this subroutine is

```
CALL SETSIZ(NROW,NCOL)
```

The variables NROW and NCOL represent the desired plotting surface size. NROW gives the number of character rows (the y direction) and valid sizes for it are 11, 21, 31, 41, 51. NCOL gives the number of character columns (the x direction) and valid sizes are 11, 21, 31, . . . ,91, 101. If invalid values for NROW or NCOL are given, the subroutine automatically forces the size to be the next higher valid value or the maximum value.

M.3 STOPNT

This subroutine stores the points to be plotted until it comes time to actually generate the plot. It must be executed at least once for each point that is to appear on the plot. For example, if the statement

    CALL STOPNT(X,Y,'A')

is executed, then the letter A (it must be a single character) will be plotted at the point X,Y on the graph. X and Y are the real cartesian coordinates of the point and must be assigned values in the program. This subroutine will store only the first 1000 points for plotting. If more than 1000 calls are made to STOPNT, the subroutine will issue a warning message and then ignore all points in excess of that number.

M.4 PLOTC

This subroutine causes the stored points to be printed. It should be executed after all points have been given to the STOPNT routine. The statement to use this subroutine is

    CALL PLOTC(I)

The variable I controls whether or not a grid is printed with the graph. If I has the value 0, no grid is printed. If I has any other value, a grid is superimposed on top of the graph.

Note that more than one curve may be plotted on the same graph by simply calling STOPNT with a different character as the third argument. If two different curves are being plotted on the same graph with different symbols, and the symbols coincide, an * will be printed in that position.

```
C Figure M.1 -- Subroutine SETPLT
C                     This subroutine initializes the plotting grid
C                     (for PLOTC) and a counter for the number of
C                     points to be plotted (for STOPNT).  A maximum
C                     of 1000 points will be stored by the programs
C                     as they are defined.
C*****************************************************************
C GRAPH  - stores the image of the graph to be plotted
C GRAPH1 - an alternate to access GRAPH to speed up processing
C NROW   - number of row positions in GRAPH
C NCOL   - number of column positions in GRAPH
C XARRAY - storage for X position of point to be plotted
C YARRAY - storage for Y position of point to be plotted
C ZARRAY - storage for character to be plotted at corresponding
C          (XARRAY,YARRAY) position
C N      - number of points submitted for plotting
C INIT   - switch to insure proper initialization is done
C 12121  - a number used to detect when the plotting system
C          has not been initialized. (No special significance
C          to that value.)
C*****************************************************************
        SUBROUTINE SETPLT

        CHARACTER*1 GRAPH(101,51)
        COMMON/ZGRIDZ/ NROW,NCOL,GRAPH

        INTEGER N,INIT
        REAL XARRAY(1000),YARRAY(1000)
        CHARACTER*1 ZARRAY(1000)
        COMMON/POINTZ/N,INIT,XARRAY,YARRAY,ZARRAY

        CHARACTER*1 SPACE/' '/
        CHARACTER*101 GRAPH1(51)
        EQUIVALENCE (GRAPH,GRAPH1)

        INIT = 12121
        NROW = 51
        NCOL = 101
        N = 0
        I = 1
        WHILE(I .LE. 51) DO
           GRAPH1(I) = SPACE
           I = I  + 1
        END WHILE
        RETURN
        END
```

```
C Figure M.2 -- Subroutine SETSIZ
C                 This subroutine allows the grid size to be set
C                 according to user requirements.  It restricts
C                 the user specified grid sizes to the following
C                     NROWS = 11, 21, 31, 41, 51
C                     NCOLS = 11, 21, 31, ... , 91, 101
C                 If invalid values are given, the next highest
C                 valid size or the maximum size is used.

C****************************************************************

C GRAPH  - stores the image of the graph to be plotted
C NROW   - number of row positions in GRAPH
C NCOL   - number of column positions in GRAPH
C NCHARX - requested number of character positions along x-axis
C NCHARY - requested number of character positions along y-axis

C****************************************************************

      SUBROUTINE SETSIZ(NCHARY,NCHARX)

      CHARACTER*1 GRAPH(101,51)
      COMMON/ZGRIDZ/ NROW,NCOL,GRAPH
 9000 FORMAT(' **** PLOTTING ERROR **** NUMBER OF COLUMNS TOO SMALL OR T
     1OO LARGE - SET TO 101')
 9010 FORMAT(' **** PLOTTING ERROR **** NUMBER OF ROWS TOO SMALL OR TOO
     1LARGE - SET TO 51')

      NCOL = (NCHARX+8)/10*10+1
      NROW = (NCHARY+8)/10*10+1
      IF(NCOL.LE.1 .OR. NCOL.GT.101) THEN DO
          NCOL = 101
          WRITE(6,9000)
      END IF
      IF(NROW.LE.1 .OR. NROW.GT.51) THEN DO
          NROW = 51
          WRITE(6,9010)
      END IF
      RETURN
      END
```

```
C Figure M.3 -- Subroutine STOPNT
C                   This subroutine stores up to 1000 X,Y points for
C                   plotting later by PLOTC.  When the 1001th point
C                   is received by STOPNT, it issues a warning
C                   message. All points in excess of 1000 are ignored.
C***************************************************************
C X       - X value of point to be plotted
C Y       - Y value of point to be plotted
C Z       - character to be plotted at (X,Y)
C XARRAY - storage for X position of point to be plotted
C YARRAY - storage for Y position of point to be plotted
C ZARRAY - storage for character to be plotted at corresponding
C            (XARRAY,YARRAY) position
C N       - number of points submitted for plotting
C INIT    - switch to insure proper initialization is done
C***************************************************************
      SUBROUTINE STOPNT(X,Y,Z)

      REAL X,Y
      CHARACTER*1 Z

      INTEGER N,INIT
      REAL XARRAY(1000),YARRAY(1000)
      CHARACTER*1 ZARRAY(1000)
      COMMON/POINTZ/N,INIT,XARRAY,YARRAY,ZARRAY
 9000 FORMAT(' **** PLOTTING ERROR **** SUBROUTINE SETPLT HAS NOT BEEN C
     1ALLED BEFORE STOPNT')
 9010 FORMAT('1 **** PLOTTING WARNING **** TOO MANY CALLS OF STOPNT - FI
     1RST 1000 TAKEN')
C Turn off WATFIV 'undefined variable' checking such that a
C recoverable error message may be issued from this
C subroutine instead.
C$NOCHECK
      IF(INIT .NE. 12121) THEN DO
         WRITE(6,9000)
         RETURN
      END IF
C$CHECK
      N = N + 1
      IF(N.LT.1001) THEN DO
            XARRAY(N) = X
            YARRAY(N) = Y
            ZARRAY(N) = Z
        ELSE DO
            IF(N.EQ.1001) THEN DO
                 WRITE(6,9010)
            END IF
      END IF
      RETURN
      END
```

```
C Figure M.4 -- Subroutine PLOTC
C                 This subroutine performs the actual plotting of
C                 the points.  If two different user characters
C                 intersect, then the routine prints an asterisk
C                 in that position.
C******************************************************************
C CODE    - 1 = plot a grid, ~1 = no grid
C GRAPH   - stores the image of the graph to be plotted
C GRAPH1  - an alternate to access GRAPH to speed up processing
C NROW    - number of row positions in GRAPH
C NCOL    - number of column positions in GRAPH
C XARRAY  - storage for X position of point to be plotted
C YARRAY  - storage for Y position of point to be plotted
C ZARRAY  - storage for character to be plotted at corresponding
C           (XARRAY,YARRAY) position
C N       - number of points submitted for plotting
C INIT    - switch to ensure proper initialization is done
C DUMMY1  - to set up array L1 for easy initialization of LINE1
C DUMMY2  - to set up array L2 for easy initialization of LINE2
C L1      - array to help blank out parts of LINE1 easily
C L2      - array to help blank out parts of LINE2 easily
C LINE1, LINE2 - used for storing characters for the grid
C LIMIT   - contains the number of points actually plotted
C XLOW, XHIGH - min and max of all x data point coordinates
C YLOW, YHIGH - min and max of all y data point coordinates
C IXFACT, IYFACT - scaling factors for the data points
C ORD     - y coordinates for printing
C ABSCIS  - x coordinates for printing
C******************************************************************
      SUBROUTINE PLOTC(CODE)

      INTEGER CODE

      CHARACTER*1 GRAPH(101,51)
      COMMON/ZGRIDZ/ NROW,NCOL,GRAPH

      INTEGER N,INIT
      REAL XARRAY(1000),YARRAY(1000)
      CHARACTER*1 ZARRAY(1000)
      COMMON/POINTZ/N,INIT,XARRAY,YARRAY,ZARRAY

      CHARACTER*1 BAR/'-'/,VBAR/'¦'/,SPACE/' '/,PLUS/'+'/,
     1            STAR/'*'/

      INTEGER LIMIT
      REAL ABSCIS(11)

      CHARACTER*1 C
      CHARACTER*101 GRAPH1(51)
      EQUIVALENCE (GRAPH,GRAPH1)

      CHARACTER*1 DUMMY1(2),DUMMY2(2)
      CHARACTER*10 L1(10),L2(10)
      CHARACTER*101 LINE1,LINE2
      EQUIVALENCE (DUMMY1(1),LINE1),(DUMMY1(2),L1(1))
      EQUIVALENCE (DUMMY2(1),LINE2),(DUMMY2(2),L2(1))
```

```
 9000 FORMAT(' **** PLOTTING ERROR **** SUBROUTINE SETPLT HAS NOT BEEN C
     1ALLED BEFORE PLOTC')
 9010 FORMAT('0**** PLOTTING ERROR **** ATTEMPT TO PLOT 0 POINTS')
 9020 FORMAT('1')
 9030 FORMAT('  - NUMBER OF POINTS: SUBMITTED ',I5,', PLOTTED ',I5)
 9040 FORMAT(' **** PLOTTING WARNING **** ALL POINTS TO BE PLOTTED HAVE
     1THE SAME X VALUE')
 9050 FORMAT(' **** PLOTTING WARNING **** ALL POINTS TO BE PLOTTED HAVE
     1THE SAME Y VALUE')
 9060 FORMAT(' ')
 9070 FORMAT(6X,F9.4,A101)
 9080 FORMAT(15X,A101)
 9090 FORMAT(11X,11(F9.4,1X))
 9100 FORMAT('0 - SCALE FACTORS: ORDINATE 10**',I2,', ABSCISSA 10**',I2)
 9110 FORMAT(///)
C Turn off WATFIV 'undefined variable' checking such that a
C recoverable error message may be issued from this
C subroutine instead.

C$NOCHECK
      IF(INIT .NE. 12121) THEN DO
            WRITE(6,9000)
            RETURN
      END IF
C$CHECK

C Check the number of points to be plotted. If n > 1000
C only 1000 points have been stored, and a top-of-form has
C already been done.

      IF(N .EQ. 0) THEN DO
            WRITE(6,9010)
            RETURN
      END IF
      LIMIT = N
      IF(LIMIT .GT. 1000) THEN DO
            LIMIT = 1000
        ELSE DO
            WRITE(6,9020)
      END IF
      WRITE(6,9030) N,LIMIT

C Determine the high and low values of the points to be plotted.

      XLOW = XARRAY(1)
      XHIGH = XLOW
      YLOW = YARRAY(1)
      YHIGH = YLOW

      I = 1
      WHILE(I .LE. LIMIT) DO
         XPOINT = XARRAY(I)
         YPOINT = YARRAY(I)
         IF(XPOINT.LT.XLOW) THEN DO
               XLOW = XPOINT
         END IF
         IF(XPOINT.GT.XHIGH) THEN DO
               XHIGH = XPOINT
         END IF
         IF(YPOINT.LT.YLOW) THEN DO
               YLOW = YPOINT
         END IF
         IF(YPOINT.GT.YHIGH) THEN DO
               YHIGH = YPOINT
         END IF
         I = I + 1
      END WHILE
```

```
C If upper and lower limits are the same for either X or Y axis,
C alter the high and low values so high-low is not zero.
      IF(XHIGH .EQ. XLOW) THEN DO
            XHIGH = XHIGH + 1.0
            XLOW = XLOW - 1.0
            WRITE(6,9040)
         ELSE DO
            WRITE(6,9060)
      END IF
      IF(YHIGH .EQ. YLOW) THEN DO
            YHIGH = YHIGH + 1.0
            YLOW = YLOW - 1.0
            WRITE(6,9050)
         ELSE DO
            WRITE(6,9060)
      END IF
C Calculate the size of the abscissa and ordinate values such
C that they may be scaled if necessary to fit in available
C space on the plot.
      XSIZE = XHIGH-XLOW
      YSIZE = YHIGH-YLOW
      XUNIT = XSIZE/(NCOL-1)
      YUNIT = YSIZE/(NROW-1)

      TEN3 = 10.0**3
      TEN4 = 10.0**4
      IF(XHIGH .LT. TEN4) THEN DO
            MAXEXP = 0
         ELSE DO
            MAXEXP = ALOG10(XHIGH)
      END IF
      IF(XLOW .GT. -TEN3) THEN DO
            MINEXP = 0
         ELSE DO
            MINEXP = ALOG10(-XLOW)
      END IF
      IXFACT = MAX0(MAXEXP-3, MINEXP-2, 0)
      XFACT = 10.0**IXFACT
      IF(YHIGH .LT. TEN4) THEN DO
            MAXEXP = 0
         ELSE DO
            MAXEXP = ALOG10(YHIGH)
      END IF
      IF(YLOW .GT. -TEN3) THEN DO
            MINEXP = 0
         ELSE DO
            MINEXP = ALOG10(-YLOW)
      END IF
      IYFACT = MAX0(MAXEXP-3, MINEXP-2, 0)
      YFACT = 10.0**IYFACT
```

```
C If a grid is required, build up the grid pattern. When the grid
C size requested is less than the maximum size, blank out the
C unwanted portion of the grid pattern. Then insert it in the
C graph.
      IF(CODE .EQ. 1) THEN DO
            LINE1 = '+---------+---------+---------+---------+---------+
     1---------+---------+---------+---------+---------+'
            LINE2 = '¦         ¦         ¦         ¦         ¦
     1         ¦         ¦         ¦         ¦         ¦'
            IF(NCOL .NE. 101) THEN DO
                  IPOS = NCOL/10 + 1
                  I = IPOS
                  WHILE(I .LE. 10) DO
                      L1(I) = SPACE
                      L2(I) = SPACE
                      I = I + 1
                  END WHILE
            END IF

            I = 1
            WHILE(I .LE. NROW) DO
                IREM = MOD(I,5)
                IF(IREM .EQ. 1) THEN DO
                      GRAPH1(I) = LINE1
                    ELSE DO
                      GRAPH1(I) = LINE2
                END IF
                I = I + 1
            END WHILE
      END IF
C Now generate the plot in the buffer. If the character position
C contains a character other than a space, "-", "¦", "+", or the
C current character, two curves have intersected. Place a "*".
      NROW1 = NROW+1
      I = 1
      WHILE(I .LE. LIMIT) DO
          IX = IFIX((XARRAY(I)-XLOW)/XUNIT+1.5)
          IY = IFIX((YARRAY(I)-YLOW)/YUNIT+1.5)
          IY = NROW1-IY
          C = GRAPH(IX,IY)
          IF(C.NE.SPACE .AND. C.NE.BAR .AND. C.NE.VBAR .AND.
     *        C.NE.PLUS  .AND. C.NE.ZARRAY(I)) THEN DO
                GRAPH(IX,IY) = STAR
            ELSE DO
                GRAPH(IX,IY) = ZARRAY(I)
          END IF
          I = I + 1
      END WHILE
C Output the plot to the printer.
      WRITE(6,9060)
      I = 1
      WHILE(I .LE. NROW) DO
          IF(MOD(I,5).NE.1) THEN DO
              WRITE(6,9080) GRAPH1(I)
            ELSE DO
              ORD = (YLOW+(NROW-I)*YUNIT)/YFACT
              WRITE(6,9070) ORD,GRAPH1(I)
          END IF
          I = I + 1
      END WHILE
```

```
C Generate the abscissa coordinates.
      J = 0
      I = 1
      WHILE(I .LE. NCOL) DO
          J = J+1
          ABSCIS(J) = (XLOW+(I-1)*XUNIT)/XFACT
          I = I + 10
      END WHILE
      WRITE(6,9090) (ABSCIS(I),I = 1,J)
      WRITE(6,9100) IYFACT,IXFACT
C Advance to the next page to get rid of compiler statistics.
C Note: a top-of-form will still be on this page.
      WRITE(6,9110)
      RETURN
      END
```

N
Data Files

This appendix contains six data files for use with questions in the main body of this book. The six data files are as follows:

1) Ages and marks for a group of first-year university students;
2) Year of graduation for a group of physicians;
3) Winning speeds at the Indianapolis 500 race;
4) Tar and nicotine deliveries of some cigarette brands;
5) National Hockey League player performance and estimated salaries for 1977/1978;
6) Mileage figures for North American and foreign cars.

The information in these files is real data since it is more interesting to work with this data than contrived data. It is not intended that the data be used for purposes other than this. The authors have attempted to reproduce the original source data as carefully as possible and apologize if any errors have crept into these files. These data files are set up for use with free-format READ statements. Machine readable copies of the data files may be obtained through the publisher.

N.1 Student Data File

This file contains the identification numbers, birthdates and marks for a group of first-year university students. The C#n notation refers to a course number.

Student Identification Number	Birthdate	Marks C#1	C#2	C#3	C#4	C#5	C#6
77046106	22 08 52	88	65	83	69	60	70
77909691	21 02 55	98	76	80	83	71	85
77908418	02 09 55	62	79	62	72	69	68
77908227	18 09 54	95	95	93	90	92	94
77997936	15 11 54	95	85	82	73	73	81
77980681	19 11 54	50	52	65	70	65	71
77980778	03 11 53	98	91	77	85	75	82
77985368	11 12 54	100	100	99	100	95	90

77981705	03	02	54	85	95	95	83	76	88
77940532	13	02	55	89	81	73	72	78	83
77949973	22	10	54	84	72	72	68	68	70
77949275	29	07	54	78	95	67	88	83	65
77945924	31	05	54	78	78	80	71	79	70
77938416	22	05	55	51	55	47	65	80	70
77935063	01	05	54	78	89	80	86	80	80
77932244	03	05	54	60	82	95	78	75	68
77931240	28	06	54	72	78	70	72	72	69
77963635	05	04	53	81	93	84	91	93	86
77965832	23	07	54	75	95	70	84	71	69
77961977	14	04	55	88	69	75	92	80	83
77957512	15	06	55	80	96	79	95	88	73
77974880	25	12	54	92	90	83	80	79	81
77972844	31	10	54	83	72	80	89	90	64
77910855	13	10	54	100	100	71	78	77	88
77919961	26	05	54	73	95	65	73	65	61
77904633	24	03	55	58	45	61	60	55	70
77902922	27	02	55	79	81	67	59	78	75
77999877	04	08	55	62	69	60	71	59	61
77988276	29	08	56	83	68	79	71	74	80
77949305	20	06	56	73	90	94	82	79	83
77943620	27	06	55	75	60	88	81	58	76
77946946	03	11	55	68	53	67	79	76	74
77942214	06	09	55	96	85	75	83	80	76
77941467	01	04	56	83	82	87	75	83	79
77137228	11	01	54	80	95	73	90	81	78
77998659	19	05	57	80	77	83	78	87	81
77994160	21	01	56	77	83	60	77	75	68
77993361	26	05	56	77	81	82	64	76	75
77996573	07	09	56	92	89	97	82	75	79
77992740	25	01	57	54	60	60	75	39	59
77980707	12	05	57	93	90	82	76	80	75
77989277	31	10	56	72	83	72	72	65	77
77983096	06	02	57	90	95	100	79	78	83
77986726	28	07	56	67	67	65	68	65	87
77981351	21	10	56	45	50	46	21	57	68
77981731	03	10	56	67	75	66	78	78	75
77981750	18	07	56	87	65	82	87	78	75
77940392	11	09	56	67	77	95	75	75	75
77948531	16	10	56	96	83	70	62	76	75
77944146	01	09	56	87	80	78	99	75	66
77947837	16	11	56	43	70	50	70	75	72
77942038	22	05	56	63	76	67	55	75	68
77941176	27	11	57	89	62	75	75	67	88
77936352	09	01	57	85	96	80	75	78	83
77937050	07	12	57	95	95	91	85	83	96
77937646	05	09	57	100	78	78	88	87	83
77823862	24	07	49	70	58	75	74	75	72
77821091	10	01	55	52	68	43	84	75	69
77997106	16	01	57	70	61	74	83	75	72
77986424	27	03	57	90	75	75	85	76	78
77944847	15	03	59	90	89	82	78	88	89
77968629	14	01	57	83	79	71	91	58	82
77963181	08	06	57	58	75	72	69	76	72
77965843	30	04	57	86	72	84	80	75	59
77961309	29	06	57	71	68	78	72	83	74
77953950	26	12	57	82	77	78	78	65	62
77956564	01	09	57	78	75	73	76	58	68
77957447	01	04	57	72	54	82	88	82	70
77974973	21	10	57	67	83	65	76	74	75
77919888	20	08	57	87	77	74	76	75	78

N.2   Physician Data File

This file contains information concerning the graduation date of a group of local physicians. The data is given by graduation year and the number of graduates in that year.

1901	1	1934	1	1944	4	1954	6	1964	1
1910	1	1935	2	1945	3	1955	6	1965	3
1921	1	1936	2	1946	3	1956	1	1967	7
1922	2	1937	2	1947	2	1957	5	1968	7
1923	1	1938	1	1948	3	1958	5	1969	3
1924	1	1939	1	1949	3	1959	3	1970	6
1926	1	1940	3	1950	3	1960	7	1971	4
1929	2	1941	3	1951	3	1961	3	1972	2
1930	1	1942	3	1952	7	1962	4	1973	3
1932	3	1943	2	1953	5	1963	4		

N.3   Indianapolis 500 Data

This file contains the winning speeds (in miles per hour) for the Indianapolis 500 race for the years 1919 through 1977. The race was not run during the war years 1942-1945.

1919	88.05	1938	117.20	1960	138.77
1920	88.62	1939	115.04	1961	139.13
1921	89.62	1940	114.28	1962	140.29
1922	94.48	1941	115.11	1963	143.14
1923	90.95	1946	114.82	1964	147.35
1924	98.23	1947	116.34	1965	151.39
1925	101.13	1948	119.81	1966	144.32
1926	95.90	1949	121.33	1967	151.21
1927	97.55	1950	124.00	1968	152.88
1928	99.48	1951	126.24	1969	156.87
1929	97.56	1952	128.92	1970	155.75
1930	100.45	1953	128.74	1971	157.74
1931	96.62	1954	130.84	1972	162.96
1932	104.11	1955	128.21	1973	159.04
1933	104.16	1956	128.49	1974	158.59
1934	104.86	1957	135.90	1975	149.21
1935	106.24	1958	133.79	1976	148.73
1936	109.07	1959	138.86	1977	161.33
1937	113.58				

N.4   Cigarette Tar and Nicotine Data

This file contains information about several brands of cigarettes and the amount of tar and nicotine that they deliver. The measurements were taken from the cigarette packages as of April 1, 1978. The type classifications are as follows:

```
R  - regular size    KS - king size      PR - premium size
P  - plain           F  - filter         C  - cork tip
M  - menthol
```

The length measurements are in millimeters (mm), and the following diagram illustrates their meaning.

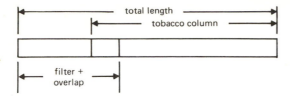

The tar and nicotine measurements are in milligrams (mg). The cigarettes were smoked to a butt length of either 30mm or (filter + overlap)+3mm, whichever is larger. these data were collected by Labstat Incorporated, Kitchener Ontario and are reprinted here with their permission.

Brand Name	Type			Dry Tar	Nic	Filter+ Overlap	Tobacco Column	Total Length
'Alpine	'KS'	'F'	'M'	17.	1.3	24	64	84
'Belmont Mild	'KS'	'F'	' '	11.	.9	30	64	84
'Belmont Mild	'R '	'F'	' '	7.	.6	23	52	72
'Belmont Mild	'KS'	'F'	'M'	13.	1.1	30	63	83
'Belvedere	'KS'	'F'	' '	27.	1.3	21	67	84
'Belvedere	'R '	'F'	' '	15.	1.1	17	59	72
'Belvedere	'KS'	'F'	'M'	17.	1.3	21	67	84
'Belvedere E.M.	'KS'	'F'	' '	11.	1.0	30	59	84
'Belvedere E.M.	'R '	'F'	' '	10.	.8	17	59	72
'Benson & Hedges	'PR'	'F'	' '	15.	1.1	30	74	99
'Benson & Hedges	'PR'	'F'	'M'	15.	1.1	30	74	99
'Black Cat	'R '	'P'	' '	18.	1.0	0	72	72
'Black Cat Cork	'C '	'P'	' '	18.	1.1	12	72	72
'Black Cat	'R '	'F'	' '	14.	.9	19	57	72
'Number 7	'KS'	'F'	' '	17.	1.1	21	67	84
'British Consols	'R '	'F'	' '	18.	1.3	18	59	72
'British Consols	'R '	'P'	' '	19.	1.2	0	71	71
'Buckingham	'KS'	'P'	' '	17.	1.0	0	84	84
'Buckingham	'R '	'P'	' '	17.	.9	0	72	72
'Cameo	'KS'	'F'	'M'	18.	1.2	20	66	83
'Cameo E.M.	'KS'	'F'	'M'	12.	.8	24	64	84
'Cavalier	'KS'	'F'	' '	18.	1.3	21	63	84
'Contessa Slims	'KS'	'F'	' '	13.	.8	24	63	83
'Craven A	'KS'	'F'	' '	15.	1.0	21	67	83
'Craven A	'R '	'F'	' '	8.	.5	19	57	73
'Craven A E.M.	'KS'	'F'	' '	5.	.4	30	64	84
'Craven A E.M.	'R '	'F'	' '	5.	.4	22	51	71
'Craven M	'KS'	'F'	'M'	11.	.8	21	66	83
'Du Maurier	'KS'	'F'	' '	18.	1.2	21	67	84
'Du Maurier	'KS'	'F'	'M'	13.	.8	21	67	84
'Du Maurier	'R '	'F'	' '	14.	.9	18	58	72
'Du Maurier	'KS'	'F'	' '	13.	.9	24	64	84
'Du Maurier S.M.	'PR'	'F'	' '	14.	1.0	24	79	99
'Dudes	'KS'	'F'	' '	19.	1.3	21	67	84
'Du Mont Select	'KS'	'F'	' '	9.	.6	25	64	84
'Dunhill	'KS'	'F'	' '	18.	1.2	21	62	83
'Embassy	'KS'	'F'	' '	18.	1.2	21	66	83
'Embassy	'R '	'F'	' '	16.	1.1	18	57	71
'Export	'R '	'F'	' '	19.	1.2	0	77	77
'Export A	'KS'	'F'	' '	19.	1.3	21	67	84
'Export A	'R '	'F'	' '	18.	1.2	18	57	72
'Export A L.	'KS'	'F'	' '	14.	1.0	25	63	84
'Export A L.	'R '	'F'	' '	14.	1.0	19	56	71
'Gauloises	'R '	'F'	' '	13.	.9	15	59	70
'Gauloises	'R '	'P'	' '	18.	1.2	0	70	70
'Gitaues	'R '	'F'	' '	12.	.8	15	59	70
'Gitanes	'R '	'P'	' '	19.5	1.2	0	70	70
'Goldcrest	'PR'	'F'	' '	15.	1.1	25	80	100
'John Player Spec.	'KS'	'F'	' '	16.	1.2	21	67	84
'Kool	'KS'	'F'	'M'	14.	.9	24	64	84
'MacDonald	'KS'	'F'	'M'	16.	1.1	21	67	84

'MacDonald	' 'R '	'F'	'M'	15.	1.0	18	57	72
'Mark Ten	' 'KS'	'F'	' '	17.	1.2	21	66	83
'Mark Ten	' 'KS'	'F'	'M'	17.	1.3	21	67	83
'Mark Ten	' 'R '	'F'	' '	16.	1.2	17	58	71
'Mark Ten	' 'KS'	'P'	' '	18.	1.3	0	84	84
'Mark Ten	' 'R '	'P'	' '	15.	1.0	0	72	72
'Matinee E. M.	' 'KS'	'F'	' '	4.	.4	30	64	84
'Matinee	' 'KS'	'F'	' '	12.	.8	21	64	83
'Matinee	' 'R '	'F'	' '	8.	.5	19	57	72
'Matinee S.F.	' 'KS'	'F'	' '	10.	.7	30	59	84
'Matinee S.F.	' 'PR'	'F'	' '	11.	.8	31	69	99
'Maverick	' 'KS'	'F'	' '	17.	1.3	21	66	83
'Medallion	' 'KS'	'F'	' '	1.	.1	30	64	84
'Millbank	' 'KS'	'F'	' '	19.	1.3	21	64	84
'Montclair	' 'KS'	'F'	' '	18.	1.3	21	66	83
'Pall Mall	' 'KS'	'P'	' '	17.	1.0	0	83	83
'Peter Jackson	' 'KS'	'F'	' '	18.	1.2	21	66	83
'Peter Jackson E. L.'	'R '	'F'	' '	7.	.7	24	51	71
'Peter Stuyvesant	' 'KS'	'F'	' '	18.	1.2	21	67	84
'Peter Stuyvesant	' 'PR'	'F'	' '	16.	1.1	21	79	99
'Peter Stuyvesant	' 'PR'	'F'	'M'	16.	1.1	21	80	100
'Perillys	' 'KS'	'F'	' '	16.	1.1	21	68	84
'Phillip Morris	' 'R '	'P'	' '	16.	.9	0	69	69
'Plus	' 'PR'	'F'	' '	19.	1.6	35	84	119
'Players	' 'KS'	'F'	' '	18.	1.2	21	67	84
'Players	' 'R '	'F'	' '	18.	1.2	18	58	72
'Players L.	' 'KS'	'F'	' '	11.	1.1	20	67	83
'Players L.	' 'R '	'F'	' '	14.	.9	18	58	72
'Players Navy	' 'R '	'F'	' '	19.	1.3	18	56	72
'Players Navy	' 'R '	'P'	' '	18.	1.1	0	72	72
'Players	' 'R '	'P'	' '	19.	1.2	0	72	72
'Rothmans	' 'KS'	'F'	' '	17.	1.1	21	68	84
'Rothmans	' 'KS'	'F'	' '	12.	.9	24	63	83
'Rothmans S.	' 'R '	'F'	' '	12.	.9	19	57	72
'Sportsman	' 'KS'	'F'	' '	18.	1.2	21	66	83
'Sportsman	' 'R '	'F'	' '	14.	.9	19	57	72
'Sportsman	' 'R '	'P'	' '	18.	1.0	0	72	72
'Sweet Caporal	' 'KS'	'F'	' '	18.	1.2	21	66	83
'Sweet Caporal	' 'R '	'F'	' '	14.	.9	18	58	72
'Sweet Caporal	' 'R '	'P'	' '	19.	1.1	0	72	72
'Tabac Leger	' 'KS'	'F'	' '	14.	.8	21	67	83
'Tabac Leger	' 'R '	'F'	' '	12.	.8	17	59	72
'Turret	' 'KS'	'F'	' '	18.	1.2	24	64	84
'Turret	' 'R '	'F'	' '	14.	1.0	18	58	72
'Vantage	' 'KS'	'F'	' '	11.	.8	29	58	83
'Vantage	' 'R '	'F'	' '	11.	.8	25	51	71
'Viceroy	' 'KS'	'F'	' '	15.	.9	24	64	84
'Viscount	' 'R '	'F'	' '	4.	.3	25	52	72
'Viscount	' 'KS'	'F'	'M'	5.	.4	30	64	84
'Viscount #1	' 'KS'	'F'	' '	1.	.1	30	63	83
'Viscount #1	' 'R '	'F'	' '	1.	.1	25	52	72
'Winston	' 'KS'	'F'	' '	16.	1.1	25	63	84

N.5   National Hockey League Statistics

This section contains two data files for the National Hockey League. The first file contains the final league standings for 1977/1978, and the second file contains the player performance and estimated salaries for most of the players.

a) Final League Standings   The final standings table contains the team name, their playing conference and division, the number of games they played, their win-loss-tie record, the total number of goals the team scored, the number of goals scored against the team and the number of points the team earned. The column and symbols in the table have the following meanings.

```
Con - conference: W - Wales, C - Campbell
Div - division:    A - Adams, N - Norris,
                   P - Patrick, S - Smythe
GP  - games played
W   - number of wins
L   - number of losses
T   - number of ties
GF  - number of goals scored for this team
GA  - number of goals scored against other teams
Pts - number of points
```

Team		Con	Div	GP	W	L	T	GF	GA	Pts
'Boston	'	'W'	'A'	80	51	18	11	333	218	113
'Buffalo	'	'W'	'A'	80	44	19	17	288	215	105
'Toronto	'	'W'	'A'	80	41	29	10	271	237	92
'Cleveland	'	'W'	'A'	80	22	45	13	230	325	57
'Montreal	'	'W'	'N'	80	59	10	11	359	183	129
'Detroit	'	'W'	'N'	80	32	34	14	252	266	78
'Los Angeles	'	'W'	'N'	80	31	34	15	243	245	77
'Pittsburgh	'	'W'	'N'	80	25	37	18	254	321	68
'Washington	'	'W'	'N'	80	17	49	14	195	321	48
'NY Islanders'	'C'	'P'	80	48	17	15	334	210	111
'Philadelphia'	'C'	'P'	80	45	20	15	296	200	105
'Atlanta	'	'C'	'P'	80	34	27	19	274	252	87
'NY Rangers	'	'C'	'P'	80	30	37	13	279	280	73
'Chicago	'	'C'	'S'	80	32	29	19	230	220	83
'Colorado	'	'C'	'S'	80	19	40	21	257	305	59
'Vancouver	'	'C'	'S'	80	20	43	17	239	320	57
'St. Louis	'	'C'	'S'	80	20	47	13	195	304	53
'Minnesota	'	'C'	'S'	80	18	53	9	218	325	45

b) Player Performance and Estimated Salaries   The player performance statistics given below list the players, their team, and their position along with the number of games played and goals and assists scored. The total number of points, number of penalty minutes, and estimated salary are also given. The majority of these salary figures are from a copyrighted article which appeared in the Globe and Mail newspaper. This information is reprinted with permission of the Globe and Mail Publishers, Toronto, Ontario, Canada. Salaries for players not in the article were estimated by the authors. The following legend describes the column titles and symbols in the table.

```
Pos - position played
GP  - games played
G   - goals scored
A   - assists scored
TP  - points scored
PIM - penalties in minutes
W   - wing position
C   - center position
D   - defense position
G   - goalie
```

Player		Team		Pos	GP	G	A	TP	PIM	Estimated Salary
'MacMillan, Bob	'	'Atlanta	'	'W'	80	38	33	71	49	85000
'Lysiak, Tom	'	'Atlanta	'	'C'	80	27	42	69	54	130000
'Chouinard, Guy	'	'Atlanta	'	'C'	73	28	30	58	8	65000
'Vail, Eric	'	'Atlanta	'	'W'	79	22	36	58	16	65000
'Phillipoff, Harold	'	'Atlanta	'	'W'	67	17	36	53	128	50000
'Clement, Bill	'	'Atlanta	'	'C'	70	20	30	50	34	85000
'Gould, John	'	'Atlanta	'	'W'	79	19	28	47	21	70000
'Plett, Willi	'	'Atlanta	'	'W'	78	22	21	43	171	70000
'Houston, Ken	'	'Atlanta	'	'W'	74	22	16	38	51	45000

Name		Team		Pos	GP	G	A	PTS	PIM	Salary
'Lalonde, Bobby	'	'Atlanta	'	'W'	73	14	23	37	28	40000
'Redmond, Dick	'	'Atlanta	'	'D'	70	11	22	33	32	125000
'Comeau, Rey	'	'Atlanta	'	'C'	79	10	22	32	20	50000
'Mulhern, Richard	'	'Atlanta	'	'D'	76	9	23	32	47	60000
'Kea, Ed	'	'Atlanta	'	'D'	60	3	23	26	40	45000
'Shand, Dave	'	'Atlanta	'	'D'	80	2	23	25	94	55000
'Zaharko, Miles	'	'Atlanta	'	'D'	71	1	19	20	26	45000
'Simpson, Bob	'	'Atlanta	'	'W'	53	10	8	18	49	50000
'Ribble, Pat	'	'Atlanta	'	'D'	80	5	12	17	68	55000
'Fox, Greg	'	'Atlanta	'	'W'	16	1	2	3	25	45000
'Bouchard, Daniel	'	'Atlanta	'	'G'	58	0	3	3	6	100000
'Ecclestone, Tim	'	'Atlanta	'	'W'	11	0	2	2	2	45000
'Belanger, Yves	'	'Atlanta	'	'G'	20	0	1	1	0	60000
'O Reilly, Terry	'	'Boston	'	'O'	77	29	61	90	211	70000
'Ratelle, Jean	'	'Boston	'	'C'	80	25	59	84	10	150000
'McNab, Peter	'	'Boston	'	'C'	79	41	39	80	4	100000
'Park, Brad	'	'Boston	'	'D'	80	22	57	79	79	250000
'Cashman, Wayne	'	'Boston	'	'W'	76	24	38	62	69	110000
'Middleton, Rick	'	'Boston	'	'W'	79	25	35	60	8	100000
'Sheppard, Gregg	'	'Boston	'	'C'	54	23	36	59	24	85000
'Marcotte, Don	'	'Boston	'	'W'	77	20	34	54	16	70000
'Schmautz, Bob	'	'Boston	'	'W'	54	27	27	54	87	75000
'Jonathan, Stan	'	'Boston	'	'W'	68	27	25	52	116	50000
'Miller, Bob	'	'Boston	'	'C'	76	20	20	40	41	40000
'Milbury, Mike	'	'Boston	'	'D'	80	8	30	38	151	50000
'Wensink, John	'	'Boston	'	'W'	80	16	20	36	181	40000
'Smith, Rick	'	'Boston	'	'D'	79	7	29	36	69	100000
'Bucyk, John	'	'Boston	'	'W'	53	5	13	18	4	115000
'Doak, Gary	'	'Boston	'	'D'	61	4	13	17	50	70000
'OBrien, Dennis	'	'Boston	'	'D'	68	2	10	12	104	40000
'Sims, Al	'	'Boston	'	'D'	43	2	8	10	6	60000
'Foster, Dwight	'	'Boston	'	'W'	14	2	1	3	6	50000
'Cheevers, Gerry	'	'Boston	'	'G'	21	0	1	1	14	160000
'Gilbert, Gilles	'	'Boston	'	'G'	25	0	1	1	8	135000
'Grahame, Ron	'	'Boston	'	'G'	40	0	1	1	0	80000
'Perreault, Gilbert	'	'Buffalo	'	'C'	79	41	48	89	20	200000
'Gare, Danny	'	'Buffalo	'	'W'	69	39	38	77	95	105000
'Robert, Rene	'	'Buffalo	'	'W'	67	25	48	73	25	100000
'Ramsay, Craig	'	'Buffalo	'	'W'	80	28	43	71	18	70000
'Martin, Richard	'	'Buffalo	'	'W'	65	28	35	63	16	170000
'Luce, Don	'	'Buffalo	'	'C'	78	26	35	61	24	65000
'McAdam, Gary	'	'Buffalo	'	'W'	79	19	22	41	44	60000
'Korab, Jerry	'	'Buffalo	'	'D'	77	7	34	41	119	80000
'Savard, Andre	'	'Buffalo	'	'C'	80	19	20	39	40	75000
'Seiling, Rick	'	'Buffalo	'	'W'	80	19	19	38	33	50000
'Guevremont, J.	'	'Buffalo	'	'D'	66	7	28	35	46	100000
'Lorentz, Jim	'	'Buffalo	'	'W'	70	9	15	24	12	60000
'Fogolin, Lee	'	'Buffalo	'	'D'	76	0	23	23	98	85000
'Schoenfeld, Jim	'	'Buffalo	'	'D'	60	2	20	22	89	115000
'Hajt, Bill	'	'Buffalo	'	'D'	76	4	18	22	30	80000
'Stanfield, Fred	'	'Buffalo	'	'C'	57	3	8	11	2	90000
'Martin, Terry	'	'Buffalo	'	'D'	21	3	2	5	9	50000
'Schock, Ron	'	'Buffalo	'	'C'	40	4	4	8	0	85000
'Smith, Derek	'	'Buffalo	'	'D'	36	3	3	6	0	50000
'Carriere, Larry	'	'Buffalo	'	'D'	180	3	3	6	29	50000
'Edwards, Don	'	'Buffalo	'	'G'	72	0	3	3	12	50000
'Stewart, Bill	'	'Buffalo	'	'D'	13	2	0	2	15	50000
'Desjardins, Gerry	'	'Buffalo	'	'G'	3	0	0	0	0	90000
'Sauve, Bob	'	'Buffalo	'	'G'	11	0	1	1	0	50000
'Boldirev, Ivan	'	'Chicago	'	'C'	80	35	45	80	34	100000
'Mikita, Stan	'	'Chicago	'	'C'	76	18	41	59	35	200000
'Bulley, Ted	'	'Chicago	'	'W'	79	23	28	51	141	60000
'Bordeleau, J.P.	'	'Chicago	'	'W'	76	15	25	40	32	75000
'Mulvey, Grant	'	'Chicago	'	'W'	78	14	24	38	135	80000
'Rota, Darcy	'	'Chicago	'	'W'	78	17	20	37	67	70000
'Marks, John	'	'Chicago	'	'W'	80	15	22	37	26	85000
'Wilson, Doug	'	'Chicago	'	'D'	77	14	20	34	72	55000
'Koroll, Cliff	'	'Chicago	'	'W'	73	16	15	31	19	95000
'Murray, Bob	'	'Chicago	'	'D'	70	14	17	31	41	60000

```
'Plante, Pierre       '  'Chicago     '  'W'  77  10  18   28   59    70000
'Russell, Phil        '  'Chicago     '  'D'  57   6  20   26  139   105000
'Tallon, Dale         '  'Chicago     '  'D'  75   4  20   24   66   150000
'Hicks, Doug          '  'Chicago     '  'D'  74   3  16   19   53    70000
'Kelly, Bob           '  'Chicago     '  'W'  75   7  11   18   95    80000
'Daigle, Alain        '  'Chicago     '  'W'  53   6   6   12   13    80000
'Harrison, Jim        '  'Chicago     '  'C'  26   2   8   10   31   125000
'Magnuson, Keith      '  'Chicago     '  'D'  67   2.  4    6  145   110000
'Logan, Dave          '  'Chicago     '  'D'  54   1   5    6   77    50000
'Bowman, Kirk         '  'Chicago     '  'W'  33   1   4    5   13    45000
'Esposito, Tony       '  'Chicago     '  'G'  64   0   4    4    0   200000
'O Connell, T.        '  'Chicago     '  'W'   6   1   1    2    2    55000
'Hoffmeyer, Bob       '  'Chicago     '  'W'   5   0   1    1   12    50000
'Veisor, Mike         '  'Chicago     '  'G'  12   0   0    0    0    70000
'Johnston, Ed         '  'Chicago     '  'G'  16   0   0    0    0   105000
'Maruk, Dennis        '  'Cleveland   '  'C'  74  33  33   66   50    95000
'Fidler, Mike         '  'Cleveland   '  'W'  78  23  28   51   38    60000
'Parise, J.P.         '  'Cleveland   '  'W'  79  21  29   50   39    80000
'Manery, Kris         '  'Cleveland   '  'C'  78  22  27   49   14    45000
'Arnason, Chuck       '  'Cleveland   '  'W'  69  25  21   46   18    60000
'MacAdam, Al          '  'Cleveland   '  'W'  80  16  32   48   42    85000
'Gardner, Dave        '  'Cleveland   '  'C'  75  19  25   44   10    55000
'Murdoch, Robert      '  'Cleveland   '  'W'  71  14  26   40   27    50000
'McKechnie, Walt      '  'Cleveland   '  'C'  69  16  23   39   12    85000
'Smith, Greg          '  'Cleveland   '  'D'  80   7  30   37   92    60000
'Hampton, Rick        '  'Cleveland   '  'D'  77  18  18   36   19    95000
'Potvin, Jean         '  'Cleveland   '  'D'  74   4  24   28   38    70000
'Neilson, Jim         '  'Cleveland   '  'D'  68   2  21   23   20   125000
'Shinske, Rick        '  'Cleveland   '  'C'  47   5  12   17    6    45000
'Stewart, Bob         '  'Cleveland   '  'W'  72   2  15   17   84    50000
'Jodzio, Rick         '  'Cleveland   '  'W'  70   2   8   10   71    40000
'Kuzyk, Ken           '  'Cleveland   '  'C'  28   5   4    9   36    45000
'Baby, John           '  'Cleveland   '  'D'  24   2   7    9   26    40000
'Crombeen, Mike       '  'Cleveland   '  'W'  48   3   4    7   18    40000
'Holt, Randy          '  'Cleveland   '  'D'  54   1   4    5  249    55000
'Edwards, Gary        '  'Cleveland   '  'G'  30   0   1    1    4    90000
'Allan, Jeff          '  'Cleveland   '  'W'   4   0   0    0    2    40000
'Meloche, Gilles      '  'Cleveland   '  'G'  54   0   0    4  125000
'Paiement, Wilf       '  'Colorado    '  'W'  60  31  56   87  114   160000
'Beck, Barry          '  'Colorado    '  'D'  75  22  38   60   89    60000
'Van Boxmeer, John    '  'Colorado    '  'D'  80  12  42   54   87    65000
'Gardner, Paul        '  'Colorado    '  'C'  46  30  22   52   29    55000
'Owchar, Dennis       '  'Colorado    '  'D'  82  10  31   41   48    65000
'Spruce, Andy         '  'Colorado    '  'W'  74  19  21   40   43    35000
'Croteau, Gary        '  'Colorado    '  'W'  62  17  22   39   24    55000
'Andruff, Ron         '  'Colorado    '  'C'  78  15  18   33   31    55000
'Hudson, Dave         '  'Colorado    '  'C'  60  10  22   32   12    45000
'Dupere, Dennis       '  'Colorado    '  'W'  54  15  15   30    4    50000
'Ahern, Fred          '  'Colorado    '  'W'  74   8  17   25   67    55000
'Pyatt, Nelson        '  'Colorado    '  'C'  71   9  12   21    8    55000
'Delorme, Ron         '  'Colorado    '  'W'  68  10  11   21   47    35000
'Contini, Joe         '  'Colorado    '  'W'  37  12   9   21   28    30000
'Suzor, Mark          '  'Colorado    '  'D'  60   4  15   19   56    65000
'Kitchen, Mike        '  'Colorado    '  'D'  61   2  17   19   45    45000
'Pierce, Randy        '  'Colorado    '  'W'  35   9  10   19   15    35000
'Klassen, Ralph       '  'Colorado    '  'C'  57   8  10   18   14    75000
'Christie, Mike       '  'Colorado    '  'D'  69   3  14   17   77    85000
'Lefley, Bryan        '  'Colorado    '  'D'  67   4  12   16   10    50000
'Neely, Bob           '  'Colorado    '  'W'  33   3   7   10    2    50000
'Skinner, Larry       '  'Colorado    '  'W'  14   3   5    8    0    40000
'Favell, Doug         '  'Colorado    '  'G'  47   0   2    2    2   155000
'McKenzie, Bill       '  'Colorado    '  'D'  12   0   0    0    2    40000
'Plasse, Michel       '  'Colorado    '  'G'  25   0   0    0   12    90000
'McCourt, Dale        '  'Detroit     '  'C'  76  33  39   72   10    65000
'St. Laurent, Andre   '  'Detroit     '  'C'  79  31  39   70  108    65000
'Larson, Reed         '  'Detroit     '  'D'  75  19  41   60   95    60000
'Hextall, Dennis      '  'Detroit     '  'C'  78  16  33   49  195   120000
'Libett, Nick         '  'Detroit     '  'W'  80  23  22   45   46   110000
'Thompson, Errol      '  'Detroit     '  'W'  73  22  23   45   12    55000
```

'Woods, Paul	'	'Detroit	'	'C'	80	19	23	42	52	50000
'Lochead, Bill	'	'Detroit	'	'W'	77	20	16	36	47	75000
'Polonich, Dennis	'	'Detroit	'	'W'	79	16	19	35	254	60000
'Nedomansky, V.	'	'Detroit	'	'C'	63	11	17	28	2	150000
'Joly, Greg	'	'Detroit	'	'D'	79	7	20	27	73	100000
'Miller, Perry	'	'Detroit	'	'D'	62	4	17	21	120	55000
'Harper, Terry	'	'Detroit	'	'D'	80	2	17	19	85	110000
'Bowness, Rick	'	'Detroit	'	'W'	61	8	11	19	76	50000
'Hull, Dennis	'	'Detroit	'	'W'	55	5	9	14	6	90000
'Cameron, Al	'	'Detroit	'	'D'	63	2	7	9	94	60000
'Wright, Larry	'	'Detroit	'	'W'	66	3	6	9	13	45000
'Hamel, Jean	'	'Detroit	'	'D'	32	2	6	8	34	55000
'Bergman, Thommie	'	'Detroit	'	'D'	14	1	6	7	16	45000
'Rutherford, Jim	'	'Detroit	'	'G'	43	0	2	2	2	135000
'Low, Ron	'	'Detroit	'	'G'	32	0	1	1	0	90000
'Dionne, Marcel	'	'Los Angeles	'	'C'	70	36	43	79	37	320000
'Goring, Butch	'	'Los Angeles	'	'C'	80	37	36	73	2	100000
'Murphy, Mike	'	'Los Angeles	'	'W'	72	20	36	56	48	120000
'Apps, Syl	'	'Los Angeles	'	'C'	79	19	33	52	18	150000
'Taylor, Dave	'	'Los Angeles	'	'W'	64	22	21	43	47	45000
'Sargent, Gary	'	'Los Angeles	'	'D'	72	7	34	41	52	60000
'Williams, Tommy	'	'Los Angeles	'	'W'	58	15	22	37	9	70000
'Manery, Randy	'	'Los Angeles	'	'D'	79	6	27	33	61	70000
'Grant, Danny	'	'Los Angeles	'	'W'	54	12	21	33	8	110000
'Goldup, Glenn	'	'Los Angeles	'	'W'	66	14	18	32	66	90000
'Stemkowski, Pete	'	'Los Angeles	'	'C'	80	13	18	31	33	65000
'Wilson, Bert	'	'Los Angeles	'	'W'	79	7	16	23	127	55000
'Monahan, Hartland	'	'Los Angeles	'	'W'	71	12	9	21	47	80000
'Murdoch, Bob	'	'Los Angeles	'	'D'	76	2	17	19	68	85000
'Kozak, Don	'	'Los Angeles	'	'W'	43	8	5	13	45	85000
'Venasky, Vic	'	'Los Angeles	'	'C'	71	3	10	13	6	65000
'Hutchison, Dave	'	'Los Angeles	'	'D'	44	0	10	10	71	50000
'Brown, Larry	'	'Los Angeles	'	'D'	57	1	8	9	23	70000
'Palmer, Rob	'	'Los Angeles	'	'W'	48	0	3	3	27	45000
'Edestrand, Darryl	'	'Los Angeles	'	'D'	14	0	2	2	15	45000
'Simmons, Gary	'	'Los Angeles	'	'G'	14	0	0	0	6	85000
'Vachon, Rogie	'	'Los Angeles	'	'G'	70	0	0	0	2	120000
'Eriksson, Roland	'	'Minnesota	'	'C'	78	21	39	60	12	70000
'Young, Tim	'	'Minnesota	'	'C'	78	23	35	58	64	65000
'Brasar Per Olov	'	'Minnesota	'	'W'	77	20	37	57	6	60000
'Sharpley, Glen	'	'Minnesota	'	'C'	79	22	33	55	42	75000
'Maxwell, Brad	'	'Minnesota	'	'D'	75	18	29	47	100	75000
'Anderson, Kent	'	'Minnesota	'	'W'	73	15	18	33	4	60000
'Zanussi, Ron	'	'Minnesota	'	'W'	68	15	17	32	89	50000
'Jensen, Steve	'	'Minnesota	'	'W'	74	13	17	30	73	60000
'Talafous, Dean	'	'Minnesota	'	'W'	75	13	17	30	73	60000
'Bennett, Harvey	'	'Minnesota	'	'W'	66	12	10	22	98	70000
'Beverley, Nick	'	'Minnesota	'	'D'	57	7	14	21	18	80000
'Younghans, Tom	'	'Minnesota	'	'W'	72	10	8	18	100	55000
'Roberts, Jimmy	'	'Minnesota	'	'W'	42	4	14	18	19	50000
'Pirus, Alex	'	'Minnesota	'	'W'	61	9	6	15	38	50000
'Barrett, Fred	'	'Minnesota	'	'D'	79	0	15	15	59	80000
'Maxwell, Bryan	'	'Minnesota	'	'D'	18	2	5	7	41	55000
'Reid, Tom	'	'Minnesota	'	'D'	36	1	6	7	21	100000
'Engele, Jerome	'	'Minnesota	'	'D'	52	1	5	6	105	50000
'LoPresti, Pete	'	'Minnesota	'	'G'	53	0	2	2	0	80000
'Butters, Bill	'	'Minnesota	'	'W'	23	1	0	1	30	50000
'Nannie, Lou	'	'Minnesota	'	'D'	26	0	1	1	8	80000
'Jackson, Don	'	'Minnesota	'	'D'	2	0	0	0	2	50000
'McGee, Dean	'	'Minnesota	'	'D'	7	0	0	0	4	50000
'Harrison, Paul	'	'Minnesota	'	'G'	27	0	0	0	10	55000
'Lafleur, Guy	'	'Montreal	'	'W'	78	60	72	132	26	180000
'Lemaire, Jacques	'	'Montreal	'	'C'	76	36	61	97	14	135000
'Shutt, Steve	'	'Montreal	'	'W'	80	49	37	86	24	120000
'Robinson, Larry	'	'Montreal	'	'D'	80	13	52	65	39	125000
'Larouche, Pierre	'	'Montreal	'	'C'	64	23	37	60	11	100000
'Houle, Rejean,	'	'Montreal	'	'W'	76	30	28	58	50	80000
'Cournoyer, Yvan	'	'Montreal	'	'W'	68	24	29	53	12	160000
'Mondou, Pierre	'	'Montreal	'	'C'	71	19	30	49	8	70000

'Savard, Serge	'	'Montreal	'	'D'	77	8	34	42	24	155000
'Risebrough, Doug	'	'Montreal	'	'W'	72	18	23	41	97	80000
'Lapointe, Guy	'	'Montreal	'	'D'	49	13	29	42	19	175000
'Lambert, Yvon	'	'Montreal	'	'W'	77	18	22	40	20	85000
'Jarvis, Doug	'	'Montreal	'	'C'	80	11	28	39	23	70000
'Gainey, Bob	'	'Montreal	'	'W'	66	15	16	31	57	80000
'Nyrop, Bill	'	'Montreal	'	'D'	72	5	21	26	37	70000
'Tremblay, Mario	'	'Montreal	'	'W'	56	10	14	24	44	75000
'Chartraw, Rick	'	'Montreal	'	'W'	68	4	12	16	64	75000
'Bouchard, Pierre	'	'Montreal	'	'D'	59	4	6	10	29	80000
'Lupien, Gilles	'	'Montreal	'	'D'	46	1	3	4	108	55000
'Larocque, Michel	'	'Montreal	'	'G'	30	0	4	4	0	105000
'Engblom, Brian	'	'Montreal	'	'D'	28	1	2	3	23	55000
'Dryden, Ken	'	'Montreal	'	'G'	52	0	2	2	0	180000
'Wilson, Murray	'	'Montreal	'	'W'	12	0	1	1	0	75000
'Trottier, Bryan	'	'NY Islanders'	'C'	77	46	77	123	46	90000
'Potvin, Denis	'	'NY Islanders'	'D'	80	30	64	94	81	150000
'Bossy, Mike	'	'NY Islanders'	'W'	73	53	38	91	6	50000
'Gillies, Clark	'	'NY Islanders'	'W'	80	35	50	85	76	95000
'Harris, Bill	'	'NY Islanders'	'W'	80	22	38	60	40	125000
'Bourne, Bob	'	'NY Islanders'	'C'	80	30	33	63	31	75000
'Nystrom, Bob	'	'NY Islanders'	'W'	80	30	29	59	94	90000
'Persson, Stefan	'	'NY Islanders'	'D'	66	6	50	56	54	60000
'Kaszycki, Mike	'	'NY Islanders'	'C'	58	13	29	42	24	55000
'Merrick, Wayne	'	'NY Islanders'	'C'	55	12	19	31	16	80000
'Henning, Lorne	'	'NY Islanders'	'C'	79	12	15	27	6	75000
'Hart, Gerry	'	'NY Islanders'	'D'	78	2	23	25	94	75000
'Drouin, Jude	'	'NY Islanders'	'C'	56	5	17	22	12	75000
'Westfall, Ed	'	'NY Islanders'	'W'	71	5	19	24	14	110000
'Howatt, Garry	'	'NY Islanders'	'W'	61	7	12	19	146	75000
'Bergeron, Michel	'	'NY Islanders'	'W'	28	10	6	16	2	55000
'Lewis, Dave	'	'NY Islanders'	'D'	77	3	11	14	58	70000
'Price, Pat	'	'NY Islanders'	'D'	52	2	10	12	27	70000
'Marshall, Bert	'	'NY Islanders'	'D'	58	0	7	7	44	80000
'Resch, Glenn	'	'NY Islanders'	'G'	45	0	1	1	12	100000
'McKendry, Alex	'	'NY Islanders'	'D'	4	0	0	0	2	50000
'Smith, Bill	'	'NY Islanders'	'G'	38	0	0	0	35	90000
'Esposito, Phil	'	'NY Rangers	'	'C'	79	38	43	81	53	325000
'Hickey, Pat	'	'NY Rangers	'	'W'	80	40	33	73	47	80000
'Greschner, Ron	'	'NY Rangers	'	'D'	78	24	48	72	100	80000
'Tkaczuk, Walt	'	'NY Rangers	'	'C'	80	26	40	66	30	250000
'Vickers, Steve	'	'NY Rangers	'	'W'	79	19	44	63	30	105000
'Murdoch, Don	'	'NY Rangers	'	'W'	66	27	28	55	41	75000
'Vadnais, Carol	'	'NY Rangers	'	'C'	80	6	40	46	115	120000
'Duguay, Ron	'	'NY Rangers	'	'C'	71	20	20	40	43	70000
'DeBlois, Lucien	'	'NY Rangers	'	'W'	71	22	8	30	27	65000
'Johnstone, Ed	'	'NY Rangers	'	'W'	53	13	13	26	34	60000
'Polis, Greg	'	'NY Rangers	'	'W'	37	7	16	23	12	50000
'Maloney, Dave	'	'NY Rangers	'	'D'	56	2	19	21	63	110000
'Dillon, Wayne	'	'NY Rangers	'	'C'	59	5	13	18	13	175000
'McEwen, Mike	'	'NY Rangers	'	'D'	57	5	13	18	52	50000
'Newman, Don	'	'NY Rangers	'	'W'	59	5	13	18	22	50000
'Heaslip, Mark	'	'NY Rangers	'	'W'	29	5	10	15	34	55000
'Awrey, Don	'	'NY Rangers	'	'D'	78	2	8	10	38	100000
'Fotiu, Nick	'	'NY Rangers	'	'W'	59	2	7	9	105	65000
'Farrish, Dave	'	'NY Rangers	'	'D'	66	3	5	8	66	65000
'Smith, Dallas	'	'NY Rangers	'	'D'	29	1	4	5	25	75000
'Thomas, Wayne	'	'NY Rangers	'	'G'	41	0	1	1	9	100000
'Davidson, John	'	'NY Rangers	'	'G'	34	0	0	0	10	100000
'Clarke, Bobby	'	'Philadelphia'	'C'	71	21	68	89	83	160000
'Barber, Bill	'	'Philadelphia'	'W'	80	41	31	71	34	150000
'Macleish, Rick	'	'Philadelphia'	'C'	76	31	39	70	33	150000
'Kindrachuk, O.	'	'Philadelphia'	'C'	73	17	45	62	128	90000
'Dailey, Bob	'	'Philadelphia'	'D'	76	21	36	57	62	110000
'Leach, Reggie	'	'Philadelphia'	'W'	72	24	28	52	24	90000
'Bridgman, Mel	'	'Philadelphia'	'C'	76	16	32	48	203	80000
'Lonsberry, Ross	'	'Philadelphia'	'W'	78	18	30	48	45	90000
'Saleski, Don	'	'Philadelphia'	'W'	70	27	18	45	44	80000
'Bladon, Tom	'	'Philadelphia'	'C'	79	11	24	35	57	80000

Name		Team		Pos	GP	G	A	PTS	PIM	Salary
'Holmgren, Paul	'	'Philadelphia'	'W'	62	16	18	34	190	70000
'Kelly, Bob	'	'Philadelphia'	'W'	74	19	13	32	95	75000
'Dean, Barry	'	'Philadelphia'	'W'	56	7	18	25	34	60000
'Lapointe, Rick	'	'Philadelphia'	'D'	47	4	16	20	91	80000
'McCarthy, Kevin	'	'Philadelphia'	'D'	62	2	15	17	32	55000
'Watson, Jimmy	'	'Philadelphia'	'D'	71	5	12	17	62	115000
'Watson, Joe	'	'Philadelphia'	'D'	65	5	9	14	22	100000
'Dupont, Andre	'	'Philadelphia'	'D'	69	2	12	14	225	80000
'Dornhoefer, Gary	'	'Philadelphia'	'W'	47	7	5	12	62	120000
'Hoyda, Dave	'	'Philadelphia'	'W'	41	1	3	4	119	45000
'Stephenson, Wayne	'	'Philadelphia'	'G'	26	0	0	0	0	95000
'Parent, Bernie	'	'Philadelphia'	'G'	49	0	0	0	4	140000
'Mahovlich, Peter	'	'Pittsburgh	'C'	74	28	41	69	41	125000
'Pronovost, Jean	'	'Pittsburgh	'W'	79	40	25	65	50	135000
'Malone, Greg	'	'Pittsburgh	'C'	78	18	43	61	80	50000
'Carr, Gene	'	'Pittsburgh	'C'	75	19	37	56	80	75000
'Edur, Tom	'	'Pittsburgh	'D'	78	10	45	55	28	75000
'Kehoe, Rick	'	'Pittsburgh	'W'	70	29	21	50	10	110000
'Chapman, Blair	'	'Pittsburgh	'W'	75	24	20	44	37	60000
'Schultz, Dave	'	'Pittsburgh	'W'	74	11	25	36	405	100000
'Bianchin, Wayne	'	'Pittsburgh	'W'	61	20	13	33	40	70000
'Corrigan, Mike	'	'Pittsburgh	'W'	25	8	12	20	10	75000
'Stackhouse, Ron	'	'Pittsburgh	'D'	50	5	15	20	36	110000
'Spencer, Brian	'	'Pittsburgh	'W'	79	9	11	20	81	60000
'Burrows, Dave	'	'Pittsburgh	'D'	67	4	15	19	24	125000
'Lee, Peter	'	'Pittsburgh	'W'	60	5	13	18	19	55000
'Anderson, Russ	'	'Pittsburgh	'D'	74	2	16	18	150	60000
'Macdonald, Lowell	'	'Pittsburgh	'W'	19	5	8	13	2	80000
'Flesch, John	'	'Pittsburgh	'W'	29	7	5	12	19	40000
'Paradise, Bob	'	'Pittsburgh	'D'	64	2	10	12	53	60000
'Campbell, Colin	'	'Pittsburgh	'D'	55	1	9	10	103	60000
'Cassidy, Tom	'	'Pittsburgh	'W'	26	3	4	7	15	50000
'Faubert, Mario	'	'Pittsburgh	'D'	18	0	6	6	11	50000
'Sanderson, Derek	'	'Pittsburgh	'C'	13	3	1	4	0	50000
'Wilson, Dunc	'	'Pittsburgh	'G'	21	0	1	1	0	90000
'Herron, Denis	'	'Pittsburgh	'G'	60	0	1	1	6	90000
'Laxton, Gord	'	'Pittsburgh	'G'	2	0	0	0	0	50000
'Unger, Garry	'	'St. Louis	'C'	80	32	20	52	66	175000
'Federko, Bernie	'	'St. Louis	'C'	72	17	24	41	27	70000
'Hammarstrom, Inge	'	'St. Louis	'W'	73	20	20	40	4	95000
'Berenson, Red	'	'St. Louis	'C'	80	13	25	38	12	125000
'Patey, Larry	'	'St. Louis	'C'	80	17	17	34	29	90000
'Bennett, Curt	'	'St. Louis	'W'	75	10	24	34	64	85000
'Fairbairn, Bill	'	'St. Louis	'W'	66	14	17	31	10	100000
'Gibbs, Barry	'	'St. Louis	'D'	78	7	17	24	69	100000
'Sutter, Brian	'	'St. Louis	'W'	78	9	13	22	123	55000
'Larose, Claude	'	'St. Louis	'W'	69	8	13	21	20	85000
'Affleck, Bruce	'	'St. Louis	'D'	75	4	14	18	26	80000
'Brownschidle, Jack	'	'St. Louis	'D'	40	2	15	17	23	50000
'Komadoski, Neil	'	'St. Louis	'D'	58	2	14	16	97	70000
'Ogilvie, Brian	'	'St. Louis	'C'	32	6	8	14	12	65000
'Roberts, Jim	'	'St. Louis	'D'	75	4	10	14	39	100000
'Hess, Bob	'	'St. Louis	'D'	55	2	12	14	16	60000
'Seiling, Rod	'	'St. Louis	'D'	78	1	11	12	40	105000
'Holt, Gary	'	'St. Louis	'W'	49	7	4	11	81	60000
'Currie, Tony	'	'St. Louis	'W'	22	4	5	9	4	45000
'Richardson, Ken	'	'St. Louis	'W'	12	2	5	7	0	45000
'Myre, Phil	'	'St. Louis	'G'	53	0	2	2	12	105000
'Grant, Doug	'	'St. Louis	'D'	9	0	0	0	0	60000
'Sittler, Darryl	'	'Toronto	'C'	80	45	72	117	100	165000
'McDonald, Lanny	'	'Toronto	'W'	74	47	40	87	54	145000
'Salming, Borje	'	'Toronto	'D'	80	16	60	76	70	155000
'Turnbull, Ian	'	'Toronto	'D'	77	14	47	61	77	120000
'Ellis, Ron	'	'Toronto	'W'	80	26	24	50	17	140000
'Williams, Dave	'	'Toronto	'W'	78	19	31	50	351	105000
'Maloney, Dan	'	'Toronto	'W'	79	19	33	52	176	105000
'Boutette, Pat	'	'Toronto	'W'	80	17	19	36	120	50000
'Boudreau, Bruce	'	'Toronto	'C'	40	11	18	29	12	40000
'Ferguson, George	'	'Toronto	'C'	73	7	16	23	37	80000

'Valiquette, Jack	'	'Toronto	'	'C'	60	8	13	21	15	85000
'Butler, Jerry	'	'Toronto	'	'W'	82	9	9	18	54	60000
'Glennie, Brian	'	'Toronto	'	'D'	77	2	15	17	62	80000
'Weir, Stan	'	'Toronto	'	'C'	30	12	5	17	4	70000
'Johansen, Trevor	'	'Toronto	'	'D'	79	2	14	16	82	50000
'Jones, Jimmy	'	'Toronto	'	'W'	78	4	9	13	23	40000
'Carlyle, Randy	'	'Toronto	'	'D'	49	2	11	13	31	60000
'Pelyk, Mike	'	'Toronto	'	'D'	41	1	11	12	14	75000
'McKenny, Jim	'	'Toronto	'	'D'	15	2	2	4	8	40000
'Walker, Kurt	'	'Toronto	'	'W'	40	2	2	4	69	40000
'Wilson, Ron	'	'Toronto	'	'W'	13	2	1	3	0	40000
'Ashby, Don	'	'Toronto	'	'D'	12	1	2	3	0	40000
'Anderson, John	'	'Toronto	'	'W'	17	1	2	3	2	40000
'Palmateer, Mike	'	'Toronto	'	'G'	63	0	1	1	12	75000
'McRae, Gord	'	'Toronto	'	'G'	18	0	0	0	2	70000
'Walton, Mike	'	'Vancouver	'	'C'	65	29	37	66	30	100000
'Blight, Rick	'	'Vancouver	'	'W'	80	25	38	63	33	75000
'Ververgaert, D.	'	'Vancouver	'	'W'	80	21	33	54	23	120000
'Lever, Don	'	'Vancouver	'	'W'	75	17	32	49	58	120000
'Martin, Pit	'	'Vancouver	'	'C'	74	16	32	48	36	140000
'Kearns, Dennis	'	'Vancouver	'	'D'	80	4	43	47	27	90000
'Graves, Hilliard	'	'Vancouver	'	'W'	80	21	26	47	18	100000
'Gillis, Jere	'	'Vancouver	'	'W'	79	23	18	41	35	65000
'Oddleifson, C.	'	'Vancouver	'	'C'	78	17	22	39	64	80000
'Sedlbauer, Ron	'	'Vancouver	'	'W'	62	18	12	30	25	80000
'Monahan, Garry	'	'Vancouver	'	'W'	67	10	19	29	28	85000
'Alexander, Claire	'	'Vancouver	'	'D'	32	8	18	26	6	60000
'Snepsts, Harold	'	'Vancouver	'	'D'	75	4	16	20	118	70000
'Manno, Bob	'	'Vancouver	'	'D'	49	5	14	19	29	50000
'O Flaherty, Gerry	'	'Vancouver	'	'W'	59	6	11	17	15	60000
'Gassoff, Brad	'	'Vancouver	'	'W'	47	9	6	15	70	50000
'Grisdale, John	'	'Vancouver	'	'D'	42	0	9	9	47	60000
'McLlhargey, Jack	'	'Vancouver	'	'D'	69	3	5	8	172	65000
'Kannegiesser, S.	'	'Vancouver	'	'D'	42	1	7	8	36	70000
'Ridley, Curt	'	'Vancouver	'	'G'	40	0	1	1	9	75000
'Hanlon, Glen	'	'Vancouver	'	'D'	4	0	0	0	2	40000
'Maniago, Cesare	'	'Vancouver	'	'G'	46	0	0	0	18	105000
'Charron, Guy	'	'Washington	'	'C'	80	38	35	73	12	85000
'Sirois, Bob	'	'Washington	'	'W'	72	24	37	61	6	70000
'Meehan, Gerry	'	'Washington	'	'C'	78	19	24	43	10	70000
'Picard, Robert	'	'Washington	'	'D'	75	10	27	37	101	60000
'Girard, Bob	'	'Washington	'	'W'	77	9	18	27	17	60000
'Riley, Bill	'	'Washington	'	'W'	57	13	12	25	125	55000
'Forbes, Dave	'	'Washington	'	'W'	77	11	11	22	119	60000
'Rowe, Tom	'	'Washington	'	'W'	63	13	8	21	82	50000
'Collins, Bill	'	'Washington	'	'W'	74	10	9	19	18	75000
'Green, Rick	'	'Washington	'	'D'	60	5	14	19	67	60000
'Bailey, Garnet	'	'Washington	'	'W'	40	7	12	19	28	70000
'Bragnalo, Bryan	'	'Washington	'	'D'	44	2	13	15	22	55000
'Watson, Bryan	'	'Washington	'	'D'	79	3	11	14	167	80000
'Smith, Gord	'	'Washington	'	'D'	80	4	7	11	78	55000
'Lane, Gord	'	'Washington	'	'D'	69	2	9	11	195	50000
'Lynch, Jack	'	'Washington	'	'D'	29	1	8	9	4	70000
'Marson, Mike	'	'Washington	'	'W'	46	4	4	8	101	60000
'Labre, Yvon	'	'Washington	'	'D'	22	0	8	8	41	65000
'Lalonde, Ron	'	'Washington	'	'W'	67	1	5	6	16	55000
'Bedard, Jim	'	'Washington	'	'G'	42	0	2	2	4	50000
'Wolfe, Bernie	'	'Washington	'	'G'	25	0	0	0	0	65000

N.6   Gas Mileage Data File

This file gives the gas mileage figures for North American and foreign cars along with their model type, engine size, number of cylinders, whether they have a catalytic converter, and their transmission type. The following legend applies to the data list:

```
Mt    - manufacturer type: A - American Motors,
                           C - Chrysler,
                           F - Ford,
                           G - General Motors,
                           O - other (foreign)
Disp  - engine displacement
Dt    - units of displacement: L - litres
                               I - cubic inches
Cyl   - number of cylinders in the engine
Tran  - transmission type:
        M - manual (M4 - 4 speed manual)
        A - automatic (A2 - 2 speed automatic)
Carb  - type of carburetor:
        FI - fuel injection
        n  - number of carburetor barrels
Cat   - catalytic converter
        X - yes
        b - no
C     - city mileage (KPG)
H     - highway mileage (KPG)
Comb  - combined mileage (KPG)
```

Mt	Manufacturer	Model	Disp	Dt	Cyl	Tran	Carb	Cat	C	H	Comb
'O'	'Alfa Romeo	' 'Alfetta	' 2.0	'L'	4	'M5'	'FI'	'X'	37	56	44
'O'	'Alfa Romeo	' 'Spider	' 2.0	'L'	4	'M5'	'FI'	'X'	35	50	41
'A'	'AMC	' 'Concord	' 232.0	'I'	6	'A3'	' 1'	' '	29	41	34
'A'	'AMC	' 'Concord	' 232.0	'I'	6	'M3'	' 1'	' '	33	47	38
'A'	'AMC	' 'Concord	' 232.0	'I'	6	'M4'	' 1'	' '	29	50	36
'A'	'AMC	' 'Concord	' 258.0	'I'	6	'A3'	' 2'	'X'	31	44	36
'A'	'AMC	' 'Concord	' 258.0	'I'	6	'M4'	' 2'	'X'	32	48	37
'A'	'AMC	' 'Concord	' 304.0	'I'	8	'A3'	' 2'	'X'	26	37	30
'A'	'AMC	' 'Concord Wagon	' 232.0	'I'	6	'A3'	' 1'	' '	29	41	34
'A'	'AMC	' 'Concord Wagon	' 232.0	'I'	6	'M3'	' 1'	' '	33	47	38
'A'	'AMC	' 'Concord Wagon	' 232.0	'I'	6	'M4'	' 1'	' '	29	50	36
'A'	'AMC	' 'Concord Wagon	' 258.0	'I'	6	'A3'	' 2'	'X'	31	44	36
'A'	'AMC	' 'Concord Wagon	' 258.0	'I'	6	'M4'	' 2'	'X'	32	48	37
'A'	'AMC	' 'Concord Wagon	' 304.0	'I'	8	'A3'	' 2'	'X'	26	37	30
'A'	'AMC	' 'Gremlin	' 121.0	'I'	4	'A3'	' 2'	'X'	39	56	45
'A'	'AMC	' 'Gremlin	' 121.0	'I'	4	'M4'	' 2'	'X'	43	67	51
'A'	'AMC	' 'Gremlin	' 232.0	'I'	6	'A3'	' 1'	' '	30	42	35
'A'	'AMC	' 'Gremlin	' 232.0	'I'	6	'M3'	' 1'	' '	33	48	38
'A'	'AMC	' 'Gremlin	' 232.0	'I'	6	'M4'	' 1'	' '	30	49	36
'A'	'AMC	' 'Gremlin	' 258.0	'I'	6	'A3'	' 2'	'X'	31	44	36
'A'	'AMC	' 'Gremlin	' 258.0	'I'	6	'M4'	' 2'	'X'	32	48	37
'A'	'AMC	' 'Matador	' 360.0	'I'	8	'A3'	' 2'	'X'	23	32	26
'A'	'AMC	' 'Matador Wagon	' 360.0	'I'	8	'A3'	' 2'	'X'	23	32	26
'A'	'AMC	' 'Pacer	' 232.0	'I'	6	'A3'	' 1'	' '	29	41	34
'A'	'AMC	' 'Pacer	' 232.0	'I'	6	'M3'	' 1'	' '	33	47	38
'A'	'AMC	' 'Pacer	' 232.0	'I'	6	'M4'	' 1'	' '	29	50	36
'A'	'AMC	' 'Pacer	' 258.0	'I'	6	'A3'	' 2'	'X'	31	44	36
'A'	'AMC	' 'Pacer	' 258.0	'I'	6	'M4'	' 2'	'X'	32	48	37
'A'	'AMC	' 'Pacer	' 304.0	'I'	8	'A3'	' 2'	'X'	26	37	30
'A'	'AMC	' 'Pacer Wagon	' 232.0	'I'	6	'A3'	' 1'	' '	29	41	34
'A'	'AMC	' 'Pacer Wagon	' 232.0	'I'	6	'M3'	' 1'	' '	33	47	38
'A'	'AMC	' 'Pacer Wagon	' 232.0	'I'	6	'M4'	' 1'	' '	29	50	36
'A'	'AMC	' 'Pacer Wagon	' 258.0	'I'	6	'A3'	' 2'	'X'	31	44	36
'A'	'AMC	' 'Pacer Wagon	' 258.0	'I'	6	'M4'	' 2'	'X'	32	48	37
'A'	'AMC	' 'Pacer Wagon	' 304.0	'I'	8	'A3'	' 2'	'X'	26	37	30
'O'	'Audi	' ' 'Fox Sedan	' 1.6	'L'	4	'A3'	'FI'	' '	39	56	45

```
'O'  'Audi        '  'Fox Sedan       '    1.6 'L' 4 'M4' 'FI' '  ' 'X ' 45 72 55
'O'  'Audi        '  'Fox Wagon       '    1.6 'L' 4 'A3' 'FI' '  ' '  ' 39 56 45
'O'  'Audi        '  'Fox Wagon       ' '  ' 1.6 'L' 4 'M4' 'FI' '  ' '  ' 45 72 55
'O'  'Audi        '  '5000            '    2.2 'L' 5 'A3' 'FI' '  ' '  ' 32 46 37
'O'  'Audi        '  '5000            '    2.2 'L' 5 'M4' 'FI' '  ' '  ' 29 43 34
'O'  'Austin/MG   '  'MG Midget       '    1.5 'L' 4 'M4' ' 1' 'X'    45 66 53
'O'  'Austin/MG   '  'MGB             '    1.8 'L' 4 'M4' ' 1' '  '    40 58 48
'O'  'Austin/MG   '  'MGB (O/D)       '    1.8 'L' 4 'M4' ' 1' '  '    40 70 53
'O'  'Austin/MG   '  'Mini            '    1.0 'L' 4 'M4' ' 1' '  '    59 82 70
'O'  'Bentley     '  'Corniche        '  412.0 'I' 8 'A3' ' 2' 'X'    20 26 22
'O'  'Bentley     '  'T II/LG.WB      '  412.0 'I' 8 'A3' ' 2' 'X'    20 26 22
'O'  'BMW         '  '320I            '    2.0 'L' 4 'M4' 'FI' '  '    37 55 43
'O'  'BMW         '  '320IA           '    2.0 'L' 4 'A3' 'FI' '  '    35 50 40
'O'  'BMW         '  '530I            '    3.0 'L' 6 'M4' 'FI' 'X'    27 46 33
'O'  'BMW         '  '530IA           '    3.0 'L' 6 'A3' 'FI' 'X'    27 41 32
'G'  'Buick       '  'Century         '  231.0 'I' 6 'A3' ' 2' 'X'    37 50 42
'G'  'Buick       '  'Century         '  231.0 'I' 6 'M4' ' 2' 'X'    30 54 38
'G'  'Buick       '  'Century         '  305.0 'I' 8 'A3' ' 2' 'X'    36 50 41
'G'  'Buick       '  'Century         '  305.0 'I' 8 'A3' ' 4' 'X'    34 50 40
'G'  'Buick       '  'Century         '    3.2 'L' 6 'A3' ' 2' 'X'    35 52 41
'G'  'Buick       '  'Century         '    3.2 'L' 6 'M3' ' 2' 'X'    36 64 45
'G'  'Buick       '  'Century Wagon   '  231.0 'I' 6 'A3' ' 2' 'X'    37 52 42
'G'  'Buick       '  'Century Wagon   '  305.0 'I' 8 'A3' ' 2' 'X'    32 48 38
'G'  'Buick       '  'Century Wagon   '  305.0 'I' 8 'A3' ' 4' 'X'    31 44 35
'G'  'Buick       '  'Century-Turbo   '    3.8 'L' 6 'A3' ' 4' 'X'    33 48 38
'G'  'Buick       '  'Electra         '  350.0 'I' 8 'A3' ' 4' 'X'    30 42 34
'G'  'Buick       '  'Electra         '  403.0 'I' 8 'A3' ' 4' 'X'    27 38 31
'G'  'Buick       '  'Estate Wagon    '  350.0 'I' 8 'A3' ' 4' 'X'    30 42 34
'G'  'Buick       '  'Estate Wagon    '  403.0 'I' 8 'A3' ' 4' 'X'    27 38 31
'G'  'Buick       '  'LeSabre         '  231.0 'I' 6 'A3' ' 2' 'X'    32 47 37
'G'  'Buick       '  'LeSabre         '  301.0 'I' 8 'A3' ' 2' 'X'    32 47 38
'G'  'Buick       '  'LeSabre         '  350.0 'I' 8 'A3' ' 4' 'X'    30 43 35
'G'  'Buick       '  'LeSabre         '  403.0 'I' 8 'A3' ' 4' 'X'    28 39 32
'G'  'Buick       '  'LeSabre-Turbo   '    3.8 'L' 6 'A3' ' 4' 'X'    31 43 36
'G'  'Buick       '  'Regal           '  231.0 'I' 6 'A3' ' 2' 'X'    37 50 42
'G'  'Buick       '  'Regal           '  231.0 'I' 6 'M4' ' 2' 'X'    30 54 38
'G'  'Buick       '  'Regal           '  305.0 'I' 8 'A3' ' 2' 'X'    36 50 41
'G'  'Buick       '  'Regal           '  305.0 'I' 8 'A3' ' 4' 'X'    34 50 40
'G'  'Buick       '  'Regal           '    3.2 'L' 6 'A3' ' 2' 'X'    35 52 41
'G'  'Buick       '  'Regal           '    3.2 'L' 6 'M3' ' 2' 'X'    36 64 45
'G'  'Buick       '  'Regal-Turbo     '    3.2 'L' 6 'A3' ' 2' 'X'    35 49 40
'G'  'Buick       '  'Regal-Turbo     '    3.8 'L' 6 'A3' ' 4' 'X'    33 48 38
'G'  'Buick       '  'Riviera         '  350.0 'I' 8 'A3' ' 4' 'X'    30 42 34
'G'  'Buick       '  'Riviera         '  403.0 'I' 8 'A3' ' 4' 'X'    27 38 31
'G'  'Buick       '  'Skyhawk         '  231.0 'I' 6 'A3' ' 2' 'X'    37 52 42
'G'  'Buick       '  'Skyhawk         '  231.0 'I' 6 'M ' ' 2' 'X'    30 54 38
'G'  'Buick       '  'Skylark         '  231.0 'I' 6 'A3' ' 2' 'X'    36 50 41
'G'  'Buick       '  'Skylark         '  231.0 'I' 6 'M3' ' 2' 'X'    31 50 37
'G'  'Buick       '  'Skylark         '  305.0 'I' 8 'A3' ' 2' 'X'    32 48 38
'G'  'Cadillac    '  'Cadillac        '  425.0 'I' 8 'A3' ' 4' 'X'    25 36 29
'G'  'Cadillac    '  'Cadillac        '  425.0 'I' 8 'A3' 'FI' 'X'    24 35 28
'G'  'Cadillac    '  'Eldorado        '  425.0 'I' 8 'A3' ' 4' 'X'    21 32 25
'G'  'Cadillac    '  'Seville         '  350.0 'I' 8 'A3' 'FI' 'X'    26 39 31
'G'  'Cadillac    '  'Limousine       '  425.0 'I' 8 'A3' ' 4' 'X'    20 28 23
'G'  'Chevrolet   '  'Camaro          '  250.0 'I' 6 'A3' ' 1' 'X'    35 49 40
'G'  'Chevrolet   '  'Camaro          '  250.0 'I' 6 'M3' ' 1' 'X'    35 52 41
'G'  'Chevrolet   '  'Camaro          '  305.0 'I' 8 'A3' ' 2' 'X'    32 48 38
'G'  'Chevrolet   '  'Camaro          '  305.0 'I' 8 'M4' ' 2' 'X'    28 41 33
'G'  'Chevrolet   '  'Camaro          '  350.0 'I' 8 'A3' ' 4' 'X'    31 44 36
'G'  'Chevrolet   '  'Camaro          '  350.0 'I' 8 'M4' ' 4' 'X'    27 36 30
'G'  'Chevrolet   '  'Camaro Z28      '  350.0 'I' 8 'A3' ' 4' 'X'    27 36 30
'G'  'Chevrolet   '  'Chevette        '    1.6 'L' 4 'A3' ' 1' 'X'    49 63 54
'G'  'Chevrolet   '  'Chevette        '    1.6 'L' 4 'M4' ' 1' 'X'    59 78 67
'G'  'Chevrolet   '  'Chevrolet       '  250.0 'I' 6 'A3' ' 1' 'X'    35 49 40
'G'  'Chevrolet   '  'Chevrolet       '  305.0 'I' 8 'A3' ' 2' 'X'    32 48 38
'G'  'Chevrolet   '  'Chevrolet       '  350.0 'I' 8 'A3' ' 4' 'X'    31 44 36
'G'  'Chevrolet   '  'Chevrolet Wagon '  305.0 'I' 8 'A3' ' 2' 'X'    30 45 35
'G'  'Chevrolet   '  'Chevrolet Wagon'  350.0 'I' 8 'A3' ' 4' 'X'    28 41 33
'G'  'Chevrolet   '  'Corvette        '  350.0 'I' 8 'A3' ' 4' 'X'    27 36 30
```

'G'	'Chevrolet	'	'Corvette	'	350.0	'I'	8	'M4'	'	4'	'X'	27	36	30
'G'	'Chevrolet	'	'Malibu	'	305.0	'I'	8	'A3'	'	2'	'X'	36	50	41
'G'	'Chevrolet	'	'Malibu	'	305.0	'I'	8	'M4'	'	2'	'X'	31	44	36
'G'	'Chevrolet	'	'Malibu	'	3.3	'L'	6	'A3'	'	2'	'X'	38	54	44
'G'	'Chevrolet	'	'Malibu	'	3.3	'L'	6	'M3'	'	2'	'X'	41	57	47
'G'	'Chevrolet	'	'Malibu Wagon	'	305.0	'I'	8	'A3'	'	2'	'X'	31	44	36
'G'	'Chevrolet	'	'Malibu Wagon	'	305.0	'I'	8	'M4'	'	2'	'X'	28	41	33
'G'	'Chevrolet	'	'Malibu Wagon	'	3.3	'L'	6	'A3'	'	2'	'X'	38	51	43
'G'	'Chevrolet	'	'Malibu Wagon	'	3.3	'L'	6	'M3'	'	2'	'X'	41	57	47
'G'	'Chevrolet	'	'Monte Carlo	'	231.0	'I'	6	'A3'	'	2'	'X'	37	50	42
'G'	'Chevrolet	'	'Monte Carlo	'	231.0	'I'	6	'M '	'	2'	'X'	30	54	38
'G'	'Chevrolet	'	'Monte Carlo	'	365.0	'I'	8	'A3'	'	2'	'X'	36	50	41
'G'	'Chevrolet	'	'Monte Carlo	'	305.0	'I'	8	'M4'	'	2'	'X'	31	44	36
'G'	'Chevrolet	'	'Monza	'	151.0	'I'	4	'A3'	'	2'	'X'	42	55	47
'G'	'Chevrolet	'	'Monza	'	151.0	'I'	4	'M '	'	2'	'X'	46	67	53
'G'	'Chevrolet	'	'Monza	'	305.0	'I'	8	'A3'	'	2'	'X'	33	47	38
'G'	'Chevrolet	'	'Monza	'	305.0	'I'	8	'M4'	'	2'	'X'	31	44	36
'G'	'Chevrolet	'	'Monza	'	3.2	'L'	6	'A3'	'	2'	'X'	35	52	41
'G'	'Chevrolet	'	'Monza	'	3.2	'L'	6	'M '	'	2'	'X'	36	64	45
'G'	'Chevrolet	'	'Monza Wagon	'	151.0	'I'	4	'A3'	'	2'	'X'	42	55	47
'G'	'Chevrolet	'	'Monza Wagon	'	151.0	'I'	4	'M '	'	2'	'X'	46	67	53
'G'	'Chevrolet	'	'Monza Wagon	'	3.2	'L'	6	'A3'	'	2'	'X'	35	52	41
'G'	'Chevrolet	'	'Monza Wagon	'	3.2	'L'	6	'M '	'	2'	'X'	36	64	45
'G'	'Chevrolet	'	'Nova	'	250.0	'I'	6	'A3'	'	1'	'X'	35	48	40
'G'	'Chevrolet	'	'Nova	'	250.0	'I'	6	'M3'	'	1'	'X'	36	50	41
'G'	'Chevrolet	'	'Nova	'	305.0	'I'	8	'A3'	'	2'	'X'	32	48	38
'G'	'Chevrolet	'	'Nova	'	305.0	'I'	8	'M4'	'	2'	'X'	28	41	33
'C'	'Chrysler	'	'Cordoba	'	318.0	'I'	8	'A3'	'	2'	'X'	29	44	35
'C'	'Chrysler	'	'Cordoba	'	318.0	'I'	8	'A3'	'	4'	' '	25	44	31
'C'	'Chrysler	'	'Cordoba	'	360.0	'I'	8	'A3'	'	2'	' '	22	42	28
'C'	'Chrysler	'	'Cordoba	'	360.0	'I'	8	'A3'	'	2'	'X'	28	44	34
'C'	'Chrysler	'	'Cordoba	'	400.0	'I'	8	'A3'	'	4'	' '	23	39	28
'C'	'Chrysler	'	'LeBaron	'	225.0	'I'	6	'A3'	'	2'	'X'	34	47	38
'C'	'Chrysler	'	'LeBaron	'	225.0	'I'	6	'M4'	'	2'	'X'	34	52	40
'C'	'Chrysler	'	'LeBaron	'	318.0	'I'	8	'A3'	'	2'	'X'	29	43	34
'C'	'Chrysler	'	'LeBaron	'	318.0	'I'	8	'A3'	'	4'	'X'	25	47	32
'C'	'Chrysler	'	'LeBaron	'	318.0	'I'	8	'M4'	'	2'	'X'	27	49	34
'C'	'Chrysler	'	'LeBaron	'	360.0	'I'	8	'A3'	'	2'	' '	23	42	29
'C'	'Chrysler	'	'LeBaron	'	360.0	'I'	8	'A3'	'	2'	'X'	28	42	33
'C'	'Chrysler	'	'LeBaron Wagon	'	225.0	'I'	6	'A3'	'	2'	'X'	33	45	38
'C'	'Chrysler	'	'LeBaron Wagon	'	225.0	'I'	6	'M4'	'	2'	'X'	34	52	40
'C'	'Chrysler	'	'LeBaron Wagon	'	318.0	'I'	8	'A3'	'	2'	'X'	28	41	32
'C'	'Chrysler	'	'LeBaron Wagon	'	318.0	'I'	8	'A3'	'	4'	' '	25	43	31
'C'	'Chrysler	'	'LeBaron Wagon	'	360.0	'I'	8	'A3'	'	2'	' '	22	42	28
'C'	'Chrysler	'	'LeBaron Wagon	'	360.0	'I'	8	'A3'	'	2'	'X'	28	44	34
'C'	'Chrysler	'	'Newport	'	400.0	'I'	8	'A3'	'	4'	' '	22	37	27
'C'	'Chrysler	'	'Newport	'	440.0	'I'	8	'A3'	'	4'	' '	20	33	24
'C'	'Chrysler	'	'New Yorker	'	400.0	'I'	8	'A3'	'	4'	' '	22	37	27
'C'	'Chrysler	'	'New Yorker	'	440.0	'I'	8	'A3'	'	4'	' '	20	33	24
'O'	'Datsun	'	'B210	'	1.4	'L'	4	'A3'	'	2'	' '	56	69	61
'O'	'Datsun	'	'B210	'	1.4	'L'	4	'M4'	'	2'	' '	60	80	68
'O'	'Datsun	'	'B210	'	1.4	'L'	4	'M5'	'	2'	' '	60	87	69
'O'	'Datsun	'	'F10	'	1.4	'L'	4	'M4'	'	2'	' '	58	77	65
'O'	'Datsun	'	'F10	'	1.4	'L'	4	'M5'	'	2'	' '	58	77	65
'O'	'Datsun	'	'F10 Wagon	'	1.4	'L'	4	'M4'	'	2'	' '	58	77	65
'O'	'Datsun	'	'200SX	'	2.0	'L'	4	'A3'	'	2'	' '	46	59	51
'O'	'Datsun	'	'200SX	'	2.0	'L'	4	'M5'	'	2'	' '	49	65	55
'O'	'Datsun	'	'280Z	'	2.8	'L'	6	'A3'	'FI'	'	' '	33	44	37
'O'	'Datsun	'	'280Z	'	2.8	'L'	6	'M5'	'FI'	'	' '	36	53	42
'O'	'Datsun	'	'510	'	2.0	'L'	4	'A3'	'	2'	' '	49	59	53
'O'	'Datsun	'	'510	'	2.0	'L'	4	'M4'	'	2'	' '	53	67	58
'O'	'Datsun	'	'510	'	2.0	'L'	4	'M5'	'	2'	' '	53	67	58
'O'	'Datsun	'	'510 Wagon	'	2.0	'L'	4	'A3'	'	2'	' '	46	59	51
'O'	'Datsun	'	'510 Wagon	'	2.0	'L'	4	'M4'	'	2'	' '	52	65	57
'C'	'Dodge	'	'Aspen	'	225.0	'I'	6	'A3'	'	1'	'X'	40	53	45
'C'	'Dodge	'	'Aspen	'	225.0	'I'	6	'A3'	'	2'	'X'	35	52	41
'C'	'Dodge	'	'Aspen	'	225.0	'I'	6	'M3'	'	1'	'X'	39	52	44
'C'	'Dodge	'	'Aspen	'	225.0	'I'	6	'M3'	'	2'	'X'	35	50	41
'C'	'Dodge	'	'Aspen	'	225.0	'I'	6	'M4'	'	1'	'X'	38	60	46

'C'	'Dodge	'	'Aspen	'	225.0	'I'	6	'M4'	'	2'	'X'	36 58 44
'C'	'Dodge	'	'Aspen	'	318.0	'I'	8	'A3'	'	2'	'X'	29 44 35
'C'	'Dodge	'	'Aspen	'	318.0	'I'	8	'A3'	'	4'	' '	25 48 32
'C'	'Dodge	'	'Aspen	'	318.0	'I'	8	'M4'	'	2'	'X'	27 49 34
'C'	'Dodge	'	'Aspen	'	360.0	'I'	8	'A3'	'	2'	' '	23 43 29
'C'	'Dodge	'	'Aspen	'	360.0	'I'	8	'A3'	'	2'	'X'	28 43 33
'C'	'Dodge	'	'Aspen	'	360.0	'I'	8	'A3'	'	4'	' '	22 38 27
'C'	'Dodge	'	'Aspen Wagon	'	225.0	'I'	6	'A3'	'	2'	'X'	33 45 38
'C'	'Dodge	'	'Aspen Wagon	'	225.0	'I'	6	'M3'	'	2'	'X'	34 47 39
'C'	'Dodge	'	'Aspen Wagon	'	225.0	'I'	6	'M4'	'	2'	'X'	34 52 40
'C'	'Dodge	'	'Aspen Wagon	'	318.0	'I'	8	'A3'	'	2'	'X'	29 43 34
'C'	'Dodge	'	'Aspen Wagon	'	318.0	'I'	8	'A3'	'	4'	' '	25 45 32
'C'	'Dodge	'	'Aspen Wagon	'	318.0	'I'	8	'M4'	'	2'	'X'	27 49 34
'C'	'Dodge	'	'Aspen Wagon	'	360.0	'I'	8	'A3'	'	2'	' '	23 42 29
'C'	'Dodge	'	'Aspen Wagon	'	360.0	'I'	8	'A3'	'	2'	'X'	28 42 33
'C'	'Dodge	'	'Diplomat	'	225.0	'I'	6	'A3'	'	2'	'X'	34 47 39
'C'	'Dodge	'	'Diplomat	'	225.0	'I'	6	'M4'	'	2'	'X'	34 52 40
'C'	'Dodge	'	'Diplomat	'	318.0	'I'	8	'A3'	'	2'	'X'	29 43 34
'C'	'Dodge	'	'Diplomat	'	318.0	'I'	8	'A3'	'	4'	' '	25 47 32
'C'	'Dodge	'	'Diplomat	'	318.0	'I'	8	'M4'	'	2'	'X'	27 49 34
'C'	'Dodge	'	'Diplomat	'	360.0	'I'	8	'A3'	'	2'	' '	23 42 29
'C'	'Dodge	'	'Diplomat	'	360.0	'I'	8	'A3'	'	2'	'X'	28 42 33
'C'	'Dodge	'	'Arrow GS	'	1.6	'L'	4	'A3'	'	2'	' '	54 72 61
'C'	'Dodge	'	'Arrow GS	'	1.6	'L'	4	'M4'	'	2'	' '	56 83 66
'C'	'Dodge	'	'Arrow GS	'	2.0	'L'	4	'A3'	'	2'	' '	45 60 51
'C'	'Dodge	'	'Arrow GS	'	2.0	'L'	4	'M5'	'	2'	' '	50 74 58
'C'	'Dodge	'	'Arrow GT	'	1.6	'L'	4	'A3'	'	2'	' '	54 72 61
'C'	'Dodge	'	'Arrow GT	'	1.6	'L'	4	'M5'	'	2'	' '	51 80 61
'C'	'Dodge	'	'Arrow GT	'	2.0	'L'	4	'A3'	'	2'	' '	45 60 51
'C'	'Dodge	'	'Arrow GT	'	2.0	'L'	4	'M5'	'	2'	' '	50 74 58
'C'	'Dodge	'	'Challenger	'	2.0	'L'	4	'A3'	'	2'	' '	42 59 48
'C'	'Dodge	'	'Challenger	'	2.0	'L'	4	'M5'	'	2'	' '	45 68 53
'C'	'Dodge	'	'Challenger	'	2.6	'L'	4	'A3'	'	2'	' '	42 58 48
'C'	'Dodge	'	'Challenger	'	2.6	'L'	4	'M5'	'	2'	' '	45 65 52
'C'	'Dodge	'	'Colt Coupe	'	1.6	'L'	4	'A3'	'	2'	' '	54 72 61
'C'	'Dodge	'	'Colt Coupe	'	1.6	'L'	4	'M4'	'	2'	' '	64 92 74
'C'	'Dodge	'	'Colt Sedan	'	1.6	'L'	4	'A3'	'	2'	' '	54 72 61
'C'	'Dodge	'	'Colt Sedan	'	1.6	'L'	4	'M4'	'	2'	' '	58 86 68
'C'	'Dodge	'	'Colt Wagon	'	2.0	'L'	4	'A3'	'	2'	' '	42 59 48
'C'	'Dodge	'	'Colt Wagon	'	2.0	'L'	4	'M5'	'	2'	' '	45 68 53
'C'	'Dodge	'	'Colt Wagon	'	2.6	'L'	4	'A3'	'	2'	' '	42 58 48
'C'	'Dodge	'	'Colt Wagon	'	2.6	'L'	4	'M5'	'	2'	' '	45 65 52
'C'	'Dodge	'	'Magnum XE	'	318.0	'I'	8	'A3'	'	2'	'X'	29 44 35
'C'	'Dodge	'	'Magnum XE	'	318.0	'I'	8	'A3'	'	4'	' '	25 44 31
'C'	'Dodge	'	'Magnum XE	'	360.0	'I'	8	'A3'	'	2'	' '	22 45 29
'C'	'Dodge	'	'Magnum XE	'	360.0	'I'	8	'A3'	'	2'	'X'	28 45 34
'C'	'Dodge	'	'Magnum XE	'	400.0	'I'	8	'A3'	'	4'	' '	22 39 27
'C'	'Dodge	'	'Monaco	'	225.0	'I'	6	'A3'	'	2'	'X'	33 45 38
'C'	'Dodge	'	'Monaco	'	225.0	'I'	6	'M3'	'	2'	'X'	34 47 39
'C'	'Dodge	'	'Monaco	'	318.0	'I'	8	'A3'	'	2'	'X'	29 44 35
'C'	'Dodge	'	'Monaco	'	318.0	'I'	8	'A3'	'	4'	' '	25 44 31
'C'	'Dodge	'	'Monaco	'	360.0	'I'	8	'A3'	'	2'	' '	22 42 28
'C'	'Dodge	'	'Monaco	'	360.0	'I'	8	'A3'	'	2'	'X'	28 44 34
'C'	'Dodge	'	'Monaco	'	400.0	'I'	8	'A3'	'	4'	' '	29 39 28
'C'	'Dodge	'	'Monaco Wagon	'	360.0	'I'	8	'A3'	'	2'	' '	24 40 29
'C'	'Dodge	'	'Monaco Wagon	'	360.0	'I'	8	'A3'	'	2'	'X'	26 39 30
'C'	'Dodge	'	'Monaco Wagon	'	400.0	'I'	8	'A3'	'	4'	' '	21 34 26
'C'	'Dodge	'	'Omni	'	1.7	'L'	4	'A3'	'	2'	' '	48 63 54
'C'	'Dodge	'	'Omni	'	1.7	'L'	4	'M4'	'	2'	' '	46 68 54
'O'	'Fiat	'	'X1/9	'	1.3	'L'	4	'M4'	'	2'	' '	39 60 44
'O'	'Fiat	'	'124 Spyder	'	1.8	'L'	4	'M5'	'	2'	' '	37 54 43
'O'	'Fiat	'	'128	'	1.3	'L'	4	'M4'	'	2'	' '	43 66 50
'O'	'Fiat	'	'131 Sedan	'	1.8	'L'	4	'A3'	'	2'	' '	35 44 39
'O'	'Fiat	'	'131 Sedan	'	1.8	'L'	4	'M5'	'	2'	' '	33 52 41
'O'	'Fiat	'	'131 Wagon	'	1.8	'L'	4	'A3'	'	2'	' '	35 44 39
'O'	'Fiat	'	'131 Wagon	'	1.8	'L'	4	'M5'	'	2'	' '	33 52 41
'F'	'Ford	'	'Fairmont	'	200.0	'I'	6	'A3'	'	1'	'X'	37 50 42
'F'	'Ford	'	'Fairmont	'	200.0	'I'	6	'M3'	'	1'	'X'	40 56 46
'F'	'Ford	'	'Fairmont	'	302.0	'I'	8	'A3'	'	2'	'X'	31 45 36

'F'	'Ford	'	'Fairmont	'	2.3	'L'	4	'A3'	'	2'	' '	41	59 48
'F'	'Ford	'	'Fairmont	'	2.3	'L'	4	'A3'	'	2'	'X'	42	59 48
'F'	'Ford	'	'Fairmont	'	2.3	'L'	4	'M4'	'	2'	'X'	43	65 51
'F'	'Ford	'	'Fairmont Wagon	'	200.0	'I'	6	'A3'	'	1'	'X'	35	45 39
'F'	'Ford	'	'Fairmont Wagon	'	200.0	'I'	6	'M3'	'	1'	'X'	37	56 44
'F'	'Ford	'	'Fairmont Wagon	'	302.0	'I'	8	'A3'	'	2'	'X'	31	45 36
'F'	'Ford	'	'Fairmont Wagon	'	2.3	'L'	4	'M4'	'	2'	'X'	43	65 51
'F'	'Ford	'	'Fiesta	'	1.6	'L'	4	'M4'	'	2'	'X'	65	88 74
'F'	'Ford	'	'Ford	'	302.0	'I'	8	'A3'	'	2'	'X'	28	42 33
'F'	'Ford	'	'Ford	'	351.0	'I'	8	'A3'	'	2'	' '	23	37 28
'F'	'Ford	'	'Ford	'	400.0	'I'	8	'A3'	'	2'	'X'	25	38 30
'F'	'Ford	'	'Ford	'	460.0	'I'	8	'A3'	'	2'	'X'	23	34 27
'F'	'Ford	'	'Ford	'	351.0	'I'	8	'A3'	'	2'	'X'	29	43 34
'F'	'Ford	'	'Ford Wagon	'	351.0	'I'	8	'A3'	'	2'	'X'	26	40 31
'F'	'Ford	'	'Ford Wagon	'	400.0	'I'	8	'A3'	'	2'	'X'	25	38 30
'F'	'Ford	'	'Ford Wagon	'	460.0	'I'	8	'A3'	'	2'	'X'	22	34 26
'F'	'Ford	'	'Granada	'	250.0	'I'	6	'A3'	'	1'	'X'	36	51 41
'F'	'Ford	'	'Granada	'	250.0	'I'	6	'M4'	'	1'	'X'	40	55 46
'F'	'Ford	'	'Granada	'	302.0	'I'	8	'A3'	'	2'	'X'	31	45 36
'F'	'Ford	'	'Granada	'	302.0	'I'	8	'M4'	'	2'	'X'	31	43 35
'F'	'Ford	'	'LTD II	'	302.0	'I'	8	'A3'	'	2'	'X'	28	42 33
'F'	'Ford	'	'LTD II	'	351.0	'I'	8	'A3'	'	2'	' '	22	36 27
'F'	'Ford	'	'LTD II	'	400.0	'I'	8	'A3'	'	2'	'X'	25	39 30
'F'	'Ford	'	'LTD II	'	351.0	'I'	8	'A3'	'	4'	'X'	27	39 31
'F'	'Ford	'	'LTD II	'	351.0	'I'	8	'A3'	'	2'	'X'	28	43 33
'F'	'Ford	'	'Mustang II	'	302.0	'I'	8	'A3'	'	2'	'X'	31	45 36
'F'	'Ford	'	'Mustang II	'	302.0	'I'	8	'M4'	'	2'	'X'	30	42 35
'F'	'Ford	'	'Mustang II	'	2.3	'L'	4	'A3'	'	2'	' '	41	59 48
'F'	'Ford	'	'Mustang II	'	2.3	'L'	4	'A3'	'	2'	'X'	42	59 48
'F'	'Ford	'	'Mustang II	'	2.3	'L'	4	'M4'	'	2'	'X'	43	65 51
'F'	'Ford	'	'Mustang II	'	2.8	'L'	6	'A3'	'	2'	'X'	31	39 34
'F'	'Ford	'	'Mustang II	'	2.8	'L'	6	'M4'	'	2'	'X'	38	50 43
'F'	'Ford	'	'Pinto	'	2.3	'L'	4	'A3'	'	2'	' '	40	59 47
'F'	'Ford	'	'Pinto	'	2.3	'L'	4	'A3'	'	2'	'X'	42	57 48
'F'	'Ford	'	'Pinto	'	2.3	'L'	4	'M4'	'	2'	'X'	49	69 56
'O'	'FOrd	'	'Pinto	'	2.8	'L'	6	'A3'	'	2'	'X'	35	42 38
'F'	'Ford	'	'Pinto Wagon	'	2.3	'L'	4	'A3'	'	2'	' '	41	59 48
'F'	'Ford	'	'Pinto Wagon	'	2.3	'L'	4	'A3'	'	2'	'X'	42	59 48
'F'	'Ford	'	'Pinto Wagon	'	2.3	'L'	4	'M4'	'	2'	'X'	43	65 51
'F'	'Ford	'	'Pinto Wagon	'	2.8	'L'	6	'A3'	'	2'	'X'	35	42 38
'F'	'Ford	'	'Thunderbird	'	302.0	'I'	8	'A3'	'	2'	'X'	28	42 33
'F'	'Ford	'	'Thunderbird	'	351.0	'I'	8	'A3'	'	2'	' '	22	36 27
'F'	'Ford	'	'Thunderbird	'	400.0	'I'	8	'A3'	'	2'	'X'	25	39 30
'F'	'Ford	'	'Thunderbird	'	351.0	'I'	8	'A3'	'	4'	'X'	27	39 31
'F'	'Ford	'	'Thunderbird	'	351.0	'I'	8	'A3'	'	2'	'X'	28	43 33
'O'	'Honda	'	'Accord	'	1.6	'L'	4	'A2'	'	2'	' '	48	66 55
'O'	'Honda	'	'Accord	'	1.6	'L'	4	'M5'	'	2'	' '	64	85 72
'O'	'Honda	'	'Civic CVCC	'	1.5	'L'	4	'M5'	'	3'	' '	69	86 76
'O'	'Honda	'	'Civic	'	1.2	'L'	4	'A2'	'	2'	' '	54	65 59
'O'	'Honda	'	'Civic	'	1.2	'L'	4	'M4'	'	2'	' '	63	78 69
'O'	'Honda	'	'Civic	'	1.2	'L'	4	'M5'	'	2'	' '	65	80 71
'O'	'Honda	'	'Civic Wagon	'	1.5	'L'	4	'A2'	'	2'	' '	54	64 58
'O'	'Honda	'	'Civic Wagon	'	1.5	'L'	4	'M4'	'	2'	' '	63	75 68
'O'	'Lancia	'	'Beta Coupe	'	1.8	'L'	4	'M5'	'	2'	' '	33	48 39
'O'	'Lancia	'	'Beta HPE	'	1.8	'L'	4	'M5'	'	2'	' '	33	48 39
'O'	'Lancia	'	'Beta Sedan	'	1.8	'L'	4	'M5'	'	2'	' '	33	48 39
'F'	'Lincoln-Merc'		'Bobcat	'	2.3	'L'	4	'A3'	'	2'	' '	40	59 47
'F'	'Lincoln-Merc'		'Bobcat	'	2.3	'L'	4	'A3'	'	2'	'X'	42	57 48
'F'	'Lincoln-Merc'		'Bobcat	'	2.3	'L'	4	'M4'	'	2'	'X'	49	69 56
'F'	'Lincoln-Merc'		'Bobcat	'	2.8	'L'	6	'A3'	'	2'	'X'	35	42 38
'F'	'Lincoln-Merc'		'Bobcat Wagon	'	2.3	'L'	4	'A3'	'	2'	' '	41	59 48
'F'	'Lincoln-Merc'		'Bobcat Wagon	'	2.3	'L'	4	'A3'	'	2'	'X'	42	59 48
'F'	'Lincoln-Merc'		'Bobcat Wagon	'	2.3	'L'	4	'M4'	'	2'	'X'	43	65 51
'F'	'Lincoln-Merc'		'Bobcat Wagon	'	2.8	'L'	6	'A3'	'	2'	'X'	35	42 38
'F'	'Lincoln-Merc'		'Mark V	'	400.0	'I'	8	'A3'	'	2'	'X'	25	39 30
'F'	'Lincoln-Merc'		'Mark V	'	460.0	'I'	8	'A3'	'	2'	'X'	23	34 27
'F'	'Lincoln-Merc'		'Cougar/XR-7	'	302.0	'I'	8	'A3'	'	2'	'X'	28	42 33
'F'	'Lincoln-Merc'		'Cougar/XR-7	'	351.0	'I'	8	'A3'	'	2'	' '	22	36 27
'F'	'Lincoln-Merc'		'Cougar/XR-7	'	400.0	'I'	8	'A3'	'	2'	'X'	25	39 30

'F'	'Lincoln-Merc'	'Cougar/XR-7	'	351.0	'I'	8	'A3'	' 4'	'X'	27 39 31
'F'	'Lincoln-Merc'	'Cougar/XR-7	'	351.0	'I'	8	'A3'	' 2'	'X'	28 43 33
'F'	'Lincoln-Merc'	'Lincoln	'	400.0	'I'	8	'A3'	' 2'	'X'	25 38 30
'F'	'Lincoln-Merc'	'Lincoln	'	460.0	'I'	8	'A3'	' 2'	'X'	22 34 26
'F'	'Lincoln-Merc'	'Versailles	'	302.0	'I'	8	'A3'	' 2'	'X'	31 45 36
'F'	'Lincoln-Merc'	'Mercury	'	351.0	'I'	8	'A3'	' 2'	' '	23 37 28
'F'	'Lincoln-Merc'	'Mercury	'	351.0	'I'	8	'A3'	' 2'	'X'	26 40 31
'F'	'Lincoln-Merc'	'Mercury	'	400.0	'I'	8	'A3'	' 2'	'X'	25 38 30
'F'	'Lincoln-Merc'	'Mercury	'	460.0	'I'	8	'A3'	' 2'	'X'	23 34 27
'F'	'Lincoln-Merc'	'Mercury Wagon	'	351.0	'I'	8	'A3'	' 2'	'X'	26 40 31
'F'	'Lincoln-Merc'	'Mercury Wagon	'	400.0	'I'	8	'A3'	' 2'	'X'	25 38 30
'F'	'Lincoln-Merc'	'Mercury Wagon	'	460.0	'I'	8	'A3'	' 2'	'X'	22 34 26
'F'	'Lincoln-Merc'	'Monarch	'	250.0	'I'	6	'A3'	' 1'	'X'	36 51 41
'F'	'Lincoln-Merc'	'Monarch	'	250.0	'I'	6	'M4'	' 1'	'X'	40 55 46
'F'	'Lincoln-Merc'	'Monarch	'	302.0	'I'	8	'A3'	' 2'	'X'	31 45 36
'F'	'Lincoln-Merc'	'Monarch	'	302.0	'I'	8	'M4'	' 2'	'X'	31 43 35
'F'	'Lincoln-Merc'	'Zephyr	'	200.0	'I'	6	'A3'	' 1'	'X'	37 50 42
'F'	'Lincoln-Merc'	'Zephyr	'	200.0	'I'	6	'M3'	' 1'	'X'	40 56 46
'F'	'Lincoln-Merc'	'Zephyr	'	302.0	'I'	8	'A3'	' 2'	'X'	31 45 36
'F'	'Lincoln-Merc'	'Zephyr	'	2.3	'L'	4	'A3'	' 2'	' '	41 59 48
'F'	'Lincoln-Merc'	'Zephyr	'	2.3	'L'	4	'A3'	' 2'	'X'	42 59 48
'F'	'Lincoln-Merc'	'Zephyr	'	2.3	'L'	4	'M4'	' 2'	'X'	43 65 51
'F'	'Lincoln-Merc'	'Zephyr Wagon	'	200.0	'I'	6	'A3'	' 1'	'X'	35 45 39
'F'	'Lincoln-Merc'	'Zephyr Wagon	'	200.0	'I'	6	'M3'	' 1'	'X'	37 56 44
'F'	'Lincoln-Merc'	'Zephyr Wagon	'	302.0	'I'	8	'A3'	' 2'	'X'	31 45 36
'F'	'Lincoln-Merc'	'Zephyr Wagon	'	2.3	'L'	4	'M4'	' 2'	'X'	43 65 51
'O'	'Mazda	'	'GLC	'	1.3	'L'	4	'A3'	' 1'	' '	59 69 63
'O'	'Mazda	'	'GLC	'	1.3	'L'	4	'M4'	' 1'	' '	63 78 69
'O'	'Mazda	'	'GLC	'	1.3	'L'	4'	M5	' 1'	' '	63 83 71
'O'	'Mazda	'	'929	'	1.8	'L'	4	'A3'	' 1'	' '	47 63 53
'O'	'Mazda	'	'929	'	1.8	'L'	4	'M4'	' 1'	' '	46 67 53
'O'	'Mazda	'	'929 Wagon	'	1.8	'L'	4	'A3'	' 1'	' '	47 63 53
'O'	'Mazda	'	'929 Wagon	'	1.8	'L'	4	'M4'	' 1'	' '	46 67 53
'O'	'Mercedes	'	'230	'	2.3	'L'	4	'A4'	' 1'	'X'	33 42 37
'O'	'Mercedes	'	'240D	'	2.4	'L'	4	'A4'	'FI'	' '	50 58 53
'O'	'Mercedes	'	'240D	'	2.4	'L'	4	'M4'	'FI'	' '	51 66 57
'O'	'Mercedes	'	'280E/280CE	'	2.8	'L'	6	'A4'	'FI'	'X'	27 36 31
'O'	'Mercedes	'	'300/CD	'	3.0	'L'	5	'A4'	'FI'	' '	43 54 48
'O'	'Mercedes	'	'450SEL	'	4.5	'L'	8	'A3'	'FI'	'X'	23 35 28
'O'	'Mercedes	'	'450SL/SLC	'	4.5	'L'	8	'A3'	'FI'	'X'	23 36 28
'G'	'Oldsmobile	'	'Custom Cruiser	'	350.0	'I'	8	'A3'	' 4'	'X'	29 41 33
'G'	'Oldsmobile	'	'Custom Cruiser	'	403.0	'I'	8	'A3'	' 4'	'X'	27 38 31
'G'	'Oldsmobile	'	'Cruiser-Diesel	'	5.7	'L'	8	'A3'	'FI'	' '	37 52 43
'G'	'Oldsmobile	'	'Cutlass	'	231.0	'I'	6	'A3'	' 2'	'X'	37 50 42
'G'	'Oldsmobile	'	'Cutlass	'	231.0	'I'	6	'M	' 2'	'X'	30 54 38
'G'	'Oldsmobile	'	'Cutlass	'	260.0	'I'	8	'A3'	' 2'	'X'	37 52 43
'G'	'Oldsmobile	'	'Cutlass	'	260.0	'I'	8	'M5'	' 2'	'X'	39 56 45
'G'	'Oldsmobile	'	'Cutlass	'	305.0	'I'	8	'A3'	' 2'	'X'	36 50 41
'G'	'Oldsmobile	'	'Cutlass	'	305.0	'I'	8	'A3'	' 4'	'X'	34 50 40
'G'	'Oldsmobile	'	'Cutlass	'	305.0	'I'	8	'M4'	' 2'	'X'	31 44 36
'G'	'Oldsmobile	'	'Cutlass Cruiser	'	231.0	'I'	6	'A3'	' 2'	'X'	37 52 42
'G'	'Oldsmobile	'	'Cutlass Cruiser	'	260.0	'I'	8	'A3'	' 2'	'X'	35 48 40
'G'	'Oldsmobile	'	'Cutlass Cruiser	'	305.0	'I'	8	'A3'	' 2'	'X'	32 48 38
'G'	'Oldsmobile	'	'Cutlass Cruiser	'	305.0	'I'	8	'A3'	' 4'	'X'	31 44 35
'G'	'Oldsmobile	'	'Cutlass Supreme'	231.0	'I'	6	'A3'	' 2'	'X'	37 50 42
'G'	'Oldsmobile	'	'Cutlass Supreme'	231.0	'I'	6	'M '	' 2'	'X'	30 54 38
'G'	'Oldsmobile	'	'Cutlass Supreme'	260.0	'I'	8	'A3'	' 2'	'X'	37 52 43
'G'	'Oldsmobile	'	'Cutlass Supreme'	260.0	'I'	8	'M5'	' 2'	'X'	39 56 45
'G'	'Oldsmobile	'	'Cutlass Supreme'	305.0	'I'	8	'A3'	' 2'	'X'	36 50 41
'G'	'Oldsmobile	'	'Cutlass Supreme'	305.0	'I'	8	'A3'	' 4'	'X'	34 50 40
'G'	'Oldsmobile	'	'Cutlass Supreme'	305.0	'I'	8	'M4'	' 2'	'X'	31 44 36
'G'	'Oldsmobile	'	'Delta 88	'	231.0	'I'	6	'A3'	' 2'	'X'	32 47 37
'G'	'Oldsmobile	'	'Delta 88	'	260.0	'I'	8	'A3'	' 2'	'X'	35 48 40
'G'	'Oldsmobile	'	'Delta 88	'	350.0	'I'	8	'A3'	' 4'	'X'	32 44 36
'G'	'Oldsmobile	'	'Delta 88	'	403.0	'I'	8	'A3'	' 4'	'X'	28 39 32
'G'	'Oldsmobile	'	'Delta 88-Diesel	'	5.7	'L'	8	'A3'	'FI'	' '	41 58 47
'G'	'Oldsmobile	'	'Ninety Eight	'	350.0	'I'	8	'A3'	' 4'	'X'	29 41 33
'G'	'Oldsmobile	'	'Ninety Eight	'	403.0	'I'	8	'A3'	' 4'	'X'	27 38 31
'G'	'Oldsmobile	'	'98-Diesel	'	5.7	'L'	8	'A3'	'FI'	' '	41 58 47

'G'	'Oldsmobile	'	'Omega	'	231.0	'I'	6	'A3'	' 2'	'X'	37 50 42	
'G'	'Oldsmobile	'	'Omega	'	231.0	'I'	6	'M '	' 2'	'X'	30 53 38	
'G'	'Oldsmobile	'	'Omega	'	305.0	'I'	8	'A3'	' 2'	'X'	32 48 38	
'G'	'Oldsmobile	'	'Omega	'	305.0	'I'	8	'M4'	' 2'	'X'	28 41 33	
'G'	'Oldsmobile	'	'Toronado	'	403.0	'I'	8	'A3'	' 4'	'X'	25 34 28	
'O'	'Peugeot	'	'504	'	2.0	'L'	4	'A3'	' 2'	' '	35 46 39	
'O'	'Peugeot	'	'504	'	2.0	'L'	4	'M4'	' 2'	' '	37 52 44	
'O'	'Peugeot	'	'504 Diesel	'	2.3	'L'	4	'A3'	'FI'	' '	48 60 53	
'O'	'Peugeot	'	'504 Diesel	'	2.3	'L'	4	'M4'	'FI'	' '	54 68 59	
'O'	'Peugeot	'	'504 Diesel Wag	'	2.3	'L'	4	'A3'	'FI'	' '	48 60 53	
'O'	'Peugeot	'	'504 Diesel Wag	'	2.3	'L'	4	'M4'	'FI'	' '	54 68 59	
'O'	'Peugeot	'	'504 Wagon	'	2.0	'L'	4	'A3'	' 2'	' '	35 44 39	
'O'	'Peugeot	'	'504 Wagon	'	2.0	'L'	4	'M4'	' 2'	' '	37 50 42	
'O'	'Peugeot	'	'604	'	2.7	'L'	6	'A3'	' 2'	' '	35 46 39	
'O'	'Peugeot	'	'604	'	2.7	'L'	6	'M4'	' 2'	' '	33 48 38	
'C'	'Plymouth	'	'Caravelle	'	225.0	'I'	6	'A3'	' 2'	'X'	34 47 39	
'C'	'Plymouth	'	'Caravelle	'	225.0	'I'	6	'M4'	' 2'	'X'	34 52 40	
'C'	'Plymouth	'	'Caravelle	'	318.0	'I'	8	'A3'	' 2'	'X'	29 43 34	
'C'	'Plymouth	'	'Caravelle	'	318.0	'I'	8	'A3'	' 4'	'X'	25 47 32	
'C'	'Plymouth	'	'Caravelle	'	318.0	'I'	8	'M4'	' 2'	'X'	27 49 34	
'C'	'Plymouth	'	'Caravelle	'	360.0	'I'	8	'A3'	' 2'	' '	23 42 29	
'C'	'Plymouth	'	'Caravelle	'	360.0	'I'	8	'A3'	' 2'	'X'	28 42 33	
'C'	'Plymouth	'	'Fury	'	225.0	'I'	6	'A3'	' 2'	'X'	33 45 38	
'C'	'Plymouth	'	'Fury	'	225.0	'I'	6	'M3'	' 2'	'X'	34 47 39	
'C'	'Plymouth	'	'Fury	'	318.0	'I'	8	'A3'	' 2'	'X'	29 44 35	
'C'	'Plymouth	'	'Fury	'	318.0	'I'	8	'A3'	' 4'	' '	25 44 31	
'C'	'Plymouth	'	'Fury	'	360.0	'I'	8	'A3'	' 2'	' '	22 42 28	
'C'	'Plymouth	'	'Fury	'	360.0	'I'	8	'A3'	' 2'	'X'	28 44 34	
'C'	'Plymouth	'	'Fury	'	400.0	'I'	8	'A3'	' 4'	' '	23 39 28	
'C'	'Plymouth	'	'Fury Wagon	'	360.0	'I'	8	'A3'	' 2'	' '	24 40 29	
'C'	'Plymouth	'	'Fury Wagon	'	360.0	'I'	8	'A3'	' 2'	'X'	26 39 30	
'C'	'Plymouth	'	'Fury Wagon	'	400.0	'I'	8	'A3'	' 4'	' '	21 34 26	
'C'	'Plymouth	'	'Horizon	'	1.7	'L'	4	'A3'	' 2'	' '	48 63 54	
'C'	'Plymouth	'	'Horizon	'	1.7	'L'	4	'M4'	' 2'	' '	46 68 54	
'C'	'Plymouth	'	'Ply Arrow GS	'	1.6	'L'	4	'A3'	' 2'	' '	54 72 61	
'C'	'Plymouth	'	'Ply Arrow GS	'	1.6	'L'	4	'M4'	' 2'	' '	56 83 66	
'C'	'Plymouth	'	'Ply Arrow GS	'	2.0	'L'	4	'A3'	' 2'	' '	45 60 51	
'C'	'Plymouth	'	'Ply Arrow GS	'	2.0	'L'	4	'M5'	' 2'	' '	50 74 58	
'C'	'Plymouth	'	'Ply Arrow GT	'	1.6	'L'	4	'A3'	' 2'	' '	54 72 61	
'C'	'Plymouth	'	'Ply Arrow GT	'	1.6	'L'	4	'M5'	' 2'	' '	51 80 61	
'C'	'Plymouth	'	'Ply Arrow GT	'	2.0	'L'	4	'A3'	' 2'	' '	45 60 51	
'C'	'Plymouth	'	'Ply Arrow GT	'	2.0	'L'	4	'M5'	' 2'	' '	50 74 58	
'C'	'Plymouth	'	'Ply Colt Coupe	'	1.6	'L'	4	'A3'	' 2'	' '	54 72 61	
'C'	'Plymouth	'	'Ply Colt Coupe	'	1.6	'L'	4	'M4'	' 2'	' '	64 92 74	
'C'	'Plymouth	'	'Ply Colt Sedan	'	1.6	'L'	4	'A3'	' 2'	' '	54 72 61	
'C'	'Plymouth	'	'Ply Colt Sedan	'	1.6	'L'	4	'M4'	' 2'	' '	58 86 68	
'C'	'Plymouth	'	'Ply Colt Wagon	'	2.0	'L'	4	'A3'	' 2'	' '	42 59 48	
'C'	'Plymouth	'	'Ply Colt Wagon	'	2.0	'L'	4	'M5'	' 2'	' '	45 68 53	
'C'	'Plymouth	'	'Ply Colt Wagon	'	2.6	'L'	4	'A3'	' 2'	' '	42 58 48	
'C'	'Plymouth	'	'Ply Colt Wagon	'	2.6	'L'	4	'M5'	' 2'	' '	45 65 52	
'C'	'Plymouth	'	'Ply Sapporo	'	2.0	'L'	4	'A3'	' 2'	' '	42 59 48	
'C'	'Plymouth	'	'Ply Sapporo	'	2.0	'L'	4	'M5'	' 2'	' '	45 68 53	
'C'	'Plymouth	'	'Ply Sapporo	'	2.6	'L'	4	'A3'	' 2'	' '	42 58 48	
'C'	'Plymouth	'	'Ply Sapporo	'	2.6	'L'	4	'M5'	' 2'	' '	45 65 52	
'C'	'Plymouth	'	'Volare	'	225.0	'I'	6	'A3'	' 1'	'X'	40 53 45	
'C'	'Plymouth	'	'Volare	'	225.0	'I'	6	'A3'	' 2'	'X'	35 52 41	
'C'	'Plymouth	'	'Volare	'	225.0	'I'	6	'M3'	' 1'	'X'	39 52 44	
'C'	'Plymouth	'	'Volare	'	225.0	'I'	6	'M3'	' 2'	'X'	35 50 41	
'C'	'Plymouth	'	'Volare	'	225.0	'I'	6	'M4'	' 1'	'X'	38 60 46	
'C'	'Plymouth	'	'Volare	'	225.0	'I'	6	'M4'	' 2'	'X'	36 58 44	
'C'	'Plymouth	'	'Volare	'	318.0	'I'	8	'A3'	' 2'	'X'	29 44 35	
'C'	'Plymouth	'	'Volare	'	318.0	'I'	8	'A3'	' 4'	' '	25 44 32	
'C'	'Plymouth	'	'Volare	'	318.0	'I'	8	'M4'	' 2'	'X'	27 49 34	
'C'	'Plymouth	'	'Volare	'	360.0	'I'	8	'A3'	' 2'	' '	23 43 29	
'C'	'Plymouth	'	'Volare	'	360.0	'I'	8	'A3'	' 2'	'X'	28 43 33	
'C'	'Plymouth	'	'Volare	'	360.0	'I'	8	'A3'	' 4'	' '	22 38 27	
'C'	'Plymouth	'	'Volare Wagon	'	225.0	'I'	6	'A3'	' 2'	'X'	33 45 38	
'C'	'Plymouth	'	'Volare Wagon	'	225.0	'I'	6	'M3'	' 2'	'X'	34 47 39	
'C'	'Plymouth	'	'Volare Wagon	'	225.0	'I'	6	'M4'	' 2'	'X'	34 52 40	

'C'	'Plymouth	'	'Volare Wagon	'	318.0	'I'	8	'A3'	'	2'	'X'	29 43 34
'C'	'Plymouth	'	'Volare Wagon	'	318.0	'I'	8	'A3'	'	4'	' '	25 45 32
'C'	'Plymouth	'	'Volare Wagon	'	318.0	'I'	8	'M4'	'	2'	'X'	27 49 34
'C'	'Plymouth	'	'Volare Wagon	'	360.0	'I'	8	'A3'	'	2'	' '	23 42 29
'C'	'Plymouth	'	'Volare Wagon	'	360.0	'I'	8	'A3'	'	2'	'X'	28 42 33
'G'	'Pontiac	'	'Acadian	'	1.6	'L'	4	'A3'	'	1'	'X'	49 63 54
'G'	'Pontiac	'	'Acadian	'	1.6	'L'	4	'M4'	'	1'	'X'	59 78 67
'G'	'Pontiac	'	'Firebird	'	231.0	'I'	6	'A3'	'	2'	'X'	32 47 37
'G'	'Pontiac	'	'Firebird	'	231.0	'I'	6	'M3'	'	2'	'X'	31 48 37
'G'	'Pontiac	'	'Firebird	'	305.0	'I'	8	'A3'	'	2'	'X'	32 48 38
'G'	'Pontiac	'	'Firebird	'	305.0	'I'	8	'M4'	'	2'	'X'	28 41 33
'G'	'Pontiac	'	'Firebird	'	350.0	'I'	8	'A3'	'	4'	'X'	31 44 36
'G'	'Pontiac	'	'Firebird	'	350.0	'I'	8	'M4'	'	4'	'X'	27 36 30
'G'	'Pontiac	'	'Firebird	'	400.0	'I'	8	'A3'	'	4'	'X'	26 34 29
'G'	'Pontiac	'	'Firebird	'	400.0	'I'	8	'M4'	'	4'	'X'	23 32 27
'G'	'Pontiac	'	'Grand Prix	'	231.0	'I'	6	'A3'	'	2'	'X'	37 52 42
'G'	'Pontiac	'	'Grand Prix	'	231.0	'I'	6	'M3'	'	2'	'X'	30 54 38
'G'	'Pontiac	'	'Grand Prix	'	301.0	'I'	8	'A3'	'	2'	'X'	34 48 39
'G'	'Pontiac	'	'Grand Prix	'	301.0	'I'	8	'A3'	'	4'	'X'	33 47 38
'G'	'Pontiac	'	'Lemans	'	231.0	'I'	6	'A3'	'	2'	'X'	37 50 42
'G'	'Pontiac	'	'Lemans	'	231.0	'I'	6	'M '	'	2'	'X'	30 54 38
'G'	'Pontiac	'	'Lemans	'	301.0	'I'	8	'A3'	'	2'	'X'	34 48 39
'G'	'Pontiac	'	'Lemans	'	301.0	'I'	8	'A3'	'	4'	'X'	33 47 38
'G'	'Pontiac	'	'Lemans	'	305.0	'I'	8	'A3'	'	2'	'X'	36 50 41
'G'	'Pontiac	'	'Lemans	'	3.3	'L'	6	'A3'	'	2'	'X'	38 54 44
'G'	'Pontiac	'	'Lemans	'	3.3	'L'	6	'M3'	'	2'	'X'	41 57 47
'G'	'Pontiac	'	'Lemans Wagon	'	231.0	'I'	6	'A3'	'	2'	'X'	37 52 42
'G'	'Pontiac	'	'Lemans Wagon	'	305.0	'I'	8	'A3'	'	2'	'X'	31 44 36
'G'	'Pontiac	'	'Lemans Wagon	'	305.0	'I'	8	'A3'	'	4'	'X'	31 44 35
'G'	'Pontiac	'	'Phoenix	'	151.0	'I'	4	'A3'	'	2'	'X'	43 55 47
'G'	'Pontiac	'	'Phoenix	'	231.0	'I'	6	'A3'	'	2'	'X'	36 50 41
'G'	'Pontiac	'	'Phoenix	'	231.0	'I'	6	'M3'	'	2'	'X'	31 50 37
'G'	'Pontiac	'	'Phoenix	'	305.0	'I'	8	'A3'	'	2'	'X'	32 48 38
'G'	'Pontiac	'	'Phoenix	'	305.0	'I'	8	'M4'	'	2'	'X'	28 41 33
'G'	'Pontiac	'	'Pontiac	'	250.0	'I'	6	'A3'	'	1'	'X'	35 49 40
'G'	'Pontiac	'	'Pontiac	'	305.0	'I'	8	'A3'	'	2'	'X'	32 48 38
'G'	'Pontiac	'	'Pontiac	'	350.0	'I'	8	'A3'	'	4'	'X'	31 44 36
'G'	'Pontiac	'	'Pontiac Wagon	'	305.0	'I'	8	'A3'	'	2'	'X'	30 45 35
'G'	'Pontiac	'	'Pontiac Wagon	'	350.0	'I'	8	'A3'	'	4'	'X'	28 41 33
'G'	'Pontiac	'	'Sunbird	'	151.0	'I'	4	'A3'	'	2'	'X'	42 55 47
'G'	'Pontiac	'	'Sunbird	'	151.0	'I'	4	'M '	'	2'	'X'	46 67 53
'G'	'Pontiac	'	'Sunbird	'	231.0	'I'	6	'A3'	'	2'	'X'	37 52 42
'G'	'Pontiac	'	'Sunbird	'	231.0	'I'	6	'M '	'	2'	'X'	31 55 38
'G'	'Pontiac	'	'Sunbird	'	305.0	'I'	8	'A3'	'	2'	'X'	33 47 38
'G'	'Pontiac	'	'Sunbird	'	305.0	'I'	8	'M4'	'	2'	'X'	31 44 36
'G'	'Pontiac	'	'Sunbird Wagon	'	151.0	'I'	4	'A3'	'	2'	'X'	42 55 47
'G'	'Pontiac	'	'Sunbird Wagon	'	151.0	'I'	4	'M '	'	2'	'X'	46 67 53
'G'	'Pontiac	'	'Sunbird Wagon	'	231.0	'I'	6	'A3'	'	2'	'X'	37 52 42
'G'	'Pontiac	'	'Sunbird Wagon	'	231.0	'I'	6	'M '	'	2'	'X'	32 56 40
'O'	'Porsche	'	'Turbo Carrera	'	3.3	'L'	6	'M4'	'FI'		'X'	22 43 28
'O'	'Porsche	'	'911SC	'	3.0	'L'	6	'M5'	'FI'		'X'	29 51 36
'O'	'Porsche	'	'924	'	2.0	'L'	4	'A3'	'FI'		'X'	36 51 41
'O'	'Porsche	'	'924	'	2.0	'L'	4	'M4'	'FI'		'X'	38 58 45
'O'	'Porsche	'	'928	'	4.5	'L'	8	'A3'	'FI'		'X'	22 32 25
'O'	'Porsche	'	'928	'	4.5	'L'	8	'M5'	'FI'		'X'	23 36 28
'O'	'Renault	'	'12 TL	'	85.0	'I'	4	'A3'	'	2'	' '	40 53 45
'O'	'Renault	'	'12 TL	'	85.0	'I'	4	'M4'	'	2'	' '	51 68 57
'O'	'Renault	'	'30	'	163.0	'I'	6	'A3'	'	2'	' '	29 38 32
'O'	'Renault	'	'30	'	163.0	'I'	6	'M4'	'	2'	' '	27 43 33
'O'	'Renault	'	'5 GTL	'	79.0	'I'	4	'M4'	'	2'	' '	63 82 71
'O'	'Rolls Royce	'	'Camargue	'	412.0	'I'	8	'A3'	'	2'	'X'	20 26 22
'O'	'Rolls Royce	'	'Corniche	'	412.0	'I'	8	'A3'	'	2'	'X'	20 26 22
'O'	'Rolls Royce	'	'Shadow II	'	412.0	'I'	8	'A3'	'	2'	'X'	20 26 22
'O'	'Rolls Royce	'	'Silver Wraith	'	412.0	'I'	8	'A3'	'	2'	'X'	20 26 22
'O'	'Saab	'	'Saab 99	'	2.0	'L'	4	'A3'	'FI'		' '	35 44 39
'O'	'Saab	'	'Saab 99	'	2.0	'L'	4	'M4'	'FI'		' '	40 49 43
'O'	'Saab	'	'Saab 99 Turbo	'	2.0	'L'	4	'M4'	'FI'		'X'	38 53 43
'O'	'Subaru	'	'Sed & HTP	'	1.6	'L'	4	'A3'	'	2'	' '	50 64 56
'O'	'Subaru	'	'Sed & HTP	'	1.6	'L'	4	'M4'	'	2'	' '	60 79 68

'O'	'Subaru	'	'Sed & HTP	'	1.6	'L'	4	'M5'	'	2'	'	'	61 90 71
'O'	'Subaru	'	'Wagon	'	1.6	'L'	4	'A3'	'	2'	'	'	48 64 55
'O'	'Subaru	'	'Wagon	'	1.6	'L'	4	'M4'	'	2'	'	'	55 71 60
'O'	'Subaru	'	'Wagon	'	1.6	'L'	4	'M5'	'	2'	'	'	55 77 61
'O'	'Subaru	'	'Wagon 4 x 4	'	1.6	'L'	4	'M4'	'	2'	'	'	50 69 56
'O'	'Subaru	'	'FE Coupe	'	1.6	'L'	4	'M5'	'	2'	'	'	64 96 75
'O'	'Toyota	'	'Celica	'	134.0	'I'	4	'A3'	'	2'	'	'	42 52 46
'O'	'Toyota	'	'Celica	'	134.0	'I'	4	'M '	'	2'	'	'	40 65 48
'O'	'Toyota	'	'Corolla	'	71.0	'I'	4	'M4'	'	2'	'	'	54 83 64
'O'	'Toyota	'	'Corolla	'	97.0	'I'	4	'A3'	'	2'	'	'	48 62 53
'O'	'Toyota	'	'Corolla	'	97.0	'I'	4	'M '	'	2'	'	'	53 72 60
'O'	'Toyota	'	'Corolla Wagon	'	97.0	'I'	4	'A3'	'	2'	'	'	48 62 53
'O'	'Toyota	'	'Corolla Wagon	'	97.0	'I'	4	'M '	'	2'	'	'	53 72 60
'O'	'Toyota	'	'Corona	'	134.0	'I'	4	'A3'	'	2'	'	'	37 45 40
'O'	'Toyota	'	'Corona	'	134.0	'I'	4	'M5'	'	2'	'	'	38 54 44
'O'	'Toyota	'	'Corona	'	134.0	'I'	4	'A3'	'	2'	'	'	37 45 40
'O'	'Toyota	'	'Corona Wagon	'	134.0	'I'	4	'M5'	'	2'	'	'	38 54 44
'O'	'Toyota	'	'Cressida	'	156.0	'I'	6	'A4'	'	2'	'X'	'	38 52 43
'O'	'Triumph	'	'Spitfire	'	1.5	'L'	4	'M4'	'	1'	'X'	'	41 61 48
'O'	'Triumph	'	'Spitfire (O/D)	'	1.5	'L'	4	'M4'	'	1'	'X'	'	43 68 52
'O'	'Triumph	'	'TR-7	'	2.0	'L'	4	'A3'	'	2'	'	'	38 52 43
'O'	'Triumph	'	'TR-7	'	2.0	'L'	4	'M5'	'	2'	'	'	42 53 46
'O'	'Volkswagen	'	'Rabbit	'	1.5	'L'	4	'A3'	'FI'	'	'	43 61 49
'O'	'Volkswagen	'	'Rabbit	'	1.5	'L'	4	'M4'	'FI'	'	'	47 72 56
'O'	'Volkswagen	'	'Rabbit Diesel	'	1.5	'L'	4	'M4'	'FI'	'	'	76 01 85
'O'	'Volkswagen	'	'Scirocco	'	1.5	'L'	4	'A3'	'FI'	'	'	43 61 49
'O'	'Volkswagen	'	'Scirocco	'	1.5	'L'	4	'M4'	'FI'	'	'	47 72 56
'O'	'Volkswagen	'	'Beetle Conv.	'	1.6	'L'	4	'M4'	'FI'	'	'	41 58 46
'O'	'Volvo	'	'242A	'	2.1	'L'	4	'A3'	'	1'	'	'	38 51 43
'O'	'Volvo	'	'242 GT(O/D)	'	2.1	'L'	4	'M4'	'FI'	'	'	38 63 46
'O'	'Volvo	'	'242 M	'	2.1	'L'	4	'M4'	'FI'	'	'	36 59 44
'O'	'Volvo	'	'244 A	'	2.1	'L'	4	'A3'	'	1'	'	'	38 51 43
'O'	'Volvo	'	'244 GL(O/D)	'	2.1	'L'	4	'M4'	'FI'	'	'	38 63 46
'O'	'Volvo	'	'244 GLA	'	2.1	'L'	4	'A3'	'FI'	'	'	37 50 42
'O'	'Volvo	'	'244 M	'	2.1	'L'	4	'M4'	'	1'	'	'	36 59 44
'O'	'Volvo	'	'245 A	'	2.1	'L'	4	'A3'	'	1'	'	'	36 50 41
'O'	'Volvo	'	'245 O(O/D)	'	2.1	'L'	4	'M4'	'	1'	'	'	37 62 45
'O'	'Volvo	'	'264 GLA	'	2.7	'L'	6	'A3'	'FI'	'X'	31 43 35
'O'	'Volvo	'	'264 GLO(O/D)	'	2.7	'L'	6	'M4'	'FI'	'X'	29 52 36
'O'	'Volvo	'	'265 GLA	'	2.7	'L'	6	'A3'	'FI'	'X'	31 43 35
'O'	'Volvo	'	'265 GLO(O/D)	'	2.7	'L'	6	'M4'	'FI'	'X'	29 52 36

O
Areas Under the Standard Normal Curve

The following table gives the percentage area under the standard normal (z) curve between 0 and z as indicated in the diagram. Since the curve is symmetric, the area for a given value of z also applies for $-z$. The values given in the table are rounded to the number of digits shown.

Figure O.1   Standard normal (z) curve showing area given by table.

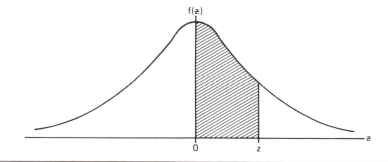

Figure O.2   Table of the area under the standard normal curve.

z	.00	.01	.02	.03	.04	.05	.06	.07	.08	.09
0.0	.0000	.0040	.0080	.0120	.0160	.0199	.0239	.0279	.0319	.0359
0.1	.0398	.0438	.0478	.0517	.0557	.0596	.0636	.0675	.0714	.0753
0.2	.0793	.0832	.0871	.0910	.0948	.0987	.1026	.1064	.1103	.1141
0.3	.1179	.1217	.1255	.1293	.1331	.1368	.1406	.1443	.1480	.1517
0.4	.1554	.1591	.1628	.1664	.1700	.1736	.1772	.1808	.1844	.1879
0.5	.1915	.1950	.1985	.2019	.2054	.2088	.2123	.2157	.2190	.2224
0.6	.2257	.2291	.2324	.2357	.2389	.2422	.2454	.2486	.2518	.2549
0.7	.2580	.2612	.2642	.2673	.2704	.2734	.2764	.2794	.2823	.2852
0.8	.2881	.2910	.2939	.2967	.2995	.3023	.3051	.3078	.3106	.3133
0.9	.3159	.3186	.3112	.3238	.3264	.3289	.3315	.3340	.3365	.3389
1.0	.3413	.3438	.3461	.3485	.3508	.3531	.3554	.3577	.3599	.3621
1.1	.3643	.3665	.3686	.3708	.3729	.3749	.3770	.3790	.3810	.3830
1.2	.3849	.3869	.3888	.3907	.3925	.3944	.3962	.3980	.3997	.4015
1.3	.4032	.4049	.4066	.4082	.4099	.4115	.4131	.4147	.4162	.4177
1.4	.4192	.4207	.4222	.4236	.4251	.4265	.4279	.4292	.4306	.4319
1.5	.4332	.4345	.4357	.4370	.4382	.4394	.4406	.4418	.4429	.4441
1.6	.4452	.4463	.4474	.4484	.4495	.4505	.4515	.4525	.4535	.4545
1.7	.4554	.4564	.4573	.4582	.4591	.4599	.4608	.4616	.4625	.4633
1.8	.4641	.4649	.4656	.4664	.4671	.4678	.4686	.4693	.4699	.4706
1.9	.4713	.4719	.4726	.4732	.4738	.4744	.4750	.4756	.4761	.4767
2.0	.4772	.4778	.4783	.4788	.4793	.4798	.4803	.4808	.4812	.4817
2.1	.4821	.4826	.4830	.4834	.4838	.4842	.4846	.4850	.4854	.4857
2.2	.4861	.4864	.4868	.4871	.4875	.4878	.4881	.4884	.4887	.4890
2.3	.4893	.4896	.4898	.4901	.4904	.4906	.4909	.4911	.4913	.4916
2.4	.4918	.4920	.4922	.4925	.4927	.4929	.4931	.4932	.4934	.4936
2.5	.4938	.4940	.4941	.4943	.4945	.4946	.4948	.4949	.4951	.4952
2.6	.4953	.4955	.4956	.4957	.4959	.4960	.4961	.4962	.4963	.4964
2.7	.4965	.4966	.4967	.4968	.4969	.4970	.4971	.4972	.4973	.4974
2.8	.4974	.4975	.4976	.4977	.4977	.4978	.4979	.4979	.4980	.4981
2.9	.4981	.4982	.4982	.4983	.4984	.4984	.4985	.4985	.4986	.4986
3.0	.49865	.4987	.4987	.4988	.4988	.4989	.4989	.4989	.4990	.4990
3.1	.49903	.4991	.4991	.4991	.4992	.4992	.4992	.4992	.4993	.4993
3.2	.4993129	.4993	.4994	.4994	.4994	.4994	.4994	.4995	.4995	.4995
3.3	.4995166	.4995	.4995	.4996	.4996	.4996	.4996	.4996	.4996	.4997
3.4	.4996631	.4997	.4997	.4997	.4997	.4997	.4997	.4997	.4998	.4998
3.5	.4997674	.4998	.4998	.4998	.4998	.4998	.4998	.4998	.4998	.4998
3.6	.4998409	.4998	.4999	.4999	.4999	.4999	.4999	.4999	.4999	.4999
3.7	.4998922	.4999	.4999	.4999	.4999	.4999	.4999	.4999	.4999	.4999
3.8	.4999277	.4999	.4999	.4999	.4999	.4999	.4999	.5000	.5000	.5000
3.9	.4999519	.5000	.5000	.5000	.5000	.5000	.5000	.5000	.5000	.5000
4.0	.4999683									
4.5	.4999966									
5.0	.4999997133									

P
Built-in WATFIV-S Functions

This appendix describes the built-in functions which are part of the WATFIV-S compiler. These functions are supplied automatically by the compiler whenever a program references them. The following notation is used in the tables to describe the type of the function arguments and the type of the function itself:

> i2 - an INTEGER*2 expression (half-word integer)
> i4 - an INTEGER*4 expression (full-word integer)
> r4 - a REAL*4 expression (single-precision real)
> r8 - a REAL*8 expression (double-precision real)
> c8 - a COMPLEX*8 expression (single-precision complex)
> c16 - a COMPLEX*16 expression (double-precision complex)

In the definition of the function the following notation is used:

> a - argument (used when only one argument eists)
> a_1 - argument number 1
> a_2 - argument number 2
> . . . - many arguments

Purpose	Function name and type of arguments	Definition	Result
Absolute value	IABS(i4)	$\lvert a \rvert$	i4
	ABS(r4)		r4
	DABS(r8)		r8
	CABS(c8)	$\sqrt{a^2+b^2}$ for $a+bi$	r4
	CDABS(c16)		r8

Purpose	Function name and type of arguments	Definition	Result
Truncation	INT(r4) AINT(r4) DINT(r8)	sign of a times largest integer $\leq |a|$	i4 r4 r8
Modular arithmetic	MOD(i4,i4) AMOD(r4,r4) DMOD(r8,r8)	$a_1 \pmod{a_2} = a_1 - a_2 \times \text{int}(a_1/a_2)$	i4 r4 r8
Largest value	MAX0(i4,i4,...) MAX1(r4,r4,...) AMAX0(i4,i4,...) AMAX1(r4,r4,...) DMAX1(r8,r8,...)	$\max(a_1, a_2, \dots)$	i4 i4 r4 r4 r8
Smallest value	MIN0(i4,i4,...) MIN1(r4,r4,...) AMIN0(i4,i4,...) AMIN1(r4,r4,...) DMIN1(r8,r8,...)	$\min(a_1, a_2, \dots)$	i4 i4 r4 r4 r8
Square root	SQRT(r4) DSQRT(r8) CSQRT(c8) CDSQRT(c16)	$\sqrt{a}$	r4 r8 c8 c16
Type conversion	IFIX(r4) HFIX(r4)	Convert from REAL to INTEGER	i4 i2
	FLOAT(i4) DFLOAT(i4)	Convert from INTEGER to REAL	r4 r8
	SNGL(r8) DBLE(r4)	Truncate REAL*8 to REAL*4 Convert REAL*4 to REAL*8	r4 r8
	CMPLX(r4,r4) DCMPLX(r8,r8)	Convert two REAL values to COMPLEX	c8 c16
	REAL(c8)	Obtain real part of COMPLEX value	r4
	AIMAG(c8)	Obtain imaginary part of COMPLEX value	r4
Complex conjucate	CONJG(c8) DCONJG(c16)	$(x, -y)$ for $a = (x, y)$	c8 c16
Transfer of Sign	ISIGN(i4,i4) SIGN(r4,r4) DSIGN(r8,r8)	Sign of a_2 times $|a_1|$ $\text{sign}(a_2) = \begin{cases} +1, & a_2 \geq 0 \\ -1, & a_2 < 0 \end{cases}$	i4 r4 r8
Positive difference	IDIM(i4,i4) DIM(r4,r4)	$a_1 - \min(a_1, a_2)$	i4 r4
Exponential	EXP(r4) DEXP(r8) CEXP(c8) CDEXP(c16)	e^a where $e \simeq 2.718282$	r4 r8 c8 c16

Purpose	Function name and type of arguments	Definition	Result
Natural logarithm	ALOG(r4)	$\log_e a$	r4
	DLOG(r8)		r8
	CLOG(c8)		c8
	CDLOG(c16)		c16
Common logarithm	ALOG10(r4)	$\log_{10} a$	r4
	DLOG10(r8)		r8
Sine	SIN(r4)	sine a (a must be in radians)	r4
	DSIN(r8)		r8
	CSIN(c8)		c8
	CDSIN(c16)		c16
Cosine	COS(r4)	cosine a (a must be in radians)	r4
	DCOS(r8)		r8
	CCOS(c8)		c8
	CDCOS(c16)		c16
Tangent	TAN(r4)	tangent a (a must be in radians)	r4
	DTAN(r8)		r8
Cotangent	COTAN(r4)	cotangent a (a must be in radians)	r4
	DCOTAN(r8)		r8
Arcsine	ARSIN(r4)	$x = \text{arcsine } a\ (-\pi/2 \leq x \leq +\pi/2$	r4
	DARSIN(r8)		r8
Arccosine	ARCOS(r4)	$x = \text{arccosine } a\ (-\pi/2 \leq x \leq +\pi/2)$	r4
	DARCOS(r8)		r8
Arctangent	ATAN(r4)	$x = \text{arctangent } a\ (-\pi/2 \leq x \leq +\pi/2)$	r4
	DATAN(r8)		r8
	ATAN2(r4,r4)	$x = \text{arctangent}(a1/a2)\ (-\pi/2 \leq x \leq +\pi/2)$	r4
	DATAN2(r8,r8)		r8
Hyperbolic sine	SINH(r4)	sinh a	r4
	DSINH(r8)		r8
Hyberbolic cosine	COSH(r4)	cosh a	r4
	DCOSH(r8)		r8
Hyperbolic tangent	TANH(r4)	tanh a	r4
	DTANH(r8)		r8
Error function	ERF(r4)		r4
	DERF(r8)	$\text{erf}(a) = \dfrac{2}{\sqrt{\pi}} \displaystyle\int_0^a e^{-t^2} dt$	r8
	ERFC(r4)	$1 - \text{erf}(a)$	r4
	DERFC(r8)		r8
Gamma function	GAMMA(r4)		r4
	DGAMMA(r8)	$g(a) = \displaystyle\int_0^\infty t^{a-1} e^{-t} dt$	r8
Log-gamma	ALGAMA(r4)	$\log_e (g(a))$	r4
	DLGAMA(r8)		r8

Q
WATFIV-S Error Messages

The type of error messages output by the WATFIV-S compiler varies from installation to installation. Although it usually prints out the following error messages in their entirety, some institutions restrict the message to the left code only. For this reason, a complete set of error messages is included in this Appendix.

Messages for Accounting and UOW Version
AC-0   ACCOUNT NUMBER INVALID
AC-1   ACCOUNT TYPE INVALID
AC-2   PROJECT NAME INVALID
AC-3   ACCOUNT HAS EXPIRED
AC-4   ALLOWED TIME HAS EXPIRED
AC-5   THE NUMBER OF STATEMENTS TO BE EXECUTED HAS BEEN EXCEEDED

Assembler Language Subprogrammes
AL-0   MISSING END CARD ON ASSEMBLY LANGUAGE OBJECT DECK
AL-1   ENTRY-POINT OR CSECT NAME IN AN OBJECT DECK WAS PREVIOUSLY DEFINED. FIRST DEFINITION USED

BLOCK DATA Statements
BD-0   EXECUTABLE STATEMENTS ARE ILLEGAL IN BLOCK DATA SUBPROGRAMS
BD-1   IMPROPER BLOCK DATA STATEMENT

Card Format and Contents
CC-0   COLUMNS 1-5 OF CONTINUATION CARD ARE NOT BLANK.
       PROBABLE CAUSE: STATEMENT PUNCHED TO LEFT OF COLUMN 7
CC-1   LIMIT OF 5 CONTINUATION CARDS EXCEEDED
CC-2   INVALID CHARACTER IN FORTRAN STATEMENT. A '$' WAS INSERTED IN THE SOURCE LISTING
CC-3   FIRST CARD OF A PROGRAM IS A CONTINUATION CARD.
       PROBABLE CAUSE: STATEMENT PUNCHED TO LEFT OF COLUMN 7
CC-4   STATEMENT TOO LONG TO COMPILE (SCAN-STACK OVERFLOW)
CC-5   A BLANK CARD WAS ENCOUNTERED
CC-6   KEYPUNCH USED DIFFERS FROM KEYPUNCH SPECIFIED ON JOB CARD
CC-7   THE FIRST CHARACTER OF THE STATEMENT WAS NOT ALPHABETIC
CC-8   INVALID CHARACTER(S) ARE CONCATENATED WITH THE FORTRAN KEYWORD
CC-9   INVALID CHARACTERS IN COLUMNS 1-5. STATEMENT NUMBER IGNORED.
       PROBABLE CAUSE: STATEMENT PUNCHED TO LEFT OF COLUMN 7

CC-A   CONTROL CARDS MAY NOT BE CONTINUED
CC-B   CONTROL CARDS MUST BE IN PROGRAM SEGMENT

COMMON Statement

CM-0   THE VARIABLE IS ALREADY IN COMMON
CM-1   OTHER COMPILERS MAY NOT ALLOW COMMONED VARIABLES TO BE INITIALIZED IN
         OTHER THAN A BLOCK DATA SUBPROGRAM
CM-2   ILLEGAL USE OF A COMMON BLOCK OR NAMELIST NAME

FORTRAN Type Constants

CN-0   MIXED REAL*4, REAL*8 IN COMPLEX CONSTANT; REAL*8 ASSUMED FOR BOTH
CN-1   AN INTEGER CONSTANT MAY NOT BE GREATER THAN 2,147,483,647 (2**31-1)
CN-2   EXPONENT ON A REAL CONSTANT IS GREATER THAN 2 DIGITS
CN-3   A REAL CONSTANT HAS MORE THAN 16 DIGITS. IT WAS TRUNCATED TO 16
CN-4   INVALID HEXADECIMAL CONSTANT
CN-5   ILLEGAL USE OF A DECIMAL POINT
CN-6   CONSTANT WITH MORE THAN 7 DIGITS BUT E-TYPE EXPONENT, ASSUMED TO BE
         REAL*4
CN-7   CONSTANT OR STATEMENT NUMBER GREATER THAN 99999
CN-8   AN EXPONENT OVERFLOW OR UNDERFLOW OCCURRED WHILE CONVERTING A CONSTANT
         IN A SOURCE STATEMENT

Compiler Errors

CP-0   COMPILER ERROR - LANDR/ARITH
CP-1   COMPILER ERROR. LIKELY CAUSE: MORE THAN 255 DO STATEMENTS
CP-2   COMPILER ERROR
CP-4   COMPILER ERROR - INTERRUPT AT COMPILE TIME, RETURN TO SYSTEM

CHARACTER Variable

CV-0   A CHARACTER VARIABLE IS USED WITH A RELATIONAL OPERATOR
CV-1   LENGTH OF A CHARACTER VALUE ON RIGHT OF EQUAL SIGN EXCEEDS THAT ON
         LEFT. TRUNCATION WILL OCCUR
CV-2   UNFORMATTED CORE-TO-CORE I/O NOT IMPLEMENTED

DATA Statement

DA-0   REPLICATION FACTOR IS ZERO OR GREATER THAN 32767.
         IT IS ASSUMED TO BE 32767
DA-1   MORE VARIABLES THAN CONSTANTS
DA-2   ATTEMPT TO INITIALIZE A SUBPROGRAM PARAMETER IN A DATA STATEMENT
DA-3   OTHER COMPILERS MAY NOT ALLOW NON-CONSTANT SUBSCRIPTS IN DATA
         STATEMENTS
DA-4   TYPE OF VARIABLE AND CONSTANT DO NOT AGREE. (MESSAGE ISSUED ONCE FOR
         AN ARRAY)
DA-5   MORE CONSTANTS THAN VARIABLES
DA-6   A VARIABLE WAS PREVIOUSLY INITIALIZED. THE LATEST VALUE IS USED.
         CHECK COMMONED AND EQUIVALENCED VARIABLES
DA-7   OTHER COMPILERS MAY NOT ALLOW INITIALIZATION OF BLANK COMMON
DA-8   A LITERAL CONSTANT HAS BEEN TRUNCATED
DA-9   OTHER COMPILERS MAY NOT ALLOW IMPLIED DO-LOOPS IN DATA STATEMENTS
DA-A   MORE THAN 255 CONSTANTS IN A DATA STATEMENT SUBLIST

DEFINE FILE Statements

DF-0   THE UNIT NUMBER IS MISSING
DF-1   INVALID FORMAT TYPE
DF-2   THE ASSOCIATED VARIABLE IS NOT A SIMPLE INTEGER VARIABLE
DF-3   NUMBER OF RECORDS OR RECORD SIZE IS ZERO OR GREATER THAN 32767

DIMENSION Statements

DM-0   NO DIMENSIONS ARE SPECIFIED FOR A VARIABLE IN A DIMENSION STATEMENT
DM-1   THE VARIABLE HAS ALREADY BEEN DIMENSIONED
DM-2   CALL-BY-LOCATION PARAMETERS MAY NOT BE DIMENSIONED
DM-3   THE DECLARED SIZE OF ARRAY EXCEEDS SPACE PROVIDED BY CALLING ARGUMENT

DO **Loops**

DO-0   THIS STATEMENT CANNOT BE THE OBJECT OF A DO-LOOP
DO-1   ILLEGAL TRANSFER INTO THE RANGE OF A DO-LOOP
DO-2   THE OBJECT OF THIS DO-LOOP HAS ALREADY APPEARED
DO-3   IMPROPERLY NESTED DO-LOOPS
DO-4   ATTEMPT TO REDEFINE A DO-LOOP PARAMETER WITHIN THE RANGE OF THE LOOP
DO-5   INVALID DO-LOOP PARAMETER
DO-6   ILLEGAL TRANSFER TO A STATEMENT WHICH IS INSIDE THE RANGE OF A DO-LOOP
DO-7   A DO-LOOP PARAMETER IS UNDEFINED OR OUT OF RANGE
DO-8   BECAUSE OF ONE OF THE PARAMETERS, THIS DO-LOOP WILL TERMINATE AFTER THE
        FIRST TIME THROUGH
DO-9   A DO-LOOP PARAMETER MAY NOT BE REDEFINED IN AN INPUT LIST
DO-A   OTHER COMPILERS MAY NOT ALLOW THIS STATEMENT TO END A DO-LOOP

EQUIVALENCE **and/or** COMMON

EC-0   EQUIVALENCED VARIABLE APPEARS IN A COMMON STATEMENT
EC-1   A COMMON BLOCK HAS A DIFFERENT LENGTH THAN IN A PREVIOUS
        SUBPROGRAM: GREATER LENGTH USED
EC-2   COMMON AND/OR EQUIVALENCE CAUSES INVALID ALIGNMENT.
        EXECUTION SLOWED. REMEDY: ORDER VARIABLES BY DECREASING LENGTH
EC-3   EQUIVALENCE EXTENDS COMMON DOWNWARDS
EC-4   A SUBPROGRAM PARAMETER APPEARS IN A COMMON OR EQUIVALENCE STATEMENT
EC-5   A VARIABLE WAS USED WITH SUBSCRIPTS IN AN EQUIVALENCE STATEMENT BUT HAS
        NOT BEEN PROPERLY DIMENSIONED

END **Statements**

EN-0   MISSING END STATEMENT:END STATEMENT GENERATED
EN-1   AN END STATEMENT WAS USED TO TERMINATE EXECUTION
EN-2   AN END STATEMENT CANNOT HAVE A STATEMENT NUMBER. STATEMENT NUMBER
        IGNORED
EN-3   END STATEMENT NOT PRECEDED BY A TRANSFER

Equal Signs

EQ-0   ILLEGAL QUANTITY ON LEFT OF EQUALS SIGN
EQ-1   ILLEGAL USE OF EQUAL SIGN
EQ-2   OTHER COMPILERS MAY NOT ALLOW MULTIPLE ASSIGNMENT STATEMENTS
EQ-3   MULTIPLE ASSIGNMENT IS NOT IMPLEMENTED FOR CHARACTER VARIABLES
EQ-4   ILLEGAL QUANTITY ON RIGHT OF EQUALS SIGN

EQUIVALENCE **Statements**

EV-0   ATTEMPT TO EQUIVALENCE A VARIABLE TO ITSELF
EV-1   THERE ARE LESS THAN 2 VARIABLES IN AN EQUIVALENCE LIST
EV-2   A MULTI-SUBSCRIPTED EQUIVALENCED VARIABLE HAS BEEN INCORRECTLY
        RE-EQUIVALENCED. REMEDY: DIMENSION THE VARIABLE FIRST

Powers and Exponentiation

EX-0   ILLEGAL COMPLEX EXPONENTIATION
EX-1   I**J WHERE I=J=0
EX-2   I**J WHERE I=0, J.LT.0
EX-3   0.0**Y WHERE Y.LE.0.0
EX-4   0.0**J WHERE J=0
EX-5   0.0**J WHERE J.LT.0
EX-6   X**Y WHERE X .LT. 0.0, Y IS NOT TYPE INTEGER OR .NE. 0.0

ENTRY **Statement**

EY-0   ENTRY-POINT NAME WAS PREVIOUSLY DEFINED
EY-1   PREVIOUS DEFINITION OF FUNCTION NAME IN AN ENTRY IS INCORRECT
EY-2   THE USAGE OF A SUBPROGRAM PARAMETER IS INCONSISTENT WITH A PREVIOUS
        ENTRY-POINT
EY-3   A PARAMETER HAS APPEARED IN A EXECUTABLE STATEMENT BUT IS NOT A
        SUBPROGRAM PARAMETER
EY-4   ENTRY STATEMENTS ARE INVALID IN THE MAIN PROGRAM
EY-5   ENTRY STATEMENT INVALID INSIDE A DO-LOOP

FORMAT Statement

Some FORMAT error messages give characters in which error was detected.

FM-0	IMPROPER CHARACTER SEQUENCE OR INVALID CHARACTER IN INPUT DATA
FM-1	NO STATEMENT NUMBER ON A FORMAT STATEMENT
FM-2	FORMAT CODE AND DATA TYPE DO NOT MATCH
FM-4	FORMAT PROVIDES NO CONVERSION SPECIFICATION FOR A VALUE IN I/O LIST
FM-5	AN INTEGER IN THE INPUT DATA IS TOO LARGE. (MAXIMUM=2,147,483,647=2**31-1)
FM-6	A REAL NUMBER IN THE INPUT DATA IS OUT OF MACHINE RANGE (1.E-78,1.E+75)
FM-7	UNREFERENCED FORMAT STATEMENT
FT-0	FIRST CHARACTER OF VARIABLE FORMAT IS NOT A LEFT PARENTHESIS
FT-1	INVALID CHARACTER ENCOUNTERED IN FORMAT
FT-2	INVALID FORM FOLLOWING A FORMAT CODE
FT-3	INVALID FIELD OR GROUP COUNT
FT-4	A FIELD OR GROUP COUNT GREATER THAN 255
FT-5	NO CLOSING PARENTHESIS ON VARIABLE FORMAT
FT-6	NO CLOSING QUOTE IN A HOLLERITH FIELD
FT-7	INVALID USE OF COMMA
FT-8	FORMAT STATEMENT TOO LONG TO COMPILE (SCAN-STACK OVERFLOW)
FT-9	INVALID USE OF P FORMAT CODE
FT-A	INVALID USE OF PERIOD(.)
FT-B	MORE THAN THREE LEVELS OF PARENTHESES
FT-C	INVALID CHARACTER BEFORE A RIGHT PARENTHESIS
FT-D	MISSING OR ZERO LENGTH HOLLERITH ENCOUNTERED
FT-E	NO CLOSING RIGHT PARENTHESIS
FT-F	CHARACTERS FOLLOW CLOSING RIGHT PARENTHESIS
FT-G	WRONG QUOTE USED FOR KEY-PUNCH SPECIFIED
FT-H	LENGTH OF HOLLERITH EXCEEDS 255
FT-I	EXPECTING COMMA BETWEEN FORMAT ITEMS
FT-J	HOLLERITH STRING EXTENDS BEYOND END OF STATEMENT
FT-K	CHARACTERS FOLLOW CLOSING RIGHT PARENTHESIS FOR VARIABLE FORMAT

Functions and Subroutines

FN-1	A PARAMETER APPEARS MORE THAN ONCE IN A SUBPROGRAM OR STATEMENT FUNCTION DEFINITION
FN-2	SUBSCRIPTS ON RIGHT-HAND SIDE OF STATEMENT FUNCTION. PROBABLE CAUSE: VARIABLE TO LEFT OF EQUAL SIGN NOT DIMENSIONED
FN-4	ILLEGAL LENGTH MODIFIER
FN-5	INVALID PARAMETER
FN-6	A PARAMETER HAS THE SAME NAME AS THE SUBPROGRAM

GO TO Statements

GO-0	THIS STATEMENT COULD TRANSFER TO ITSELF
GO-1	THIS STATEMENT TRANSFERS TO A NON-EXECUTABLE STATEMENT
GO-2	ATTEMPT TO DEFINE ASSIGNED GOTO INDEX IN AN ARITHMETIC STATEMENT
GO-3	ASSIGNED GOTO INDEX MAY BE USED ONLY IN ASSIGNED GOTO AND ASSIGN STATEMENTS
GO-4	INDEX OF AN ASSIGNED GOTO IS UNDEFINED OR OUT OF RANGE, OR INDEX OF COMPUTED GOTO OR CASE IS UNDEFINED
GO-5	ASSIGNED GOTO INDEX MAY NOT BE AN INTEGER*2 VARIABLE

Hollerith Constants

HO-0	ZERO LENGTH SPECIFIED FOR H-TYPE HOLLERITH
HO-1	ZERO LENGTH QUOTE-TYPE HOLLERITH
HO-2	NO CLOSING QUOTE OR NEXT CARD NOT A CONTINUATION CARD
HO-3	UNEXPECTED HOLLERITH OR STATEMENT NUMBER CONSTANT

IF Statements (Arithmetic and Logical)

IF-0	AN INVALID STATEMENT FOLLOWS THE LOGICAL IF
IF-1	ARITHMETIC OR INVALID EXPRESSION IN LOGICAL IF OR WHILE
IF-2	LOGICAL, COMPLEX OR INVALID EXPRESSION IN ARITHMETIC IF

IMPLICIT Statement

IM-0	INVALID DATA TYPE
IM-1	INVALID OPTIONAL LENGTH
IM-3	IMPROPER ALPHABETIC SEQUENCE IN CHARACTER RANGE
IM-4	A SPECIFICATION IS NOT A SINGLE CHARACTER. THE FIRST CHARACTER IS USED

IM-5   IMPLICIT STATEMENT DOES NOT PRECEDE OTHER SPECIFICATION STATEMENTS
IM-6   ATTEMPT TO DECLARE THE TYPE OF A CHARACTER MORE THAN ONCE
IM-7   ONLY ONE IMPLICIT STATEMENT PER PROGRAM SEGMENT ALLOWED. THIS ONE
        IGNORED

Input/Output
IO-0   I/O STATEMENT REFERENCES NON-FORMAT STATEMENT. PROBABLE CAUSE:
        STATEMENT DEFINED AS NON-FORMAT
IO-1   A VARIABLE FORMAT MUST BE AN ARRAY NAME
IO-2   INVALID ELEMENT IN INPUT LIST OR DATA LIST
IO-3   OTHER COMPILERS MAY NOT ALLOW EXPRESSIONS IN OUTPUT LISTS
IO-4   ILLEGAL USE OF END= OR ERR= PARAMETERS
IO-5   INVALID UNIT NUMBER
IO-6   INVALID FORMAT
IO-7   ONLY CONSTANTS, SIMPLE INTEGER*4 VARIABLES, AND CHARACTER VARIABLES ARE
        ALLOWED AS UNIT
IO-8   ATTEMPT TO PERFORM I/O IN A FUNCTION WHICH IS CALLED IN AN OUTPUT
        STATEMENT
IO-9   UNFORMATTED WRITE STATEMENT MUST HAVE A LIST
IO-A   EXPECTING STATEMENT TO BE A FORMAT. PREVIOUSLY REFERENCED IN I/O
        STATEMENT

Job Control Cards
JB-0   CONTROL CARD ENCOUNTERED DURING COMPILATION;
        PROBABLE CAUSE: MISSING C$ENTRY CARD
JB-1   MIS-PUNCHED JOB OPTION

Job Termination
KO-0   SOURCE ERROR ENCOUNTERED WHILE EXECUTING WITH RUN=FREE
KO-1   LIMIT EXCEEDED FOR FIXED-POINT DIVISION BY ZERO
KO-2   LIMIT EXCEEDED FOR FLOATING-POINT DIVISION BY ZERO
KO-3   EXPONENT OVERFLOW LIMIT EXCEEDED
KO-4   EXPONENT UNDERFLOW LIMIT EXCEEDED
KO-5   FIXED-POINT OVERFLOW LIMIT EXCEEDED
KO-6   JOB-TIME EXCEEDED
KO-7   COMPILER ERROR - EXECUTION TIME: RETURN TO SYSTEM
KO-8   TRACEBACK ERROR. TRACEBACK TERMINATED
KO-9   CANNOT OPEN WATFIV.ERRTEXTS. RUN TERMINATED
KO-A   I/O ERROR ON TEXT FILE

Logical Operations
LG-0   .NOT. WAS USED AS A BINARY OPERATOR

Library Routines
LI-0   ARGUMENT OUT OF RANGE DGAMMA OR GAMMA. (1.382E-76 .LT. X .LT. 57.57)
LI-1   ABS(X) .GE. 175.366 FOR SINH, COSH, DSINH OR DCOSH OF X
LI-2   SENSE LIGHT OTHER THAN 0,1,2,3,4 FOR SLITE OR 1,2,3,4 FOR SLITET
LI-3   REAL PORTION OF ARGUMENT .GT. 174.673, CEXP OR CDEXP
LI-4   ABS(AIMAG(Z)) .GT. 174.673 FOR CSIN, CCOS, CDSIN OR CDCOS OF Z
LI-5   ABS(REAL(Z)) .GE. 3.537E15 FOR CSIN, CCOS, CDSIN OR CDCOS OF Z
LI-6   ABS(AIMAG(Z)) .GE. 3.537E15 FOR CEXP OR CDEXP OF Z
LI-7   ARGUMENT .GT. 174.673, EXP OR DEXP
LI-8   ARGUMENT OF CLOG OR CDLOG IS ZERO
LI-9   ARGUMENT IS NEGATIVE OR ZERO, ALOG, ALOG10, DLOG OR DLOG10
LI-A   ABS(X) .GE. 3.537E15 FOR SIN, COS, DSIN OR DCOS OF X
LI-B   ABSOLUTE VALUE OF ARGUMENT .GT. 1, FOR ARSIN, ARCOS, DARSIN OR DARCOS
LI-C   ARGUMENT IS NEGATIVE, SQRT OR DSQRT
LI-D   BOTH ARGUMENTS OF DATAN2 OR ATAN2 ARE ZERO
LI-E   ARGUMENT TOO CLOSE TO A SINGULARITY, TAN, COTAN, DTAN OR DCOTAN
LI-F   ARGUMENT OUT OF RANGE DLGAMA OR ALGAMA. (0.0 .LT. X .LT. 4.29E73)
LI-G   ABSOLUTE VALUE OF ARGUMENT .GE. 3.537E15, TAN, COTAN, DTAN, DCOTAN

Mixed Mode
MD-0	RELATIONAL OPERATOR HAS LOGICAL OPERAND
MD-1	RELATIONAL OPERATOR HAS COMPLEX OPERAND
MD-2	MIXED MODE - LOGICAL OR CHARACTER WITH ARITHMETIC
MD-3	OTHER COMPILERS MAY NOT ALLOW SUBSCRIPTS OF TYPE COMPLEX, LOGICAL OR CHARACTER

Memory Overflow
MO-0	INSUFFICIENT MEMORY TO COMPILE THIS PROGRAM. REMAINDER WILL BE ERROR CHECKED ONLY
MO-1	INSUFFICIENT MEMORY TO ASSIGN ARRAY STORAGE. JOB ABANDONED
MO-2	SYMBOL TABLE EXCEEDS AVAILABLE SPACE, JOB ABANDONED
MO-3	DATA AREA OF SUBPROGRAM EXCEEDS 24K -- SEGMENT SUBPROGRAM
MO-4	INSUFFICIENT MEMORY TO ALLOCATE COMPILER WORK AREA OR WATLIB BUFFER
MO-5	INSUFFICIENT MEMORY TO PRODUCE CROSS REFERENCE. COMPILATION CONTINUING.

NAMELIST Statements
NL-0	NAMELIST ENTRY MUST BE A VARIABLE, NOT A SUBPROGRAM PARAMETER
NL-1	NAMELIST NAME PREVIOUSLY DEFINED
NL-2	VARIABLE NAME TOO LONG
NL-3	VARIABLE NAME NOT FOUND IN NAMELIST
NL-4	INVALID SYNTAX IN NAMELIST INPUT
NL-6	VARIABLE INCORRECTLY SUBSCRIPTED
NL-7	SUBSCRIPT OUT OF RANGE
NL-8	NESTED BLANKS ARE ILLEGAL IN NAMELIST INPUT

Parentheses
PC-0	UNMATCHED PARENTHESIS
PC-1	INVALID PARENTHESIS NESTING IN I/O LIST

PAUSE, STOP Statements
PS-0	OPERATOR MESSAGES NOT ALLOWED:SIMPLE STOP ASSUMED FOR STOP, CONTINUE ASSUMED FOR PAUSE

RETURN Statement
RE-1	RETURN I, WHERE I IS OUT OF RANGE OR UNDEFINED
RE-2	MULTIPLE RETURN NOT VALID IN FUNCTION SUBPROGRAM
RE-3	VARIABLE IS NOT A SIMPLE INTEGER
RE-4	A MULTIPLE RETURN IS NOT VALID IN THE MAIN PROGRAM

Arithmetic and Logical Statement Functions
Probable cause of SF errors - variable on left of = was not dimensioned
SF-1	A PREVIOUSLY REFERENCED STATEMENT NUMBER APPEARS ON A STATEMENT FUNCTION DEFINITION
SF-2	STATEMENT FUNCTION IS THE OBJECT OF A LOGICAL IF STATEMENT
SF-3	RECURSIVE STATEMENT FUNCTION DEFINITION: NAME APPEARS ON BOTH SIDES OF EQUAL SIGN. LIKELY CAUSE: VARIABLE NOT DIMENSIONED
SF-4	A STATEMENT FUNCTION DEFINITION APPEARS AFTER THE FIRST EXECUTABLE STATEMENT
SF-5	ILLEGAL USE OF A STATEMENT FUNCTION NAME

Structured Programming Blocks
SP-0	AT END STATEMENT MUST FOLLOW IMMEDIATELY AFTER A READ
SP-1	AT END FOLLOWS CORE TO CORE, DIRECT ACCESS OR INVALID READ STATEMENT
SP-2	AT END NOT VALID WHEN 'END=' SPECIFIED IN THE READ STATEMENT
SP-3	MISSING OR INVALID DO CASE, WHILE, AT END, OR IF-THEN STATEMENT
SP-4	IMPROPER NESTING OF BLOCK OR CONSTRUCT
SP-5	IMPROPER NESTING OF DO-LOOP
SP-6	IMPROPER NESTING WITH DO-LOOP
SP-7	MISSING END CASE, END WHILE, END AT END, OR END IF STATEMENT
SP-8	OTHER COMPILERS MAY NOT ALLOW IF-THEN-ELSE, DO CASE, WHILE, EXECUTE, REMOTE BLOCK OR AT END STATEMENTS
SP-9	IF NONE BLOCK ALREADY DEFINED FOR CURRENT DO CASE CONSTRUCT
SP-A	IF NONE BLOCK MUST FOLLOW ALL CASE BLOCKS
SP-B	ATTEMPT TO TRANSFER CONTROL ACROSS REMOTE BLOCK BOUNDARIES
SP-C	REMOTE BLOCK NOT PRECEDED BY A TRANSFER

```
SP-D    REMOTE BLOCK PREVIOUSLY DEFINED
SP-E    REMOTE BLOCK STATEMENT MISSING OR INVALID
SP-F    LAST REMOTE BLOCK NOT COMPLETED
SP-G    REMOTE BLOCK IS NOT DEFINED
SP-H    REMOTE BLOCK IS NOT REFERENCED
SP-I    ATTEMPT TO NEST REMOTE BLOCK DEFINITIONS
SP-J    MISSING OR INVALID REMOTE BLOCK NAME
SP-K    ATTEMPT TO EXECUTE A REMOTE BLOCK RECURSIVELY
SP-L    NUMBER OF REMOTE BLOCKS EXCEEDS 255
SP-M    RETURN STATEMENTS ARE INVALID WITHIN REMOTE BLOCKS
```

Subprograms
```
SR-0    MISSING SUBPROGRAM
SR-1    SUBPROGRAM REDEFINES A CONSTANT, EXPRESSION, DO-PARAMETER OR ASSIGNED
        GOTO INDEX
SR-2    THE SUBPROGRAM WAS ASSIGNED DIFFERENT TYPES IN DIFFERENT PROGRAM
        SEGMENTS
SR-3    ATTEMPT TO USE A SUBPROGRAM RECURSIVELY
SR-4    INVALID TYPE OF ARGUMENT IN REFERENCE TO A SUBPROGRAM
SR-5    WRONG NUMBER OF ARGUMENTS IN A REFERENCE TO A SUBPROGRAM
SR-6    A SUBPROGRAM WAS PREVIOUSLY DEFINED. THE FIRST DEFINITION IS USED
SR-7    NO MAIN PROGRAM
SR-8    ILLEGAL OR MISSING SUBPROGRAM NAME
SR-9    LIBRARY PROGRAM WAS NOT ASSIGNED THE CORRECT TYPE
SR-A    METHOD FOR ENTERING SUBPROGRAM PRODUCES UNDEFINED VALUE FOR
        CALL-BY-LOCATION PARAMETER
SR-B    MAINLINE PROGRAM NOT IN LIBRARY
```

Subscripts
```
SS-0    ZERO SUBSCRIPT OR DIMENSION NOT ALLOWED
SS-1    ARRAY SUBSCRIPT EXCEEDS DIMENSION
SS-2    INVALID SUBSCRIPT FORM
SS-3    SUBSCRIPT IS OUT OF RANGE
SS-4    SUBSCRIPTS EXCEED BOUNDS OF ACTUAL ARRAY
```

Statements and Statement Numbers
```
ST-0    MISSING STATEMENT NUMBER
ST-1    STATEMENT NUMBER GREATER THAN 99999
ST-2    STATEMENT NUMBER HAS ALREADY BEEN DEFINED
ST-3    UNDECODEABLE STATEMENT
ST-4    UNNUMBERED EXECUTABLE STATEMENT FOLLOWS A TRANSFER
ST-5    STATEMENT NUMBER IN A TRANSFER IS A NON-EXECUTABLE STATEMENT
ST-6    ONLY CALL STATEMENTS MAY CONTAIN STATEMENT NUMBER ARGUMENTS
ST-7    STATEMENT SPECIFIED IN A TRANSFER STATEMENT IS A FORMAT STATEMENT
ST-8    MISSING FORMAT STATEMENT
ST-9    SPECIFICATION STATEMENT DOES NOT PRECEDE STATEMENT FUNCTION DEFINITIONS
        OR EXECUTABLE STATEMENTS
ST-A    UNREFERENCED STATEMENT FOLLOWS A TRANSFER
ST-B    STATEMENT NUMBER MUST END WITH COLON. STATEMENT NUMBER WAS IGNORED
```

Subscripted Variables
```
SV-0    THE WRONG NUMBER OF SUBSCRIPTS WERE SPECIFIED FOR A VARIABLE
SV-1    AN ARRAY OR SUBPROGRAM NAME IS USED INCORRECTLY WITHOUT A LIST
SV-2    MORE THAN 7 DIMENSIONS ARE NOT ALLOWED
SV-3    DIMENSION OR SUBSCRIPT TOO LARGE (MAXIMUM 10**8-1)
SV-4    A VARIABLE USED WITH VARIABLE DIMENSIONS IS NOT A SUBPROGRAM PARAMETER
SV-5    A VARIABLE DIMENSION IS NOT ONE OF SIMPLE INTEGER VARIABLE, SUBPROGRAM
        PARAMETER, IN COMMON
SV-6    PSEUDO VARIABLE DIMENSIONING ASSUMED FOR ARRAY
```

Syntax Errors
```
SX-0    MISSING OPERATOR
SX-1    EXPECTING OPERATOR
SX-2    EXPECTING SYMBOL
SX-3    EXPECTING SYMBOL OR OPERATOR
SX-4    EXPECTING CONSTANT
SX-5    EXPECTING SYMBOL OR CONSTANT
```

SX-6   EXPECTING STATEMENT NUMBER
SX-7   EXPECTING SIMPLE INTEGER VARIABLE
SX-8   EXPECTING SIMPLE INTEGER VARIABLE OR CONSTANT
SX-9   ILLEGAL SEQUENCE OF OPERATORS IN EXPRESSION
SX-A   EXPECTING END-OF-STATEMENT
SX-B   SYNTAX ERROR
SX-C   EXPECTING '(' OR END-OF-STATEMENT

Type Statements
TY-0   THE VARIABLE HAS ALREADY BEEN EXPLICITLY TYPED
TY-1   THE LENGTH OF THE EQUIVALENCED VARIABLE MAY NOT BE CHANGED.
        REMEDY: INTERCHANGE TYPE AND EQUIVALENCE STATEMENTS

I/O Operations
UN-0   CONTROL CARD ENCOUNTERED ON UNIT 5 AT EXECUTION.
        PROBABLE CAUSE: MISSING DATA OR INCORRECT FORMAT
UN-1   END OF FILE ENCOUNTERED (IBM CODE IHC217)
UN-2   I/O ERROR (IBM CODE IHC218)
UN-3   NO DD STATEMENT WAS SUPPLIED (IBM CODE IHC219)
UN-4   REWIND, ENDFILE, BACKSPACE REFERENCES READER, PRINTER, OR PUNCH
UN-5   ATTEMPT TO READ ON UNIT 5 AFTER IT HAS HAD END-OF-FILE
UN-6   AN INVALID VARIABLE UNIT NUMBER WAS DETECTED (IBM CODE IHC220)
UN-7   PAGE-LIMIT EXCEEDED
UN-8   ATTEMPT TO DO DIRECT ACCESS I/O ON A SEQUENTIAL FILE OR VICE VERSA.
        POSSIBLE MISSING DEFINE FILE STATEMENT (IBM CODE IHC231)
UN-9   WRITE REFERENCES READER, OR READ REFERENCES PRINTER OR PUNCH
UN-A   DEFINE FILE REFERENCES A UNIT PREVIOUSLY USED FOR SEQUENTIAL I/O (IBM
        CODE IHC235)
UN-B   RECORD SIZE FOR UNIT EXCEEDS 32767, OR DIFFERS FROM DD STATEMENT
        SPECIFICATION (IBM CODES IHC233, IHC237)
UN-C   FOR DIRECT ACCESS I/O THE RELATIVE RECORD POSITION IS NEGATIVE, ZERO, OR
        TOO LARGE (IBM CODE IHC232)
UN-D   ATTEMPT TO READ MORE INFORMATION THAN LOGICAL RECORD CONTAINS (IBM CODE
        IHC213)
UN-E   FORMATTED LINE EXCEEDS BUFFER LENGTH (IBM CODE IHC212)
UN-F   I/O ERROR - SEARCHING LIBRARY DIRECTORY
UN-G   I/O ERROR - READING LIBRARY
UN-H   ATTEMPT TO DEFINE THE OBJECT ERROR FILE AS A DIRECT ACCESS FILE
        (IBM CODE IHC234)
UN-I   RECFM IS NOT V(B)S FOR I/O WITHOUT FORMAT CONTROL (IBM CODE IHC214)
UN-J   MISSING DD CARD FOR WATLIB. NO LIBRARY ASSUMED
UN-K   ATTEMPT TO READ OR WRITE PAST THE END OF CHARACTER VARIABLE BUFFER
UN-L   ATTEMPT TO READ ON AN UNCREATED DIRECT ACCESS FILE (IHC236)
UN-M   DIRECT ACCESS SPACE EXCEEDED
UN-N   UNABLE TO OPEN WATLIB DUE TO I/O ERROR; NO LIBRARY ASSUMED
UN-P   ATTEMPT TO WRITE ON A READ ONLY FILE
UN-Q   DIRECT ACCESS UNAVAILABLE IN DEBUG MODE
UN-R   NAME ON C$COPY CARD NOT FOUND IN LIBRARY
UN-S   MISSING OR INVALID NAME ON C$COPY CARD
UN-T   C$COPY CONTROL CARD OR 'PGM=' OPTION FOUND IN LIBRARY
UN-U   ATTEMPT TO DO UNFORMATTED (BINARY) I/O ON READER, PRINTER, OR PUNCH

Undefined Variables
UV-0   VARIABLE IS UNDEFINED
UV-3   SUBSCRIPT IS UNDEFINED
UV-4   SUBPROGRAM IS UNDEFINED
UV-5   ARGUMENT IS UNDEFINED
UV-6   UNDECODABLE CHARACTERS IN VARIABLE FORMAT
UV-7   VARIABLE UNIT NUMBER IS UNDEFINED

Variable Names
VA-0   A NAME IS TOO LONG. IT HAS BEEN TRUNCATED TO SIX CHARACTERS
VA-1   ATTEMPT TO USE AN ASSIGNED OR INITIALIZED VARIABLE OR DO-PARAMETER IN A
        SPECIFICATION STATEMENT
VA-2   ILLEGAL USE OF A SUBROUTINE NAME
VA-3   ILLEGAL USE OF A VARIABLE NAME
VA-4   ATTEMPT TO USE THE PREVIOUSLY DEFINED NAME AS A FUNCTION OR AN ARRAY
VA-5   ATTEMPT TO USE A PREVIOUSLY DEFINED NAME AS A SUBROUTINE

VA-6   ATTEMPT TO USE A PREVIOUSLY DEFINED NAME AS A SUBPROGRAM
VA-7   ATTEMPT TO USE A PREVIOUSLY DEFINED NAME AS A COMMON BLOCK
VA-8   ATTEMPT TO USE A FUNCTION NAME AS A VARIABLE
VA-9   ATTEMPT TO USE A PREVIOUSLY DEFINED NAME AS A VARIABLE
VA-A   ILLEGAL USE OF A PREVIOUSLY DEFINED NAME

EXTERNAL **Statement**
XT-0   A VARIABLE HAS ALREADY APPEARED IN AN EXTERNAL STATEMENT

Index